PROP

D1047189

NOTES

ON THE

OLD TESTAMENT

EXPLANATORY AND PRACTICAL

BY

ALBERT BARNES

ENLARGED TYPE EDITION

EDITED BY

ROBERT FREW, D.D.

JOB

VOLUME I

BAKER BOOK HOUSE
Grand Rapids, Michigan

Library of Congress Catalog Card Number: **55-11630**

ISBN: 0-8010-0529-9

First Printing, December 1949
Second Printing, August 1955
Third Printing, February 1958
Fourth Printing, November 1960
Fifth Printing, January 1963
Sixth Printing, October 1965
Seventh Printing, September 1967
Eighth Printing, September 1969
Ninth Printing, April 1971
Tenth Printing, September 1971
Eleventh Printing, April 1973
Twelfth Printing, March 1974
Thirteenth Printing, August 1975
Fourteenth Printing, January 1977
Fifteenth Printing, February 1978
Sixteenth Printing, April 1979
Seventeenth Printing, September 1980
Eighteenth Printing, November 1981
Nineteenth Printing, October 1982

PHOTOLITHOPRINTED BY CUSHING - MALLOY, INC.
ANN ARBOR, MICHIGAN, UNITED STATES OF AMERICA

EDITOR'S PREFACE.

In presenting these Volumes to the British Public, it may not be amiss to state, that they have been subjected to the same careful scrutiny with the Volumes on the Epistles. To these last Supplementary Notes were added in many places, where the opinions of the Author were supposed to be at variance with the orthodox theology. The general acceptance with which these Notes had been favoured, determined the Editor to adopt the same plan in his revision of the Volumes on Job. Ultimately, however, various circumstances seemed to demand a modification of that plan. The Book of Job does not, or at all events very rarely, lead a commentator to the discussion of those points in doctrinal theology, which seemed to render additional Notes desirable in former Volumes. Consequently the Editor could not but feel, while reading the delightful comments and disquisitions on the many interesting points, relating to art, science, and religion, which this " the oldest book in the world " presents to view—that his vocation, as formerly exercised at all events, was well nigh gone. He entertained the conviction, that the learning and research displayed in the introduction, and indeed throughout the commentary ; the full and luminous statements on almost every point of difficulty, leaving nothing to be desired in the way of further elucidation ; the general fidelity of the translation, and the charm which the peculiar genius of the Author has, *more solito*, thrown around the whole—would place his work in the first rank among English commentaries on Job. Sufficiently critical, it is at the same time full and popular. Indeed, no criticism of any value seems to have escaped the Author's notice, nor is the least fear entertained, that the judicious reader will ever have occasion to consult him in vain. In fine, the distinguishing excellence, to which attention has been drawn in a prefatory notice affixed to a former volume,* and which, for purposes of general utility, gives a commentary higher claims than originality even—the excellence, namely, of writing under full and digested knowledge of all that has been said on a subject, is throughout apparent in these volumes. " The Author is fully up to the modern mark, and never leaves the reader to complain, that a judgment has been formed. in ignorance of what the more recent authorities have alleged, while his independence is everywhere manifest." There is, however, one point, in regard to which, very many will be found to differ from the Author, and that point, in the Book of Job, is brought into great

* Volume on the Hebrews.

a

and frequent prominence, viz., *the state of knowledge, in patriarchal times, on the doctrine of a future world.* The views presented in the commentary and introduction on this subject, are not such as have been generally entertained in this country, and, on that account, are likely to startle many readers. Expression is given to them in almost every case where the passage furnishes occasion, and that is not unfrequently. As, however, the point is but *one*, it seemed better so far to modify the plan adopted in former volumes, as to present a general view of the subject in a prefatory notice, rather than insert detached Notes under the passages specially touching the question.

The Author's views on this subject may be seen at length in his introduction,* and in his commentary, under the texts that affect it. The substance of them is, that the resurrection of the body was a doctrine utterly unknown to Job and his times, and that the celebrated passage in the nineteenth chapter, with other places that have been confidently appealed to in evidence of knowledge of it, have been quite misinterpreted, and are, when rightly explained, silent on the subject. He allows that there existed an idea of the soul's separate or disembodied existence, but in a region, "where only a few scattered rays of light would exist, and where the whole aspect of the dwelling was in strong contrast with the cheerful region of the land of the living. To that dark world," he continues, "even Job felt that it would be a calamity to descend, for though there was an expectation, that there would be a distinction there between the good and the evil, yet compared with the present world of light and beauty, it was a sad and gloomy place."† He appeals, in corroboration of these remarks, to Hezekiah and to David,‡ with what success there may possibly be room to inquire towards the close of this notice. He allows that the idea of future retribution obtained, though faintly and inefficiently. Such is a fair though brief account of the view of the future state, which the Author professes to have found in the Book of Job. It embraces the ideas entertained of the resurrection, the separate existence of the soul, and future retribution. But as no good purpose could be served by examining these points separately, since very nearly the same passages would require to be appealed to, it will be deemed sufficient to subject to a careful scrutiny those texts, or the more important of them, that have a bearing on the general question of the knowledge of the future world in the times of Job, noting, as they pass under review, to what extent they furnish evidence on one or all of the points embraced. These passages may be divided into two classes; first, those which indicate, or seem to indicate, clearer light in regard to the future world, than the Author supposes then existed; second, those which seem to countenance the dark views which he imagines to have prevailed.

Before entering on an examination of the evidence contained in these passages, it is proper to notice a presumption in favour of the opinion

* vii. 10.   † Introduction.   ‡ In Isa. xxxviii. 11, 18, 19; and Psal. vi. 5.

which attributes more knowledge to Job on the subject of a future world, than those who think with our Author imagine he could possibly possess. That presumption arises from the improbability—the high improbability— that God, in any age, should have left the church, or the saints, in utter ignorance of the resurrection of the body, and with just so much knowledge of the separate existence of the soul in another world, as made them look on their admission to it rather in the light of a calamity to be deplored, than a blessing to be desired ; with such ideas too of future retribution as could serve little or no practical purpose. It is of no use to allege in opposition to this presumption, that we must allow something for the gradual progress of truth, and for the development of the science of theology, which, like other sciences, has had its infancy and early stages, during which we in vain look for the fulness, the breadth, the precision, that are at length attained in the ripened and perfected system. For while there are certain points of analogy between human science and the science of theology ; and between the mode in which the truth in both cases is advanced in the world, there are, in this very respect, points of strong dissimilarity and contrast. The knowledge of the true religion was not discovered by man, imperfectly apprehended at first, and gradually brought by him to perfection. It was originally matter of divine revelation, and subsequently preserved by tradition. The early ancestors of the human family were in direct communication with God, and were not inventors of religious science at all. It is true indeed, that revelation becomes more full and explicit as ages roll on ; and that Jesus by his gospel hath brought life and immortality to light. But this on all hands must be understood comparatively, and not absolutely. And a consistent enough sense of it is given, when it is allowed, that on the great doctrine of a future state, a fulness of light, unknown before, has been shed by Christianity. It is not necessary to suppose, that the resurrection of the body, or the immortality of the soul, were absolutely unknown. The presumption, on the other hand, is, that they must have been known from the earliest times. Man could not discover them, but God could reveal them, just as he did the rite of sacrifice to Adam or to Abel. Moreover, while the general law of increasing fulness as ages pass away, according to which the measure of revelation seems to be regulated, might account for *less* knowledge on the part of Job, than on the part of Paul, it cannot account for *contradictory* belief. It is difficult to conceive of the one regarding death as a departure to be with Christ, which is far better than to remain alive, and of the other regarding it as a calamity, *because* introducing to a gloomier world than the present. Nay, this general law does not forbid the supposition, that, on certain occasions, Job, or saints in his day, might go beyond the knowledge of their times, and, as it were, anticipate the revelations of the future. How highly evangelical, and *Christian* even, does David become, in many of his Psalms, speaking in them in such manner as argues a measure of knowledge, that would be no discredit to any one in the fulness of New Testament light !

Yet a host of eminent critics, on examination of the Book of Job, have substantially agreed with the Author, as Grotius, Le Clerc, Michaelis, Warburton, Rosenmüller, Patrick, Kennicott, and others.   It is time, therefore, that we examine particularly one or two passages belonging to the first class noticed above, viz., the class indicating clearer light on the future world, than these critics will allow to have existed in Job's day.*

An important passage under this class is Chap. xiv. 7—15, "There is hope of a tree if it be cut down that it will sprout again. . . . But man dieth and wasteth away ; yea, man giveth up the ghost, and where is he ? As the waters fail from the sea, and the flood decayeth and drieth up ; so man lieth down and riseth not : till the heavens be no more, they shall not awake, nor be raised out of their sleep. O that thou wouldest hide me in the grave, . . until thy wrath be past, that thou wouldest appoint me a set time, and remember me ! If a man die, shall he live again ? all the days of my appointed time will I wait, till my change come. Thou shalt call and I will answer thee, thou wilt have a desire to the work of thine hands." The Author, in his Introduction, places this passage among those which argue ignorance of the doctrine of the resurrection, and that strangely enough, since it is very confidently appealed to on the other side. Dr. Good, who is not at all disposed to push his views on this subject to extremes, after remarking that nothing can be inferred either for or against resurrection belief, from the use of the image of sleep in the 12th verse, farther observes, under the same verse, that " it has been a subject of dispute among the commentators, whether Job, in the present place, refers to a definite term in which a resurrection will take place, or denies it by the strongest figure he could command. Yet I think the latter part of the sentence in ver. 14, 15, is so strongly in favour of the former opinion, that no man can refuse his assent to it, who gives it the attention it is entitled to; *nor do I well know how a full persuasion of such a belief could be more definitely drawn up.* It appears to me so strong as to settle the question of itself, and without the concurrence of other passages that might be called in to its aid." The testimony of the passage indeed seems most explicit and full. Anything in it that *seems* to oppose resurrection belief may consistently enough be explained of man's no longer appearing *in the present scene*, without at all affecting the question of his again appearing in *another* scene, and this principle of explanation is admitted again and again in the commentary, as will immediately be seen. Some, indeed, find *no use* for this principle here, but on the contrary, find in ver. 7—10, a beautiful analogical argument in favour of the resurrection. " He (Job) toucheth upon the argument from the analogy of things, which has so often been made use of in treating upon this subject, as if he had said, After a tree is cut down, we see nevertheless the old stock flourish again and send forth new

---

* In the course of this examination, passages belonging to the second class will necessarily be introduced and discussed, thus rendering needless any further or more formal notice. The plan of this preface is to embrace all that is essential to its subject, under the two leading texts, chap. xiv. 7—15, and xix. 25—27.

branches, and shall man then, when he once expires, be extinct for ever? Is there no hope that he shall revive, and be raised again hereafter? Yes there is, according to the doctrine delivered to us from our ancestors ; but then they inform us, that this resurrection shall not be, but with the desolation of the world."* The reading of the Septuagint, with the point of interrogation, favours this view—πεσὼν δὲ Βροτὸς οὐκ ἔτι ἐστί ; There seems not, however, sufficient evidence to establish this as the true sense ; and it appears more natural to understand the comparison with the tree introduced, not to furnish an analogical argument, but to set off, by way of contrast, the brief existence of man *on the present stage*, and the impossibility of his reappearing on it. The passage is a lament over the comparative brevity of human existence, yet, as shall by and by be seen, the doctrine of the resurrection looks through the gloom, and inspires the mourner with gladness and triumph. It should be remarked, however, while thus abandoning the analogical argument, that it has appeared satisfactory to very high authorities. The Author has himself introduced the beautiful poetical paraphrase of Dr. Dwight, in which that argument is embodied, and though he will not allow that anything of the kind is intended by the comparison in the passage, he admits, notwithstanding, that " such comparisons must have early occurred to mankind, and hence *led* to the inquiry whether he (man) would not live in a future state. Other things that are cut down spring up again and live. But man is cut down, and does not spring up again. Will he not be likely, therefore, to have an existence in some future state, and to spring up and flourish there?" But the advocates of resurrection belief can well afford to waive this point. Their cause finds enough in the passage without it.

First, A term is appointed when the slumbers of the grave shall be broken. These shall not continue for ever, but only TILL the heavens be no more. It is indeed confidently asserted, that this is simply a strong poetical or rhetorical figure, the meaning of which is NEVER—as if Job had said, These heavens will never pass ; they are the most durable things we know. Man rise from the grave ! He may, when the everlasting heavens pass away, but not till then ; that is, the resurrection is impossible. Finally, it is affirmed, that " it does not follow from this passage, that he believed that the heavens ever *would* be no more." Yet the Author is not disposed to use the emphatic " *never* " thus obtained, for the purpose of bringing out of it a positive denial of the resurrection on the part of Job. He seeks but to neutralize the evidence in favour of the doctrine. The question of the resurrection, according to his comment, *is not touched*, since Job simply asserts, that man, when he dies, " dies to live *no more on the earth*." " Whether he believed in a *future* state, or in the future resurrection, is another question, and one that cannot be determined from this passage." In this ingenious decision, one might be disposed more readily to acquiesce, if the Author himself were found always to abide by it. But in his Introduc-

---

* Peters' Critical Dissertation on the Book of Job.

tion, he adduces *this very passage* and others, which, in the commentary, he
has in like manner disposed of, as not touching the question—in evidence of
" *disbelief* of the doctrine of the resurrection, or *ignorance* of it.'* How can
passages which " determine nothing " on a question, be evidence of ignorance and unbelief regarding it ? It is said, indeed, that had Job known of
the resurrection he would have expressed himself differently. But according
to the Author, in the comment, Job just speaks of death and the grave
as Christian poets and Christian people do every day, when they intimate
that by them an end is put to all the present pursuits of man, and he is for
ever removed from this life.† It is still needful, therefore, to inquire into
the validity of the criticism that explains away the famous clause " till the
heavens be no more," and substitutes " never " in its room. Such an interpretation, to say the least of it, is not natural, is not (as the Author
himself frequently speaks in his commentaries on the epistles) what would
first occur to any unbiassed mind, what would at once strike an unpreju-
diced reader. There is nothing in the words, nothing in the sentiment
they are commonly understood to express, forcing one to seek about for a
non-literal interpretation. That truth or sentiment is just what might very
naturally be expected in such a connection, and nothing but the idea, that
the knowledge of the resurrection was too much for Job and his times,
could ever have raised a question about it. It is a corroboration of these
remarks, that, in very early times, the knowledge of the doctrine regarding
the final dissolution of all things prevailed, so that the literal interpretation cannot be said to proceed on what was inconsistent with the belief of
the period, on that important article.‡ Moreover, on considering the
other parts of the passage, the literal interpretation of this clause will be
found essential to the unity and coherence of the whole. So convinced
was Mr. Scott of the truth of this view, that he expresses himself with a
severity scarce justifiable, considering that the question is not about the
truth of the resurrection, but about the amount of knowledge obtained in
regard to it, in a particular age or book. " When a man is cut off by
death, he is for ever removed from his place in this world ; no one expects
to see him again, and his body returns to the earth whence it was taken.
. . . Thus he lieth down till the consummation of all things, when he
shall awake at the general resurrection. All these expressions imply Job's
belief of that great doctrine, though both ancient and modern Sadducees
have contrived to misunderstand him. Why else should he speak of death
as ' *sleep*,' and mention a *period* to it, when he shall *awake*, even ' when
the heavens be no more ? ' "

Secondly, Job wishes to be hidden in the grave, or in the state of the
dead, till God's wrath should be past, but he has no idea of remaining in
that state for ever ; and therefore *desires an appointed time in which he
might be remembered and restored.* It is allowed in the commentary, that

---

* vii. (10) (c).
† See this point further discussed in the remarks that follow under xix. 25—27.
‡ Good, *in loco.*

here is an " expectation that he should live at some future period ;" and that he had " unconsciously worked himself up almost to the belief that man might live again on earth," although it is added, he immediately " checks himself," and abandons the hope as " visionary and vain." And well he might, if his hope regarded restoration to the present life, with its occupations and enjoyments. But he felt that such restoration could not be, and expresses himself everywhere so strongly on that point, that he has been supposed to deny the resurrection altogether. When, then, he asserts that his hope regarded something that should take place after his body had long slumbered in the dust, and his spirit had inhabited Sheol; according to every legitimate principle of interpretation, he must be understood as referring to the future life and the resurrection. It remains to be seen, moreover, whether the clause in which he is supposed to abandon his hope; viz., " If a man die, shall he live again ?" will admit of such a sense being put on it, or will not equally admit of another.

Thirdly, Let it be noticed, meantime, that Job expressly mentions his *renovation,* חֲלִיפָה, in our translation rendered *change,* though with less propriety. The word is most frequently, if not always, used of a change to the better, a renewal.* It is the same word, in its verbal form, which, in the preceding context, is applied to the reviving of trees, and in Psal. xc. 5, to the springing of the grass. Anticipating this blessed *revival,* Job intimates that he would wait with patience all the days appointed to him in the grave, or in Sheol, till at last it arrived—עַד בּוֹא חֲלִיפָתִי, *i. e.* as the Seventy beautifully render, εως παλιν γενωμαι—till I am made anew. It is somewhat remarkable, that the argument so very generally founded on this significant word is in the commentary passed over in silence. It is certainly worthy of notice. And now, as to the introductory clause of this 14th verse, " If a man die, shall he live again ?" there seems just as good reason to interpret of joyful assurance, as of gloomy doubt, and better reason, if we take the connection into account. Job had expressed " an expectation that he should live at some future period. He had wrought himself up to the belief that man *might* live again." Is it not then as natural to suppose the clause in question an exclamation of glad surprise —" Yea, is it so, shall man live again !" as to suppose it a sudden and emphatic denial of his fondly cherished hopes, involving a transition in a moment from the joys of faith to the horrors of despair ? If we understand it in this way, there is a beautiful connection between the two parts of the verse, " Shall man indeed live again ! *then* all the days of my appointed time will I wait till my renovation come." " Here," says Dr. Adam Clarke, remarking on this clause, " is *no doubt,* but a strong persuasion of the certainty of the general resurrection."†

Fourthly, In exact consistency with his previously expressed expectations, Job addressing God says, " Thou shalt call and I will answer thee ; thou wilt have a desire to the work of thine hands "—referring obviously

---

* Peters' Dissertation. † See also Parkhurst, Heb. Lex. *sub voce* חֲלַף,

to the resurrection and the general judgment, when his innocence should
be established, and his sufferings terminated for ever. The proposed rendering, " call thou now," &c., alters the sense indeed, and supposes Job
to express his anxiety to come to *immediate* trial.* But is it natural?
Is not the reference obviously to the set time, the period of renovation?
Else, what becomes of the connection of the passage? According to this
rendering, the striking contrast between what God *would do* at the set
time, and what he *now did*, would in like manner be entirely lost. *Then*
God would have a desire toward him. But *now* (ver. 16) he " numbered
his steps, and watched over his sin." On the whole, if the resurrection
and the future life be excluded from this celebrated passage, it seems
nothing but a collection of disjointed fragments, or a rhapsody of passionate
contradictions, which, it may be said, the intensity of Job's sufferings must
excuse. Yet certainly if the sufferer utter beautiful and connected speech,
or a fair interpretation can be found according to which he does so, there
is no need of resorting to such apologies.

   The next passage requiring consideration, is that celebrated one, chap.
xix. 25, 27. " For I know that my Redeemer liveth, and that he shall stand
at the latter day upon the earth," &c. It is impossible, in a brief notice of
this kind, to present any thing like a full view of the controversy to which
these remarkable words have given rise. Such a task would require a volume.
The sense that would at once spring up in the mind of a reader ignorant of
the disputations of the learned, is that which supposes Job to speak of the
resurrection. And not a few, rising from the study of these disputations,
have, notwithstanding, been heartily disposed to subscribe, with some little
abatement, to the opinion of Jerome, " Quid hac prophetia manifestius?
Nullus tam aperte post Christum, quam iste ante Christum, de resurrectione
loquitur. What can be clearer than this prophecy? No one living after
Christ has spoken more plainly of the resurrection than Job, who lived
before him." Such, indeed, is the opinion of the Fathers generally, of our
venerable translators, and of the larger part both of ancient and modern
critics. It is not denied, that interpreters of great note are opposed to this
view, the chief of whom are Grotius, Le Clerc, and Warburton. Allured
by the lustre of these names, and supported by their authority, a certain
class of critics have been but too proud to follow in their wake. Yet though
these great chiefs are distinguished for vast and varied learning, and for
critical acumen, no one acquainted with them will expect the evangelical
or spiritual view to be taken, if it can be avoided, or a loftier sense to be
received, if a meaner one can be obtained. Grotius is famed as the
expositor that can find Christ nowhere. Nor is Le Clerc distinguished for
greater elevation of view. To both may be applied the celebrated stricture
of Robert Hall on a recent commentator. " He never sets his foot," said
Hall, " in the other world, if he can get a hole to step into in this ; and he

* See the Commentary.

never gives a passage a meaning which would render it applicable and useful in all ages, if he can find in it any local or temporary allusion."* Warburton's love of paradox is as well known as his fondness for controversy, and rare ability in the conducting of it. It is true that opinions are entitled to considerations on their own merits, irrespective of the character of their authors. But when great names are put forward as authority (and in no question has the argument from authority been put forward more frequently, or more confidently, than in this), it is but just to inquire what are their claims to sober, judicious, evangelical exposition; while at the same time the profoundest respect is entertained for genius and learning.

Those who deny the reference to the resurrection in this passage, are not exactly at one in regard to the sense that ought to be assigned to it. It was first asserted, and long confidently maintained, that Job expresses a firm persuasion of *temporal deliverance from suffering, and restorat on to his former state of prosperity and happiness.* The absurdity, however, of attributing such an expectation to one who nowhere else gives the slightest hint of it ; and who uniformly, both before and after this time, expresses himself in the language of despair in regard to hopes of happiness on earth ; and who maintained the position against his friends, that, in the providence of God, a good man might be overwhelmed with adversity, and, in this world, never be relieved from it ;—has induced many to abandon this untenable position, and adopt in its stead the modified hypothesis of Kennicott. "The conviction," says that critic, "which I suppose Job to express here, is this : that though his dissolution was hastening on, amidst the unjust accusations of his pretended friends ; and though, while he was thus singularly oppressed with anguish of mind, he was also tortured with pains of body, torn by sores and ulcers from head to foot, and sitting upon dust and ashes ; yet still out of that miserable body, in his flesh thus stripped of skin, and really dropping into the grave, HE SHOULD SEE GOD, who would *appear in his favour,* and vindicate the INTEGRITY of his character." According to this modified view, Job had an expectation, not of temporal deliverance, but of vindication only. He believed that, ere he died, however low he might be reduced, his God would appear to dispel the clouds that had for a time obscured his reputation, and to assert his innocence in the face of the world. The opinion ably maintained by the author in his exposition of the passage, is substantially the same, unless the writer has misapprehended him. Job had an expectation that God would come forth as his vindicator in some such way as he is declared afterwards to have done. The events at the close of the book, it is further stated, fully meet all that is implied in the words. He would be vindicated *on earth;* of that he was assured, in whatever manner it might be effected.† It will afterwards appear, that this theory of interpretation, though less gross than that

---

* Hall's Works, Vol. VI., p. 148 of Life.

† See the commentary, chapter xix. 25, seq. Compare Notes on chapter xvi. 22, and xxx. 23.

of temporal *deliverance*, is exposed to very nearly the same objections with it. Meantime the passage must be subjected to some little examination.

It is asserted that our English translators have given a turn to the text by the use of certain supplementary words, which carry the mind forward to the resurrection, though there be no such idea in the original. It is very true, as any one consulting the English Bible may see without the help of critics, that the words "day," "though," "body," and "worms," are supplied in the translation. But the addition of these words is not at all essential to bring out the idea of the resurrection. That idea will be manifest in any translation that is accurate, however literal or severe. The following is a close rendering of the Hebrew. " I surely do know my REDEEMER, the LIVING ONE. And He, the LAST, will arise over the dust. And after the disease has cut down my skin, even from my flesh, I shall see God; whom I shall see on my behalf; and mine eyes shall behold him, and not estranged. The thoughts of my bosom are accomplished."* Job's hope of the resurrection, instead of being obscured, seems to brighten, the more faithfully the original is followed. It were easy to shew further, by an analysis of the words, that they are just such as would have been used, or might properly have been used, had it been the intention of Job, or of the Spirit speaking by him, to point to that glorious scene, when the Redeemer shall arise over the ruins of the grave and reanimate its dust. It is not needful, however, to enter largely on any such task, as the reader will observe that all that is contended for on the other side of the question, is that the words do not NECESSARILY bear the resurrection sense, but are capable of another, to which certain circumstances, different entirely from those which depend on the meaning of the words or terms, compel the critic to resort. This, at all events, is what will be found stated by the author in his commentary. He does not say that the sense usually put upon the words is such as they will not bear. He does not contend for another sense, on the ground that it better suits the meaning of the original text. He attempts to prove that the words will equally suit the idea of vindication, in some such way as ultimately happened, and then proceeds to settle the controversy on other ground than that of verbal criticism. To that ground it will be necessary to follow him. Meanwhile, it may be observed, that though certain of the words and phrases may possibly be explained on the theory that excludes the resurrection, yet the passage, taken as a whole, cannot very consistently, or without an appearance of force, be so explained; while some of the more important clauses have a dignity and energy about them, that disappears the moment the attempt is made If the English translation in this place be supposed, in some of its renderings, more favourable to a particular view than faithful to its original, there is one instance in which it has departed from the original much to the disadvantage of that

---

* Dr. Pye Smith. He has adopted Dr. Good's emendation, by which the original text is read עוֹרִי נִקְּפוּ instead of זֹאת נִקְּפוּ־עוֹרִי "*disease* (so זֹאת, an Arabic term, signifies) hath destroyed my skin," instead of "after my skin *they* destroy *this,* זֹאת, *i.e.,* body."

view.   The words על עפר יקום literally signify, " He shall arise over the dust." That עפר dust is sometimes used to denote " the earth," as in chap. xli. 3, is allowed. But while those who reject the idea of the resurrection cannot understand why *this* word should be used, rather than the ordinary term for earth, ארץ, that rejected idea sufficiently explains it. By a beautiful and obvious figure, "the dust" is put for " the dead," as in Ps. xxx. 9, where the same Hebrew term is used. " What profit is there in my blood, when I go down to the pit?   Shall the DUST praise thee?" It should be noticed also, that יקים is clearly a forensic term,* indicating a rising to the judgment-seat ; and, although taken by itself it may not determine whether that judgment should be " visible or not," yet when conjoined with " the dust," or " dead," to what other judgment can it refer than that which is connected with the resurrection?   See also chap. xxxi. 14, for a similar use of the word.   As to מבשרי, *from* my flesh ; if it be contended that this means *out of* my body,—*absque carne mea*,—*without* my body, then it is clear Job did *not* expect to " see God " in *this* world, unless, indeed, the improbable hypothesis of Dr. Stock be admitted, (a hypothesis which never could have been invented, but from the great difficulty the ingenious author felt in explaining the words in accordance with the principle he had adopted), viz., " that the irritated patriarch roused himself to an expectation that he should be miraculously restored from the grave, *for a time*, even in this present world, to the vindication of his own character, and the utter confusion of his enemies !!" How hard pressed the critic must have been, ere he fled to a resort of this kind ! The idea of a resurrection looked out on him so clearly from this famous text, that he knows not what to do, and he will rather *invent a temporary resurrection* for Job, than allow that the distressed patriarch could be acquainted with *the true doctrine*. The invention is instructive, and shows, among other things, that men of learning and sense have found no small difficulties in their way as soon as they departed from the common understanding of this text.

But since, as has just been stated, it is not contended that the words will not bear the ordinary sense, the only question that remains is, on what other grounds a sense that it is allowed to be the most obvious is set aside   The first, and perhaps the principal ground, is that the doctrine of the resurrection, introduced on this occasion, must have solved the whole difficulty, and at once have decided the controversy in favour of Job.   It must have finally settled the long pending question.   The frequency with which this objection is introduced, and the various forms in which it is put, by Warburton and his followers, shews the importance attached to it.   In their view, the very mention of this grand article of the faith, on the part of Job, must have given him an immediate and triumphant victory, and left no room for his adversaries to utter another word.   All this proceeds on the supposition, that the question under discussion in this patriarchal debate is, how the

---

* For the same use of it see Psal. lxxiv. 22 ; lxxxii. 8 ; and Job xxxi. 13, 14 ; with Dr. Good's remarks in Intro. Dis. p. 82.

afflictions of the righteous, and the prosperity of the wicked, can be reconciled with the equity of Divine providence ? The doctrine of the resurrection is supposed to furnish a complete solution of this question. It may
be so. But what evidence is there that Job's friends must necessarily have
regarded it in that light ? Certainly *they* may be excused though they
manifested some little dulness of apprehension, and presumed to continue
the controversy, even after this decisive settlement, when certain eminent
modern critics, though not disposed to admit Job's knowledge of the resurrection, profess themselves equally dull.* What wonder if men living in
this early age could not see the bearing of Job's doctrine, on the discussion
in which they were engaged, when men of learning and abilities cannot see
it, under all the advantages of Christian times! It is possible, moreover,
that critics and philosophical interpreters may have erred in laying down
a problem about providence, and asserting that the book of Job was designed
to furnish a solution of it. The simple question, according to Peters, was
not *how* the sufferings of good men might be reconciled with the equity of
Divine providence ? but whether Job was an innocent man or not, and in
order to ascertain this, whether great sufferers were not necessarily great
sinners ? But what is the bearing of the resurrection on these questions ?
At best, it could only furnish a reason WHY good men suffered (on the supposition that the suffering of such *was admitted to be fact*), but could give
no answer to the inquiry regarding the *fact* whether they *did* suffer, *i. e.*,
of course under such heavy trials as had been imposed on Job.† Job's

* Hengstenberg, in Kitto's Cyclopedia of Biblical Literature, article "Job." He remarks
on two great errors into which he thinks most commentators on Job have fallen. The
second is thus introduced, "There is another fundamental error which has led nearly all
modern interpreters to a mistaken idea of the design of this book. Pareau (*De Immortali-
tatis Not. in libro Jobi*, Deventer, 1807, p. 207,) is the only one who saw the error adverted
to, and combated it with success. They assume that the problem could be satisfactorily
solved only when the doctrine of immortality and retribution had been first established. . .
On nearer examination, however, it appears that the doctrine of retribution after death
is not of itself alone calculated to lead to a solution of the problem. . . The belief in a final
judgment is firm and rational only when it rests on the belief in God's continued providential government of the world, and in his acting as sovereign Lord in all the events of
human life. If God is holy and just, he must also have the will to manifest these qualities
in our present life. Woe to him who expects in a future world to be supplied with every
thing he missed here, and with redress for all injuries sustained. He deceives himself.
His God was during his life on earth, inactive, shutting himself up in heaven; is he sure
that his God will hereafter be better disposed, or more able to protect him ? As his essence
remains the same, and the nature of sin and virtue is unchanged, how should he, then, in
a future life, punish the former and reward the latter, if he does not do so in this life!
Temporary injustice is still injustice, and destroys the idea of a holy and just God." They
who have leisure and inclination may examine the theology of this extract. To have quoted
it is enough to establish what is said above.

† The following passage from Peters is worthy of being quoted entire. "It will appear
plain to any one that reads this book with care, that the main point debated betwixt those
friends was, whether Job was an upright or religious man, or, on the contrary, a wicked
man and a hypocrite ? And this very naturally brought on another question, not *why* good
men are afflicted ? (as Le Clerc has wrongly put it,) but *whether* they are so or not ? Or,
whether it was usual with God to afflict in so extraordinary a manner as they saw Job
afflicted, but for sins of an extraordinary size. This, then, being the truth of the case, it is

friends, too, would have their own mode of regarding the resurrection and the judgment. Instead of looking forward to these events for an explanation of inequalities in providence, *the existence of which they did not believe,* they may have regarded them as in reality fitted to strengthen their favourite position ; for if God *in the end* deal with men, in respect of imposing suffering and exempting from it, according to character, *i. e.,* if *then* the righteous alone are rewarded and the wicked alone punished, must it not be so in this world also ? The ruler is the same. And it is remarkable, that this is exactly the line of reasoning adopted by the critics referred to above, as not allowing that the resurrection furnishes any solution of the difficulty.

It is further alleged, that "the interpretation which refers this (passage) to the resurrection of the dead, is inconsistent with numerous passages where Job expresses a contrary belief." The passages cited are vii. 9, 21 ; x. 21, 22 ; xiv. 7—12 ; xvi. 22. The first of these obviously intimates only, that man shall appear no more *in this present scene,* when once the grave has closed on him. " As the cloud is consumed and vanisheth away, so he that goeth down to the grave shall come up no more." If further evidence of this being the true sense were needed, the very next verse would furnish it. " He shall return no more *to his house,* neither shall his place know him any more." But this is admitted in the commentary, under vii. 9, where the author informs his readers that " it would be pressing this too far, to adduce it as proving that Job did not believe in the doctrine of the resurrection ;" and under xix. 25 – 27, where the above list of texts is given, he says of the passages contained in it generally, that they "imply that when he (man) should die, he would not appear again on the earth," and adds, "this is not such *language as one would use* who believed in the resurrection of the dead ;" so that although he immediately asks, " How is it *possible* to believe that a man in his circumstances would ever *deny* the doctrine of the resurrection if he held it," &c., and has cited the passage as " *expressing* contrary belief," yet he seems to intend no more than that Job's faith in the resurrection must have prevented the use of so melancholy strains. Thus, in the introduction, he says, too, " *It may be said* (he comes to say it himself in his commentary) that these passages only teach that man would not appear again *on the earth.* This may be so ; but still, if they had known of the resurrection at all, these sentiments would not have been uttered. *That* doctrine would have relieved all the difficulty as effectually as the belief that man would be raised up to dwell on the earth would have done." It is not, however, by any means clear that

easy to observe that the doctrine of the resurrection and a future state, supposing they had received an obscure tradition of it, as it is evident to me they had, will afford no solution to either of these questions. The friends might still judge rashly of poor Job (as we know some Christians do of one another with as little reason, notwithstanding they believe a life to come), and then there could be no room for their urging this doctrine to him by way of consolation, for it can be only such to good men, and he, in their opinion, was quite otherwise. Job, indeed, might take some consolation to himself from it, and it appears that he does do so in more places than one."—*Page* 220, *Ed. London,* 1751.

the knowledge of the resurrection must have prevented Job from speaking
as he has done in these places.   That doctrine might have removed what
is supposed to have been the grand difficulty, viz., that regarding the equity
of the Divine administration.   Yet Job might, notwithstanding, speak of
man dying and returning no more *to the earth*, and even lament that such
should soon be his own case, since it could not but grieve him, that he must
die under a cloud, and leave a tarnished name behind him.   The vindication and recompense at the "resurrection of the just," would not render
him altogether indifferent to this.   In this view his expostulation with God
in chap. vii. 7—10, ought evidently to be understood, the 8th verse of which
is thus paraphrased by Dr. Adam Clarke, " If I die in my present state,
with all this load of undeserved odium which is cast upon me by my friends,
I shall never have an opportunity of vindicating my character and regain-
ing the good opinion of mankind."   It should be noticed, too, that these
lamentations, on the part of Job, are for the most part introduced in connection with the cruel aspersions of his friends, which entered his very soul,
and formed the chief cause of his mental agony.   He was not afraid to die
because of the gloom of *Sheol*, but he desired to die with a spotless name,
and accordingly, in the 21st verse, he passionately appeals to God for
immediate assistance, if it were to be granted at all, otherwise it might
come too late ; "for now," says he, " I shall sleep in the dust, and thou
shalt seek me in the morning, but I shall not be."   Such is the sense which
the author himself attaches to chap. xvi. 22.   In the 21st verse the afflicted
patriarch says, " Oh that one might plead for a man with God, as a man
pleadeth for his neighbour," and then in the 22d verse subjoins, " When a
few years are come, then I shall go the way whence I shall not return."
" He was overwhelmed," says the author, "with calamities and reproaches.
He did not wish to die thus.   He wished that the reproaches might be
wiped off, and if he obtained that he was not unwilling to die.   It is the
expression of such a wish as *every man* has that his sun may not go down
under a cloud, and that his name, if remembered at all when he is dead,
may go untarnished down to future times, and be such that his friends might
repeat it without a blush."   It appears then that Job, though supported
by the knowledge of the resurrection, might, notwithstanding, very well
use the language in question.   To suppose that he might not, or that the
idea of a future state of rewards and punishments must have "kept him
from murmuring and complaining under his severe trials,"[*] is to expect
from him what perhaps *no Christian* under similar suffering, with all the
advantage of life and immortality brought fully to light, would be able to
exhibit.

Nor is there anything in the two remaining places, viz., xiv. 7—12, and
x. 21, 22, that might not have been uttered by one acquainted with the
doctrine of the resurrection, or that can be produced as evidence of " contrary belief."   The first of these passages has already been claimed as

---

* Introduction, vii. 10 , d).

proof of Job's faith in a coming חֲלִיפָה, or renovation, in which the body of
man should rise from the grave, as the grass of the field from the earth,
when the breath of Spring revisits its.   The last is a description of the
grave, or of the region of departed spirits. " I go," says Job, " whence I
shall not return, even to the land of darkness, and the shadow of death ; a
land of darkness, as darkness itself ; and of the shadow of death, without
any order, and where the light is as darkness."   It is not necessary to remark on the almost endlessly varied renderings by which this passage has
been distracted.   Suffice it to say, that it does not touch the doctrine of
the resurrection, either directly or by implication.   No possible construction can bring anything more out of the words, than that they present a
most doleful view of the state of separate existence, or of Sheol.   Many,
however, are of opinion that they do *not* refer to that state.   In any view,
the anguish and distraction of the speaker must be taken into account.
" The description," says Mr. Scott, " seems to be only intended for the
grave, and not to relate to the invisible world.   Coherency or exactness
in the discourse of one who spoke in the bitterness of his spirit, was not
to be expected ; yet Job certainly believed that there would be a future
state, and had some hope of happiness in it, though now exceedingly
clouded and discouraged.   But he here described the state of dead bodies
in the grave, as darkness and disorder ; and he used many repetitions,
meaning in general, that they know nothing of the vicissitudes of day and
night, or of the order established among the living ; and that men are cited
thither, and arraigned there, without respect to age, rank, or character."
Others, who understand the passage of the unseen world, regard it as descriptive of the " obscurity and uncertainty that hangs over it," of the
small amount of knowledge which men possess in regard to it.   There are
a multitude of questions bearing on the intermediate state, to which no
answer can be returned, and which men shall never be able to resolve, till
they find themselves in the midst of its disclosures.*

---

* " There are here a crowd of obscure and dislocated terms, admirably expressive of the
obscurity and uncertainty of the subject. What do we know of the state of separate
spirits? What do we know of the spiritual world? How do souls exist separate from
their respective bodies? Of what are they capable, and what is their employment? Who
can answer these questions? Perhaps nothing can be said much better of the state than
is here said, *a land of obscurity, like darkness*. . . . It is the *state of the dead!* The
place of separate spirits! It is *out of time, out of probation, beyond change or mutability.*
It is on the *confines of eternity.* But *what* is THIS? and where? *Eternity!* how can I
form any conception of thee? In thee there is no order, no bound, no substance, no pro-
gression, no change, no past, no present, no future! Thou art an indescribable something, to which there is no analogy in the compass of creation. Thou art infinity and
incomprehensibility to all finite beings. Thou art what living, I know not, and what I
must die to know; and even then I shall apprehend no more of thee than that thou art
ETERNITY."—*Dr. Adam Clarke, in loco.* The readers of John Foster will be reminded
by this passage of his frequent questionings in regard to the intermediate state, and his
inextinguishable desire to penetrate the gloom which he felt to hang over it. In a long
letter on the subject to the Rev. F. Clowes, the following passage occurs:—" But that
mysterious hereafter! We must submit to feel that we are in the dark, and have to walk
by faith in the mere general fact of a conscious and retributive state immediately after

Chap. xvii. 15, 16, is another of the same class of passages, though not cited on the list given above. It is supposed to carry in it more of gloom than could have been admitted into the mind of Job, had he known the cheering doctrine of the resurrection. Care should be taken, however, not to throw over it a gloomier sense than Job, under all his despondency, ever intended. The interpreters of Job are not unfrequently more gloomy than himself. His words are, "And where is now my hope? as for my hope, who shall see it? They, (my hopes,) shall go down to the bars of the pit, בדי שׁאל when our rest together is in the dust," i. e. of me and my hopes. But what hopes? Confessedly the hopes which he might have entertained of temporal deliverance or vindication. He felt he was about to descend into the grave. Already he claimed kindred with corruption and the worms, and should soon be beyond the reach of deliverance on earth. Therefore he had said to his friends in introducing this doleful complaint, "Do ye return and come now," i. e. reinvestigate my cause. Reconsider your judgment. It will soon be too late. The talons of the all-devouring grave will soon enclose me fast, and opportunity of reversal on your part be for ever gone! There is certainly nothing in the passages entitling one to say, that in Job's opinion the place of souls after death was "a gloomy and wretched world," which, "though not properly a place of punishment(!) yet was not a place of positive joy;" or that the certainty of his going to it, filled Job "not with joy, but with anguish and distress of heart." It is admitted that the hopes which Job abandoned were temporal hopes only, hopes of life and happiness here, and the whole of this lugubrious exposition is founded on an erroneous, or at all events very doubtful sense of the expression בדי שׁאל, according to which בדי means bars; and these suggest the idea of a prison, in which the souls of men after death were by Job supposed to be confined; and thus in a moment the deep gloom of a nether dungeon gathers around the text and its interpreter! The radical idea of the word is separated, disjoined, branched off, hence it signifies branches as of a tree, and limbs of the leviathian or crocodile, Ezek. xvii. 6; Job xli. 3, or 12. The other word שׁאל, meaning either the grave or the invisible state, is with great probability here explained of the former, since Job, immediately before, had been contemplating it. In this view Parkhurst renders the phrase "bars of the sepulchre;" others, adhering still more closely to the radical idea, "sepulchral cells branching off from the main subterraneous grot." But the rendering which at once gives the best sense, and is at the same time the most faithful, is that of "limbs or talons," according to which, in the true spirit of poetry, the grave is personified as a huge monster enclosing his prey within his deadly

death, revealed without definitions, illustrations, expansion into a field of varieties and specific forms. Still a contemplative spirit hovers with insuppressible inquisitiveness about the dark frontier beyond which it knows that wonderful realities are existing, realities of greater importance to it than the whole world on this side of that limit. We watch for some glimmer through any part of the solemn shade; but still are left to the faint, dubious resources of analogy, imagination, and conjecture."—Life and Correspondence of John Foster, vol. ii., page 369.

gripe.* On the whole there seems nothing in this passage that argues a belief on the part of Job, contrary to that of the resurrection; nor indeed any thing that countenances the idea that he had no more cheering views of the invisible state than the heroes of Virgil and Homer.

Another objection against the common interpretation of chap. xix. 25, 27, is drawn from the supposed fact that the doctrine of the resurrection is nowhere else introduced in the poem. It is not, it is said, referred to by Job, either before or after this memorable occasion; it is neither noticed by his friends, nor by Elihu; while in the speech of God himself, with which the controversy is closed and settled, the same neglect appears of a doctrine which would have cleared up all the difficulties that perplexed the Arabian sages. It will not be necessary to make many observations on an argument of this kind; for even admitting the truth of the representation on which it is built, the conclusion does not follow. It is quite possible that the resurrection may be introduced here, though elsewhere in the book there be no reference to it. On such a supposition it might be alleged, that the author had studied effect, by reserving, for one particular occasion and place, the sublime doctrine of the resurrection, and the equally sublime expression he has given to it. Such a mode of presenting a subject of this nature is in perfect keeping with the poetical usage, in which the "matter is disposed, (to use the language of an eminent living critic,) according to the taste and choice of the writer; and that a more vivid impression might be made, by presenting a capital circumstance with its brightness and force collected into one point, than would be produced if it were dispersed through the general composition." † But the representation in the objection is not according to fact. Job *does* elsewhere introduce the resurrection. The most competent judges find the doctrine in chap. xiv. 7—12, expressed with a distinctness and force which no language could have surpassed. There are, moreover, in the speeches of Job, frequent allusions to the future state of retribution, as in chap. xxi. 27, 30; xxvii. 8, 9; xxx. 1—4, 13. True indeed, the friends of Job make scarcely any allusion to this doctrine, yet there is no evidence that they denied it; nay, in one of the passages quoted above, viz., xxi. 27, 30, Job ascribes to them the same belief entertained by himself. That they should not have recurred to the doctrine of the resurrection after Job's famous appeal, may appear wonderful, but it cannot be regarded as of any great consequence in the present controversy, unless it can be proved that Job must have alleged the resurrection, if he introduced it at all, as a solution of a

* "The image is peculiarly bold, and true to the general character under which the grave is presented to us in the figurative language of sacred poetry—as a monster ever greedy to devour; with horrid jaws wide gaping for his prey; and in the passage before us, with limbs in unison with his jaws, and ready to seize hold of the victims allotted to him, with a strength and violence from which none can extricate themselves. The common rendering of *fulcra, vectes,* or *bars,* as of a prison, is as unnecessary a departure from the proper figure, as it is from the primary meaning of the original term."—*Dr. Good.*

† Dr. J. Pye Smith.

particular difficulty in regard to the arrangements of providence, or that his friends must so have understood him. There is no evidence of either of these things. Job seems to have intended by a solemn appeal to convince his friends of his innocence, and in this light they understood him, and continued the controversy as before. The same remarks apply to the omission on the part of *Elihu*. Nor can it appear unaccountable that *God* should not introduce the doctrine of the resurrection. That doctrine, according to the views of some, was alone wanting to solve the entire difficulty; but the Almighty has his own way of solving the question. He attests the innocence of Job, and in doing so, for ever establishes the position that great sufferings are not always evidence of corresponding guilt. He does not indeed condescend to *vindicate* his providence, but asserts his sovereignty, and claims the submission of his creatures; and thus while the *real* question in dispute is solved by the *dictate* of the Almighty, a practical lesson is furnished of the highest moment, and of equal importance to men in all ages.

The last objection requiring notice is derived from the supposed inconsistency between the common opinion, and the amount of knowledge that obtained in Job's time, regarding the resurrection and the future world. This objection may be dealt with precisely in the same way with the preceding one. Admitting it to be true that Job on this grand occasion uttered sentiments in advance of his times, if we suppose him to refer to the resurrection of the dead; it will not follow that such reference is therefore impossible, or even improbable. It must first be proved that when he exclaimed, "Oh that my words were now written! oh that they were printed in a book, that they were graven with an iron pen and lead in the rock for ever,"—he was not under *immediate inspiration*, or that the doctrine and the occasion were alike unworthy of this. It must be proved too that saints and prophets have never uttered any thing beyond the general knowledge of their times, or that the morning twilight of revelation has never for a moment been lit up with a gleam, that partook of the character of its noon-day splendours. But the patriarchal knowledge of a future state may not have been so scanty as some imagine. The doctrine of the resurrection was involved in the covenant made with Abraham, by which Jehovah engaged to be "a God unto him and his seed after him."* Under this covenant name of the "God of Abraham," the Almighty made himself known to Moses at the bush.† And our Lord has thus expounded it: "Now that the dead are raised, even Moses shewed at the bush, when he called the Lord the God of Abraham, and the God of Isaac, and the God of Jacob. For he is not a God of the dead but of the living; for all live unto him."‡ There is no evading of the fact that the covenant name is cited in proof of the resurrection of the body. The resurrection was the subject in dispute, and the Scribes on the occasion held the argument from Moses decisive, while the objectors were silenced. The *bearing* of the

---

* Gen. xvii. 7.   † Exod. iii. 6.   ‡ Luke xx. 37, 38.

argument may be differently explained; it may be said that the covenant relation extends to the entire person, to the body as well as to the soul, or that the immortality of the soul was so connected in the minds of the Jews with the resurrection of the body, that the one doctrine involved the other. But the fact is the same. The covenant name *was* produced in proof of the resurrection. Nor were the minds of the patriarchs occupied by so gloomy views of the state after death as is sometimes supposed. They "confessed that they were strangers and pilgrims on the earth. They that say such things declare plainly that they seek a country. And truly if they had been mindful of that country from whence they came out, they might have had opportunity to have returned. But now they desire a better country, that is an heavenly : wherefore God is not ashamed to be called their God: for he hath prepared for them a city."* The writer of the epistle to the Hebrews was evidently unacquainted with that part of the patriarchal belief, according to which the patriarchs regarded leaving this world and entering on the next, as a serious calamity. There is no hint here of intermediate gloom. " If we may believe the papists," says Dr. Owen, " they (the patriarchs) were deceived in their expectation. For whereas the apostle teacheth, that when they died, they looked to go to heaven, they affirm that they came short of it, and fell into a *limbus* they know not where."

Such are the principal objections against the resurrection view of Job's sublime testimony. None of them is fatal to it, or indeed of very great weight ; certainly not of so great weight as to justify the assertion that *feeling* and not *judgment*, *piety* and not *argument*, have originated it. On the other hand, the opposite view is inconsistent with Job's uniform despair of such temporal deliverance or vindication as he ultimately enjoyed; vi. 8—11; ix. 21—24; x. 15 — 22; xxx. 16—23. It is inconsistent with the principles which Job maintained regarding what have been called the unequal distributions of providence. At all events, maintaining these principles he could have no assurance that *he* any more than other

* Heb. xi. 13, 16. It was at first intended to extend this inquiry so far as to embrace a very brief view of the principal texts that cast light on the amount of knowledge that obtained in patriarchal times, and in subsequent times, under the ancient economy, on the doctrine of the resurrection and the intermediate state. This must have led to an examination of the views of David and Hezekiah, noticed in the opening of this preface, in the course of which it would have been attempted to shew that Ps. vi. 5, and Isa. xxxviii. 11, 18, 19, are to be interpreted on very nearly the same principles with the gloomy passages in Job.—David and Hezekiah felt that death closed all opportunity of praising God, or serving man on earth; and that, therefore, it was painful to leave the world without having accomplished the good they intended. If this be thought an improbable view of their state of feeling, the same liberty may be allowed them, that in certain moods of mind is taken by good Christians, when they speak of death in somewhat mournful strains, as shutting them out from the light of the sun and the society of friends, &c. This is *but one side of their view*: ask them for the other, and they will reply in the language of the Psalmist, " Thou shalt guide me with thy counsel, and *afterwards receive me to glory*," Ps. lxxiii. 24 The whole Psalm is instructive, as shewing the Psalmist's views of the future world.—The length to which this preface has already extended, however, renders it necessary to abandon the design originally entertained.

righteous men would be vindicated and recompenced on earth, unless he obtained it by express revelation—a supposition not in itself improbable, but which cannot consistently be resorted to by those who urge the objections that have just been reviewed, since the same supposition, on the other side, would at once account for Job's views being beyond those of his age. Finally, when the grandeur and solemnity of its introduction is taken into account, along with the obvious—confessedly obvious—sense of the words, and the general consent of interpreters—this much disputed passage will appear to be most consistently explained of that glorious occasion, when all that are in their graves shall hear the voice of the Son of man, and shall come forth; they that have done good, unto the resurrection of life; and they that have done evil, unto the resurrection of damnation!* May the writer and reader of these pages alike see God on that day. as Job believed he should see him, not estranged, but his Friend and Redeemer!

* John v. 28; Dan. xii. 2.

THE BOOK OF JOB.

INTRODUCTION.

In reference to no part of the Scriptures have so many questions arisen as to the Book of Job. The time of its composition ; the author ; the country where the scene was laid ; the question whether Job was a real person ; the nature and design of the poem ; have been points on which a great variety of opinion has been entertained among expositors, and on which different views still prevail. It is important, in order to a correct understanding of the Book, that all the light should be thrown on these subjects which can be ; and though amidst the variety of opinion which prevails among men of the highest distinction in learning absolute certainty cannot be hoped for, yet such advances have been made in the investigation that on some of these points we may arrive to a high degree of probability.

§ 1. *The question whether Job was a real person.*

The first question which presents itself in the examination of the Book is, whether Job had a real existence. This has been doubted on such grounds as the following. (1.) The Book has been supposed by some to have every mark of an allegory. Allegories and parables, it is said, are not uncommon in the Scriptures where *a case is supposed,* and then the narrative proceeds as if it were real. Such an instance, it has been maintained, occurs here, in which the author of the poem designed to illustrate important truths, but instead of stating them in an abstract form, chose to present them in the more graphic and interesting form of a supposed case—in which we are led to sympathize with a sufferer ; to see the ground of the difficulty in the question under discussion in a more affecting manner than could be presented in an abstract form ; and where the argument has all to interest the mind which one has when occurring in real life. (2.) It has been maintained that some of the transactions in the Book *must* have been of this character, or are such as could not have actually occurred. Particularly it has been said that the account of the interview of Jehovah (chap. i. 6—12 ; ii. 1—7) must be regarded merely as a supposed case, it being in the highest degree improbable that such an interview would occur, and such a conversation be held. (3.) The same conclusion has been drawn from the artificial character of the statements about the possessions of Job, both before and after his trials—statements which appear as if the case were merely supposed, and which would not be likely to occur in reality. Thus we have only round numbers mentioned in enumerating his possessions—as seven thousand sheep, three thousand camels, five hundred yoke of oxen, and five hundred she-asses. So, also, there is something artificial in the manner in which the sacred numbers *seven* and *three* are used. He had *seven* thousand sheep, *seven* sons—both before and after his trials ; his *three* friends came and sat down *seven* days and *seven* nights without saying a word to condole with him (chap. ii. 13) ; and both before and after his trials he had *three* daughters. The same artificial and parabolical appearance, it is said, is seen in the fact that after his recovery his possessions were exactly *doubled*, and he had again in his old age exactly the same number of *seven* sons and *three* daughters which he had before his afflictions. (4.) That the whole narration is allegorical or parabolical has been further argued from the conduct of the friends of Job. Their sitting down seven days and seven nights without saying any thing, when they had come expressly to condole with him, it is said, is a wholly improbable circumstance, and looks as if the whole were a supposed case. (5.) The same thing has been inferred from the manner in which the Book is written. It is of the highest order of poetry. The speeches are most elaborate ; are filled with accurate and carefully prepared argument ; are arranged with great care ; are expressed in the most sententious manner ; embody the results of long and careful observation, and are wholly unlike what would be uttered in unpremeditated and extemporary debate. No men, it is said, *talk* in this manner ; nor can it be supposed that beautiful poetry and sublime argument, such as abound in this book, ever fell in animated debate from the lips of men. See Eichhorn, Einleitung in das Alte Tes. V. Band. 129—131. From considerations such as these the historical character of the Book has been doubted, and the whole has been regarded as *a supposed case* designed to illustrate the great question which the author of the poem proposed to examine.

It is important, therefore, to inquire what reasons there are for believing that such a person as Job lived, and how far the transactions referred to in the Book are to be regarded as historically true.

(1.) The fact of his existence is expressly declared, and the narrative has all the appearance of being a simple record of an actual occurrence. The first two chapters of the Book, and a part of the last chapter, are simple historical records. The remainder of the Book is indeed poetic, but these portions have none of the characteristics of poetry. There are not to be found in the Bible more simple and plain historical statements than these ; and there are none which, in themselves considered, might not be as properly set aside as allegorical. This fact should be regarded as decisive, unless there is some reason which does not appear on the face of the narrative for regarding it as allegorical.

(2.) The account of the existence of such a man is regarded as historically true by the inspired writers of the Scriptures. Thus in Eze. xiv. 14, God says, " Though these three men, Noah, Daniel, and Job, were in it [the land], they should deliver but their own souls by their righteousness, saith the Lord God." Comp. ver. 16, 20, of the same chapter. Here Job is referred to as a real character as distinctly as Noah and Daniel, and all the circumstances are just such as they would be on the supposition that he had a real existence. They are alike spoken of as real " men ;" as having souls —" they should deliver *but their own souls* by their own righteousness ;" as having sons and daughters—" they shall deliver neither sons nor daughters, they only shall be delivered " (ver. 16), and are in all respects mentioned alike as real characters. Of the historic fact that there were such men as Noah and Daniel there can be no doubt, and it is evident that Ezekiel as certainly regarded Job as a real character as he did either of the others. A parallel passage, which will illustrate this, occurs in Jer. xv. 1 : " Then said the Lord unto me, Though Moses and Samuel stood before me, yet my mind could not be towards this people." Here Moses and Samuel are spoken of as real characters, and there is no doubt of their having existed. Yet they are mentioned in the same manner as Job is in the passage in Ezekiel. In either case it is incredible that a reference should have been made to a fictitious character. The appeal is one that could have been made only to a real character, and there can be no reasonable doubt that Ezekiel regarded Job as having really existed ; or rather, since it is *God* who speaks and not Ezekiel, that *he* speaks of Job as having actually existed. The same thing is evident from a reference to Job by the apostle James : "Ye have heard of the patience of Job, and have seen the end of the Lord ; that the Lord is very pitiful and of tender mercy" (chap. v. 11) ; that is, the happy issue to which the Lord brought all his trials, showing that he was pitiful to those in affliction, and of great mercy. There can be no doubt that there is reference here to the sufferings of a *real* man, as there is to the *real* compassion which the Lord shows to one in great trials. It is incredible that this sacred writer should have appealed in this instance to the case of one whom *he* regarded as a fictitious character ; and if the views of Ezekiel and James are to be relied on, there can be no doubt that Job had a real existence. Ezekiel mentions him just as he does Noah and Daniel, and James mentions him just as he does Elijah (chap. v. 17) ; and so far as this historical record goes there is the same evidence of the actual existence of the one as of the other.

(3.) The specifications of places and names in the Book are not such as would occur in an allegory. Had it been merely a "supposed case," to illustrate some great truth, these specifications would have been unnecessary, and would not have occurred. In the acknowledged parables of the Scripture, there are seldom any very minute specifications of names and places. Thus, in the parable of the prodigal son, neither the name of the father, nor of the sons, nor of the place where the scene was laid, is mentioned. So of the nobleman who went to receive a kingdom ; the unjust steward ; the ten virgins, and of numerous others. But here we have distinct specifications of a great number of things which are in no way necessary to illustrate the main truth in the poem. Thus we have not only the name of the sufferer, but the place of his residence mentioned, as if it were well known. We have the names of his friends, and the places of their residence mentioned— "Eliphaz the *Temanite*," and "Bildad the *Shuhite*," and "Zophar the *Naamathite*," and Elihu "the son of Barachel the *Buzite*, of the kindred of Ram." Why are the places of residence of these persons mentioned unless it be meant to intimate that they were real persons, and not allegorical characters ? In like manner we have express mention of the Sabeans and the Chaldeans—specifications wholly unnecessary if not improbable if the work is an allegory. The single word "robbers" would have answered all the purpose, and would have been such as an inspired writer would have used unless the transaction were real, for an inspired writer would not have charged this offence on any class of men, thus holding them up to lasting reproach, unless an event of this kind had actually occurred. When the Saviour, in the parable of the good Samaritan, mentions a robbery that occurred between Jerusalem and Jericho, the word "thieves," or more properly *robbers*, is the only word used. No names are mentioned, nor is any *class* of men referred to, who would *by* such a mention of the name be held up to infamy. Thus also we have the particular statement respecting the feasting of the sons and daughters of Job ; his sending for and admonishing them ; his offering up special sacrifices on their behalf ; the account of the destruction of the oxen, the sheep, the camels, and the house where the sons and daughters of Job were —all statements of circumstances which would not be likely to occur in an allegory. They are such *particular* statements as we expect to find respecting the real transactions, and they bear on the face of them the simple impression of truth. This is not the kind of information which we look for in a parable. In the parable of the rich man and Lazarus, almost the only one spoken by the Saviour where a *name* is mentioned, we have not

that of the rich man; and though the name *Lazarus* is mentioned, yet that
is all. We have no account of his family, of his place of residence, of his
genealogy, of the time when he lived; and the name itself is so common that
it would be impossible even to suspect whom the Saviour had in his eye, if
he had any real individual at all. Far different is this in the account of Job.
It is true that in a romance, or in an extended allegory like the Pilgrim's
Progress, we expect a detailed statement of names and places; but there is
no evidence that there is any such extended fictitious narrative in the Bible,
and unless the Book of Job be one there is no such extended allegory.

(4.) The objections urged against this view are not such as to destroy the
positive proof of the reality of the existence of Job. The objections which
have been urged against the historical truth of the narrative, and which have
already been in part alluded to, are principally the following.

The first is, the account of the interview between God and Satan in chap.
i. and ii. It is alleged that this is so improbable a transaction as to throw
an air of fiction over all the historical statements of the book. In reply to
this, it may be observed, first, that even if this were not to be regarded as
a literal transaction, it does not prove that no such man as Job lived, and
that the transactions in regard to *him* were not real. He might have had
an existence, and been stripped of his possessions, and subjected to these
long and painful trials of his fidelity, even if this *were* a poetic ornament, or
merely a figurative representation. But, secondly, it is impossible to *prove*
that no such transaction occurred. The existence of such a being as Satan
is everywhere recognized in the Scriptures; the account which is here given
of his character accords entirely with the uniform representation of him; he
exerts no power over Job which is not expressly conceded to him; and it is
impossible to prove that he does not even now perform the same things in
the trial of good men, which it is said that he did in the case of Job. And
even if it be admitted that there is somewhat of poetic statement in the
form in which he is introduced, still this does not render the main account
improbable and absurd. The Bible, from the necessity of the case, abounds
with representations of this sort; and when it is said that God "speaks" to
men, that he conversed with Adam, that he spake to the serpent (Gen. iii.),
we are not necessarily to suppose that all this is strictly literal, nor does the
fact that it is *not* strictly literal invalidate the main facts. There were *results*, or there was a series of FACTS following, *as if* this had been literally
true; see Notes on chap. i. 6–12.

A second objection to the historical truth of the transactions recorded in
the book is, the poetic character of the work, and the strong improbability
that addresses of this kind should ever have been made in the manner here
represented. See Eichhorn, Einleit. v. 123, 124. They are of the highest
order of poetry; they partake not at all of the nature of extemporaneous
effusions; they indicate profound and close thinking, and are such as must
have required much time to have prepared them. Especially it is said that
it is in the highest degree improbable that Job, in the anguish of his body
and mind, should have been capable of giving utterance to poetry and argument of this highly finished character. In regard to this objection, it may
be observed, (1.) that even if this were so, and it were to be supposed that
the arguments of the various speakers have a poetic character, and were in
reality never uttered in the form in which we now have them, still this would
not invalidate the evidence which exists of the historic truth of the facts
stated about the existence and trials of Job. It might be true that he lived
and suffered in this manner, and that a discussion of this character actually
occurred, and that substantially these arguments were advanced, though
they were afterwards wrought by Job himself or by some other hand into
the poetic form in which we now have them. Job himself lived after his
trials one hundred and forty years, and, in itself considered, there is no

improbability in the supposition, that when restored to the vigorous use of his powers, and in the leisure which he enjoyed, he should have thought it worthy to present the argument which he once held on this great subject in a more perfect form, and to give to it a more poetic cast. In this case, the main historic truth would be retained, and the real argument would in fact be stated—though in a form more worthy of preservation than could be expected to fall extemporaneously from the lips of the speakers. But (2.) all the difficulty may be removed by a supposition which is entirely in accordance with the character of the book and the nature of the case. It is, that the several speeches succeeded each other at such intervals as gave full time for reflection, and for carefully framing the argument. There is no evidence that the whole argument was gone through with *at one sitting;* there are no proofs that one speech followed immediately on another, or that a sufficient interval of time may not have elapsed to give opportunity for preparation to meet the views which had been suggested by the previous speaker. Every thing in the book bears the marks of the most careful deliberation, and is as free as possible from the hurry and bustle of an extemporaneous debate. The sufferings of Job were evidently of a protracted nature. His friends sat down " seven days and seven nights" in silence before they said any thing to him. The whole subject of the debate seems to be arranged with most systematic care and regularity. The speakers succeed each other in regular order in a *series* of arguments—in each of these series following the same method, and no one of them out of his place. No one is ever interrupted while speaking; and no matter how keen and sarcastic his invectives, how torturing his reproaches, how bold or blasphemous what he said was thought to be, he is patiently heard till he has said all that he designed to say; and then all that he said is carefully weighed and considered in the reply. All this looks as if there might have been ample time to arrange the reply before it was uttered, and this supposition, of course, would relieve all the force of this objection. If this be so, then there is no more ground of objection against the supposition that these things were spoken, as it is said they were, than there is about the genuineness of the poems of the Grecian Rhapsodists, composed with a view to public recitation, or to the Iliad of Homer or the History of Herodotus, both of which, after they were composed, were recited publicly by their authors at Athens. No one can *prove* certainly that the several persons named in the book— Job, Eliphaz, Bildad, Zophar, and Elihu—were incompetent to compose the speeches which are severally assigned to them, or that all the time necessary for such a composition was not taken by them. Unless this can be done, the objection of its improbability, so confidently urged by Eichhorn (Einleit. v. 123, *seq.*), and defended by Noyes (Intro. pp. xx. xxi.), where he says that " the supposition that so beautiful and harmonious a whole, every part of which bears the stamp of the highest genius, was the casual production of a man brought to the gates of the grave by a loathsome disease, of three or four friends who had come to comfort him in his affliction, all of them expressing their thoughts in poetical and measured language ; that the Deity was actually heard to speak half an hour in the midst of a violent storm; and that the consultations in the heavenly world were actual occurrences, is too extravagant to need refutation,'' is an objection really of little force.

A third objection has been derived from the *round* and *doubled* numbers which occur in the book, and the artificial character which the whole narrative seems to assume on that account. It is alleged that this is wholly an unusual and improbable occurrence ; and that the whole statement appears *as if* it were a fictitious narrative. Thus Job's possessions of oxen and camels and sheep are expressed in round numbers; one part of these is exactly the double of another; and what is more remarkable still, all these are exactly *doubled* on his restoration to health. He had the same number of sons and the same number of daughters after his trial which he had before, and the number of each was what was esteemed among the Hebrews as a sacred number.—In regard to this objection, we may observe, (1.) That as to the *round* numbers, this is no more than what constantly occurs in historical statements. Nothing is more common in the enumeration of armies, of the people of a country, or of herds and flocks, than such statements. (2.) In regard to the fact that the possessions of Job are said to have been exactly "doubled" after his recovery from his calamities, it is not necessary to suppose that this was in all respects *literally* true. Nothing forbids us to suppose that, from the gifts of friends and other causes, the possessions of Job came so near to being just twice what they were before his trials, as to justify this general statement. In the statement itself, there is nothing improbable. Job lived an hundred and forty years after his trials. If he had then the same measure of prosperity which he had before, and with the assistance of his friends to enable him to *begin* life again, there is no improbability in the supposition that these possessions would be doubled.

These are substantially all the objections which have been urged against the historical character of the book, and if they are not well founded, then it follows that it should be regarded as historically true that such a man actually lived, and that he passed through the trials which are here described. How far, if at all, the license of poetry has been employed in the composition of the book will be considered more particularly in another part of this Introduction, § 5. A more extended statement of these objections, and a refutation of them, may be found in the following works:—Warburton's Divine Legation of Moses, Vol. V. p. 298, seq., ed. 8vo, London, 1811; Prof. Lee on Job, Intro. § 11; and Magee on Atonement and Sacrifice, p. 212, seq., ed. New-York, 1813. It should be said, however, that not a few writers admit that such a man as Job lived, and that the book has an historical basis, while they regard the work itself as in the main poetic. In the view of such critics, the poet, in order to illustrate the great truth which he proposed to consider, made use of a tradition respecting the sufferings of a well-known person of distinction, and gave to the whole argument the high poetic cast which it has now. This supposition is in accordance with the methods frequently adopted by epic and tragic poets, and which is commonly followed by writers of romance. This is the opinion of Eichhorn, Einleitung V. § 638.

§ 2. *The question where Job lived.*

In chapter i. 1, it is said that Job dwelt "in the land of Uz." The only question, then, to be settled in ascertaining where he lived, is, if possible, to determine where this place was. From the manner in which the record is made ("*the land* of Uz") it would seem probable that this was a region of country of some considerable extent, and also that it derived its name from some man of that name who had settled there. The word Uz (עוּץ), according to Gesenius, means a light, sandy soil; and if the name was given to the country with reference to this quality of the soil, it would be natural to fix on some region remarkable for its barrenness—a waste place or a desert. Gesenius supposes that Uz was in the northern part of Arabia Deserta—a place lying between Palestine and the Euphrates, called by Ptolemy Αἰσῖται (*Aisitai*). This opinion is defended by Rosenmüller (Proleg.).; and is adopted by Spanheim, Bochart, Lee, Umbreit, Noyes, and the authors of the Universal History. Dr. Good supposes that the Uz here referred to was in Arabia Petræa, on the south-western coast of the Dead sea, and that Job and all his friends referred to in the poem were Idumeans. Introductory Dissertation, § 1, pp. vii—xii. Eichhorn also supposes that the scene is laid in Idumea, and that the author of the poem shows that he had a particular acquaintance with the history, customs, and productions of

Egypt. Einleit. § 638. Bochart (in Phaleg et Canaan), Michaelis (Spicileg. Geog. Hebræo.), and Ilgen (Jobi, Antiquis. carminis Heb. natura et
indoles, p. 91), suppose that the place of his residence was the valley of
Guta near Damascus, regarded as the most beautiful of the four Paradises
of the Arabians. For a description of this valley, see Eichhorn, Einleit. V.
s. 134. The word ‎עוּץ‎ (*Uz*) occurs only in the following places in the Hebrew Bible :—Gen. x. 23; xxii. 21; xxxvi. 28, and 1 Chron. i. 17, 42, in each
of which places it is the name of a man ; and in Jer. xxv. 20 ; Lam. iv. 21,
and in Job i. 1, where it is applied to a country. The only circumstances
which furnish any probability in regard to the place where Job lived, are
the following.

(1.) Those which enable us to determine with some probability where *the
family* of Uz was settled, who not improbably gave his name to the
country—as Sheba, and Seba, and Tema, and Cush, and Misraim, and
others, did to the countries where they settled. In Gen. x. 23, Uz (‎עוּץ‎),
is mentioned as a grandson of Shem. In Gen. xxii. 21, an *Uz* (English
Bible *Huz*) is mentioned as the son of Nahor, brother of Abraham, undoubtedly a different person from the one mentioned in Gen. x. 23. . In Gen.
xxxvi. 28, an individual of this name is mentioned among the descendants of
Esau. In 1 Chron. i. 17, the name occurs among the " sons of Shem ;"
and in ver. 42, of the same chapter, the same name occurs among the descendants of Esau. So far, therefore, as the *name* is concerned, it may
have been derived from one of the family of Shem, or from one who was a
contemporary with Abraham, or from a somewhat remote descendant of
Esau. It will be seen in the course of this Introduction, that there is a
strong improbability that the name was given to the country because it was
settled by either of the two latter, as such a supposition would bring down
the time when Job lived to a later period than the circumstances recorded
in his history will allow, and it is therefore probable that the name was conferred in honour of the grandson of Shem. This fact, of itself, will do *something* to determine the place. Shem lived in Asia, and we shall find that
the settlements of his descendants originally occupied the country somewhere in the vicinity of the Euphrates ; Gen. x. 21—30. In Gen. x. 23,
Uz is mentioned as one of the sons of *Aram*, who gave name to the country
known as *Aramea*, or *Syria*, and from whom the Arameans descended. Their
original residence, it is supposed, was near the river Kir, or Cyrus, whence
they were brought, at some period now unknown, by a deliverance resembling that of the children of Israel from Egypt, and placed in the regions of
Syria ; see Amos ix. 7. The inhabitants of Syria and Mesopotamia
are always called by Moses *Arameus :* as they had their seat in and near
Mesopotamia, it is probable that *Uz* was located also not far from that
region. We should, therefore, naturally be led to look for the country of
Uz somewhere in that vicinity. In Gen. x. 30, it is further said of the sons of
Shem, that " their dwelling was from Mesha, as thou goest unto Sephar, *a
mount of the East ;*" a statement which corresponds with what is said of
Job himself, that he was " the greatest of all the men *of the East*" (chap. i.
3), manifestly implying that he was an inhabitant of the country so called.
Various opinions have been entertained of the places where Mesha and Sephar were. The opinion of Michaelis is the most probable (Spicileg. pt. 11,
p. 214), " that Mesha is the region around Passora, which the later Syrians
called *Maishon*, and the Greeks *Mesene*. Under these names they included
the country on the Euphrates and the Tigris, between Seleucia and the
Persian Gulf. Abulfeda mentions in this region two cities not far from
Passora, called *Maisan*, and *Mushan*. Here, then, was probably the north-
eastern border of the district inhabited by the Joktanites. The name of the
opposite limit, *Sephar*, signifies in the Chaldee *shore* or *coast*, and is probably the western part of Yemen, along the Arabian Gulf, now called by the

Arabs Tehâmah. The range of high and mountainous country between these
two borders, Moses calls "the Mount of the East," or eastern mountains.
It is also called by the Arabs *Djebal*, i. e. *mountains*, to the present day.
See Rosenmüller's Alterthumskunde, iii. 163, 164.

The supposition that some portion of this region is denoted by the country
where Uz settled, and is the place where Job resided is strengthened by the
fact, that many of the persons and tribes mentioned in the book resided in this
vicinity. Thus it is probable that Eliphaz the Temanite had his residence
there ; see Notes on chap. ii. 11. The Sabeans probably dwelt not very remote from that region (Notes on chap. i. 15); the Chaldeans we know had their
residence there (Notes, chap. i. 17), and this supposition will agree well with
what is said of the tornado that came from the "wilderness," or desert ; see
Notes on chap. i. 19. The residence of Job was so near to the Chaldeans
and the Sabeans that he could be reached in their usual predatory excursions ; a fact that better accords with the supposition that his residence was
in some part of Arabia Deserta, than that it was in Idumea.

(2.) This country is referred to in two places by Jeremiah, which may
serve to aid us in determining its location ; Lam. iv. 21.

> " Rejoice and be glad, O daughter of Edom,
> That dwellest in the land of Uz ;
> The cup shall pass through unto thee :
> Thou shalt be drunken, and shalt make thyself naked."

At first view, perhaps, this passage would indicate that the land of Uz was a
part of Edom, yet it more properly indicates that the land of Uz was not a
part of that land, but that the Edomites or Idumeans had gained possession
of a country which did not originally belong to them. Thus the prophet
speaks of the " daughter of Edom," not as dwelling in her own country properly, but as dwelling " in the land of Uz "—in a foreign country, of which
she had somehow obtained possession. The country of Edom, properly, was
Mount Seir and the vicinity, south of the Dead sea ; but it is known that
the Edomites subsequently extended their boundaries, and that at one period
Bozrah, on the east of the Dead sea, in the country of Moab, was their
capital ; see the Analysis of chap. xxxiv. of Isaiah, and Notes on Isa. xxxiv.
6. It is highly probable that Jeremiah refers to the period when the Idumeans, having secured these conquests, and made this foreign city their
capital, is represented as dwelling there. If so, according to this passage in
Lamentations, we should naturally look for the land of Uz somewhere in the
countries to which the conquests of the Edomites extended—and these conquests were chiefly to the *east* of their own land. A similar conclusion will
be derived from the other place where the name occurs in Jeremiah. It is
in chap. xxv. 20, seq. " And all the mingled people, *and all the kings of the
land of Uz*, and all the kings of the land of the Philistines, and Askelon, and
Azzah, and Ekron, and the remnant of Ashdod, *and Edom*, and Moab, and
the children of Ammon," &c. Two things are apparent here. One is, that
the country of Uz was distinct from the land of Edom, since they are mentioned as separate nations ; the other is, that it was a country of some considerable extent, since it is mentioned as being under several "kings."
There is, indeed, in this reference to it no allusion to its situation ; but it is
mentioned as being in the time of Jeremiah well known.

(3.) The same thing is evident from the manner in which the residence of
Job is spoken of in chap. i. 3. He is there said to have been the "greatest
of all *the men of the east.*" This implies that his residence was in the land
which was known familiarly as the country of the East. It is true, indeed,
that we have not yet determined where the poem was composed, and of
course do not know precisely what the author would understand by this phrase,
but the expression has a common signification in the Scriptures, as denoting

the country east of Palestine. The land of Idumea, however, was directly south ; and we are, therefore, naturally led to look to some other place as the land of Uz ; comp. Notes on chap. i. 3. The expression " the East," as used in the Bible, would in no instance naturally lead us to look to Idumea.

(4.) The LXX render the word *Uz* in chap. i. 1. by *Ασίτις*, *Asitis*—a word which seems to have been formed from the Hebrew עוץ *Utz*, or *Uz*. Of course, their translation gives no intimation of the place referred to. But Ptolemy (Geog. Lib. v.) speaks of a tribe or nation in the neighbourhood of Babylon, whom he calls *Αὐσῖται*, *Ausitæ* (or as it was perhaps written *Αἰσῖται*), the same word which is used by the LXX in rendering the word Uz. These people are placed by Ptolemy in the neighbourhood of the Cauchebeni—*ὑπὸ μὲν τοῖς* Καυχαβηνοις—and he speaks of them as separated from Chaldea by a ridge of mountains. See Rosenm. Proleg. p. 27. This location would place Job so near to the Chaldeans, that the account of their making an excursion into his country (chap. i. 17) would be entirely probable.—It may be added, also, that in the same neighbourhood we find a town called *Sabas* (Σάβας) in Diodorus Sic. Lib. iii. § 46. Prof. Lee, p. 32. These circumstances render it probable that the residence of the Patriarch was west of Chaldea, and somewhere in the northern part of Arabia Deserta, between Palestine, Idumea, and the Euphrates.

(5.) The monuments and memorials of Job still preserved or referred to in the East, may be adduced as some slight evidence of the fact that such a man as Job lived, and as an indication of the region in which he resided. It is true that they depend on mere tradition ; but monuments are not erected to the memory of any who are not *supposed* to have had an existence, and traditions usually have some basis in reality. Arabian writers always make mention of Job as a real person, and his pretended grave is shown in the East to this day. It is shown indeed in six different places : but this is no evidence that all that is said of the existence of such a man is fabulous, any more than the fact that seven cities contended for the honour of the birth of Homer is an evidence that there was no such man. The most celebrated tomb of this kind is that of the Trachonitis, towards the springs of the Jordan. It is situated between the cities still bearing the names of Teman, Shuah, and Naama—(Wemyss) ; though there is every reason to believe that these names have been given rather with reference to the fact that that was supposed to be his residence, than that they were the names of the places referred to in the book of Job. One of these tombs was shown to Niebuhr. He says (Reisebeschreib, i. 466), " Two or three hours east of Saada is a great mosque, in which, according to the opinion of the Arabs who reside there, the sufferer Job lies buried." " On the eastern limits of Arabia, they showed me the grave of Job, close to the Euphrates, and near the Helleh, one hour south from Babylon." It is of importance to remark here only that all of these tombs are *without* the limits of Idumea. Among the Arabians there are numerous traditions respecting Job, many of them indeed stories that are entirely ridiculous, but all showing the firm belief prevalent in Arabia that there was such a man. See Sale's Koran, vol. ii. pp. 174, 322 ; Magee on Atonement and Sacrifice, pp. 366, 367 ; and D'Herbelot, Bibli. Orient. tom. i. pp. 75, 76, 432, 438, as quoted by Magee.

(6.) The present belief of the Arabians may be referred to as corroborating the results to which we have approximated in this inquiry, that the residence of Job was not in Idumea, but was in some part of Arabia Deserta, lying between Palestine and the Euphrates. The Rev. Eli Smith stated to me (Nov. 1840) that there was still a place in the Houran called by the Arabians, *Uz;* and that there is a tradition among them that that was the residence of Job. It is north-east of Bozrah. Bozrah was once the capital of Idumea (Notes on Isa. xxxiv. 6), though it was situated without the limits of their natural territory. If this tradition is well founded, then Job was not probably an Idumean. There is nothing that renders the tradition improbable, and the course of the investigation conducts us, with a high degree of probability, to the conclusion that this was the residence of Job. On the residence of Job and his friends, consult also Abrahami Peritsol Itinera Mundi, in Ugolin, Thes. Sac. vii. pp. 103–106.

§ 3. The time when Job lived.

There has been quite as much uncertainty in regard to the *time* when Job lived, as there has been in regard to the place where.—It should be observed here, that this question is not necessarily connected with the inquiry when the book was composed, and will not be materially affected, whether we suppose it to have been composed by Job himself, by Moses, or by a later writer. Whenever the book was composed, if at a later period than that in which the patriarch lived, the author would naturally conceal the marks of his own time, by referring only to such customs and opinions as prevailed in the age when the events were supposed to have occurred.

On this question, we cannot hope to arrive at absolute certainty. It is remarkable that neither the genealogical record of the family of Job nor that of his three friends is given. The only record of the kind occurring in the book, is that of Elihu (chap. xxxii. 2), and this is so slight as to furnish but little assistance in determining when he lived. The only circumstances which occur in regard to this question, are the following; and they will serve to settle the question with sufficient probability, as it is a question on which no important results can depend.

(1.) The age of Job. According to this, the time when he lived, would occur somewhere between the age of Terah, the father of Abraham, and Jacob, or about one thousand eight hundred years before Christ, and about six hundred years after the deluge. For the reasons of this opinion, see the Notes on chap. xlii. 16. This estimate cannot pretend to entire accuracy, but it has a high degree of probability. If this estimate be correct, he lived not far from four hundred years before the departure of the children of Israel from Egypt, and before the giving of the law on Mount Sinai ; comp. Notes on Acts vii. 6.

(2.) As a slight confirmation of this opinion, we may refer to the traditions in reference to the time when he lived. The account which is appended to the Septuagint, that he was a son of Zare, one of the sons of Esau, and the fifth in descent from Abraham, may be seen in the Notes on chap. xlii. 16. A similar account is given at the close of the Arabic translation of Job, so similar that the one has every appearance of having been copied from the other, or of their having had a common origin. "Job dwelt in the land of Uz, between the borders of Edom and Arabia, and was before called Jobab. He married a foreign wife, whose name was Anun. Job was himself a son of Zare, one of the sons of Esau ; and his mother's name was Basra, and he was the sixth in descent from Abraham. But of the kings who reigned in Edom, the first who reigned over the land was Balak, the son of Beor ; and the name of his city was Danaba. And after him Jobab, who is called Job ; and after him the name of him who was prince of the land of Teman ; and after him his son Barak, he who slew and put to flight Madian in the plain of Moab, and the name of his city was Gjates. And of the friends of Job who came to meet him, was Elifaz, of the sons of Esau, the king of the Temanites." These traditions are worthless, except as they show the prevalent belief when these translations were made, that Job lived somewhere near the time of the three great Hebrew patriarchs.

A nearly uniform tradition also has concurred in describing this as about the age in which he lived. The Hebrew writers generally concur in describing him as living in the days of Isaac and Jacob. *Wemyss.* Eusebius places him about two "ages" before Moses. The opinions of the Eastern nations generally concur in assigning this as the age in which he lived.

(3.) From the representations in the book itself, it is clear that he lived before the departure from Egypt. This is evident from the fact that there is no direct allusion either to that remarkable event, or to the series of wonders which accompanied it, or to the journey to the land of Canaan. This silence is unaccountable on any other supposition than that he lived before it occurred, for two reasons. One is, that it would have furnished the most striking illustration occurring in history, of the interposition by God in delivering his friends and in destroying the wicked, and was such an illustration as Job and his friends could not have failed to refer to, in defence of their opinions, if it were known to them; and the other is, that this event was the great storehouse of argument and illustration for all the sacred writers, after it occurred. The deliverance from Egyptian bondage. and the divine interposition in conducting the nation to the promised land, is constantly referred to by the sacred writers. They derive from those events their most magnificent descriptions of the power and majesty of Jehovah. They refer to them as illustrating his character and government. They appeal to them in proof that he was the friend and protector of his people, and that he would destroy his foes. They draw from them their most sublime and beautiful poetic images, and are never weary with calling the attention of the people to their obligation to serve God, on account of his merciful and wonderful interposition. The very point of the argument in this book is one that would be better illustrated by that deliverance, than by any other event which ever occurred in history; and as this must have been known to the inhabitants of the country where Job lived, it is inexplicable that there is no allusion to these transactions, if they had already occurred.

It is clear, therefore, that even if the book was written at a later period than the exode from Egypt, the author of the poem *meant* to represent the patriarch as having lived before that event. He has described him as one who was ignorant of it, and in such circumstances, and with such opinions, that he could not have failed to refer to it, if he was believed to have lived after that event. It is equally probable that Job lived before the destruction of Sodom and Gomorrah. This event occurred in the vicinity of the country where he lived, and he could not have been ignorant of it. It was, moreover, a case not less in point in the argument than the deliverance from Egypt was; and it is not conceivable that a reference to so signal a punishment on the wicked by the direct judgment of the Almighty, would have been omitted in an argument of the nature of that in this book. It was the *very point* maintained by the friends of Job, that God interposed by direct judgments to cut off the wicked; and the world never furnished a more appropriate illustration of this than had occurred in their own neighbourhood, on the supposition that the calamities of Job occurred *after* that event.

(4.) The same thing is apparent also from the absence of all allusion to the Jewish rites, manners, customs, religious ceremonies, priesthood, festivals, fasts, Sabbaths, &c. There will be occasion in another part of this Introduction (§ 4. iii.) to inquire how far there is *in fact* such a want of allusion to these things. All that is now meant is, that there is an obvious and striking want of such allusions as we should expect to find made by one who lived at a later period, and who was familiar with the customs and religious rites of the Jews. The plan of the poem, it may be admitted, indeed, did not demand any frequent allusion to these customs and rites, and may be conceded to be adverse to such an allusion, even if they were known;

but it is hardly conceivable that there should not have been some reference to them of more marked character than is now found. Even admitting that Job was a foreigner, and that the author meant to preserve this impression distinctly, yet his residence could not have been far from the confines of the Jewish people ; and one who manifested such decided principles of piety towards God as he did, could not but have had a strong sympathy with that people, and could not but have referred to their rites in an argument so intimately pertaining to the government of JEHOVAH. The representation of Job, and the allusions in the book, are in all respects such as *would* occur on the supposition that he lived before the peculiar Jewish polity was instituted.

(5.) The same thing is manifest from another circumstance. The religion of Job is of the same kind which we find prevailing in the time of Abraham, and before the institution of the Jewish system. It is a religion of sacrifices, but without any officiating priest. Job himself presents the offering, as the head of the family, in behalf of his children and his friends; chap. i. 5 ; xlii. 8. There is no priest appointed for this office; no temple, tabernacle, or sacred place of any kind; no consecrated altar. Now this is just the kind of religion which we find prevailing among the patriarchs, until the giving of the law on Mount Sinai; and hence it is natural to infer that Job lived anterior to that event. Thus we find Noah building an altar to the Lord, and offering sacrifices, Gen. viii. 20; Abraham offering a sacrifice himself in the same manner, Gen. xv. 9—11 ; comp. Gen. xii. 1—13; and this was undoubtedly the earliest form of religion. Sacrifices were offered to God, and the father of a family was the officiating priest.

These circumstances combined leave little doubt as to the time when Job lived. They concur in fixing the period as not remote from the age of Abraham, and there is no other period of history in which they will be found to unite. No question of great importance, however, depends on settling this question ; and these circumstances determine the time with sufficient accuracy for all that is necessary, in an exposition of the book.

§ 4. *The Author of the Book.*

A question of more vital importance than those which have been already considered, relates to the authorship of the book. As the name of the author is nowhere mentioned, either in the book itself or elsewhere in the Bible, it is of course impossible to arrive at absolute certainty; and after all that has been written on it, it is still and must be a point of mere conjecture. Still the question, as it is commonly discussed, opens a wide range of inquiry, and claims an investigation. If the name of the author cannot be discovered with certainty, it may be possible at least to decide with some degree of probability at what period of the world it was committed to writing, and perhaps with a degree of probability that may be sufficiently satisfactory, by whom it was done.

The first inquiry that meets us in the investigation of this point is, whether the whole book was composed by the same author, or whether the historical parts were added by a later hand. The slightest acquaintance with the book is sufficient to show, that there are in it two essentially different kinds of style—the poetic and prosaic. The body of the work, chap. iii.— xlii. 1—6, is poetry; the other portion, chap. i. ii. and xlii. 7—17, is prose. The genuineness of the latter has been denied by many eminent critics, and particularly by De Wette, who regard it as the addition of some later hand. Against the prologue and the epilogue De Wette urges, "that the perfection of the work requires their rejection, because they solve the problem which is the subject of the discussion, by the idea of trial and compensation :

whereas it was the design of the author to solve the question through the idea of entire submission on the part of man to the wisdom and power of God;" see Noyes, Intro. pp. xxi. xxii.

To this objection it may be replied, (1.) That we are to learn the view of the author only by *all* that he has presented to us. It may have been a part of his plan to exhibit just this view—not to present an abstract argument, but such an argument in connection *with a real case*, and to make it more vivid by showing an actual instance of calamity falling upon a pious man, and by a state of remarkable prosperity succeeding it. The presumption is, that the author of the poem designed to throw all the light possible on a very obscure and dark subject; and in order to that, a statement of the *facts* which preceded and followed the argument seems indispensable. (2.) Without the statement in the conclusion of the prosperity of Job after his trials, the argument of the book is incomplete. The main question is not solved. God is introduced in the latter chapters, not as solving by explicit statements the questions that had given so much perplexity, but as showing the duty of unqualified submission. But when this is followed by the historical statement of the return of Job to a state of prosperity, of the long life which he afterwards enjoyed, and of the wealth and happiness which attended him for nearly a century and a half, the objections of his friends and his own difficulties are abundantly met, and the conclusion of the whole shows that God is not regardless of his people, but that, though they pass through severe trials, still they are the objects of his tender care. (3.) Besides, the prologue is necessary in order to understand the character, the language, and the arguments of Job. In the harsh and irreverent speeches which he sometimes makes, in his fearful imprecations in chap. iii. on the day of his birth, and in the outbreaks of impatience which we meet with, it would be impossible for us to have the sympathy for the sufferer which the author evidently desired we should have, or to understand the depth of his woes, unless we had a view of his previous prosperity, and of the causes of his trials, and unless we had the assurance that he had been an eminently pious and upright man. As it is, we are prepared to sympathize with a sufferer of eminent rank, a man of previous wealth and prosperity, and one who had been brought into these circumstances *for the very purpose of trial*. We become at once interested to know how human nature will act in such circumstances, nor does the interest ever flag. Under these sudden and accumulated trials, we admire, at first, the patience and resignation of the sufferer; then, under the protracted and intolerable pressure, we are not surprised to witness the outbreak of his feelings in chap. iii.; and then we watch with great interest and without weariness the manner in which he meets the ingenious arguments of his "friends" to prove that he had always been a hypocrite, and their cutting taunts and reproaches. It would be impossible to keep up this interest in the argument unless we were prepared for it by the historical statement in the introductory chapters. It should be added, that any supposition that these chapters are by a later hand, is entirely conjectural—no authority for any such belief being furnished by the ancient versions, MSS., or traditions. These remarks, however, do not forbid us to suppose, that, if the book were composed by Job himself, the last two verses in chap. xlii., containing an account of his age and death, were added by a later hand—as the account of the death of Moses (Deut. xxxiv.) must be supposed not to be the work of Moses himself, but of some later inspired writer.

If there is, therefore, reason to believe that the whole work, substantially as we have it now, was committed to writing by the same hand, the question arises, whether there are any circumstances by which it can be determined with probability who the author was. On no question, almost, pertaining to sacred criticism, have there been so many contradictory opinions as on this. Lowth, Magee, Prof. Lee. and many others, regard it as the work of Job

himself. Lightfoot and others ascribe it to Elihu; some of the Rabbinical
writers, as also Kennicott, Michaelis, Dathe, and Good, to Moses; Luther,
Grotius, and Doederlin, to Solomon; Umbreit and Noyes to some writer who
lived not far from the period of the Jewish captivity; Rosenmüller, Spanheim, Reimar, Stauedlin, and C. F. Richter, suppose that it was composed
by some Hebrew writer about the time of Solomon; Warburton regards it as
the production of Ezra; Herder (Heb. Poetry, i. 110) supposes that it was
written by some ancient Idumean, probably Job himself, and was obtained
by David in his conquests over Idumea. He supposes that in the later
writings of David he finds traces of his having imitated the style of this
ancient book.

It would be uninteresting and profitless to go into an examination of the
reasons suggested by these respective authors for their various opinions.
Instead of this, I propose to state the leading considerations which have
occurred in the examination of the book itself, and of the reasons which have
been suggested by these various authors, which may enable us to form a probable opinion. If the investigation shall result only in adding one more conjecture to those already formed, still it will have the merit of stating about
all that seems to be of importance in enabling us to form an opinion in the
case.

I. The first circumstance that would occur to one in estimating the question about the authorship of the book, is the foreign cast of the whole work—
the fact that it differs from the usual style of the Hebrew compositions. The
customs, allusions, figures of speech, and modes of thought, to one who is
familiar with the writings of the Hebrews, have a foreign air, and are such
as evidently show that the speakers lived in some other country than Judea.
There is, indeed, a common Oriental cast diffused over the whole work,
enough to distinguish it from all the modes of composition in the Occidental
world; but there is, also, scarcely less to distinguish it from the compositions
which we know had their origin among the Hebrews. The style of thought,
and the general cast of the book, is Arabian. The allusions; the metaphors; the illustrations; the reference to historical events and to prevailing
customs, are not such as an Hebrew would make; certainly not, unless in
the very earliest periods of history, and before the character of the nation
became so formed as to distinguish it characteristically from their brethren
in the great family of the East. Arabian deserts; streams failing from
drought; wadys filled in the winter and dry in the summer; moving hordes
and caravans that come regularly to the same place for water; dwellings of
tents easily plucked up and removed; the dry and stinted shrubbery of the
desert; the roaring of lions and other wild beasts; periodical rains; trees
planted on the verge of running streams; robbers and plunderers that rise
before day, and make their attack in the early morning; the rights, authority, and obligation of the *Goel*, or avenger of blood; the claims of hospitality; the formalities of an Arabic court of justice, are the images which are
kept constantly before the mind. Here the respect due to an Emir; the
courtesy of manners which prevails among the more elevated ranks in the
Arabic tribes; the profound attention which listens to the close while one
is speaking, and which never interrupts him (Herder i. 81), so remarkable
among well-bred Orientals at the present day, appear every where. It is
true, that many of these things may find a resemblance in the undoubted
Hebrew writings—for some of them are the common characteristics of the
Oriental people—but still, no one can doubt that they abound in this book
more than in any other in the Bible, and that, as we shall see more particularly soon, they are unmixed as they are elsewhere, with what is indubitably
of Hebrew origin. In connection with this, it may be remarked that there
are in the book an unusual number of words, whose root is found now only in
the Arabic, and which are used in a sense not common in the Hebrew, but

usual in the Arabic. Of this all will be convinced who, in interpreting the book, avail themselves of the light which Gesenius has thrown on numerous words from the Arabic, or who consult the Lexicon of Castell, or who examine the Commentaries of Schultens and Lee. That more importance has been attached to this by many critics than facts will warrant, no one can deny; but as little can it be denied that more aid can be derived from the Arabic language in interpreting this book, than in the exposition of any other part of the Bible. On this point Gesenius makes the following remarks: " Altogether there is found in the book much resemblance to the Arabic, or which can be illustrated from the Arabic; but this is either Hebrew, and pertains to the poetic diction, or it is at the same time Aramaish, and was borrowed by the poet from the Aramæan language, and appears here not as Aramæan but as Arabic. Yet there is not here proportionably more than in other poetic books and portions of books. It would be unjust to infer from this that the author of this book had any immediate connection with Arabia, or with Arabic literature." Geschichte der hebr. Sprache und Schrift, S. 33. The *fact* of the Arabic cast of the work is conceded by Gesenius in the above extract; the inferences in regard to the connection of the book with Arabia and with Arabic literature which may be derived from this, is to be determined from other circumstances; comp. Eichhorn, Einleitung, v. S. 163, fgg.

II. A second consideration that may enable us to determine the question respecting the authorship of the book is, the fact that there are in it numerous undoubted allusions to events which occurred *before* the departure of the children of Israel from Egypt, the giving of the law on Mount Sinai, and the establishment of the Jewish institutions. The point of this remark is, that if we shall find such allusions, and also that there are no allusions to events occurring after that period, this is a circumstance which may throw some light on the authorship. It will at least enable us to fix, with some degree of accuracy, the time when the book was committed to writing. Now that there are manifest allusions to events occurring *before* that period, the following references will show; Job x. 9, " Remember, I beseech thee, that thou hast made me as the clay, and wilt thou bring me to dust again?" Here there is an allusion in almost so many words to the statements in Gen. ii. 7, iii. 19, respecting the manner in which man was formed,—showing that Job was familiar with the account of the creation of man, Job xxvii. 3, "All the while my breath is in me, and the spirit of God is in my nostrils;" chap. xxxiii. 4, "The Spirit of God hath made me, and the breath of the Almighty hath given me life;" chap. xxxii. 8, "But there is a spirit in man, and the inspiration of the Almighty giveth them understanding." Here there are undoubted allusions, also, to the manner in which man was formed —(comp. Gen. ii. 7)—allusions which show that the *fact* must have been made known to the speakers by tradition, since it is not such a fact as man would readily arrive at by reasoning. The imbecility and weakness of man also, are described in terms which imply an acquaintance with the manner in which he was created. " How much less in them that dwell in houses of clay, whose foundation is in the dust, which are crushed before the moth;" chap. iv. 19. In chap. xxxi. 33, there is probably an allusion to the fact that Adam attempted to hide himself from God when he had eaten the forbidden fruit. " If I covered my transgressions as Adam." For the reasons for supposing that this refers to Adam, see Notes on the verse. In chap. xxii. 15, 16, there is a manifest reference to the deluge. " Hast thou marked the old way which wicked men have trodden? which were cut down out of time, whose foundation was overflown with a flood?" See the Notes on that passage. In connection with this we may refer also to the fact that the description of the modes of worship, and the views of religion, found in this book, show an acquaintance with the form in which worship was offered to God before the exode from Egypt. They are of precisely such a character as we find in the time of Abel, Noah, and Abraham. These events are not such as would occur to one who was not familiar with the historical facts recorded in the first part of the book of Genesis. They are not such as would result from a train of reasoning, but could only be derived from the knowledge of those events which would be spread over the East at that early period of the world. They demonstrate that the work was composed by one who had had an opportunity to become acquainted with what is now recorded as the Mosaic history of the creation, and of the early events of the world.

III. There are no such allusions to events occurring *after* the exode from Egypt, and the establishment of the Jewish institutions. As this is a point of great importance in determining the question respecting the authorship of the book, and as it as been confidently asserted that there *are* such allusions, and as they have been made the basis of an argument to prove that the book had an origin as late as Solomon or even as Ezra, it is of importance to examine this point with attention. The point is, that there are no such allusions as a Hebrew would make after the exode; or in other words, there is nothing in the book itself which would lead us to conclude that it was composed *after* the departure from Egypt. A few remarks will show the truth and the bearing of this observation.

The Hebrew writers were remarkable above most others for allusions to the events of their own history. The dealings of God with their nation had been so peculiar, and they were so much imbued with the conviction that the events of their own history furnished proofs of the divine favour towards their nation, that we find in their writings a constant reference to what had happened to them as a people. Particularly the deliverance from Egypt, the passage of the Red sea, the giving of the law on Sinai, the journey in the wilderness, the conquest of the land of Canaan, and the destruction of their enemies, constituted an unfailing depository of argument and illustration for their writers in all ages. All their poetry written subsequent to these events, abounds with allusions to them. Their prophets refer to them for topics of solemn appeal to the nation; and the remembrance of these things warms the heart of piety, and animates the song of praise in the temple-service. Under the sufferings of the "captivity," they are cheered by the fact that God delivered them once from much more galling oppression ; and in the times of freedom, their liberty is made sweet by the memory of what their fathers suffered in the "house of bondage."

Now it is as undeniable as it is remarkable, that in the book of Job there are no such allusions to these events as a Hebrew would make. There is no allusion to Moses; no indisputable reference to their bondage in Egypt, to the oppressive acts of Pharaoh, to the destruction of his army in the Red sea, to the rescue of the children of Israel, to the giving of the law on Mount Sinai, to the perils of the wilderness, to their final settlement in the promised land. There is no reference to the tabernacle, to the ark, to the tables of the law, to the institution and the functions of the priesthood, to the cities of refuge, or to the peculiar religious rites of the Hebrew people. There is none to the theocracy, to the days of solemn convocation, to the great national festivals, or to the names of the Jewish tribes. There is none to the peculiar judicial laws of the Hebrews, and none to the administration of justice but such as we should find in the early patriarchal times.

These omissions are the more remarkable, as has been already observed, because many of these events would have furnished the most apposite illustrations of the points maintained by the different speakers of any which had ever occurred in history. Nothing could have been more in point, on numerous occasions in conducting the argument, than the destruction of Pharaoh, the deliverance and protection of the people of God, the care evinced for them in the wilderness, and the overthrow of their enemies in the promised land. So obvious do these considerations appear, that they seem to settle the question on one point in regard to the authorship of the book, and to show that it could not have been composed by a Hebrew *after* the exode. For several additional arguments to prove that the book was written before the exode, see Eichhorn, Einleit. § 641. As, however, notwithstanding these facts, it has been held by some respectable critics—as Rosenmüller, Umbreit, Warburton, and others—that it was composed as late as the time of Solomon, or even the captivity, it is important to inquire in what way it is proposed to set this argument aside, and by what considerations they propose to defend its composition at a later date than the exode. They are, briefly, the following.

(1.) One is, that the very design of the poem, whenever it was composed, required that there should be no such allusion. The scene, it is said, is laid, not in Palestine, but in a foreign country; the time supposed is that of the patriarchs, and before the exode; the characters are not Hebrew, but are Arabian or Idumean, and the very purpose of the author required that there should be no allusion to the peculiar history or customs of the Hebrews. The same thing, it is said, occurred which would in the composition of a poem or romance now in which the scene is laid in a foreign land, or in the time of the Crusades or the Cæsars. We should expect that the characters, the costume, the habits of that foreign country or those distant times, would be carefully observed. "As they [the characters and the author of the work] were Arabians who had nothing to do with the institutions of Moses, it is plain that a writer of genius would not have been guilty of the absurdity of putting the sentiments of a Jew into the mouth of an Arabian, at least so far as relates to such tangible matters as institutions, positive laws, ceremonies, and history. The author has manifested abundant evidence of genius and skill in the structure and execution of the work, to account for his not having given to Arabians the obvious peculiarities of Hebrews who lived under the institutions of Moses, at whatever period it may have been written. Even if the characters of the book had been Hebrews, the argument under consideration would not have been perfectly conclusive; for, from the nature of the subject, we might have expected as little in it that was Levitical or grossly Jewish, as in the Book of Proverbs or Ecclesiastes." *Noyes*, Intro. p. xxviii. This supposition *assumes* that the work was written in a later age than that of Moses. It furnishes no *evidence*, however, that it was so written. It can only furnish evidence that the author had genius and skill so to throw himself back into a distant age and into a foreign land, as completely to conceal his own peculiarity of country or time, and to represent characters as living and acting in the supposed country and period, without betraying his own. So far as the question about the author, and the time when the work was composed, is concerned, the fact here admitted, that there *are* no allusions to events after the exode, is quite as strong certainly in favour of the supposition that it was composed before as after that event. There are still some difficulties on the supposition that it was written by a Hebrew of a later age, who designedly meant to give it an Arabic dress, and to make no allusion to any thing in the institutions and history of his own country that would betray its authorship. One is, *the intrinsic difficulty* of doing this. It requires rare genius for an author so to throw himself into past ages, as to leave nothing that shall betray his own times and country. We are never so betrayed as to imagine that Shakspeare lived in the time of Coriolanus or of Cæsar; that Johnson lived in the time and the country of Rasselas; or that Scott lived in the times of the Crusaders. Instances have been found, it is admitted, where the concealment has been effectual, but they have been exceedingly rare. Another objection to this view is, that such a work would have been peculiarly impracticable for a Hebrew, who of all men would have been most likely to betray his time and country. The cast of the poem is highly philosophical. The argument is in many places exceedingly abstruse. The appeal is to close and long observation ; to the recorded experience of their ancestors ; to the observed effects of divine judgments on the world. A Hebrew in such circumstances would have appealed to the authority of God ; he would have referred to the terrible sanctions of the law rather than to cold and abstract reasoning ; and he could hardly have refrained from some allusion to the events of his own history that bore so palpably on the case, It may be doubted, also, whether any Hebrew ever had such versatility of genius and character as to divest himself wholly of the proper costume of his country, and to appear throughout as an Arabic Emir, and so as never in a long argument to express any thing but such as became the assumed character of the foreigner. It should be remembered, also, that the *language* which is used in this poem is different from that which prevailed in the time of Solomon and the captivity. It has an antique cast. It abounds in words which do not elsewhere occur, and whose roots are now to be found only in the Arabic. It has much of the peculiarities of a strongly marked *dialect*—and would require all the art necessary to keep up the spirit of an ancient dialect. Yet in the whole range of literature there are not probably half a dozen instances where such an expedient as this has been resorted to—where a writer has made use of a foreign or an antique dialect for the purpose of giving to the production of his pen an air of antiquity. Aristophanes and the tragedians, indeed, sometimes introduce persons speaking the dialects of parts of Greece different from that in which they had been brought up (*Lee*), and the same is occasionally true of Shakspeare ; but except in the case of Chatterton, scarcely one has occurred where the device has been continued through a production of any considerable length. There is a moral certainty that a Hebrew would not attempt it.

(2.) A second objection to the supposition that the work was composed before the exode, or argument that it was composed by a Hebrew who lived at a much later period of the world, is derived from the supposed allusions to the historical events connected with the Jewish people, and to the peculiar institutions of Moses. It is not maintained that there is any direct mention of those events or those institutions, but that the author has undesignedly "betrayed" himself by the use of certain words and phrases such as no one would employ but a Hebrew. This argument may be seen at length in Warburton's Divine Legation of Moses, vol. v. pp. 306—319, and a full examination of it may be seen in Peters' Critical Dissertation on the Book of Job, pp. 22—36. All that can be done here is to make a very brief reference to the argument. Even the advocates for the opinion that the book was composed after the exode, have generally admitted that the passages referred to contribute but little to the support of the opinion. The passages referred to by Warburton are the following : (1.) *The allusion to the calamities which the wickedness of parents brings upon their children.* "He that speaketh flattery to his friends, even the eyes of his children shall fail ;" chap. xvii. 5. "God layeth up his iniquity for his children; he rewardeth him, and they shall know it ;" chap. xxi. 19. Here it is supposed there is a reference to the principle laid down in the Hebrew Scriptures as a part of the divine administration, that the iniquities of the fathers should be visited upon their children. But it is not necessary to suppose that there was any particular acquaintance with the laws of Moses, to understand this. Observation of the actual course of events would have suggested all that is alleged in the Book of Job on this point. The poverty, disease, and disgrace which the vicious entail on their offspring in every land, would have furnished to a careful observer all the facts necessary to suggest this remark. The opinion that children suffer as a consequence of the sins of wicked parents was common all over the world. Thus in a verse of Theocritus, delivered as a sort of oracle from Jupiter, *Idyll.* 26 :

Εὐσεβίων παῖδεσσι τὰ λώια, δυσσεβίων δ' οὐ.

" Good things happen to children of the pious, but not to those of the irreligious." (2.) *Allusion to the fact that idolatry is an offence against the
state, and is to be punished by the civil magistrate.* " This also [idolatry]
were an iniquity to be punished by the judge ; for I should have denied the
God that is above ;" chap. xxxi. 28.   This is supposed to be such a sentiment as a Hebrew only would have employed, as derived from his peculiar
institutions, where idolatry was an offence against the state, and was made a
capital crime.   But there is not the least evidence that in the patriarchal
times, and in the country where Job lived, idolatrous worship might not be
regarded as a civil offence ; and whether it were so or not, there is no reason for surprise that a man who had a profound veneration for God, and for
the honour due to his name, such as Job had, should express the sentiment,
that the worship of the sun and moon was a heinous offence, and that pure
religion was of so much importance that a violation of its principles ought
to be regarded as a crime against society.   (3.) *Allusions to certain* PHRASES
*such as only a Hebrew would use, and which would be employed only at a
later period of the world than the exode.*   Such phrases are referred to as
the following : " He shall not see the rivers, the floods, the brooks of honey
and butter;" chap. xx. 17. " Receive, I pray thee, the law from his mouth,
and lay up his words in thine heart ;" chap. xxii. 22.   " O that I were as I
was in the days of my youth, when the secret of God was upon my tabernacle ;" chap. xxix. 4.   It is maintained that these are manifest allusions to
facts referred to in the books of Moses : that the first refers to the common
description of the Holy Land ; the second, to the giving of the law on Sinai ;
and the third, to the dwelling of the *Shekinah,* or visible symbol of God, on
the tabernacle.   To this we may reply, that the first is such common language as was used in the East to denote plenty or abundance, and is manifestly
a proverbial expression.   It is used by Pindar, *Nem. iv. γ* ; and is common
in the Arabic writers.   The second is only such general language as any one
would use who should exhort another to be attentive to the law of God, and
has in it manifestly no particular allusion to the method in which the law
was given on Sinai.   And the third can be shown to have no special reference to the Shekinah or cloud of glory as resting on the tabernacle, nor is it
such language as a Hebrew would employ in speaking of it.   That cloud is
nowhere in the Scripture called " the *secret* of God," and the fair meaning
of the phrase is, that God came into his dwelling as a friend and counsellor,
and admitted him familiarly to communion with him ; see Notes on chap.
xxix. 4.   It was one of the privileges, Job says, of his earlier life that he
could regard himself as the friend of God, and that he had clear views
of his plans and purposes.   Now, those views were withheld, and he was
left to darkness and solitude.   (5.) *Supposed allusions to the miraculous
history of the Jewish people.*   " Which commandeth the sun, and it riseth
not, and sealeth up the stars ;" chap. ix. 7.   Here it is supposed there is allusion to the miracle performed by Joshua in commanding the sun and
moon to stand still.   But assuredly there is no necessity for supposing that
there is a reference to any thing miraculous.   The idea is, that God has
power to cause the sun, the moon, and the stars to shine or not, as he pleases.
He can obscure them by clouds, or he can blot them out altogether.   Besides, in the account of the miracle performed at the command of Joshua,
there is no allusion to *the stars.*   " He divideth the sea with his power, and
by his understanding he smiteth through the proud ; ' chap. xxvi. 12.   Here
it is supposed there is an allusion to the passage of the Israelites through
the Red sea.   But the language does not necessarily demand this interpretation, nor will it admit of it.   The word improperly rendered "divideth,"
means *to awe,* to cause to cower, or tremble, and then to be calm or still,
and is descriptive of the power which God has over a tempest.   See Notes

on the verse. There is not the slightest evidence that there is any allusion to the passage through the Red Sea. "He taketh away the heart of the chief of the people of the earth, and causeth them to wander in the wilderness where there is no way;" chap. xii. 24. " Who can doubt," says Warburton, "but that these words alluded to the wandering of the Israelites forty years in the wilderness, as a punishment for their cowardice and diffidence in God's promises?" But there is no necessary reference to this. Job is speaking of the control which God has over the nations. He has power to frustrate all their counsels, and to defeat all their plans. He can confound all the purposes of their princes, and throw their affairs into inextricable confusion. In the original, moreover, the word does not necessarily imply a " wilderness" or desert. The word is תֹּהוּ a word used in Gen. i. 2, to denote *emptiness*, or *chaos*, and may here refer to the *confusion* of their counsels and plans ; or if it refer to a desert, the allusion is of a general character, meaning that God had power to drive the people from their fixed habitations, and to make them wanderers on the face of the earth. " I will show thee ; hear me ; and what I have seen will I declare ; which wise men have told from their fathers, and have not hid it;" chap. xv. 17, 18. " The very way," says Warburton, " in which Moses directs the Israelites to preserve the memory of the miraculous works of God." And the very way, also, it may be replied, in which all ancient history, and all the ancient wisdom from the beginning of the world, was transmitted to posterity. There was no other method of preserving the record of past transactions, but by transmitting the memory of them from father to son ; and this was and is, in fact, the method of doing it all over the East. It was by no means confined to the Israelites. " Unto whom alone the earth was given, AND NO STRANGER PASSED AMONGST THEM;" chap. xv. 19. " A circumstance, " says Warburton, "agreeing to no people whatever but to the Israelites settled in Canaan." But there is no necessary allusion here to the Israelites. Eliphaz is speaking of the *golden age* of his country ; of the happy and pure times when his ancestors dwelt in the land without being corrupted by the intermingling of foreigners. He says that he will state the result of *their* wisdom and observation in those pure and happy days, before it could be pretended that their views were corrupted by any foreign admixture ; see the Notes on the passage. These passages are the strongest instances of what has been adduced to show that in the book of Job there are allusions to the customs and opinions of the Jews after the exode from Egypt. It would be tedious and unprofitable to go into a particular examination of all those which are referred to by Bishop Warburton. The remark may be made of them all, that they are of so *general* a character, and that they apply so much to the prevailing manners and customs of the East, that there is no reason for supposing that there is a special reference to the Hebrews. The remaining passages referred to, are chap. xxii. 6; xxiv. 7, 9, 10; xxxiii. 17, seq.; xxxiv. 20 ; xxxvi. 7—12; and xxxvii. 13. A full examination of these may be seen in Peters' Critical Dissertation, pp. 32—36.

(3.) A third objection to the supposition that the book was composed before the time of the exode, is derived from the use of the word JEHOVAH. This word occurs several times in the historical part of the book (chap. i. 6—9, 12, 21; ii. 1—4, 6; xlii. 1, 10, 12), and a few times in the body of the poem. The objection is founded on what God says to Moses, Ex. vi. 3 ; " And I appeared unto Abraham, unto Isaac, and unto Jacob, by the name of God Almighty ; but by my name JEHOVAH was I not known to them." At the burning bush, when he appeared to Moses, he solemnly assumed this name, and directed him to announce him as " *I am that I am*," or as JEHOVAH. From this it is inferred that, as the name occurs in the book of Job, that book must have been composed subsequently to the time when God appeared to Moses. But this conclusion does not follow, for the following reasons : (1.) It *might* be true that God was not known to " Abraham, Isaac, and Jacob," by this name, and still the name might have been used by others to designate him. (2.) The name JEHOVAH was actually used before this by God himself and by others ; Gen. ii. 7—9, 15, 16, 18, 19, 21 ; iii. 9, *et al;* xii. 1, 4, 7, 8, 17; xiii. 10, 13, 14 ; xv. 6, 18; xvi. 9, 10, 13, *et sæpe al.* If the argument from this, therefore, be valid to prove that the book of Job was not composed before the exode, it will demonstrate that the book of Genesis was also a subsequent production. (3.) But the whole argument is based on a misapprehension of Ex. vi. 3. The meaning of that passage, since the name JEHOVAH *was* known to the patriarchs, must be (*a*) that it was not by this name that he had promulgated his existence, or was publicly and solemnly known. It was a name used in common with other names by them, but which he had in no special way appropriated to himself, or to which he had affixed no special sacredness. The name which he had himself more commonly employed was another. Thus when he appeared to Abraham and made himself known, he said, " I am the ALMIGHTY GOD ; walk before me, and be thou perfect ;" Gen. xvii. 1. So he appeared to Jacob : " I am GOD ALMIGHTY ; be fruitful and multiply ;" Gen. xxxv. 11 ; comp. Gen. xxviii. 3; xliii. 14. (*b*) At the bush (Ex. iii. vi. 3), God publicly and solemnly assumed the name JEHOVAH. He affixed to it a peculiar sacredness. He explained its meaning, Ex. iii. 14. He said it was *the* name by which he intended peculiarly to be known as the God of his people. He invested it with a solemn sacredness, as that by which he chose ever afterwards to be known among his people as *their* God. Other nations had their divinities with different names ; the God of the children of Israel was to be known by the peculiar and sacred name JEHOVAH. But this solemn assumption of the name is by no means inconsistent with the supposition that he might have used it before, or that it might have been used before in the composition of the book of Job.

(4.) A fourth objection to the supposition that the book was composed before the time of the exode, is, that the name *Satan,* which occurs in this book, was not known to the Hebrews at so early a date, and that in fact it occurs as a proper name only at a late period of their history. See Warburton's Divine Legation, vol. v. 353, seq. In reply to this it may be observed, (1.) that the doctrine of the existence of an *evil spirit* of the character ascribed in this book to Satan, was early known to the Hebrews. It was known in the time of Ahab, when, it is said, the Lord had put a lying spirit in the mouth of the prophets, (1 Kings xxii. 22, 23,) and the belief of such an evil spirit must have been early prevalent to explain in any tolerable way the history of the fall. On the meaning of the word, see Notes on chap. i. 6. (2.) The word *Satan* early occurs in history in the sense of an adversary or accuser, and it was natural to transfer this word to the great adversary. See Num. xxii. 22. In Zech. iii. 1, 2, it is used in the same sense as in Job, to denote the great adversary of God appearing before him; see Notes on chap. i. 6. Here Satan is introduced as a being whose name and character were well known. (3.) It is admitted by Warburton himself (p. 355), that the notion of "an evil Demon," or a "Fury," was a common opinion among the heathen, even in early ages, though he says it was not admitted among the Hebrews until a late period of their history. But if it prevailed among the heathen, it is possible that the same sentiment might have been understood in Arabia, and that this might at a very early period have been incorporated into the book of Job. See this whole subject examined in Peters' Critical Dissertation, pp. 80—92. I confess, however, that the answers which Peters and Magee (pp. 322, 323) give to this objection, are not perfectly satisfactory ; and that the objection here urged against the composition of the book *before* the exode, is the most forcible of all those which I have seen. A more thorough investigation of the *history* of the opinions respecting a presiding evil being than I have had access to, seems to be necessary to a full removal of the difficulty. The real difficulty is, not that no such being is elsewhere referred to in the Scriptures; not that his existence is improbable or absurd—for the existence of Satan is no more improbable in itself than that of Nero, Tiberius, Richard III., Alexander VI., or Cæsar Borgia, than either of whom he is not much worse; and not that there are no traces of him in the early account in the Bible;—but it is, that while in the Scriptures we have, up to the time of the exode, and indeed long after, only obscure *intimations* of his existence and character—without any particular designation of his attributes, and without any *name* being given to him, in the book of Job he appears *with* a name apparently in common use; with a definitely formed character; in the full maturity of his plans—a being evidently as well defined as the Satan in the latest periods of the Jewish history. I confess myself unable to account for this, but still do not perceive that there is any impossibility in supposing that this maturity of view in regard to the evil principle might have prevailed in the country of Job at this early period, though no occasion occurred for its statement in the corresponding part of the Jewish history. There *may* have been such a prevalent belief among the patriarchs, though in the brief records of their opinions and lives no occasion occurred for a record of their belief.

(5.) A fifth objection has been derived from the fact that in the book of Job there is a strong resemblance to many passages in the Psalms, and in the book of Proverbs, from which it is inferred that it was composed subsequently to those books. Rosenmüller, who has particularly urged this objection, appeals to the following instances of resemblance; Ps. cvii. 40; comp. with Job xii. 21, 24; Ps. cvii. 42; Job v. 16; Ps. lxv. 10; cxlvii. 8; Job v. 10; Ps. cxxxvi. 25; cxlvii. 9; Job xxxviii. 41; Prov. viii. 11; Job xxviii. 12; Prov. i. 7; Job xxviii. 28; Prov. xv. 11; Job xxvi. 6; Prov. xxvi. 6; Job xv. 16; xxxiv. 7; Prov. viii. 28, 29; Job xxviii. 25; Prov. xvii. 28; Job xiii. 5; Prov. ii. 18; xxi. 16; Job xxvi. 5; Prov. xxviii. 8; Job xxvii. 16, 17; Prov. xvi. 18; xviii. 12; xxix. 23; Job xxii. 29; Prov. viii. 26—29; xxx. 4; Job xxxviii. 4—8; Prov. x. 7; Job xx. 7. It is unnecessary to go into an examination of these passages, or to attempt to disprove their similarity. There can be no doubt of their very strong resemblance, but still the question is fairly open, *which* of these books was first composed, and which, if one has borrowed from another, was the original fountain. Warburton has himself well remarked, that "if the sacred writers must needs have borrowed trite moral sentences from one another, it may be as fairly said that the authors of the Psalms borrowed from the book of Job, as that the author of Job borrowed from the book of Psalms." Works, vol. v. 320. The supposition that the book of Job was first composed will meet the whole difficulty, so far as one was derived from the other. It should be added, also, that many of these sentiments consist of the common maxims that must have prevailed among a people accustomed to close observation, and habituated to expressing their views in a proverbial form.

I have now noticed at length all the objections which have been urged, which seem to me to have any force, against the supposition that the book of Job was composed before the exode from Egypt, and have stated the arguments which lead to the supposition that it had so early an origin. The considerations suggested are such as seem to me to leave no rational doubt that the work was composed before the departure from Egypt. The train of thought pursued, therefore, if conclusive, will remove the necessity of all further inquiry into the opinion of Luther, Grotius, and Doederlin, that Solomon was the author; of Umbreit and Noyes, that it was composed by some unknown writer about the period of the captivity; of Warburton, that it was the production of Ezra; and of Rosenmüller, Spanheim, Reimer, Staeudlin, and Richter, that it was composed by some Hebrew writer about the time of Solomon. It remains then to inquire whether there are any circumstances which can lead us to determine with any degree of probability who was the author. This inquiry leads us,

IV. In the fourth place, to remark that there are no sufficient indications that the work was composed by Elihu. The opinion that he was the author was held, among others, by Lightfoot. But, independently of the want of any positive evidence which would lead to such a conclusion, there are objections to this opinion which render it in the highest degree improbable. They are found in the argument of Elihu himself. He advances, indeed, with great modesty, but still with extraordinary pretensions to wisdom. He lays claim to direct inspiration, and professes to be able to throw such light on the whole of the perplexed subject as to end the debate. But in the course of his addresses, he introduces but one single idea on the point under discussion which had not been dwelt on at length by the speakers before. That idea is, that afflictions are designed, not to demonstrate that the sufferer was eminently guilty, as the friends of Job held, *but that they might be intended for the benefit of the sufferer himself*, and might, therefore, be consistent with true piety. This idea he places in a variety of attitudes ; illustrates it with great beauty, and enforces it with great power on the attention of Job ; comp. Notes on chap. xxxiii. 14—30 ; xxxiv. 31, 32; xxxv. 10—15; xxxvi. 7—16. But in his speeches Elihu shows no such extraordinary ability as to lead us to suppose that he was the author of the work. He does not appear to have understood the design of the trials that came upon Job ; he gives no satisfactory solution of the causes of affliction ; he abounds in repetition ; his observation of the course of events had been evidently much less profound than that of Eliphaz, and his knowledge of nature was much less extensive than that of Job and the other speakers ; and he was evidently as much in the dark in the great question which is discussed throughout the book as the other speakers were. Besides, as Prof. Lee has remarked (p. 44), the belief that Elihu wrote the book is inconsistent with the supposition that the first two chapters and the last chapter were written by the same author who composed the body of the work. He who wrote these chapters manifestly "saw through the whole affair," and understood the reasons why these trials came upon the patriarch. Those reasons would have been suggested by Elihu in his speech, if he had known them.

V. The supposition that Job himself was the author of the book, though it may have been slightly modified by some one subsequently, will meet all the circumstances of the case. This will agree with its foreign cast and character ; with the use of the Arabic words now unknown in Hebrew ; with the allusions to the nomadic habits of the times, and to the modes of living, and to the illustrations drawn from sandy plains and deserts ; with the statements about the simple modes of worship prevailing, and the notice of the sciences and the arts (see Intro. § 8), and with the absence of all allusion to the exode, the giving of the law, and the peculiar customs and institutions of the Hebrews. In addition to these *general* considerations for supposing that Job was the author of the work, the following suggestions may serve to show that this opinion is attended with the highest degree of probability. (1.) Job lived after his calamities an hundred and forty years, affording ample leisure to make the record of his trials. (2.) The art of making books was known in his time, and by the patriarch himself, chap. xix. 23, 24 ; xxxi. 35. In whatever way it was done, whether by engraving on stone or lead, or by the use of more perishable materials, he was not ignorant of the art of making a record of thoughts to be preserved and transmitted to future times. Understanding this art, and having abundant leisure, it is scarcely to be conceived, that he would have failed to make a record of what had occurred during his own remarkable trials. (3.) The whole account was one that would furnish important lessons to mankind, and it is hardly probable that a man who had passed through so unusual a scene would be willing that the recollection of it should be intrusted to uncertain tradition. The strongest arguments which human ingenuity could invent, had been urged on both sides of a great question pertaining to the divine administration ; a case of a strongly marked character had happened, similar to what is constantly occurring in the world, in which similar perplexing and embarrassing questions would arise ; God had come forth to inculcate the duty of man in this case, and had furnished instruction that would be invaluable in all similar instances ; and the result of the whole trial had been such as to furnish the strongest proof that, however the righteous are afflicted, their sufferings are not proof that they are deceivers or hypocrites. (4.) The record of his own imperfections and failures is just such as we should expect from Job, on the supposition that he was the author of the book. Nothing is concealed. There is the most fair and full statement of his impatience, his murmuring, his irreverence, and of the rebuke which he received of the Almighty. Thus Moses, too, records his own failings, and, throughout the Scriptures, the sacred writers never attempt to conceal their own infirmities and faults. (5.) Job has shown in his own speeches that he was abundantly able to compose the book. In every thing he goes immeasurably beyond all the other speakers, except God ; and he who was competent, in trials so severe as his were, to give utterance to the lofty eloquence, the argument, and the poetry now found in his speeches, was not incompetent to make a record of them in the long period of health and prosperity which he subsequently enjoyed. Every circumstance, therefore, seems to me to render it probable that Job was the compiler, or perhaps we should rather say, *the editor* of this remarkable book, with the exception of the record which is made of his own age and death. The speeches were undoubtedly made substantially as they are recorded, and the work of the author was to collect and *edit* those speeches, to record his own and that of the Almighty, and to furnish to the whole the proper historical notices, that the argument might be properly understood.

VI. But one other supposition seems necessary to meet all the questions which have been raised in regard to the origin of the work. It is, that Moses adopted it and published it among the Hebrews as a part of divine revelation, and intrusted it to them, with his own writings, to be transmitted to future times. Several circumstances contribute to render this probable. (1.) Moses spent forty years in various parts of Arabia, mostly in the neighbourhood of Horeb ; and in a country where, if such a work had been in existence, it would be likely to be known. (2.) His talents and previous training at the court of Pharaoh were such as would make him likely to look with interest on any literary document ; on any work expressive of the customs, arts, sciences, and religion of another land ; and especially on any thing having the stamp of uncommon genius. (3.) The work was eminently adapted to be useful to his own countrymen, and could be employed to great advantage in the enterprise which he undertook of delivering them from bondage. It contained an extended examination of the great question which could not but come before their minds—why the people of God were subjected to calamities ; it inculcated the necessity of submission without murmuring, under the severest trials ; and it showed that God was the friend of his people, though they were long afflicted, and would ultimately bestow upon them abundant prosperity. There is every probability, therefore, that if Moses found such a book in existence, he would have adopted it as an important auxiliary in accomplishing the great work to which he was called. It may be added (4.) that there is every reason to think that Moses was not himself the author of it. This opinion rests on such considerations as these : (*a*) The style is not that of Moses. It has more allusion to proverbs, and maxims, and prevailing views of science, than occur in his poetic writings; see Lowth, Præ. Hebr. xxxii, Michaelis, Nat. et Epim. p 186, as quoted by Magee, p. 328, and Herder, Heb. Poetry, vol. i. pp. 108, 109. (*b*) Moses in his poetry almost invariably used the word JEHOVAH as the name of God, rarely that of *the Almighty* (שדי, *Shaddai*); in Job, the word JEHOVAH rarely occurs in the body of the poem, some other name for the Deity being almost uniformly employed. (*c*) In the book of Job there are numerous instances of words, the roots of which are now obsolete, or which are found only in the Arabic or Chaldee. See Prof. Lee, Intro. p. 50. (*d*) The allusions to Arabic customs, opinions, and manners, are not such as would have been likely to be familiar to the mind of Moses. All that he could have learned of them would have been what he acquired, when over forty years of age, in keeping the flocks of his father-in-law Jethro; and though it might be said with plausibility that the forty years which he spent with him might have made him familiar with the habits of Arabia, still, in a poem of this length, we should have expected that these would not have been the only allusions. The most vivid and permanent impressions on the mind are those made in youth; and on the mind of Moses, those impressions had been received in Egypt. If the work had been composed by him we should, therefore, have expected that there would have been frequent allusions that would have betrayed its Egyptian origin. But of these there are none, or if there are any which have such an origin, they are such as might have been readily learned from the common reports of travellers. But with all that pertained to the desert, to the keeping of flocks and herds, to the nomadic mode of life, to the poor and needy wanderers there, to the methods of plunder and robbery, the author of the poem shows himself to be perfectly familiar. It seems to me, therefore, that by this train of remarks, we are conducted to a conclusion attended with as much certainty as can be hoped for in the nature of the case, that the work was composed by Job himself in the period of rest and prosperity which succeeded his trials, and came to the knowledge of Moses during his residence in Arabia, and was adopted by him *to represent to the Hebrews, in their trials, the duty of submission to the will of God, and to furnish the assurance that he would yet appear to crown with abundant blessings his own people, however much they might be afflicted.*

§ 5. *The character and the design of the book.*

It has long been a question which has excited much interest among those who have written on this book, what is the *nature* of the poem? That the body of the work is poetic, admits of no doubt; and an attempt was early made to determine the department of poetry to which it belonged. With some, it has been regarded as a regular drama; with others, as an epic poem; and laborious efforts have been made to show, that in its form, spirit, and arrangement, it comes within the limits usually assigned to these kinds of composition. But it cannot be doubted that undue importance has been attached to this question; nor can it be any more doubted that it cannot fairly be classed with either. It stands by itself—a poem, framed without reference to the Grecian rules of art; composed and published long before the laws of composition were reduced to order, and having, in fact, the characteristics of neither the epic nor the drama. There is nothing that bears an exact resemblance to it in Grecian, in Roman, or in modern literature. As a composition, it has little that resembles the Iliad, the Æneid, the Jerusalem Delivered, or the Paradise Lost. The design of the author was not to excite interest in the fortunes of the principal person or hero of the poem, nor to exhibit characteristic traits in the other personages introduced, nor to conduct a regular action to a determined and important result—as in an epic poem. As little can it be regarded as a regular drama. In its dialogue, indeed, and in the tragic interest which encompasses the character of Job, it has some resemblance to the drama; but this resemblance is incidental to the purpose of the author, and not a part of his main design. "If the word" [drama], says Eichhorn, Einleit. § 640, "be taken in its most simple meaning, as denoting a dialogue, I would not contend with any one about the name. But if the word be taken according to the modern acceptation, the poem is not a drama. The drama, according to the modern conceptions, was entirely unknown to the Orientals, and is so little in accordance with their views and customs, that the Arabians, after they become acquainted with the Grecian dramatic learning, would not introduce it among themselves. Casiri, Biblioth. Arab. Escur. T. 1, p. 85. All *action* is wanting in this poem ; for the prologue and epilogue, where there *is* some action, do not pertain properly to the poem." On the question, whether it has the properties of an epic poem, the reader may consult also Eichhorn, Einleit. § 640, vol. v., pp. 139, fgg. Indeed, this whole controversy, to what particular department of poetry this work belongs, which has been waged for centuries almost, has all the characteristics of a logomachy, and, if determined, would do little in explanation of the book. Those who are disposed to prosecute the inquiry, may find a full discussion in Lowth's Lectures on Hebrew Poetry, Lecture xxxii—xxxiv ; Warburton's Divine Legation, B. VI. § 2 ; Herder's Heb. Poetry, Dial. IV. 5 ; and Dr. Good's Introduction.

Instead of entering into the controversy respecting the nature of the poem, it will be more useful to state what seems to be the design of the book, and the *form* which the poem actually presents. Having this object before the mind distinctly, it will be easy for any one to give it such a classification in the various departments of poetry, as shall seem to him to be most accordant with truth. In order to understand this poem, it is important to have before the mind a clear conception of the peculiarities of the poetry of the Hebrews. I shall, therefore, enter here into a somewhat detailed explanation of a subject that is important to every student of the Scriptures.

Much has been written on the subject of Hebrew poetry, and yet there is no department of Scriptural investigation which has been pursued with less encouraging success. Almost nothing has been done to throw light on it since the time of Lowth, and it must be admitted that he has left many questions almost entirely unsettled. It is still asked, What constitutes the peculiarity of Hebrew poetry? Is it to be found in rhythm? Are the various kinds of poetry, which occur in the writings of other nations, to be found in the compositions of the Hebrews? How does their poetry differ from the more elevated parts of their prose writings? And as the one sometimes seems to slide insensibly into the other, how shall it be known where the one ends and the other begins?

In regard to these questions, it may be observed,

(1.) That the poetry of the Hebrews is not constituted by *rhyme*. The same remark, it is obvious, might be made respecting the poetry of all other people. Rhyme, or the occurrence of similar sounds at the close of the lines, is an artifice of modern origin, and of doubtful advantage. The reader need not be informed that it does not occur in Homer or Hesiod ; in Virgil or Ovid ; in the Paradise Lost, or in the Task. The highest kind of poetry exists without rhyme, and it has been made a question whether its use might not have been dispensed with altogether.

It is certain that rhyme does not constitute the peculiarity of Hebrew poetry; for in the few cases where it occurs in the Hebrew Scriptures, it seems to have been the result of accident rather than design. Something like rhyme can, indeed, be discovered in cases like the following:

יְהוָֹה אַל־בְּאַפְּךָ תוֹכִיחֵנִי ;
וְאַל־בַּחֲמָתְךָ תְיַסְּרֵנִי

Yehováh, ãl beäppeká thokihhēni;
Veäl bahhamâtheka theyässerēni.   Ps. vi, 2,

מָה־אֱנוֹשׁ כִּי תִזְכְרֶנּוּ
וּבֶן־אָדָם כִּי תִפְקְדֶנּוּ

Mâ änosh ki thĭzkerĕnnu,
Ubĕn âdâm ki thĭphqedhĕnnu.   Ps. viii. 5.

אַל־תִּתְהַר־ בַּמְּרֵעִים
אַל־תְּקַנֵּא בְּרְשָׁעִים

Al tithkhăr bämmĕrēim,
Al tĕkännē bâreshâim.   Prov. xxiv. 19,

שָׁלַח מֶלֶךְ וַיַּתִּירֵהוּ
מֹשֵׁל עַמִּים וַיְפַתְּחֵהוּ

Shâlāhh mēlĕk vaiyattirēhu,
Mōshēl ämmim vaiyephattehhēhu.   Ps. cv. 20.

In Isa. x. 6, the two subdivisions of the first clause of the verse rhyme together :

בְּגוֹי חָנֵף אֲשַׁלְּחֶנּוּ
וְעַל עַם עֶבְרָתִי אֲצַוֶּנּוּ

Begōy hhânēph ashăllĕhhĕnnu,
Veäl am ibrâthi ätzăvvĕnnu.

So in Isa. liii. 6 :

כֻּלָּנוּ כַּצֹּאן תָּעִינוּ
אִישׁ לְדַרְכּוֹ פָּנִינוּ

Kŭllânu kättzōn tâinu
Ish lĕdhärko pâninu.

So the two last clauses in Isa. i. 9; xliv. 3, and Ps. x.v. 8.   The two principal clauses of the verse rhyme in Prov. vi. 1, 2; Job vi. 9; Isa. i. 29.   In one
instance three rhymes are to be found in a sentence, as in Isa. i, 25 :

וְאָשִׁיבָה יָדִי עָלַיִךְ
וְאֶצְרֹף כַּבֹּר סִיגָיִךְ
וְאָסִירָה כָּל־בְּדִילָיִךְ

Vĕâshibâh yâdhi âläik,
Vĕĕtzroph kăbbor siggäik,
Vĕâsirâh kŏl bĕdhilâik.

Other instances of a similar kind may be found in the dissertation of
Theodore Ebert on the rules of Hebrew measure and rhythm, in Ugolin's
Thes. Sac. Ant., tom. xxxi. pp. 20, 21.   The cases, however, which occur in
the poetry of the Hebrews where rhyme at the end of verses is apparent,
are too few to lead us to suppose that it was designed by the writers, and
they are probably only such as would occur had an effort to write in the
form of rhyme never been known.

(2.) The poetry of the Hebrews is not constituted by *rhythm*.   Rhythm
has reference to the admeasurement of the lines of poetry by feet and numbers, and relates to the length and shortness of the syllables, and to the
regular succession of one after another.   It is the rule in composition which

aims to reduce its various and resisting elements to unity and harmony. De Wette, Einlei. pp. 51, 52. The rules in regard to this pertain to quantity, inflection, accentuation, and the arrangement of the members and parts of a period. *Metre* of some kind has been regarded as almost necessary to poetry, and the care of the ancient Greek and Latin poets in regard to it is well known. It has been made a question of much interest whether such laws prevail in the Hebrew poetry; and whether, if it ever existed, it is possible to trace it now. Carpzov, Ebert, and Lowth, maintained that such metre or rhythm must have existed, though it is now lost to us. Lowth (Lectures on Hebrew Poetry, III.) maintains that "the Hebrew writings are not only animated with the true poetic spirit, but are in some degree confined to numbers;" that properties altogether peculiar to metrical composition are found; that the Hebrew poets use, like the Greeks, "glosses," or expressions taken from foreign languages, and adopt a peculiar form in the termination of words, so as to form a poetical dialect; but that as to the "quantity, rhythm, or modulation," it is hopeless now to attempt to recover it, "the true pronunciation being now lost." Similar views are expressed by Pfeiffer (Ueber d. Musik d. alten Heb. p. xvi.); Bauer (Einleit. ins A. T. p. 358, sq.); Jahn (Bibl. Arch. Th. I. B. I.); and Meyer, Hermen. des A. T. ii. 329; comp. De Wette, Einleit. p. 45. Josephus affirmed that in Hebrew poetry are to be found both hexameter and tetrameter verses. Ant. B. II. chap. xvi. § 4; B. VII. chap. xii. § 3. "Philo, in several passages of his writings, maintains that Moses was acquainted with metre." Nordheimer, Heb. Gram. vol. ii. p. 319. Gomarus, Hare, Greve, and several others of equal celebrity, have sought to ascertain the laws of metre in Hebrew poetry, but without success. If it ever existed, it is now hopeless to attempt to recover it. There is little evidence that we have the correct pronunciation of the language; the laws of metre are now unknown, and there is no way of ascertaining them. Indeed, the evidence is not satisfactory that any such laws ever existed. The assertions of Josephus and Philo can be easily accounted for. They were Jews, proud of their own language; and supposing, justly, that the poetry of their sacred bards was equal to any which could be produced in the writings of the Romans or the Greeks, they were anxious to show that it had all the properties of poetry existing among them. Yet in their time, it was a settled rule among the Greeks and Romans that poetry was known by its rhythm, by its accurate and careful admeasurement of numbers, and its harmonious and graceful flow of measure. Nothing was more natural, therefore, than that they should affirm that the same thing existed in the Hebrew poetry, and that portions of it could be adduced which for beauty and grace of measure would equal the boasted productions of Greece and Rome. That specimens *might* have been produced capable of being measured by feet, no one can disprove; and yet this may not have been at all a leading object in the poetry of the Hebrews. It should be remembered, that the Hebrew poetry is the oldest now extant; that it was composed long before the artificial rules known in Greece and Rome were in existence; that it was designed to express the sentiments of the earliest period of the world when all was fresh and new; and that we are to look for less attention to the rules of composition than in a more cultivated and artificial age. Indications of *art* there are indeed in the alphabetical poems, and in the carefully constructed parallelisms, but it is not the art of rhythm or metre.

(3.) It is not a characteristic of Hebrew poetry, that it is formed according to the regular laws of composition which fetter the poets of more modern times. There are, indeed, lyric and elegiac poems of exquisite beauty and tenderness. But there is no regular epic poem, for although their early history furnished finer materials for such a poem than the occurrences celebrated in either the Iliad or the Æneid, it seems never to have occurred to them to attempt to mould those materials into the form of a heroic poem. The Hebrews had no dramatic poetry. The stage was unknown among them, and indeed was unknown among the Greeks until long after the time when the most celebrated of the Hebrew poets lived. We are not to look, therefore, for the characteristics of Hebrew poetry in the stately modes of composition which occur in other languages.

If it be asked, then, what are the characteristics of Hebrew poetry; how does it differ from prose; how can its existence be determined, we may reply, (1.) It consists in the nature of the subjects which are treated; in the ornate and elevated character of the style; in the sententious manner of expression; and in certain peculiarities in the structure of sentences and the choice of words which are found only in poetry, which will be noticed hereafter. (2.) It is the language of nature in the early periods of the world, expressing itself in the form of surprise, astonishment, exultation, triumph,—the outpouring of a mind raised by excitement above its ordinary tone of feeling. The prose writer expresses himself in a calm and tranquil manner when free from the influence of strong excitement. His sedate emotions are reflected in the language which he uses. The poet is animated. His mind is excited. Every faculty of the soul is brought into exercise. His heart is full; his imagination glows; his associations are rapid; and the soul pours forth its emotions in language figurative, concise, abrupt. The boldest metaphors are sought; the terms expressing deepest intensity of feeling suggest themselves to the mind; or language most beautiful, tender, and soothing, expresses the emotions of sorrow or of love. It is in the Hebrew poetry more strikingly than anywhere else, that we perceive the evidence of the intensity with which objects struck the imagination in the early periods of the world; and nowhere do we find such examples of sublimity and power as there. (3.) The language of poetry is distinguished from prose by the *effort* which is made to express the ideas, and by the *form* which that effort gives. Sometimes we have merely a *glimpse* of the thought or the object, which it is left for the imagination to fill up. Sometimes the thought is repeated, thrown into a new form, modified, or merely *echoed* from the first attempt to express it. The mind, full of the conception, labours to give utterance to it, and in the effort there may be repetition, or a slight variation in the words, or an attempt to show its force by striking contrast. It is from this effort of the mind that there was originated the principal peculiarity of the Hebrew poetry, exhibited in the form of *parallelism*.

This general characteristic of poetry in all languages, manifests itself in some peculiar form in accordance with the character of a people, or with prevailing taste, or in imitation of some distinguished writer. Some *artificial* rules are adopted, in accordance with which the poetic spirit is manifested. In one country or age this may be by rhyme; in another, by the rhythm of measured feet or numbers; at one time, it may be by simple "blank verse;" at another, by the smoothness and harmony of similar endings. The elegy, the eclogue, the pastoral, the lyric, the tragic, the epic, may all be employed, and in all the poetic spirit may reign. The Greeks and Romans employed rhythm, and reduced the laws of poetic feet and numbers to the severest rules; rhyme has been since invented for similar purposes, and occupies a large place in modern poetry; while another form still may be found in the Hebrew, the Arabic, and the Persian poetry. In some countries and times the artificial rules may be few and little complicated; in others they may be numerous and wrought up with the highest skill of art. One mode may be adapted to the taste of one people, and another to that of another; and still the essential characteristics of poetry be found in all. Nay, one artificial mode of poetry that is now obsolete may be in itself as reasonable and valuable as another that is retained, and no reason can be given except that the *tastes* of men change by time, circumstances,

and fashion. The parallelism of the Hebrew may be as poetic in its character, and as rational in itself, as the rhyme; perhaps it may be better adapted
to express the conceptions of the highest kind of poetry. The apparently
cumbrous versification of Spenser may have as much poetic merit as the
numbers of Pope, and the time may come when that stanza shall be restored
to the honour which it once possessed as the medium of the poetic sentiment.

We are not, therefore, to judge Hebrew poetry by *our* artificial forms.
We are not to say, because it lacks the ornament of rhyme, or because it
cannot now be reduced to the laws of poetic numbers which are applied to
Homer or Virgil, that therefore it is destitute of the true spirit of poetry.
We are to inquire whether it have the elevated conceptions, the sublime
thoughts, the grandeur of imagery, the tenderness and sweetness, the beauty
of description, and the power to rouse the soul, which are every where recognized as the characteristic of poetry. We are then to inquire, what modes
the ancient bards chose as the forms in which they should embody their
conceptions;—perhaps as an incidental inquiry we are to ask whether *those*
forms are not adapted to the age and land in which they occur, as really
as the forms now most admired may be to our own. This inquiry has never
been pursued as it should have been, and this is not the place in which to
prosecute it. The inquiry which is proper here is, only, in what artificial
forms the spirit of poetry among the Hebrews was embodied and preserved.
What rules had they according to which to record their poetic conceptions?

Hebrew poetry appears, then, under the following artificial forms. 1. In
an alphabetical arrangement. We have something like this in the acrostic,
where each line begins with a letter of a certain word. The Hebrew poets
sometimes adopted a similar method, by commencing each line with one of
the letters of the alphabet; or where every alternate verse began with a
succeeding letter; or where a series of verses have the same initial letters.
This artificial mode of composition appears with several modifications.

(*a*.) Commonly each verse begins with one of the successive letters of
the alphabet, and the number of the verses is, therefore, the same as the
number of Hebrew letters. This occurs in Prov. xxxi. 10–31, where the
order of the letters is exactly observed, and Lam. i. This is the case, also,
in Psalm xxv., except that two verses begin with א; and none with ב; the
ו and ק are wanting, and two verses begin with ר; and at the close after the
ת a line beginning with פ occurs. So in Lam. ii. 4, except that פ and ע
are exchanged in their places. In like manner in Psalm xxxiv., which is
constructed on this plan, the ו is wanting, and the Psalm concludes with a
line beginning with פ. In Ps. cxlv. the order is exactly observed, except
that נ is wanting.

(*b*.) In Ps. xxxvii. there are evidences of a more artificial structure,
though it is not wholly regular. The Psalm consists of forty verses, and it
would seem that it was the original conception that the letter כ should
precede each of the letters of the alphabet in the beginning of the verse.
The order of letters is the following: א, ב, כ, ב, ג, י, ד, ה, כ, ו,
י, צ, פ, ת, כ, ע, ס, נ, מ, ל, כ, ל, ר, כ, ט, יח, ה, ת, א, ז,
ק, ר, ש, י, י, י, ו. The Psalm, it will at once be seen, is quite irregular,
though the general order of the letters of the alphabet is observed. It is
now impossible to explain the cause of the irregularity.

(*c*.) Another form is found in Ps. cxi. cxii. In these Psalms the half-
verses are alphabetically arranged, or every half-verse or member begins
with a new letter of the alphabet. These Psalms are regular in their structure, and the series occurs in the exact order of the letters of the alphabet.

(*d*.) In Lamentations iii. and Ps. cxix. another alphabetical form still more
artificial appears. In Lamentations three verses in succession begin with
one of the letters of the alphabet, followed by three more beginning with the
succeeding letter, and so on through the alphabet; except that, as in chap.

ii. and iv., ם and ע change places. In Psalm cxix. the same arrangement
extends through eight successive verses, dividing the whole Psalm into
alphabetical strophes of that number of verses.

What was the *design* of this arrangement is now unknown. Michaelis
supposes that it was at first a device employed in the funeral dirge to aid
mourners; and De Wette, that it was owing to a vitiated taste. Lowth
supposes that it was confined to those compositions which consisted of detached maxims, or sentiments without any express order or connection, and
that the whole arrangement was to assist the memory. It seems to me that
it must be regarded as a mere matter of *taste*—and certainly of taste quite
as elevated and rational as the rhyme or the acrostic are with moderns.
That it was not adopted to aid the memory is apparent, because it is found
in very few of the poetical compositions of the Hebrews; while if this were
the object, we should expect to find it extended to all. For a similar reason
it could not have been designed, as Michaelis supposes, to aid in funeral
dirges; for it is found in no funeral dirges, unless the "Lamentations" be regarded as such. Nor can the supposition of Lowth be correct, for in Ps. xxv.,
xxxvii., cxi., cxii., cxlv. there is as close a connection of sentiment as occurs in
any of the Psalms; and indeed some of them are quite remarkable for the con-
tinuity of thought and singleness of design. There are many artificial modes
of poetry in all languages which can be accounted for on no other principle
than that they are mere matters of taste; and they who censure this form of
Hebrew poetry, should inquire whether the censure should be withheld from
many forms of poetry existing in the best writings of modern times.

II. An artificial form of poetry is observable in a few instances where a
complex rhythmical period or strophe occurs. The peculiarity of this form
is, that the same verse or sentiment is repeated at somewhat distant intervals, or after the recurrence of about the same number of verses. Whether
this *intercalary* verse (Germ. *Schaltvers*) was designed to aid the memory,
or to be sung by a part of a choir, or was regarded as a mere poetic ornament, cannot now be determined. An instance occurs in Ps. xlii., xliii.
After the first four verses, the following occurs: "Why art thou cast down,
O my soul? and why art thou disquieted within me? Hope thou in God;
for I shall yet praise him for the help of his countenance." After five
verses, the same verse occurs with a slight variation, and after four verses
more it occurs again in the same manner, showing that it was intended to
close a strophe, or large period. The same thing occurs in Ps. cvii., where
the Psalm is divided into unequal portions by the recurrence of the same
sentiment, "O that men would praise the Lord for his goodness, and for his
wonderful works to the children of men." This occurs after ver. 1—7; ver. 9
—14; ver. 16—20; and ver. 22—30. Gesenius supposes that a part of Solomon's Song is composed in the same manner. One instance of this occurs in
Isaiah. It is in chap. ix. 8—21, x. 1—4. After each strophe, consisting of
four or five verses, the following sentiment is repeated: "For all this his anger
is not turned away, but his hand is stretched out still;" chap. ix. 12, 17, 21;
x. 4.; Amos i. 3—15; ii. 1—6, is constructed in the same artificial manner.

III. A third artificial form of poetry occurs in the *rhythm of gradation*
(De Wette, *Stufenrhythmus*), and is found mainly in the "Psalms of Degrees." It consists in this, that the thought or expression of the preceding
verse is resumed and carried forward in the next. An instance of this
occurs in Ps. cxxi.:

1. I lift up mine eyes unto the hills;
   From whence will *my help come?*
2. *My help cometh* from JEHOVAH,
   The Creator of heaven and earth.
3. He suffereth not thy foot to be moved;
   Thy keeper *slumbereth* not.
4. Lo! he *slumbereth* not, nor sleepeth
   The *keeper* of Israel.

5. Jehovah is thy *keeper;*
   Jehovah thy shade is at thy right hand:
6. The sun shall not smite thee by day,
   Nor the moon by night.
7. Jehovah *preserveth* thee from all evil,
   Preserveth thy soul.
8. Jehovah *preserveth* thy going out and thy coming in,
   From this time forth and for evermore.

These "Songs of Degrees" are fifteen in number, extending from Ps. cxx. to cxxxiv. The same characteristics may be found in them all, and it is probable that they derived their name from this artificial structure, and not because they were sung as the tribes were *going up* to Jerusalem. The song of Deborah (Judges v.) is constructed on this principle, as the following specimens will show:

4. Lord, *when thou wentest out* of Seir,
   When *thou marchedst out* of the field of Edom,
      The earth trembled,
      And the heavens *dropped,*
      The clouds also *dropped water.*
5. The mountains melted *before the Lord,*
   Even that Sinai, from *before the Lord God of Israel.*
7. The inhabitants of the villages *ceased,*
   They *ceased in Israel.*
   Until that I Deborah *arose,*
   That I *arose a mother in Israel.*
20. They *fought* from heaven.
   The *stars in their courses fought* against Sisera.
21. The *river of Kishon* swept them away,
   That *ancient river, the river Kishon.*
22. Then were the horse-hoofs broken by means of the *prancings,*
   The *prancings of their mighty ones,* etc. etc.

An instance of this artificial arrangement occurs in Isa. xxvi. 5, 6:

The lofty city *he layeth it low,*
Hath *laid it low to the ground,*
He *hath levelled it to the dust,*
The foot shall trample on it,
The feet of the poor, the steps of the needy.

IV. The grand peculiarity of the Hebrew poetry, however, is the *parallelism.* This form of composition, which seems to us to be artificial in a high degree, consists in the repetition of the main thought usually with some modification. It arose from such circumstances as the following. (1.) The Hebrew poetry, in the main, was composed at a very early period of the world, and at that point of intellectual cultivation when the mind is in a condition to seize only certain simple and general relations of things, and to express them strongly. (2.) The mind is supposed to be struck with wonder and to be highly excited. The object presented is new and strange, and fills the soul with elevated and glowing conceptions. (3.) In this state, the mind naturally expresses itself in short sentences, and is apt merely to repeat the idea. It is not in a condition to observe minute relations, but seeks to express the thought in the most impressive and forcible manner possible. The speaker struggles with language; the words are slow to adapt themselves to the thought; and the principal idea is expressed and dwelt upon with earnestness. The object is to express the glowing conception of the mind; and that object is effected by repetition, by the addition of a slight circumstance, by comparison, or by contrast with some other subject. Sometimes in this effort to express the main thought, the secondary expression will be little more than the echo of the first attempt; sometimes it will greatly excel it in force and brilliancy; sometimes some striking and beautiful conception will be appended; sometimes, to heighten the impression, the main idea will be expressed in contrast with some other. In all these cases the form of short sentences will be preserved : though the number and modes of the *efforts* made to give expression to the main thought may be greatly varied. These circumstances gave rise to the parallelism, which became the favourite form of poetry among the Hebrews, and which abounds so much in every part of the Old Testament.

Various divisions have been made of the parallelism, and to a considerable extent those divisions must be arbitrary. Lowth (Prel. Diss. to Isaiah, and Lectures on Hebrew Poetry, xix.) reduces the parallelism to three kinds— synonymous, antithetic, and synthetic. This division has been adopted by Nordheimer (Gram. vol. ii. pp. 323, seq.), and by writers on Hebrew poetry in general. De Wette (Einleit. 56—63) has suggested *four* kinds of parallelism, as embracing the forms which exist in the Old Testament. They are (I.) when there is an equality of words; (II.) when the words are not equal : divided into (1) the *simple* unequal parallelism, and (2) the *complex* unequal parallelism, embracing (*a*) the synonymous, (*b*) the antithetic, and (*c*) the synthetic; (3) instances where the simple member is disproportionably small; (4) cases where the complex member is increased to three or four propositions; and (5) cases where there is a short clause or supplement, for the most part in the second member. III. Parallelism when both the members are complex; embracing also (*a*) the synonymous; (*b*) the antithetic; and (*c*) the synthetic. IV. *Rhythmical parallelism*, when it consists not in the thought but in the form of the period. Under this last form of parallelism, De Wette supposes that the Lamentations of Jeremiah should be nearly all ranged.

Without adopting precisely either of the arrangements above referred to, the following classification will probably include all the modes in which the parallelism occurs in the Scriptures, being substantially the same as that of Lowth.

I. *The synonymous parallelism.* In this, the second clause is a repetition of the first. This occurs under considerable variety in regard to the *length* of the members.

(*a*) The repetition is nearly in the same words, or where a single word may be changed. Thus in Isa. xv. 1, where the *subject* alone is changed :

> Verily, by a nightly assault, Ar of Moab is laid waste and ruined !
> Verily, by a nightly assault, Kir of Moab is laid waste and ruined!

In Prov. vi. 2 the *verb* only is changed :

> Thou art snared with the words of thy mouth;
> Thou art taken with the words of thy mouth.

Sometimes an idea is only partially expressed in the first clause; in the second this is repeated, and the sentence brought to a close, as in Ps. xciv. 1:

> God of vengeance—JEHOVAH !
> God of vengeance—shine forth.

In Ps. xciii. 3, the entire sentence is again repeated in a varied form :

> The floods have lifted up, O JEHOVAH !
> The floods have lifted up the r voice;
> The floods lift up their waves.

(*b*) In this parallelism there is often an *equality in the words*, at least in their number. Thus in the song of Lamech, Gen. iv. 23:

> Adah and Zillah, hear my voice.
> Wives of Lamech, receive my speech !
> If I have slain a man to my wounding,
> And a young man to my hurt ;
> If Cain was avenged seven times,
> Then Lamech—seventy times seven.

Thus also in Job vi. 5:

> Doth the wild ass bray over his grass?
> Doth the ox low over his fodder?

Such instances occur often in the Scriptures, and perhaps this may be considered the *original* form of the parallelism.

(c) In the synonymous parallelism, as in other forms also, there is often a great inequality in the number of the words. These instances seem to have occurred where it was desirable to give *emphasis* to the thought by the utmost brevity in one of the members, while, perhaps, in the other member, the thought is dwelt upon or repeated. Thus in Ps. lxviii. 32:

> Sing unto God, ye kingdoms of the earth;
> O sing praises unto JEHOVAH.

So in Ps. xl. 9, where the simple member is disproportionately small, and the inequality, therefore, still more striking:

> I proclaim thy righteousness in the great congregation,
> Lo! I refrain not my lips
> O Lord, thou knowest!

So in Job x. 1, where the principal emphatic thought is followed by a parallelism, stating what was proper in view of the fact of which he complained:

> I am weary of my life:
> Therefore will I give loose to my complaints;
> I will speak in the bitterness of my soul

(d) The idea is expressed in the form of a *climax*, where the thought rises and becomes more emphatic. This climax sometimes is found in the verbs used. Thus in Ps. xxii. 27:

> All the ends of the world shall *remember*, and *turn* to the Lord;
> And all the kindreds of the nations shall WORSHIP before thee.

For the sake of emphasis, the verb of the first clause is sometimes placed at the commencement, and the corresponding one of the second at the termination. Isa. xxxv. 3:

> Strengthen the weak hands;
> And the tottering knees make firm.

A climax in thought often occurs, as in this instance, Isa. liv. 4:

> Fear not, for thou shalt not be confounded;
> And blush not, for thou shalt not be put to shame
> For thou shalt forget the shame of thy youth,
> And the reproach of thy widowhood shalt thou remember no more.

(e) We meet with double parallelisms, or cases where each clause of a verse corresponds with each clause of the member preceding, as in Ps. xxxiii. 13, 14.

> From heaven the Lord looks down,
> He sees all the sons of men;
> From his dwelling-place he looks
> Upon all the inhabitants of the earth.

So in Isa. i. 15:

> When ye spread forth your hands,
> I will hide mine eyes from you;
> When ye multiply prayers,
> I will not hearken.

Sometimes the second parallelism contains the *cause* of what is stated in the preceding. Isa. lxi. 10:

> I will greatly rejoice in JEHOVAH ;
> My soul shall exult in my God :
> For he hath clothed me with the garments of salvation ;
> He hath covered me with the mantle of righteousness.

Or the first contains a comparison, and the second the thing compared. Isa. lxi. 11 :

> For as the earth putteth for her tender shoots,
> And as a garden causes its seed to germinate ;
> So the Lord JEHOVAH will cause righteousness to germinate,
> And praise before all the nations.

(f) This form of parallelism—*the synonymous*, admits of five lines, and often employs them with great elegance. Thus in Isa. i. 15, quoted above, where the fifth line is given as *a reason* for what is affirmed in the second and fourth :

> And when ye spread forth your hands,
> I will hide mine eyes from you ;
> And when ye multiply prayers,
> I will not hear :
> Your hands are full of blood !

In the stanza of five lines the odd line may come in between the two distichs. Thus in Isa. xlvi. 7 :

> They bear him upon the shoulder, and they carry him ;
> They set him in his place, and there he standeth ;
> From his place shall he not remove—
> Yea, one cries unto him, and he does not answer ;
> Nor save him out of his trouble.

So, also, in Isa. l. 10 :

> Who is there among you that feareth JEHOVAH,
> That obeyeth the voice of his servant,
> Who walketh in darkness and seeth no light ?
> Let him trust in the name of JEHOVAH ;
> Let him stay himself upon his God.

II. A second form of the parallelism is the *antithetic*, in which the idea contained in the second clause is the converse of that in the first. This appears also with various modifications.

(a.) It occurs in a simple form. Prov. x. 1 :

> A wise son rejoiceth his father ;
> But a foolish son is the grief of his mother.

(b) A form of antithesis occurs in which the second clause is the consequence of the first. Isa. i. 19, 20 :

> If ye be willing and obedient,
> Ye shall eat the good of the land ;
> But if ye refuse and rebel,
> Ye shall be devoured with the sword.

(c.) Occasionally we meet with a double synonym and a double antithesis. Isa. i. 3 :

> The ox knoweth his owner,
> And the ass the crib of his master ;
> Israel knoweth not,
> My people understand not.

(d.) Sometimes there is an alternate correspondence in the antithesis. Ps. xliv. 2 :

> Thou didst drive out the heathen with thy hand,
> And plantedst those ;
> Didst destroy the nations,
> And enlargedst those.   *De Wette's translation.*

(e.) A double antithetical form of the parallelism is not uncommon in

the prophets. A very beautiful parallelism of this kind occurs in Habakkuk iii. 17, 18 :

> Although the fig-tree shall not blossom,
>   Neither shall fruit be in the vines ;
> The buds of the olive shall fail,
>   And the fields shall yield no bread ;
> The flock shall be cut off from the fold,
>   And there shall be no herd in the stall ;
> Yet I will rejoice in the Lord,
>   I will joy in the God of my salvation.

Comp. Isa. ix. 10.

> The bricks are fallen down,
>   But we will build with hewn stone ;
> The sycamores are cast down,
>   But we will replace them with cedars.

III. The third form of the parallelism is that which is denominated by
Lowth, the *synthetic*. In this, the parallelism consists only in the similar
form of construction ; where there is "a correspondence and equality between different propositions in respect to the shape and turn of the whole
sentence, such as noun answering to noun, verb to verb, member to member,
negative to negative, interrogative to interrogative." *Lowth.* The poet, instead of merely echoing the former sentiment, or placing it in contrast, enforces his thought by accessory ideas and modifications. A general proposition is stated, and the sentiment is amplified or dwelt upon in detail. Thus
in Isa. i. 5—9 the description of the punishment brought upon the Hebrews
is continued through several verses, each heightening the effect of the preceding :

> The whole head is sick, the whole heart faint.
> From the sole of the foot even unto the head there is no soundness in it ;
> It is wound, and bruise, and running sore ;
> They have neither pressed it nor bound it up,
> Neither hath it been softened with ointment.
> Your country is desolate ;
> Your cities are burnt with fire :
> Your land—strangers devour it in your presence,
> And it is desolation, like the overturning produced by enemies.

So in Isa. lviii. 6. seq. :

> Is not this the fast that I approve :
> To loose the bands of wickedness,
> To undo the heavy burdens,
> To free the oppressed,
> And to break asunder every yoke ?
> Is it not to deal thy bread to the hungry,
> And to bring the poor that are cast out, into thy house ?
> When thou seest the naked, that thou clothe him,
> And that thou hide not thyself from thine own kindred ?

A beautiful specimen of this kind of amplification occurs in the powerful
passage in Job iii. 3—9, where he curses the day of his birth, and where he
amplifies the thought with which he commences in the most impressive and
solemn manner :

> O that the day might have perished in which I was born,
> And the night which said, " A male child is conceived."
> Let that day be darkness,
> Let not God inquire after it from on high !
> Yea, let not the light shine upon it !
> Let darkness and the shadow of death stain it ;
> Let a cloud dwell upon it,
> Let whatever darkens the day terrify it !

Examples of this kind of parallelism occur in abundance in the Scriptures,
and especially in the Prophets.

Under this head may be included also a species of *alternate* parallelism, a form of poetic composition not uncommon. The following are specimens. Isa. li. 19 :

> These two things are come upon thee ;
> Who shall bemoan thee ?
> Desolation and destruction, famine and the sword ;
> How shall I comfort thee ?

That is, taken alternately, desolation by famine, and destruction by the sword. Cant. i. 5 :

> I am black, but yet beautiful, O daughters of Jerusalem ;
> Like the tents of Kedar, like the pavilions of Solomon.

That is, black as the tents of Kedar ; beautiful as the pavilions of Solomon.

Under this head, also, may be mentioned a form of parallelism, of a highly artificial kind, called the introverted parallelism, where the fourth member answers to the first, and the third to the second. An instance of this kind occurs in the New Testament ; Matth. vii. 6 :

> Give not that which is holy unto the dogs,
> Neither cast ye your pearls before swine ;
> Lest they trample them under their feet,
> And turn again and rend you.

Here it is the dogs mentioned in the first member which in the fourth it is said would turn and rend them ; and the swine which it is said in the third member would trample under their feet the pearls mentioned in the second.

It may be added here, that the Arabic has no parallelism of members, as the Hebrew has, though both the modern Arabic and Persian have rhyme. Pococke, however, regards the Arabic metre as a late invention, and probably everywhere *rhyme* was invented long after poetry had existence in other forms.

In reading the Bible, it is of importance to understand the laws of poetic parallelism, for it often furnishes important facilities in interpretation. One member often expresses substantially the same sense as its parallel, and difficult words and phrases are thus rendered susceptible of easy explanation. The subject of Hebrew poetry is confessedly one of the most difficult pertaining to the study of the Bible, and all that is hoped from the above observations is to furnish some principles which may be applied in the study of the sacred Scriptures. Those who are desirous of pursuing the investigation further may consult the following works :

Lowth's Introduction to Isaiah, and Lectures on Hebrew Poetry, particularly Lec. xix. ; The Spirit of Hebrew Poetry, by J. G. Herder, translated by James Marsh, 2 vols. 12mo. ; De Wette, Einleitung in die Psalmen (translated in the Biblical Repository, vol. iii. p. 445, seq.) ; Nordheimer's Hebrew Grammar, vol. ii. p. 320, seq. ; Theod. Eberti Poetica Hebraica ; Davidis Lyra, autore Francisco Gomaro ; Augusti Pfeifferi Diatribe de Poesi Heb. ; and Francis Hare on the Psalms, found in Ugolin's Thesau. ; Sac. Ant., tom. xxxi.

In reference to the poetry in the book of Job, the following characteristics are discernible.

I. The leading feature of the Hebrew poetry—*the parallelism*—is observed with great strictness and perfection. In no part of the Old Testament are there more perfect specimens of this mode of composition. The parallels are, indeed, in general, of the more simple forms—where the second member corresponds with the first with some slight modification of the meaning ; and the instances are very rare, if they occur at all, where the more laboured and artificial forms of the parallelism occur. Indeed, it may be doubted whether one instance of the *introverted* parallelism occurs in the book. This circumstance marks the early age of the poetry, and is an additional consideration to show that the book had an early origin.

II. Besides the parallelism, the poem bears the marks of a regular design or plan in its composition, and is constructed with a rigid adherence to the purpose which was in the mind of the author. I refer to the *tripartite* division of the book, and to the regularity observed in that division. The *trichotomy* appears not only in respect to the longer divisions of the book, but also in respect to most of its minuter subdivisions. Thus we have in the grand division of the book (1.) the prologue; (2.) the poem proper; and (3.) the epilogue, or the conclusion. The *poem* presents also three leading divisions, (1.) the dispute or controversy of Job and his three friends; (2.) the address of Elihu, who proffers himself as umpire; and (3.) the address of God, who decides the controversy. In the controversy between Job and his friends, we find the same artificial arrangement. There are *three* series in the controversy, each having the same order, and without any deviation, except that in the last of the series, Zophar, whose turn it was to speak, fails to respond. No poem in any language exhibits a more artificial structure than this, and as this is the most striking feature in it, it may be proper to exhibit it at one view.

> I. The first series of the argument, chap. iv.—xiv.
>
> > (1.) With Eliphaz, chap. iv.—vii.
> >   (a) Speech of Eliphaz, chap. iv., v.
> >   (b) Reply of Job, chap. vi., vii.
> > (2.) With Bildad, chap. viii.—x.
> >   (a) Speech of Bildad, chap. viii.
> >   (b) Reply of Job, chap. ix., x.
> > 3.) With Zophar, chap. xi.—xiv.
> >   (a) Speech of Zophar, chap. xi.
> >   (b) Reply of Job, chap. xii.—xiv.
>
> II. The second series of the argument, chap. xv.—xxi.
>
> > (1.) With Eliphaz, chap. xv.—xvii.
> >   (a) Speech of Eliphaz, chap. xv.
> >   (b) Reply of Job, chap. xvi., xvii.
> > (2.) With Bildad, chap. xviii., xix.
> >   (a) Speech of Bildad, chap. xviii.
> >   (b) Reply of Job, chap. xix.
> > (3.) With Zophar, chap. xx., xxi
> >   (a) Speech of Zophar, chap. xx.
> >   (b) Reply of Job, chap. xxi.
>
> III. The third series of the argument, chap. xxii.—xxxi.
>
> > (1.) With Eliphaz, chap. xxii.—xxiv.
> >   (a) Speech of Eliphaz, chap. xxii.
> >   (b) Reply of Job, chap. xxiii., xxiv.
> > (2.) With Bildad, chap xxv., xxvi.
> >   (a) Speech of Bildad, chap. xxv.
> >   (b) Reply of Job, chap. xxvi.
> > (3.) With Zophar, chap. xxvii.—xxxi.
> >   (a) *   *   *   *   *   *   *
> >   (b) Continuation of the reply of Job, chap. xxvii.—xxxi.

So also in the final address of Job (chap. xxvi.—xxxi.), there are three speeches, (a) chap. xxvi.; (b) chap. xxvii. xxviii.; (c) chap. xxix.—xxxi. In the speeches of Elihu, there is evidence of a design that a regular number of speeches should be made. The plan seems to have been, that to each of the speakers there should be assigned three speeches. But Zophar, one of the original disputants, had failed when his regular turn came, and *four* speeches are allowed to Elihu; (1.) chap. xxxii. xxxiii.; (2.) chap. xxxiv.; (3.) chap. xxxv.; and (4.) chap. xxxvi. xxxvii. In the controversy, the dispute appears to have been carried on through three days or sessions—perhaps with a considerable interval between them, and the most rigid order was observed during the debate. In like manner JEHOVAH is introduced as making three addresses, (1.) chap. xxxviii. xxxix.; (2.) chap. xl. 1, 2; and (3.) chap. xl. 6—24, chap. xli.; and last of all the epilogue contains a similar subdivision. There is (1.) an account of Job's justification; (2.) his reconciliation with his friends; (3.) his restoration to prosperity, chap. xlii.

" If." says Prof. Stuart (Intro. to the Apocalypse), " we withdraw our attention from these obvious and palpable trichotomies, in respect to the larger portions of the book, and direct it to the examination of the individual speeches which are exhibited, we shall find the like three-fold division in many of them. If we descend still lower, even down to strophes, we shall there find that a great number consist of three members."

" Thus the economy of this book exhibits a regular and all-pervading series of trichotomies, most of them so palpable that none can mistake them. This seems to settle two things that have been called in question, viz.: first, the highly artificial arrangement of the book ; and secondly, that the prologue and the epilogue are essential parts of the work. The great contest about the genuineness of these, and also of the speech of Elihu, might have been settled long ago, had due attention been paid to the trichotomy of the book. It is proper to add, that notwithstanding the highly artificial arrangement of the poem, such is the skill of the writer in the combinations, that every thing appears to proceed in a way which is altogether easy and natural."

Another circumstance evincing artificial arrangement is noticed by Eichhorn, Einleitung, § 640, vol. v. pp. 148—150. It is the *regular advance* in the argument, or the *increase* (das Wachsende) of zeal and ardour in the debaters. This is seen in the speeches of Job. " In the beginning he will not trust himself to contend with God (chap. ix. 11); then he wishes before his death to prove to him his innocence (chap. xiii. 3); then he sighs after a judicial hearing before God (chap. xvi. 18); then he affirms that it is certain that before his death God will appear to vindicate him (chap. xix. 25); and then at last he solemnly demands of him a judicial investigation." The same is true of the other speakers. " Eliphaz, who begins the controversy with Job, commences with mildness and gentleness; for the passion and heat with which he had heard Job speak, one gladly forgives to a sufferer. With Bildad, who speaks next, every thing is more severe and bitter; the heat of Job had made his friends too warm, and he could not speak to Job with the gentleness and softness evinced by Eliphaz. And so also the manner of the individual speakers rises in warmth and interest. Eliphaz, the first time that he speaks, is mild and forbearing; the second time he is more ardent, and utters reproaches against Job, yet in a manner somewhat covered; but in the third speech he hides nothing, but charges him openly with being a hypocrite. The same thing is observable in the speeches of Bildad. In the beginning of his speeches he is more heated than Eliphaz, yet he condemns him only *conditionally* (bedingnissweis); in the second he condemns him openly; and in the third, with cool contempt, he tramples the sufferer under foot."

The same artificial mode of composition prevails elsewhere in the poetry of the Hebrews. See it more fully illustrated in the Intro. to Isaiah, § 8. Thus we have seven Psalms each verse of which begins with a letter of the alphabet in succession ; Ps. xxv., xxxiv., xxxvii., cxi., cxii., cxix., cxlv. In Ps. cxix. we have this peculiarity, that each paragraph of it consists of eight verses, and these eight verses all begin with the same letter of the alphabet. In the book of Lamentations, four chapters out of the five are *alphabetic* compositions, while chap. iii. exhibits three verses in succession, each one of which begins with the same letter of the alphabet. This artificial mode of composition seems to have been one of the earliest features of Hebrew poetry, and in no part of the Bible is it more perfect than in the book of Job.

III. The true account of the book of Job, as a poem, is, that *it is* A PUB-LIC DEBATE, *conducted in a poetic form, on a very important question pertaining to the divine government.* It is not an epic poem, where the hero is placed in a great variety of interesting and perilous situations, and where the main object is to create an interest in his behalf; it is not a drama, with a regular plot to be gradually developed, and where the dialogue is adopted to inculcate some moral lesson, or to awaken a tragic interest. It is *a public discussion,* with a real case in view, where the question is one of great difficulty, and where there is all the interest of reality. The question is fairly understood. The whole arrangement appears to have been made, or tacitly fallen into from a sense of propriety. The discussion is continued, evidently, on successive days, giving a full opportunity to weigh the arguments which had been previously advanced, and to frame a reply. The most respectful attention is paid to what is advanced. There is no rude interruption; no impatience; no disposition to correct the speaker; no outbreak of excited feeling even under the most provoking remarks. The *poetic form* in the argument is adopted manifestly, because it would furnish the opportunity for expressing their sentiments in the most terse, beautiful, and sententious manner, and in a way which could be best retained in the memory, and which was most in accordance with the genius of the age. In all countries, poetry is among the earliest forms of composition; and in Arabia and the East generally, it has been customary to preserve their sentiments in the terse and somewhat proverbial form which is exhibited here.

If conjecture may be allowed in a case where it is now impossible to speak with certainty, and if we may be permitted to judge according to what *appears* to have been the fact in regard to this remarkable argument, we may imagine that the discussion assumed somewhat of this form; Job, as related in chap. i. and ii., was suddenly overwhelmed with almost unparalleled calamity. All that he possessed was suddenly swept away; and he was visited with a form of disease of the most distressing nature. Of his character hitherto there had been no doubt. His life had never given occasion to suspect him of insincerity. Three of his friends, apparently intimate with him before this—men of age, and prudence, and large experience, came to him with a full intention of sympathizing with him, and of suggesting to him the usual topics of consolation under trials. The greatness of his calamity, severe beyond what they had anticipated, struck them dumb with amazement, and they remained a long time speechless, apparently contemplating the keenness and the extent of his sufferings. It would be obvious that the *case* would present a grave one for consideration; that it would be in conflict with many of the maxims which they had cherished, as we learn from their expressions subsequently, about the methods of the divine government with the pious. Here was an individual, esteemed universally as a man of eminent piety, who was now treated as if he were the most vile and abandoned of sinners. This *fact,* thus in conflict with their settled views, appears at first to have confounded them, and to have divested them of the power of offering the topics of consolation which they had intended. But it was not until Job made his first speech (chap. iii.), bitterly cursing his day, indulging in the language of murmuring and complaint, and wishing for death, that they seem to have had any confirmed suspicion of his insincerity and hypocrisy. That speech, in connection with his remarkable sufferings, so much at variance with all their views of the manner in which God deals with the righteous, seems to have satisfied them that, so far from being, as had been supposed, a man of eminent piety, he was a man of eminent guilt. This, therefore, opened the whole field of debate, and suggested the great question whether the divine government was not conducted on equal principles here; whether a life of piety would not be attended with corresponding prosperity, and whether extraordinary sufferings like these were not demonstrative of corresponding guilt. Either tacitly, or by express arrangement, it seems to have been agreed to discuss this question. The *manner* of doing it was the best possible, and was in accordance with every principle of urbanity, justice, and refined feeling. Eliphaz, as the eldest, and as the most experienced and sagacious, led the way in the argument, to be followed, in the same order, during each *sitting* of the debate, by his two friends. Job, having no one to stand by him, and being the one most deeply concerned in the issue, is allowed to respond to each one of the speakers. Three successive series of arguments in this order gave to each one the privilege of expressing all that he desired to say on the point of debate; thus permitting each one of the friends of Job to speak three times, and Job himself to make nine addresses. It seems to have been understood that the debate should proceed in this order until the third series should be completed, or until one party should cease to speak. The debate continued in fact until Zophar, whose turn it was, failed to speak—thus tacitly acknowledging defeat, and leaving the whole field open, and conceding that no reply could be made to Job. At this stage Elihu, who appears to have been an attentive auditor, comes forward to do what the friends of Job tacitly confessed that they could not do— to reply to what had been advanced by Job. He comes modestly forward, and begs permission to state some considerations which had been suggested to him, and which he supposed would relieve all the difficulty. The divine interposition, unexpected by all except by Job (comp. chap. xix. 25—29, Notes), the indications of whose appearance in the tempest overwhelm the mind of Elihu with astonishment, and cause him abruptly to break off his address (Notes on chap. xxxvii. 19—24), closes the argument. "The whole book," says Eichhorn, "may be regarded as a dialogue of sages respecting the government of the world, with a prologue and an epilogue; a *consessus* of friends, as we find it among the Arabs of later times. In Casiri, Biblioth. Arab. Escur., t. i. p. 144, mention is made of a dialogue held by fifty-one artists, in which each one praises his own art." Einleit. § 640, vol. v. p. 142. By this supposition, it will be allowable to suppose that the debate may have occupied several days; for there is no evidence that it was completed at one sitting. By this supposition, also, some difficulties which have been felt in regard to its composition may be removed. (1.) It is not necessary to suppose that the addresses are *extemporary;* and the objection that it is incredible that men in the heat of debate should utter such finished and sublime specimens of poetry, is of no force. All the time requisite for composing each successive speech, may be allowed, and it may be presumed that each speaker came fully prepared to meet what had been advanced by the one who went before him. (2.) The same supposition will meet much of the difficulty which has been felt in regard to the speeches of Job. It has been said that it is wholly incredible that a man suffering under intolerable pain, and prostrate by long continued disease, should have uttered the sentiments which are here ascribed to him, and been able to reply as he did to the arguments of his opponents. To this difficulty it may be said in reply, that there is no evidence that his disease impaired his mental powers—for it is not *always* true that the faculties of the mind are enfeebled by bodily suffering; and further, that Job may have had ample time to mature his reflections, and to arrange them in such a manner as he would wish. (3.) This supposition may throw some light on the question of the authorship of the poem. According to this view, what would be necessary for the author to do, would be to prepare the introductory and concluding historical statements, and to collect and arrange the speeches which had been actually made. Those speeches would doubtless be preserved mostly in the memory, and the work to be done would be rather that of a *compiler* or *editor*, than that of an *author*. In the discussion pursued in the poem, the great inquiry propounded relates to the equality of the divine dealings, and this inquiry is conducted in the most interesting manner conceivable. An actual case of a pious sufferer existed, giving to the question all the interest of reality. It was not a mere abstract inquiry, examined in a cold and unfeeling manner ; but it was a case which, while it admitted of all the illustration which could be derived from experience, observation, tradition, and profound reflection, had all the interest also to be derived from the warm feelings and even excited passions which the case of an actual sufferer is fitted to produce.

The main question discussed has respect to the distribution of good and evil in the world. It is an inquiry whether there is a righteous and equal retribution in the present life, and whether the dealings of God here are according to the character. In the discussion of this question, the three friends of Job maintain the affirmative—defending the position, that the character of an individual can be determined from the events which occur to him under the divine administration ; that there is a course of things which favours the righteous, and brings calamity on the wicked ; that where there is extraordinary prosperity there is extraordinary virtue, and that when overwhelming calamities come upon a man or a community, there is proof of extraordinary wickedness. On this principle they infer that, notwithstanding Job's professions in his prosperity, the calamities which had come upon him were full proof that he had been insincere, and that he must have been at heart a man of eminent wickedness. In defence of this opinion, they refer to their own observation, appeal to revelations which they say they had had on this very point, adduce the maxims and adages which had been accumulated by their ancestors, and boldly maintain that it *must* be so under the administration of a holy God.

Job as strenuously maintains the opposite opinion, with all the interest which can be derived from the fact that it is his own case, and that it involves the whole question about his own character as well as from the fact that it is an inquiry about the general rectitude of the dealings of God with his creatures. He appeals to his consciousness of integrity ; shows by abstract arguments that the opinions of his friends are not well founded ; refers to general principles, to his own observation, and to the reports of travellers ; complains bitterly of the unkindness of his friends, and expresses an earnest desire to carry the cause up to God to get a hearing before him, with a confident assurance that he would at once decide it in his favour. He is evidently embarrassed by the arguments of his friends, and is unable to meet many things in their reasoning, and to explain *why* it is that the righteous are thus afflicted. He maintains only that their afflictions do *not* prove that they are bad men, and that the dealings of God with men are *not* a certain indication of their true moral character. There are two considerations which would have relieved his embarrassment, and which *we* would now use in such a case, but which did not occur to him ; the one is, that the afflictions of the righteous may be *disciplinary*, and may be really a proof of paternal kindness on the part of God ; the other, that in the future state all the inequalities of the present life will be adjusted ; that though the good may suffer much here, they will be abundantly recompensed hereafter ; and that however prosperous the wicked may be here, the divine dealings in the future state will be entirely according to their character.

In reading the book of Job, we must remember that these truths were not then clearly revealed. We must place ourselves in the circumstances of the speakers, and look at the argument in view of the light which they had. We must not approach the book under the feeling that they had the same knowledge of the divine government, of the design of affliction, and of the doctrine of the future state, which we now have under the Christian dispensation. *Children* now, under the light of the gospel, may easily solve many questions on moral subjects which entirely confounded these sagacious ancient sages, just as children now can answer many questions in astronomy which perplexed and embarrassed the most profound Grecian and Roman philosophers.

The manner in which the great question about the equality of the divine administration is disposed of in this book, will be understood by a brief analysis of the argument, and by a statement of the points maintained by the different speakers.

I. In the commencement of the book, the reader is made acquainted with the character and the sufferings of the principal personage referred to. We are introduced to an inhabitant of the land of Uz, in the northern part of Arabia. He is a prince or an Emir in the place where he resided—honoured and respected by all. He is a man of large property, whose life had been one of almost unexampled prosperity. He is surrounded by a large and interesting family, who are represented as enjoying themselves in the festivities usual in the place where they resided, and in a manner appropriate to their station and rank in life. The patriarch himself is a man of eminent holiness. He performs with faithfulness the duties of a pious father, evinces the deepest concern that his children should not sin, and is declared to be a perfect and upright man—a man whose character would bear the severest scrutiny. In this state of things, the scene is opened in heaven. The tribunal of the Almighty appears; an assembling of the Sons of God occurs; and the celestial spirits are summoned before the Most High. Among those who came is Satan—an evil spirit—an accuser—a dark, malignant being, who is represented as having no confidence in human integrity, and who says that he has been through the earth to look on its affairs. Being asked respecting the character of this good man, he insinuates that all his religion is mere selfishness : that he could not be otherwise than a devout worshipper of God in the circumstances in which God had placed him ; but that if his circumstances were changed, it would soon be apparent that all his professions were false and hollow. Permission is given to the evil spirit to make the trial, with the single reservation that the person of the man himself was to be untouched. Animated by this permission, Satan immediately leaves the heavenly council, and in a single day Job is stripped of his children and all his possessions. By the instrumentality of robbers, and whirlwinds, and storms, every thing which he had is swept away, and messenger after messenger comes to him in rapid succession, acquainting him with these calamities. Still the integrity of the patriarch remains. He sits down patient and resigned. Not a word of murmuring escapes from his lips, not a complaining thought seems to have been in his heart. The trial is thus far complete ; the insinuation of Satan is shown to be unfounded, and piety is triumphant.

The celestial session is held again, and Satan again appears. Foiled in his first attempt, he now insinuates that the trial had not been fair ; that there could be no real, thorough trial of the character of a man unless he were made personally to suffer, and his life were placed in jeopardy. If a man were himself spared to enjoy health, it was not yet certainly known what his true character was, for he might still be purely selfish. If he were made personally to suffer, he says that, so far from maintaining his integrity, he would curse God to his face. Permission is given to make this trial also, with the single reservation that his life was to be spared. The evil spirit again goes forth, selects the most painful and loathsome form of disease consistent with the preservation of life, and Job becomes an object of loathing and abhorrence even to his friends. Still this trial results as the former did. The integrity of the patriarch is preserved, and religion again triumphs. Satan is thus far foiled, and appears no more on the scene. The best man on the earth is made the most miserable; the man that was most prospered in the East is reduced to the lowest stage of poverty and wretchedness. But his virtue has survived it all, and it is seen that fidelity to God can be main-

tained in the most sudden reverses and in the deepest distresses which the
body can be made to endure short of death.

In this state of things, three of his friends, who had heard of his calamities,
are represented as coming by agreement to condole with him. When they
arrive, however, they have nothing to say. The sufferings of their friend
appear to be beyond any thing which they had anticipated, and the topics of
consolation which they had purposed to use are found insufficient, and they
sit down in silent astonishment. The overwhelming calamities which had
come upon an eminently good man seem to have confounded them, but still
they do not yet express a doubt, if they cherished a suspicion, about his
integrity. The subject is evidently one that, in their view, demands grave
reflection, and that presents some deep inquiries about the reason of the
divine dealings. They were probably overcome by the unexpected severity
of his sufferings and the depth of their sympathetic sorrow, but they were
perplexed also because it seems to have conflicted with their cherished views
of the divine government, that such trials should come upon so good a man;
and it is *possible* that, in accordance with these views, a *suspicion* may have
already been started in their minds that he was less holy than he had been
reputed to be. Still, if they had any doubts about the integrity of their
friend, his perfect patience and resignation seem thus far to have silenced
or removed them, or their courtesy kept them from expressing them, and
not knowing what to say, they sat down in silence. It was only the bitter
language of complaint of the sufferer himself (chap. iii.), that led them to
adopt the conclusion that their much venerated and esteemed friend *must*
have been a bad man.

II. The second, or principal part of the work, comprises the discussion
between Job and his three friends, and extends from the third to the thirty-
first chapter. The discussion is brought on by the bitter complaints of Job
as recorded in chap. iii. Up to this time his friends had been silent. If
they had had any suspicion of his integrity, they had not until then expressed
it. His complaints and murmurings, however, now gave them occasion to
express their feelings without reservation. They commence the discussion
respecting the causes of human suffering. They hold the doctrine of a strict
retribution in the present life; maintain that misery always implies corresponding guilt; defend the opinion that it is fair to infer what a man's character is from the dealings of God with him; and do not hesitate to express
the opinion that the calamities of Job must have been brought upon him in
consequence of his secret wickedness. Job repels their insinuations with
indignation, and boldly asserts his innocence. He knows not why he suffers.
He is unable to explain the causes why calamities come upon good men, but
he maintains that they are no certain indications of the character of the
sufferer. He regards himself as unkindly treated by his friends; complains
that they are not disposed to do him justice; affirms that instead of offering
him the consolation which they ought, they have taken occasion to aggravate
his woes by false and severe accusations; and expresses a desire to carry the
cause directly before God himself, assured that *he* would do him that justice
which was denied him by his friends. His friends are offended at his sentiments, and undertake to vindicate the conduct of the Deity towards him, and
repeat the charges with greater asperity, and even accuse him of particular
crimes. But the more they press the argument, the more confidently does
he assert his innocence, and the more boldly does he appeal to God to vindicate his character. His friends are finally reduced to silence; Bildad, in the
last series of the controversy, closing the discussion by a few general maxims
of great beauty, but without any pertinency to the cause, on the greatness
of God, and Zophar, who should have replied in his turn to Job, not saying
any thing.

In this controversy, as has been already remarked, there are three series, or sessions, conducted with great regularity, and carried on in the same order. Eliphaz is the first speaker, Bildad the second, and Zophar the third; and Job replies to each.

The *first* series of the discussion extends from chap. iv. to chap. xiv. Eliphaz commences it, chap. iv., v. He probably had the precedence among those engaged in the discussion, both on account of age and experience. He is more mild than either of the others, depends more on close reasoning and observation, and is less severe in his reflections on his friend. His speech commences with delicacy and an air of candour, and is conducted with artful address. After apologizing, in a tender manner, for speaking, he proceeds to point out the inconsistency of a good man's repining under discipline; says that Job had counselled and comforted many others, and ought now to show that the same considerations were sufficient to sustain himself, and that it is absurd that *he* should not bear up under trial who had so often exhorted others to fortitude. He then advances the position that the truly righteous are never overthrown, and that no one who was innocent ever perished; that the wicked are dealt with according to their sins, and that the ways of God must be just. This position he proceeds to establish by a vision which he says he himself had had, of a most remarkable character, affirming the uprightness of the divine dealings, and declaring that man could not be more just than his Maker, and that even the angels were charged with folly before God. The *object* of this, as applied by Eliphaz, is to meet the complaints of Job, and to show that God *must* be right in his ways. He admits (chap. v.) that the wicked may prosper for a while, but asserts that they will meet with sudden calamity; that their habitation will be suddenly cursed, their children crushed in the gate, and their property carried away by robbers. He does not expressly apply this to Job, but he leaves no doubt that it was intended for him, and advises Job even now to turn to God, and assures him that he may yet find happiness, and come to the grave in an honoured old age.

Job replies to Eliphaz (chap. vi., vii.), and justifies himself for complaining. He says that there was a good reason for his complaints; expresses again the earnest wish to die; declares that his strength is not equal to the weight of woes laid on him; complains severely of his friends for having wholly disappointed his reasonable expectations; and compares them to the deceitful brook of the desert, which wholly disappoints the hopes of the faint and thirsty traveller. He says that he had not *asked* them to come and sympathize with him, but that even now, if they would make use of solid argument, he would listen to them. He then (chap. vii.) proceeds to a more impassioned description of his sufferings, as being wholly beyond endurance; expresses again the wish to die; says that he is not a monster, like a whale, that God should pursue him in this manner; and complains of God in language highly irreverent, as having punished him far beyond his deserts, and as having set a special mark on *him*, and asks with impatience why he will not let him alone?

Bildad is the next one to speak, chap. viii. He commences his address in a most severe and provoking manner. He openly declares that the children of Job had been cut off for their transgressions, and that Job was a wicked man. If he were pure and upright, God would at once interpose and restore his prosperity. He exhorts him, therefore, as Eliphaz had done, to repent, and enforces his sentiments by a reference to the opinions of the men of former days. In accordance with those sentiments, he says that the hypocrite must be soon destroyed; that however flourishing and prosperous he may appear, he is like succulent plants that spring up with rapid growth and are soon withered; and that his hope will be like the spider's web. He does not expressly apply these maxims to Job, but he leaves no doubt on the mind that he intends it, and that he fully believes that this principle will fully account for all that he had suffered; or in other words, that in the midst of all his prosperity he had been a mere hypocrite.

To Bildad Job replies in his turn, chap. ix., x. He commences in a calm manner, and shows that he is superior to the acrimony of the assault. He acknowledges that all power is with God, and confesses that he has a right to universal supremacy. He controls the heavens and the earth, rules among the stars and directs them, and nothing can stand before the exertion of his power. He acknowledges that he is far from being perfect, and says that, even if this were his private feeling, he would not dare to assert it before God. He could not engage in so unequal a contest where he should regard him as guilty, but he must yield his own views to those of God. Still he maintains that the position of his friends cannot be defended; that the earth is given into the hands of the wicked; and that so far from its being true that the dealings of God are according to the character of men, and are a fair illustration of their character, it is a matter of fact that the wicked are triumphant and prosperous. Then he adverts to his own sorrows; says that his days are fast flying away amid grief, and complains bitterly that notwithstanding all his attempts *to be* innocent and holy, God holds and treats him *as if* he were a guilty man. Though he should wash himself in the purest water, yet God throws him in the ditch, and regards and treats him as if he were most vile. He complains that he has no fair opportunity of vindicating himself before God, and that he presses him down with sorrows so that he cannot make a defence; but says that if he would remove his rod from him, and give him the opportunity of a fair trial, he would speak, and would vindicate himself. Becoming more excited as he proceeds (chap. x.), he gives himself up to complaint. He becomes desperate at the idea that God has become his enemy and persecutor; speaks of him as if he were seeking an opportunity to inflict pain under some plausible pretence; complains that he had made him, as if with exquisite skill, only to torment and destroy him; says that he hunts him with the fierceness of a lion; expresses regret again that he had not died on the day of his birth; and entreats of God to let him alone only for a little time, till he should go down to the deep shades of death.

Zophar, the third speaker, now takes his place in the argument, and replies, chap. xi. He commences, as Bildad did, with violent invective. He regards Job as a man of words without sense; and reproaches him for maintaining his innocence before God. He says that the ways of God are plain, and earnestly desires that God would himself speak to Job, and is assured that he would then see that it was his own iniquities that had brought these calamities upon him. He refers, in magnificent language, to the supremacy of God; says that he fully understands the secret character of men; and, like Eliphaz and Bildad, exhorts Job to acknowledge his transgressions, and assures him that if he would do this he would be restored to prosperity and yet end his days in peace.

To Zophar Job replies, chap. xii., xiii., xiv. Yet he does not answer him personally. As they had all maintained the same sentiments, he groups them together, and commences, in turn, with a severe sarcasm. He says that no doubt wisdom would die with them, and reproaches them for their cool self-complacency and their arrogance in supposing that they were wiser than all the rest of mankind. In return for their traditionary maxims he retorts in the same manner, and shows them that he is as much at home in this kind of argument as they can be. He therefore adduces a large number of proverbial sayings (chap. xii.), of far more pertinency and point than many of those on which they relied, all going to show the majesty the power, and the supremacy of God. He then (chap. xiii.) commences a direct attack on their motives, and charges them with maintaining their opinions with the hope of propitiating the favour of God. To do this, he says, they had employed unsound arguments; had evinced partiality for God;

had been unwilling to yield the proper weight to the considerations adduced
on the other side ; and that they had really no regard for the *truth* in the
case, but were " special" and partial pleaders. He says that they ought to
be awed and to tremble in view of such a fact ; that they were really mocking God by undertaking to defend his government by such reasons as they
had adduced ; and that they had great reason to dread his investigation of
their motives, even when they were pretending to vindicate his government.
Alike in the principles of government which they ascribed to him, and the
arguments by which they undertook to vindicate him, they were offensive to
him, and must apprehend his displeasure. Weary with this mode of argumentation, he then expresses the earnest wish that he might carry his cause
directly before the tribunal of God, and manage it there, on equal terms, for
himself. He would go before God in this cause, confident that he would do
right, and resolved to trust him even though he should slay him, chap. xiii.
15. He would ask of him only two things—one was, that he would withdraw his hand from him so that he might be able to do justice to himself in
the argument ; the other was, that he would not take advantage of his great
power to overawe him, so that he could say nothing. He then reverts to his
calamities, speaks of them as overwhelming, and closes his address (chap.
xiv.) with a most beautiful and pathetic description of the frailty and the
shortness of life. He says that God removes man from all his comforts, and
hides him in the grave, hopeless of a return to the land of the living, and that
his condition is even more sad and desolate than that of the tree that is cut
down. Thus ends the *first* series in the controversy. The *second* commences
with chap. xv., and extends to the close of the twenty-first chapter. It is
pursued in the same order, and with the same question in view.

Eliphaz. as before, opens the discussion, chap. xv. He accuses Job of
vehemence and vanity ; charges him with casting off fear and restraining
prayer ; says that his own mouth condemned him ; blames him for his arrogance and presumption in speaking as if he were the first man that had lived ;
declares that with himself were men far more advanced in life than Job was,
and even older than his father ; and asks him whether he had been admitted
to the secret counsels of the Almighty, that he spoke so confidently of the
nature of his government. He then enters into a vindication of God ; proposes to adduce the observations of the sages of ancient times, in the purer
days when there was no foreign admixture in the sentiments of his country ;
and maintains that, in accordance with those sentiments, and with the settled
course of events, God deals with wicked men according to their character. This opinion he illustrates with great beauty, and by a large number
of apothegms, showing that the wicked man is subject to sudden alarms ;
that in prosperity the destroyer comes suddenly upon him ; that he wanders
abroad for bread ; that he is made to dwell in desolate cities ; that all his
prosperity fails, like the shaking off of fruit before it is ripe ; and that he is
like a tree dried up by heat.

To this speech of Eliphaz, Job replies in his turn, chap. xvi., xvii. He
renews his complaint of the severe manner in which his friends had treated
him, and says that he could easily speak as they did, but if his case were
theirs he would meet them with consolatory words. But now, he says, it
makes no difference whether he speaks or is silent. He finds no consolation
if he speaks ; he meets with no relief though he is silent. He then adverts
with new bitterness of feeling, and in still more severe and irreverent language, to the intensity of his sufferings, and to their manifest injustice. He
compares his enemies to a wild beast, gnashing his teeth and casting a furious glance upon him ; says that God had given him over to the ungodly ;
that he was at ease, when God came upon him like a hunter, and stationed
his archers around him ; that he had come upon him like an army attacking
a city, " breach upon breach ;" and that all this was *not* because he was

wicked, for his hands were pure. He then calls upon the earth to cover his blood, and says that, after all, his only appeal is to God, and before him his eyes poured out tears. In chap. xvii. he continues the description of his sufferings, and says that the record of his trials will yet be a subject of amazement to good men which they will not be able to understand, and that all his plans are now broken off, and that he *must* make the grave his house and his bed in darkness.

To this address of Job, Bildad replies in his turn, chap. xviii. He begins by repeating the accusation before made, that the argument of Job was made up merely of vain words. He accuses him of arrogance and a presumptuous idea of his own importance—as if the settled course of events were to be made to give way on his account. He says that the great laws of the divine administration are fixed, and that it is an established maxim that the wicked shall be punished in this life. This sentiment he proceeds to enforce by a number of beautiful adages or proverbs. The light of the wicked shall be put out ; the candle in his dwelling shall be extinguished ; he shall be cast down by his own counsel ; the gin shall suddenly take him ; the robber shall come upon him ; his strength shall vanish ; terrors shall surprise him ; his roots shall perish ; his memory shall perish ; he shall be chased out of the world ; he shall have neither son nor nephew ; and all that come after him shall hold him up as an example of the manner in which God deals with the wicked. Bildad advances nothing new, but he enforces what had been said before with great emphasis, and urges it as if it were so settled that it *could* not admit of dispute. He does not, in the description of the evils that come upon the wicked, refer to Job by name, but he presents his argument in such a way as to leave no doubt that he designs to have it applied to him. There is much refinement of cruelty in this, and he doubtless *meant* that it should be keenly felt by Job.

In the reply of Job to Bildad, chap. xix., he shows that he felt it deeply. His speech on this occasion is one of the most pathetic parts of the poem, and exhibits his character in a most beautiful light. He commences, as usual, with the language of sorrow, but it is with a tender and subdued spirit. He asks his friends how long they will continue to vex him, and crush him with their remarks ; says that they had reproached him ten times, and had made themselves strange to him ; and declares that *if* he had erred, his error was his own, and remained with himself. He then gives a most affecting description of his sufferings. God had overthrown him ; he had fenced up his way; he had taken the crown from his head ; he had removed all his hopes ; he had put away from him his brethren and friends, his kinsfolk and acquaintance ; he had made him an object of reproach to his servants ; his wife was estranged from him, and he was derided even by children. In most impassioned language he calls on his friends to pity him, for the hand of God had touched him. Then follows the most noble and sublime declaration, perhaps, to be found in the book. Conscious of the importance of what he was about to say, he asks that his words might be engraved on the eternal rock, and then professes his unwavering confidence in God, and his firm assurance that he would yet appear and fully vindicate his character. Though now consumed by disease, and though this process should still go on till all his flesh was wasted away, yet he had the firmest conviction that God would appear on the earth to deliver him, and that with renovated flesh, and in prosperity, he would be permitted to see God for himself. For a view of the reasons for this interpretation of this sublime passage, the reader is referred to the Notes on the chapter.

Zophar now speaks in his turn, chap. xx. But he speaks only to recapitulate the old argument under a new form. He maintains the position which had been so often before advanced, that certain and dreadful calamity must overtake the wicked. This thought he puts into new forms, and urges it with a variety of proverbial illustrations and bold statements, but without much that is new in the argument. He undoubtedly means, like the previous speakers, to have Job apply this to himself, though he does not expressly declare it.

Job replies to Zophar, chap. xxi., and his reply closes the second session of the controversy. He collects all his strength for the argument, as though he were resolved at once to answer all that had been said. He calls upon them attentively to mark what he has to urge; and says that if they will now hear him, they may then mock on. He then proceeds to answer their arguments by appealing to well-known and indisputable *facts*. He says that the wicked live—grow old—become mighty in power—are prospered in their flocks and herds—send forth their children to the dance—and spend their days in wealth and enjoyment, and then go down to the grave without long and lingering pain. He says that they openly cast off the fear of God, and live in irreligion. Yet he admits that it is not *always* so; that the candle of the wicked is sometimes put out, and that sorrows are laid up for their children; so that no universal rule can be laid down in regard to the dealings of God with men here. He alleges that in fact there is the greatest variety in the manner in which people die—one dying in full strength, cut down in his vigour, and another in the bitterness of his soul, having had no pleasure. He says that the wicked are *reserved* for the day of destruction—for some future retribution, and that they will be hereafter brought forth to wrath. By this appeal to *facts*, he evidently supposed that the controversy would be ended. Of the *facts* he had no doubt; and these facts were of more value than all speculations on the subject.

The *third* session of the discussion, like the previous ones, is opened by Eliphaz, chap. xxii. This is the last speech which Eliphaz makes, and roused by the argument of Job in the previous chapter, and excited by his appeal to *facts*, he pours forth his soul in one grand effort to confute the position which he had taken. There is great art in this speech, and greater severity than he had before used. He begins by maintaining that a man could not be profitable to God, and that he could not be influenced in his dealings with men by any claim which they had on him, or any dread which he had of them. No rank, authority, or eminence could prevent his dealing with them as he pleased. He then, in open and bold terms, charges Job with great guilt; says that these calamities *could* not have come upon a man unless there had been extraordinary iniquity, and proceeds to argue *as if* this were so, and to state what crimes Job must have committed to make it necessary to bring such calamities upon him. He accuses him of cruelty, oppression, and injustice in the performance of his duties as a magistrate; affirms that he had wronged the poor, the widow, and the fatherless; says that he had wholly disregarded the laws of hospitality, and that it was no wonder that in view of these things such heavy calamities had come upon him. It could not be otherwise. God could have dealt with him in no other way than this. He then appeals, with great force, to the deluge, and says that that was a case which demonstrated that God would deal with the wicked according to their character and deserts. In view of these things he again counsels Job to acquaint himself with God, and to be at peace with him. He assures him that if he would confess his sins and return to God, he would yet have prosperity, and be able to lay up gold as dust; and that if he prayed to God, he would be propitious to him. He would become yet a counsellor to the feeble, and be exalted to honour in the land.

Job, in his turn, replies, chap. xxiii., xxiv. He commences in a most pathetic and tender manner. He turns away from every human helper, and looks to God. He had looked to earthly friends in vain; and finding there no consolation, he expresses the most earnest wish that he might be able to carry his cause at once before his Maker. Could he come before him, as he wished, he would plead his cause there, and there he would find One who *would* hear him, and would know why it was that he was thus afflicted. He could not now explain it, yet *God* would do it, if he was permitted to carry his cause before him. Yet he could not find him. He looked in every direction for some token of his appearing, in vain. He went east, and west, and north, and south—in the quarters of the heavens where he usually manifested himself, but he could not find him; Notes on verses 9, 10. Yet he had the firmest confidence in him, and he felt assured that when he had been tried, he would come forth as gold. He asserts his consciousness of integrity, and says that it had been the great aim of his life to honour and obey God. He then proceeds, chap. xxiv., to defend his former position, and affirms that so far from its being true that the dealings of God were in accordance with the character of men here, it was *a fact* that the wicked often lived long and in great prosperity. He refers to large classes of the wicked—to those who remove the landmarks—to those who take the property of the widow and the fatherless for a pledge—to those who live by plunder—to those who oppress the poor and turn them out without shelter—to those who cause others to labour under hard exactions—to the murderer who rises early to accomplish his purpose—to the adulterer, and to all who perform deeds of darkness. He says that they often have in fact long prosperity, though he admits that they will be ultimately cut off; they are only exalted for a little time, and then they will be brought low.

These facts being undeniable, Bildad, whose turn it was to answer, does not attempt to reply to them. The argument of Job from what actually occurs had settled the question, and, so far as the friends of Job were concerned, decided the controversy. Bildad indeed, chap. xxv., attempts something like a reply; but it consists merely of a description of the power, wisdom, and majesty of God, and closes with the sentiment twice before expressed concerning the comparative impurity and insignificance of man—a reply that, however beautiful, has no relevancy to the considerations stated by Job. The manner in which he speaks is, in fact, a yielding of the argument, and a retiring from the field of debate.

Job, who next speaks, in reply to Bildad, chap. xxvi., opens his address in a strain of bitter irony. " How had the feeble, the powerless, and the ignorant [referring to himself], been strengthened, helped, and enlightened, by this wise speech!" He inquires of Bildad, by whose spirit he had spoken, and who had helped him to utter such marvellous things! He then proceeds himself to expatiate on the topic on which Bildad had proposed to enlighten him—the greatness and majesty of God, and does it in such a manner as to show that his own views were far more elevated than those of Bildad, and that he was far in advance of his professed teacher in his knowledge of the character and government of God. In this sublime description, he states his views of the creation; says that the deep, dark world of the shades is open before God ; that he stretched out the north over the immense void, and hung the earth upon nothing; that he binds up the thick clouds, holds back the face of his throne, compasses the waters with bounds so that they cannot pass, divides the sea with his power; and that by his own hands he had formed the beautiful constellations of the heavens. There is not to be found any where a more sublime description of God, nor a passage of more exquisite beauty, than that with which he closes :

> Lo ! these are but the outlines of his ways !
> And how faint the whisper which we hear of him !
> [Should he speak with] the thunder of his power, who could understand him ?

This was the appropriate place for Zophar to reply, and Job evidently paused to give him an opportunity. But he had nothing to say, and the argument on the part of the three friends of Job is closed.

Finding that no one replies to him, Job proceeds, in a more calm manner

to a full vindication of himself, chap. xxvii.—xxxi. He states further his
views about the government of God, and especially in reference to his dealings with a hypocrite (chap. xxvii.); gives a most beautiful description of the
search for wisdom, detailing many of the discoveries of science known in his
time, and saying that no one of them could disclose it, and concluding by
saying that true wisdom could be found only in the fear of the Lord (chap.
xxviii.); affectingly contrasts his present condition with his former prosperity (chap. xxix., xxx.); maintains the integrity of his life, asserting that he
was free from the crimes charged on him, and imprecating the severest punishment if he had been guilty; and closes by saying, that if God would come
forth and pronounce a just judgment on him, he would take the decision and
bind it on his head as a diadem, and march forth with it in triumph. For
the train of thought in these beautiful chapters, the reader is referred to the
"Analysis" prefixed to the Notes.

III. Thus far Job is triumphant. He has silenced his "friends," and
gained the field as a victor. At this stage a new character is introduced, who
comes with great apparent modesty, and yet with great pretensions. It is
Elihu. He had evidently listened to the debate, and feels indignant that no
one of the three friends of Job dared to reply to him. He is young and comparatively inexperienced, and hence he had thus far taken no part in the
controversy. But he professes to have had views communicated to him by
divine revelation, which clear up all the difficulties in the case; and he proceeds to state them. The single additional thought on which he dwells so
much, and which he introduces with so much pomp and parade of language,
is, *that afflictions are for the good of the sufferer*, and that if those who are
afflicted will hearken to the counsel which God sends, and turn from their
sins, they will find their afflictions to be sources of great benefit. This leading thought he exhibits in various lights, and evidently supposes that it
would be sufficient to solve the difficulties which had been felt in the discussion. It is remarkable that it had not been made more prominent by Job
and his friends; and it is from the fact that it had not been particularly adverted to, that leads Elihu to place it in such a variety of view. In the
course of his speech there is much severe reflection on Job for his rashness
and presumption, and the general tenor of the address is, undoubtedly, to
coincide with the "friends" of Job in their views, rather than in his. The
thirty-second chapter is wholly introductory, in which he expresses great
modesty, and apologizes for his speaking, by saying that he was grieved that
no one replied to Job, and that he was constrained to reply by the pressure
of important thoughts on his mind. In chap. xxxiii. he enters on his argument, and says that he was inspired of God to say what he had to communicate; that as Job had *wished* to bring his cause before God, he was now in
the place of God, and that Job need not be overawed by one of the same
nature with himself. He then adverts to what he understood Job to maintain, that he was innocent; and says that in this he could not be correct, but
that God must be more righteous than man. He then adverts to the main
thought which he had to communicate, that God speaks to man in various
ways, by dreams, by visions, and by afflictions,—to withdraw him from his
purpose, and to save him from sin. If God sends a messenger to him when
he is afflicted, and he turns from his sins, then he is merciful to him, and he
is restored to more than his former prosperity. To this fact Elihu calls the
particular attention of Job, and then pauses for a reply. As Job says nothing, Elihu in chap. xxxiv. proposes more particularly to examine his case.
He then proceeds to state that Job had manifested a very improper spirit;
that he had been irreverent, and had maintained that it was of no advantage
for a man to serve God. He then advances the position that God cannot
do wickedly, and proceeds to illustrate this by showing that he is supreme,
that it is presumptuous for man to arraign his dealings, and that in fact his

government is administered on the principles of equity. On the basis of this, and assuming that Job was a wicked man, he calls on him to confess that his chastisement was just, and to resolve to offend no more. In chap. xxxv. ho charges Job with having in fact maintained that his own righteousness was more than that of God. *This* position he proceeds to examine, and to show, which he does with great conclusiveness, that it is impossible that the right-eousness of man can be in any way profitable to God. He admits that a man's righteousness might be of advantage to his fellow-man, but maintains that it could not affect God. He then proceeds to show that the true rea-son why God did not interpose when men were afflicted, and remove their calamities, was, that they were obstinate and perverse, and that no one cried to God, who alone could give consolation. Elihu, having undertaken to vin-dicate the character of God, proceeds, in chap. xxxvi., xxxvii., to state some of the great principles of his government, and to maintain that God was right. He says that there yet remains much to be said on the part of God. Job, as he understood, had maintained that his government was adminis-tered on no settled principles. In opposition to this, Elihu asserts that God is mighty, and that his government is not to be despised ; that he will not prosper the wicked ; that in fact he protects the righteous and vindicates the cause of the poor ; and that his eye is on all. If they are in affliction, and bound in fetters, it is in order that they may see their iniquity and be brought to true repentance. The hypocrites, he says, heap up wrath, but the poor and afflicted are delivered, and Job would have found favour if he had been truly penitent. Elihu counsels him to beware lest his refusal to submit to God, and to exercise true repentance, should be the occasion of his entire destruction. To illustrate his views, and to show the necessity of submis-sion, he closes his speech (chap. xxxvi. 26—33; chap. xxxvii.) with a sublime description of the greatness of God, especially as manifested in the storm and tempest. There is in this description every indication that a storm was actually rising, and that a fearful tempest was gathering. In the midst of this approaching tempest, the address of Elihu is broken off, and the Almighty appears and closes the debate. See the Analysis to chap. xxxvii.

IV. The fourth part of the book consists of the address of the Almighty ; chap. xxxviii.—xli. This sublime discourse is represented as made from the midst of the tempest or whirlwind which Elihu describes as gathering. In this address, the principal object of God is to assert his own greatness and majesty, and the duty of profound submission under the dispensations of his government. The general thought is, that he is Lord of heaven and earth ; that all things have been made by him, and that he has a right to control them ; and that in the works of his hands he had given so much evidence of his wisdom, power, and goodness, that men ought to have unwavering con-fidence in him. He appeals to his works, and shows that in fact man could explain little, and that the most familiar objects were beyond his comprehen-sion. It was, therefore, to be expected that in his moral government there would be much that would be above the power of man to explain. In this speech, the creation of the world is first brought before the mind in lan-guage which has never been equalled. Then the Almighty refers to various things in the universe that surpass the wisdom of man to comprehend them, or his power to make them—to the laws of light ; the depths of the ocean ; the formation of the snow, the rain, the dew, the ice, the frost ; the changes of the seasons, the clouds, the lightnings ; and the instincts of animals. He then makes a particular appeal to some of the more remarkable inhabitants of the air, the forests, and the waters, as illustrating his power. He refers to the gestation of the mountain-goats ; to the wild ass, to the rhinoceros, to the ostrich, and to the horse ; chap. xxxix. The ground of the argument in this part of the address, is, that he had adapted every kind of animals to the mode of life which it was to lead ; that he had giving cunning where cunning was necessary, and where unnecessary, that he had withheld it ; that he had endowed with rapidity of foot or wing where such qualities were needful ; and that where power was demanded, he had conferred it. In reference to all these classes of creatures, there were peculiar laws by which they were governed ; and all, in their several spheres, showed the wisdom and skill of their Creator. Job is subdued and awed by these exhibitions, and confesses that he is vile ; chap. xl. 3—5. To produce, however, a more overpowering impression of his greatness and majesty, and to secure a deeper prostration before him, the Almighty proceeds to a particular description of two of the more remarkable animals which he had made—the behemoth, or hippopotamus, and the leviathan, or crocodile ; and with this description, the address of the Almighty closes.

The general impression designed to be secured by this whole address is that of awe, reverence, and submission. The general thought is, that God is supreme ; that he has a right to rule ; that there are numberless things in his government which are inexplicable by human wisdom ; that it is presumptuous in man to sit in judgment on his doings ; and that at all times man should bow before him with profound adoration. It is remarkable that in this address, the Almighty does not refer to the main point in the controversy. He does not attempt to vindicate his government from the charges brought against it of inequality, nor does he refer to the future state as a place where all these apparent inequalities will be adjusted. For the *reasons* of this, see the remarks at the close of the Notes on chap. xli.

V. The whole work now closes ; chap. xlii. Job is humbled and penitent. His confession is accepted, and his general course is approved. His three friends are reprimanded for the severity of their judgment on him, and he is directed to make intercession for them. His calamities are at an end, and he is restored to double his former prosperity, and is permitted to live long in affluence and respectability. Thus God shows himself in the end to be the friend of the righteous ; and thus the great object of the trial is fully secured—by showing that there *is* true virtue which is not based on selfishness, and that real piety will bear any trial to which it can be subjected.

§ VI. *The canonical authority and inspiration of the book.*

The canonical authority of the book of Job, or its right to a place among the inspired Scriptures, is determined on the same principles as the other books of the Old Testament. The argument for this rests mainly on two considerations, which have generally been regarded as satisfactory by those who hold to the divine mission of the Saviour and the inspiration of the apostles. The first is, that it was found in the canon of the Jewish Scriptures to which the Saviour gave his sanction as inspired ; and the other is, that it is quoted in the New Testament as of divine authority.

In regard to the first of these, there can be no doubt that it existed among the books which were regarded by the Hebrews as inspired. It has the same evidence of this kind which exists in favour of any one of the books of the Old Testament. There is the same authority—arising from the opinions of the Jews, from the existence of manuscripts, from the ancient versions, from repeated quotations, from extended commentaries, and from the enumeration of the books of divine inspiration in the ancient catalogues—in favour of the book of Job, which there is for any one of the books of Moses or of the prophets. The argument from this source is thus stated by Wemyss : " The Seventy translated it about 277 years before Christ ; Josephus places it among the historical writings ; Philo the Jew quotes a fragment of it ; part of it is evidently imitated by Baruch ; the subject of it is mentioned in the book of Tobit ; and in the catalogue of Jewish canonical books, drawn up by Melito, Bishop of Sardis, near the end of the second century, we find it inserted after the Song of Songs, on the supposition that it was written by Solomon. Jerome introduced it into the Vulgate, and almost all the Fathers of the Church have quoted it. The Talmud places it after the book of Psalms, so that Jews and Christians equally acknowledge its canonicity." p. 6. It was in reference to this entire collection that the Saviour gave to the Jews of his time the direction, "Search the Scriptures;" John v. 39. And it was of this entire collection that the apostle Paul said, "All Scripture is given by inspiration of God, and is profitable for doctrine, for reproof, for correction, for instruction in righteousness; 2 Tim. iii. 16.

The other argument for the canonical authority and inspiration of the book of Job, is the fact that it is quoted in the New Testament. It is introduced by the same formula, and evidently with the belief that it sustains the same rank as the other books of the inspired volume. It is true that it is but twice quoted directly, but that is sufficient to show that the writers of the New Testament, in common with all the Jews, regarded it as of divine authority. The quotations in the New Testament are the following:

Job v. 13 :

> "He taketh the wise in their own craftiness,"

quoted in 1 Cor. iii. 19, where Paul introduces the quotation by the words, "It is written," agreeably to the common form of quoting from the other parts of Scripture.

Job xxxix. 30 :

> "Her young ones suck up blood;
> And where the slain are, there is she," i. e. the eagle.

This is evidently referred to by the Saviour; Matt. xxiv. 28, "For wheresoever the carcass is, there will the eagles be gathered together;" and Luke xvii. 37. It must, in candour, however, be admitted that the argument from this source rests mainly on the former passage, as the remark of the Saviour may have been merely proverbial, without any *special* reference to the book of Job. Besides these places, there are a few others in which there seems to be an allusion to Job, though not so manifest as to be regarded as intentional quotations; see James iv. 10, comp. Job xxii. 29; Rom. xi. 34, 35, comp. Job xv. 8; and 1 Pet. v. 6, comp. Job xxii. 29. It is once alluded to by Philo (§ 31), but is not referred to by Josephus. *Eichhorn*, Einleit. § 645.

But if the canonical authority and inspiration of the book of Job be admitted, still a most interesting question presents itself. In what sense is it to be regarded as of divine origin? Are we to consider the whole of it as inspired? Are all the speeches made, and all the arguments used, and all the complainings uttered by Job, and all the views of science presented, to be regarded as the suggestions of the Holy Spirit? If this is not to be supposed, on what principles are we to be guided in determining what is of divine authority, and what not? And in what sense is the word *inspiration* to be used, as applied to those portions of the book? These questions, which probably occur to every reader of the book, and which create perplexity whenever they occur, make it necessary to offer a few suggestions in regard to its inspiration. The principles which are necessary to be understood in order to a correct interpretation of the book of Job, may be stated as follows:

(1.) In an inspired book there is an exact and infallible record of *facts* as they actually occur. Whether the record relates to the existence, perfections, and plans of God; to what he has done in the work of creation, providence, or redemption, or to his claims on mankind; whether to the existence and employments of angels, or to the creation, character, and destiny of man; and whether to the revolutions of kingdoms, or to the actions, words, feelings, and views of individual men, still the same principle exists in the case. The sole object is to secure *a fair record;* to state things as they are. The design of inspiration is not always to communicate new truth, or truth that was not or could not be otherwise known ; it is to make *a record* that shall be free from all error, and shall preserve the remembrance of things as they actually exist. And so far as pertains to this principle, it is unnecessary to inquire whether inspiration is by immediate suggestion or by superintendence ; the only essential thing is, that in an inspired work there is an exact and infallible statement of the truth which is professed to be recorded. As a matter of fact, in the volume of revelation, a large part of the truths are far above any power of man to discover them, and they were directly communicated to the speakers and writers by the Holy Spirit. In regard to all that is recorded in the Scriptures, it is to be held that the Holy Spirit so presided over the minds of the sacred writers, as to keep them from error, and to secure the exact record of such things as were necessary to be known to man.

In applying this principle to the book before us, the only thing which it is necessary to maintain is, that there is a correct *record* of events as they occurred to Job, and of the arguments of himself and his friends, and of the address of the Almighty. Whether either he or his friends were *inspired*, is quite another question, and is to be determined by other considerations. Whether all which *he* said was true, or whether all or any thing which *they* advanced was correct, is not to be determined by the mere position that *the book* is inspired.

(2.) It is to be admitted that there are in this book many things recorded which are in themselves wrong and false. It is not to be denied that Job uttered some sentiments which cannot be vindicated, and often manifested a spirit which was wrong. This is apparent not only from the contrariety of such sentiments and feelings to other parts of the Scriptures, but from the reproof of the Almighty himself at the close of the book. Nor can it be denied that the friends of Job uttered many erroneous sentiments, for their views are expressly condemned by God himself. chap. xlii. 7. Still, it is true that they *uttered* those sentiments, and that they entertained those opinions ; and this is properly all that inspiration is responsible for. In the records of profane history there are often things occurring just of this character. There are many things recorded which were in themselves wrong, yet *the record* is correctly made; there are many sentiments expressed by various speakers which are wrong in spirit, and yet the record that such sentiments were uttered is true. All that the fidelity of the historian is responsible for is the correctness of the record. He is not at all answerable for the propriety of the acts referred to, nor for the sentiments of the various speakers. If he gives a fair statement, he has done all that the world can demand of him as an historian—just as all that a painter can be required to do is to give a fair copy of his original. Whether that original be beautiful or otherwise, is quite another question. So in the matter before us, all that the inspired writer, whoever he may have been, is fairly responsible for, is the fairness and correctness of his record.

(3.) It is of great importance to preserve the record of things as they actually occurred, whether they were good or evil, right or wrong. This gives its value and importance to history ; and this object is not unworthy of inspiration. We wish to know what the facts were ; what were the opinions which prevailed ; what were the sentiments expressed ; what were the views of men on important subjects. Hence history has brought down to us many things that are in themselves of little value, or that cannot be depended on as guides now, but which show what has been the progress of events. So in the book before us, it was of great importance to show the opinions which prevailed in an early age of the world, and with the best opportunities for reflection, on a great and important question of the divine government. It

will make us prize more nighly the revelation which *we* have on those points;
and it will show us how much we are *really* indebted to revelation. The
discussion in this book was on one of the most important points that can come
before the mind of man. It is on a question which has occurred in all ages,
and which has been every where examined. The inquiry why the good are
afflicted, and why the wicked are prospered, is one that *must* came before
the minds of thinking men, and *must* present a great many difficulties. This
question is discussed here under every conceivable advantage. It arose from
a most interesting and afflicting *case* which had actually occurred. It was
examined by men of age, experience, and wisdom ; by men who could bring
to bear on it the result of patient thought, and who were imbued with the
wisdom of the ancients. The subject was never more fairly or fully examined ;
and nothing ever occurred that could do more to determine the just limits
of the human powers on these great inquiries pertaining to the divine government.

(4.) In a book of revelation for the guidance of mankind, it is important
not only to preserve the memory of *facts* as they actually occurred, and to
impart to men truths which the human mind could not originate ; but to
preserve, also, *a correct record of the workings of the human mind in circumstances of trial and temptation*. It is important not only *to state* in the
abstract, and by clear propositions, what man is, but *to show* what he is by
exhibiting him as placed in a great variety of situations, and by permitting
us to see how he will feel, and speak, and act in such circumstances. We
need to see what human nature is ; how it developes itself in trying situations; how the general declarations which God makes about man are illustrated in his life ; and especially, we want to see the effect of religion in
subduing, calming, and elevating the soul, and in enabling it to bear trials
and to meet with temptations. And for the same purpose, also, it is important to exhibit mind *as it actually exists* under the influence of religion—
with the imperfections of our nature—with the impatience, restlessness,
murmuring, and unguarded expressions which occur in times of calamity and
trial. Even the eminent saint is not perfect in this life. Religion does not
deliver him from all imperfection. It leaves the mind subject to conflict,
anxiety, trouble ; engaged in a fearful warfare with sin and temptation ; liable
to the outbreaks of impatience and murmuring; subject to the possibility of
being thrown off the guard, and of saying things which will be subsequently
the occasion of much regret. Now, as it is the design of revelation to exhibit
religion not only in its precepts, doctrines, and commands, but *as it actually
exists in the mind and heart*, it was important to furnish some actual illustrations of this in detail. For this purpose, nothing could be better adapted
than to select just such a case as that of Job, and to exhibit him in a condition of most extraordinary trial. He possessed undoubted piety. He had
made uncommon attainments in religion. He had been a man of calm judgment—of sober views—of eminent wisdom. His was a fair case, therefore,
in which to show the workings of human nature even under the most favourable circumstances, and when the mind is imbued with religion. It was a
case designed not to show what man *ought to be*, but what he *is;* and how
much infirmity and passion may actually exist in the soul, even when imbued
with the principles of piety. Much of this same thing also occurs in the
Book of Psalms ; and one of the principal things which which give value to
that inestimable part of the Scriptures is, that it so fully expresses the feelings of a pious man in a great variety of trying circumstances. Many of
the expressions in the Psalms, as well as in the Book of Job, we are by no
means to regard as the offspring of genuine religion, but as denoting what
human nature is, even when the prevailing feelings are those of piety. Even
in such a mind, there will be outbreakings of passion ; improper murmuring;
doubts about the safe condition of the soul; moments of darkness, when clear

visions of the divine goodness will be withdrawn; and expressions of impatience, which will give occasion of regret in the subsequent life; comp. Ps. cxvi. 11; lxxiii. 1—15. To record these is not to express approbation of them; and the record may be a source of unspeakable consolation to those who are betrayed into similar expressions, as showing that their feelings do not demonstrate that they have no true religion. One of the principal excellencies of the Book of Job is, that it preserves just such a record, and that it shows what the human mind is, even under the prevalent ascendancy of religious feeling, when it is subjected to severe trials.

(5.) In order, then, to ascertain in this book what is right and what is wrong, a careful examination is necessary, in connection with the other parts of the Bible. The views of the friends of Job, and the expressions of Job himself, must be carefully compared with the law of God, with the counsels and precepts elsewhere revealed, and with the nature of true religion as elsewhere exhibited. We are not to assume that all that Job said was right; nor are we to assume that *we* would have avoided the impatience and irreverence which he sometimes manifested. We are to compare the arguments of Job and his friends with the statements of truth elsewhere occurring in the Scriptures, and to place his feelings by the side of those of the only perfect man—the Lord Jesus. In him there was no impatience—no murmuring—no irreverence. In him was illustrated fully what religion, under the most trying circumstances, *ought* to be; in Job we see what, as human nature is constituted, it often *is*. With the New Testament in our hand, it is not difficult to form a correct estimate of what was wrong in the Patriarch of Uz; and we shall not find it difficult to determine what we ought to avoid when we are called to pass through similar trials.

(6.) It is not difficult, then, to determine the value of this book, or the place which it deserves to occupy in the sacred canon. It shows the following things :—(*a*) The operations of the human heart when under trial. (*b*) The real power of religion in restraining the mind, and in producing ultimately acquiescence in God. (*c*) It shows how far the human mind can go of itself, under the most favourable circumstances, in explaining the mysteries of the divine government. (*d*) It shows the necessity that truth should be *revealed* beyond what the human understanding has power itself to originate, to furnish support and consolation. (*e*) It shows the duty of perfect submission to the will of God, even when we cannot see the reason of his doings. In the works of creation and providence he has evinced so much wisdom and power, so much that surpasses even now all that science can do to explain it, so much that is every way superior to man, that we ought to have confidence in the wisdom of God *in all things*, and to believe that the great Governor of the universe is qualified for universal empire.

Various places have been assigned to the Book of Job in the ancient and modern arrangements. The place which it occupied at first in the Jewish canon is uncertain, for the ancient catalogues of the sacred books differ much from each other in regard to the place of this book. In that of Melito, it stands after the Canticles; in that of Origen, after Ezekiel; in that of Jerome, after the minor prophets. In Bava Bathra, c. L. f. 14, b., the books of the Hagiographa follow each other in the following order : 1 Ruth, 2 Psalms, 3 Job, 4 the writings of Solomon, Proverbs, Ecclesiastes, Canticles, 5 Lamentations, &c. According to Elias Levita, the Masorites arranged the Hagiographa in the following order : 1 Chronicles, 2 Psalms, 3 Job, 4 Proverbs, 5 the five festival books. The order in the printed editions varies as much as in the catalogues. In the Bomberg edition, in 1521, it is placed between the book of Proverbs and Daniel; in the edition of Buxtorf, it is placed between Proverbs and Canticles; see Eichhorn, Einleit. § 645, Carpzov, Introd. in V. T. p. 31. The proper place for the book of Job, in order to estimate its real value and importance, is at the commencement of the Bible, or in the early part of the book of Genesis. There is reason to suppose that it is the oldest book in the world; and there is a moral certainty that it was penned before the giving of the law on Mount Sinai, and before, in fact, any of the revelations were given which now shed so much light on the path of man. In our estimation of its design, it should stand at the commencement of the volume of revealed truth, to show how little the human mind can discover in regard to the principles of the divine government, and the necessity of revelation. The reasonings of the sages of Arabia, in the earliest period of the world, demonstrated abundantly what the reasonings of the sages of Greece afterwards did—that man needed a revelation to acquaint him with the true principles of the divine administration.

§ VII. *The patriarchal religion, as developed in the book of Job.*

On the supposition that this book was composed at the time supposed, then it is an invaluable document in regard to the nature of the patriarchal religion. We have comparatively few notices on that subject in the book of Genesis, and this volume supplies a chasm which it is of the greatest importance to fill up in order to understand the history of the world. We may suppose, without impropriety, that the mind of Job was imbued with the principles of religion, as then understood by the patriarchs; that he was acquainted with the traditions which had come down from more remote periods; that he was apprized of the revelations which had then been communicated to mankind; and that he practised the rites of religion which were then prevalent among the true worshippers of God. If this is so, then it will be of interest and importance to bring together, in a brief compass, some of the notices of the patriarchal religion scattered throughout this book.

(1.) The existence of one supreme God, the infinitely wise and glorious Creator of all things. In the entire book, God is spoken of as *one*, nor is there an intimation by any of the speakers that there is more than one God. There are no allusions to a *good* and an *evil* principle contending in the universe; nor any trace of the doctrine which subsequently became prevalent in the East, that such contending principles existed. No sentiments occur like those which were afterwards embodied in Persia respecting the existence and conflicts of Ormuzd and Ahriman (see Creuzer, Symbolik und Mythologie, Erster Band, 226, seq., and Neander, Geschichte, 2, a. 219, seq.), or what became subsequently the doctrine of the Manichæans. The religion of the book of Job is throughout a pure *theism*. This fact is remarkable, because the subject of the controversy—the mingled good and evil in the world—was such as constituted the foundation of the argument for *dualism* subsequently in a considerable portion of the Oriental world.

The characteristics ascribed to God in this book are such as are every where attributed to him in the Bible, and are far above any conceptions which prevailed of him at any time among Pagan philosophers. He is *almighty*, chap. v. 9; vi. 4; ix. 5—12, *et al.* He is *omniscient*, chap. xi. 11; xxi. 22. He is *wise*, chap. xii. 13; xxiv. 1; *inscrutable*, chap. xi. 7—9; xxxvi. 26; *invisible*, chap. ix. 11. He is *the Supreme Governor of the world, and the regulator of its concerns*, chap. v. 9—13; ix. 5—10. He is *the Creator of all things*, chap. iv. 17; x. 8—11; xxxv. 10; xxxviii. 4—10. He is *perfectly pure and holy*, chap. xv. 15, 16; xxv. 5, 6. He is *eternal*, chap. x. 5. He is *a spiritual Being*, chap. x. 4. He is *gracious*, and *is ready to forgive sin to the penitent*, chap. v. 17—27; xi. 13—19; xxii. 21—23; xxxiii. 23—28. He is *a hearer of prayer*, chap. xxxiii. 26; xii. 4; xxii. 27. He is *the dispenser of life and death*, chap. iv. 9; x. 12; xxxiii. 4. He *communicates his will by revelation to mankind*, chap. iv. 12—17; xxxiii. 14—17. In these and in numerous other passages in the book, the existence and attributes of the One Supreme God are stated with perhaps as much clearness as in any part of the Bible, and in a manner infinitely superior to any statements respecting the divine character and perfections in any other ancient books except those of the Scriptures.

(2.) The universe was created by this one great and glorious God. It was not the work of chance ; it was not the creation of any inferior beings ; it was not eternal. A single passage is all that is necessary to be referred to on this point—a passage of unequalled sublimity, chap. xxxviii. 4—11.

> Where wast thou when I laid the foundations of the earth ?
> Declare, if thou hast understanding.
> Who hath laid the measures thereof, if thou knowest ?
> Or who hath stretched the line upon it ?
> Whereupon are the foundations thereof fastened ?
> Or who laid the corner-stone thereof,
> When the morning stars sang together,
> And all the sons of God shouted for joy ?
> Or who shut up the sea with doors,
> When it brake forth, as if it had issued out of the womb ?
> When I made the cloud the garment thereof,
> And thick darkness a swaddling-band for it,
> And brake it up for my decreed place
> And set bars and doors,
> And said, " Hitherto shalt thou come, but no further ;
> And here shall thy proud waves be stayed ?"

(3.) He is the moral Governor of all his intelligent creatures, dispensing rewards and punishments according to their character. It is unnecessary to refer to particular passages demonstrating this, as the whole of the controversy in the book turns on it. The *fact* that God thus governs the universe, and that he punishes the evil and rewards the good, is assumed on both sides in the controversy, and is never called in question. The point of inquiry is, In what manner is it done ? One of the parties maintains that the dispensations of God here are strictly according to human character, and that character may be fairly inferred from those dispensations ; the other denies this, but maintains that there will be a *future* retribution, which will be strictly in accordance with justice ; comp. Notes on chap. xix. 23—27. *Somewhere*, and *somehow*, it seems to have been held by all parties, God would show himself the friend of the righteous and the punisher of the wicked.

(4.) The existence of *angels*, or a superior rank of holy intelligences, is asserted. In chap. i. 6, it cannot be denied that by " the sons of God," who came to present themselves before God, holy beings superior to men are denoted, and that it is designed to represent this scene as occurring in heaven. It is further implied there, that they came together from an important service, *as if* they had been absent engaged in some ministry to other parts of the universe, and returned now to render an account, and to receive a fresh commission in their work. The term " son of God " is used in Daniel iii. 25, comp. 28, to denote an angel. Angels also are, undoubtedly, referred to in chap. xv. 15 :

> Behold, he putteth no trust in his saints ;
> Yea, the heavens are not clean in his sight.

The express mention of " the heavens " in the parallelism, as well as the contrast between the " saints " or holy ones, here referred to, and with *man* (ver. 14, 16), proves that the " holy ones " are angels. It is possible also that in a parallel expression in chap. xxv. 5, there may be a reference to angels :

> Behold even to the moon, and it shineth not ;
> Yea, the stars are not pure in his sight.

The declaration in chap. xv. 15, demonstrates that the received opinion then was that the angels were far inferior to God. They are spoken of as

holy beings ; as superior to men ; as eminently holy in comparison with the
most holy men, but still as so far inferior to God that they were comparatively impure.

In chap. v. 1, also, there is probably an allusion to angels :

> Call now, if there be any to answer thee ;
> And to which of the saints wilt thou turn ?

And in chap. xxxviii. 7, they are mentioned as having been present at the
creation of the earth, and as celebrating that great event with a song of
praise :

> When the morning stars sang together,
> And all the sons of God shouted for joy.

If the book of Job was composed in the time which I have supposed, as
stated in the previous parts of this Introduction, then these are among the
earliest notices of the heavenly hierarchy that we have in the sacred volume.
They imply that the existence of superior intelligences was an undisputed
fact that might be used for the sake of argument and illustration ; that they
were eminently holy, though far inferior to God ; that they performed important offices in the administration of the universe, and that they were
under the control of the Almighty, and assembled together before him from
time to time to give their account, and to receive afresh his commands.
Early notices of the existence of angelic beings may be found also in Gen.
xix. 1, 15 ; xxii. 11 ; xxiv. 7, 40 ; xxviii. 12 ; xlviii. 16 ; Ex. xxiii. 20 ; Judg.
xiii. 19 ; 2 Sam. xxiv. 16, *et al.*

It would be impossible now to trace the origin of the belief in the existence of superior ranks of holy intelligences, and it would be inappropriate
here to attempt to follow out the *development* of the idea as it occurs in the
Scriptures, or as it is found in the early views of the Orientals. The belief,
however, has always pervaded the Oriental world, of a series of ascending
orders of intelligences, employed for various purposes in the administration
of the affairs of the universe. See Creuzer, Sym. u. Myth. and Neander, as
quoted above. "The ancient Persians," says Mr. Sale, Pre. Dis. to the
Koran, sect. iv., "firmly believed the ministry of angels, and their superintendence over the affairs of the world (as the Magians still do), and therefore assign them distinct charges and provinces, giving their names to the
months and the days of the months." The Mohammedans probably derived
their views on this subject from the Old Testament, intermingled with the
fables of the Jews ; but it is an interesting fact that in the country of Mohammed, in the days of Job, the doctrine of the existence of a superior order
of intelligences was held in its purity, and without any of the intermixtures
of puerility with which the doctrine is intermingled in the Jewish traditions,
and in the Koran. See Sale, Pre. Dis., sect. iv.

(5.) The doctrine of the existence of evil spirits was believed with as much
certainty. The introduction of the character of Satan, chap. i. 11, is conclusive proof on that point. He is a dark, malignant, accusing spirit ; one
who lives to spy out the conduct of others ; who is suspicious of the sincerity of all virtue ; who delights in the opportunity of putting virtue to the
severest test with a view to show that it is false and hollow ; who delights
to give pain. Satan is introduced in chap. i. 11, as if it were generally admitted that there were such evil spirits, and as if their character was so well
understood that it was unnecessary to offer a remark on the subject. The
book of Job, however, furnishes no information as to the prevalent belief
whether those spirits were originally evil, or whether they had apostatized
from a former state of holiness and happiness. The character of Satan,
however, in the book of Job, is such as to render it in the highest degree
probable that it was a matter of tradition that *he* had been the agent in the
temptation of Adam, and in the introduction of sin into the world. There

is a strong resemblance between the feelings with which he looked on Job, and those with which he must have regarded man in Paradise ; and the general distrust which he is represented as having in the piety of Job, and the conviction which he expresses that if the proper test were applied it would be found to be insincere, is such as we might expect from one emboldened by the successful attempt to alienate man as he was created, from his Creator. There is, indeed, a slight intimation in the poem itself, that Satan was a fallen spirit that had been once holy and happy. It is found in the expression of the belief of Eliphaz in two places, that entire confidence could not be put even in the holy angels—as if there had been some revolt or apostasy among them, which rendered it possible that there might be more :

> Behold, he put no trust in his servants,
> And his angels he charged with folly.
> How much less in them that dwell in houses of clay,
> Whose foundation is in the dust ? Chap. iv. 18, 19.

And again :
> Behold, he putteth no trust in his saints;
> Yea, the heavens are not clean in his sight. Chap. xv. 15.

Comp. chap. xxv. 5. Language like this would hardly be employed unless there was a belief that even the holiness of the angels was not incorruptible, and that there had been some revolt there among a part, which rendered it *possible* that others might revolt also ; comp. Jude 6, " And the angels which kept not their first estate." These passages taken together lead to a clear intimation of a belief that there had been a defection among the heavenly hosts, which was of such a character as to make it *possible* that they who remained there might apostatize also. They are not represented, indeed, as *sinful* (see the Notes on those passages); they have a degree of holiness which nothing human can equal ; but still it is not of the same character as that of God ; it is not so exalted as to put it above the suspicion that it *might* fall.

(6.) Man, in the time of Job, was regarded as a fallen being, and as wholly depraved. Of the belief that man is fallen, the following passages are full proof:

> Shall mortal man be more just than God?
> Shall a man be more pure than his Maker ?
> Behold, he put no trust in his servants,
> And his angels he charged with folly.
> How much less in them that dwell in houses of clay,
> Whose foundation is in the dust ? Chap. iv. 17—19.

> Man that is born of a woman, is of few days,
> And full of trouble.
> Who can bring a clean thing out of an unclean ?
> Not one. Chap. xiv. 1, 4.

> What is man, that he should be clean ?
> And he that is born of a woman, that he should be righteous ?
> Behold, he putteth no trust in his saints ;
> Yea, the heavens are not clean in his sight,
> How much more abominable and filthy is man,
> Who drinketh iniquity like water ? Chap. xv. 14—16.

There is also an allusion to the manner in which this depravity was introduced into the world :
> If I covered my transgressions as Adam,
> By hiding mine iniquity in my bosom. Chap. xxxi. 33.

In chap. i. 21, there seems also to be a reference to the sentence pronounced on man in consequence of the apostasy, and in chap. x. 9, it is possible that there may be the same allusion. As the language there used, however, is such as is common in all languages, and such as may be suggested by mere observation, it is not conclusively certain that the reference is to the sentence pronounced on man on account of his sin.

(7.) The necessity of reconciliation with God in order that peace may be enjoyed, is abundantly stated and enforced :

> Acquaint now thyself with him, and be at peace ;
> Thereby good shall come unto thee.
> Receive, I pray thee, the law from his mouth,
> And lay up his words in thine heart. Chap. xxii. 21, 22.

Comp. chap. v. 17—27 ; xi. 13—19.

(8.) The doctrine is taught that if man was penitent under the divine chastisement, God would receive the true penitent to his favour. See the passages quoted above (7), and the following :

> If thou return to the Almighty, thou shalt be built up,
> Thou shalt put away iniquity far from thy tabernacles. Chap. xxii. 23.
>
> If there be a messenger with him, an interpreter,
> One among a thousand, to show unto man his uprightness,
> Then he is gracious unto him, and saith,
>   Deliver him from going down to the pit ;
>   I have found a ransom.
> His flesh shall be fresher than a child's ;
> He shall return to the days of his youth ;
> He shall pray unto God, and he will be favourable unto him,
> And he shall see his face with joy ;
> For he will render unto man his righteousness.
> He looketh upon men ; and if any say, I have sinned,
> And perverted that which was right, and it profited me not,
> He will deliver his soul from going unto the pit,
> And his life shall see the light. Chap. xxxiii. 23—28.

(9.) The doctrine was held that man would not live again on the earth ; that when he died, he departed to return no more. See this opinion presented with great beauty and force in chap. xiv.

(10.) A very important inquiry next meets us in reference to the question whether man would live after death ; and if he did, what would be his condition then. This inquiry is of special importance, if, as has been supposed, this is the oldest book in the world. It will thus throw important light on the development of the idea of the future state, and the belief of the early ages on that point. On this important subject, the following remarks will probably comprise all the views presented in the book of Job.

(a) There is no distinct and formal statement of the doctrine of the immortality of the soul. Indeed, it would be difficult, if not impossible, to make out from this book that there were any settled views on that subject then prevailing.

(b) There is no mention made of heaven, as a place of rest, or as an abode of holiness. The angels are referred to, and God is often mentioned, and there is, as we shall see, a reference to a future state of being ; but there is no distinct conception of heaven, as a place where the righteous would dwell together for ever.

(c) There is no belief expressed of the resurrection. The only passage which can, by any persons, be regarded as teaching this doctrine, is the celebrated passage, chap. xix. 25—27. But that this does not refer to the resurrection of the body, seems to me to be clear, for the reasons which are suggested in the Notes on that passage. The remarks also in chap. xiv. seem to be conclusive proof that Job did not suppose that the body would be raised up again after it had once been laid in the dust.

> For there is hope of a tree,
> If it be cut down, that it will sprout again,
> And that the tender branch thereof will not cease.
> Though the root thereof wax old in the earth,
> And the stock thereof die in the ground ;
> Yet through the scent of water it will bud,
> And bring forth boughs like a plant.
> But man dieth and wasteth away ;
> Yea, man giveth up the ghost, and where is he ? Verses 7—10.

The same disbelief of the doctrine of the resurrection, or ignorance of it, appears from the following passages :

> As the cloud is consumed and vanisheth away ,
> So he that goeth down to the grave shall come up no more :
> He shall return no more to his house,
> Neither shall his place know him any more.   Chap. vii. 9, 10.

> As the waters fail from the sea,
> And the flood decayeth and drieth up ;
> So man lieth down and riseth not :
> Till the heavens be no more they shall not awake,
> Nor be raised out of their sleep.   Chap. xiv. 11, 12.

> If a man die, shall he live again?   Ver. 14.

It may be said that these passages only teach that man would not appear again *on the earth;* that he would not rise as the tree sprouts up and lives again.   This may be so ; but still, if they had known of the resurrection at all, these sentiments would not have been uttered.   *That* doctrine would have relieved all the difficulty as effectually as the belief that man would be raised up to dwell on the earth would have done.

(*d*) The doctrine of future retribution is not brought forward as it would have been, if it was clearly understood.   The reference to a future state of rewards and punishments would have removed all the embarrassment which was felt by Job and his friends.   It would have explained the mysterious events in the unequal distribution of rewards and punishments in this life ; relieved the difficulty arising from the fact that the righteous suffer and the wicked are prospered here ; and would have kept Job from murmuring and complaining under his severe trials.   And though there is an occasional allusion to a future state, yet it is by no means such as would be made now in arguing on the difficulties which perplexed the minds of Job and his friends.

(*e*) Yet still, there *was* a belief that man would live after death, or that the grave would not be the end of existence.   It is remarkable that the only passages which refer to the subject, or express the belief at all, occur in the speeches of Job ; and the manner in which he brings forward the doctrine seems to have made no impression on the minds of the other speakers.   Even the reference to the future state by Job himself does not appear to have been designed to turn aside the force of their arguments.   The views which he presented on the subject do not seem to have excited any curiosity in their minds, or to have been regarded as of sufficient importance to demand a reply.   The views which were entertained by Job on the subject are the following :

1. The grave was a quiet resting-place ; a place where toil and woe and care would cease:

> For now should I have lain still and been quiet ;
> I should have slept ;
> Then had I been at rest
> With kings and counsellors of the earth.
> Or as an hidden untimely birth I had not been ;
> As infants which never saw the light.
> There the wicked cease from troubling,
> And there the weary be at rest.   Chap. iii. 13—17.

> My days are passed ;
> My plans are at an end—
> The cherished purposes of my heart.
> Night has become day to me ;
> The light bordereth on darkness.
> Truly, I look to Sheol as my home ;
> My bed I spread in the place of darkness.
> To corruption I say, " Thou art my father ;"
> To the worm, "My mother and my sister."

> And where now is my hope?
> And who will see my hope fulfilled?
> To the bars of Sheol they must descend;
> Yea, we shall descend together to the dust.   Chap. xvii. 1.—16.

> For the numbered years pass away;
> And I am going the way whence I shall not return.
> My spirit is exhausted;
> My days are at an end;
> The grave waits for me.   Chap. xvi. 22; xvii. 1.

> And surely the mountain falling comes to nought;
> And the rock is removed from his place;
> The waters wear away the stones,
> The floods wash away the dust of the earth,
> And the hope of man thou dost destroy.
> Thou dost overpower him for ever, and he passes off;
> Thou dost change his countenance, and sendest him away.
> His sons are honoured, but he knoweth it not;
> Or they are brought low, but he perceiveth it not.   Chap. xiv. 18—21.

2. But though the grave is thus the termination of man's earthly hopes, yet it is not the end of man. There is an abode to which the grave is but the entrance; a world where there is still consciousness, and susceptibility of happiness or woe. In that world the Shades or the *Rephaim* reside—the spirits of departed men:

> The shades tremble from beneath;
> The waters and their inhabitants.
> Sheol is naked before him;
> And Destruction hath no covering.   Chap. xxvi. 5, 6.

It is clear here that that world is supposed to be "beneath;" that it is under the waters; that it is the region of "Sheol" to which the grave is the entrance; and that there is a dominion of God over those departed Shades or Rephaim, so that he has power to make them tremble. There can be no doubt that by the Shades or Rephaim here, there is an allusion to the *Manes Mortuorum*, the spirits of the dead confined in Sheol; comp. Isa. xiv. 9; Prov. ii. 18; Ps. lxxxviii. 10; Prov. ix. 18; Isa. xxvi. 19. That world is dark and dismal. There is an obscure light there, but it serves only to heighten the gloom:

> Are not my days few?
> O spare me, and let me alone, that I may take a little ease,
> Before I go whence I shall not return,
> To the land of darkness, and the shadow of death—
> The land of darkness, like the blackness of the shadow of death,
> Where there is no order, and where its shining is like blackness.   Chap. x. 20—22.

For the bearing of this passage on the belief of the future state, the reader is referred to the Notes. This view of the future world is remarkably obscure and gloomy, and shows that even the mind of Job had not such anticipations of the future state as to cheer and support him in the time of trial. The apprehension seems to have been that all the dead would descend through the grave to a region where only a few scattered rays of light would exist, and where the whole aspect of the dwelling was in strong contrast with the cheerful regions of the "land of the living." To that dark world even Job felt that it would be a calamity to descend, for though there was an expectation that there would be a distinction there between the good and the evil, yet compared with the present world of light and beauty, it was a sad and gloomy dwelling-place.

3. That world was regarded by the ancients as less desirable as a place of residence than this in several respects. It was dark and gloomy. It was entered through the grave, and the grave was only its outer court. They who dwelt there were cut off from the enjoyments of the present life. It

was a land of silence. Thus Hezekiah, speaking of that world to which he had a prospect of descending when so sick, says:

> I said, " I shall not see JEHOVAH ;
> JEHOVAH in the land of the living :
> I shall see man no more,
> Among the inhabitants of the land of stillness." Isa. xxxviii. 11.

In like manner, it would be a place where the worship of God could not be appropriately celebrated. Thus Hezekiah says:

> For Sheol cannot praise thee ;
> Death cannot celebrate thee ;
> They that go down into the pit cannot hope for thy truth.
> The living, the living, he shall praise thee, as I do this day ;
> The father to the children shall make known thy faithfulness. Isa. xxxviii. 18, 19.

A similar sentiment is expressed by David, Ps. vi. 5 :

> For in death there is no remembrance of thee ;
> In the grave who shall give thee thanks?

A similar view of that world appears to have been taken by Job. Indeed, it is not improbable that the view of Job was even more gloomy in regard to that future world, as he lived at a period so much earlier than David and Hezekiah. Successive revelations imparted new light, and the idea of the future state was more and more developed, though in the time of Hezekiah it was accompanied with much that was dark and gloomy. It was reserved for the gospel fully to " bring life and immortality to light." Yet,

4. In that future world there was some belief that there would be a separation between the good and the bad ; or that the wicked would be visited with *punishment*—though the belief of this is represented as received from travellers, the faith of foreign lands :

> Have ye not inquired of the travellers?
> And will you not admit their testimony ?
> That the wicked man is kept for the day of destruction ?
> And that he shall be brought forth in the day of fierce wrath ? Chap. xxi. 29, 30.

That this "wrath" refers to punishment which the wicked will experience after death, is apparent from what Job immediately adds, that he well knows that his present life may be one of prosperity, and that he may lie down with honour in the grave, and that the clods of the valley will be sweet unto him :

> Who charges him with his way to his face ?
> And who recompenses to him that which he hath done ?
> And he shall be borne [with honour] to the grave,
> And [friends] shall watch tenderly over his tomb.
> Sweet to him shall be the clods of the valley ;
> Every man shall go out to honour him,
> And of those before him there shall be no number. Chap. xxi. 31—33.

Comp. Notes on Isa. xiv. 15—19. It will be apparent from these illustrations, that the views of the future state in the time of Job were very obscure, and this is the reason of the remarkable fact that no particular reference is made in the argument to it, in order to remove the difficulties that were felt in regard to the divine administration here.

(11.) God was to be worshipped by sacrifice and burnt-offerings. It was in this way that Job sought to make expiation for the sins which his children might inadvertently have committed (chap. i. 4, 5.), and that the sins of his friends were to be expiated (chap. xlii. 8). This was evidently among the earliest modes of worship (comp. Gen. iv. 4; viii. 20, 21), and there was, therefore, some idea of the nature of an atonement, or of expiation for sin. I do not see any reason to doubt that Job, in common with all the patriarchs, may have had some conception that these bloody offerings were designed to point to the one great Sacrifice that was to be made for the sins of the world ; but there is no intimation of any such belief in the book itself. Of the modes of worship, besides the offering of sacrifice, nothing can be learned from this book, except that sacrifices were to be accompanied with prayer, and that prayer was acceptable to God and would be heard ; chap. xlii. 8 ; xxxiii. 26; 27, 28; xi 13—15. Repentance was also demanded, and where there was a penitent heart, the offender would be accepted.

> If thou prepare thine heart,
> And stretch out thine hands towards him ;
> If the iniquity which is in thine hands thou wilt put far away,
> And will not suffer evil to dwell in thy habitation,
> Then shalt thou lift up thy countenance [bright] without spot,
> And thou shalt be firm, and shalt not fear.
> And thy life shall be bright above the noonday,
> — Now thou art in darkness—but thou shalt be as the morning.
> Chap. xi. 13—17.

The religion of the time of Job was a pure theism. It consisted in the worship of one God, with appropriate sacrifices, and with acts of confidence and adoration, and with dependence on his mercy to lost sinners. There is, indeed, no express mention of convocations for public worship, nor of the Sabbath, nor of the office of priest. As in the time of Noah (Gen. viii.) the father of a family was the officiating priest who laid the victim on the altar, so it was in the time of Job, chap. i. 4, 5. In these services there was the most profound veneration for the one God, and the deepest abhorrence of idolatry in all its forms.

> If I have made gold my trust,
> Or said to the fine gold, Thou art my confidence ;
> If I rejoiced because my wealth was great,
> And because mine hand had found much ;
> If I beheld the sun when it shined,
> And the moon advancing in its brightness,
> And my heart has been secretly enticed,
> And my mouth has kissed my hand ;
> This also were a crime to be punished by the judge,
> For I should have denied the God who is above. Chap. xxxi. 24—28.

There is nowhere in the book an intimation that the sun, the moon, the stars, or any created being, was to be honoured as God.

(12.) We have in the book of Job an interesting view of the nature and effects of true piety. The necessity of holiness of life, of trust in God, of integrity and truth, is every where insisted on as essential to true religion. To transcribe the particular places where these are dwelt upon, would be to copy a considerable part of the book. We may just advert to the beautiful manner in which the necessity of *sincerity* in the service of God is urged, and in which the sin and danger of *hypocrisy* are expressed :

> Can the paper reed grow up without mire ?
> Can the bulrush grow up without water ?
> Even yet in its greenness, and uncut,
> It withereth before any other herb.
> Such are the ways of all who forget God ;
> So perishes the hope of the hypocrite.
> His hope shall rot,
> And his trust shall be the building of the spider.
> He shall lean upon the building, and it shall not stand ;
> He shall grasp it, but it shall not endure. Chap. viii. 11—15.

> Knowest thou not that from the most ancient times,
> From the time when man was placed upon the earth,
> That the triumphing of the wicked is short,
> And the joy of the hypocrite is but for a moment ?
> Though his greatness mount up to the heavens,
> And his excellency unto the clouds,
> Yet he shall perish for ever as the vilest substance
> They who have seen him shall say, Where is he ?
> He shall flee away as a dream, and not be found,
> Yea, he shall vanish as a vision of the night. Chap. xx. 4—8.

> For what is the hope of the hypocrite when [God] cuts him off;
> When he taketh away his life ?
> Will God listen to his cry
> When trouble cometh upon him ?
> Will he delight himself in the Almighty ?
> Will he call at all times upon God ?   Chap. xxvii. 8—10.

(13.) An interesting view of the religion of the time of Job is seen in its influence on morals and manners.   Customs in the Oriental world change little, and in Arabia at the present time we have still interesting illustrations of what existed in the days of Job.   In the patriarchal times all this was identified with their religion, and there is scarcely even now to be found any where more beautiful illustrations of the nature and effects of religion in these respects, than occur in the book of Job, and nowhere are there more happy descriptions of the simplicity, the purity, the urbanity of early manners and customs.   This is seen in the book of Job in the following respects :

(a) In the perfect respectfulness of manner in their treatment of each other.   In all the long controversy recorded in this book, and in all that was said that was harsh and adapted to irritate, there is no *interruption* of the speaker.   There is no passionate outbreak.   It was a conceded and well-understood matter that the speaker was to be heard patiently through, and then that the reply was to be heard *as* patiently.   No matter how much misapprehension of the meaning of the one who had spoken there might be, no matter what reflection there might be on his motives or character, and no matter how severe and withering the sarcasm, yet there is no attempt to break in upon the speaker.   This is understood still to be courtesy in the Oriental world ; this was regarded as courtesy among the aborigines of N. America; and in this respect the more civilized and polished people of our times might learn something from even the wandering Arab, or the " wild untutored Indian."   Thus Dr. Franklin (Works, vol. ii. 455), speaking of the " Savages of North America," says, " Having frequent occasions to hold public councils, they have acquired great order and decency in conducting them.   The old men sit in the foremost ranks, the warriors in the next, and the women and children in the hindmost.   The business of the women is to take exact notice of what passes, imprint it on their memories, and communicate it to their children.   He that would speak, rises.   The rest observe a profound silence.   When he has finished, and sits down, they leave him five or six minutes to recollect, that if he has omitted any thing he intended to say, or has any thing to add, he may rise again and deliver it.   To interrupt another, even in common conversation, is reckoned highly indecent.   How different this is from the conduct of a polite British House of Commons, where scarce a day passes without some confusion, that makes the Speaker hoarse in calling *to order*," &c.   " It is one of the Indian rules of politeness not to answer a public proposition the same day that it is made ; they think it would be treating it as a light matter, and that they show it respect by taking time to consider it, as of a matter important." Ibid. p. 454.

(b) Respect for age.   More beautiful instances of this can nowhere be found than in the modesty of Elihu, and in the deference which Job said was paid to him in his days of prosperity.   Elihu says :

> I am young, and ye are very old ;
> Therefore I was afraid,
> And durst not make known to you mine opinion.
> I said, Days should speak,
> And multitude of years should teach wisdom.
> But there is a spirit in man :
> And the inspiration of the Almighty giveth him understanding.
> Great men are not always wise ;
> Neither do the aged always understand what is right.
> Therefore I said, Hearken unto me ;
> I also will declare mine opinion.

> Behold, I waited for your words,
> I listened to your arguments,
> While ye searched out what to say.
> Yea, I attended to you ;
> And behold, there is no one that hath refuted Job,
> Or answered his words.
> They were confounded ; they answered no more ;
> They put words far from them.
> And I waited, although they did not speak ;
> Although they stood still, and answered no more.
> Now will I answer on my part ;
> Even I will show mine opinion.   Chap. xxxii. 6—17.

So Job speaks of the respect that was shown him in the days of his prosperity :

> When I went forth to the gate through the city,
> And prepared my seat in the public place,
> The young men saw me, and respectfully retired before me ;
> The aged arose, and stood.
> The princes refrained from speaking,
> And laid their hand upon their mouth.
> The voice of counsellors was silent,
> And their tongue cleaved to the roof of their mouth.
> For the ear heard, and it blessed me ;
> And the eye saw, and it bore witness to me.   Chap. xxix. 7—11.

(c) One of the virtues then much dwelt on, as an act of piety, was that of hospitality. This is frequently alluded to with great beauty in the poem, as it is in all the poetry of Arabia now, and in the days of Job was esteemed to be a virtue as essential as it is now in the East.

> If I have withheld the poor from their desire,
> Or caused the eyes of the widow to fail ;
> If I have eaten my morsel alone,
> And the fatherless hath not eaten of it ;
> —For from my youth he grew up with me as with a father,
> And I was her guide from my earliest days—
> If I have seen any one perish for want of clothing,
> Or any poor man without covering ;
> If his loins have not blessed me,
> And if he have not been warmed with the fleece of my sheep ;
> Then may my shoulder fall from the blade,
> And mine arm be broken from the upper bone.   Chap. xxxi. 16—22.

> If my domestics could not at all times say,
> " Let them show one who has not been satisfied from his hospitable table,"
> (The stranger did not lodge in the street,
> My doors I opened to the traveller,)
> Then let me be confounded before a great multitude !
> Let the contempt of families crush me !   Chap. xxxi. 31—34.

See also chap. xviii. 5, 6 ; xxi. 17, and the Notes on those places.

(d) In like manner, piety then consisted much in kindness to the poor, the widow, and the fatherless, and to those in the humbler ranks of life.   Job s beautiful description of his own piety in the days of his prosperity is all that is needful to illustrate this :

> For I rescued the poor when they cried,
> And the fatherless when there was none to help him.
> The blessing of him that was ready to perish came upon me,
> And I caused the heart of the widow to sing for joy.
>
> Chap. xxix. 12, 13.

> I was eyes to the blind,
> And feet was I to the lame.
> I was a father to the poor :
> And the cause of the unknown I searched out.
> And I broke the teeth of the wicked,
> And from their teeth I plucked away the spoil.   Chap. xxix. 15—17.

> Did not I weep for him that was in trouble,
> Was not my soul grieved for the poor ?   Chap. xxx. 25.

If I have refused justice to my man-servant or maid-servant,
When they had a cause with me,
What shall I do when God riseth up?
When he visiteth, what shall I answer him?
Did not he that made me in the womb make him?
Did not the same One fashion us in the womb? Chap. xxxi. 13—15.

If my land cry out against me,
And the furrows likewise complain;
If I have eaten its fruits without payment,
And extorted the living of its owners;
Let thistles grow up instead of wheat,
And noxious weeds instead of barley. Chap. xxxi. 38—40.

§ VIII. *The state of the arts and sciences in the time of Job.*

There is one important aspect still in which the book of Job may be contemplated. It is as an illustration of the state of the arts and sciences of
the period of the world when it was composed. We are not indeed, in a
poem of this nature, to look for formal treatises on any of the arts or sciences as then understood, but all that we can expect to find must be incidental allusions, or *hints*, that may enable us to determine with some degree of
accuracy what advances society had then made. Such allusions are also of
much more value in determining the progress of society, than extended descriptions of conquests and sieges would be. The latter merely change the
boundaries of empire; the former indicate *progress* in the condition of man.
Inventions in the arts and discoveries in science are *fixed points*, from which
society does not go backward. I propose, then, as an illustration of the progress which society had made in the time of Job, as well as to prepare the
mind to read the book in the most intelligent manner, to bring together the
scattered notices of the state of the arts and sciences contained in this poem.
No exact *order* can be observed in this; nor is there any thing in the poem
to indicate which of the things specified had the priority in point of time, or
when the invention or discovery was made. The order of the arrangement
chosen will have some reference to the importance of the subjects, and also
some to what may be supposed to have first attracted attention. For a more
full view of the various points that will be referred to, reference may be made
to the *Notes* on the various passages adduced.

I. ASTRONOMY.

The stars were early observed in Chaldea, where the science of astronomy
had its origin. A pastoral people always have some knowledge of the heavenly bodies. The tending of flocks by night, under a clear Oriental sky,
gave abundant opportunity for observing the motions of the heavenly bodies,
and names would soon be given to the most important of the stars; the difference between the planets and the fixed stars would be observed, and the
imagination would be employed in grouping the stars into fanciful resem-
blances to animals and other objects. In like manner, as caravans travelled
much at night through the deserts, on account of the comparative coolness
then, they would have an opportunity of observing the stars, and some knowledge of the heavenly bodies became necessary to guide their way. The
notices of the heavenly bodies in this poem show chiefly that *names* were
given to some of the stars; that they were grouped together in constellations; and that the times of the appearance of certain stars had been carefully observed, and their relation to certain aspects of the weather had been
marked. There is no express mention of the planets as distinguished from
the fixed stars; and nothing to lead us to suppose that they were acquainted
with the true system of astronomy.

He commandeth the sun, and it riseth not,
And he sealeth up the stars.
He alone stretcheth out the heavens

And walketh upon the high waves of the sea.
He maketh Arcturus, Orion,
The Pleiades, and the secret chambers of the south.   Chap. ix. 7–9.

Canst thou bind the sweet influences of Pleiades,
Or loose the bands of Orion ?
Canst thou bring forth Mazzaroth in his season,
Or lead forth the Bear with her young ?
Knowest thou the laws of the heavens,
Or hast thou appointed their dominion over the earth ?
                         Chap. xxxviii. 31—33.

It would seem from these passages, that the allusion to the clusters of
stars here, is made to them as the harbingers of certain *seasons.* " It is
well known, that, in different regions of the earth, the appearance of certain
constellations before sunrise or after sunset, marks the distinction of seasons,
and regulates the labours of the husbandman." *Wemyss.* It is also known
that the appearance of certain constellations—as Orion—was regarded by
mariners as denoting a stormy and tempestuous season of the year. See
the Notes on the passages quoted above. This seems to be the knowledge of
the constellations referred to here, and there is no certain evidence that the
observation of the heavens in the time of Job had gone beyond this.

A somewhat curious use has been made of the reference to the stars in
the book of Job, by an attempt to determine the time when he lived. Supposing the principal stars here mentioned to be those of Taurus and Scorpio, and that these were the cardinal constellations of spring and autumn in
the time of Job, and calculating their positions by the precession of the
equinoxes, the time referred to in the book of Job was found to be 818 years
after the deluge, or 184 years before the birth of Abraham. " This calculation, made by Dr. Brinkley of Dublin, and adopted by Dr. Hales, had been
made also in 1765 by M. Ducontant in Paris, with a result differing only in
being forty-two years less." The coincidence is remarkable, but the proof
that the constellations referred to are Taurus and Scorpio, is too uncertain
to give much weight to the argument.

II. COSMOLOGY.

The intimations about the structure, the size, and the support of the
earth, are also very obscure, and the views entertained would seem to have
been very confused. Language is used, doubtless, such as would express the
popular belief, and it resembles that which is commonly employed in the
Scriptures. The common representation is, that the heavens are stretched
out as a curtain or tent, or sometimes as a solid concave sphere in which the
heavenly bodies are *fixed* (see Notes on Isa. xxxiv. 4), and that the earth is
an immense plain, surrounded by water, which reached the concave heavens
in which the stars were fixed. Occasionally the earth is represented as supported by pillars, or as resting on a solid foundation ; and once we meet
with an intimation that it is globular, and suspended in space.

In the following passages the earth and the sky are represented as supported by pillars :

He shaketh the earth out of her place,
And the pillars thereof tremble.   Chap. ix. 6.

The pillars of heaven tremble,
And are astonished at his rebuke.   Chap. xxvi. 11.

In the latter passage the reference is to mountains, which seem to uphold
the sky as pillars, in accordance with the common and popular representation among the ancients. Thus Mount Atlas, in Mauritania, was represented
as a pillar on which heaven was suspended :

"Atlas' broad shoulders prop th' incumbent skies,
Around his cloud-girt head the stars arise."

In the following passage the earth is represented as suspended on nothing, and there would seem to be a slight evidence that the true doctrine about the form of the earth was then known :

> He stretcheth out the North over the empty space,
> And hangeth the earth upon nothing. Chap. xxvi. 7.

See particularly the Notes on that passage. Though the belief seems to have been that the earth was thus "self-balanced," yet there is no intimation that they were acquainted with the fact that it revolves on its axis, or around the sun as a centre.

III. GEOGRAPHY.

There are few intimations of the prevalent knowledge of geography in the time of Job. In one instance foreign regions are mentioned, though there is no certainty that the countries beyond Palestine are there referred to :

> Have ye not inquired of the travellers?
> And will ye not hear their testimony ? Chap. xxi. 29.

In the close of the book, in the mention of the hippopotamus and the crocodile, there is evidence that there was some knowledge of the land of Egypt, though no intimation is given of the situation or extent of that country.

The cardinal points are referred to, and there is evidence in this book, as well as elsewhere in the Scriptures, that the geographer then regarded himself as looking towards the East. The South was thus the "right hand," the North the left hand, and the West the region "behind :"

> Behold, I go to the East, and he is not there;
> And to the West, but I cannot perceive him;
> To the North, where he doth work, but I cannot behold him ;
> He hideth himself on the South, that I cannot see him.   Chap. xxiii. 8, 9.

See the Notes on this verse for an explanation of the terms used ; comp. the following places, where similar geographical terms occur; Judges xviii. 12; Deut. xi. 24; Zech. xiv. 8; Ex. x. 19; Josh. xvii. 7; 2 Kings xxiii. 13; 1 Sam. xxiii. 24; Gen. xiv. 15; Josh. xix. 27.

Whatever was the form of the earth, and the manner in which it was sustained, it is evident from the following passage that the land was regarded as surrounded by a waste of waters, whose outer limit was deep and impenetrable darkness:

> He hath drawn a circular bound upon the waters,
> To the confines of the light and darkness. Chap. xxvi. 10.

Yet the whole subject is represented as one with which man was then unacquainted, and which was beyond his grasp:

> Hast thou observed the breadths of the earth?
> Declare, if thou knowest it all. Chap. xxxviii. 18.

For a full illustration of this passage, and the views of geography which then prevailed, the reader is referred to the Notes. It is evident that the knowledge of geography, so far as is indicated by this book, was then very limited, though it should also be said that in the argument of the poem there was little occasion to refer to knowledge of this kind, and that few intimations are to be expected on the subject.

IV. METEOROLOGY.

There are much more frequent intimations of the state of knowledge on the various subjects embraced under this head, than of either astronomy or geography. These intimations show that these subjects had excited much attention, and had been the result of careful observation; and in regard to some of them there are indications of a plausible theory of their causes, though most of them are appealed to as among the inscrutable things of God. The *facts* excited the wonder of the Arabian observers, and they clothed their conceptions of them in the most beautiful language of poetry; but they do not often attempt to explain them. On the contrary, these obvious and undisputed *facts*, so inscrutable to them, are referred to as full proof that we cannot hope to comprehend the ways of God, and as a reason why we should bow before him with profound adoration. Among the things referred to are the following :

(*a*) The Aurora Borealis, or Northern lights. Thus the magnificent description of the approach of the Almighty to close the controversy (chap. xxxvii. 21—23), seems to have been borrowed by Elihu from the beautiful lights of the North, in accordance with the common opinion that the North was the seat of the Divinity :

> And now—man cannot look upon the bright splendour that is on the clouds:
> For the wind passeth along and maketh them clear.
> Golden splendour approaches from the North :—
> How fearful is the majesty of God !
> The Almighty ! we cannot find him out !
> Great in power and in justice, and vast in righteousness !

Comp. Notes on Isa. xiv. 13, and on Job xxiii. 9.

(*b*) Tornadoes, whirlwinds, and tempests, were the subject of careful observation. The sources whence they usually came were attentively marked, and the various phenomena which they exhibited were so observed that the author of the poem was able to describe them with the highest degree of poetic beauty :

> With his hands he covereth the lightning
> And commandeth it where to strike.
> He pointeth out to it his friends—
> The collecting of his wrath is upon the wicked.
> At this also my heart palpitates,
> And is moved out of its place.
> Hear, O hear, the thunder of his voice !
> The muttering thunder that goes forth from his mouth '
> He directeth it under the whole heaven,
> And his lightning to the ends of the earth.
> He thundereth with the voice of his majesty,
> And he will not restrain the tempest when his voice is heard.
>   Chap. xxxvi. 32, 33 ; xxxvii. 1—4.

> Terrors come upon him like waters,
> In the night a tempest stealeth him away.
> The east wind carrieth him away, and he departeth,
> And it sweeps him away from his place.   Chap. xxvii 20, 21.

(*c*) The *dew* had been carefully observed, yet the speakers did not understand its phenomena. How it was produced ; whether it descended from the atmosphere, or ascended from the earth, they did not profess to be able to explain. It was regarded as one of the things which God only could understand ; yet the manner in which it is spoken of shows that it had attracted deep attention, and led to much inquiry :

> Hath the rain a father ?
> And who hath begotten the drops of the dew?   Chap. xxxviii. 28.

(*d*) The same remarks may be made of the formation of the hoar-frost, of snow, of hail, and of ice. There is no *theory* suggested to account for them but they are regarded as among the things which God alone could comprehend, and which evinced his wisdom. There had been evidently much careful observation of the facts, and much inquiry into the cause of these things ; but the speakers did not profess to be able to explain them. To this day, also, there is much about them which is unexplained, and the farther the investigation is carried, the more occasion is there to admire the wisdom of God in the formation of these things.   See the Notes on the passages that will now be referred to :

> From whose womb came the ice;
> The hoar-frost of heaven, who gave it birth ?   Chap. xxxviii. 29.

> By the breath of God frost is produced,
> And the broad waters become compressed.   Chap. xxxvii. 10.

> For he saith to the snow, " Be thou on the earth."   Chap. xxxvii. 6.

> Hast thou been into the storehouses of snow ?
> Or seen the storehouses of hail,
> Which I have reserved until the time of trouble,
> To the day of battle and war ?   Chap. xxxviii. 22, 23.

(*e*) The dawning of the morning is described with great beauty, and is re-presented as wholly beyond the power of man to produce or explain :

> Hast thou, in thy life, given commandment to the morning ?
> Or caused the dawn to know his place ?
> That it may seize on the far corners of the earth,
> And scatter the robbers before it ?
> It turns itself along like clay under the seal,
> And all things stand forth as if in gorgeous apparel.*
> > Chap. xxxviii. 12—14.

(*f*) So all the phenomena of light are represented as evincing the wisdom of God, and as wholly beyond the ability of man to explain or comprehend them ; yet so represented as to show that it had been a subject of careful observation and reflection :

> Where is the way to the dwelling-place of light ?
> And the darkness, where is its place ?
> That thou couldest conduct it to its limits,
> And that thou shouldest know the path to its dwelling ?
> > Chap. xxxviii. 19, 20.

(*g*) The clouds and rain also had been carefully observed, and the laws which governed them were among the inscrutable things of God :

> Who can number the clouds by wisdom ?
> And who can empty the bottles of heaven ?   Chap. xxxviii. 37.

The clouds seem to have been regarded as a solid substance capable of holding rain like a leathern bottle, and the rain was caused by their emptying themselves on the earth.   Yet the whole phenomena were considered to be beyond the comprehension of man.   The laws by which the clouds were suspended in the air, and the reason why the rain descended in small drops, instead of gushing floods, were alike incomprehensible :

> Who also can understand the outspreading of the clouds,
> And the fearful thunderings in his pavilion ?   Chap. xxxvi. 29.

> For he draweth up the drops of water ;
> They distil rain in his vapour,
> Which the clouds pour down ;
> They pour it upon man in abundance.   Chap. xxxvi. 27, 28.

> He bindeth up the waters in the thick clouds,
> And the cloud is not rent under them.   Chap. xxvi. 8.

(*h*) The sea had also attracted the attention of these ancient observers and there were phenomena there which they could not explain :

> Who shut up the sea with doors,
> In its bursting forth as from the womb ?
> When I made the cloud its garment,

---

* For the meaning of this uncommonly beautiful imagery, see the Notes on this place.

And swathed it in thick darkness?
I measured out for it its limits,
And fixed its bars and doors,
And said, Thus far shalt thou come, but no farther.
And here shall thy proud waves be stayed !   Chap. **xxxviii**. 8—11.

There is a reference here, undoubtedly, to the creation ; but as this is the language of God describing that event, it cannot be determined with certainty that a knowledge of the method of creation had been communicated to them by tradition.   But language like this implies that there had been a careful observation of the ocean, and that there were things in regard to it which were to them incomprehensible.   The passage is a most sublime description of the creation of the mighty mass of waters, and while it is entirely consistent with the account in Genesis, it supplies some important circumstances not recorded there.

V. MINING OPERATIONS.

The twenty-eighth chapter of the book—one of the most beautiful portions of the Bible—contains a statement of the method of mining then practised, and shows that the art was well understood.   The mechanical devices mentioned, and the skill with which the process was carried on, evince considerable advance in the arts :

Truly there is a vein for silver,
And a place for gold where they refine it.
Iron is obtained from the earth,
And ore is fused into copper.
Man putteth an end to darkness,
And completely searches every thing—
The rocks, the thick darkness, and the shadow of death
He sinks a shaft far from a human dwelling ;
They, unsupported by the feet, hang suspended ;
Far from men they swing to and fro.
The earth—out of it cometh bread ;
And when turned up beneath, it resembles fire.
Its stones are the places of sapphires,
And gold dust pertains to it.
The path thereto no bird knoweth,
And the vulture's eye hath not seen it.
The fierce wild beasts have not trodden it,
And the lion hath not walked over it.
Man layeth his hand upon the flinty rock ;
He overturneth mountains from their foundations ;
He cutteth out canals among the rocks,
And his eye seeth every precious thing.
He restraineth the streams from trickling down,
And bringeth hidden things to light.   Ver. 1—11.

The operation of mining must have early attracted attention, for the art of working metals, and of course their value, was understood in a very early age of the world.   Tubal Cain is described as an " instructor of every artificer in brass and iron ;" Gen. iv. 22.   The description in Job shows that this art had received much attention, and that in his time it had been carried to a high degree of perfection ; see Notes on chap. xxviii. 1—11.

VI. PRECIOUS STONES.

There is frequent mention of precious stones in the book of **Job**, and it is evident that they were regarded as of great value, and were used for ornament.   The following are mentioned, as among the precious stones, though some of them are now ascertained to be of little value.   There is evidence that they judged, as was necessarily the case in the early age of the world, rather from appearances than from any chemical knowledge of their nature. The onyx and sapphire :

It [wisdom] cannot be estimated by the gold of Ophir ;
By the precious onyx, or the sapphire.   Chap. xxviii. 16.

Coral, crystal, and rubies :

> No mention shall be made of coral or of crystal ;
> For the price of wisdom is above rubies. Chap. xxviii. 18.

The topaz found in Ethiopia, or Cush :

> The topaz of Cush cannot equal it,
> Nor can it be purchased with pure gold. Chap. xxviii. 19.

These were found as the result of the processes of mining, though it is not known that the art of engraving on them was known. It is, moreover, not entirely easy to fix the signification of the original words used here. See Notes on chap. xxviii.

VII. COINING, WRITING, ENGRAVING.

It is not quite certain, though there is some evidence, that the art of coining was known in the days of Job. The solution of this question depends on the meaning of the word rendered "a piece of money," in chap. xlii. 11. For an examination of this, the reader is referred to the Notes on that verse. There is the fullest evidence that the art of writing was then known :

> O that my words were now written !
> O that they were engraved on a tablet !
> That with an iron graver, and with lead,
> They were engraven upon a rock for ever. Chap. xix. 23, 24.

> O that He would hear me :
> Behold my defence ! May the Almighty answer me !
> Would that he who contends with me would write down his charge !
> Truly upon my shoulder would I bear it ;
> I would bind it upon me as a diadem. Chap. xxxi. 35, 36.

The materials for writing are not indeed particularly mentioned, but it is evident that permanent records on stone were made; that this was done sometimes by making use of lead ; and also that it was common to make use of portable materials, and as would seem of *flexible* materials, since Job speaks (chap. xxxi.) of binding the charge of his adversary, when written down, around his head like a turban or diadem ; comp. Notes on Isa. viii. 1; xxx. 8. Though the papyrus, or "paper reed," of Egypt, seems to be once alluded to (see Notes on chap. viii. 11), yet there is no evidence that it was known as a material for writing.

VIII. THE MEDICAL ART.

Physicians are once mentioned .

> For truly are ye forgers of fallacies ;
> Physicians of no value, all of you. Chap. xiii. 4.

But there is no intimation of the methods of cure, or of the remedies that were applied. It is remarkable that, so far as appears, no methods were taken to cure the extraordinary malady of Job himself. He excluded himself from society, sat down in dust and ashes, and merely attempted to re-move the offensive matter that the disease collected on his person ; chap. ii. 8. So far as appears from the Scriptures, the means of cure resorted to in early times were chiefly external applications. See Notes on Isa. i. 6; xxxviii. 21, 22. " Physicians" are mentioned in Gen. l. 2, but only in connection with embalming, where it is said that " Joseph commanded his servants the physicians to embalm his father, and the physicians embalmed Israel."

IX. MUSIC.

Musical instruments are mentioned in the book of Job in such a manner as to show that the subject of music had attracted attention, though we may not be able now to ascertain the exact form of the instruments which were employed:

> They excite themselves with the tabor and the harp,
> And rejoice at the sound of the pipe.   Chap. xxi. 12.

> My harp also is turned to mourning,
> And my pipes to notes of grief.   Chap. xxx. 31.

For an explanation of these terms, the reader is referred to the Notes on these passages.   We have evidence that music was cultivated long before the time in which it is supposed Job lived (Gen. iv. 21), though there is no certainty that even in his time it had reached a high degree of perfection.

X.   HUNTING.

One of the earliest arts practised in society would be that of taking and destroying wild beasts, and we find several allusions to the methods in which this was done, in the book of Job.   Nets, gins, and pitfalls, were made use of for this purpose, and in order to drive the wild beasts into the nets or pit-falls, it was customary for a number of persons to extend themselves in a forest, inclosing a large space, and gradually drawing near to each other and to the centre:

> His strong steps shall be straitened,
> And his own plans shall cast him down.
> For he is brought into his net by his own feet,
> And into the pitfall he walks.
> The snare takes him by the heel,
> And the gin takes fast hold of him.
> A net is secretly laid for him in the ground,
> And a trap for him in the pathway.   Chap. xviii. 7—10.

The howling of dogs, and the shouts of the hunters, are represented as filling the wild animal with dismay, and as harassing him as he attempts to escape:

> Terrors alarm him on every side,
> And harass him at his heels.   Chap. xviii. 11.

While spent with hunger and fatigue, he is entangled in the spread nets, and becomes an easy prey for the hunter:

> His strength shall be exhausted by hunger,
> And destruction shall seize upon his side.
> It shall devour the vigour of his frame,
> The first-born of Death shall devour his limbs.   Chap. xviii. 12, 13.

Comp. Ps. cxl. 4, 5; Ezek. xix. 6—9.

XI.   METHODS OF HUSBANDRY.

The customs of the pastoral life, one of the chief employments of early ages, are often referred to; chap. i. 3, 16; xlii. 12.

> He shall never look upon the rivulets—
> The streams of the valleys—of honey and butter.   Chap. xx. 17.

> When I washed my steps with cream,
> And the rock poured me out rivers of oil.   Chap. xxix. 6.

Ploughing with oxen is mentioned, chap. i. 14. So also chap. xxxi. 38—40

> If my land cry out against me,
> And the furrows likewise complain;
> If I have eaten its fruits without payment,
> And extorted the living of its owners;
> Let thistles grow up instead of wheat,
> And noxious weeds instead of barley.   Chap. xxxi. 38—40.

The cultivation of the vine and the olive, and the pressure of grapes and olives, is mentioned:

> He shall cast his unripe fruit as the vine,
> And shed his blossoms like the olive.   Chap. xv. 33.

> They reap their grain in the field [of others],
> And they gather the vintage of the oppressor.   Chap. xxiv. 6.

> They cause them to express oil within their walls;
> They tread their wine-presses, and yet they suffer thirst.
> Chap. xxiv. 11.

It is remarkable that in the book of Job there is no mention of the palm, the pomegranate, or any species of flowers.   In a country like Arabia, where the date now is so important an article of food, it would have been reasonable to anticipate that there would have been some allusion to it.   Little is known, from what is said, of the implements of husbandry, and nothing forbids us to suppose that they were of the rudest sort.

XII.   MODES OF TRAVELLING.

From the earliest period in the East the mode of travelling to any distance appears to have been by caravans, or companies.   Two objects seem to have been contemplated by this in making long journeys across pathless deserts that were much infested by robbers; the one was the purpose of self-defence, the other mutual accommodation.   For the purposes of those travelling companies, camels are admirably adapted by nature, alike from their ability to bear burdens, from the scantiness of food which they require, and for their being able to travel far without water.   Caravans are first mentioned in Gen. xxxvii. 25, " And they sat down to eat bread, and they lifted up their eyes and looked, and behold a company of Ishmaelites came from Gilead, with their camels bearing spicery, and balm, and myrrh, going to carry it down to Egypt."   A beautiful notice of this mode of travelling occurs in Job (vi. 15—20), as being common in his time:

> My brethren are faithless as a brook,
> Like the streams of the valley that pass away;
> Which are turbid by means of the [melted] ice,
> In which the snow is hid [by being dissolved].
> In the time when they become warm they evaporate.
> When the heat cometh, they are dried up from their place;
> The channels of their way wind round about;
> They go into nothing, and are lost.
> The caravans of Tema look;
> The travelling companies of Sheba expect to see them.
> They are ashamed that they have relied on them,
> They come even to the place, and are confounded.

There is, in one place in Job, a slight intimation that runners or carriers were employed to carry messages when extraordinary speed was demanded, though there is no evidence that this was a settled custom, or that it was regulated by law:

> And my days are swifter than a runner;
> They flee away, and they see no good.   Chap. ix. 25.

Connected with the subject of travelling, we may remark, that the art of making light boats or skiffs from reeds appears to have been known, though there is no mention of ships, or of distant navigation:

> They pass on like the reed-skiffs;
> As the eagle darting on its prey.   Chap. ix. 26.

XIII.   THE MILITARY ART.

There are in the book of Job frequent allusions to weapons of war, and to

modes of attack and defence, such as to show that the subject had attracted
much attention, and that war then was by no means unknown.   In the poem
we find the following allusions to the weapons used, and to the methods of
attack and defence.

To poisoned arrows :

> For the arrows of the Almighty are within me,
> Their poison drinketh up my spirit ;
> The terrors of God set themselves in array against me.   Chap. vi. 4.

To the shield :

> He runneth upon him with outstretched neck,
> With the thick bosses of his shields.   Chap. xv. 26.

To the methods of attack, and the capture of a walled town :

> He set me up for a mark,
> His archers came around me ;
> He transfixed my reins, and did not spare ;
> My gall hath he poured out upon the ground.
> He breaketh me with breach upon breach ;
> He rusheth upon me like a mighty man.   Chap. xvi. 12—14.

To the iron weapon and the bow of brass :

> He shall flee from the iron weapon,
> But the bow of brass shall pierce him through.   Chap. xx. 24.

To the works cast up by a besieging army for the annoyance of a city by
their weapons of war :

> His troops advanced together against me ;
> They throw up their way against me,
> And they encamp round about my dwelling.   Chap. xix. 12.

In this connection, also, should be mentioned the sublime description of the
war-horse in chap. xxxix. 19, seq.   The horse was undoubtedly used in war,
and a more sublime description of this animal caparisoned for battle, and
impatient for the contest, does not occur in any language :

> Hast thou given the horse his strength ?
> Hast thou clothed his neck with thunder ?
> Dost thou make him to leap as the locust ?
> How terrible is the glory of his nostrils !
> He paweth in the valley ; he exulteth in his strength ;
> He goeth forth into the midst of arms.
> He laugheth at fear, and is nothing daunted ;
> And he turneth not back from the sword.
> Upon him rattleth the quiver ;
> The glittering spear and the lance.
> In his fierceness and rage he devoureth the ground,
> And will no longer stand still when the trumpet sounds.
> When the trumpet sounds, he saith, "Aha !"
> And from afar he snuffeth the battle—
> The war-cry of the princes, and the battle-shout.

XIV. ZOOLOGY.

The references to zoology in this book, which are numerous, and which
show that the habits of many portions of the animated creation had been
observed with great care, may be ranked under the heads of insects, reptiles,
birds, and beasts.

1. Of insects, the only two that are mentioned are the spider and the moth:

> His hope shall rot,
> And his trust shall be the building of the spider.
> He shall lean upon his dwelling, and it shall not stand ;
> He shall grasp it, but it shall not endure.   Chap. viii. 14, 15.

> Behold, in his servants he putteth no confidence,
> And his angels he chargeth with frailty ;

How much more true is this of those who dwell in houses of clay,
Whose foundation is in the dust
They are crushed before the moth-worm! Chap. iv. 18, 19.

He buildeth his house like the moth,
Or like a shed which the watchman maketh. Chap. xxvii. 18.

2. Of reptiles, we find the asp and the viper mentioned :

He shall suck the poison of asps ;
The viper's tongue shall destroy him. Chap. xx. 16.

3. The birds or fowls that are mentioned in this book, are much more numerous. They are the following, nearly all so mentioned as to show that their habits had been the subject of careful observation.

The vulture :

The path thereto no bird knoweth,
And the vulture's eye hath not seen it. Chap. xxviii. 7.

The raven :

Who provideth for the raven his food,
When his young ones cry unto God,
And wander for lack of food ? Chap. xxxviii. 41.

The stork and the ostrich :

A wing of exulting fowls moves joyfully !
Is it the wing and plumage of the stork ?
For she leaveth her eggs upon the ground,
And upon the dust she warmeth them,
And forgetteth that her foot may crush them,
And that the wild beast may break them.
She is hardened towards her young, as if they were not hers,
In vain is her travail, and without solicitude ;
Because God hath withheld wisdom from her,
And hath not imparted to her understanding.
In the time when she raiseth herself up on high,
She laugheth at the horse and his rider. Chap. xxxix. 13–18.

The eagle and the hawk :

Is it by thy understanding that the hawk flieth,
And spreadeth his wings toward the south ?
Is it at thy command that the eagle mounteth up,
And that he buildeth his nest on high ?
He inhabiteth the rock and abideth there—
Upon the crag of the rock, and the high fortress.
From thence he spieth out his prey,
His eyes discern it from afar.
His young ones greedily gulp down blood ;
And where the slain are, there is he. Chap. xxxix. 26–30.

4. The beasts that are mentioned are, also, quite numerous, and the description of some of them constitutes the most magnificent part of the poem. The descriptions of the various animals are also more minute than any thing else referred to, and but a few of them can be copied without transcribing whole chapters. The beasts referred to are the following.

The camel, sheep, ox, and she-ass, chap. i. 3; xlii. 12.

The lion :

The roaring of the lion, and the voice of the fierce lion [are silenced],
And the teeth of young lions are broken out.
The old lion perishes for want of prey,
And the whelps of the lioness are scattered abroad. Chap. iv. 10, 11.

The wild ass :

Doth the wild ass bray in the midst of grass ?
Or loweth the ox over his fodder ? Chap. vi. 5.

Who hath sent forth the wild ass free;
Or who hath loosed the bonds of the wild ass ?
Whose home I have made the wilderness,

And his dwellings the barren land.
He scorneth the uproar of the city ;
The cry of the driver he heedeth not.
The range of the mountains is his pasture :
He searcheth after every green thing.   Chap. xxxix. 5–8.

The dog :

But now they who are younger than I have me in derision,
Whose fathers I would have disdained to set with the dogs of my flock.
Chap. xxx. 1.

The jackal :

I am become a brother to the jackal,
And a companion to the ostrich.   Chap. xxx. 29.

The mountain-goat and the hind :

Knowest thou the time when the wild goats of the rock bring forth ?
Or canst thou observe the birth-throes of the hind ?
Canst thou number the months that they fulfil ?
Knowest thou the season when they bring forth ?
They bow themselves ; they give birth to their young ;
They cast forth their sorrows.
Their young ones increase in strength,
They grow up in the wilderness,
They go from them, and return no more.   Chap. xxxix. 1–4.

The unicorn :

Will the unicorn be willing to serve thee ?
Will he abide through the night at thy crib ?
Wilt thou bind him with his band to the furrow ?
And will he harrow the valleys after thee ?
Wilt thou trust him because his strength is great ?
Or wilt thou commit thy labour to him ?
Wilt thou have confidence in him to bring in thy grain ?
Or to gather it to thy threshing-floor ?   Chap. xxxix. 9–12.

The war-horse, in a splendid passage already quoted, chap. xxxix. 19—25. And, finally, the behemoth or hippopotamus, and the leviathan or crocodile, in chap. xl. 15—24 ; xli.—perhaps the most splendid descriptions of animals to be found any where in poetry. For the nature and habits of the animals there described, as well as of those already referred to, the reader is referred to the Notes.

Such is a mere reference to the various topics of science and the arts referred to in the book of Job. Though brief, yet they furnish us with an invaluable account of the progress which society had then made ; and in order to obtain an estimate of the state of the world on these subjects at an early period, there is no better means now at command than a careful study of this book. The scene of the book is laid in the vicinity of those portions of the earth which had made the greatest progress in science and the arts, and from this poem we may learn with considerable accuracy, probably, what advances had then been made in Babylon and in Egypt.

§ IX.   *Exegetical helps to the book of Job.*

I.   THE ANCIENT VERSIONS.

The Vulgate, Septuagint, Syriac, and the Chaldee Paraphrase. For the general character of these versions, and their value in interpreting the Old Testament, see Introduction to Isaiah, § 8. Of the book of Job, the Vulgate is, in general, a very fair and correct version. The translation of the Septuagint is much inferior to what it is on the Pentateuch, and some of the other books of the Bible, though superior to the translation of Isaiah. There are various attempts at explanation of difficulties in it, and statements of things as *facts,* for which there is no authority in the original—showing that if these were inserted by the translators themselves, there was an effort to make it as clear as possible. Whether these, however, were inserted by the translators, or have been interpolated by later hands, it is not easy now to determine. The same attempt at explanation occurs, but much more frequently, in the Targum, or Chaldee Paraphrase. In that work, however, this is much more excusable than in what was designed as a strict translation, for the word *Targum* (תרגום *interpretation, translation, explanation of one language by another*) will admit with propriety considerable latitude of explanation in the attempt to render a work from one language into another. See Buxtorf, Lex. Chald. Talmud. The old Syriac version is literal, and, so far as I can judge, is incomparably the best ancient version of the Scriptures which has been made. Its aid is of great value in the exposition of the Bible.

II. HEBREW WRITERS.

Abraham Ben Juda, published under the name of חרוזי לכם, i. e. *Compositiones Collectaneæ*, a commentary on the Prophets, Megilloth, and Hagiographa, collected chiefly from Jarchi, Aben-Ezra, and Levi Ben Gersom. 1593 and 1612, fol.

Abraham Ben Meir, Aben-Esræ, Commentary on Job. Found in the Rabbinic editions of the Bible, Venice, 1525, 1526, Basle, 1618, 1619, and Amsterdam, 1724. "In multifarious erudition, and accurate knowledge of the Hebrew language, and in a happy tact of hitting the sense of his author, Aben-Ezra greatly surpasses all his contemporaries." *Rosenmüller.* He has made much use of the Arabic language; but on account of his conciseness, he is often obscure.

Abraham Ben Mardochai Perizol, Commentary on Job in the Bible published at Venice, 1517, and Amsterdam, 1724.

Isaac Cohen, Ben Schelomoh, Commentary on Job with the Hebrew text, Constantinople, 1545.

Isaac Ben Schelomoh Jabez, who lived at Constantinople in the 16th century, also published a commentary on Job, inscribed שדי ידאה, "The fear of the Almighty," which is found in the edition of the Bible at Amsterdam, 1724.

Levi Ben Gerschom, born 1288, died 1370. In 1326 he wrote a commentary on Job, which was first published in 1477. It was republished at Naples in 1487, and is found in the Rabbinical Bibles. This is the most copious and clear of the Rabbinical commentaries. He gives an explanation of the words and phrases in the book, and accompanies it with a paraphrase.

Meir Ben Isaac Arama, born 1492, died at Thessalonica 1556. He wrote a commentary on Job, called מאור איוב , "Illustrating Job," which was published in fol. at Thessalonica, in 1516, and subsequently at Venice, 1567 and 1603.

Moseh Alscheh, of Galilee. He died about 1601. He wrote a commentary on Job, called חלקת מהוקק , "The Portion of the Legislator." It was published at Venice, 1603-4. Again in 1722 and 1725.

Moses Nachmanides. He lived in the 13th century. A commentary of his on Job is found in the Rabbinical Bible, Venice, 1517, and Amsterdam, 1724.

Obadiah Ben Jacob Sphorno. He wrote a commentary on Job with the title. משפט צדק, "The Judgment of the Just." Venice, 1590, and Amsterdam, 1724.

Schelomoh Jarchi Ben Jizchak, commonly called *Rasche.* He lived in Campania in the 11th century. His commentary on Job, and on the other books of the Old Testament, is found in the Rabbinical Bible published at Venice and Amsterdam. This work of Jarchi is of great authority among the Hebrews. He has collected and preserved most of the interpretations handed down by tradition.

Schelomoh Ben Melech. He lived at Constantinople in the 16th century. He published a commentary on the whole of the Old Testament under the title of מכלל יופי, " Perfection of Beauty." Amsterdam, 1661 and 1663, fol. In this work he was much aided by the celebrated David Kimchi.

Schimeon Ben Zemach Duran, a Spanish Jew of the 15th century. He wrote a commentary on Job called איהב משפט, " Loving Judgment." Venice, 1590, 1594.

III. THE FATHERS.

Catena in beatissimum Job absolutissima e xxiv. Græciæ doctorum explanationibus, contexta a PAULO COMITOLO Perusiano. Lyons, 1586 ; Venice, 1587.

The same published under the title of Catena Græcorum Patrum in beatum Job, etc., by Niceta. He revised the work, and amended it, and greatly increased it. This was published under the care of P. Junius, Royal Librarian, in London, 1637, fol.

Ephrem the Syrian. Commentary, or Scholia on Job, in Syriac. Found in his works.

Jerome. Commentary found in his works. It is of very little value. The principles of interpretation are fanciful. Jerome held that Job was a type of Christ ; that the land of Uz represents the Virgin Mary ; that his seven sons were the seven-form spirit of grace ; that his daughters were the law, the prophets, and the gospel ; that the sheep represented the church, and the camels the depravity of the Gentiles ; the oxen, which are clean animals, represent the Jews ! Notes on chap. i. 3.

Augustine. Found in his works.

Philip Presbyter lived about A. D. 440. Basle, 1527. His commentary is allegorical and mystical.

Gregory the Great, A. D. 590. Expositiones in Job. Rome, 1475 ; Paris, 1495, fol. ; and in French, Paris, 1666, 1669.

IV. CATHOLIC VERSIONS AND COMMENTARIES.

Thomæ de Vio Caietani (Cardinal and Bishop) Commentarii in Librum Jobi. Rome, 1535, fol. Cardinal Cajetan was ignorant of the Hebrew language, but a man of distinguished talent. Had he been as much acquainted with the Hebrew, says Rosenmüller, as he was distinguished for genius and the power of judgment, he would have greatly excelled all who went before him in the explication of Job.

Franc. Titelmanni Elucidatio paraphastica in Jobum. Antwerp, 1547, 1550, 1553, 1556. Lyons, 1554.

Augustini Steuchi Enarrationes in Librum Jobi. Venice, 1567. He was well acquainted with the Hebrew and Chaldee languages.

Joa. Merceri Commentarii in Job. Geneva, 1573

C. Sanctii Commentarius in Job. Lugd. Bat. 1625, fol.

Cypriani de Huerga Commentaria in xviii. priora Capita Jobi. 1582, fol.

Didaci de Zuniga Commentaria in Librum Jobi. Rome, 1591. This professes to explain and reconcile the Hebrew, Latin Vulgate, and Septuagint.

J. de Pineda Commentariorum in Librum Jobi Libri xiii. With a paraphrase. 1597, 1602, fol. Often reprinted. 1600, 1605, 1609, 1613, 1619, 1627, 1631, 1685, 1701, 1710. This work is highly commended by Schultens.

Liber Job paraphrastice explicatus a Joanne a Jesu Maria. Rome, 1611.

Jacobi Jansonii Enarrationes in propheticum Librum Job. 1623, 1643, fol.

Gasparis Sanctii in Librum Jobi Commentarii, cum Paraphrasi. 1625, fol. Lyons. 1712, Leipsic.

Jacob Bolducii Commentaria in Librum Job. Paris, 1638.

Balthas. Corderii Jobus explicatus. Antwerp, 1646 and 1656, fol.

Philippi Codurci Scholia seu Adnotationes in Jobum. Paris, 1651.

Job brevi commentario et Metaphrasi poetica illustratus. Scripsit Franciscus Vavassor. Paris, 1638.

Analyse du livre de Job (par Laur. Daniel). Lyon, 1710.

Le Livre de Job, selon la Vulgate, Paraphrase, avec des remarques, par Jean Hardouin. 2 vol. Paris, 1729.

Explication du Livre de Job, etc. 4 vol. Paris, 1732. Il Libro de Giobbe dal testo Ebreo in versi Italiani dall' Giacinto Ceruti. Rome, 1773.

v. PROTESTANT VERSIONS AND COMMENTARIES.

Jo. Bugenhagii Adnotationes in Jobum. 1526.

Mart. Buceri Commentaria in Librum Job. 1528, fol.

Jo. Œcolampadii Exegemata in Job et Danielem. Basle, 1532, 1533, 1536. Geneva, 1532, 1533, 1567, 1578, fol. French at Geneva, 1562.

Mart. Borrhai, alias Cellarii, Commentarius in Jobum. 1532, 1539, 1610.

Reinhardi Lutzi Adnotationes in Librum Jobi. 1539, 1563.

Jo. Calvini Conciones in Jobum. 1569, 1593. French, 1563, 1611. German, 1587. English, London, 1584, fol.

Victorini Strigellii Liber Job, ad Ebraicam veritatem recognitus, et Argumentis atque Scholiis illustratus. 1566, 1571.

Ivan. Merceri Commentarii in Librum Job. Geneva, 1573, fol. With a letter from Beza appended.

Jobus Commentario et Paraphrasi illustratus a Theodoro Beza. Geneva, 1583, 1589, 1599, 1600.

Roberti Rolloci (a minister at Edinburgh) Commentarius in Jobum. Geneva, 1610.

Jo. Piscatoris Commentarius in Librum Job. 1612.

Joh. Drusius, Nova Versio et Scholia in Jobum. Amsterdam, 1636. A posthumous work.

Explications sur le livre de Job, Pseaumes, Proverbes, Ecclésiaste, et Cantique, par Jean Diodati. Geneva, 1638.

Exposition of the Book of Job, by George Abbott. London, 1640.

Abbott's Paraphrase of the Book of Job. 1640, 4to. It is formed on the basis of the English version, and contains no notes.

Christophori Schulteti Analysis typica concionum habitarum in Job, etc. 1647, fol.

Joh. Cocceii Commentarius in Librum Jobi. 1644, fol. "A diffuse work, and filled with numerous disputations merely theological." *Rosenmüller.*

Jo. Meiern, Commentaria in Job, Proverbia, Ecclesiasten, et in Canticum Canticorum. 1651, fol.

Ed. Leigh, Annotations on the five poetical Books of the Old Testament. London, 1657. fol.

Terenti, Liber Jobi, Chald. Græc. et Lat. 1663, 4to.

Spanheim, Historia Jobi. 1672.

Joh. cour. Zelleri, Auslegung des Büchleins Hiob. Hamburgh, 1667.

Exposition of the Book of Job, being the sum of 316 Lectures, by George Hutcheson (of Edinburgh). London, 1669, fol.

Caryl's Exposition of the Book of Job, two vols. fol. 1669. This work was originally published in six vols. 4to. "The author was a respectable scholar, a useful preacher, and an exemplary man. He was a non-conformist minister. He was concerned in an English-Greek Lexicon." The work is too voluminous to be much consulted, or to be generally useful.

Sebast. Schmidii in Librum Jobi Commentarius, etc. 1670, 1680, 1690, 1705. Commended by Schultens for the careful comparison of the different versions, the accurate examination of words, and the clearness of the method. There is, however, too constant a reference to theological questions debated in the time of the author between the Lutherans and the Reformed.

Petr. Van Hoecke on Job. Leyden, 1697.

Theod. Antonis (a Dutch commentator) on Job. Frankfort, 1702. He holds that the book of Job is a representation or a type of the church in its afflictions and persecutions.

A parpahrase on the Book of Job, by Richard Blackmore. London, 1700.

Das Buch Hiob aus dem Hebräischen Grundtext aufs neue getreulich ins Teusche übersetzt u. s. w. von Renato Andrea Kortüm. Leips. 1708.

Pauli Egerdi Erläuterung des Buches Hiob. u. s. w. von Joh. Hein. Michaelis. 1716. Published after the death of the author.

Animadversiones philologicæ in Jobum, etc. Auc. Albert Schultens. 1708.

Joh. Hen. Michaelis Notæ uberiores in Librum Jobi, in vol. ii. of his Annotations on the Hagiographa. Halle, 1720.

Herm. Von der Hardt, on Job. 1728, fol.

Jobi Physica Sacra, oder Hiobs Naturwissenschaft verglichen mit der heutigen, von Joh. Jac. Scheutzer. 1721. The author sometimes attributes views of science to the speakers in the book of Job which there is no certain evidence that they possessed. Still the work of Scheutzer contains much that is valuable. It extends to the whole Bible, and is in 8 vols. fol. in Latin and German, with numerous valuable plates.

Theodore de Hase, de Leviathan Jobi et Ceto Jonæ. Bremen, 1723, 8vo.

Le Livre de Job, traduit en Francois, sur l' original Hébreu, par Theod. Criusoz. Rotterdam, 1729.

Veteris Testamenti Libri Hagiographi, ex translatione Joannis Clerici. Amsterdam, 1731, fol. He regards the book of Job as written *after* the return from the Babylonish exile.

Annotations on the Book of Job and the Psalms, by Thomas Fenton. London, 1732.

Joh. Adolf Hoffmaus Neue Erklärung des Buchs Hiob u. s. w. Hamburgh, 1734. This work professes to illustrate Job from the remains of antiquity, and from the Oriental philosophy. The author found deep mysteries in the book, and is much addicted to the allegorical mode of interpretation. The work is now of little value.

Samuel Wesley Dissertationes et Conjecturæ in Librum Jobi, tabulis geographicis et figuris æneis illustratæ. London, 1736, fol.

Liber Jobi, cum nova versione, ad Hebræum fontem, et commentario perpetuo, in quo veterum et recentiorum interpretum cogitata præcipua expenduntur; genuinus sensus ad priscum linguæ genium indagatur, atque ex filo, et nexu universo, argumenti nodus intricatissimus evolvitur. Curavit et edidit ALBERTUS SCHULTENS. Lugd. Batav. 1737. The same work abridged by Richard Grey, London, 1741, 8vo; and a more full abridgment, Halæ, 1773, 1774, 8vo. This great work of Schultens on Job deserves the first place, on many accounts, in the list of those illustrative of this book. It is the most elaborate commentary which has been published, and contains a full statement of the opinions which have been entertained by critics on different parts of the work. Schultens brought to the interpretation of the book of Job a more accurate and extensive knowledge of the Hebrew and Arabic than was possessed by any one who preceded him in this department of labour. The leading faults of the work are, a too minute and tedious detail of the opinions of other commentators—amounting in many instances to a statement of more than twenty opinions on the meaning of a verse or phrase, and, in determining the meaning of Hebrew words, too great a proneness to rely on etymological conjectures.

Liber Jobi in versiculos metrice divisus, cum versione Alberti Schultens Notisque ex ejus Commentario excerptis. Richard Grey. London, 1741.

Sigmund Jacob Baumgartens Auslegung des Buchs Hiob. Halle, 1740.

Recht beleuchtetes Buch Hiobs, mit vielen dabey gemachten neuen Entduckungen, nöthigen Anmerkungen und erbaulichen Nutzanwendungen. Herausgegeben von Jacob Koch. 1743, 1744, 1747.

Kleine Geographisch-historische Abhandlungen zur Erläuterung einiger Stellen Mosis und vornehmlich des ganzen Buchs Hiob. von Jac. Koch. 1747.

Costard's Observations on the Book of Job. 1747, 8vo.

A Dissertation on the Book of Job, &c., by John Garnett, D. D., quarto, London, 1749. According to Garnett, the book of Job is a drama, or allegory; the Babylonish captivity is the main subject of the allegory; the three friends who came to visit Job are the children of Edom coming to condole with the Hebrews in their captivity. The work is of very little value.

Das richte Gericht in dem kurz und verständlich erklarten, übersetzten und zergliederten Buch Hiob u.s.w. durch Christoph Friedrich Oetinger. 1743.

Elihu, or an inquiry into the principal scope and design of the Book of Job, by Walter Hodges, D. D. London, quarto, 1750. According to Dr. Hodges, the Book of Job relates to patriarchal times, and the design is to give a summary of the patriarchal religion. The particular purpose of the book, according to the view of this author, is, to reveal and establish the doctrine of *justification.* Job was a type of the Saviour, and by Job's friends being directed to offer sacrifices for themselves, is "intimated that each national church ought to have an independent power in such matters." In the opinion of this author, Elihu was the Son of God himself! The nature and value of the work may be easily seen from these views. The author was a divine of the Hutchinsonian school.

The Book of Job, with a Paraphrase from the third verse of the third chapter to the seventh verse of the forty-second chapter. By Leonard Chappelow, B. D., Arabic Professor. Cambridge, 1752. "A mere paraphrase, verbose, and without annotations."

Observationes Miscellaneæ in Librum Job, etc., by David Renat. Bouillier. Amsterdam, 1758.

The Divine Legation of Moses demonstrated, by Bishop Warburton. 1758. In this great work there is an examination of the book of Job which has attracted much attention on account of the learning and talent of the author. The theory of Warburton is, that the book of Job is a drama; that it relates to the Jews in the time of the captivity; that it was written some time between the return and the thorough settlement of the Jews in their own land; that the drama is allegorical in its character; that the character of Job is designed to represent the Jewish people; that his wife is a representation of the heathen influence which led the Hebrews on their return to marry "strange wives;" that the three friends of Job represent the three capital enemies of the Jews who hindered their efforts to rebuild the temple on their return from Babylon, Sanballat, Tobiah, and Geshem; that under the character of Elihu the writer or author of the poem is himself designated. Div. Lega. B. vi. § 2. After the view which Bishop Warburton gives of the book of Job, there is more real point and force than he himself intended in what he says in a letter to his friend Dr. Hurd. "Poor Job! It was his eternal fate to be persecuted by his friends. His three friends passed sentence of condemnation upon him, and he has been executed in effigy ever since. He was first bound to the stake by a long catena of Greek Fathers; then tortured by Pineda; then strangled by Caryl; and afterwards cut up by Wesley and anatomized by Garnett. I only acted the tender part of his wife, and was for making short work with him. But he was ordained, I think, by a fate like that of Prometheus, to lie still upon his dunghill, and to have his brains sucked out by owls."

An Essay towards a new English version of the Book of Job from the original Hebrew, with a commentary, and some account of his life.   By Thomas Heath, Esq., of Exeter.   Quarto.   London, 1756.   There is little in this work that can now be regarded as of value.   The knowledge of Hebrew by the author was quite limited, and the notes throw little light on the meaning of the text.

A Critical Dissertation on the Book of Job, by Charles Peters, A. M. London, 1751, quarto.   This work is designed particularly to examine the theory of Bishop Warburton; to vindicate the antiquity of the book; to show that the passage in chap. xix. 25—27 refers to the resurrection and the future judgment; and that the doctrine of the future state was the popular belief among the Hebrews.   It is a work of considerable learning and value.   It contains much valuable matter, though all its reasonings may not be satisfactory.

Paraphrastische Erklärung des Buchs Hiob, von Joh. Fried. Bahrdt. Leips. 1764.

Das Buch Hiob, in einer poetischen Uebersetzung nach Schultens Erklärung mit Anmerkungen, von Simon Grynæus.   1767.

Joh. Dav. Cube poetische und prosaische Uebersetzung des Buchs Hiob. Berlin, 1769.

Paul Bauldri, Critical Remarks on Job.

Kurze doch grundliche Erklarung des Buchs Hiob, u. s. w. von Joh. Georg. Meintel.   Nürnberg, 1771.

Velthusen, Exercitationes Criticæ in Jobum, cap xix.   1772, 12mo.

Scott's Book of Job in English verse, with Notes.   1773, 8vo. " A very valuable work."   *Wemyss.*

Metaphrasis libri Jobi, sive Job metricus, vario carminis genere, primo ejulans, post jubilans, interprete Jo. Georg. Meintel.   1775.

Versuch einer neuen poetischen Uebersetzung des Buches Hiob, u. s. w. von J. C. R. Eckermann.   1778.

Animadversiones in Librum Job.   Scripsit Jas. Christ. Rud. Eckermann. Lubeck, 1779.

Jo. Christoph. Doederlein Scholia in libros vet. Testam. poeticos, Jobum, Psalmos, et tres Salomonis.   Halle, 1779.

Joa. Jac. Reiske, Conjecturæ in Jobum et Proverbia Salomonis.   Leips. 1779.   He takes great liberty with the Hebrew text, transposing, changing, or rejecting whole verses at pleasure.

Hiob. übersetzt von Dan. Gotthilf Moldenhawer.   Leips. 1780.

Das Buch Hiob zum allgemeinen Gebrauch, von Heinr. Sander. Leips. 1780, 8vo.

Hiob, neu übersetzt mit Anmerkungen, von W. F. Hufnagel.   1781, 8vo.

Hiob, aus dem Hebräischen Original neu übersetzt, u. s. w. von Christ. Dav. Kessler.   1784, 8vo.

Hiob, aus dem Hebräischen Original neu übersetzt und mit erklärenden Anmerkungen versehen, zum allgemeinen Gebrauch, von Chr. Dan. Kessler.   Tubingen, 1784, 8vo.

Greve, Ultima Capita Jobi.   1788, 4to.

Jobi, antiquissimi carminis Hebraici, natura atque virtus.   Scripsit Car. Dav. Ilgen.   Leips. 1789, 8vo.

Jobus, Proverbia Salomonis, etc. a Joh. Aug. Dathio.   Halle, 1789, 8vo.

Job oversat [with brief critical and philological remarks], by And. Heins. In the Dutch language.   Amsterdam, 1794, 8vo.

Het Bock Job, etc. [also in the Dutch language.]   By Herrman Muntinghe.   Amsterdam, 1794, 8vo.

Garden's improved version of the Book of Job.   1796, 8vo.

The same work translated into German by J. P. Berg.   Leips. 1797, 8vo.

Hiob, übersetzt; ein Versuch von Samuel Christian Pape. Göttingen, 1797, 8vo.

Das Buch Hiob metrisch ubersetzt. Ein Versuch von A. S. Block. Ratzeburg, 1799, 8vo.

Hiob, übersetzt von J. G. Eichhorn. Leips. 1800, 8vo. Neue verbesserte Ausgabe. Göttingen, 1824.

Exegetische und kritische versuche über die schwersten stellen des Buchs Hiob. Leips. 1801, 8vo.

Discourses and Dissertations on the Scriptural Doctrine of Atonement and Sacrifice. By William Magee, D. D. 1801. In this important work on the atonement, there is a very valuable dissertation on the book of Job. Bishop Magee supposes that Moses was the author, or that it was written by Job himself, or by some contemporary, and that it fell into the hands of Moses, and was adopted by him as an important help to encourage the Israelites in their trials.

Die heilige Schrift des Alten Testaments, zweiten Theils. dritten Bandes zweite Hälfte, welche das Buch Hiob euthalt, von D. Brentano und Th. A. Dereser. Frankfort, 1804, 8vo.

Hiob. Ein religioses Gedicht Aus dem Hebräischen neu übersetzt, geprüft und erläubert von Matthias Heinr. Stuhlmann. Hamburg, 1804, 8vo.

Stock's Book of Job; a new version, with Notes. 1805, 4to. See this work examined with great severity in Magee on the Atonement.

Pareau, Commentatio, &c. 1807, 8vo.

Das Buch Hiob, bearbeitet von Gaab. Tübingen, 1809, 8vo.

Die Schriften des Alten Testaments. Neu übersetzt von J. C. W. Augusti und W. M. L. de Wette. Dritter Band Hiob. Heidelberg, 1809, 8vo.

Jobus: Latine vertit, et annotatione perpetua illustravit, Ern. Frid. Car. Rosenmüller, Ling. Arab. in Acad. Leips. Prof. Leips. 1806. The commentary of Rosenmüller is, on the whole, probably the most valuable of all the expositions of this book. One who wishes to *explain* and *understand* the book of Job will find more valuable materials collected there than in any other of the commentaries. Nothing is passed over without an attempt at explanation; and nothing collected by his predecessors that would throw light on the meaning of the book, seems to have been unnoticed by him. For the most part, also, the exposition is distinguished by sound sense, by correct and sober views, as well as by eminent learning.

The Book of Job, translated by Eliz. Smith. 1810, 8vo. "This work was completed before the twenty-sixth year of the authoress, with little help except from Parkhurst's Lexicon, and the revision of her friend Dr. Randolph, who annexed to it a few critical notes. She left a fine example to her sex; and though self-taught, with little access to books, she left behind her some monuments of learning and piety, calculated to make many blush for their own idleness." *Wemyss.*

The Book of Job literally translated from the original Hebrew, and restored to its natural arrangement, with notes critical and illustrative, and an introduction on its scene, scope, language, author, and object. By John Mason Good, F. R. S., &c. 1812. The "Introduction" by Dr. Good is very valuable. In the Notes there is much learning, but it is more extensive than accurate. The translation cannot be relied on as correct. The work, however, is a valuable contribution to sacred literature, and deserves a place in every theological library.

Das Buch Hiob, aus dem Grundtext metrisch übersetzt und erläutert von J. Rud. Schärer. Bern, 1818, 8vo.

Bridel, Le Livre de Job. 1818, 8vo.

Hiob, fur gebildete Leser bearbeitet von C. G. A. Bückel. Berlin, 1821, 8vo.

Das Burch Hiob, aus dem Hebräischen metrisch übersetzt und durch kurze philologische Anmerkungen erläutert von L. F. Melsheimer. Mannheim, 1823.

Buch Hiob. Uebersetzung und Anslegung, von D. Friedrich Wilhelm Carl Umbreit, Professor an der Universität zu Heidelberg. Heidelberg, 1824, 8vo. This is the production of an acute and sharp-sighted critic. The translation is very accurate, and the Notes, though brief, are very valuable. The Introduction is less brief than is desirable, and the views maintained in it are not such as seem to me to be correct.

Middledorff, curæ Hexaplares in Jobum. 1837, 4to.

The Book of the Patriarch Job, translated from the original Hebrew, as nearly as possible, in the terms and style of the authorized English version, to which is prefixed an introduction on the History, Times, Country, Friends, and Book of the Patriarch, &c. By Samuel Lee, D. D., etc. London, 1837. This work is not what might have been expected from the learning and reputation of Prof. Lee. It abounds with Arabic learning, which is scattered with ostentatious profuseness through the volume, but which often contributes little to the elucidation of the text. It is designed for the critical scholar rather than the general reader.

A new translation of the Book of Job, with an Introduction and Notes chiefly explanatory. By George R. Noyes. Boston, 1838. This is an elegant and a very accurate translation. Dr. Noyes is understood to be a Unitarian, but neither in this work nor in the translation of Isaiah, have I observed any attempt to accommodate the translation to the views of that denomination. His aim has evidently been to give the exact sense of the original, and this, so far as I can judge, has been accomplished with great accuracy. The Notes are very brief, but they are pithy and valuable. The Introduction is less valuable than the other parts of the work.

Job and his times, or a picture of the Patriarchal age during the period between Noah and Abraham, as regards the state of morality, arts and sciences, manners and customs, &c., and a new version of that most ancient poem, accompanied with Notes and Dissertations. The whole adapted to the English reader. By Thomas Wemyss, author of Biblical Gleanings, Symbolical Dictionary, and other works. London, 1839. This is designed to be a popular work. It is not so much of the nature of a commentary as a collection of fragments and brief essays on various topics referred to in the book of Job. It is chiefly valuable from its illustration of the religion of the time of Job, the arts and sciences, the manners and customs, &c. It lacks lucid arrangement, and furnishes comparatively little illustration of the difficulties of the text.

GENERAL ANALYSIS OF THE BOOK OF JOB.

PART FIRST.

THE HISTORICAL INTRODUCTION, IN PROSE, CHAP. I. II.

PART SECOND.

THE ARGUMENT, OR CONTROVERSY, IN VERSE, CHAP. III.—XLII. 6.

I. The first series in the controversy, chap. iii.—xiv.

(1.) Job opens the discussion by cursing his birth-day, and by a bitter complaint of his calamity, chap. iii.
(2.) Speech of Eliphaz, chap. iv. v.
(3.) Answer of Job, chap. v. vi.
(4.) Speech of Bildad, chap. viii.
(5.) Answer of Job, chap. ix. x.
(6.) Speech of Zophar, chap. xi.
(7.) Answer of Job, chap. xii.—xiv.

II. The second series in the controversy, chap. xv.—xxi.

(1.) Speech of Eliphaz, chap. xv.
(2.) Answer of Job, chap. xvi. xvii.
(3.) Speech of Bildad, chap. xviii.
(4.) Answer of Job, chap. xix.
(5.) Speech of Zophar, chap. xx.
(6.) Answer of Job, chap. xxi.

III. The third series in the controversy, chap. xxii.—xxxi.

(1.) Speech of Eliphaz, chap. xxii.
(2.) Answer of Job, chap. xxiii. xxiv.
(3.) Speech of Bildad, chap. xxv.
(4.) Answer of Job, chap. xxvi.—xxxi.

IV. Speech of Elihu, chap. xxxii.—xxxvii.

V. The close of the discussion, chap. xxxviii.—xlii. 1—6.

(1.) The speech of the Almighty, chap. xxxviii.—xli.
(2.) The response and penitent confession of Job, chap. xlii. 1—6.

PART THIRD.

THE CONCLUSION, IN PROSE, CHAP. XLII. 7—17.

THE BOOK OF JOB.[1]

CHAPTER I.

ANALYSIS OF THE CHAPTER.

Brief history of Job; his piety and prosperity, ver. 1—5. The tribunal of the Almighty, and the assembling there of the sons of God. Satan appears among them, ver. 6. The inquiry of the Almighty of Satan where he had been, and his answer, ver. 7. His remark respecting the fidelity of Job, ver. 8. Satan insinuates that all his fidelity is the mere result of selfishness, produced by the favours that God had bestowed on him, and that if his blessings were taken away he would curse God to his face, ver. 10, 11. The Almighty consents to the trial of Job, only making it a condition that his person should not be touched, ver. 12, and Satan goes out from the presence of JEHOVAH to afflict Job. The calamities that came upon the family of Job, ver. 13—19. Job's deep affliction, but perfect resignation, ver. 20—22.

THERE was a man in the land of *a* Uz, whose name *was* Job; *b* and that man was perfect and upright, and one that *c* feared God, and eschewed evil.

1 Moses is thought to have wrote the Book of *Job* whilst among the *Midianites*, B. C. 1520.
a 1 Ch.1.17,42; La.4.21.   *b* Eze.14.14,20.
c Pr.16.6.

CHAPTER I.

There was a man. This has all the appearance of being a true history. Many have regarded the whole book as a fiction, and have supposed that no such person as Job ever lived. But the book opens with the appearance of reality; and the express declaration that there was such a man, the mention of his name and of the place where he lived, show that the writer meant to affirm that there was in fact such a man. On this question see the Introduction, § 1. ¶ *In the land of Uz.* On the question where Job lived, see also the Introduction, § 2. ¶ *Whose name was Job.* The name Job (Heb. אִיּוֹב, Gr. 'Ιὼβ) means properly, according to Gesenius, *one persecuted*, from a root (עָיַב) meaning to be an enemy to any one, to persecute, to hate. The primary idea, according to Gesenius, is to be sought in breathing, blowing, or puffing at, or upon any one, as expressive of anger or hatred, Germ. *Anschnauben.* Eichhorn (Einleit. § 638. 1,) supposes that the name denotes a man who turns himself penitently to God, from a sense of the verb still found in Arabic *to repent.* On this supposition, the name was given to him, because, at the close of the book, he is represented as exercising repentance for the improper expressions in which he had indulged during his sufferings. The verb occurs only once in the Hebrew Scriptures, Ex. xxiii. 22: "But if thou shalt indeed obey his voice, and do all that I speak, then *I will be an enemy* (וָאֹיַבְתִּי) *unto thine enemies* (אֶת־אֹיְבֶיךָ)." The participle אֹיֵב *Oyēb* is the common word to denote an enemy in the Old Testament, Ex. xv. 6, 9; Lev. xxvi.25; Num. xxxv. 23; Deut. xxxii. 27, 42; Ps. vii. 5; viii. 2; xxxi. 8; Lam. ii. 4, 5; Job xiii. 24; xxvii. 7; xxxiii. 10, *et sœpe al.* If this be the proper meaning of the word *Job*, then the name would seem to have been given him by anticipation, or by common consent, as a much persecuted man. Significant names were very common among the Hebrews—given either by anticipation (see Notes on Isa. viii. 18), or subsequently, to denote some leading or important event in the life; comp. Gen. iv. 1, 2, 25; v.29; 1 Sam. i. 20. Such, too, was the case among the Romans, where the *agnomen* thus bestowed became the appellation by which the individual was best

2 And there were born unto him | seven sons and three daughters.

known. Cicero thus received his name from a wart which he had on his face, resembling a *vetch*, and which was called by the Latins, *cicer.* Thus also Marcus had the name *Ancus*, from the Greek word αγκων, *ancon*, because he had a crooked arm ; and thus the names Africanus, Germanicus, &c., were given to generals who had distinguished themselves in particular countries ; see Univer. Hist. Anc. Part ix. 619, ed. 8vo, Lond. 1779. In like manner it is possible that the name *Job* was given to the Emir of Uz by common consent, as the man much persecuted or tried, and that this became afterwards the appellation by which he was best known. The name occurs once as applied to a son of Issachar, Gen. xlvi. 13, and in only two other places in the Bible except in this book; Ezek. xiv. 14 ; James v. 11. ¶ *And that man was perfect* (תּם). The LXX. have greatly expanded this statement, by giving a paraphrase instead of a translation. " He was a man who was true (ἀληθινὸς), blameless (ἄμεμπτος), just (δίκαιος), pious (θεοσεβὴς), abstaining from every evil deed." Jerome renders it, *simplex—simple*, or *sincere*. The Chaldee, שׁלים, *complete, finished, perfect.* The idea seems to be that his piety, or moral character, was *proportionate* and was *complete in all its parts.* He was a man of integrity in all the relations of life—as an Emir, a father, a husband, a worshipper of God. Such is properly the meaning of the word תּם *tâm* as derived from תּמם *tâmim, to complete, to make full, perfect* or *entire*, or *to finish.* It denotes that in which there is no part lacking to complete the whole—as in a watch in which no wheel is wanting. Thus he was not merely upright as an Emir, but he was pious towards God ; he was not merely kind to his family, but he was just to his neighbours and benevolent to the poor. The word is used to denote integrity as applied to the heart, Gen. xx. 5 : בתם לבבי, " In the honesty, simplicity, or sincerity of

my heart (see the margin) have I done this." So 1 Kings xxii. 34, " One drew a bow לתמו in the simplicity [or perfection] of his heart ;" i. e. without any evil intention ; comp. 2 Sam. xv. 11 ; Prov. x. 9. The proper notion, therefore, is that of simplicity, sincerity, absence from guile or evil intention, and completeness of parts in his religion. That he was a man absolutely sinless, or without any propensity to evil, is disproved alike by the spirit of complaining which he often evinces, and by his own confession, chap. ix. 20 :

If I justify myself, mine own mouth shall
    condemn me ;
If I say I am perfect, it shall prove me per-
    verse.

So also chap. xlii. 5, 6 :

I have heard of thee by the hearing of the ear,
But now mine eye seeth thee ;
Wherefore I abhor myself,
And repent in dust and ashes.

Comp. Eccl. vii. 20. ¶ *And upright.* The word ישׁר *yâshâr*, from ישׁר *yishâr*, to be straight, is applied often to a road which is straight, or to a path which is level or even. As here used it means upright or righteous ; comp. Ps. xi. 7 ; xxxvii. 14 ; Deut. xxxii. 4 ; Ps. xxxiii. 4. ¶ *And one that feared God.* Religion in the Scriptures is often represented as the fear of God ; Prov. i. 7, 29 ; ii. 5 ; viii. 13 ; xiv. 26, 27 ; Isa. xi. 2 ; Acts ix. 31, *et sæpe al.* ¶ *And eschewed evil.* " And departed from (סר) evil." Sept. " Abstaining from every evil thing." These then are the four characteristics of Job's piety—he was sincere ; upright ; a worshipper of God ; and one who abstained from all wrong. These are the essential elements of true religion everywhere ; and the whole statement in the book of Job shows Job was, though not absolutely free from the sins which cleave to our nature, eminent in each of these things.

2. *And there were born unto him seven sons and three daughters.* The same number was given to him again after these were lost, and his severe trials had been endured ; see chap. xlii. 13. Of his second family the

3 His [1] substance also was seven thousand sheep, and three thousand camels, and five hundred yoke of oxen, and five hundred

1 or, *cattle.*

dred she-asses, and a very great [2] household ; so that this man was the greatest of all the [3] men of the east.

2 or, *husbandry.*   3 *sons.*

names of the daughters are mentioned, chap. xlii. 14. Of his first, it is remarkable that neither the names of his wife, his sons nor his daughters are recorded. The Chaldee, however, on what authority is unknown, says that the name of his wife was דינה *Dinah,* chap. ii. 9.

3. *His substance.* Marg., or *cattle.* The word here used (מקנה) is derived from קנה, *kânâh,* to gain or acquire, to buy or purchase, and properly means any thing acquired or purchased — property, possessions, riches. The wealth of nomadic tribes, however, consisted mostly in flocks and herds, and hence the word in the Scripture signifies, almost exclusively, property in cattle. The word, says Gesenius, is used *strictly* to denote sheep, goats, and neat cattle, excluding beasts of burden (comp. Gr. κτῆνος, *herd,* used here by the LXX.), though sometimes the word includes asses and camels, as in this place. ¶ *Seven thousand sheep.* In this verse we have a description of the wealth of an Arab ruler or chief, similar to that of those who are at this day called *Emirs.* Indeed the whole description in the book is that which is applicable to the chief of a tribe. The possessions referred to in this verse would constitute no inconsiderable wealth anywhere, and particularly in the nomadic tribes of the East. Land is not mentioned as a part of his wealth ; for among nomadic tribes living by pasturage, the right to the soil in fee simple is not claimed by individuals, the right of pasturage or a temporary possession being all that is needed. For the same reason, and from the fact that their circumstances require them to live in movable tents, houses are not mentioned as a part of the wealth of this Emir. To understand this book, as well as most of the books of the Old Testament, it is necessary for us to lay aside our notions of living, and transfer ourselves in imagination to

the very dissimilar customs of the East.—The Chaldee has made a very singular explanation of this verse, which must be regarded as the work of fancy, but which shows the character of that version : " And his possessions were seven thousand sheep—a thousand for each of his sons ; and three thousand camels—a thousand for each of his daughters ; and five hundred yoke of oxen—for himself ; and five hundred she-asses—for his wife." ¶ *And three thousand camels.* Camels are well-known beasts of burden, extensively used still in Arabia. The Arabs employed these animals anciently in war, in their caravans, and for food. They are not unfrequently called " ships of the desert," particularly valuable in arid plains because they go many days without water. They carry from three to five hundred pounds, in proportion to the distance which they have to travel. Providence has adapted the camel with wonderful wisdom to sandy deserts, and in all ages the camel must be an invaluable possession there. The driest thistle and the barest thorn is all the food that he requires, and this he eats while advancing on his journey without stopping or causing a moment's delay. As it is his lot to cross immense deserts where no water is found, and where no dews fall, he is endowed with the power of laying in a store of water that will suffice him for days—Bruce says for thirty days. To effect this, nature has provided large reservoirs or stomachs within him, where the water is kept pure, and from which he draws at pleasure as from a fountain. No other animal is endowed with this power, and were it not for this, it would be wholly impracticable to cross those immense plains of sand. The Arabians, the Persians, and others, eat the flesh of camels, and it is served up at the best tables in the country. One of the ancient Arab poets, whose hospitality grew into a proverb, is reported to have killed yearly, in a certain month, ten camels every day for the entertainment of his friends. In regard to the hardihood of camels, and their ability to live on the coarsest fare, Burckhardt has stated a fact which may furnish an illustration. In a journey which he made from the country south of the Dead Sea to Egypt, he says, "During the whole of this journey, the camels had no other provender than the withered shrubs of the desert, my dromedary excepted, to which I gave a few handfuls of barley each evening." Trav. in Syria, p. 451; comp. Bruce's Travels, vol. iv. p. 596; Niebuhr, Reisebeschreibung nach Arabien, 1 Band, s. 215; Sandys, p. 138; Harmer's Obs. iv. 415, ed. Lond. 1808, 8vo; and Rob. Cal. ¶ *And five hundred yoke of oxen.* The fact that Job had so many oxen implies that he devoted himself to the cultivation of the soil as well as to keeping flocks and herds; comp. ver. 14. So large a number of oxen would constitute wealth anywhere. ¶ *And five hundred she-asses.* Bryant remarks (Observations, p. 61) that a great part of the wealth of the inhabitants of the East often consisted of she-asses, the males being few and not held in equal estimation. She-asses are early mentioned as having been in common use to ride on; Num. xxii. 25; Judges v. 10; 2 Kings iv. 24 (Hebrew). One reason why the ass was chosen in preference to the horse, was that it subsisted on so much less than that animal, there being no animal except the camel that could be so easily kept as the ass. She-asses were also regarded as the most valuable, because, in traversing the deserts of the country they would furnish travellers with milk. It is remarkable that *cows* are not mentioned expressly in this enumeration of the articles of Job's wealth, though *butter* is referred to by him subsequently as having been abundant in his family, chap. xxix. 6. It is possible, however, that *cows* were included as a part of the "five hundred yoke of בקר *Bâkâr,*" here rendered "oxen;" but which would be quite as appropriately rendered *cattle.* The word is in the common gender, and is derived from בקר, in Arab. to cleave, to divide, to lay open, and hence to plough, to cleave the soil. It denotes properly the animals used in ploughing; and it is well known that cows are employed as well as oxen for this purpose in the East; see Judges xiv. 18; Hos. iv. 16; comp. Deut. xxxii. 14, where the word בקר *Bâkâr* is used to denote a cow—"milk of *kine,*" Gen. xxxiii. 13. (Heb.) ¶ *And a very great household;* marg., *husbandry.* The Hebrew word here (עבדה) ambiguous. — It may denote service rendered, i. e., work, or the servants who performed it; comp. Gen. xxvi. 14, *marg.* The LXX. render it ὑπηρεσία, Aquhe. δουλεία, and Symmachus, οἰκετία; all denoting *service,* or *servitude,* or that which pertained to the domestic service of a family. The word refers doubtless to those who had charge of his camels, his cattle, and of his husbandry; see ver. 15. It is not implied by the word here used, nor by that in ver. 15, that they were *slaves.* They may have been, but there is nothing to indicate this in the narrative. The LXX. add to this, as if explanatory of it, "and his works were great in the land." ¶ *So that this man was the greatest.* Was possessed of the most wealth, and was held in the highest honour. ¶ *Of all the men of the East;* marg. as in Heb. *sons.* The sons of the East denote those who lived in the East. The word *East* (קדם) is commonly employed in the Scriptures to denote the country which lies east of Palestine. For the places intended here, see Intro. § 2, (3.) It is of course impossible to estimate with accuracy the exact amount of the value of the property of Job. Compared with many persons in modern times, indeed, his possessions would not be regarded as constituting very great riches. The Editor of the Pictorial Bible supposes that on a fair estimate his property might be considered as worth from thirty to forty thousand pounds sterling—equivalent to some two hundred thousand dollars. In this estimate the camel is reckoned as worth about forty-five

4 And his sons went and feast- | ed *in their* houses, every one his

dollars, the oxen as worth about five dollars, and the sheep at a little more than one dollar, which it is said are about the average prices now in Western Asia. Prices, however, fluctuate much from one age to another; but at the present day such possessions would be regarded as constituting great wealth in Arabia. The value of the property of Job may be estimated from this fact, that he had almost half as many camels as constituted the wealth of a Persian king in more modern times. Chardin says, "as the king of Persia in the year 1676 was in Mesandera, the Tartars fell upon the camels of the king and took away three thousand of them, which was to him a great loss, for he had only seven thousand."—Rosenmüller, Morgenland, *in loc.* The condition of Job we are to regard as that of a rich Arabic Emir, and his mode of life as between the nomadic pastoral life, and the settled manner of living in communities like ours. He was a princely shepherd, and yet he was devoted to the cultivation of the soil. It does not appear, however, that he claimed the right of the soil in *fee simple,* nor is his condition inconsistent with the supposition that his residence in any place was regarded as temporary, and that all his property might be easily removed. "He belonged to that condition of life which fluctuated between that of the wandering shepherd, and that of a people settled in towns. That he resided, or had a residence, in a town is obvious; but his flocks and herds evidently pastured in the deserts, between which and the town his own time was probably divided. He differed from the Hebrew patriarchs chiefly in this, that he did not so much wander about "without any certain dwelling place." This mixed condition of life, which is still frequently exhibited in Western Asia, will, we apprehend, account sufficiently for the diversified character of the allusions and pictures which the book contains—to the pastoral life and the scenes and products of the wilderness; to the scenes and circumstan-

ces of agriculture; to the arts and sciences of settled life and of advancing civilization."—Pict. Bib. It may serve somewhat to illustrate the different ideas in regard to what constituted wealth in different countries, to compare this statement respecting Job with a remark of Virgil respecting an inhabitant of ancient Italy, whom he calls the most wealthy among the Ausonian farmers :—

> Seniorque Galæsus,
> Dum paci medium se offert ; justissimus unus
> Qui fuit, *Ausoniisque olim ditissimus arvis:*
> Quinque greges illi balantum, quina redibant
> Armenta, et terram centum vertebat aratris.
> Æn. vii. 535—539.

> Among the rest, the rich Galæsus lies ;
> A good old man, while peace he preached in vain.
> Amid the madness of the unruly train :
> Five herds, five bleating flocks his pasture filled,
> His lands a hundred yoke of oxen tilled.
>   DRYDEN.

4. *And his sons went and feasted* in their *houses.* Dr. Good renders this, "and his sons went to hold a banquet house." Tindal renders it, "made bankettes." The Hebrew means, they went and made a "house-feast;" and the idea is, that they gave an entertainment in their dwellings, in the ordinary way in which such entertainments were made. The word here used (משתה) is derived from שתה *shâthâh, to drink;* and then to drink together, to banquet. Schultens supposes that this was merely designed to keep up the proper familiarity between the different branches of the family, and not for purposes of revelry and dissipation ; and this seems to accord with the view of Job. He, though a pious man, was not opposed to it, but he apprehended merely that they might have sinned in their hearts, ver. 5. He knew the danger, and hence he was more assiduous in imploring for them the divine guardianship. ¶ *Every one his day.* In his proper turn, or when his day came round. Perhaps it refers only to their birth-days; see chap. iii. 1, where the word "day" is used to denote a birthday. In early times the birth-day was observed with great solemnity and re-

day; and sent and called for their three sisters to eat and to drink with them.

5 And it was so, when the days of *their* feasting were gone about, that Job sent and sanctified them, and rose up early in the morn-

ing, and offered burnt offerings *according* to the number of them all : for Job said, It may be that my sons have sinned, and *a* cursed God in their hearts. Thus did Job [1] continually.

a Le.24.15,16.　　1 *all the days.*

joicing. Perhaps in this statement the author of the Book of Job means to intimate that his family lived in entire harmony, and to give a picture of his domestic happiness strongly contrasted with the calamities which came upon his household. It was a great aggravation of his sufferings that a family thus peaceful and harmonious was wholly broken up.—The Chaldee adds, "until seven days were completed," supposing that each one of these feasts lasted seven days, a supposition by no means improbable, if the families were in any considerable degree remote from each other. ¶ *And sent and called for their three sisters.* This also may be regarded as a circumstance showing that these occasions were not designed for revelry. Young men, when they congregate for dissipation, do not usually invite their *sisters* to be with them ; nor do they usually desire the presence of virtuous females at all. The probability, therefore, is, that this was designed as affectionate and friendly family intercourse. In itself there was nothing wrong in it, nor was there necessarily any danger; yet Job felt it *possible* that they might have erred and forgotten God, and hence he was engaged in more intense and ardent devotion on their account ; ver. 5.

5. *And it was so, when the days of* their *feasting were gone about.* Dr. Good renders this, "as the days of such banquets returned." But this is not the idea intended. It is, when the banquets had gone round as in a circle through all the families, *then* Job sent and sanctified them. It was not from an anticipation that they *would* do wrong, but it was from the apprehension that they *might* have sinned. The word rendered "were gone about" (נקף) means properly to join together, and then to move round in a circle, to

revolve, as festivals do ; see Notes on Isaiah, xxix. 1 : "Let the festivals go round." Here it means that the days of their banqueting had gone round the circle, or had gone round the several families. Sept. " When the days of the entertainment (or drinking, πότου) were finished." A custom of feasting similar to this prevails in China. "They have their fraternities which they call the brotherhood of the months ; this consists of months according to the number of the days therein, and in a circle they go abroad to eat at one another's houses by turns. If one man has not conveniences to receive the fraternity in his own house, he may provide for them in another; and there are many public houses well furnished for this purpose." See Semedo's History of China, i. chap. 13, as quoted by Burder in Rosenmüller's Morgenland. *in loc.* ¶ *That Job sent.* Sent for them, and called them around him. He was apprehensive that they might have erred, and he took every measure to keep them pure, and to maintain the influence of religion in his family. ¶ *And sanctified them.* This expression, says Schultens, is capable of two interpretations. It may either mean that he *prepared* them by various lustrations, ablutions, and other ceremonies to offer sacrifice ; or that he offered sacrifices for the purpose of procuring expiation for sins which they might actually have committed. The former sense, he remarks, is favoured by the use of the word in Ex. xix. 10 ; 1 Sam. xvi. 5, where the word means to prepare themselves by ablutions to meet God and to worship him. The latter sense is demanded by the connection. Job felt as every father should feel in such circumstances, that there was reason to fear that God had not been remembered as he ought to have been, and he was therefore more fervent in his devotions, and called them around him, that their own minds might be affected in view of his pious solicitude. What father is there who loves God, and who feels anxious that his children should also, who does not feel special solicitude if his sons and his daughters are in a situation where successive days are devoted to feasting and mirth? The word here rendered *sanctified* (קִדֵּשׁ) means properly to be pure, clean, holy; in Pihel, the form used here, to make holy, to sanctify, to consecrate, as a priest; and here it means, that he took measures to make them holy on the apprehension that they had sinned; that is, he took the usual means to procure for them forgiveness. The LXX. render it ἐκάθαριζεν, he purified them. ¶ *And rose up early in the morning.* For the purpose of offering his devotions, and procuring for them expiation. It was customary in the patriarchal times to offer sacrifice early in the morning. See Gen. xxii. 3; Ex. xxxii. 6. ¶ *And offered burnt-offerings.* Heb. "and caused to ascend;" that is, by burning them so that the smoke ascended towards heaven. The word rendered *burnt-offerings* (עֹלָה) is from עָלָה *âlàh*, *to ascend* (the word used here and rendered "*offered*"), and means that which was made to ascend, to wit, by burning. It is applied in the Scriptures to a sacrifice that was wholly consumed on the altar, and answers to the Greek word ὁλόκαυστον, *Holocaust.* See Notes on Isa. i. 11. Such offerings in the patriarchal times were made by the father of a family, officiating as priest in behalf of his household. Thus Noah officiated, Gen. viii. 20; and thus also Abraham acted as the priest to offer sacrifice, Gen. xii. 7, 8; xiii. 18; xxii. 13. In the earliest times, and among heathen nations, it was supposed that pardon might be procured for sin by offering sacrifice. In Homer there is a passage which remarkably corresponds with the view of Job before us; Il. ix. 493:

The gods (the great and only wise)
Are moved by offerings, vows, and sacrifice;

Offending man their high compassion wins,
And daily prayers atone for daily sins.
PoPE.

¶ *According to the number of them all.* Sons and daughters. Perhaps an additional sacrifice for each one of them. The LXX. render this, "according to their numbers, καὶ μόσχον ἕνα περὶ ἁμαρτίας περὶ τῶν ψυχῶν αὐτῶν—a young bullock for sin [or a sin-offering] for their souls." ¶ *It may be that my sons have sinned.* He had no positive or certain proof of it. He felt only the natural apprehension which every pious father must, that his sons might have been overtaken by temptation, and perhaps, under the influence of wine, might have been led to speak reproachfully of God, and of the necessary restraints of true religion and virtue. ¶ *And cursed God in their hearts.* The word here rendered *curse* is that which is usually rendered *bless* (בָּרַךְ). It is not a little remarkable that the same word is used in senses so directly opposite as *to bless* and *to curse.* Dr. Good contends that the word should be always rendered *bless,* and so translates it in this place, "peradventure my sons may have sinned, *nor blessed* God in their hearts," understanding the ו (vau) as a disjunctive or negative participle. So too in chap. ii. 9, rendered in our common translation, "curse God and die," he translates it, "blessing God and dying." But the interpretation which the connection demands is evidently that of cursing, renouncing, or forgetting; and so also it is in chap. ii. 9. This sense is still more obvious in 1 Kings xxi. 10: "Thou didst *blaspheme* (בֵּרַכְתָּ) God and the king." So also ver. 13 of the same chapter—though here Dr. Good contends that the word should be rendered *bless,* and that the accusation was that Naboth *blessed* or worshipped the gods, even Moloch—where he supposes the word מֶלֶךְ *mélech,* should be pointed מֹלֶךְ and read *Molech.* But the difficulty is not removed by this, and after all it is probable that the word here, as in chap ii. 9, means *to curse.* So it is understood by nearly all interpreters. The Vulgate indeed renders it singularly enough, "Lest perhaps my sons have sinned, and have blessed God (et be-nedixerint Deo) in their hearts." The LXX, " Lest perhaps my sons in their mind have thought evil towards God" —κακὰ ἐνενόησαν πρὸς Θεόν. The Chaldee, " Lest my sons have sinned and provoked JEHOVAH (וארגיזד קדם יי) in their hearts." Assuming that this is the sense of the word here, there are three ways of accounting for the fact that the same word should have such opposite significations. (1.) One is that proposed by Taylor (Concor.), that pious persons of old regarded blasphemy as so abominable that they abhorred to express it by the proper name, and that therefore by an *euphemism* they used the term *bless* instead of *curse.* But it should be said that nothing is more common in the Scriptures than words denoting cursing and blasphemy. The word אלה *álah,* in the sense of cursing or execrating, occurs frequently. So the word גדף *ghádhăph,* means to blaspheme, and is often used ; 2 Kings xix. 6, 22 ; Isa. xxxvii. 6, 23 ; Ps. xliv. 16. Other words also were used in the same sense, and there was no necessity of using a mere *euphemism* here. (2.) A second mode of accounting for this double use of the word is, that this was the common term of salutation between friends at meeting and parting. It is then supposed to have been used in the sense of the English phrase *to bid farewell to.* And then, like that phrase, to mean *to renounce, to abandon, to dismiss from the mind, to disregard.* The words χαίρειν in Greek, and *valere* in Latin, are used in this way. This explanation is suggested by Schultens, and is adopted by Rosenmüller and Noyes, who refer to the following places as parallel instances of the use of the word. Virg. Ecl. 8. 58. *Vivite Sylvæ*—a form, says the Annotator on Virgil (Delphin), of bidding farewell to, like the Greek χαίρετε, *gaudete* —"a form used against those whom we reject with hatred, and wish to depart." Thus Catull. 11. 17: Cum suis vivat, valeatque mœchis. So Æsch. Agam. 574:

Καὶ πολλὰ χαίρειν ξυμφοραῖς καταξιῶ.

Thus Plut. Dion. p. 975. So Ci-

cero in a letter to Atticus (viii. 8), in which he complains of the disgraceful flight of Pompey, applies to him a quotation from Aristophanes ; πολλὰ χαίρειν εἰπὼν τῷ καλῷ—"bidding farewell to honour he fled to Brundusium ;" comp. Ter. And. iv. 2. 14. Cicero de Nat. Deor. 1. 44. According to this interpretation, it means that Job apprehended they had renounced God in their hearts. i. e., had been unmindful of him, and had withheld from him the homage which was due.—This is plausible ; but the difficulty is in making out the use of this sense of the word in Hebrew. That the word was used as a mode of *parting salutation* among the Hebrews is undoubted. It was a solemn form of invoking the divine blessing when friends separated ; comp. Gen. xxviii. 3 ; xlvii. 10. But I find no use of the word where it is applied to separation in the sense of *renouncing,* or bidding farewell to *in a bad sense;* and unless some instances of this kind can be adduced, the interpretation is unsound, and though similar phrases are used in Greek, Latin, and other languages, it does not demonstrate that this use of the word obtained in the Hebrew. (3.) A third, and more simple explanation is that which supposes that the original sense of the word was *to kneel.* This, according to Gesenius, is the meaning of the word in Arabic. So Castell gives the meaning of the word—" to bend the knees for the sake of honour ;" that is, as an act of respect. So in Syriac, "*Genua flexit, procubuit.*" So *Genu,* the *knee.* Then it means to bend the knee for the purpose of invoking God, or worshipping. In Piel, the form used here, it means (1) to bless God, to celebrate, to adore ; (2) to bless men—i. e., to *invoke* blessings on them ; to greet or salute them—in the sense of invoking blessings on them when we meet them ; 1 Sam. xv. 13 ; Gen. xlvii. 7 ; 2 Sam. vi. 20 ; or when we part from them ; Gen. xlvii. 10 ; 1 Kings viii. 66 ; Gen. xxiv. 60 ; (3) *to invoke evil,* in the sense of *cursing others.* The idea is, that punishment or destruction is from God, and hence it is *imprecated* on others. In one word, the term is used, as derived from the

6 ¶ Now there was a day *a* when the sons of God came *b* to present themselves before the

a chap. 2.1, &c.   *b* 1 Ki.22.19 ; chap.38.7.

Lord, and [1] Satan came also among [2] them.

1 *the adversary;* 1 Ch.21.1 ; Zec.3.1 ; Re.12. 9,10.   2 *in the midst of them.*

general sense of kneeling, in the sense of *invoking* either blessings or curses; and then in the general sense of blessing or cursing. This interpretation is defended by Selden, de jure Nat. et Gent. Lib. II. c. xi. p. 255, and by Gesenius, *Lex.* The idea here is, that Job apprehended that his sons, in the midst of mirth, and perhaps revelry, had been guilty of irreverence, and perhaps of reproaching God inwardly for the restraints of virtue and piety.— What is more common in such scenes ? What was more to be apprehended? ¶ *Thus did Job continually.* It was his regular habit whenever such an occasion occurred. He was unremitted in his pious care ; and his solicitude lest his sons should have sinned never ceased —a beautiful illustration of the appropriate feelings of a pious father in regard to his sons. The Heb. is, "all day ;" i. e., at all times.

6. *Now there was a day.* Dr. Good renders this, " And the day came." Tindal, " Now upon a time." The Chaldee Paraphrast has presumed to specify the time, and renders it, " Now it happened in the day of judgment [or scrutiny, בדינא דיומא], *in the beginning of the year,* that hosts of angels came to stand in judgment before Jehovah, and Satan came." According to this, the judgment occurred once a year, and a solemn investigation was had of the conduct even of the angels. In the Hebrew there is no intimation of the frequency with which this occurred, nor of the time of the year when it happened. The only idea is, that "the sons of God" on a set or appointed day came to stand before God to give an account of what they had done, and to receive further orders in regard to what they were to do.—This is evidently designed to introduce the subsequent events relating to Job. It is language taken from the proceedings of a monarch who had sent forth messengers or ambassadors on important errands through the different provinces of his

empire, who now returned to give an account of what they had observed, and of the general state of the kingdom. Such a return would, of course, be made on a fixed day when, in the language of the law, their report would be "returnable," and when they would be required to give in an account of the state of the kingdom. If it be said that it is inconsistent with the supposition that this book was inspired to suppose such a poetic fiction, I reply, (1.) That it is no more so than the parables of the Saviour, who often supposes cases, and states them as real occurrences, in order to illustrate some important truth. Yet no one was ever led into error by this. (2.) It is in accordance with the language in the Scripture everywhere to describe God as a monarch seated on his throne, surrounded by his ministers, and sending them forth to accomplish important purposes in different parts of his vast empire. It is not absolutely necessary, therefore, to regard this as designed to represent an actual occurrence. It is one of the admissible ornaments of poetry ;—*as* admissible as any other poetic ornament. To represent God as a king is not improper ; and if so, it is not improper to represent him with the usual accompaniments of royalty, — surrounded by ministers, and employing angels and messengers for important purposes in his kingdom. This supposition being admitted, all that follows is merely in *keeping*, and is designed to preserve the verisimilitude of the conception.—This idea, however, by no means militates against the supposition that angels are in fact really employed by God in important purposes in the government of his kingdom, nor that Satan has a real existence, and is permitted by God to employ an important agency in the accomplishment of his purposes towards his people. On this verse, however, see the Introduction, § 1, (4.) ¶ *The sons of God.* Angels;

comp. chap. xxxviii. 7. The whole narrative supposes that they were celestial beings. ¶ *Came to present themselves.* As having returned from their embassy, and to give an account of what they had observed and done. ¶ *Before the Lord.* Before JEHOVAH. On the meaning of this word, see Notes on Isa. i. 2. A scene remarkably similar to this is described in 1 Kings xxii. 19—23. JEHOVAH is there represented as "sitting on his throne, and all the host of heaven standing by him on his right hand and on his left." He inquires who would go and persuade Ahab that he might go up and fall at Ramoth-gilead? "And there came forth a spirit and stood before the LORD, and said, I will persuade him." This he promised to do by being "a lying spirit in the mouth of all his prophets." ¶ *And Satan came also among them.* Marg. "The adversary" came "in the midst of them." On the general meaning of this passage, and the reasons why Satan is introduced here, and the argument thence derived respecting the age and authorship of the book of Job, see Introduction, § 4, (4.) The Vulgate renders this by the name *Satan.* The LXX, ὁ διάβολος—the devil, or the accuser. The Chaldee, אטן *Satan.* So the Syriac. Theodotion, ὁ ἀντι-κείμενος — *the adversary.* The word rendered *Satan* (שטן) is derived from שטן *Satan,* to lie in wait, to be an adversary, and hence it means properly an adversary, an accuser. It is used to denote one who *opposes,* as in war (1 Kings xi. 14, 23, 25 ; 1 Sam. xxix. 4) ; one who is an adversary or an accuser in a court of justice (Ps. cix. 6), and one who stands in the way of another ; Num. xxii. 22, "And the angel of JEHOVAH stood in the way for an adversary against him" (לשטן), *to oppose him.* It is then used by way of eminence, to denote THE *adversary,* and assumes the form of a proper name, and is applied to the great foe of God and man—the malignant spirit who seduces men to evil, and who accuses them before God. Thus in Zech. iii. 1, 2, "And he showed me Joshua the priest standing before the angel of the LORD, and Satan

standing at his right hand to resist him. And the LORD said unto Satan, The LORD rebuke thee, O Satan ;" comp. Rev. xii. 10, "Now is come salvation —for the accuser (ὁ κατηγορῶν—i. e., Satan, see ver. 9) of our brethren is cast down, which accused them before our God day and night."—The word does not often occur in the Old Testament. It is found in the various forms of a verb and a noun in only the following places. As a verb, in the sense of being an adversary, Ps. lxxi. 13; cix. 4, 20, 29; Zech. iii. 1 ; Ps. xxxviii. 20; as a noun, rendered *adversary* and *adversaries,* 1 Kings v. 4 ; xi. 14, 23, 25 ; Num. xxii. 22, 32 ; 1 Sam. xxix. 4 ; 2 Sam. xix. 22 ; rendered *Satan,* 1 Chron. xxi. 1 ; Ps. cix. 6 ; Job i. 6, 7, 8, 9, 12 ; ii. 1, 2, 3, 4, 6, 7; Zech. iii. 2 ; and once rendered *an accusation,* Ezra iv. 6. It was a word, therefore, early used in the sense of an adversary or accuser, and was applied to any one who sustained this character, until it finally came to be used as a proper name, to denote, by way of eminence, the prince of evil spirits, as the adversary or accuser of men. An opinion has been adopted in modern times by Herder, Eichhorn, Dathe, Ilgen, and some others, that the being here referred to by the name of Satan is not the malignant spirit, the enemy of God, the Devil, but is one of the sons of God, "a faithful, but too suspicious servant of JEHOVAH." According to this, God is represented as holding a council to determine the state of his dominions. In this council, Satan, a zealous servant of JEHO-VAH, to whom had been assigned the honourable office of visiting different parts of the earth, for the purpose of observing the conduct of the subjects of JEHOVAH, makes his appearance on his return with others. Such was the piety of Job, that it had attracted the special attention of JEHOVAH, and he puts the question to Satan, whether in his journey he had remarked this illustrious example of virtue. Satan, who, from what he has observed on earth, is supposed to have lost all confidence in the reality and genuineness of the virtue which man may exhibit, suggests that he doubts whether even

7 And the LORD said unto Satan, Whence comest thou? Then Satan answered the LORD, and said, From going [a] to and fro in the earth, and from walking up and down in it.

a Mat.12.43; 1 Pe.5.8.

Job serves God from a disinterested motive; that God had encompassed him with blessings, and that his virtue is the mere result of circumstances; and that if his comforts were removed he would be found as destitute of principle as any other man. Satan, according to this, is a suspicious minister of JEHOVAH, not a malignant spirit; he inflicts on Job only what he is ordered to by God, and nothing because he is himself malignant. Of this opinion Gesenius remarks (Lex.), that it "is now universally exploded." An insuperable objection to this view is, that it does not accord with the character usually ascribed to Satan in the Bible, and especially that the disposition attributed to him in the narrative before us is wholly inconsistent with this view. He is a malignant being; an accuser; one delighting in the opportunity of charging a holy man with hypocrisy, and in the permission to inflict tortures on him, and who goes as far in producing misery as he is allowed—restrained from destroying him only by the express command of God.—In Arabic the word Satan is often applied to a serpent. Thus Gjauhari, as quoted by Schultens, says, "The Arabs call a serpent Satan, especially one that is conspicuous by its crest, head, and odious appearance." It is applied also to any object or being that is evil. Thus the Scholiast on Hariri, as quoted by Schultens also, says, "Every thing that is obstinately rebellious, opposed, and removed from good, of genii, men, and beasts, is called Satan."— The general notion of an adversary and an opponent is found everywhere in the meaning of the word.—Dr. Good remarks on this verse, "We have here another proof that, in the system of patriarchal theology, the evil spirits, as well as the good, were equally amenable to the Almighty, and were equally cited, at definite periods, to answer for their conduct at his bar." Rosenmüller remarks well on this verse, "It is to be observed, that Satan, no less than the other celestial spirits, is subject to the government of God, and dependent on his commands (comp. chap. ii. 1); where Satan equally with the sons of God (בני אלהים) is said to present himself before God (להתיצב; i. e., λειτουργεῖν) to minister. Jehovah uses the ministry of this demon [hujus dæmonis] to execute punishment, or when from any other cause it seemed good to him to send evil upon men. But he, although incensed against the race of mortals, and desirous of injuring, is yet described as bound with a chain, and never dares to touch the pious unless God relaxes the reins. Satan, in walking round the earth, could certainly attentively consider Job, but to injure him he could not, unless permission had been given him."

7. *And the Lord said unto Satan, Whence comest thou?* This inquiry does not appear to have been made as if it was improper that Satan should have appeared there, for no blame seems to have been attached to him for this. He came as a spirit that was subject to the control of JEHOVAH; he came with others, not to mingle in their society, and partake of their happiness, but to give an account of what he had done, and of what he had observed. The poetic idea is, that this was done periodically, and that *all* the spirits employed by JEHOVAH to dispense blessings to mortals, to inflict punishment, or to observe their conduct, came and stood before him. Why the inquiry is directed particularly to *Satan,* is not specified. Perhaps it is not meant that there was any *special* inquiry made of him, but that, as he was to have so important an agency in the transactions which follow, the inquiry that was made of him only is recorded In respect to the others, nothing occurred pertaining to Job, and their examination is not adverted to. Or it may be, that, as Satan was known to be malignant, suspicious,

4

8 And the Lord said unto Satan, Hast thou¹ considered my servant Job, that *there is* none like him in the earth, a perfect and an upright man, one that feareth God and escheweth evil?

¹ *set thine heart on.*

and disposed to think evil of the servants of God, the design was to direct his attention particularly to Job as an illustrious and indisputable example of virtue and piety. ¶ *From going to and fro in the earth.* Dr. Good renders this, "from roaming round." Noyes, "from wandering over." The word which is here used (שוט) means properly, (1.) to whip, to scourge, to lash; (2.) to row, i. e., to lash the sea with oars; (3.) to run up and down, to go hither and thither, or to and fro, so as to lash the air with one's arms as with oars, and hence to travel over a land, or to go through it in order to see it, 2 Sam. xxiv. 2, 8. Dr. Good, in conformity with the interpretation proposed by Schultens, says that "the word imports, not so much the act of going forwards and backwards, as of making a circuit or circumference; of going round about. The Hebrew verb is still in use among the Arabic writers, and in every instance implies the same idea of gyration or circumambulation." In Arabic, according to Castell, the word means *to heat, to burn, to cause to boil, to consume:* then to propel to weariness, as e. g. a horse, and then to make a circuit, to go about at full speed, to go with diligence and activity. Thus in *Carnuso*, as quoted by Schultens, "a course made at one impulse to the goal is called שוט *shot.* In 2 Sam. xxiv. 2, the word is used in the sense of passing around through different places for the purpose of taking a census. "Go now (Marg. *compass*) through all the tribes of Israel." In Num. xi. 8, it is applied to the Israelites going about to collect manna,— passing rapidly and busily in the places where it fell for the purpose of gathering it. In Zech. iv. 10, it is applied to "the eyes of Jehovah," which are said to "run to and fro through the earth," i. e., he surveys all things as one does whose eye passes rapidly from object to object. The same phrase occurs in 2 Chron. xvi. 9. In Jer. v. 1, it is applied to the action of a man passing rapidly through the streets of a city. "Run ye to and fro through the streets of Jerusalem;" comp. Jer. xlix. 3. From these passages it is clear that the idea is not that of going *in a circuit* or circle, but it is that of passing rapidly; of moving with alacrity and in a hurry; and it is not improbable that the *original* idea is that suggested in the Arabic of *heat*—and thence applied to a whip or scourge because it produces a sensation like burning, and also to a rapid journey or motion, because it produces heat or a glow. It means that Satan had been active and diligent in passing from place to place in the earth to survey it. The Chaldee adds to this, "to examine into the works of the sons of men." ¶ *And from walking.* That is, to investigate human affairs. On this verse it is observed by Rosenmüller, that in the life of Zoroaster (see Zendavesta by J. G. Kleukner, vol. iii. p. 11,) the prince of the evil demons, the angel of death, whose name is *Engremeniosch,* is said to go far and near through the world for the purpose of injuring and opposing good men.

8. *Hast thou considered my servant Job?* Marg. *Set thine heart on.* The margin is a literal translation of the Hebrew. Schultens remarks on this, that it means more than merely to observe or to look at—since it is abundantly manifest from the following verses that Satan *had* attentively considered Job, and had been desirous of injuring him. It means, according to him, to set himself against Job, to fix the heart on him with an intention to injure him, and Jehovah means to ask whether Satan had done this. But it seems more probable that the phrase means to consider *attentively,* and that God means to ask him whether he had carefully observed him. Satan is represented as having no confidence in human virtue, and as maintaining that there was none which would resist

9 Then Satan answered the LORD, and said, Doth Job fear God for nought?

10 Hast thou not made an hedge*a* about him, and about his

a Ps. 34. 7.

house, and about all that he hath on every side? thou hast blessed the work of his hands, and his ¹ substance is increased in the land.

1 or, *cattle*.

---

temptation, if presented in a form sufficiently alluring. God here appeals to the case of Job as a full refutation of this opinion. The trial which follows is designed to test the question whether the piety of Job was of this order. ¶ *That* there is *none like him in the earth.* That he is the very highest example of virtue and piety on earth. Or might not the word כִּי *ki* here be rendered *for?* " For there is none like him in the earth." Then the idea would be, not that he had considered *that* there was none like him, but God directs his attention to him *because* he was the most eminent among mortals. ¶ *A perfect and an upright man;* see Notes on verse 1. The LXX. translate this verse as they do verse 1.

9. *Doth Job fear God for nought?* " Is his religion disinterested? Would not any one be willing to worship God in such circumstances?" The idea is, that there was nothing genuine about his piety; that religion could not be tried in prosperity; that Job had an abundant compensation for serving God, and that if the favours conferred on him were taken away, he would be like the rest of mankind. Much of the apparent virtue and religion of the world is the result of circumstances, and the question here proposed *may*, it is to be feared, be asked with great propriety of many professors of religion who are rich; it *should* be asked by every professed friend of the Most High, whether his religion is not selfish and mercenary. Is it because God has blessed us with great earthly advantages? Is it the result of mere gratitude? Is it because he has preserved us in peril, or restored us from sickness? Or is it merely because we hope for heaven, and serve God because we trust he will reward us in a future world? All this may be the result of mere selfishness; and of all such persons it may

be appropriately asked, " Do they fear God for nought?" True religion is not mere gratitude, nor is it the result of circumstances. It is the love of religion for its own sake—not for reward; it is because the service of God is right in itself, and not merely because heaven is full of glory; it is because God is worthy of our affections and confidence, and not merely because he will bless us—and this religion will live through all external changes, and survive the destruction of the world. It will flourish in poverty as well as when surrounded by affluence; on a bed of pain as well as in vigorous health; when we are calumniated and despised for our attachment to it, as well as when the incense of flattery is burnt around us, and the silvery tones of praise fall on our ear; in the cottage as well as the palace; on the pallet of straw as well as on the bed of down.

10. *Hast thou not made an hedge about him?* Dr. Good remarks, that to give the original word here its full force, it should be derived from the science of engineering, and be rendered, " Hast thou not raised a palisado about him?" The Hebrew word here used (שׂוּךְ) properly means to hedge; to hedge in or about; and hence to protect, as one is defended whose house or farm is hedged in either with a fence of thorns, or with an inclosure of stakes or palisades. The word in its various forms is used to denote, as a noun, *pricks in the eyes* (Num. xxxiii. 55); that is, that which would be like thorns; *barbed irons* (Job xli. 7), that is, the barbed iron used as a spear to take fish; and a hedge, and thorn hedge, Mic. vii. 4; Prov. xv. 19; Isa. v. 5. The idea here is, that of making an inclosure around Job and his possessions to guard them from danger. The LXX. render it περιέφραξας, to " make a defence around," to *circumvallate* or inclose,

11 But put forth thine hand now, and touch *a* all that he hath, and[1] he will *b* curse thee to thy face.

12 And the LORD said unto

a chap. 19. 21.   1 *if he curse thee not.*

Satan, Behold, all that he hath *is* in thy power,[2] only upon himself put not forth thine hand. So Satan went forth from the presence of the LORD.

b Is. 8. 21.   2 *hand,* Ge. 16. 6.

as a camp is in war. In the Syriac and Arabic it is rendered, "Hast thou not protected him with thy hand?" The Chaldee, "Hast thou protected him with thy word?" The LXX. render the whole passage, "Hast thou not encircled the things which are without him" (τὰ ἔξω αὐτοῦ), i. e., the things abroad which belong to him, "and the things within his house." The sense of the whole passage is, that he was eminently under the divine protection, and that God had kept himself, his family, and property from plunderers, and that *therefore* he served and feared him. ¶ *Thou hast blessed the work of his hands.* Thou hast greatly prospered him. ¶ *And his substance is increased in the land.* His property, verse 3. Marg. *cattle.* The word *increased* here by no means expresses the force of the original. The word פרץ means properly to break, to rend, then to break or burst forth as waters do that have been pent up; 2 Sam. v. 20, comp. Prov. iii. 10, "So shall thy barns be filled with plenty, and thy presses *shall burst out* (יִפְרֹצוּ) with new wine;" i. e., thy wine-fats shall be so full that they shall overflow, or *burst* the barriers, and the wine shall flow out in abundance. The Arabians, according to Schultens, employ this word still to denote the mouth or *embouchure*—the most rapid part of a stream. So Golius, in proof of this, quotes from the Arabic writer Gjauhari, a couplet where the word is used to denote the mouth of the Euphrates :

" His rushing wealth o'erflowed him with its heaps;
So at its mouth the mad Euphrates sweeps."

According to Schultens, the word denotes a place where a river bursts forth, and makes a new way by rending the hills and rocks asunder. In like manner the flocks and herds of

Job had burst, as it were, every barrier, and had spread like an inundation over the land; comp. Gen. xxx. 43 ; 2 Chron. xxxi. 5 ; Ex. i. 7 ; Job xvi. 14.

11. *But put forth thine hand now.* That is, for the purpose of injuring him, and taking away his property. ¶ *And touch all that he hath.* Dr. Good renders this, "and smite." The Vulg. and the LXX. "touch." The Hebrew word used here (נגע) means properly to *touch ;* then to touch any one with violence (Gen. xxvi. 11 ; Josh. ix. 19), and then to smite, to injure, to strike ; see Gen. xxxii. 26, 33 ; 1 Sam. vi. 9 ; Job xix. 21 ; comp. Notes on Isa. liii. 4. Here it means evidently to smite or strike ; and the idea is, that if God should take away the property of Job, he would take away his religion with it—and the trial was to see whether this effect would follow. ¶ *And he will curse thee to thy face.* He will do it openly and publicly. The word rendered *curse* here (ברך) is the same as that used in verse 5, and which is usually rendered *bless ;* see Notes on verse 5. Dr. Good contends that it should be rendered here "bless," and translates it as a question : " Will he then, indeed, bless thee to thy face ?" But in this he probably stands alone. The evident sense is, that Job would openly renounce God, and curse him on his throne ; that all his religion was caused merely by his abundant prosperity, and was mere gratitude and selfishness ; and that if his property were taken away, he would become the open and avowed enemy of him who was now his benefactor.

12. *All that he hath is in thy power.* Marg. as in Heb. *hand.* That is, all this is now committed to thee, for it is manifest that hitherto Satan had no power to injure even his property. He complained that God had made a

13 And there was a day*ᵃ* when his sons and his daughters *were* eating and drinking wine in their eldest brother's house :

14 And there came a messenger unto Job, and said, The oxen were

a Ec. 9.12.

ploughing, and the asses feeding beside them :

15 And the Sabeans fell *upon them*, and took them away ; yea, they have slain the servants with the edge of the sword ; and I only am escaped alone to tell thee.

hedge around all that Job possessed. Now it was all intrusted to him in order that he might make full trial of the faith of Job. The grant extended to his sons and daughters as well as to his property. ¶ *Only upon himself put not forth thine hand.* Job himself was not to be visited with sickness, nor was his life to be taken. The main accusation of Satan was, that Job was virtuous only because God encompassed him with so many blessings, and especially because he had endowed him with so much property. The trial, therefore, only required that it should be seen whether his piety was the mere result of these blessings. ¶ *So Satan went forth from the presence of the* LORD. That is, from the council which had been convened ; see Notes on verse 6.

13. *And there was a day.* That is, on the day on which the regular turn came for the banquet to be held in the house of the elder brother ; comp. Notes on verse 4. ¶ *And drinking wine.* This circumstance is omitted in verse 4. It shows that wine was regarded as an essential part of the banquet, and it was from its use that Job apprehended the unhappy results referred to in verse 5.

14. *And there came a messenger unto Job,* Heb. מלאך ; the word usually rendered *angel,* appropriately rendered " messenger" here. The word properly means *one who is sent.* ¶ *The oxen were ploughing.* Heb. *the cattle* (הבקר) including not merely *oxen,* but probably also *cows;* see Notes on ver. 3. ¶ *And the asses.* Heb. האתנות *she-asses.* The *sex* is here expressly mentioned, and Dr. Good maintains that it should be in the translation. So it is in the LXX. αἱ θήλειαι ὄνοι. So Jerome, *asinæ.* The reason why the sex is specified is, that female asses, on account of their milk, were much more valuable than males. On this account

they were preferred also for travelling ; see Notes on ver. 3. ¶ *Beside them.* Heb. " By their hands," i. e., by their sides, for the Heb. יד is often used in this sense ; comp. Notes on Isa. xxxiii. 21.

15. *And the Sabeans.* Heb. שבא, Vulg. *Sabæi.* The LXX. give a paraphrase, καὶ ἐλθόντες οἱ αἰχμαλωτεύοντες ᾐχμαλώτευσαν, " And the plunderers coming, plundered them," or made them captive. On the situation of Sheba and Seba, see Notes on Isa. xliii. 3 ; xlv. 14 ; lx. 6. The people here referred to were, undoubtedly, inhabitants of some part of Arabia Felix. There are three persons of the name of Sheba mentioned in the Scriptures. (1.) A grandson of Cush ; Gen. x. 7. (2.) A son of Joktan ; Gen. x. 28. (3.) A son of Jokshan, the son of Abraham by Keturah. *Calmet.* The Sheba here referred to was probably in the southern part of Arabia, and from the narrative it is evident that the Sabeans here mentioned were a predatory tribe. It is not improbable that these tribes were in the habit of wandering for purposes of plunder over the whole country, from the banks of the Euphrates to the outskirts of Egypt. The Bedawin Arabs of the present day resemble in a remarkable manner the ancient inhabitants of Arabia, and for many centuries the manners of the inhabitants of Arabia have not changed, for the habits of the Orientals continue the same from age to age. The Syriac renders this simply, " *a multitude rushed* upon them ;" omitting the word *Sabean.* ¶ *Fell* upon them. With violence ; or rushed unexpectedly upon them. This is the way in which the Arab tribes now attack the caravan, the traveller, or the village, for plunder. ¶ *And took them away.* As plunder. It is common now to make such sudden incursions, and to

16 While he *was* yet speaking, there came also another, and said [1] The fire of God is fallen from heaven, and hath burned up the

1 or, *a great fire.*

sheep and the servants, and consumed them ; and I only am escaped alone to tell thee.

17 While he was yet speak-

carry off a large booty. ¶ *They have slain the servants.* Heb. בְּנַעֲרֵי, *the young men.* The word נַעַר, *naär,* properly means *a boy,* and is applied to an infant just born, Ex. ii. 6 ; Judg. xiii. 5, 7 ; or to a youth, Gen. xxxiv. 19 ; xli. 12. It came then to denote a servant or slave, like the Greek παῖς; Gen. xxiv. 2 ; 2 Kings v. 20 ; comp. Acts v. 6. So the word *boy* is often used in the Southern States of North America to denote a slave. Here it evidently means the servants that were employed in cultivating the lands of Job, and keeping his cattle. There is no intimation that they were slaves. Jerome renders it *pueros, boys;* so the LXX. τοῦς παῖδας. ¶*And I only am escaped alone.* By myself, לְבַדִּי. There is no other one with me. It is remarkable that the same account is given by each one of the servants who escaped, ver. 16, 17, 19. The Chaldee has given a very singular version of this—apparently from the desire of accounting for every thing, and of mentioning the *names* of all the persons intended. "The oxen were ploughing, and Lelath, queen of Zamargad, suddenly rushed upon them, and carried them away."

16. *While he* was *yet speaking.* All this indicates the rapidity of the movement of Satan, and his desire to *overwhelm* Job with the suddenness and greatness of his calamities. The object seems to have been to give him no time to recover from the shock of one form of trial before another came upon him. If an interval had been given him he might have rallied his strength to bear his trials ; but afflictions are much more difficult to be borne when they come in rapid succession.—It is not a very uncommon occurrence, however, that the righteous are tried by the rapidity and accumulation as well as the severity of their afflictions. It has passed into a proverb that "afflictions do not come

alone." ¶ *The fire of God.* Marg. *A great fire:* evidently meaning a flash of lightning, or a thunderbolt. The Hebrew is "fire of God;" but it is probable that the phrase is used in a sense similar to the expression, "cedars of God," meaning lofty cedars ; or "mountains of God," meaning very high mountains. The lightning is probably intended; comp. Num. xvi. 35; Note on Isa. xxix. 6. ¶ *From heaven.* From the sky, or the air. So the word heaven is often used in the Scriptures; see Notes on Matth. xvi. 1. ¶ *And hath burnt up the sheep.* That lightning might destroy herds and men no one can doubt ; though the fact of their being actually consumed or burnt up may have been an exaggeration of the much affrighted messenger.—The narrative leads us to believe that these things were under the control of Satan, though by the permission of God ; and his power over the lightnings and the winds (ver. 19) may serve to illustrate the declaration, that he is the "Prince of the power of the air," in Eph. ii. 2.

17. *The Chaldeans.* The LXX. translate this, οἱ ἱππεῖς, *the horsemen.* Why they thus expressed it is unknown. It may be possible that the Chaldeans were supposed to be distinguished as horsemen, and were principally known as such in their predatory excursions. But it is impossible to account for all the changes made by the LXX. in the text. The Syriac and the Chaldee render it correctly, *Chaldeans.* The Chaldeans (Heb. כַּשְׂדִּים *Kasdim*) were the ancient inhabitants of Babylonia. According to Vitringa (Comm. in Isa. tom. i. p. 412, c. xiii. 19), Gesenius (Comm. zu Isa. xxiii. 13), and Rosenmüller (Bib. Geog. 1, 2, p. 36 seq), the Chaldees or Casdim were a warlike people who orignally inhabited the Carduchian mountains, north of Assyria, and the northern part of

ing, there came also another, and said, The Chaldeans made out three bands, and ¹ fell upon the camels, and have carried them

1 *rushed.*

away, yea, and slain the servants with the edge of the sword; and I only am escaped alone to tell thee.

Mesopotamia. According to Xenophon (Cyrop. iii. 2, 7) the Chaldees dwelt in the mountains adjacent to Armenia, and they were found in the same region in the campaign of the younger Cyrus, and the retreat of the ten thousand Greeks. Xen. Anaba. iv. 3, 4; v. 5, 9; viii. 8, 14. They were allied to the Hebrews, as appears from Gen. xxii. 22, where *Chesed* (כשד, whence *Casdim*) the ancestor of the people is mentioned as a son of Nahor, and was consequently the nephew of Abraham. And further, Abraham himself emigrated to Canaan from Ur of the Chaldees (אור כשדים, *Ur of the Casdim*), Gen. xi. 28; and in Judith v. 6, the Hebrews themselves are said to be descended from the Chaldeans. The region around the river Chaboras, in the northern part of Mesopotamia, is called by Ezekiel (i. 3) *the land of the Chaldeans;* Jeremiah (v. 15) calls them "an ancient nation;" see Notes on Isa. xxiii. 13. The Chaldeans were a fierce and warlike people, and when they were subdued by the Assyrians, a portion of them appear to have been placed in Babylon to ward off the incursions of the neighbouring Arabians. In time *they* gained the ascendency over their Assyrian masters, and grew into the mighty empire of Chaldea or Babylonia. A part of them, however, appear to have remained in their ancient country, and enjoyed under the Persians some degree of liberty. Gesenius supposes that the Kurds who have inhabited those regions, at least since the middle ages, are probably the descendants of that people.—A very vivid and graphic description of the Chaldeans is given by the prophet Habakkuk, which will serve to illustrate the passage before us, and show that they retained until his times the predatory and fierce character which they had in the days of Job; chap. i. 6—11:

For lo I raise up the Chaldeans,
A bitter and hasty nation,
Which marches far and wide in the earth,
To possess the dwellings which are not theirs.
They are terrible and dreadful,
Their judgments proceed only from themselves.
Swifter than leopards are their horses,
And fiercer than the evening wolves.
Their horsemen prance proudly around;
And their horsemen shall come from afar and fly,
Like the eagle when he pounces on his prey.
They all shall come for violence,
In troops—their glance is ever *forward!*
They gather captives like the sand!
And they scoff at kings,
And princes are a scorn unto them.
They deride every strong hold;
They cast up [mounds of] earth and take it.

This warlike people ultimately obtained the ascendency in the Assyrian empire. About the year 597 B. C. Nabopolassar, a viceroy in Babylon, made himself independent of Assyria, contracted an alliance with Cyaxares, king of Media, and with his aid subdued Nineveh, and the whole of Assyria. From that time the Babylonian empire rose, and the history of the Chaldeans becomes the history of Babylon.—*Rob. Calmet.* In the time of Job, however, they were a predatory race that seem to have wandered far for the sake of plunder. They came from the North, or the East, as the Sabeans came from the South. ¶ *Made out three bands.* Literally, "three *heads.*" That is, they divided themselves, for the sake of plunder, into three parties. Perhaps the three thousand camels of Job (ver. 3) occupied three places remote from each other, and the object of the speaker is to say that the whole were taken. ¶ *And fell upon the camels.* Marg. "And *rushed.*" The word is different from that which in ver. 15 is rendered *fell.* The word here used (פשט) means to spread out, to expand. It is spoken of hostile troops, 1 Chron. xiv. 9, 13; of locusts which spread over a country, Nah. iii. 15; and of an army or company of marauders, Judg. ix. 33, 44; 1 Sam. xxvii. 8. This is its sense here.

18 While he *was* yet speaking, there came also another, and said, Thy sons and thy daughters *were* eating and drinking wine in their eldest brother's house:

19 And behold, there came a great wind from [1] the wilderness, and smote the four corners of the house, and it fell upon the young men, and they are dead; and I only am escaped alone to tell thee.

20 Then Job arose and *a* rent

1 *from aside.*   a Ge.37.29.

---

18. *Eating and drinking wine;* Notes on ver. 4, 13.

19. *There came a great wind.* Such tornadoes are not less common in Oriental countries than in the United States. Indeed they abound more in regions near the equator than they do in those which are more remote ; in hot countries than in those of higher latitude. ¶ *From the wilderness.* Marg. *From aside.* That is, from aside the wilderness. The word here rendered "from aside" in the margin (מעבר) means properly *from across,* and is so rendered by Dr. Good. The word עבר *ōbēr* means literally a region or country beyond, or on the other side, *sc.* of a river or a sea, which one must *pass;* Judg. xi. 18; Gen. ii. 10, 11 ; Deut. i. 1, 5. Then it means on the other side, or beyond ; see Notes on Isa. xviii. 1. Here it means that the tornado came sweeping across the desert. On the ample plains of Arabia it would have the opportunity of accumulating its desolating power, and would sweep every thing before it. The Hebrew word here rendered *wilderness,* מדבר, does not express exactly what is denoted by our word. We mean by it usually, a region wholly uncultivated, covered with forests, and the habitation of wild beasts. The Hebrew word more properly denotes *a desert;* an uninhabited region, a sterile, sandy country, though sometimes adapted to pasture. In many places the word would be well translated by the phrases *open fields,* or *open plains;* comp. Joel ii. 22 ; Ps. lxv. 13 ; Jer. xxiii. 10 ; Isa. xlii. 11 ; Gen. xiv. 6 ; xvi. 7 ; Ex. iii. 1 ; xiii. 18 ; Deut. xi. 24 ; comp. Isa. xxxii. 15 ; xxxv. 1. 2. ¶ *And smote the four corners of the house.* Came as a tornado usually does, or like a whirlwind. It seemed to come from all points of the com-

pass, and prostrated every thing before it. ¶ *And it fell upon the young men.* The word here rendered "young men" is the same which is rendered in ver. 15, 17, *servants* (הנערים) There can be no reasonable doubt, however, that the messenger by the word here refers to the children of Job. It is remarkable that his daughters are not particularly specified, but they may be included in the word here used (נערים), which may be the same in signification as our phrase " *young people,*" including both sexes. So it is rendered by Eichhorn : Es stürzte über den jungen Leuten zusammen.

20. *Then Job arose.* The phrase *to arise,* in the Scriptures is often used in the sense of beginning to do any thing. It does not necessarily imply that the person had been previously sitting ; see 2 Sam. xiii. 13. ¶ *And rent his mantle.* The word here rendered *mantle* (מעיל) means an upper or outer garment. The dress of Orientals consists principally of an under garment or tunic—not materially differing from the *shirt* with us—except that the sleeves are wider, and under this large and loose pantaloons. Niebuhr, Reisebescreib. 1. 157. Over these garments they often throw a full and flowing mantle or robe. This is made without sleeves ; it reaches down to the ankles; and when they walk or exercise it is bound around the middle with a girdle or sash. When they labour it is usually laid aside. The robe here referred to was worn sometimes by women, 2 Sam. xiii. 18 ; by men of birth and rank, and by kings, 1 Sam. xv. 27; xviii. 4 ; xxiv. 5, 11 ; by priests, 1 Sam. xxviii. 14, and especially by the High Priest under the ephod, Ex. xxviii. 31. See Braun de vest Sacerd. ii. 5. Schroeder de vest. mulier. Heb. p. 267; Hartmann Hebräerin, iii. p. 512, and

his [1] mantle, and shaved his head,
1 or, *robe*.   *a* 1Pe.5.5.

Thesau. Antiq. Sacra. by Ugolin, Tom. i. 509, iii. 74, iv. 504, viii. 90, 1000, xii. 788, xiii 306 ; comp. Notes on Matt. v. 40, and Niebuhr, as quoted above. The custom of rending the garment as an expression of grief prevailed not only among the Jews but also among the Greeks and Romans. Suetonius, in *Jul. Cæs.* 33. It prevailed also among the Persians. Curtius, B. x. c. 5, § 17. See Christian Boldich, in Thesau. Antiq. Sacra. Tom. xii. p. 145 ; also Tom. xiii. 551, 552, 560, xxxiii. 1105, 1112. In proof also that the custom prevailed among the Heathen, see Diod. Sic. Lib. i. p. 3, c. 3, respecting the Egyptians ; Lib. xvii. respecting the Persians ; Quin. Curt. iii. 11 ; Herod. Lib. iii. in Thalia, Lib. viii. in Urania, where he speaks of the Persians. So Plutarch in his life of Antony, speaking of the deep grief of Cleopatra, says, περιὶρ-ρήξατο τοὺς πίπλους επ' αὐτῷ. Thus Herodian, Lib. i.: καῖ ρηξαμένη εσϑῆτα. So Statius in Glaucum :

Tu modo fusus humi, lucem aversaris iniquam,
Nunc torvus pariter vestes, et pectora rumpis.

So Virgil :

Tunc pius Æneas humeris abscindere vestem,
Auxilioque vocare Deos, et tendere palmas.
Æn. v. 685.

Demittunt mentes ; it scissa veste Latinus,
Conjugis attonitus fatis, urbisque ruina.
Æn. xii. 609.

So Juvenal, Sat. x. :
ut primos edere planctus
Cassandra inciperet, scissaque Polyxena palla.

Numerous other quotations from the classic writers, as well as from the Jewish writings, may be seen in Ugolin's Sacerdotium Hebraicum, cap. vi. Thesau. Antiq. Sacrar. Tom. xiii. p. 550, seq. ¶ *And shaved his head.* This was also a common mode of expressing great sorrow. Sometimes it was done by formally cutting off the hair of the head ; sometimes by plucking it violently out by the roots, and sometimes also the beard was plucked out, or cut off. The idea seems to have been that mourners should divest themselves of that which was usually deemed most ornamental ; comp. Jer. vii. 29 ; Isa. vii. 20.

and fell *a* down upon the ground, and worshipped,

Lucian says that the Egyptians expressed their grief by cutting off their hair on the death of their god Apis, and the Syrians in the same manner at the death of Adonis. Olympiodorus remarks on this passage, that the people among whom long hair was regarded as an ornament, cut it off in times of mourning ; but those who commonly wore short hair, suffered it on such occasions to grow long. See Rosenmüller, Morgenland, *in loc.* A full description of the customs of the Hebrews in times of mourning, and particularly of the custom of plucking out the hair, may be seen in Martin Geier, de Hebræorum Luctu, especially in chap. viii. Thesau. Antiq. Sacra. xxxiii. p. 147, seq. The meaning here is that Job was filled with excessive grief, and that he expressed that grief in the manner that was common in his day. Nature demands that there should be *some* external expression of sorrow ; and religion does not forbid it. He pays a tribute to the nature with which God has endowed him who gives an appropriate expression to sorrow ; he wars against that nature who attempts to remove from his countenance, conversation, dress, and dwelling, every thing that is indicative of the sorrows of his soul in a time of calamity. Jesus wept at the grave of Lazarus ; and religion is not designed to make the heart insensible or incapable of grief. Piety, like every kind of virtue, always increases the susceptibility of the soul to suffering. Philosophy and sin destroy sensibility ; but religion deepens it. Philosophy does it on principle—for its great object is to render the heart dead to all sensibility ; sin produces the same effect naturally. The drunkard, the licentious man, and the man of avarice, are incapable of being affected by the tender scenes of life. Guilt has paralyzed their feelings and rendered them dead. But religion allows men to feel, and then shows its power in sustaining the soul, and in imparting

21 And said, Naked came I out of my mother's womb, and naked shall I return thither : the [a] LORD [b] gave, and the LORD hath taken away ; blessed [c] be the name of the LORD.

a 1 Ti.6.7.   *b* La.3.38.   *c* Ps.89.38,52.

its consolations to the heart that is broken and sad. It comes to dry up the tears of the mourner, not to forbid those tears to flow ; to pour the balm of consolation into the heart, not to teach the heart to be unfeeling. ¶ *And fell down upon the ground.* So Joshua in a time of great calamity prostrated himself upon the earth and worshipped, Josh. vii. 6.—The Orientals were then in the habit, as they are now, of prostrating themselves on the ground as an act of homage. Job seems to have done this partly as an expression of grief, and partly as an act of devotion—solemnly bowing before God in the time of his great trial. ¶ *And worshipped.* Worshipped God. He resigned himself to his will. A pious man has nowhere else to go in trial ; and he will desire to go nowhere else than to the God who has afflicted him.

21. *And said, Naked came I out.* That is, destitute of property, for so the connection demands ; comp. 1 Tim. vi. 7 ; "For we brought nothing into this world, and it is certain we can carry nothing out." A similar expression also occurs in Pliny, *Hominem natura tantum nudum.* Nat. Hist. proem. L. vii. Job felt that he was stripped of all, and that he must leave the world as destitute as he entered it. ¶ *My mother's womb.* The earth—the universal mother. That he refers to the earth is apparent, because he speaks of returning thither again. The Chaldee adds לבית קברהא — *to the house of burial.* The earth is often called the mother of mankind ; see Cic. de Nat. Deor. ii. 26 ; comp. Ps. cxxxix. 15. Dr. Good remarks, that "the origin of all things from the earth introduced, at a very early period of the world, the superstitious worship of the earth, under the title of Dameter, or the *Mother-goddess,* a Chaldee term, probably common to Idumea at the time of the existence of Job himself. It is

hence the Greeks derive their Δημήτηρ (Demeter), or as they occasionally wrote it Γημήτηρ (Ge-meter), or mother earth, to whom they appropriated annually two religious festivals of extraordinary pomp and solemnity. Thus Lucretius says,

> Linquitur, ut merito maternum nomen adepta
> Terra sit, e terra quoniam sunt cuncta creata.   v. 793.
> ———— " Whence justly EARTH
> Claims the dear name of mother, since alone
> Flowed from herself whate'er the sight enjoys."

For a full account of the views of the ancients in regard to the *marriage* (ἱερὸς γάμος) of the "heaven" and the "earth," from which union all things were supposed to proceed, see Creuzer's Symbolik und Mythologie der alt. Völk. Erst. Theil, p. 26, fg. ¶ *And naked.* Stripped of all, I shall go to the common mother of the race. This is exceedingly beautiful language ; and in the mouth of Job it was expressive of the most submissive piety. It is not the language of complaint ; but was in him connected with the deep feeling that the loss of his property was to be traced to God, and that he had a right to do as he had done. ¶ *The Lord gave.* Heb. JEHOVAH. He had nothing when he came into the world, and all that he had obtained had been by the good providence of God. As *he* gave it, he had a right to remove it. Such was the feeling of Job, and such is the true language of submission everywhere. He who has a proper view of what he possesses will feel that it is all to be traced to God, and that he has a right to remove it when he pleases. ¶ *And the Lord hath taken away.* It is not by accident ; it is not the result of hap-hazard ; it is not to be traced to storms and winds and the bad passions of men. It is the result of intelligent design, and whoever has been the agent or instrument in it, it is to be referred to the overruling providence of God. Why

22 In *a* all this Job sinned not, | nor [1] charged God foolishly.

a chap. 2.10. | 1 or, *attributed folly to God.*

did not Job vent his wrath on the Sabeans? Why did he not blame the Chaldeans? Why did he not curse the tempest and the storm? Why did he not blame his sons for exposing themselves? Why not suspect the malice of Satan? Why not suggest that the calamity was to be traced to bad fortune, to ill-luck, or or to an evil administration of human affairs? None of these things occurred to Job. He traced the removal of his property and his loss of children at once to God, and found consolation in the belief that an intelligent and holy Sovereign presided over his affairs, and that he had removed only what he gave. ¶ *Blessed be the name of the Lord.* That is, blessed be JEHOVAH—the *name* of any one in Hebrew being often used to denote the person himself. The Syriac, Arabic, and some MSS. of the LXX. here add "*for ever.*"—" Here, says Schmid, "the contrast is observable between the object of Satan, which was to induce Job to renounce God, and the result of the temptation which was to lead Job to *bless* God." Thus far Satan had been foiled, and Job had sustained the shock of the calamity, and showed that he did not serve God on account of the benefits which he had received from him.

22. *In all this.* In all his feelings and expressions on this occasion. ¶ *Job sinned not.* He expressed just the feelings and manifested just the submission which he ought to do. ¶ *Nor charged God foolishly.* Marg. *Attributed folly to God.* Vulg. "Neither did he speak any foolish thing against God." The LXX. render it, "and he did not impute [or give, ἔδωκεν] folly (ἀφροσύνην) [indiscretion, *Thompson*] to God." Good renders this, "nor vented a murmur against God;" and remarks that the literal rendering would be, "nor vented FROTH against God." Tindal renders it, "nor murmured foolishly against God." The Hebrew word תִּפְלָה is derived from the obsolete root תָּפֵל *tăphăl, to spit out;* and hence to be insi-

pid, tasteless, not seasoned. The noun, therefore, means properly that which is spit out; then that which is insipid or tasteless; and then folly. Wit and wisdom are represented by Oriental writers as pungent and seasoned; comp. the expression among the Greeks of "Attic *salt*," meaning wit or wisdom. The word *folly* in the Scriptures often means wickedness, for this is supreme folly. Here it has this sense, and means that Job did not say any thing *wrong.* Satan was disappointed and had borne a false accusation before God. He did *not* charge God foolishly, and he did *not* curse him to his face.

From this instructive narrative of the manner in which Job received afflictions, we may learn (1.) That true piety will bear the removal of property and friends without murmuring. Religion is not based on such things, and their removal cannot shake it. It is founded deeper in the soul, and mere external changes cannot destroy it. (2.) When we are afflicted, we should not vent our wrath on winds and waves; on the fraud and perfidy of our fellow-men; on embarrassments and changes in the commercial world; on the pestilence and the storm. Any or all of these may be employed as instruments in taking away our property or our friends, but we should trace the calamity ultimately to God. Storms and winds and waves, malignant spirits and our fellow-men, do no more than God permits They are all restrained and kept within proper limits. They are not directed by chance, but they are under the control of an intelligent Being, and are the wise appointment of a holy God. (3.) God has a right to remove our comforts. He gave them—not to be our permanent inheritance, but to be withdrawn when he pleases. It is a proof of goodness that we have been permitted to tread his earth so long—though we should be allowed to walk it no more; to breathe his air so long—though we should be permitted to inhale it no more; to look upon his sun and moon

CHAPTER II.

ANALYSIS OF THE CHAPTER.

The second trial of Job. The day returns when the sons of God come to present themselves before God, ver. 1.—Jehovah inquires of Satan whence he came, and particularly whether he had attentively considered the case of Job, and that he held fast his integrity notwithstanding his afflictions, ver. 2, 3.—Satan answers that it was because he had not been afflicted enough; that if he was subjected to bodily sufferings he would curse JEHOVAH to his face, ver. 4, 5.—God consents that Job should be subjected to a second trial, only on the condition that his life should be spared, ver. 6.—Job's sore affliction, ver. 7, 8.—His wife conjures him to curse God and die, ver. 9.—Job's stern rebuke of his wife, and calm submission to God, ver. 10.—The visit of his three friends to condole with him, and their amazement at the extent of his sufferings, ver. 11–13.

A GAIN [a] there was a day when the sons of God came to present themselves before the LORD, and Satan came also among them to present himself before the LORD.

2 And the LORD said unto Satan, From whence comest thou?   And

  a chap. 1. 6, &c.

---

and stars so long—though we should be permitted to walk by their light no more ; to enjoy the society of the friends whom he has given us so long —though we should enjoy that society no longer.   A temporary gift may be removed at the pleasure of the giver, and we hold all our comforts at the mere good pleasure of God.   (4.) We see the nature of true resignation.   It is not because we can always see the *reason* why we are afflicted ; it consists in bowing to the will of a holy and intelligent God, and in the feeling that he has a *right* to remove what he has given us.   It is his ; and may be taken away when he pleases. It may be, and should be yielded, without a murmur—and to do this *because* God wills it, is true resignation. (5.) We see the true source of *comfort* in trials.   It is not in the belief that things are regulated by chance and hap-hazard ; or even that they are controlled by physical laws.   We may have the clearest philosophical view of the mode in which tempests sweep away property, or the pestilence our friends ; we may understand the laws by which all this is done, but this affords no consolation. It is only when we perceive an *intelligent Being* presiding over these events, and see that they are the result of plan and intention on his part, that we can find comfort in trial. What satisfaction is it for me to understand the law by which fire burns when my property is swept away ; or to know *how* disease acts on the human frame when my child dies ; or how the plague produces its effects on the body when friend after friend is laid in the grave ?   This is *philosophy ;* and this is the consolation which this world furnishes.   I want some higher consolation than that which results from the knowledge of unconscious laws.   I want to have the assurance that it is the result of intelligent design, and that this design is connected with a benevolent end—and that I find only in religion.   (6.) We see the *power* of religion in sustaining in the time of trial.   How calm and submissive was this holy man !   How peaceful and resigned !   Nothing else but piety could have done this. Philosophy blunts the feelings, paralyses the sensibilities, and chills the soul ; but it does not give consolation.   It is only confidence in God ; a feeling that he is right ; and a profound and holy acquiescence in his will, that can produce support in trials like these. This we may have as well so Job ; and this is indispensable in a world so full of calamity and sorrow as this is.

CHAPTER II.

1. *Again there was a day,* &c. ; see Notes, chap. i. 6.   These seasons are represented as periodical, when the angels came, as it were, to make report to God of what they had observed and done.   The Chaldee renders this, " And there was a day of the great judgment (יום דינא רבא), a day of the remission of sins (סרחניא יום שבוק) and there came bands (כתי) of angels." ¶ *To present himself before the* LORD. This does not occur in the former statement in chap. i. 6.   It here means that he came before the Lord after he had had permission to afflict Job.   The Chaldee renders it " that he might stand in judgment (בדינא) before the Lord."

2. *And the Lord said unto Satan,* &c. ; see Notes on chap. i. 7.

Satan answered the LORD, and said, From going to and fro in the earth, and from walking up and down in it.

3 And the LORD said unto Satan, Hast thou considered my servant Job, that *there is* none like him in the earth, a perfect and an upright man, one that feareth God, and es-

cheweth evil ? and still he holdeth fast his integrity, *a* although thou movedst me against him, to ¹ destroy him without cause.

4 And Satan answered the LORD, and said, Skin for skin, yea, all that a man hath will he give *b* for his life.

a chap.27.5,6; Ps. 26.1; 41.12.

1 *swallow him up.*   *b* Matt.6.25.

3. *Hast thou considered;* Notes, chap. i. 8. ¶ *That* there is *none like him in the earth.* The same addition is made here by the Septuagint which occurs in chap. i. 1 ; see Notes on that verse. ¶ *And still he holdeth fast his integrity.* Notwithstanding all the efforts made to show that his piety was the result of mere selfishness. The word *integrity* here תֻּמָּתוֹ means *perfection;* another form of the word which is rendered "perfect" in chap. i. 1 ; see Notes on that verse. ¶ *Although thou movedst me.* The word rendered "movedst" (סוּת) means to incite, to impel, to urge, to irritate against any one; Josh. xv. 18; Judg. i. 14; 2 Chron. xviii. 2 ; 1 Sam. xxvi. 19; Jer. xliii. 3. The LXX. render this in a peculiar manner, "And thou hast ordered (εἶπας) his property to be destroyed in vain" (διακενῆς), i. e., without accomplishing the purpose intended. ¶ *To destroy him.* The word here used (from בלע) means properly to swallow, to devour, with the idea of eagerness or greediness. It is then used in the sense of to consume, or destroy; comp. Job xx. 18; Prov. i. 12; Num. xvi. 30 ; Ps. lxix. 15. In the margin it is rendered "swallow him up." ¶ *Without cause.* Without any sufficient reason. The cause assigned by Satan (chap. i. 9—11) was, that the piety of Job was selfish, and that if God should remove his possessions, he would show that he had no true religion. God says now that it was demonstrated that there was no reason for having made the trial. The result had shown that the charge was unfounded, and that his piety still remained, though he was stripped of all that he had. This passage may remind us of the speech of Neptune in favour of Æneas, Iliad v. 297:

And can ye see this righteous chief atone With guiltless blood for vices not his own ? To all the gods his constant vows were paid: Sure though he wars for Troy he claims our aid.
Fate wills not this—   POPE.

4. *Skin for skin.* This is a proverbial expression, whose origin is unknown, nor is its meaning *as a proverb* entirely clear. The general sense of the passage here is plain, for it is immediately explained that a man would give every thing which he had to save his life ; and the idea here is, that if Job was so afflicted in his body that he was likely to die, he would give up all his religion in order to purchase life. His religion, which had borne the comparatively trifling test before applied to it, would not bear the severer trial if his life was endangered. In regard to the proverb itself, a great variety of explanations has been given. The ancient versions throw no light on it. The Vulgate renders it, *Pellem pro pelle.* The LXX. Δέρμα ὑπὲρ δέρματος—skin for, or instead of, skin. The Chaldee renders it, "member for member," אבָרָא אמָטוּל אבָרָא —and the author of that paraphrase seems to have supposed that it means that a man would give the members of his body or his limbs to preserve his life. Parkhurst renders it, "skin after skin," meaning, as he explains it, that a man may bear to part with all that he has, and even to have his skin, as it were, stripped off again and again, provided only that his life is safe. Noyes supposes that it means that any man will give the skin or life of another, whether animal or man, to save his own; and that Job gave up all, without complaint, from the selfish fear of exposing his own life to danger. Dr. Good remarks on the passage, that the skins or spoils of

beasts, in the rude and early ages of man, were the most valuable property he could acquire, and that for which he most frequently combated. Thus Lucretius says,

Tum igitur *pelles*, nunc aurum et purpura, curis
Exercent hominum vitam, belloque fatigant.
                                        v. 1422.
" Then man for *skins* contended ; purple now,
And gold, for ever plunge him into war."

In various parts of the book of Job, however, Dr. Good remarks, the word *skin* imports the *person* of a man as well as his *property*, the whole living body which it envelopes, as in chap. xviii. 13 ; xix. 26. " It is," says he, " upon the double meaning of the same term, and the play which is here given to it, by employing the term first in one sense and then in the other, that the gist of the proverb, as of a thousand others similarly constructed, depends. ' Skin for skin' is in this view, in plain English, ' property for person,' or ' the skin forming property for the skin forming person.' " See a somewhat similar view presented by Callaway, in Bush's Illustrations, *in loco.* The editor of the Pictorial Bible coincides mainly with this view, and supposes that the reference is to the time when trade was conducted by barter, and when the skins of animals, being a most frequent and valuable commodity, were used to represent property. Tributes, ransoms, &c., he observes, were paid in skins. According to this, it means that a man would give "skin upon skin ;" that is, would pile one piece of property upon another, and give *all* that he had, in order to save his life. It refers to the necessity of submitting to one great evil rather than incur a greater, answering to the Turkish proverb, " We must give our beards to save our heads." According to Gesenius, it means "life for life." Drusius explains it as meaning, that he would give the skin of others, as of his sons, to save his own ; that is, that he was unmoved so long as his own skin or life was safe. The same view is given by Ephrem the Syrian. " Skin for skin ; the skin not only of flocks, but even of his sons will he give, in order to save his own."

This view also is adopted by Umbreit. That is, his religion was supremely selfish. The loss of property and even of children he could bear, provided his person was untouched. His own health, and life ; his own skin and body were dearer to him than any thing else. Other men would have been afflicted by the loss of children and property. But Job was willing to part with any or all of these, provided he himself was safe. Rosenmüller supposes that the word skin here is used for the whole body ; and says that the sense is, that he would give the body of another for his own, as in Ex. xxi. 23. " The meaning of this proverbial formula," says he, " is, that any one would redeem his own safety by the skin of others ; that is, not only by the skins or lives of oxen, camels, servants, but even of his own children." Schultens supposes it means that a man would submit to any sufferings in order to save his life ; that he would be willing to be flayed alive ; to be repeatedly excoriated ; to have, so to speak. one skin stripped off after another, if he might save his own life. According to this, the idea is, that the loss of life was the great calamity to be feared, and that a man would give *any* thing in order to save it. Umbreit says, " there is nothing so valuable to a man that he will not exchange it—one thing for another ; one outward good for another, *skin for skin.* But life, the inward good, is to him of no value that can be estimated. That he will give for nothing ; and much more, he will offer every thing for that." Another solution is offered in the Biblische Untersuchungen ii. Th. s. 88. " Before the use of gold, traffic was conducted chiefly by barter. Men exchanged what was valuable to themselves for what others had which they wanted. Those who hunted wild beasts would bring their skins to market, and would exchange them for bows and arrows. Since these traffickers were exposed to the danger of being robbed, they often took with them those who were armed, who agreed to defend them on condition that they should have a part of the skins which they took, and in

5 But put forth thine hand now, and touch his bone and his flesh, and he will curse thee to thy face.

6 And the LORD said unto Satan, Behold, he *is* in thine hand ; [1] but save his life.

1 or, *only.*

this way they purchased their property and life." That is, they gave the skins of animals for the safety of their own ; all that they had they would surrender, in order that their lives might be saved. See Rosenmuller's Morgenland, *in loc.* None of these solutions appear to me perfectly satisfactory, and the proverb is involved in perplexity still. It seems to refer to some kind of barter or exchange, and to mean that a man would give up one thing for another ; or one piece of property of less value in order to save a greater ; and that in like manner he would be willing to surrender *every thing*, in order that his life, the most valuable object, might be preserved. But the exact meaning of the proverb, I suspect, has not yet been perceived. ¶ *Yea, all that a man hath.* This is evidently designed to express the same thing as the proverb, "skin for skin," or to furnish an illustration of that. The meaning is plain. A man is willing to surrender all that he has, in order to preserve his life. He will part with property and friends, in order that he may be kept alive. If a man therefore is to be reached in the most tender and vital part ; if any thing is to be done that shall truly reveal his character, his life must be put in danger, and his true character will then be revealed. The object of Satan is to say, that a test had not been applied to Job of sufficient severity to show what he really was. What he had lost was a mere trifle compared with what would be if he was subjected to severe bodily sufferings, so that his life would be in peril. It is to be remembered that these are the words of Satan, and that they are not necessarily true. Inspiration is concerned only in securing *the exact record* of what is said, not in affirming that all that is said is true. We shall have frequent occasion to illustrate this sentiment in other portions of the book. In regard to the sentiment here expressed, however, it is in gene-

ral true. Men will surrender their property, their houses, and lands, and gold, to save their lives. Many, too, would see their friends perish, in order that they might be saved. It is not universally true, however. It is possible to conceive that a man might so love his property as to submit to any torture, even endangering life, rather than surrender it. Many, too, if endangered by shipwreck, would give up a plank in order to save their wives or children, at the risk of their own lives. Many will give their lives rather than surrender their liberty ; and many would die rather than abandon their principles. Such were the noble Christian martyrs ; and such a man was Job. Satan urged that if his life were made wretched, he would abandon his integrity, and show that his professed piety was selfish, and his religion false and hollow. The Syriac and Arabic add, "that he may be safe."

5. *But put forth thine hand now.* Satan felt that he had no power to afflict Job without permission. Malignant as he was, he knew that God only could subject the holy man to this trial—another proof that Satan is under the control of the Almighty, and acts only as he is *permitted* to act in tempting and trying the good. ¶ *And touch his bone.* See Note on chap. i. 11. Afflict his body so as to endanger his life. The words "bone" and " flesh" denote the whole body. The idea was, that the whole body should be subjected to severe pain. ¶ *And he will curse thee to thy face ;* Notes on chap. i. 11.

6. *Behold, he is in thine hand.* He is at thy disposal ; see chap. i. 12, Margin. ¶ *But save his life.* Marg. *only.* This was to be the only limitation. It would seem that he had the power to make any selection of disease, and to afflict him in any manner, provided it did not terminate fatally. The keen sorrows which Job afterwards endured showed the malignancy

7 So went Satan forth from the presence of the Lord, and smote Job with sore boils from the sole of his foot unto his crown.

---

of the tempter; evinced his ingenuity in inflicting pain, and his knowledge of what the human frame *could* be made to bear.

7. *So went Satan forth;* chap. i. 12. ¶ *And smote Job with sore boils.* The English word *boil* denotes the well-known tumour upon the flesh, accompanied with severe inflammation; a sore angry swelling. *Webster.* The Hebrew word, however, is in the singular number (שְׁחִין), and should have been so rendered in our translation. Dr. Good renders it "a burning ulceration." The Vulgate translates it, *ulcere pessimo.* The Septuagint, ἕλκει πονηρῷ—*with a foul ulcer.* The Hebrew word שׁחין means a burning sore, an inflamed ulcer, a bile. *Gesenius.* It is derived from שׁחן *shâh-hăn*, an obsolete root, retained in Arabic, and meaning to be hot or inflamed. It is translated *bile* or *boil*, in Ex. ix. 9—11; Lev. xiii. 18; 2 Kings xx. 7; Isa. xxxviii. 21, (see Notes on that place), Lev. xiii. 19, 20; Job ii. 7; and *botch*, Deut. xxviii. 27, 35. The word does not occur elsewhere in the Scriptures. In Deut. xxviii. 27, it means "the botch of Egypt," some species of leprosy, undoubtedly, which prevailed there. In regard to the disease of Job, we may learn some of its characteristics, not only from the usual meaning of the word, but from the circumstances mentioned in the book itself. It was such that he took a potsherd to scrape himself with, chap. ii. 8; such as to make his nights restless, and full of tossings to and fro, and to clothe his flesh with clods of dust, and with worms, and to break his flesh, or to constitute a running sore or ulcer, chap. vii. 4, 5; such as to make him bite his flesh for pain, chap. xiii. 14, and to make him like a rotten thing, or a garment that is moth eaten, chap. xiii. 28; such that his face was foul with weeping, chap. xvi. 16, and such as to fill him with wrinkles, and to make his flesh lean, chap. xvi. 8; such as to make his breath corrupt, chap. xvii. 1, and his bones cleave to his skin, chap. xix. 20, 26; such as to pierce his bones with pain in the night, chap. xxx. 17, and to make his skin black, and to burn up his bones with heat, chap. xxx. 30. It has been commonly supposed that the disease of Job was a species of black leprosy commonly called *Elephantiasis*, which prevails much in Egypt. This disease received its name from ἐλέφας, *an elephant*, from the swelling produced by it, causing a resemblance to that animal in the limbs; or because it rendered the skin like that of the elephant, scabrous and dark coloured. It is called by the Arabs *judhăm* (Dr. Good), and is said to produce in the countenance a grim, distorted, and *lion-like* set of features, and hence has been called by some *Leontiasis.* It is known as the *black* leprosy, to distinguish it from a more common disorder called *white leprosy*—an affection which the Greeks call *Leuce*, or *whiteness.* The disease of Job seems to have been a universal ulcer; producing an eruption over his entire person, and attended with violent pain, and constant restlessness. A universal bile or groups of biles over the body would accord with the account of the disease in the various parts of the book. In the elephantiasis the skin is covered with incrustations like those of an elephant. It is a chronic and contagious disease, marked by a thickening of the legs, with a loss of hair and feeling, a swelling of the face, and a hoarse nasal voice. It affects the whole body; the bones as well as the skin are covered with spots and tumours, at first red, but afterwards black. *Coxe, Ency. Webster.* It should be added that the leprosy in all its forms was regarded as contagious, and of course involved the necessity of a separation from society; and all the circumstances attending this calamity were such as deeply to humble a man of the former rank and dignity of Job.

8. *And he took him a potsherd.* The word here used (חֶרֶשׂ) means a fragment of a broken vessel; see Notes

8 And he took him a potsherd to scrape himself withal; and he sat down among the ashes.[a]

a Matt. 11. 21.

9 Then said his wife unto him, Dost thou still retain thine integrity? curse God, and die.

on Isa, xlv. 9. The LXX. render it ὄστρακον—a shell. One object of taking this was to remove from his body the filth accumulated by the universal ulcer, comp. chap. vii. 4, 5; and another design probably was, to *indicate* the greatness of his calamity and sorrow. The ancients were accustomed to show their grief by significant external actions (comp. Notes on chap. i. 20), and nothing could more strongly denote the greatness of the calamity, than for a man of wealth, honour, and distinction, to sit down in the ashes, to take a piece of broken earthen-ware, and begin to scrape his body covered over with undressed and most painful sores. It does not appear that any thing was done to heal him, or any kindness shown in taking care of his disease. It would seem that he was at once separated from his home, as a man whom none would venture to approach, and was doomed to endure his suffering without sympathy from others. ¶ *To scrape himself withal.* The word here used (גרד) has the sense of grating, scraping, sawing; or to scrape or rasp with an edged tool. The same word identically, as to letters, is used at present among the Arabs; meaning to rasp or scrape with any kind of tool. The idea here seems to be, that Job took the pieces of broken pottery that he found among the ashes to scrape himself with. ¶ *And he sat down among the ashes.* On the expressions of grief among the ancients, see Notes on chap. i. 20. The general ideas of mourning among the nations of antiquity seem to have been, to strip off all their ornaments; to put on the coarsest apparel, and to place themselves in the most humiliating positions. To sit on the ground (see Note on Isa. iii. 26), or on a heap of ashes, or a pile of cinders, was a common mode of expressing sorrow; see Note on Isa. lviii. 5. To wear sackcloth, to shave their heads and their beards, and to abstain from pleasant food and

from all cheerful society, and to utter loud and long exclamations or shrieks, was also a common mode of indicating grief. The Vulgate renders this *sedens in sterquilinio*, "sitting on a dunghill." The LXX. "and he took a shell to scrape off the ichor (ἰχῶρα), the *sanies*, or filth produced by a running ulcer, and sat upon the ashes *out of the city*," implying that his grief was so excessive that he left the city and his friends, and went out to weep alone.

9. *Then said his wife unto him.* Some remarkable additions are made by the ancient versions to this passage. The Chaldee renders it, "and *Dinah* (דינה), his wife, said to him." The author of that paraphrase seems to have supposed that Job lived in the time of Jacob, and had married his daughter Dinah; Gen. xxx. 21. Drusius says, that this was the opinion of the Hebrews, and quotes a declaration from the Gemara to this effect: "Job lived in the days of Jacob, and was born when the children of Israel went down into Egypt; and when they departed thence he died. He lived therefore 210 years, as long as they were into Egypt." This is mere tradition, but it shows the ancient impression as to the time when Job lived. The LXX. have introduced a remarkable passage here, of which the following is a translation. "After much time had elapsed, his wife said unto him, How long wilt thou persevere, saying, Behold, I will wait a little longer, cherishing the hope of my recovery? Behold, the memorial of thee has disappeared from the earth—those sons and daughters, the pangs and sorrows of my womb, for whom I toiled laboriously in vain. Even thou sittest among loathsome worms, passing the night in the open air, whilst I, a wanderer and a drudge, from place to place, and from house to house, watch the sun till his going down, that I may rest from the toils and sorrows that now oppress me. But speak some

word towards the Lord ($\tau\iota$ $\dot{\rho}\tilde{\eta}\mu\alpha$ $\epsilon\dot{\iota}\varsigma$ $\varkappa\dot{\nu}\rho\iota o\nu$) and die." Whence this addition had its origin, it is impossible now to say. Dr. Good says it is found in Theodotion, in the Syriac, and the Arabic (in this he errs, for it is not in the Syriac and Arabic in Walton's Polyglott), and in the Latin of St. Ambrose. Dathe suggests that it was probably added by some person who thought it incredible that an angry woman could be content with saying so *little* as is ascribed in the Hebrew to the wife of Job. It may have been originally written by some one in the margin of his Bible by way of paraphrase, and the transcriber, seeing it there, may have supposed it was omitted accidentally from the text, and so inserted it in the place where it now stands. It is one of the many instances, at all events, which show that implicit confidence is not to be placed in the Septuagint. There is not the slightest evidence that this was ever in the Hebrew text. It is not wholly unnatural, and as an exercise of the fancy is not without ingenuity and plausibility, and yet the simple but abrupt statement in the Hebrew seems best to accord with nature. The evident distress of the wife of Job, according to the whole narrative, is not so much that she was subjected to trials, and that she was compelled to wander about without a home, as that Job should be so patient, and that he did not yield to the temptation. ¶ *Dost thou still retain thine integrity?* Notes ver. 3. The question implies that, in her view, he ought not to be expected to manifest patience and resignation in these circumstances. He had endured evils which showed that confidence ought not to be reposed in a God who would thus inflict them. This is all that we know of the wife of Job. Whether this was her general character, or whether *she* yielded to the temptation of Satan and cursed God, and thus heightened the sorrows of Job by her unexpected impropriety of conduct, is unknown. It is not conclusive evidence that her general character was bad; and it may be that the strength of her usual virtue and piety was overcome by accumulated calamities. She expressed, however, the feelings of corrupt human nature everywhere when sorely afflicted. The suggestion *will* cross the mind, often with almost irresistible force, that a God who thus afflicts his creatures is not worthy of confidence; and many a time a child of God is *tempted* to give vent to feelings of rebellion and murmuring like this, and to renounce all his religion. ¶ *Curse God;* see Notes on chap. i. 11. The Hebrew word is the same. Dr. Good renders it, "And yet dost thou hold fast thine integrity, blessing God and dying?" Noyes translates it, "Renounce God, and die,' Rosenmüller and Umbreit, "Bid farewell to God, and die." Castellio renders it, "Give thanks to God and die." The response of Job, however (ver. 10), shows that he understood her as exciting him to reject, renounce, or curse God. The sense is, that she regarded him as unworthy of confidence, and submission as unreasonable, and she wished Job to express this and be relieved from his misery. Roberts supposes that this was a heathen sentiment, and says that nothing is more common than for the heathen, under certain circumstances, to curse their gods. "That the man who has made expensive offerings to his deity, in hope of gaining some great blessing, and who has been disappointed, will pour out all his imprecations on the god whose good offices have (as he believes) been prevented by some superior deity. A man in reduced circumstances says, 'Yes, yes, my god has lost his eyes; they are put out; he cannot look after my affairs.' 'Yes,' said an extremely rich devotee of the supreme god Siva, after he had lost his property, ' Shall I serve him any more? What! make offerings to him! No, no. He is the lowest of all gods!'" ¶ *And die.* Probably she regarded God as a stern and severe Being, and supposed that by indulging in blasphemy Job would provoke him to cut him off at once. She did not expect him to lay wicked hands on himself. She expected that God would at once interpose and destroy him. The sense is, that nothing but

10 But he said unto her, Thou speakest as one of the foolish women speaketh. What! shall *a* we receive good at the hand of God,

a Ja.5.10,11.

and shall we not receive evil? In all this did not Job sin *b* with his lips.

11 Now when Job's three friends heard of all this evil that was come

b Ps.39.1.

death was to be expected, and the sooner he provoked God to cut him off from the land of the living, the better.

10. *As one of the foolish women speaketh.* The word here rendered *foolish* (נְבָלוּת, from נָבָל), means properly stupid or foolish, and then wicked, abandoned, impious—the idea of sin and *folly* being closely connected in the Scriptures, or sin being regarded as supreme folly; 1 Sam. xxv. 25 ; 2 Sam. iii. 33 ; Ps. xiv. 1 ; liii. 2. The Arabs still use the word with the same compass of signification. *Gesenius.* The word is here used in the sense of *wicked;* and the idea is, that the sentiment which she uttered was impious, or was such as were on the lips of the wicked. Sanctius supposes that there is a reference here to Idumean females, who, like other women, reproached and cast away their gods, if they did not obtain what they asked when they prayed to them. Homer represents Achilles and Menelaus as reproaching the gods. Il. i. 353, iii. 365. See Rosenmüller, Morgenland, *in loc.* ¶ *What! shall we receive good at the hand of God.* Having received such abundant tokens of kindness from him, it was unreasonable to complain when they were taken away, and when he sent calamity in their stead. ¶ *And shall we not receive evil?* Shall we not expect it? Shall we not be willing to bear it when it comes? Shall we not have sufficient confidence in him to believe that his dealings are ordered in goodness and equity? Shall we at once lose all our confidence in our great Benefactor the moment he takes away our comforts, and visits us with pain? This is the true expression of piety. It submits to all the arrangements of God without a murmur. It receives blessings with gratitude; it is resigned when calamities are sent in their place. It esteems it as a mere favour to be permitted to breathe the air which God has made, to look upon the light of his sun, to tread upon his earth, to inhale the fragrance of his flowers, and to enjoy the society of the friends whom he gives ; and when he takes one or all away, it feels that he has taken only what belongs to him, and withdraws a privilege to which we had no claim. In addition to that, true piety feels that all claim to any blessing, if it had ever existed, has been forfeited by sin. What right has a sinner to complain when God withdraws his favour, and subjects him to suffering? What claim has he on God, that should make it wrong for Him to visit him with calamity ?

Wherefore doth a living man complain,
A man for the punishment of his sins ?
Lam. iii. 39.

¶ *In all this did not Job sin with his lips;* see Notes chap. i. 22. This remark is made here perhaps in contrast with what occurred afterwards. He subsequently did give utterance to improper sentiments, and was rebuked accordingly, but thus far what he had expressed was in accordance with truth, and with the feelings of most elevated piety.

11. *Now when Job's three friends heard.* It would seem from this that these men were his particular friends. ¶ *They came every one from his own place.* His residence. This was the result of agreement or appointment thus to meet together. ¶ *Eliphaz the Temanite.* This was the most prominent of his friends. In the ensuing discussion he regularly takes the lead, advances the most important and impressive considerations, and is followed and sustained by the others. The LXX. render this Ελιφὰζ ὁ Θαιμαινῶν βασιλεὺς—"Eliphaz, the king of the Themanites." The Hebrew does not intimate that he held any office or rank. The word rendered *Temanite* (תֵּימָנִי) is a patronymic from תֵּימָן *Teman,* meaning properly *at the right hand,* and then *the South.*

upon him, they came every one from his own place : Eliphaz the
a Ge.36.11 ; Je.49 7.

Temanite, *a* and Bildad the Shuhite, *b* and Zophar the Naamathite:
b Ge.25.2.

The Hebrew geographers are always represented as looking to the East, and not towards the North, as we do; and hence, with them, the right hand denotes the South. Teman or Theman was a son of Eliphaz, and grandson of Esau ; see Gen. xxxvi. 15, where he is spoken of as "duke " or prince (אלוף), a head of a family or tribe, a chieftain. He is supposed to have lived on the east of Idumea. Eusebius places Thaeman in Arabia Petræa, five miles from Petra (see Notes on Isa. xvi. 1), and says that there was a Roman garrison there. The Temanites were celebrated for wisdom. " Is wisdom no more in Teman ?" Jer. xlix. 7. The country was distinguished also for producing men of strength : " And thy mighty men, O Teman, shall be dismayed ;" Obad. 9. That this country was a part of Idumea is apparent, not only from the fact that Teman was a descendant of Esau, who settled there, but from several places in the Scriptures. Thus in Ezek. xxv. 13, it is said, " I will also stretch out mine hand upon Edom, and I will make it desolate from Teman, and they of Dedan shall fall by the sword." In Amos i. 12, Teman is mentioned as in the vicinity of Bozrah, at one time the capital of Idumea : "But I will send a fire upon Teman, which shall devour the palaces of Bozrah ;" see Notes on Isa. xxi. 14. The inhabitants of this country were distinguished in early times for wisdom, and particularly for that kind of wisdom which is expressed in close observation of men and manners, and the course of events, and which was expressed in proverbs. Thus they are mentioned in the book of Baruch, iii. 23 : " The merchants of Meran and of Theman, the authors of fables, and searchers out of understanding," οἱ μυθολόγοι καὶ οἱ ἐκζητηταὶ τῆς συνίσεως. ¶ *And Bildad the Shuhite.* The second speaker uniformly in the following argument. The LXX. render this, " Bildad the sovereign of the Saucheans," Σαυχέων τύραννος. Shuah

שׁוּחַ (meaning a pit) was the name of a son of Abraham, by Keturah, and also of an Arabian tribe, descended from him, Gen. xxv. 2. " The country of the Shuhites," says Gesenius, "was not improbably the same with the Σακχαία of Ptolemy, v. 15, eastward of Batanea." But the exact situation of the Shuhites is unknown. It is difficult to determine the geography of the tribes of Arabia, as many of them are migratory and unsettled. It would seem that Bildad did not reside very far from Eliphaz, for they made an *agreement* to go and visit Job. ¶ *And Zophar the Naamathite.* An inhabitant of Naamah, whose situation is unknown. The LXX. render this, " Zophar, king of the Minaians—Μιναίων βασιλεύς. A place by the name of Naamah is mentioned in Josh. xv. 41, as in the limits of the tribe of Judah. But this was a considerable distance from the residence of Job, and it is not probable that Zophar was far from that region. Conjecture is useless as to the place where he lived. The Editor of the Pictorial Bible, however, supposes that Zophar was from the town in Judah mentioned in Josh. xv. 41. He observes that this town is " mentioned in a list of the uttermost cities of Judah's lot, ' towards the coast of Edom *southward ;*' it is farther among that portion of those towns that lay ' in the valley' (Josh. xv. 33), which valley is the same that contained Joktheel (Josh. xv. 38), which is supposed to have been Petra. Naamah was probably, therefore, in or near the Ghor or valley which extends from the Dead Sea to the Gulf of Akaba.—These considerations," he adds, " seem to establish the conclusion that the scene of this book is laid in the land of Edom." In the first part of this verse, a remarkable addition occurs in the Chaldee paraphrase.—It is as follows: " And the three friends of Job heard of all the evil which had come upon him, and when they saw the trees of his gardens (Chald. *Paradise* for they had made an appointment together to come *a* to mourn with him, and to comfort him.

12 And when they lifted up their eyes afar off, and knew him

a Ro.12.15.

not, they lifted up their voice and wept; and they rent every one his mantle, and sprinkled dust *b* upon their heads toward heaven.

13 So they sat down *c* with him

b Ne.9.1; La.2.10.　　*c* Ezr. 9. 3—5.

פרדסיהון) that they were dried up, and the bread of his support that it was turned into living flesh (אתהפך לבסרא חיא ולהם סעודתהון), and the wine of his drink turned into blood (אתהפך לדמא והמר משתיהון)." Here is evidently the doctrine of *transubstantiation*, the change of bread into flesh, and of wine into blood, and bears the marks of having been interpolated by some friend of the Papacy. But when or by whom it was done is unknown. It is a most stupid forgery. The evident intention of it was to sustain the doctrine of transubstantiation, by the plea that it was found far back in the times of Job, and that it could not be regarded, therefore, as an absurdity. To what extent it has ever been used by the advocates of that doctrine, I have no means of ascertaining. Its interpolation here is a pretty sure proof of the conviction of the author of it that the doctrine is not found in any fair interpretation of the Bible. ¶ *For they had made an appointment together.* They had agreed to go together, and they evidently set out on the journey together. The Chaldee—or some one who has interpolated a passage in the Chaldee—has introduced a circumstance in regard to the design of their coming, which savours also of the Papacy. It is as follows: "They came each one from his place, *and for the merit of this they were freed from the place destined to them in Gehenna*" (בגיהנם), a passage evidently intended to defend the doctrine of *purgatory*, by the authority of the ancient Chaldee Paraphrase. ¶ *To come to mourn with him, and to comfort him.* To show the appropriate sympathy of friends in a time of peculiar calamity. They did not come with an intention to reproach him, or to charge him with being a hypocrite.

12. *And when they lifted up their eyes afar off.* "When they saw him at the distance at which they could

formerly recognize him without difficulty, disease had so altered his appearance that at first sight they knew him not." *Noyes.* ¶ *They lifted up their voice.* This is a common expression in the Scriptures, to denote grief; Gen. xxvii. 38; xxix. 11; Judg. ii. 4; Ruth i. 9; 1 Sam. xxiv. 16, *et sæpe al. We* learn to suppress the expressions of grief. The ancients gave vent to their sorrows aloud.—They even hired persons to aid them in their lamentations; and it became a professional business of women to devote themselves to the office of making an outcry on occasions of mourning. The same thing prevails in the East at present. Friends sit around the grave of the dead, or go there at different times, and give a long and doleful shriek or howl, as expressive of their grief. ¶ *And they rent every one his mantle;* see Notes on chap. i. 20. ¶ *And sprinkled dust upon their heads towards heaven.* Another expression of sorrow; comp. Lam. ii. 10; Neh. ix. 1; 1 Sam. iv. 12; Josh. vii. 6; Ezek. xxvii. 30. The indications of grief here referred to, were such as were common in ancient times. They resemble, in a remarkable manner, the mode in which Achilles gave utterance to his sorrow, when informed of the death of Patroclus. Iliad xviii. 21—27.

A sudden horror shot through all the chief,
And wrapp'd his senses in the cloud of grief;
Cast on the ground, with furious hands he spread
The scorching ashes o'er his graceful head,
His purple garments, and his golden hairs,
Those he deforms with dust, and these he tears:
On the hard soil his groaning breast he threw,
And roll'd and grovell'd as to earth he grew.
                                                POPE.

Thus far the feelings of the three friends were entirely kind, and all that they did was expressive of sympathy for the sufferer.

13. *So they sat down with him upon the ground;* see Notes on chap. i.

upon the ground seven *a* days and
seven nights, and none spake a word

20 ; ii. 8 ; comp. Ezra ix. 3, " I rent
my garment and my mantle, and
plucked off the hair of my head, and
my beard, and sat down astonished."
¶ *Seven days and seven nights.* Seven days was the usual time of mourning among the Orientals. Thus they
made public lamentation for Jacob
seven days, Gen. l. 10. Thus, on the
death of Saul, they fasted seven days,
1 Sam. xxxi. 13. So the author of
the book of Ecclesiasticus says, " Seven days do men mourn for him that
is dead;" chap. xxii. 12. It cannot be
supposed that they remained in the
same place and posture for seven days
and nights, but that they mourned
with him during that time in the usual
way. An instance of grief remarkably similar to this, continuing through
a period of six days, is ascribed by
Euripides to Orestes:

Ἐντεῦθεν ἀγρίᾳ ξυνταχεὶς νόσῳ νοσεῖ
Τλήμων Ὀρέστης· ὁ δὲ πεσὼν ἐν δεμνίοις
Κεῖται.
Ἕκτον δὲ δὴ τόδ' ἦμαρ, κ. τ. λ.

"'Tis hence Orestes, agonized with griefs
And sore disease, lies on his restless bed
Delirious. Now six morns have winged their
      flight,
Since by his hands his parent massacred
Burnt on the pile in expiatory flames.
Stubborn the while he keeps a rigid fast,
Nor bathes, nor dresses; but beneath his robes
He skulks, and if he steals a pause from rage,
'Tis but to feel his weight of wo and weep."

¶ *And none spake a word to him.*—
That is, on the subject of his grief.
They came to condole with him, but
they had now nothing to say. They
saw that his affliction was much
greater than they had anticipated.
¶ *For they saw that* his *grief was very
great.* This is given as a reason why
they were silent. But *how* this produced silence, or why his great grief was
a cause of their silence, is not intimated.
Perhaps one or all of the following
considerations may have led to it.
(1.) They were amazed at the extent
of his sufferings. Amazement is often
expressed by silence. We look upon
that which is out of the usual course
of events without being able to ex-

unto him : for they saw that *his*
grief was very great.

press any thing. We are "struck
dumb" with wonder. (2.) The effect
of great calamity is often to prevent
utterance. Nothing is more natural
or common than profound silence when
we go to the house of mourning. " It
is the lesser cares only that speak ;
the greater ones find not language."
Curæ leves loquuntur, ingentes stupent.
(3.) They might not have known what
to say. They had come to sympathize
with him, and to offer consolation.
But their anticipated topics of consolation may have been seen to be inappropriate. The calamity was greater
than they had before witnessed. The
loss of property and children ; the deep
humiliation of a man who had been
one of the most distinguished of the
land ; the severity of his bodily sufferings, and his changed and haggard
appearance, constituted so great a
calamity, that the usual topics of conversation did not meet the case. What
they had to say, was the result of careful observation on the usual course of
events, and it is by no means improbable that they had never before witnessed sorrows so keen, and that they
now saw that their maxims would by
no means furnish consolation for *such*
a case. (4.) They seem to have been
very early thrown into doubt in regard
to the real character of Job. They
had regarded him as a pious man, and
had come to him under that impression. But his great afflictions seem
soon to have shaken their confidence
in his piety, and to have led them to
ask themselves whether so great a
sufferer *could* be the friend of God.
Their subsequent reasonings show
that it was with them a settled opinion that the righteous would be prospered, and that very great calamities
were proof of great criminality in the
sight of God. It was not inconsistent
with this belief to suppose that the
righteous might be slightly afflicted,
but when they saw *such* sorrows, they
supposed they were altogether beyond
what God could send upon his friends;
and with this doubt on their minds,

CHAPTER III.

ANALYSIS OF THE CHAPTER.

Job's Complaint.

This chapter introduces the argument of the poem, which continues to chap. xlii. 6. The pathetic lamentation of Job, and his bitter complaint, furnishes an occasion for the reply of Eliphaz in chap. iv., and gives rise to the argument which follows. Thus far his friends, overwhelmed with astonishment and grief, had said nothing. They knew not what to say to comfort him, and they felt that if they said any thing, and expressed the convictions of their own minds, it could only give him pain. They were, therefore, silent. The lamentation and complaint of Job, however, furnished them with an opportunity to express their convictions fully, and in the following chapters they enter on the argument with great earnestness.

This chapter contains Job's complaint. At the end of seven days, when he saw no prospect of relief from his sufferings, and when his friends did not utter one word of condolence, he unburdens his heart in the language of bitter lamentation and despair. This complaint comprises the following parts or subjects:—

He curses the day in which he was born, using a great variety of strong, rash, and violent language, to show the deep detestation with which he regarded it—wishing that that day had perished, that night had rested on it, that it should not be numbered among the days of the year, and that it should be an accursed day never to be mentioned but with some expression of abhorrence; ver. 1—9.

He states the reason why he regarded it as accursed. It was because it did not prevent his birth, and thus save him from sorrow and despair; ver. 10.

He asks with impatience, why he did not die as soon as he was born ? Why were any pains taken to keep him alive ? Why was he reserved to endure these bitter sorrows ? ver. 11, 12.

He states with great beauty, what would have occurred if he had died as soon as he was born. Then he would have been at rest. He would have slept as princes and kings do. He would have been as unconscious of suffering as infants are who are not born. He would have been in that peaceful abode where the wicked cease from troubling, and where the weary are at rest ; where the chains of slavery are broken, and the servant is as free as his master; ver. 13—19.

He asks, in the language of bitter complaint, why life is given to a man in misery, who does not desire it, and who longs impatiently for death ? This implies a bitter complaint against God. Before this nothing had escaped him reflecting on God ; but here, in the language of deep and excited feeling, he allows himself to insinuate that God is unjust and unkind ; ver. 20—23.

---

and this change in their views, they knew not what to say. How *could* they console him when it was their settled belief that great sufferings were proof of great guilt ? They could say nothing which would not seem to be a departure from this, unless they assumed that he had been a hypocrite, and should administer reproof and rebuke for his sins. (5.) In this state of things, to administer *rebuke* would seem to be cruel. It would aggravate the sorrows which already were more than he could bear. They did, therefore, what the friends of the afflicted are often compelled to do in regard to specific sufferings; they kept silence. As they could not comfort him, they would not aggravate his grief. All they could have said would probably have been unmeaning generalities which would not meet his case, or would have been sententious maxims which would imply that he was a sinner and a hypocrite ; and they were therefore dumb, until the bitter complaint of Job himself (chap. iii.) gave them an opportunity to state the train of thought which had passed through their minds during this protracted silence. How often do similar cases occur now—cases where consolation seems almost impossible, and where *any* truths which might be urged, except the most abstract and unmeaning generalities, would tend only to aggravate the sorrows of the afflicted ! When calamity comes upon a person as the result of his sins ; when property is taken away which has been gained in an unlawful manner ; when a friend dies, leaving no evidence that he was prepared ; when it is impossible to speak of that friend without recalling the memory of his irreligious, prayerless, or dissolute life, how difficult is it to administer consolation ! How often is the Christian friend constrained to close his lips in silence, or utter only *torturing* general truths that can give no consolation, or refer to facts which will tend only to open the wound in the heart deeper ! To be silent at such times is all that can be done ; or to commend the sufferer in humble prayer to God, an expedient which seems not to have been resorted to either by Job or his friends, It is remarkable that Job is not represented as calling upon God for support, and it is as remarkable that his friends during these seven days of silent grief did not commend the case of their much afflicted friend to the Father of mercies. Had *Job* prayed, he might have been kept from much of the improper feeling to which he gave vent in the following chapter ; had *they* prayed, they might have obtained much more just views of the government of God than they had hitherto possessed.

In the close of his complaint, he discloses the fact that he had greatly feared these sufferings, and that in the time of his prosperity he had not felt that he was secure. He had had an apprehension of a reverse of circumstances, and now the worst that he had dreaded had come ; ver. 24—26.

There is, undoubtedly, much in this complaint that is irreverent, impatient, and improper. Yet the author of the poem has contrived to secure our sympathy in favour of the sufferer. He has been subjected to trials of the severest nature, and has found no one to condole with him, or to express a sentiment of kindness in his favour. Under this excess of suffering, and wrought up to this height of feeling, we are more inclined to pity him than to censure him for his obviously irreverent language. Such is the art of

the poem that these complaints do not strike us as coming from a bad man, but as being the effect of momentary impatience and passion. They are not expressions indicating settled character and principles but they are the result of the circumstances in which he was placed. They are felt to be such as not to demonstrate that he is a hypocrite, but such as to show that while he was in the main "a man of integrity, he was too confident of it ; a man oppressed with almost every imaginable evil, both corporeal and mental, and hurried beyond the limits of virtue by the strong influence of pain and affliction." *Lowth's Lectures on Hebrew poetry*, xxxiv.

AFTER this opened Job his mouth, and cursed his day.

2 And Job [1] spake, and said,

3 Let *a* the day perish wherein

1 *answered.*   *a* chap. 10.18, &c.; Je.20.

CHAPTER III.

1. *After this.* Dr. Good renders this, "at length." It means after the long silence of his friends, and after he saw that there was no prospect of relief or of consolation. ¶ *Opened Job his mouth.* The usual formula in Hebrew to denote the commencement of a speech ; see Matt. v. 2. Schultens contends that it means boldness and vehemency of speech, παῤῥησία, or an opening of the mouth for the purpose of accusing, expostulating, or complaining ; or to begin to utter some sententious, profound, or sublime maxim ; and in support of this he appeals to Ps. lxxviii. 2, and Prov. viii. 6. There is probably, however, nothing more intended than to begin to speak. It is in accordance with Oriental views, where an act of speaking is regarded as a grave and important matter, and is entered on with much deliberation. Blackwell (Life of Homer, p. 43) remarks that the Turks, Arabs, Hindoos, and the Orientals in general, have little inclination to society and to general conversation, that they seldom speak, and that their speeches are sententious and brief, unless they are much excited. With such men, to make a speech is a serious matter, as is indicated by the manner in which their discourses are commonly introduced : " I will open my mouth," or they " opened the mouth," implying great deliberation and gravity. This phrase occurs often in Homer, Hesiod, Orpheus, and in Virgil (comp. Æn. vi. 75), as well as in the Bible.

See Burder, in Rosenmüller's Morgenland, *in loc.* ¶ *And cursed his day.* The word rendered *curse* here (וַיְקַלֵּל) is different from that used in chap. i. 11 ; ii. 9. It is the proper word to denote *to curse.* The Syriac adds, " the day in which he was born." A similar expression occurs in Klopstock's Messias, Ges. iii.

Wenn nun, aller Kinder beraubt, die verzweifelnde Mutter,
Wuthend dem Tag, an dem sie gebahr, und gebohren ward, fluchet.
" When now of all her children robb'd, the desperate mother enraged curses the day in which she bare, and was borne."

2. *And Job spake.* Marg. as in Hebrew, *answered.* The Hebrew word here used (עָנָה) *to answer,* is often employed when one commences a discourse, even though no question had preceded. It is somewhat in the sense of replying to a subject, or of speaking in a case where a question *might* appropriately be asked ; Isa. xiv. 10 (Heb.), Zech. iii. 4 ; Deut. xxvi. 5 (Heb.), xxvii. 14 (Heb.). The word *to answer* (ἀποκρίνομαι) is frequently used in this way in the New Testament ; Matt. xvii. 4, 17 ; xxviii. 5 ; Mark ix. 5 ; x. 51, *et al.*

3. *Let the day perish.* " Perish the day ! O that there had never been such a day ! Let it be blotted from the memory of man ! There is something singularly bold, sublime, and *wild* in this exclamation. It is a burst of feeling where there had been long restraint, and where now it breaks forth in the most vehement and impassioned manner. The word *perish* here (יֹאבַד) expresses the *optative,*

I was born, and the night *in which* it | was said, There is a man child conceived.

---

and indicates strong desire. So the LXX., 'Απόλοιτο, *may it perish,* or be destroyed; comp. chap. x. 18. "O that I had given up the ghost." Dr. Good says of this exclamation, "There is nothing that I know of, in ancient or modern poetry, equal to the entire burst, whether in the wildness and horror of the imprecations, or the terrible sublimity of its imagery." The boldest and most animated of the Hebrew poets have imitated it, and have expressed themselves in almost the same language, in scenes of distress. A remarkably similar expression of feeling is made by Jeremiah.

Cursed be the day wherein I was born!
Let not the day wherein my mother bare me
be blessed!
Cursed be the man who brought tidings to my
father, saying,
" A man child is born unto thee,"
Making him very glad.
Be that man as the cities which JEHOVAH overthrew and repented not!
Yea, let him hear the outcry in the morning,
And the lamentation at noon day!
                                    Chap. xx 14—16.

The sense of this expression in Job is plain. He wished there never had been such a day, and then he would not have been born. It is impossible to vindicate these expressions in Job and Jeremiah, unless it be on the supposition that it is highly wrought poetic language, caused by sorrow so acute that it could not be expressed in prose. We are to remember, however, if this seems to us inconsistent with the existence of true piety, that Job had far less light than we have; that he lived at an early period of the world, when the views of the divine government were obscure, and that he was not sustained by the hopes and promises which the Christian possesses now. What light he had was probably that of tradition, and of the result of careful observation on the course of events. His topics of consolation must have been comparatively few. He had few or no promises to sustain him. He had not had before him, as we have, the example of the patient Redeemer. His faith was not sustained by those

strong assurances which we have of the perfect rectitude of the divine government. Before we blame him too severely, we must place ourselves in imagination in his circumstances, and ask what *our* piety would have done under the trials which afflicted *him.* Yet with all allowances, it is not possible to vindicate this language; and while we cannot but admire its force and sublimity, and its unequalled power and boldness in expressing strong passion, we at the same time feel that there was a want of proper submission and patience.—It is the impassioned language of a man who felt that he could bear no more; and there can be no doubt that it gave to Satan the hope of his anticipated triumph. ¶ *And the night* in which *it was said.* Dr. Good renders this, " And the night which shouted." Noyes, " And the night which said." So Gesenius and Rosenmüller, "Perish the night which said, a man child is conceived." The Vulgate renders it, " The night in which it was said;" the LXX., " That night in which they said." The Chaldee paraphrases the verse, " Perish the day in which I was born, and the angel who presided over my conception." Scott, quoted by Good, translates it, " The night which hailed the new-born man." The language throughout this imprecation is that in which the night is *personified,* and addressed as if it were made glad by the birth of a son. So Schultens says, " Inducitur enim *Nox* illa quasi *conscia mysterii, et exultans ob spem prolis virilis.'* Such personifications of day and night are common among the Arabs; see Schultens. It is a representation of day and night as " sympathizing with the joys and sorrows of mankind, and is in the truest vein of Oriental poetry.' ¶ *There is a man child conceived.* Heb. גבר—*a man;* comp. John xvi. 21. The word " conceived " Dr. Good renders " brought forth." So Herder translates it. The LXX., 'Ιδοὺ ἄρσεν—*lo, a male.* The common translation expresses the true sense

4 Let that day be darkness; let not God regard it from above, neither let the light shine upon it.

---

of the original. The joy at the birth of a male in Oriental countries is much greater than that at the birth of a female. A remarkable instance of an imprecation on the day of one's birth is found in a Mohammedan book of modern times, in which the expressions are almost precisely the same as in Job. "Malek er Nasser Daub, prince of some tribes in Palestine, from which however he had been driven, after many adverse fortunes, died in a village near Damascus in the year 1258. When the crusaders had desolated his country, he deplored its misfortunes and his own in a poem, from which Abulfeda (Annals, p. 560) has quoted the following passage : ' O that my mother had remained unmarried all the days of her life ! That God had determined no lord or consort for her ! O that when he had destined her to an excellent, mild, and wise prince, she had been one of those whom he had created barren ; that she might never have known the happy intelligence that she had born a man or woman ! Or that when she had carried me under her heart, I had lost my life at my birth ; and if I had been born, and had seen the light, that, when the congratulating people hastened on their camels, I had been gathered to my fathers.' " The Greeks and the Romans had their unlucky days (ἡμέραι ἀποφράδες, dies infausti) ; that is, days which were unpropitious, or in which they expected no success in any enterprise or any enjoyment. Tacitus (Annals, xiv. 12) mentions that the Roman Senate, for the purpose of flattering Nero, decreed that the birth-day of Agrippina should be regarded as an accursed day ; ut dies natalis Agrippinæ inter nefastos esset. See Rosenmüller, Alt. u. neue Morgenland, in loc. Expressions also similar to those before us, occur in Ovid, particularly in the following passage, Epist. ad Ibin:

Natus es infelix (ita Dii voluere), nec ulla
    Commoda nascenti stella, levisve fuit.

Lux quoque natalis, ne quid nisi tristo videres,
    Turpis, et inductis nubibus atra fuit.
Sedit in adverso nocturnus culmine bubo,
    Funereoque graves edidit ore sonos.

We have now similar days, which by common superstition are regarded as unlucky or inauspicious. The wish of Job seems to be, that the day of his birth might be regarded as one of those days.

4. *Let that day be darkness.* Let it not be day ; or, O, that it had not been day, that the sun had not risen, and that it had been night. ¶ *Let not God regard it from above.* The word rendered here "regard" (שׁרדּ) means properly to seek or inquire after, to ask for or demand. Dr. Good renders it here, "Let not God inclose it," but this meaning is not found in the Hebrew. Noyes renders it literally, "Let not God seek it." Herder, "Let not God inquire after it." The sense may be, either that Job wished the day sunk beneath the horizon, or in the deep waters by which he conceived the earth to be surrounded, and prays that God would not seek it and bring it from its dark abode ; or he desired that God would never inquire after it, that it might pass from his remembrance and be forgotten. What we value, we would wish God to remember and bless ; what we dislike, we would wish him to forget. This seems to be the idea here. Job hated that day, and he wished all other beings to forget it. He wished it blotted out, so that even God would never inquire after it, but regard it as if it had never been. ¶ *Neither let the light shine upon it.* Let it be utter darkness ; let not a ray ever reveal it. It will be seen here that Job first curses *the day.* The amplification of the curse with which he commenced in the first part of ver. third, continues through the fourth and fifth verses ; and then he returns to the *night,* which also (in the latter part of ver. 3) he wished to be cursed. His desires in regard to that unhappy night, he expresses in ver. 6—10.

5 Let darkness and the shadow of death stain ¹ it ; let a cloud dwell upon it ; ² let the blackness of the day terrify it.

1 or, *challenge.*

2 or. *let them terrify it, as those who have a bitter day,* Am. 8. 10.

---

5. Let darkness and the shadow of death. The Hebrew word צלמות *tzălmăvĕth* is exceedingly musical and poetical. It is derived from צל *tzel,* a shadow, and מות *măv'th, death;* and is used to denote the deepest darkness ; see Notes on Isa. ix. 2. It occurs frequently in the sacred Scriptures ; comp. Job x. 21, 22 ; Ps. xxiii. 4 ; Job xii. 22 ; xvi. 16 ; xxiv. 17 ; xxxiv. 22 ; xxxviii. 17 ; Amos v. 8 ; Jer. ii. 6. It is used to denote the abode of departed spirits, described by Job as " a land of darkness, as darkness itself ; of the shadow of death without any order, and where the light is as darkness ;" Job x. 21, 22. The idea seems to have been, that *death* was a dark and gloomy object that obstructed all light, and threw a baleful shade afar, and that that melancholy shade was thrown afar over the regions of the dead. The sense here is, that Job wished the deepest conceivable darkness to rest upon it. ¶ *Stain it.* Marg., or *challenge.* Vulg. *obscure it.* LXX., " take or occupy it," Ἐκλάβοι. Dr. Good, *crush it.* Noyes, *redeem it.* Herder, *seize it.* This variety of interpretation has arisen in part from the twofold signification of the word here used, גאל. The word means either to *redeem,* or to *defile, pollute, stain.* These senses are not very closely connected, and I know not how the one has grown out of the other, unless it be that redemption was accomplished with blood, and that the frequent sprinkling of blood on an altar rendered it defiled, or unclean. In one sense, blood thus sprinkled would purify, when it took away sin ; in another, it would render an object unclean or polluted. Gesenius says, that the latter signification occurs only in the later Hebrew. If the word here means to *redeem,* the sense is, that Job wished darkness to resume its dominion over the day, and redeem it to itself, and thus wholly to exclude the light. If the word means to defile or pollute, the sense is, that he desired the death-shade to stain the day wholly black ; to take out every ray of light, and to render it wholly obscure. Gesenius renders it in the former sense. The sense which Reiske and Dr. Good give to the word, " crush it," is not found in the Hebrew. The word means to defile, stain, or pollute, in the following places, viz. : it is rendered *pollute* and *polluted* in Mal. i. 7, 12 ; Zeph. iii. 1 ; Lam. iv. 14 ; Ezra ii. 62 ; Neh. vii. 64 ; *defile* or *defiled* in Isa. lix. 3 ; Dan. i. 8 ; Neh. xiii. 29 ; and *stain* in Isa. lxiii. 3. It seems to me that this is the sense here, and that the meaning has been well explained by Schultens, that Job wished that his birth-day should be involved in a deep *stain,* that it should be covered with clouds and storms, and made dark and dismal. This imprecation referred not only to the day on which he was born, but to each succeeding birth-day. Instead of its being on its return a bright and cheerful day, he wished that it might be annually a day of tempests and of terrors ; a day so marked that it would excite attention as peculiarly gloomy and inauspicious. It was a day whose return conveyed no pleasure to his soul, and which he wished no one to observe with gratitude or joy. ¶ *Let a cloud dwell upon it.* There is, as Dr. Good and others have remarked, much sublimity in this expression. The Hebrew word rendered *a cloud* (עננה) occurs nowhere else in this form. It is the feminine form of the word ענן, *a cloud,* and is used *collectively* to denote *clouds;* that is, clouds piled on clouds ; clouds " condensed, impacted, heaped together" (Dr. Good), and hence the gathered tempest, the clouds assembled deep and dark, and ready to burst forth in the fury of a storm. Theodotion renders it συννεφία, *assembled clouds ;* and hence darkness. Tho

LXX. render it γνόφος, *tempest,* or *thick darkness.* So Jerome, *caligo.* The word rendered "dwell upon it" (תשכן), means properly to *settle down,* and there to abide or dwell. Perhaps the original notion was that of fixing a tent, and so Schultens renders it, *Tentorium figat super eo Nubes,* "Let the cloud pitch its tent over it;" rendered by Dr. Good, "The gathered tempest pavilion over it!" "This is an image," says Schultens, "common among the Arabs." The sense is, that Job wished clouds piled on clouds to settle down on the day permanently, to make that day their abode, and to involve it in deep and eternal night. ¶ *Let the blackness of the day terrify it.* Marg. "Or, *Let them terrify it as those who have a bitter day.*" There has been great variety in the interpretation of this passage. Dr. Good renders it, "The blasts of noontide terrify it." Noyes, "Let whatever darkens the day terrify it." Herder, "The blackness of misfortune terrify it." Jerome, Et involvatur amaritudine, "let it be involved in bitterness." The LXX, καταραθείη ἡ ἡμέρα, "let the day be cursed." This variety has arisen from the difficulty of determining the sense of the Hebrew word used here and rendered "blackness," כמרירי. If it is supposed to be derived from the word כמר *kâmăr,* to be warm, to be hot, to burn, then it would mean the deadly heats of the day, the dry and sultry blasts which prevail so much in sandy deserts. Some writers suppose that there is a reference here to the poisonous wind Samum or Samiel, which sweeps over those deserts, and which is so much dreaded in the heat of summer. "Men as well as animals are often suffocated with this wind. For during a great heat, a current of air often comes which is still hotter; and when men and animals are so exhausted that they almost faint away with the heat, it seems that this little addition quite deprives them of breath. When a man is suffocated with this wind, or when, as they say, his heart is burst, blood is said to flow from his nose and ears two hours after his death. The body is said to remain long warm, to swell, to turn blue and green, and if the arm or leg is taken hold of to raise it up, the limb is said to come off." Burder's Oriental customs, No. 176. From the testimony of recent travellers, however. it would seem that the injurious effects of this wind have been greatly exaggerated. If this interpretation be the true one, then Job wished the day of his birth to be frightful and alarming, as when such a poisonous blast should sweep along all day, and render it a day of terror and dread. But this interpretation does not well suit the parallelism. Others, therefore, understand by the word, *obscurations,* or whatever darkens the day. Such is the interpretation of Gesenius, Bochart, Noyes, and some others. According to this, the reference is to eclipses or fearful storms which cover the day in darkness. The noun here is nootide found elsewhere; but the *verb* (כמר) is used in the sense of being black and dark in Lam. v. 10: "Our skin was black like an oven, because of the terrible famine;" or perhaps more literally, "Our skin is scorched as with a furnace, from the burning heat of famine." That which is burnt becomes black, and hence the word may mean that which is dark, obscure, and gloomy. This meaning suits the parallelism, and is a sense which the Hebrew will bear. Another interpretation regards the כ *kaph* as a prefix before the word מרירי *bitterness,* and then the sense is, "according to the bitterness of the day;" that is, the greatest calamities which can happen to a day. This sense is found in several of the ancient versions, and is adopted by Rosenmüller. To me it seems that the second interpretation proposed best suits the connection, and that the meaning is, that Job wished that every thing which could render the day gloomy and obscure might rest upon it. The Chaldee adds here, "Let it be as the bitterness of day—the grief with which Jeremiah was afflicted in being cut off from the house of the sanctuary, and Jonah in being cast into the sea of Tarshish."

6 *As for* that night, let darkness seize upon it; let it not be [1] joined unto the days of the year; let it not come into the number of the months.

7 Lo, let that night be soli-

---

6. As for *that night.* Job, having cursed the *day,* proceeds to utter a malediction on the *night* also; see ver. 3. This malediction extends to ver. 9. ¶ *Let darkness seize upon it.* Heb. Let it take it. Let deep and horrid darkness seize it as its own. Let no star arise upon it; let it be unbroken and uninterrupted gloom. The word *darkness,* however, does not quite express the force of the original. The word here used (אֵל) is poetic, and denotes darkness more intense than is denoted by the word which is usually rendered darkness (חֹשֶׁךְ). It is a darkness accompanied with clouds and with a tempest. Herder understands it as meaning, that darkness should seize upon that night and bear it away, so that it should not be joined to the months of the year. So the Chaldee. But the true sense is, that Job wished so deep darkness to possess it, that no star would rise upon it; no light whatever be seen. A night like this Seneca beautifully describes in Agamemnon, vs. 465, seq.

Nox prima cœlum sparserat stellis,
Cum subito luna conditur, stellæ cadunt;
In astra pontus tollitur, et cœlum petit.
Nec una nox est, densa tenebras obruit
Caligo, et omni luce subducta, fretum
Cœlumque miscet. . . .
Premunt tenebræ lumina, et diræ Stygis
Inferna nox est.

¶ *Let it not be joined unto the days of the year.* Marg. *rejoice among.* So Good and Noyes render it. The word used here (יַחַדְ), according to the present pointing, is the apocopated future of חָדָה, to *rejoice, to be glad.* If the pointing were different (יַחַד) it would be the future of יָחַד, to be one; to be united, or joined to. The Masoretic points are of no authority, and the interpretation which supposes that the word means here to exult or rejoice, is more poetical and beautiful. It is then a representation of the days of the year as rejoicing together, and a wish is expressed that *that* night

might never be allowed to partake of the general joy while the months rolled around. In this interpretation Rosenmüller and Gesenius concur. Dodwell supposes that there is an allusion to a custom among the ancients, by which inauspicious days were stricken from the calendar, and their place supplied by intercalary days. But there is no evidence of the existence of such a custom in the time of Job. ¶ *Let it not come,* &c. Let it never be reckoned among the days which go to make up the number of the months. Let there be always a blank there; let its place always be wanting.

7. Lo, let that night be solitary. Dr. Good, " O! that night! Let it be a barren rock!" Noyes, " O let that night be unfruitful!" Herder, " Let that night be set apart by itself." The Hebrew word used here (גַּלְמוּד) means properly *hard;* then sterile, barren, as of a hard and rocky soil. It does not mean properly solitary, but that which is unproductive and unfruitful. It is used of a woman who is barren, Isa. xlix. 21, and also of that which is lean, famished, emaciated with hunger; Job xv. 34; xxx. 3. According to this it means that that should be a night in which none would be born—a night of loneliness and desolation. According to Jerome, it means that the night should be solitary, lonely, and gloomy; a night in which no one would venture forth to make a journey, and in which none would come together to rejoice. Thus interpreted, the night would resemble that which is so beautifully described by Virgil, Æn. vi. 268:

Ibant obscuri sola sub nocte per umbras,
Perque domos Ditis vacuas et inania regna.

It is probable, however, that the former is the correct interpretation. ¶ *Let no joyful voice come therein.* Let there be no sound of praise and rejoicing. The Chaldee paraphrases this, " Let not the crowing of a cock be heard in it." The sense of the

tary; let no joyful voice come therein.

8 Let them curse it that curse

the day, who [a] are ready to raise up [1] their mourning.

a Je. 9. 17, 20.   1 or, a *leviathan*.

whole is, that Job wished that night to be wholly desolate. He wished there might be no assembling for amusement, congratulation, or praise, no marriage festivals, and no rejoicing at the birth of children ; he would have it as noiseless, solitary, and sad, as if all animals and men were dead, and no voice were heard. It was a night hateful to him, and he would have it in no way remembered.

8. *Let them curse it who curse the day.* This entire verse is exceedingly difficult, and many different expositions have been given of it. It seems evident that it refers to some well-known class of persons, who were accustomed to utter imprecations, and were supposed to have the power to render a day propitious or unpropitious—persons who had the power of divination or enchantment. A belief in such a power existed early in the world, and has prevailed in all savage and semi-barbarous nations, and even in nations considerably advanced in civilization. The origin of this was a desire to look into futurity ; and in order to accomplish this, a league was supposed to be made with the spirits of the dead, who were acquainted with the events of the invisible world, and who could be prevailed on to impart their knowledge to favoured mortals. It was supposed, also, that by such union there might be a power exerted which would appear to be miraculous. Such persons also claimed to be the favourites of heaven, and to be endowed with control over the elements, and over the destiny of men; to have the power to bless and to curse, to render propitious or calamitous. Balaam was believed to be endowed with this power, and hence he was sent for by Balak, king of Moab, to curse the Israelites ; Num. xxii. 5, 6 ; see Notes on Isa. viii. 19. The practice of cursing the day, or cursing the sun, is said by Herodotus to have prevailed among a people of Africa, whom he calls the Atlantes, living in the vicinity of Mount Atlas.

" Of all mankind," says he, " of whom we have any knowledge, the Atlantes alone have no distinction of names ; the body of the people are termed Atlantes, but their individuals have no appropriate appellation. When the sun is at the highest they heap on it reproaches and execrations, because their country and themselves are parched by its rays ;" book iv. 184. The same account of them is found in Pliny, Nat. His. v. 8: Solem orientem occidentemque dira imprecatione contuentur, ut exitialem ipsis agrisque. See also Strabo, Lib. xvii. p. 780. Some have supposed, also, that there may be an allusion here to a custom which seems early to have prevailed of hiring people to mourn for the dead, and who probably in their official lamentation bewailed or cursed the day of their calamity; comp. Jer. ix. 17; 2 Chron. xxxv. 25. But the correct interpretation is doubtless that which refers it to pretended prophets, priests, or diviners—who were supposed to have power to render a day one of ill omen. Such a power Job wished exerted over that unhappy night when he was born. He desired that the curses of those who had power to render a day unpropitious or unlucky, should rest upon it. ¶ *Who are ready to raise up their mourning.* This is not very intelligible, and it is evident that our translators were embarrassed by the passage. They seem to have supposed that there was an allusion here to the practice of employing professional mourners, and that the idea is, that Job wished that they might be employed to howl over the day as inauspicious, or as a day of ill omen. The margin is, as in the Heb., *a leviathan.* The word rendered *ready* (עֲרִידָי‎), means properly ready, prepared; and then practised or skilful. This is the idea here. that they were practised or skilful in calling up the *leviathan;* see Schultens *in loc.* The word rendered in the text *mourning,* and in the margin *leviathan* (לִוְיָתָן‎), in all other parts of the sa-

9 Let the stars of the twilight thereof be dark; let it look for light, but *have* none; neither let it see the [1] dawning of the day;

10 Because it shut not up the doors of my *mother's* womb, nor hid sorrow from mine eyes.

[1] *eyelids of the morning.*

---

cred Scriptures denotes an animal; see it explained in the Notes on Isa. xxvii. 1, and more fully in the Notes on Job xli. It usually denotes the crocodile, or some huge sea monster. Here it is evidently used to represent the most fierce, powerful and frightful of all the animals known, and the allusion is to some power claimed by necromancers to call forth the most terrific monsters at their will from distant places, from the "vasty deep," from morasses and impenetrable forests. The general claim was, that they had control over all nature: that they could curse the day, and make it of ill omen, and that the most mighty and terrible of land or sea monsters were entirely under their control. If they had such a power, Job wished that they would exercise it to curse the night in which he was born. On what pretensions they founded this claim is unknown. The power, however, of taming serpents, is practised in India at this day; and jugglers bear around with them the most deadly of the serpent race, having extracted their fangs, and creating among the credulous the belief that they have control over the most noxious animals. Probably some such art was claimed by the ancients, and to some such pretension Job alludes here.

9. *Let the stars of the twilight thereof be dark.* That is, be extinguished, so that it shall be total darkness—darkness not even relieved by a single star. The word here rendered *twilight* (נֶשֶׁף) means properly a breathing; and hence the evening, when cooling breezes *blow*, or gently breathe. It is used however to denote both the morning and the evening twilight, though here probably it means the latter. He wishes that the evening of that night, instead of being in any way illuminated, should *set in* with total darkness and continue so. The LXX. render it, *night.* ¶ *Let it look for light, but have none.* Personify-

ing the night, and representing it as looking out anxiously for some ray of light. This is a beautiful poetic image—the image of *Night*, dark and gloomy and sad, anxiously looking out for a single beam or a star to break in upon its darkness and diminish its gloom. ¶ *Neither let it see the dawning of the day.* Margin, more literally and more beautifully, *eyelids of the morning.* The word rendered "dawning" (עַפְעַפֵּי) means properly *the eyelashes* (from עוּף *to fly*), and it is given to them from their flying or fluttering. The word rendered "day" (שַׁחַר) means the aurora, the morning. The sun when he is above the horizon is called by the poets the eye of day; and hence his earliest beams, before he is risen, are called the eyelids or eyelashes of the morning opening upon the world. This figure is common in the ancient classics, and occurs frequently in the Arabic poets; see Schultens *in loc.* Thus in Soph. Antiq. 104, the phrase occurs, Ἀμέρας βλέφαρον. So in Milton's Lycidas,

"——Ere the high lawns appeared
Under the opening eyelids of the dawn,
We drive afield."

Job's wish was, that there might be no star in the evening twilight, and that no ray might illuminate that of the morning; that it might be enveloped in perpetual, unbroken darkness.

10. *Because it shut not up,* &c. That is, because the accursed day and night did not do it. Aben Ezra supposes that God is meant here, and that the complaint of Job is that he did not close his mother's womb. But the more natural interpretation is to refer it to the Νυχθήμερον—the night and the day which he had been cursing, on which he was born. Throughout the description the day and the night are personified, and are spoken of as active in introducing him into the world. He here curses them because they did not wholly prevent his birth. ¶ *Nor hid sorrow*

11 Why died I not from the
womb? *why* did I *not* give up the
ghost when I came out of the belly?
12 Why did the knees *a* prevent

a Is.66.12.

me? or why the breasts that I
should suck?
13 For now should I have lain
still and been quiet, I should have
slept: then had I been at rest,

from mine eyes. By preventing my
being born. The meaning is, that he
would not have known sorrow if he
had then died.

11. *Why died I not from the womb?*
Why did I not die as soon as I was
born? Why were any pains taken to
keep me alive? The suggestion of this
question leads Job in the following
verses into the beautiful description
of what he would have been if he had
then died. He complains, therefore,
that any pains were taken by his friends
to keep him alive, and that he was
not suffered peacefully to expire.
¶ *Gave up the ghost.* A phrase that
is often used in the English version
of the Bible to denote death; Gen.
xlix. 33; Job xi. 20; xiv. 10; Jer. xv.
9; Matt. xxvii. 50; Acts v. 10. It
conveys an idea, however, which is
not necessarily in the original, though
the idea in itself is not incorrect. The
idea conveyed by the phrase is that of
yielding up the *spirit* or *soul,* while
the sense of the original here and elsewhere is simply *to expire, to die.*

12. *Why did the knees prevent me?*
That is, the lap of the nurse or of
the mother, probably the latter. The
sense is, that if he had not been deli-
cately and tenderly nursed, he would
have died at once. He came helpless
into the world, and but for the attention of others he would have soon
died. Jahn supposes (Archæ. § 161)
that it was a common custom for the
father, on the birth of a son, to clasp
the new-born child to his bosom,
while music was heard to sound, and
by this ceremony to declare it as his
own. That there was some such
recognition of a child or expression
of paternal regard, is apparent from
Gen. l. 23. Probably, however, the
whole sense of the passage is expressed by the tender care which is necessarily shown to the new-born infant
to preserve it alive. The word rendered "prevent" here (קִדֵּם), means
properly to anticipate, to go before,

as the English word *prevent* formerly
did; and hence it means to go to meet
any one in order to aid him in any
way. There is much beauty in the
word here. It refers to the provision
which God has made in the tender
affection of the parent to *anticipate*
the wants of the child. The arrangement has been made beforehand.
God has taken care when the feeble
and helpless infant is born, that tender
affection has been already created and
prepared to meet it. It has not to be
created then; it is not to be excited
by the suffering of the child; it is
already in existence as an active,
powerful, and self-denying principle,
to *anticipate* the wants of the new-
born babe, and to save it from death.

13. *For now should I have lain still.*
In this verse Job uses *four* expressions to describe the state in which
he would have been if he had been
so happy as to have died when an
infant. It is evidently a very pleasant subject to him, and he puts it in
a great variety of form. He uses the
words which express the most quiet
repose, a state of perfect rest, a gentle
slumber; and then in the next verses
he says, that instead of being in the
miserable condition in which he then
was, he would have been in the same
state with kings and the most illustrious men of the earth. ¶ *I should
have lain still*—שָׁכַבְתִּי. I should have
been *lying down,* as one does who is
taking grateful repose. This is a
word of less strength than any of those
which follow. ¶ *And been quiet*—
אֶשְׁקוֹט. A word of stronger signification than that before used. It means
to rest, to lie down, to have quiet. It
is used of one who is never troubled,
harassed, or infested by others, Judg.
iii. 11; v. 31; viii. 28; and of one who
has no fear or dread, Ps. lxxvi. 9.
The meaning is, that he would not
only have lain down, but would have
been perfectly tranquil. Nothing
would have harassed him, nothing

14 With kings and counsellors of the earth, which built deso-

late ^a places for themselves;
a ch. 15.28.

would have given him any annoyance. ¶ *I should have slept*—רשנתי. This expression also is in advance of those before used. There would not only have been *quiet*, but there would have been a calm and gentle slumber. Sleep is often represented as "the kinsman of death." Thus Virgil speaks of it:

"Tum consanguineus Leti sopor—"
Æn. vi. 278.

So Homer:

Ενθ' ύπνῳ ξύμβλητο κασιγνήτῳ θανάτοιο—
Iliad, xiv. 231.

This comparsion is an obvious one, and is frequently used in the classic writers. It is employed to denote the calmness, stillness, and quiet of death. In the Scriptures it frequently occurs, and with a significancy far more beautiful. It is there employed not only to denote the tranquillity of death, but also to denote the Christian hopes of a resurrection and the prospect of being awakened out of the long sleep. We lie down to rest at night with the hopes of awaking again. We sleep calmly, with the expectation that it will be only a temporary repose, and that we shall be aroused, invigorated for augmented toil, and refreshed for sweeter pleasure. So the Christian lies down in the grave. So the infant is committed to the calm slumber of the tomb. It may be a sleep stretching on through many nights and weeks and years and centuries, and even cycles of ages, but it is not eternal. The eyes will be opened again to behold the beauties of creation; the ear will be unstopped to hear the sweet voice of friendship and the harmony of music; and the frame will be raised up beautiful and immortal to engage in the service of the God that made us; comp. Ps. xiii. 3; xc. 5; John xi. 11.; 1 Cor. xv. 51; 1 Thess. iv. 14; v. 10. Whether *Job* used the word in this sense and with this understanding, has been made a matter of question, and will be considered more fully in the examination of the passage in chap. xix. 25—27. ¶ *Then had I been at rest.* Instead of the troubles and anxieties which I

now experience. That is, he would have been lying in calm and honourable repose with the kings and princes of the earth. 14. *With kings.* Reposing as they do. This is the language of calm meditation on what would have been the consequence if he had died when he was an infant. He seems to delight to dwell on it. He contrasts it with his present situation. He pauses on the thought that that would have been an honourable repose. He would have been numbered with kings and princes. Is there not here a little spice of ambition even in his sorrows and humiliation? Job had been an eminently rich man; a man greatly honoured; an emir; a magistrate; one in whose presence even princes refrained talking, and before whom nobles held their peace; chap. xxix. 9. Now he was stripped of his honours, and made to sit in ashes. But had he died when an infant, he would have been numbered with kings and counsellors, and would have shared their lot. Death is repulsive; but Job takes comfort in the thought that he would have been associated with the most exalted and honourable among men. There is some consolation in the idea that when an infant dies he is associated with the most honoured and exalted of the race; there *is* consolation in the reflection that when we die we shall lie down with the good and the great of all past times, and that though our bodies shall moulder back to dust, and be forgotten, we are sharing the same lot with the most beautiful, lovely, wise, pious, and mighty of the race. To Christians there is the richest of all consolations in the thought that they will sleep as their Saviour did in the tomb, and that the grave, naturally so repulsive, has been made sacred and even attractive by being the place where the Redeemer reposed.

Why should we tremble to convey
Their bodies to the tomb?
There the dear flesh of Jesus lay,
And left a long perfume.

15 Or with princes that had gold, who filled their houses with silver: [a] Ps.58.8.

16 Or as an hidden untimely birth [a] I had not been ; as infants *which* never saw light.

The graves of all his saints he blessed,
And softened every bed :
Where should the dying members rest
But with the dying Head ?

¶ *And counsellors of the earth.* Great and wise men who were qualified to give counsel to kings in times of emergency. ¶ *Which built desolate places for themselves.* Gesenius supposes that the word here used (הרבות) means palaces which would soon be in ruins. So Noyes renders it, " Who build up for themselves —ruins !" That is, they build splendid palaces, or perhaps tombs, which are destined soon to fall to ruin. Dr. Good renders it, "Who restored to themselves the ruined wastes ;" that is, the princes who restored to their former magnificence the ruins of ancient cities, and built their palaces in them. But it seems to me that the idea is different. It is, that kings constructed for their own burial, magnificent tombs or mausoleums, which were lonely and desolate places, where they might lie in still and solemn grandeur ; comp. Notes on Isa. xiv. 18. Sometimes these were immense excavations from rocks ; and sometimes they were stupendous structures built as tombs. What more desolate and lonely places could be conceived than the pyramids of Egypt —reared probably as the burial places of kings ? What more lonely and solitary than the small room in the centre of one of those immense structures, where the body of the monarch is supposed to have been deposited ? And what more emphatic than the expression—though " so nearly pleonastic that it may be omitted " *(Noyes)* —"for themselves"? To my view, that is far from being pleonastic. It is full of emphasis. The immense structure was made for *them.* It was not to be a common burial-place ; it was not for the public good ; it was not to be an abode for the living and a contributor to their happiness : it was a matter of supreme selfishness and pride—an immense structure built only FOR THEMSELVES. With such persons lying in their places of lonely

grandeur, Job felt it would be an honour to be associated. Compared with his present condition it was one of dignity ; and he earnestly wished that it might have been his lot thus early to have been consigned to the fellowship of the dead. It may be some confirmation of this view to remark, that the land of Edom, near which Job is supposed to have lived, contains at this day some of the most wonderful sepulchral monuments of the world ; comp. Notes on Isa. xvii.1.

15. *Or with princes that had gold.* That is, he would have been united with the rich and the great. Is there not here too also a slight evidence of the fondness for wealth, which might have been one of the errors of this good man ? Would it not seem that such was his estimate of the importance of being esteemed rich, that he would count it an honour to be united with the affluent in death, rather than be subjected to a condition of poverty and want among the living ? ¶ *Who filled their houses with silver.* Rosenmüller supposes that there is reference here to the custom among the ancients of burying treasures with the dead, and that the word *houses* refers to the tombs or mausoleums which they erected. That such a custom prevailed, there can be no doubt. Josephus informs us that large quantities of treasure were buried in the tomb with David, which afterwards was taken out for the supply of an army ; and Schultens *(in loc.)* says that the custom prevailed extensively among the Arabs. The custom of burying valuable objects with the dead was practised also among the aborigines of N. America, and is to this day practised in Africa. If this be the sense here, then the idea of Job was, that he would have been in his grave united with those who even there were accompanied with wealth, rather than suffering the loss of all his property as he was among the living.

16. *Or as an hidden untimely birth.* As an abortion which is hid, or con-

17 There the wicked cease *from* troubling; and there the [1] weary be at rest.

1 *wearied in strength.*

18 *There* the prisoners rest together; they hear not the voice of the oppressor.

cealed; that is, which is soon removed from the sight. So the Psalmist, lviii. 8:

As a snail which melteth, let them dissolve;
As the untimely birth of a woman, that they
may not see the sun.

Sept. ἔκτρωμα, the same word which is used by Paul in 1 Cor. xv. 8, with reference to himself; see Notes on that place. ¶ *I had not been.* I should have perished; I should not have been a man, as I now am, subject to calamity. The meaning is, that he would have been taken away and concealed, as such an untimely birth is, and that he would never have been numbered among the living and the suffering. ¶ *As infants* which *never saw light.* Job expresses here no opinion of their future condition, or on the question whether such infants had immortal souls. He is simply saying that his lot would have been as theirs was, and that he would have been saved from the sorrows which he now experienced.

17. *There the wicked cease* from *troubling.* In the grave — where kings and princes and infants lie. This verse is often applied to heaven, and the language is such as will express the condition of that blessed world. But as used by Job it had no such reference. It relates only to the grave. It is language which beautifully expresses the condition of the dead, and the *desirableness* even of an abode in the tomb. They who are there, are free from the vexations and annoyances to which men are exposed in this life. The wicked cannot torture their limbs by the fires of persecution, or wound their feelings by slander, or oppress and harass them in regard to their property, or distress them by thwarting their plans, or injure them by impugning their motives. All is peaceful and calm in the grave, and *there* is a place where the malicious designs of wicked men cannot reach us. The object of this verse and the two following is,

to show the *reasons* why it was desirable to be in the grave, rather than to live and to suffer the ills of this life. We are not to suppose that Job referred exclusively to his own case in all this. He is describing, in general, the happy condition of the dead, and we have no reason to think that he had been particularly annoyed by wicked men. But the pious often are, and hence it should be a matter of gratitude that there is *one* place, at least, where the wicked cannot annoy the good; and where the persecuted, the oppressed, and the slandered may lie down in peace. ¶ *And there the weary be at rest.* Marg. *Wearied in strength.* The margin is in accordance with the Hebrew. The meaning is, those whose strength is exhausted; who are worn down by the toils and cares of life, and who feel the need of rest. Never was more beautiful language employed than occurs in this verse. What a charm such language throws even over the grave — like strewing flowers, and planting roses around the tomb! Who should fear to die, if prepared, when such is to be the condition of the dead? Who is there that is not in some way troubled by the wicked — by their thoughtless, ungodly life; by persecution, contempt, and slander? comp. 2 Pet. ii. 8; Ps. xxxix. 1. Who is there that is not at some time weary with his load of care, anxiety, and trouble? Who is there whose strength does not become exhausted, and to whom rest is not grateful and refreshing? And who is there, therefore, to whom, if prepared for heaven, the grave would not be a place of calm and grateful rest? And though true religion will not prompt us to wish that we had lain down there in early childhood, as Job wished, yet no dictate of piety is violated when we look forward with calm delight to the time when *we* may repose where the wicked cease from troubling, and where the weary be at rest. O grave, thou art a peaceful

19 The small and great are there; and the servant *is* free from his master.

spot! Thy rest is calm: thy slumbers are sweet.

Nor pain, nor grief, nor anxious fear
Invade thy bounds. No mortal woes
Can reach the peaceful sleeper here,
Wh le angels watch the soft repose.

So Jesus slept; God's dying Son
Passed through the grave, and blest the bed.

18. There *the prisoners rest together*. Herder translates this, "There the prisoners rejoice in their freedom." The LXX. strangely enough, "There they of old (οἱ αἰώνιοι) assembled together (ὁμοθυμαδόν) have not heard the voice of the exactor." The Hebrew word שׁאן means to rest, to be quiet, to be tranquil; and the sense is, that they are in the grave freed from chains and oppressions. ¶ *They hear not the voice of the oppressor.* Of him who exacted taxes, and who laid on them heavy burdens, and who imprisoned them for imaginary crimes. He who is bound in chains, and who has no other prospect of release, can look for it in the grave and will find it there. Similar sentiments are found respecting death in Seneca *ad Marciam*, 20: "Mors omnibus finis, multis remedium, quibusdam votum; hæc servitutem invito domino remittit; hæc captivorum catenas levat; hæc a carcere reducit, quos exire imperium impotens vetuerat; hæc exulibus, in patriam semper animum oculosque tendentibus, ostendit, nihil interesse inter quos quisque jaceat; hæc, ubi res communes fortuna male divisit, et æquo jure genitos alium alii donavit, exæquat omnia; hæc est, quæ nihil quidquam alieno fecit arbitrio; hæc est, ea quâ nemo humilitatem suam sensit; hæc est, quae nulli paruit." The sense in Job is, that all are at liberty in death. Chains no longer bind; prisons no longer incarcerate; the voice of oppression no longer alarms.

19. *The small and the great are there.* The old and the young, the high and the low. Death levels all. It shows no respect to age; it spares

20 Wherefore is light given to him that is in misery, and life unto the bitter *in* soul;

none because they are vigorous, young, or beautiful. This sentiment has probably been expressed in various forms in all languages, for all men are made deeply sensible of its truth. The classic reader will recall the ancient proverb,

Mors sceptra ligonibus æquat,

and the language of Horace:

Æquæ lege Necessitas
Sortitur insignes et imos.
Omne capax movet urna nomen.
Tristis unda scilicet omnibus,
Quicunque terræ munere vescimur,
Enaviganda, sive reges,
Sive inopes erimus coloni.
Divesne prisco natus ab Inacho
Nil interest, an pauper et infima
De gente sub dio moreris
Victima nil miserantis Orci.
Omnes eodem cogimur. Omnium
Versatur urna. Serius, ocyus,
Sors exitura.
—Omnes una manet nox,
Et calcanda semel via leti. [Nullum
Mista senum ac juvenum densantur funera.
Sæva caput Proserpina fugit. [tabernas
Pallida mors æquo pulsat pede pauperum
Regumque turres.

¶ *And the servant* is *free from his master.* Slavery is at an end in the grave. The master can no longer tax the powers of the slave, can no longer scourge him or exact his uncompensated toil. Slavery early existed, and there is evidence here that it was known in the time of Job. But Job did not regard it as a desirable institution; for assuredly that is not desirable from which death would be regarded as a *release*, or where death would be preferable. Men often talk about slavery as a valuable condition of society, and sometimes appeal even to the Scriptures to sustain it; but Job felt that *it was worse than death*, and that the grave was to be preferred because there the slave would be free from his master. The word here used and rendered "free" (חפשׁי) properly expresses manumission from slavery. See it explained at length in my Notes on Isa. lviii. 6.

20. *Wherefore is light given to him that is in misery?* The word *light* here is used undoubtedly to denote *life*. This verse commences a new

21 Which [1] long [a] for death, but it *cometh* not ; and dig for it more than for hid treasures ;

22 Which rejoice exceedingly, *and*

1 *wait.*   *a* Re.9.6.   *b* chap. 19.8 ; La.3.7.

are glad when they can find the grave ?

23 *Why is light given* to a man whose way is hid, and whom God hath hedged [b] in ?

---

part of Job's complaint. It is that God keeps men alive who would prefer to die ; that he furnishes them with the means of sustaining existence, and actually preserves them, when they would consider it an inestimable blessing to expire. Schultens remarks, on this part of the chapter, that the tone of Job's complaint is considerably modified. He has given vent to his strong feelings, and the language here is more mild and gentle. Still it implies a reflection on God. It is not the language of humble submission. It contains an implied charge of cruelty and injustice ; and it laid the foundation for some of the just reproofs which follow. ¶ *And life unto the bitter* in *soul.* Who are suffering bitter grief. We use the word *bitter* yet to denote great grief and pain.

21. *Which long for death.* Whose pain and anguish are so great that they would regard it as a privilege to die. Much as men dread death, and much as they have occasion to dread what is beyond, yet there is no doubt that this often occurs. Pain becomes so intense, and suffering is so protracted, that they would regard it as a privilege to be permitted to die. Yet that sorrow *must* be intense which prompts to this wish, and usually must be long continued. In ordinary cases such is the love of life, and such the dread of death and of what is beyond, that men are willing to bear all that human nature can endure rather than meet death ; see Notes on chap. ii. 4. This idea has been expressed with unsurpassed beauty by Shakspeare :

For who would bear the whips and scorns of
    time,
The oppressor's wrong, the proud man's con-
    tumely.
The pangs of despised love, the law's delay,
The insolence of office, and the spurns
That patient merit of the unworthy takes,
When he himself might his quietus make
With a bare bodkin ? Who would fardels bear,
To grunt and sweat under a weary life,

But that the dread of something after death—
The undiscovered country, from whose bourne
No traveller returns—puzzles the will ;
And makes us rather bear those ills we have,
Than fly to others that we know not of.
                                        HAMLET.

¶ *And dig for it.* That is, express a stronger desire for it than men do who dig for treasures in the earth. Nothing would more forcibly express the intense desire to die than this expression.

22. *Which rejoice exceedingly.* Heb. " Who rejoice upon joy or exultation " (אֱלֵי־גִיל), that is, with exceedingly great joy. ¶ *When they can find the grave.* What an expression ! How strikingly does it express the intense desire to die, and the depth of a man's sorrow, when it becomes a matter of exultation for him to be permitted to lie down in the corruption and decay of the tomb ! A somewhat similar sentiment occurs in Euripides, as quoted by Cicero, Tusc. Quæst. Lib. 1, cap. 48 :

Nam nos decebat, domum
Lugere, ubi esset aliquis in lucem editus,
Humanæ vitæ varia reputantes mala ;
At, qui labores morte finisset graves
Hunc omni amicos laude et lætitia exsequi.

23. Why is light given *to a man whose way is hid ?* That is, who does not know what way to take, and who sees no escape from the misery that surrounds him. ¶ *Whom God hath hedged in;* see Notes, chap. i. 10. The meaning here is, that God had surrounded him as with a high wall or hedge, so that he could not move freely. Job asks with impatience, why light, i. e. life, should be given to such a man ? Why should he not be permitted to die ? This closes the complaint of Job, and the remaining verses of the chapter contain a statement of his sorrowful condition, and of the fact that he had now been called to suffer all that he had ever apprehended.—In regard to the questions here proposed by Job (ver 20—23), we may remark, that there was

24 For my sighing cometh be-

1 *my meat.*

fore [1] I eat, and my roarings are poured out like the waters

1 *my meat.*

doubtless much impatience on his part, and not a little improper feeling. The language shows that Job was not absolutely sinless ; but let us not harshly blame him. What he says, is a *statement* of feelings which often pass through the mind, though they are not often expressed. Who, in deep and protracted sorrows, has not found such questions rising up in his soul—questions which required all his energy and all his firmness of principle, and all the strength which he could gain by prayer, to suppress? To the questions themselves, it may be difficult to give an answer ; and it is certain that none of the friends of Job furnished a solution of the difficulty. When it is asked, why a man is kept in misery on earth, when he would be glad to be released by death, perhaps the following, among others, may be the reasons: (1.) Those sufferings may be the very means which are needful to develope the true state of the soul. Such was the case with Job. (2.) They may be the proper punishment of sin in the heart, of which the individual was not fully aware, but which may be distinctly seen by God. There may be pride, and the love of ease, and self-confidence, and ambition, and a desire of reputation. Such appear to have been some of the besetting sins of Job. (3.) They are needful to teach true submission, and to show whether a man is willing to resign himself to God. (4.) They may be the very things which are necessary to prepare the individual to die. At the same time that men often desire death, and feel that it would be a relief, it might be to them the greatest possible calamity. They may be wholly unprepared for it. For a sinner, the grave contains no rest; the eternal world furnishes no repose. One design of God in such sorrows may be, to show to the wicked how *intolerable* will be future pain, and how important it is for them to be ready to die. If they cannot bear the pains and sorrows of a few hours in this short life, how can they endure

eternal sufferings? If it is so desirable to be released from the sorrows of the body here,—if it is felt that the grave, with all that is repulsive in it, would be a place of repose, how important is it to find some way to be secured from everlasting pains! The true place of release from suffering for a sinner, is not the grave ; it is in the pardoning mercy of God, and in that pure heaven to which he is invited through the blood of the cross. In that holy heaven is the only real repose from suffering and from sin ; and heaven will be all the sweeter in proportion to the extremity of pain which is endured on earth.

24. *For my sighing cometh before I eat.* Marg. *My meat.* Dr. Good renders this, " Behold ! my sighing takes the place of my daily food, ' and refers to Ps. xlii. 3, as an illustration:

My tears are my meat day and night.

So substantially Schultens renders it, and explains it as meaning, " My sighing comes in the manner of my food," *Suspirium ad modum panis veniens*—and supposes it to mean that his sighs and groans were like his daily food ; or were constant and unceasing. Dr. Noyes explains it as meaning, " My sighing comes on when I begin to eat, and prevents my taking my daily nourishment;' and appeals to a similar expression in Juvenal. Sat. xiii. 211:

Perpetua anxietas, nec mensæ tempore cessat.

Rosenmüller gives substantially the same explanation, and remarks, also, that some suppose that the mouth, hands, and tongue of Job were so affected with disease, that the effort to eat increased his sufferings, and brought on a renewal of his sorrows. The same view is given by Origen ; and this is probably the correct sense. ¶ *And my roarings.* My deep and heavy groans. ¶ *Are poured out like the waters.* That is, (1.) *in number* — they were like rolling billows, or like the heaving deep. (2.) Perhaps also in *sound* like them. His groans were like the troubled ocean, that can

25 For [1] the thing which I greatly feared is come upon me, and that which I was afraid of is come unto me.

26 I was not in safety, neither had I rest, neither was I quiet ; yet trouble came.

1 *I feared a fear, and it came upon me.*

be heard afar. Perhaps, also, (3.) he means to say that his groans were attended with " a flood of tears," or that his tears were like the waves of the sea. - There is some hyperbole in the figure, in whichever way it is understood ; but we are to remember that his feelings were deeply excited, and that the Orientals were in the habit of expressing themselves in a mode, which to us, of more phlegmatic temperament, may seem extravagant in the extreme. We have, however, a similar expression when we say of one that " he burst into a *flood of tears.*"

25. *For the thing which I greatly feared.* Marg. As in the Hebrew, " I feared a fear, and it came upon me." This verse, with the following, has received a considerable variety of exposition. Many have understood it as referring to his whole course of life, and suppose that Job meant to say that he was always apprehensive of some great calamity, such as that which had now come upon him, and that in the time of his highest prosperity he had lived in continual alarm lest his property should be taken away, and lest he should be reduced to penury and suffering. This is the opinion of Drusius and Codurcus. In reply to this, Schultens has remarked, that such a supposition is contrary to all probability ; that there was no reason to apprehend that such calamities as he now suffered, would come upon him ; that they were so unusual that they could not have been anticipated ; and that, therefore, the alarm here spoken of, could not refer to the general tenor of his life. That seems to have been happy and calm, and perhaps, if any thing, too tranquil and secure. Most interpreters suppose that it refers to the state in which he was *during* his trial, and that it is designed to describe the rapid succession of his woes. Such is the interpretation of Rosenmüller,

Schultens, Drs. Good, Noyes, Gill, and others. According to this, it means that his calamities came on him in quick succession. He had no time after one calamity to become composed before another came. When he heard of one misfortune, he naturally dreaded another, and they came on with overwhelming rapidity. If this be the correct interpretation, it means that the source of his lamentation is not merely the greatness of his losses and his trials considered in the *aggregate,* but the extraordinary rapidity with which they succeeded each other, thus rendering them much more difficult to be borne ; see chap. i. He apprehended calamity, and it came suddenly. When one part of his property was taken, he had deep apprehensions respecting the rest ; when all his property was seized or destroyed, he had alarm about his children ; when the report came that they were dead, he feared some other affliction still. The sentiment is in accordance with human nature, that when we are visited with severe calamity in one form, we naturally dread it in another. The mind becomes exquisitely sensitive. The affections cluster around the objects of attachment which are left, and they become dear to us. When one child is taken away, our affections cling more closely to the one which survives, and any little illness alarms us, and the value of one object of affection is more and more increased—like the Sybil's leaves —as another is removed. It is an instinct of our nature, too, to apprehend calamity in quick succession when one comes. " Misfortunes seldom come alone ;" and when we suffer the loss of one endeared object, we instinctively feel that there may be a succession of blows that will remove all our comforts from us. Such seems to have been the apprehension of Job.

26. *I was not in safety.* That is,

I have, or I had no peace. שלותי
Sept. οὔτε εἰρήνευσα—*I had no peace.*
The sense is, that his mind had been
disturbed with fearful alarms; or perhaps that at that time he was filled
with dread. ¶ *Neither had I rest.*
Trouble comes upon me in every
form, and I am a stranger wholly to
peace. The accumulation of phrases
here, all meaning nearly the same
thing, is descriptive of a state of great
agitation of mind. Such an accumulation is not uncommon in the Bible
to denote any thing which language
can scarcely describe. So in Isa.
viii. 22:

> And they shall look upward;
> And to the earth shall they look;
> And lo! trouble and darkness,
> Gloom, oppression, and deepened darkness.

So Job x. 21, 22:

> To the land of darkness and the death-shade,
> The land of darkness like the blackness of the
>   death-shade,
> Where is no order, and where the light is as
>   darkness.

Thus in the Hamasa (quoted by Dr.
Good), "Death, and devastation, and
a remorseless disease, and a still
heavier and more terrific family of
evils." The Chaldee has made a remarkable addition here, arising from
the general design in the author of
that Paraphrase, to explain every
thing. "Did I not dissemble when
the annunciation was made to me respecting the oxen and the asses?
Was I not stupid [unalarmed, or unmoved, שדיכית], when the report came
about the conflagration? Was I not
quiet, when the report came respecting the camels? And did not indignation come, when the report was
made respecting my sons?" ¶ *Yet
trouble came.* Or rather, "and trouble
comes." This is one of the cumula-
tive expressions to denote the rapidity and the intensity of his sorrows.
The word rendered *trouble* (רגז) means
properly trembling, commotion, dis-
quiet. Here it signifies such misery
as made him tremble. Once the word
means wrath (Hab. iii. 2); and it is
so understood here by the LXX, who
render it ὀργή.

In regard to this chapter, containing the first speech of Job, we may
remark, that it is impossible to approve the spirit which it exhibits, or
to believe that it was acceptable to
God. It laid the foundation for the
reflections—many of them exceedingly just—in the following chapters, and
led his friends to doubt whether such
a man could be truly pious. The
spirit which is manifested in this chapter, is undoubtedly far from that calm
submission which religion should have
produced, and from that which Job
had before evinced. That he was, in
the main, a man of eminent holiness
and patience, the whole book demonstrates; but this chapter is one of the
conclusive proofs that he was not absolutely free from imperfection. From
the chapter we may learn, (1.) That
even eminently good men sometimes
give utterance to sentiments which
are a departure from the spirit of religion, and which they will have occasion to regret. Such was the case
here. There was a language of complaint, and a bitterness of expression,
which religion cannot sanction, and
which no pious man, on reflection,
would approve. (2.) We see the effect of heavy affliction on the mind.
It sometimes becomes overwhelming.
It is so great that all the ordinary
barriers against impatience are swept
away. The sufferer is left to utter
language of murmuring, and there is
the impatient wish that life was closed, or that he had not existed. (3.)
We are not to infer that because a
man in affliction makes use of some
expressions which we cannot approve,
and which are not sanctioned by the
word of God, that therefore he is not
a good man. There may be true piety,
yet it may be far from perfection;
there may be in general submission to
God, yet the calamity may be so overwhelming as to overcome the usual
restraints on our corrupt and fallen
nature: and when we remember how
feeble is our nature at best, and how
imperfect is the piety of the holiest of
men, we should not harshly judge him
who is left to express impatience in
his trials, or who gives utterance to
sentiments different from those which
are sanctioned by the word of God.
There has been but one model of pure
submission on earth—the Lord Jesus

CHAPTER IV.

ANALYSIS OF CHAPTERS IV. AND V.

The first Speech of Eliphaz.

THE fourth and fifth chapters comprise the speech of Eliphaz in reply to the intemperate language of Job. Hitherto his friends had maintained a profound silence in regard to his afflictions—amazed by the magnitude of his sorrows, and unwilling to break in upon his grief, and perhaps pondering the question whether one who suffered so much could be a good man; see Notes on chap ii. 13. The bitter complaint of Job, however; his rash and intemperate language; his implied charges against God, seem to have settled the question in the minds of his friends that he could not be a good man—and they proceed to address him in accordance with this belief. Eliphaz—as in the whole series of arguments—opens the discussion. He is the most mild of Job's accusers; yet, though his accusations are conducted with great art, and with a studious regard to urbanity of manner, they are terribly severe. It is not improbable that he was the oldest of the friends of Job, as great respect was shown to the aged in those times, and they were expected to speak first; see chap. xxxii. 6. The speech of Eliphaz consists mainly of the statement of his own observations, that the righteous are prospered, and the wicked punished, in this world; and in solemn advice to Job to return to God, and commit his cause to him. There is not a direct charge of hypocrisy, but it is implied throughout the argument, and the discussion which it brings on leads to this direct charge in some of the subsequent speeches. The argument, which is one of great beauty and power, consists of the following parts:

1. After duly apologizing for speaking at all, he proceeds to point out the inconsistency of a good man's repining under calamity, and the absurdity of *his* complaining and murmuring, who had so often exhorted others to fortitude. This, to him, is strange and unaccountable, and inevitably leads to the question, whether Job could be a good man, chap. iv. 1—6.

2. He then advances the sentiment that no one ever perished who was innocent, and that the righteous were not cut off, chap iv. 7—11. He states, as the result of his own observation, that they that plow wickedness and sow iniquity, reap the same. They are destroyed by the blast of God, and consumed by the breath of his nostrils. This sentiment he illustrates by his observation of the ways in which the fierce lion is destroyed; or, perhaps, using the word lion to denote savage and cruel men, he shows how they are cut off, chap iv. 7—11. This is the main doctrine which he and his friends defend. It is, that misery implies guilt, that great calamities are a proof of hypocrisy or sin; and thus it is insinuated that the wickedness of Job is the cause of his present afflictions.

3. This position Eliphaz proceeds to defend, not only by his own observation, but by a remarkable revelation which he says he had formerly had on this very subject, chap. iv. 12—21. That vision was in the silence of the night. A spirit, whose form he could not discern, was before him, which proclaimed, in a deep and solemn voice, that man could not be more just than God; that even the angels were charged with folly; that men were deeply guilty before him, and that he crushed and destroyed them on account of their transgressions.

4. In confirmation of his views, Eliphaz appeals to the observation of the saints, and again urges his own experience on the subject, chap. v. 1—5. He says that he himself had seen the wicked flourishing, but soon he had occasion to observe that they were overwhelmed with calamity. Their children were crushed with sudden death, and their harvest was consumed or laid waste by the robber. Though they *seemed* to be prosperous, yet he maintained that this was no exception to his general remark that God would punish the wicked in this world, and that calamity was proof of guilt.

5. In regard to affliction in general, he maintains that it is not the work of chance. It does not, says he, spring from the ground. It is appointed and directed by an intelligent Being; and, therefore, he infers it must be designed to punish the wicked, chap. v. 6, 7.

6. In view of the doctrine which he had now advanced, Eliphaz advises Job to commit his cause to

Christ; and after the contemplation of the best of men in their trials, we can see that there is imperfection *in them*, and that if we would survey absolute perfection in suffering, we must go to Gethsemane and to Calvary. (4.) Let us not make the expressions used by Job in this chapter *our* model in suffering. Let us not suppose that because *he* used such language, that therefore we may also. Let us not infer that because they are found *in the Bible*, that therefore they are right; or that because he was an unusually holy man, that it would be proper for us to use the same language that he did. The fact that this book is a part of the inspired truth of revelation, does not make such language right. All that inspiration does, in such a case, is to secure an exact record of what was actually said; it does not, of necessity, sanction it any more than an accurate historian can be supposed to approve all that he records. There may be important rea-

sons why it should be preserved, but he who makes the record is not answerable for the truth or propriety of what is recorded. The *narrative* is true; the *sentiment* may be false. The historian may state exactly what was said or done: but what was said or done, may have violated every law of truth and justice; and unless the historian expresses some sentiment of approbation, he can in no sense be held answerable for it. So with the narratives in the Bible. Where a sentiment of approbation or disapprobation is expressed, there the sacred writer is answerable for it; in other cases he is answerable only for the correctness of the record. This view of the nature of inspiration will leave us at liberty freely to canvass the speeches made in the book of Job, and make it more important that we compare the sentiments in those speeches with other parts of the Bible, that we may know what to approve, and what was erroneous in Job or his friends.

God, chap. **v. 8—16.** He says that he would himself do it; and proceeds to show that submission to God was a duty; that God was great, and did wonderful things, that his Providence was over all events; that he took the wise in their own craftiness, but that he was the protector and defender of him who trusted in him.

7. The argument of Eliphaz concludes with a statement of the happy consequences which would follow from making God his friend, chap. v. 17—27. If there was sincere piety, there would be great benefit in trials. God would support and comfort him; he would deliver him in trouble, and would keep him alive in famine; he would make even the stones of the field and the beasts tributary to his happiness; his family would be preserved and prospered, and he would come to the grave in peace and honour. Eliphaz says that he had seen instances like this, and commends that course to Job—strongly implying throughout that he showed in his trials that he had not the true spirit of religion.

CHAPTER IV.

1. *Then Eliphaz the Temanite answered.* See Notes, chap. ii. 11.

2. If *we assay to commune with thee.* Marg. *A word.* Heb.—דָּבָר הֲנִסָּה. "*May we attempt a word with thee?*" This is a gentle and polite apology at the beginning of his speech—an inquiry whether he would take it as unkind if one should adventure on a remark in the way of argument. Jahn, in characterizing the part which Job's three friends respectively take in the controversy, says: "Eliphaz is superior to the others in discernment and delicacy. He begins by addressing Job mildly; and it is not until irritated by opposition that he reckons him among the wicked." ¶ *Wilt thou be grieved?* That is, Wilt thou take it ill? Will it be offensive to you, or weary you, or tire your patience? The word used here (לָאָה) means to labour, to strive, to weary, to exhaust; and hence, to be weary, to try one's patience, to take any thing ill. Here it is the language of courtesy, and is designed to introduce the subsequent remarks in the kindest manner. Eliphaz knew that he was about to make observations which might implicate Job, and he introduced them in as kind a manner as possible. There is nothing abrupt or harsh in his beginning. All is courteous in the highest degree, and is a model for debaters. ¶ *But who can withhold himself from speaking?* Marg. *Refrain from words.* That is, "the subject is so important, the sentiments advanced by Job are so extraordinary, and the principles involved are so momentous, that it is impossi-

---

THEN Eliphaz the Temanite answered and said,

2 If we assay [1] to commune with thee, wilt thou be grieved? but who can [2] withhold himself from speaking?

3 Behold, thou hast instructed many, and thou hast strengthened[a] the weak hands.

4 Thy words have upholden him that was falling; and thou hast strengthened the [3] feeble knees.

> 1 *a word.*   2 *refrain from words.*
> *a* Is.35.3.   3 *bowing;* He.12.12.

---

ble to refrain." There is much delicacy in this. He did not begin to speak merely to make a speech. He professes that he would not have spoken, if he had not been pressed by the importance of the subject, and had not been full of matter. To a great extent, this is a good rule to adopt: not to make a speech unless there are sentiments which weigh upon the mind, and convictions of duty which cannot be repressed.

3. *Behold, thou hast instructed many.* That is, thou hast instructed many how they ought to bear trials, and hast delivered important maxims to them on the great subject of the divine government. This is not designed to be irony, or to wound the feelings of Job. It is intended to recall to his mind the lessons which he had inculcated on others in times of calamity, and to show him how important it was now that he should reduce his own lessons to practice, and show their power in sustaining himself. ¶ *Thou hast strengthened the weak hands.* That is, thou hast aided the feeble. The hands are the instruments by which we accompli h any thing, and when they are weak, it is an indication of helplessness.

4. *Thy words have upholden him that was falling.* That is, either falling into sin, or sinking under calamity and trial. The Hebrew will bear either interpretation, but the connection seems to require us to understand it of one who was sinking under the weight of affliction. ¶ *The feeble knees.* Marg. *bowing.* The knees support the frame. If they fail, we

5 But now it is come upon thee, and thou faintest ; it toucheth thee, and thou art troubled.

6 Is not *this* thy fear, thy confidence, the uprightness of thy ways, and thy hope ?

are feeble and helpless. Hence, their being weak, is so often used in the Bible to denote imbecility. The sense is, that Job, in the days of his own prosperity, had exhorted others to submit to God ; had counselled them in such a manner as actually to give them support, and that the same views should now have sustained him which he had so successfully employed in comforting others.

5. *But now it is come upon thee.* That is, calamity ; or, the same trial which others have had, and in which thou hast so successfully exhorted and comforted them. A similar sentiment to that which is here expressed, is found in Terence :

Facile omnes, cum valemus, recta consilia
    ægrotis damus.   And. ii. i. 9.

¶ *It toucheth thee.* That is, affliction has come to yourself. It is no longer a thing about which you can coolly sit down and reason, and on which you can deliver formal exhortations. ¶ *And thou art troubled.* Instead of evincing the calm submission which you have exhorted others to do, your mind is now disturbed and restless. You vent your complaints against the day of your birth, and you charge God with injustice. A sentiment resembling this, occurs in Terence, as quoted by Codurcus :

Nonne id flagitium est, te aliis consilium dare,
Foris sapere, tibi non posse te auxiliarier?

Something similar to this not unfrequently occurs. It is an easy thing to give counsel to others, and to exhort them to be submissive in trial. It is easy to utter general maxims, and to suggest passages of Scripture on the subject of affliction, and even to impart consolation to others ; but when trial comes to ourselves, we often fail to realize the power of those truths to console us. Ministers of the gospel are called officially to impart such consolations, and are enabled to do it. But when the trial comes on *them*, and when they ought by every solemn consideration to be able to show the

power of those truths in their own case, it sometimes happens that they evince the same impatience and want of submission which they had rebuked in others ; and that whatever truth and power there may have been in their instructions, they themselves little felt their force. It is often necessary that he who is appointed to comfort the afflicted, should be afflicted himself. Then he can " weep with those who weep ;" and hence it is that ministers of the gospel are called quite as much as any other class of men to pass through deep waters. Hence, too, the Lord Jesus became so pre-eminent in suffering, that he might be touched with the feelings of our infirmity, and be qualified to sympathize with us when we are tried ; Heb. ii. 14, 17, 18 ; iv. 15, 16. It is exceedingly important that when they whose office it is to comfort others *are* afflicted, they should exhibit an example of patience and submission. Then is the time to try their religion ; and then they have an opportunity to convince others that the doctrines which they preach are adapted to the condition of weak and suffering man.

6. Is *not* this *thy fear, thy confidence?* There has been considerable variety in the interpretation of this verse. Dr. Good renders it,

Is thy piety then nothing? thy hope
Thy confidence? or the uprightness of thy
    ways?

Noyes renders it,

Is not thy fear of God thy hope,
And the uprightness of thy ways thy confi-
    dence?

Rosenmüller translates it,

Is not in thy piety and integrity of life
Thy confidence and hope?

In the Vulgate it is translated, " Where is thy fear, thy fortitude, thy patience, and the integrity of thy ways?" In the Sept., " Is not thy fear founded on folly, and thy hope, and the evil of thy way?"

Castellio translates it,

7 Remember, I pray thee, who *ever* perished, being innocent? or where were the righteous cut off?

Nimirum tantum religionis, quantum expectationis;
Quantum spei, tantum habebas integritatis morum;

and the idea according to his version is, that he had as much religion as was prompted by the hope of reward; that his piety and integrity were sustained only by his hope, and were not the result of principle; and that of course his religion was purely selfish. If this be the sense, it is designed to be a reproach, and accords with the charge in the question of Satan (chap. i. 9), "Doth Job fear God for naught?" Rosenmüller adopts the opinion of Ludovicus de Dieu, and explains it as meaning, "You seemed to be a man fearing God, and a man of integrity, and you were led hence to cherish high hopes and expectations; but now you perceive that you were deceived. Your piety was not sincere and genuine, for the truly pious do not thus suffer. Remember therefore that no one perishes being innocent." Codurcus renders it, "All thy hope was placed in thy religion, and thy expectation in the rectitude of thy ways; consider now, who perishes being innocent?" The true sentiment of the passage has undoubtedly been expressed by Good, Noyes. and Codurcus. The Hebrew rendered *thy fear* יִרְאָתֶךָ means doubtless *religious fear*, veneration, or piety, and is a word synonymous with εὐλάβεια, εὐσέβεια, *religion*. The sentiment is, that his confidence or hope was placed in his *religion*—in his fear of God, his respect and veneration for him, and in reliance on the equity of his government. This had been his stay in times past; and this was the subject which was naturally brought before him then. Eliphaz asks whether he should not put his trust in that God still, and not reproach him as unequal and unjust in his administration. ¶ *The uprightness of thy ways.* Heb. The perfection of thy ways. Note chap. i. 1. The idea is, that his hope was founded on the integrity of his life, and on the belief that the upright would be rewarded. The passage may be rendered,

Is not thy confidence and thy expectation
   founded on thy religion,
And on the integrity of thy ways?

This is the general sentiment which Eliphaz proceeds to illustrate and apply. If this was a just principle, it was natural to ask whether the trials of Job did not prove that he had no well-grounded reason for such confidence.

7. *Remember, I pray thee, who ever perished, being innocent?* The object of this question is manifestly to show to Job the inconsistency of the feelings which he had evinced. He claimed to be a righteous man. He had instructed and counselled many others. He had professed confidence in God, and in the integrity of his own ways. It was to have been expected that one with such pretensions would have evinced resignation in the time of trial, and would have been sustained by the recollection of his integrity. The fact, therefore, that Job had thus "fainted," and had given way to impatient expressions, showed that he was conscious that he had not been altogether what he had professed to be. "There must have been," is the meaning of Eliphaz, "something wrong, when such calamities come upon a man, and when his faith gives way in such a manner. It would be contrary to all the analogy of the divine dealings to suppose that such a man as Job had professed to be, could be the subject of overwhelming judgments; for who, I ask, ever perished, being innocent? It is a settled principle of the divine government, that no one ever perishes who is innocent. and that great calamities are a proof of great guilt." This declaration contains the essence of all the positions held by Eliphaz and his colleagues in this argument. This they considered as so established that no one could call it in question, and on the ground of this they inferred that one who experienced such afflictions, no matter what his professions or his

8 Even as I have seen, they [a] that plow iniquity, and sow wickedness, reap the same.

a Ga.6.7,8.

apparent piety had been, could not be a good man. This was a point about which the minds of the friends of Job were settled; and though they seem to have been disposed to concede that *some* afflictions might happen to good men, yet when sudden and overwhelming calamities such as they now witnessed came upon them, they inferred that there must have been corresponding guilt. Their reasoning on this subject—which runs through the book —perplexed but did not satisfy Job, and was obviously based on a wrong principle.—The word *perished* here means the same as cut off, and does not differ much from being overwhelmed with calamity. The whole sentence has a proverbial cast; and the sense is, that when persons were suddenly cut off it proved that they were not innocent. Job, therefore, it was inferred, could not be a righteous man in these unusual and very peculiar trials. ¶ *Or where were the righteous cut off?* That is, by heavy judgment; by any special and direct visitation. Eliphaz could not mean that the righteous did not die—for he could not be insensible to that fact; but he must have referred to sudden calamities. This kind of reasoning is common—that when men are afflicted with great and sudden calamities they must be peculiarly guilty. It prevailed in the time of the Saviour, and it demanded all his authority to settle the opposite principle; see Luke xiii. 1—5. It is that into which men naturally and easily fall; and it required much observation, and long experience, and enlarged views of the divine administration, to draw the true lines on this subject. To a certain extent, and in certain instances, calamity certainly does prove that there is peculiar guilt. Such was the case with the old world that was destroyed by the deluge; such was the case with the cities of the plain; such is the case in the calamities that come upon the drunkard, and such too in the special curse produced by indulgence in licentiousness. But this principle

does not run through *all* the calamities which fall on men. A tower may fall on the righteous as well as the wicked; an earthquake may destroy the innocent as well as the guilty; the pestilence sweeps away the holy and the unholy, the profane and the pure, the man who fears God and him who fears him not; and the inference is now seen to be too broad when we infer, as the friends of Job did, that *no* righteous man is cut off by special calamity, or that great trials demonstrate that such sufferers are less righteous than others are. Judgments are *not* equally administered in this world, and hence the necessity for a future world of retribution; see Notes on Luke xiii. 2, 3.

8. *Even as I have seen.* Eliphaz appeals to his own observation, that men who had led wicked lives were suddenly cut off. Instances of this kind he might doubtless have observed —as all may have done. But his inference was too broad when he concluded that *all* the wicked are punished in this manner. It is true that wicked men *are* thus cut off and perish; but it is not true that *all* the wicked are thus punished in this life, nor that any of the righteous are not visited with similar calamities. His reasoning was of a kind that is common in the world —that of drawing universal conclusions from premises that are too narrow to sustain them, or from too few carefully observed facts. ¶ *They that plow iniquity.* This is evidently a proverbial expression; and the sense is, that as men sow they reap. If they sow wheat, they reap wheat; if barley, they reap barley; if tares, they reap tares. Thus in Prov. xxii. 8 :

He that soweth iniquity shall reap also vanity.

So in Hosea viii. 7 :

For they have sown the wind,
And they shall reap the whirlwind :
It hath no stalk ; the bud shall yield no meal :
If so be it yield, strangers shall swallow it up.

Thus in the Persian adage :

"He that planteth thorns shall not gather roses."   [DR. GOOD.

So Æschylus :

JOB L.   K

9 By the blast of God they perish, and by [1] the breath of his nostrils are they consumed.

1 i. e. *his anger*, chap.15.30; Is.11.4.

"Άτης ἄρουρα θάνατον ἐκκαρπίζεται.
The field of wrong brings forth death as its fruit.

The meaning of Eliphaz is, that men who form plans of wickedness must reap appropriate fruits. They cannot expect that an evil life will produce ultimate happiness.

9. *By the blast of God.* That is, by the judgment of God. The figure is taken from the hot and fiery wind, which, sweeping over a field of grain, dries it up and destroys it. In like manner Eliphaz says the wicked perish before God. ¶ *And by the breath of his nostrils.* By his anger. The Scripture often speaks of *breathing out* indignation and wrath; Acts ix. 1; Ps. xxvii. 12: 2 Sam. xxii. 16; Ps. xviii. 15; xxxiii. 6; Notes on Isa. xi. 4; xxx. 28; xxxiii. 11. The figure was probably taken from the violent breathing which is evinced when the mind is under any strong emotion, especially anger. It refers here to any judgment by which God cuts off the wicked, but especially to sudden calamity —like a tempest or the pestilence.

10. *The roaring of the lion.* This is evidently a continuation of the argument in the preceding verses, and Eliphaz is stating what had occurred under his own observation. The expressions have much of a proverbial cast, and are designed to convey in strong poetic language what he supposed usually occurred. There can be no reasonable doubt here that he refers to *men* in these verses, for (1.) It is not true that the *lion* is destroyed in this manner. No more frequent calamity comes upon him than upon other animals, and perhaps he is *less* frequently overcome than others. (2.) Such a supposition only would make the remarks of Eliphaz pertinent to his argument. He is speaking of the divine government in regard to *wicked men*, and he uses this language to convey the idea that they are often destroyed. (3.) It is common in the Scriptures, as in all Oriental writings,

10 The roaring of the lion, and the voice of the fierce lion, and the teeth [a] of the young lions, are broken.

a Ps.58.6.

and indeed in Greek and Roman poetry, to compare unjust, cruel, and rapacious men with wild animals; see Notes on Isa. xi; comp. Ps. x. 9; lviii. 6. Eliphaz, therefore, here by the use of the words rendered *lion*, means to say that men of savage temper, and cruel dispositions, and untamed ferocity, were cut off by the judgments of God. It is remarkable that he employs so many words to designate the *lion* in these two verses. No less than *five* are employed, all of them probably denoting originally some peculiar and striking characteristics of the lion. It is also an illustration of the copiousness of the Hebrew language in this respect, and is a specimen of the custom of speaking in Arabia. The Arabic language is so copious that the Arabs boast that they have four hundred terms by which to designate *the lion.* A large part of them are, indeed, figurative expressions, derived from some quality of the animal, but they show a much greater copiousness in the language than can be found in Western dialects. The words used here by Eliphaz are about all the terms by which the lion is designated in the Scriptures. They are אריה, שחל, כפיר, ליש, and לביא. The word שחץ *elation, pride*, is given to the lion, Job xxviii. 8; xli. 34, from his proud gait; and perhaps the word אריאל *ariel*, 1 Sam. xvii. 10; 1 Chron. xi. 22. But Eliphaz has exhausted the usual epithets of the lion in the Hebrew language. It may be of some interest to inquire, in a few words, into the meaning of those which he has used. ¶ *The roaring of the lion.* The word here used (אריה, or in a more usual form ארי, is from אָרָה *árâh*, to *pull*, to *pluck*, and is probably given to the lion as the *puller in pieces*, on account of the mode in which he devours his prey. Bochart, however, contends that the name is not from א־ה, because, says he, the lion does not bite or crop his food like grass, which, he says, the word

11 The old lion perisheth for lack of prey, and the stout lion's whelps are scattered abroad.

12 Now a thing was [1] secretly brought to me, and mine ear received a little thereof.

[1] by stealth.

---

properly means, but is from the verb רָאָה *rââh, to see*, because, says he, the lion is the most keen-sighted of the animals; or rather from the fire of his eyes—the terror which the glance of his eye inspires. So the Greeks derive the word *lion*, λέοντα, from λάω, *to see*. See Bochart, Hieroz. Lib. iii. c. 1, p. 715. ¶ *The voice of the fierce lion.* The word here translated *fierce lion* (שַׁחַל) is from שָׁחַל, *shâhhal, to roar*, and hence given for an obvious reason to a lion. Bochart understands by it the swarthy lion of Syria; the lion which the Arabians call *adlamon.* This lion, says he, is dark and dingy. The usual colour of the lion is yellow, but Oppian says that the lion in Æthiopia is sometimes found of a dark colour, μελανόχροος; see Bochart, Hieroz. Lib. i. c. 1, p. 717, 718. ¶ *The teeth of the young lions.* The word here used, כְּפִיר, means a "young lion already weaned, and beginning to hunt for prey."—*Gesenius.* It thus differs from the גּוּר *gûr*, which means *a whelp*, still under the care of the dam; see Ezek. xix. 2, 3; comp. Bochart, Hieroz. Lib. iii. c. 1, p. 714. Some expression is here evidently to be understood that shall be applicable to the voice, or the roaring of the lion. Noyes supplies the words, "are silenced." The words "are broken" can be applicable only to the *teeth* of the young lions. It is unnatural to say that the "roaring" and the "voice" are *broken*. The sense is, that the lion roars in vain, and that calamity and destruction come notwithstanding his growl; and as applied to men, it means that men who resemble the lion are disappointed and punished.

11. *The old lion.* The word here used, לַיִשׁ, denotes a lion, "so called," says Gesenius, "from his strength and bravery," or, according to Umbreit, the lion in the strength of his old age; see an examination of the word in Bochart, Hieroz. P. i. Lib. iii. c. 1, p. 720. ¶ *Perisheth for lack*

of prey. Notwithstanding his strength and power. That is, such a thing sometimes occurs. Eliphaz could not maintain that it always happened. The meaning seems to be, that as the strength of the lion was no security that he would not perish for want, so it was with men who resembled the lion in the strength of mature age. ¶ *And the stout lion's whelps.* The word here rendered "stout lion," לָבִיא, is probably derived from the obsolete root לָבָא, *lâbâ', to roar*, and it is given to the lion on account of his roaring. Bochart, Hieroz. P. i. Lib. iii. c. 1, p. 719, supposes that the word means a *lioness.* These words complete the description of the lion, and the sense is, that the lion in no condition, or whatever name indicative of strength might be given to it, had power to resist God when he came forth for its destruction. Its roaring, its strength, its teeth, its rage, were all in vain. ¶ *Are scattered abroad.* That is, when the old lion is destroyed, the young ones flee, and are unable to offer resistance. So it is with men. When the divine judgments come upon them, they have no power to make successful resistance. God has them under control, and he comes forth at his pleasure to restrain and subdue them, as he does the wild beasts of the desert, though so fearful and formidable.

12. *Now a thing.* To confirm his views, Eliphaz appeals to a vision of a most remarkable character which he says he had had on some former occasion on the very point under consideration. The object of the vision was, to show that mortal man could not be more just than God, and that such was the purity of the Most High, that he put no confidence comparatively even in the angels. The design for which this is introduced here is, evidently, to reprove what he deemed the unfounded self-confidence of Job. He supposed that he had been placing an undue reliance on his own integrity; that he had not a just view of

the infinite holiness of God, and had not been aware of the true state of his own heart. The highest earthly excellency, is the meaning of Eliphaz, fades away before God, and furnishes no ground for self-reliance. It is so imperfect, so feeble, so far from what it should be, that it is no wonder that a God so holy and exalted should disregard it. He designed also, by describing this vision, to reprove Job for seeming to be more wise than his Maker in arraigning him for his dealings, and uttering the language of complaint. The word "thing" here means a word (Heb.), a communication, a revelation. ¶ *Was secretly brought to me.* Marg. *by stealth.* The Hebrew word (גנב) means *to steal;* to take away by stealth, or secretly. Here it means, that the oracle was brought to him as it were by stealth. It did not come openly and plainly, but in secrecy and silence—as a thief approaches a dwelling. An expression similar to this occurs in Lucian, in *Amor.* p. 884, as quoted by Schultens, κλεπτομένη λαλιὰ καὶ ψιθυρισμός. ¶ *And mine ear received a little thereof.* Dr. Good translates this, " And mine ear received a whisper along with it." Noyes, " And mine ear caught a whisper thereof." The Vulgate, " And my ear received secretly the pulsations of its whisper"—*venas susurri ejus.* The word rendered "a little," שֵׁמֶץ, occurs only here and in chap. xxvi. 14, where it is also rendered *little*. It means, according to Gesenius, a transient sound rapidly uttered and swiftly passing away. Symm. ψιθυρισμός.—*a whisper*. According to Castell, it means a sound confused and feeble, such as one receives when a man is speaking in a hurried manner, and when he cannot catch all that is said. This is probably the sense here. Eliphaz means to say that he did not get *all* that might have been said in the vision. It occurred in such circumstances, and what was said was delivered in such a manner, that he did not hear it all distinctly. But he heard an important sentiment, which he proceeds to apply to the case of Job.—It has been made a question whether Eliphaz really had such a vision, or whether he only supposed such a case, and whether the whole representation is not poetic. The fair construction is, that he had had such a vision. In such a supposition there is nothing inconsistent with the mode in which the will of God was made known in ancient times; and in the sentiments uttered there is nothing inconsistent with what might have been spoken by a celestial visitant on such an occasion. All that was spoken was in accordance with the truth everywhere revealed in the Scriptures, though Eliphaz perverted it to prove that Job was insincere and hypocritical. The general sentiment in the oracle was, that man was not pure and holy compared with his Maker ; that no one was free from guilt in his sight ; that there was no virtue in man in which God could put entire confidence ; and that, therefore, all were subjected to trials and to death. But this general sentiment he proceeds to apply to Job, and regards it as teaching, that since he was overwhelmed with such peculiar afflictions, there must have been some *secret sin* of which he was guilty, which was the cause of his calamities.

13. *In thoughts.* Amidst the tumultuous and anxious thoughts which occur in the night. The Hebrew word rendered *thoughts,* (שְׂעִפִּים), means thoughts which *divide* and *distract* the mind. ¶ *From the visions of the night.* On the meaning of the word *visions,* see Notes on Isa. i. 1. This was a common mode in which the will of God was made known in ancient times. For an extended description of this method of communicating the will of God, the reader may consult my Introduction to Isaiah, § 7. ¶ *When deep sleep falleth on men.* The word here rendered *deep sleep,* תַּרְדֵּמָה, commonly denotes a profound repose or slumber brought upon man by divine agency. So Schultens *in loc.* It is the word used to describe the " deep sleep " which God brought upon Adam when he took from his side a rib to form Eve, Gen. ii. 21 ; and that, also, which came upon Abraham, when an horror of great darkness fell upon him ; Gen. xv. 12. It

13 In thoughts from the visions of the night, when deep sleep falleth on men,

14 Fear [1] came upon me, and trembling, which made [2] all my bones to shake.

1 *met me.*   2 *the multitude of.*

means here profound repose, and the vision which he saw was at that solemn hour when the world is usually locked in slumber. Umbreit renders this, "In the time of thoughts, before the night-visions," and supposes that Eliphaz refers to the time that was especially favourable to meditation and to serious contemplation *before* the time of sleep and of dreams. In support of this use of the preposition מִן, *min,* he appeals to Hag. ii. 16, and Noldius Concord. Part. p. 546. Our common version, however, has probably preserved the true sense of the passage. It is impossible to conceive any thing more sublime than this whole description. It was midnight. There was solitude and silence all around. At that fearful hour this vision came, and a sentiment was communicated to Eliphaz of the utmost importance, and fitted to make the deepest possible impression. The time; the quiet; the form of the image; its passing along, and then suddenly standing still; the silence, and then the deep and solemn voice —all were fitted to produce the profoundest awe. So graphic and so powerful is this description, that it would be impossible to read it—and particularly at midnight and alone— without something of the feeling of awe and horror which Eliphaz says it produced on his mind. It is a description which for power has probably never been equalled, though an attempt to describe an apparition from the invisible world has been often made. Virgil has attempted such a description, which, though exceedingly beautiful, is far inferior to this of the Sage of Teman. It is the description of the appearance of the wife of Æneas:

Infelix simulacrum atque ipsius umbra Creusæ
Visa mihi ante oculos, et nota major imago.
Obstupui, steteruntque comæ, et vox faucibus hæsit.   Æn. ii. 772.
——— " At length she hears,
And sudden through the shades of night appears;

Appears no more Creusa, nor my wife,
But a pale spectre, larger than the life.
Aghast, astonished, and struck dumb with fear,
I stood: like bristles rose my stiffened hair."
                              DRYDEN.

In the poems of Ossian, there are several descriptions of apparitions or ghosts, probably more sublime than are to be found in any other uninspired writings. One of the most magnificent of these, is that of the Spirit of Loda, which I will copy, in order that it may be compared with the one before us. " The wan cold moon rose in the east. Sleep descended on the youths. Their blue helmets glitter to the beam; the fading fire decays. But sleep did not rest on the king. He rose in the midst of his arms, and slowly ascended the hill, to behold the flame of Sarno's tower. The flame was dim and distant: the moon hid her red flame in the east. A blast came from the mountain; on its wings was the SPIRIT OF LODA. He came to his place in his terrors, and shook his dusky spear. His eyes appear like flames in his dark face; his voice is like distant thunder. Fingal advanced his spear amid the night, and raised his voice on high. 'Son of Night, retire: call thy winds, and fly! Why dost thou come to my presence with thy shadowy arms? Do I fear thy gloomy form, spirit of dismal Loda? Weak is thy shield of clouds: feeble is that meteor, thy sword! The blast rolls them together; and thou thyself art lost. Fly from my presence, Son of Night! Call thy winds and fly!' 'Dost thou force me from my place?' replied the hollow voice. ' The people bend before me. I turn the battle in the field of the brave. I look on the nations, and they vanish; my nostrils pour the blast of death. I come abroad on the winds; the tempests are before my face, but my dwelling is calm above the clouds; the fields of my rest are pleasant.' " Comp. also, the description of the Ghost in Hamlet.

15 Then a spirit passed before my face ; the hair of my flesh stood up:

16 It stood still, but I could not

discern the form thereof: an image *was* before mine eyes ; [1] *there was* silence, and I heard a voice, *saying,*

1 or, *I heard a still voice.*

14. *Fear came upon me.* Marg. *Met me.* The Chaldee Paraphrase renders this, "a tempest," זַעַר. The LXX, Φρίκη—*shuddering,* or *horror.* The sense is, that he became greatly alarmed at the vision. ¶ *Which made all my bones to shake.* Marg. as in Hebrew, *the multitude of my bones.* A similar image is employed by Virgil,

Obstupuere animis, gelidusque per ima cucurrit
Ossa tremor ; . . . . Æn. ii. 120.

" A cold tremor ran through all their bones."

15. *Then a spirit passed before my face.* He does not intimate whether it was the spirit of a man, or an angel who thus appeared. The belief in such apparitions was common in the early ages, and indeed has prevailed at all times. No one can demonstrate that God *could* not communicate his will in such a manner as this, or by a messenger deputed from his immediate presence to impart valuable truth to men. ¶ *The hair of my flesh stood up.* This is an effect which is known often to be produced by fear. Sometimes the hair is made to turn white almost in an instant, as an effect of sudden alarm ; but usually the effect is to make it stand on end. Seneca uses language remarkably similar to this in describing the effect of fear, in *Hercule Œtæo:*

Vagus per artus errat excussos tremor ;
Erectus horret crinis. Impulsis adhuc
Stat terror animis, et cor attonitum salit,
Pavidumque trepidis palpitat venis jecur.

So Virgil,

Steteruntque comæ, et vox faucibus hæsit.
Æn. ii. 774.

See also Æn. iii. 48, iv. 289.

So also Æn. xii. 868:

Arrectæque horrore comæ.

A similar description of the effect of fear is given in the Ghost's speech to Hamlet:

———— " But that I am forbid
To tell the secrets of my prison-house,
I could a tale unfold, whose lightest word
Would harrow up thy soul, freeze thy young blood,
Make thy two eyes, like stars, start from their spheres,

Thy knotty and combined locks to part,
And each particular hair to stand on end,
Like quills upon the fretful porcupine."

The *fact* here referred to—that fear or fright causes the hair to stand on end—is too well established, and too common to admit a doubt. The *cause* may be, that sudden fear has the effect to drive the blood to the heart, as the seat of vitality, and the extremities are left cold, and the skin thus contracts, and the effect is to raise the hair.

16. *It stood still.* It took a fixed position and looked on me. It at first glided by, or towards him, then stood in an immovable position, as if to attract his attention, and to prepare him for the solemn announcement which it was about to make. This was the point in which most horror would be felt. We should be less alarmed at any thing which a strange messenger should *say,* than to have him stand and fix his eyes steadily and silently upon us. Hence Horatius, in " Hamlet," tortured by the imperturbable silence of the Ghost, earnestly entreated it to give him relief by speaking.

Hor—What art thou that usurp'st this time of night,
Together with that fair and warlike form
In which the majesty of buried Denmark
Did sometime march ? By heaven, I charge thee, speak.
Mar.—It is offended.
Ber.—See! It stalks away.
Hor.—Stay ; speak : speak, I charge thee speak. Act i. Sc. i.

Re-enter Ghost.

Hor.—But, soft ; behold ! lo, where it comes again !
I'll cross it, though it blast me.—Stay, illusion !
If thou hast any sound, or use of voice,
Speak to me :
If there be any good thing to be done,
That may to thee do ease, and grace to me,
Speak to me :
If thou art privy to thy country's fate,
Which, happily, foreknowing may avoid,
O speak !
Or if thou hast uphoarded in thy life
Extorted treasure in the womb of earth,
For which, they say, you spirits oft walk in death,
Speak of it ; stay, and speak. Act i.Sc.i.

17 Shall *a* mortal man be more

a chap.9.2.

Enter Ghost.

Hor.—Look, my lord, it comes!
Ham.—Angels and ministers of grace, defend us!
Be thou a spirit of health, or goblin damn'd,
Bring with thee airs from heaven, or blasts from hell,
Be thy intents wicked or charitable.
Thou com'st in such a questionable shape,
That I will speak to thee: I'll call thee, Hamlet,
King, father, royal Dane: O, answer me;
Let me not burst in ignorance! Act i. Sc. iv.

¶ *But I could not discern the form thereof.* This might have arisen from fear, or from the darkness of the night, or because the spirit was not distinct enough in its outline to enable him to do it. There is here just the kind of *obscurity* which is essential to the sublime, and the statement of this circumstance is a master-stroke in the poet. A less perfect imagination would have attempted to describe the form of the spectre, and would have given an account of its shape, and eyes, and colour. But none of these are here hinted at. The subject is left so that the imagination is most deeply impressed, and the whole scene has the aspect of the highest sublimity. Noyes very improperly renders this, " Its *face* I could not discern." But the word used, מראה, does not mean *face* here merely; it means the form, figure, aspect, of the spectre. ¶ *An image was before mine eyes.* Some form ; some appearance was before me, whose exact figure I could not mark or describe. ¶ There was *silence.* Marg. *I heard a still voice.* So Rosenmüller says that the word here, דממה, does not mean silence, but a gentle breeze, or air—*auram lenem*—such as Elijah heard after the tempest had gone by, and when God spoke to him, 1 Kings xix. 12, 13. Grotius supposes that it means here the בת-קול *Bath-Kol*, or "daughter of the voice," of which the Jewish Rabbins speak so often—the still and gentle voice in which God spoke to men. The word used (דממה) usually means silence, stillness, as of the winds after a storm, *a calm*, Ps. cvii. 29. The LXX. render it, " I heard *a gentle breeze*, αυραν, and a voice," και φωνήν.

just than God? Shall a man be more pure than his Maker?

But it seems to me that the common reading is preferable. There was stillness—a solemn, awful silence, and *then* he heard a voice impressively speaking. The stillness was designed to fix the attention, and to prepare the mind for the sublime announcement which was to be made.

17. *Shall mortal man.* Or, shall *feeble* man. The idea of *mortal* is not necessarily implied in the word here used, אנוש. It means *man;* and is usually applied to the lower classes or ranks of men ; Notes on Isa. viii. 1. The common opinion in regard to this word is, that it is derived from אנש, to be sick, or ill at ease ; and then desperate, or incurable—as of a disease or wound ; Jer. xv. 18 ; Mic. i. 9 ; Job xxxiv. 6. Gesenius (Lex.) calls this derivation in question ; but if it be the correct idea, then the word here used originally referred to man as feeble, and as liable to sickness and calamity. I see no reason to doubt that the common idea is correct, and that it refers to man as weak and feeble. The other word here used to denote man (גבר) is given to him on account of his *strength.* The two words, therefore, embrace man whether considered as feeble or strong—and the idea is, that *none of the race* could be more pure than God. ¶ *Be more just than God.* Some expositors have supposed that the sense of this expression in the Hebrew is, " Can man be pure before God, or in the sight of God?" They allege that it could not have been made a question whether man could be *more* pure than God, or more just than his Maker. Such is the view presented of the passage by Rosenmüller, Good, Noyes, and Umbreit:

" Shall mortal man be just before God ?
Shall man be pure before his Maker ?"

In support of this view, and this use of the Hebrew preposition מ, Rosenmüller appeals to Jer. li. 5; Num. xxxii. 22 ; Ezek. xxxiv. 18. This, however, is not wholly satisfactory. The more literal translation is that which occurs in the common version,

18 Behold, he put no trust in his servants ; [1] and his angels *a* he charged with folly.

[1] or, *nor in his angels,* in whom *he put light.*
a 2 Pe. 2.4.

19 How much less *in* them that dwell in houses of clay, whose foundation *is* in the dust, *which* are crushed before the moth ?

and this accords with the Vulgate and the Chaldee. If so understood, it is designed to repress and reprove the pride of men, which arraigns the equity of the divine government, and which *seems* to be wiser and better than God. Thus understood, it would be a pertinent reproof of Job, who in his complaint (chap. iii.) had *seemed* to be wiser than God. He had impliedly charged him with injustice and want of goodness. All men who murmur against God, and who arraign the equity and goodness of the divine dispensations, claim to be wiser and better than he is. They would have ordered things more wisely, and in a better manner. They would have kept the world from the disorders and sins which actually exist, and would have made it pure and happy. How pertinent, therefore, was it to ask whether man could be more pure or just than his Maker ! And how pertinent was the solemn question propounded in the hearing of Eliphaz by the celestial messenger—a question that seems to have been originally proposed in view of the complaints and murmurs of a self-confident race!

18. *Behold, he put no trust in his servants.* These are evidently the words of the oracle that appeared to Eliphaz ; see Schultens, *in loc.* The word *servants* here refers to angels ; and the idea is, that God was so pure that he did not confide even in the exalted holiness of angels—meaning that *their* holiness was infinitely inferior to his. The design is to state that God had the highest possible holiness, such as to render the holiness of all others, no matter how exalted, as nothing—as all lesser lights are as nothing before the glory of the sun. The Chaldee renders this, " Lo, in his servants, the prophets, he does not confide ;" but the more correct reference is undoubtedly to the angels. ¶ *And his angels he charged with folly.* Marg. Or, *Nor in his angels,*

in whom *he put light.* The different rendering in the text and in the margin, has arisen from the supposed ambiguity of the word employed here —הלָהֳתָ. It is a word which occurs nowhere else, and hence it is difficult to determine its true signification. Walton renders it, *gloriatio glorying;* Jerome, *pravitas, wickedness;* the LXX., σκολιόν, *fault, blemish:* Dr. Good, *default,* or *defection;* Noyes, *frailty.* Gesenius says that the word is derived from הלָל, *hâlăl* (No. 4), to be foolish. So also Kimchi explains it. According to this, the idea is that of foolishness—*i. e.* they are far inferior to God in wisdom ; or, as the word folly in the Scriptures is often synonymous with sin, it might mean that their purity was so far inferior to his as to appear like impurity and sin. The essential idea is, that even the holiness of angels was not to be compared with God. It is not that they were polluted and unholy, for, in their measure, they are perfect ; but it is that their holiness was as nothing compared with the infinite perfection of God. It is to be remembered that a part of the angels had sinned, and *they* had shown that their integrity was not to be confided in ; and whatever might be the holiness of *a creature,* it was possible to conceive that he might sin. But no such idea could for a moment enter the mind in regard to God. The object of this whole argument is to show, that if confidence could not be reposed in the angels, and if all their holiness was as nothing before God, little confidence could be placed in man ; and that it was presumption for him to sit in judgment on the equity of the divine dealings.

19. *How much less* (אַף). This particle has the general sense of *addition, accession,* especially of something more important ; *yea more, besides, even.* Gesenius. The meaning here is, " how much more true is this of

man !" He puts no confidence in his angels; he charges them with frailty; how much more strikingly true must this be of man! It is not merely, as our common translation would seem to imply, that he put much less confidence in man than in angels; it is, that all he had said must be more strikingly true of man, who dwelt in so frail and humble a habitation. ¶ In *them that dwell in houses of clay.* In man. The phrase " houses of clay " refers to the body made of dust. The sense is, that man, from the fact that he dwells in such a tabernacle, is far inferior to the pure spirits that surround the throne of God, and much more liable to sin. The body is represented as a temporary tent, tabernacle, or dwelling for the soul. That dwelling is soon to be taken down, and its tenant, the soul, to be removed to other abodes. So Paul (2 Cor. v. 1) speaks of the body as ἡ ἐπίγειος ἡμῶν οἰκία τοῦ σκήνους—" our earthly house of this tabernacle." So Plato speaks of it as γήινον σκήνος—an *earthly tent;* and so Aristophanes (Av. 587), among other contemptuous expressions applied to men, calls them πλάσματα πηλοῦ, "vessels of clay." The idea in the verse before us is beautiful, and as affecting as it is beautiful. A house of *clay* (חֹמֶר) was little fitted to bear the extremes of heat and cold, of storm and sunshine, of rain, and frost, and snow, and would soon crumble and decay. It must be a frail and temporary dwelling. It could not endure the changes of the seasons and the lapse of years like a dwelling of granite or marble. So with our bodies. They can bear little. They are frail, infirm, and feeble. They are easily prostrated, and soon fall back to their native dust. How can they who dwell in *such* edifices, be in any way compared with the Infinite and Eternal God? ¶ *Whose foundation* is *in the dust.* A house to be firm and secure should be founded on a rock; see Matt. vii. 25. The figure is kept up here of comparing man with a house; and as a house that is built on the sand or the dust may be easily washed away (comp. Matt. vii. 26, 27), and could not be

confided in, so it was with man. He was like such a dwelling; and no more confidence could be reposed in him than in such a house. ¶ Which *are crushed.* They are broken in pieces, trampled on, destroyed (יְדַכְּאוּם), by the most insignificant objects. ¶ *Before the moth;* see Notes on Isa. l. 9 ; li. 8. The word moth (עָשׁ), Gr. σὴς, Vulg. *tinea,* denotes properly an insect which flies by night, and particularly that which attaches itself to woollen cloth and consumes it. It is possible, however, that the word here denotes the *moth-worm.* This "moth-worm is one state of the creature, which first is inclosed in an egg, and thence issues in the form of a worm ; after a time, it quits the form of a worm, to assume that of the complete state of the insect, or the moth." *Calmet.* The comparison here, therefore, is not that of a moth flying against a house to overset it, nor of the moth consuming man as it does a garment, but it is that of a feeble worm that preys upon man and destroys him ; and the idea is, that the most feeble of all objects may crush him. The following remarks from Niebuhr (Reisebeschreibung von Arabien, S. 133), will serve to illustrate this passage, and show that so feeble a thing as a worm may destroy human life. " There is in Yemen, in India, and on the coasts of the South sea, a common sickness caused by the Guinea, or nerve-worm, known to European physicians by the name of *vena Medinensis.* It is supposed in Yemen that this worm is drunk in from the bad water which the inhabitants of those countries are under a necessity of using. Many of the Arabians on this account take the precaution to strain the water which they drink. If any one has by accident swallowed an egg of this worm, no trace of it is to be seen until it appears on the skin ; and the first indication of it there, is the irritation which is caused. On our physician, a few days before his death, five of these worms made their appearance, although we had been more than five months absent from Arabia. On the island of Charedsch, I saw a French officer, whose name was Le

20 They are [1] destroyed from morning to evening : they perish for ever, without any regarding *it*.

1 *beaten in pieces.*

21 Doth *a* not their excellency *which is* in them go away? they die, *b* even without wisdom.

a Ps.146.3,4.   b Is.2.22.

Page, who after a long and arduous journey, which he had made on' foot, from Pondicherry to Surat, through the heart of India, found the traces of such a worm in him, which he endeavoured to extract from his body. He believed that he had swallowed it when drinking the waters of Mahratta. The worm is not dangerous, if it can be drawn from the body without being broken. The Orientals are accustomed, as soon as the worm makes its appearance through the skin, to wind it up on a piece of straw, or of dry wood. It is finer than a thread, and is from two to three feet in length. The winding up of the worm frequently occupies a week; and no further inconvenience is experienced, than the care which is requisite not to break it. If, however, it is broken, it draws itself back into the body, and then becomes dangerous. Lameness, gangrene, or the loss of life itself is the result." See Notes on Isaiah referred to above. The comparison of man with a worm, or an insect, on account of his feebleness and shortness of life, is common in the sacred writings, and in the classics. The following passage from Pindar, quoted by Schultens, hints at the same idea :

Ἐπάμεροι, τί δέ τις; τί δ' οὖ τις;

Σκιᾶς ὄναρ ἄνθρωποι.

" Things of a day ! What is any one ? What is he not ? Men are the dream of a shadow !"—The idea in the passage before us is, that men are exceedingly frail, and that in such creatures no confidence can be placed. How should such a creature, therefore, presume to arraign the wisdom and equity of the divine dealings ? How *can* he be more just or wise than God ?

20. *They are destroyed from morning to evening.* Marg. *beaten in pieces.* This is nearer to the Hebrew. The phrase " from morning to evening" means between the morning and the evening; that is, they live scarcely a single day ; see Notes on Isaiah xxxviii. 12. The idea is, not

the continuance of the work of destruction from morning to evening ; but that man's life is exceedingly short, so short that he scarce seems to live from morning to night. What a beautiful expression, and how true ! How little qualified is such a being to sit in judgment on the doings of the Most High ! ¶ *They perish for ever.* Without being restored to life. They pass away, and nothing is ever seen of them again ! ¶ *Without any regarding* it. Without its being noticed. How strikingly true is this ! What a narrow circle is affected by the death of a man, and how soon does even that circle cease to be affected ! A few relatives and friends feel it and weep over the loss ; but the mass of men are unconcerned. It is like taking a grain of sand from the sea-shore, or a drop of water from the ocean. There is indeed *one less*, but the place is soon supplied, and the ocean rolls on its tumultuous billows as though none had been taken away. So with human life. The affairs of men will roll on ; the world will be as busy, and active, and thoughtless as though we had not been ; and soon, O how painfully soon to human pride, will our names be forgotten ! The circle of friends will cease to weep, and then cease to remember us. The last memorial that we lived, will be gone. The house that we built, the bed on which we slept, the counting-room that we occupied, the monuments that we raised, the books that we made, the stone that we directed to be placed over our graves, will all be gone ; and the last memento that WE ever lived, will have faded away ! How vain is man ! How vain is pride ! How foolish is ambition ! How important the announcement that there is another world, where we may live on for ever !

21. *Doth not their excellency, &c.* Dr. Good renders this, " Their fluttering round is over with them," by a very forced construction of the passage. Translators and expositors

CHAPTER V.

CHAPTER V.

CALL now, if there be any
that will answer thee; and

have been very much divided in opinion as to its meaning; but the sense seems to be, that whatever is excellent in men is torn away or removed. Their excellence does not keep them from death, and they are taken off before they are truly wise. The word "excellency" here refers not only to moral excellency or virtue, but every thing in which they excel others. Whatever there is in them of strength, or virtue, or influence, is removed. The word here used (יֶתֶר) means, literally, something hanging over or redundant (from יָתַר, to hang over, be redundant, or to remain), and hence it means abundance or remainder, and then that which exceeds or abounds. It is thus applied to any distinguished virtue or excellency, as that which *exceeds* the ordinary limits or bounds. Men perish; and however eminent they may have been, they are soon cut off, and vanish away. The object here is to show how weak, and frail, and unworthy of confidence are men even in their most elevated condition. ¶ *They die, even without wisdom.* That is, before they become truly wise. The object is to show, that men are so short-lived compared with angels, that they have no opportunity to become distinguished for wisdom. Their days are few; and however careful may be their observation, before they have had time to become truly wise they are hurried away. They are, therefore, wholly disqualified to sit in judgment on the doings of God, and to arraign, as Job had done, the divine wisdom.

Here closes the oracle which was addressed to Eliphaz. It is a description of unrivalled sublimity. In the sentiments that were addressed to Eliphaz, there is nothing that is contradictory to the other communications which God has made to men, or to what is taught by reason. Every reader of this passage must feel that the thoughts are singularly sublime, and that they are such as are adapted

to which of the saints wilt thou
¹ turn?

1 or, *look.*

to make a deep impression on the mind. The error in Eliphaz consisted in the *application* which he makes of them to Job, and in the inference which he draws, that he must have been a hypocrite. This inference is drawn in the following chapter. As the oracle stands here, it is pertinent to the argument which Eliphaz had commenced, and just fitted to furnish a reproof to Job for the irreverent manner in which he had spoken, and the complaints which he had brought (chap. iii.) against the dealings of God. Let us learn from the oracle: (1.) That man cannot be more just than God; and let this be an abiding principle of our lives; (2.) Not to murmur at his dispensations, but to confide in his superior wisdom and goodness; (3.) That our opportunities of observation, and our rank in existence, are as nothing compared with those of the angels, who are yet so inferior to God as to be charged with folly; (4.) That our foundation is in the dust, and that the most insignificant object may sweep us away; and (5.) That in these circumstances humility becomes us. Our proper situation is in the dust; and whatever calamities may befall us, we should confide in God, and feel that he is qualified to direct our affairs, and the affairs of the universe.

CHAPTER V.

1. *Call now.* The expressions here used, as Noyes has well observed, seem to be derived from the law, where the word *call* denotes the language of the complainant, and *answer* that of the defendant. According to this, the meaning of the words "call now" is, *in jus voca:* that is, call the Deity to account, or bring an action against him; or more properly, enter into an argument or litigation, as before a tribunal; see Notes on Isa. xli. 1, where similar language occurs. ¶ *If there be any that will answer thee.* If there is any one who will respond to thee in such a trial. Noyes renders

2 For wrath killeth the foolish | man, and ¹ envy slayeth the silly
1 or, *indignation.* | one.

this, " See if He will answer thee ;" that is, " See if the Deity will condescend to enter into a judicial controversy with thee, and give an account of his dealings towards thee." Dr. Good renders it, " Which of these can come forward to thee ; *i. e.* " Which of these weakly, ephemeral, perishing insects —which of these nothings can render thee any assistance?" The meaning is probably, " Go to trial, if you can find *any* respondent ; if there is any one willing to engage in such a debate ; and let the matter be fairly adjudicated and determined. Let an argument be entered into before a competent tribunal, and the considerations *pro* and *con* be urged on the point now under consideration." The desire of Eliphaz was, that there should be a fair investigation, where all that could be said on one side or the other of the question would be urged, and where there would be a decision of the important point in dispute. He evidently felt that Job would be foiled in the argument before whomsoever it should be conducted, and whoever might take up the opposite side ; and hence he says that he could get no one of " the saints " to assist him in the argument. In the expression, " if there be any that will answer thee," he may mean to intimate that he would find no one who would be willing even to go into an investigation of the subject. The case was so plain, the views of Job were so obviously wrong, the arguments for the opinion of Eliphaz were so obvious, that he doubted whether any one could be found who would be willing to make it the occasion of a set and formal trial, as if there could be any doubt about it. ¶ *And to which of the saints wilt thou turn?* Marg. as in Heb. *look.* That is, to which of them wilt thou look to be an advocate for such sentiments, or which of them would be willing to go into an argument on so plain a subject ? Grotius supposes that Eliphaz, having boasted that he had produced a divine revelation in his favour (chap. iv.), now calls upon Job to produce,

if he can, something of the same kind in his defence, or to see if there were any of the heavenly spirits who would give a similar revelation in *his* favour. The word here rendered " saints " (קְדֹשִׁים) means properly those who are sanctified or holy ; and it may be either applied to holy men, or to angels. It is generally supposed that it here refers to angels. So Schultens, Rosenmüller, Noyes, Good, and others, understand it. The word is often used in this sense in the Scriptures. So the LXX. understand it here — ἢ εἴ τινα ἀγγέλων ἁγίων ὄψῃ. Such is probably its meaning ; and the sense of the passage is, " Call now upon any one, and you will find none willing to be the advocate of such sentiments as you have urged. No holy beings—men or angels—would defend them." By this, probably, Eliphaz designed to show Job that he differed from all holy beings, and that his views were not those of a truly pious man. If he could find no one, either among holy angels or pious men, to be the advocate of his opinions, it followed that he *must* be in error.

2. *For wrath killeth the foolish man.* That is, the wrath of God. The word *foolish* here is used as synonymous with *wicked*, because wickedness is supreme folly. The general proposition here is, that the wicked are cut off, and that they are overtaken with heavy calamities in this life. In proof of this, Eliphaz appeals in the following verses to his own observation. The implied inference is, that Job, having had all his possessions taken away, and having been overwhelmed with unspeakably great personal calamities, was to be regarded as having been a great sinner. Some suppose, however, that the word *wrath* here relates to the indignation or the repining of the individual himself, and that the reference is to the fact that such wrath or repining preys upon the spirit, and draws down the divine vengeance. This is the view of Schultens, and of Noyes. But it seems more probable that Eliphaz means to state

3 I ^a have seen the foolish tak-

a Ps.37.35.

ing root ; but suddenly I cursed his habitation.

the proposition, that the wrath of God burns against the wicked, and that the following verses are an illustration of this sentiment, derived from his own observation. ¶ *And envy.* Marg. *indignation.* Jerome, *invidia, envy.* Sept. ζῆλος. Castellio, *severitas ac vehementia.* The Hebrew word קִנְאָה means jealousy, envy, ardour, zeal. It may be applied to any strong affection of the mind ; any fervent, glowing, and burning emotion. Gesenius supposes it means here *envy,* as excited by the prosperity of others. To me it seems that the connection requires us to understand it of wrath, or indignation, as in Deut. xxix. 20; Ps. lxxix. 5. As applied to God, it often means his jealousy, or his anger, when the affections of men are placed on other objects than himself ; Num. xxv. 11 ; Zeph. i. 18, *et al.* ¶ *Slayeth the silly one.* Good and Noyes render this, " the weak man." Jerome, *parvulum, the little one.* The LXX., πεπλανημένον, *the erring.* Walton, *ardelionem, the busy-body.* The Hebrew word פָּתָה is from פָּתָה *Páthâh, to open, to expand;* and hence the participle is applied to one who opens his lips, or whose mouth is open ; that is, a garrulous person, Prov. xx. 19 ; and also to one who is *open-hearted,* frank, ingenuous, unsuspicious ; and hence one who is easily influenced by others, or whose heart may be easily enticed. Thus it comes to mean one who is simple and foolish. In this sense it is used here, to denote one who is so simple and foolish as to be drawn aside by weak arguments and unfounded opinions. I have no doubt that Eliphaz meant, by insinuation, to apply this to Job, as being a weak-minded man, for having allowed the views which he entertained to make such an impression on his mind, and for having expressed himself as he had done. The proposition is general; but it would be easy to understand how he intended it to be applied.

3. *I have seen the foolish.* The wicked. To confirm the sentiment which he had just advanced, Eliphaz

appeals to his own observation, and says that though the wicked for a time seem to be prosperous, yet he had observed that they were soon overtaken with calamity and cut down. He evidently means that prosperity was no evidence of the divine favour ; but that when it had continued for a little time, and was then withdrawn, it was proof that the man who had been prospered was at heart a wicked man. It was easy to understand that he meant that this should be applied to Job, who, though he had been favoured with temporary prosperity, was now revealed to be at heart a wicked man. The sentiment here advanced by Eliphaz, as the result of his observation, strikingly accords with the observation of David, as expressed in the thirty-seventh Psalm :

I have seen the wicked in great power,
And spreading himself like a green bay-tree ;
Yet he passed away, and, lo, he was not :
Yea, I sought him, but he could not be found.
               Ver. 35, 36.

¶ *Taking root.* This figure, to denote prosperous and rapid growth, is often used in the Scriptures. Thus in Psalm i. 3 :

And he shall be like a tree planted by the rivers
      of water,
That bringeth forth his fruit in his season.

So Isa. xxvii. 6 :

Those that come out of Jacob shall he cause to
      take root ;
Israel shall blossom and bud,
And shall fill the face of the world with fruit.

So Ps. lxxx. 9, 10 :

Thou preparedst room before it,
And didst cause it to take deep root,
And it filled the land.
The hills were covered with the shadow of it,
And the boughs thereof were like the goodly
      cedars.

¶ *But suddenly.* Meaning either that calamity came upon him *suddenly*—as it had upon Job, that is, without any apparent preparation, or that calamity came *before a great while,* that is, that this prosperity did not continue. Probably there is an implied reference here to the case of Job, meaning that he had known just such instances before ; and as the case of Job accorded with what he had before seen, he hastened to the conclusion

4 His children are far from safety, and they are crushed in the gate, neither *is there* any to deliver *them*.

5 Whose harvest the hungry eateth up, and taketh it even out of the thorns, and the robber swalloweth up their substance.

that Job must have been a wicked man. ¶ *I cursed his habitation.* I had occasion to regard it as accursed; that is, I witnessed the downfall of his fortunes, and pronounced his habitation accursed. I saw that God regarded it as such, and that he had suddenly punished him. This accords with the observation of David, referred to above.

4. *His children are far from safety.* That is, this is soon manifest by their being cut off or subjected to calamity. The object of Eliphaz is, to state the result of his own observation, and to show how calamity overtook the wicked though they even prospered for a time. He begins with that which a man would feel most—the calamity which comes upon his children, and says that God would punish him in them. Every word of this would go to the heart of Job; for he could not but feel that it was aimed at him, and that the design was to prove that the calamities that had come upon his children were a proof of his own wickedness and of the divine displeasure. It is remarkable that Job listens to this with the utmost patience. There is no interruption of the speaker; no breaking in upon the argument of his friend; no mark of uneasiness. Oriental politeness required that a speaker should be heard attentively through whatever he might say. See the Intro. § 7. (13). Cutting and severe, therefore, as this strain of remark must have been, the sufferer sat meekly and heard it all, and waited for the appropriate time when an answer might be returned. ¶ *And they are crushed in the gate.* The gate of a city in ancient times was the chief place of concourse, and was the place where public business was usually transacted, and where courts of justice were held; see Gen. xxiii. 10; Deut. xxi. 19; xxv. 6, 7; Ruth iv. 1, seq.; Ps. cxxvii. 5; Prov. xxii. 22. The Greeks also held their courts in some public place of business. Hence the *forum*, αγορα, was also a place for fairs. See Jahn's

Archæology, § 247. Some suppose that the meaning here is, that they were oppressed and trodden down by the concourse in the gate. But the more probable meaning is, that they found no one to advocate their cause; that they were subject to oppression and injustice in judicial decisions; and then when their parent was dead, no one would stand up to vindicate them from respect to his memory. The idea is, that though there might be temporary prosperity, yet that it would not be long before heavy calamities would come upon the children of the wicked.

5. *Whose harvest the hungry eateth up.* That is, they are not permitted to enjoy the avails of their own labour. The harvest field is subject to the depredations of others, who contrive to possess themselves of it, and to consume it. ¶ *And taketh it even out of the thorns.* Or, he seizes it to the very thorns. That is, the famished robber seizes the whole of the harvest. He takes it all away, even to the thistles, and chaff, and cockle, and whatever impure substances there may be growing with the grain. He does not wait to separate the grain from the other substances, but consumes it all. He spares nothing. ¶ *And the robber swalloweth up their substance.* Noyes renders this, as Gesenius proposes to do, " and a snare gapeth after his substance;" Dr. Good, "and rigidly swoopeth up their substance." Rosenmüller much better,

Cujusque facultates exhauriebant sitibundi,

copying exactly the version of Castellio. The Vulgate in a similar manner, Et bibent sitientes divitias ejus —*And the thirsty drink up his wealth.* The LXX., ἐκσιφωνισθείη αὐτῶν ἡ ἰσχύς — *should their power be absorbed.* The true sense, as I conceive, is, "the thirsty gasp, or pant, after their wealth;" that is, they consume it. The word rendered in our common version "the robber (צמים) is, according to the ancient versions, the

6 Although [1] affliction cometh not forth of the dust, neither doth trouble spring out of the ground;

1 or, *iniquity.*

7 Yet *a* man is born unto [2] trouble, as the [3] sparks fly upward.

a 1 Co. 10. 13.   2 or, *labour.*

3 *sons of the burning coal lift up to fly.*

---

same as בְּמֵאֵי, *the thirsty,* and this sense the parallelism certainly requires. So obvious is this, that it is better to suppose a slight error in the Hebrew text, than to give it the signification of a "snare," as Noyes does, and as Gesenius (Lex.) proposes. The word rendered "swalloweth up" (שָׁאַף) means, properly, to breathe hard, to pant, to blow; and then to yawn after, to desire, to absorb; and the sense here is, that *the thirsty* consume their property. The whole figure is taken from robbers and freebooters ; and I have no doubt that Eliphaz meant impliedly to allude to the case of Job, and to say that he had known just such cases, where, though there was great temporary prosperity, yet before long the children of the man who was prospered, and who professed to be pious, but was not, were crushed, and his property taken away by robbers. It was this similarity of the case of Job to the facts which he had observed, that staggered him so much in regard to his character.

6 *Although affliction cometh not forth of the dust.* Marg. or *iniquity.* The marginal reading here has been inserted from the different meanings attached to the Hebrew word. That word (אָוֶן) properly means nothingness, or vanity ; then nothingness as to worth, unworthiness, wickedness, iniquity ; and then the consequences of iniquity—adversity, calamity, affliction ; Ps. lv. 4 ; Prov. xxii. 8 ; Ps. xc. 10 ; Job xv. 35. The LXX. render it κόπος, *labour,* or *trouble.* The Vulgate, *Nihil in terra, sine causa—* "there is nothing on the earth without a cause." The general sense is plain. It is, that afflictions are not to be ascribed to chance, or that they are not without intelligent design. They do not come up like thistles, brambles, and thorns, from the unconscious earth. They have a cause. They are under the direction of God. The *object* of Eliphaz in the statement is, to show to Job that it was

improper to murmur, and that he should commit his cause to a God of infinite power and wisdom; ver. 8, seq. Afflictions, Eliphaz says, could not be avoided. Man was born unto them. He ought to expect them, and when they come, they should be submitted to as ordered by an intelligent, wise, and good Being. This is *one* true ground of consolation in afflictions. They do not come from the unconscious earth : they do not spring up of themselves. Though it is true that man is born to them, and must expect them, yet it is also true that they are ordered in infinite wisdom, and that they always have a design. ¶ *Neither doth trouble spring out of the ground.* The LXX. render this, "Nor will affliction spring up from the mountains."

7. *Yet man is born unto trouble.* All this is connected with the sentiment in ver. 8, seq. The meaning is, that "since afflictions are ordered by an intelligent Being, and since man is born unto trouble as the sparks fly upward, *therefore* it is wise to commit our cause to God, and not to murmur against him." Marg. or *labour.* The word here (עָמָל) rather means *trouble,* or *affliction,* than *labour.* The sense is, that as certainly as man is born, so sure is it that he will have trouble. It follows from the condition of our being, as certainly as that unconscious objects will follow the laws of their nature—that sparks will ascend. This seems to have a proverbial cast, and was doubtless regarded as a sentiment universally true. It is as true now as it was then ; for it is still the great law of our being, that trouble as certainly comes sooner or later, as that material objects obey the laws of nature which God has impressed on them. ¶ *As the sparks fly upward.* The Hebrew expression here is very beautiful—"as בְּנֵי רֶשֶׁף—*the sons of flame* fly." The word used (רֶשֶׁף) means flame, lightning ; the sons, or children of the flame, are that which it pro-

8 I would seek unto God, and unto God would I commit my cause ;

1 *there is no search.*

9 Which doeth great things and [1] unsearchable ; marvellous things [2] without number :

2 *till there be no number.*

duces ; *i. e.* sparks. Gesenius strangely renders it, "*sons of the lightning; i. e.* birds of prey which fly as swift as the lightning." So Dr. Good, " As the bird-tribes are made to fly upwards." So Umbreit renders it, Gleichwie die Brut des Raubgeflügels sich hoch in Fluge hebt—" as a flock of birds of prey elevate themselves on the wing." Noyes adopts the construction of Gesenius ; partly on the principle that man would be more likely to be compared to birds, living creatures, than to sparks. There is considerable variety in the interpretation of the passage. The LXX. render it, *νεοσσοι δε γυπος*—*the young of the vulture.* The Chaldee, קני מזיקין *בני מזיקי—the sons of demons.* Syriac, *Sons of birds.* Jerome, Man is born to labour, *and the bird to flight* —*et avis ad volatum.* Schultens renders it, " glittering javelins," and Arius Montanus, "sons of the live coal." It seems to me that our common version has expressed the true meaning. But the idea is not essentially varied whichever interpretation is adopted. It is, that as sparks ascend, or as birds fly upward—following the laws of their being—so is trouble the lot of man. It certainly comes ; and comes under the direction of a Being who has fixed the laws of the inferior creation. It would be wise for man, therefore, to resign himself to God in the times when those troubles come. He should not sit down and murmur at this condition of things, but should submit to it as the law of his being, and should have sufficient confidence in God to believe that he orders it aright.

8. *I would seek unto God.* Our translators have omitted here the adversative particle אולם *but, yet, nevertheless,* and have thus marred the connection. The meaning of Eliphaz, I take to be, "that since affliction is ordered by an intelligent Being, and does not spring out of the ground, *therefore* he would commit his cause to God, and look to him." Jerome

has well expressed it, *Quam ob rem ego deprecabor Dominum.* Some have understood this as meaning that Eliphaz himself was in the habit of committing his cause to God, and that he exhorted Job to imitate his example. But the correct sense is that which regards it as counsel given to Job to look to God *because* afflictions are the result of intelligent design, and *because* God had shown himself to be worthy of the confidence of men. The latter point Eliphaz proceeds to argue in the following verses.

9. *Which doeth great things.* The object of this is, to show why Job should commit his cause to God. The reason suggested is, that he had showed himself qualified to govern the world by the great and wonderful acts which he performed. Eliphaz, therefore, proceeds to expatiate on what God had done, and thus states the ancient belief in regard to his sovereignty over the world. This strain of reasoning continues to the end of the chapter. There is great beauty and force in it ; and though we have, through the revelations of the New Testament, some more enlarged views of the government of God and of the design of affliction, yet perhaps there can be found nowhere a more beautiful argument to lead men to put confidence in God. The reason here stated is, that God does "great things," and, therefore, we should commit ourselves to him. His works are vast and boundless ; they are such as to impress the mind with a sense of his own immensity ; and in such a being we should confide rather than in a feeble creature's arm. Who, when he contemplates the vast universe which God has made, and surveys the starry world under the light of the modern astronomy, can doubt that God does " great things," and that the interests which we commit to him are safe? ¶ *And unsearchable.* Marg. "There is *no search.*" Sept. *ανεξιχνιαστα*— *whose footsteps cannot be traced.* The

Hebrew word חקר means searching out or examining; and the idea is here, that it is impossible fully to search out and comprehend what God does. See chap. xi. 7. This is stated as a reason why we should look to him. We should expect things in his administration which we cannot understand. The argument of Eliphaz seems to be, that it was a matter of indisputable fact that there are many things in the government of God which are above our comprehension; and when he afflicts us, we should feel that this is a part of the doings of the incomprehensible God. Such mysterious dealings are to be expected, and they should not be allowed for a moment to shake our confidence in him. ¶ *Marvellous things.* Things that are wonderful, and are fitted to excite amazement. See Notes on Isa. ix. 6. ¶ *Without number.* Marg. " *Till* there be *no number.*" The sense is, that it is impossible to estimate the number of those things in the universe over which he presides, which are adapted to excite admiration. If the view of the universe entertained in the time of Eliphaz was fitted to overwhelm the mind by its vastness and by the number of the objects which were created, this astonishment is much greater now that the telescope has disclosed the wonders of the heavens above to man, and the microscope the not less amazing wonders of the world beneath him. Leuwenhoeck, by the aid of the microscope, discovered, he supposed, a thousand million animalculæ, whose united bulk did not exceed the size of a grain of sand—all of whom are distinct formations, with all the array of functions necessary to life. Of the *number* also of the larger works of God, much interesting and overpowering truth is presented by the science of modern astronomy. As an instance of this, we may refer to the *Milky Way,* or the whitish, irregular zone, that goes round the whole heavens, and that can be seen at any season of the year, but particularly in the months of August, September, and November. " This vast portion of the heavens is found to consist wholly of stars, crowded into immense clusters.

On first presenting a telescope of considerable power to this splendid zone, we are lost in astonishment at the number, the variety, and the beautiful configuration of the stars of which it is composed. In certain parts of it, every slight motion of the telescope presents new groups and new configurations; and the new and wondrous scene is continued over a space of many degrees in succession. In several fields of view, occupying a space of not more than twice the breadth of the moon, you perceive more of these twinkling luminaries, than all the stars visible to the naked eye throughout the whole canopy of heaven. The late Sir W. Herschel, in passing his telescope along a space of this zone fifteen degrees long, and two broad, descried at least fifty thousand stars, large enough to be distinctly counted; besides which, he suspected twice as many more, which could be seen only now and then by faint glimpses for want of sufficient light; that is, fifty times more than the acutest eye can discern in the whole heavens during the clearest night; and the space which they occupy is only the one thousand three hundred and seventy-fifth part of the visible canopy of the sky. On another occasion this astronomer perceived nearly six hundred stars in *one* field of view of his telescope ; so that in the space of a quarter of an hour, one hundred and sixteen thousand stars passed in review before him. Now, were we to suppose every part of this zone equally filled with stars as the places now alluded to, there would be found in the Milky Way alone, no less than twenty millions one hundred and ninety thousand stars. In regard to the *distance* of some of these stars, it has been ascertained that some of the more remote are not less than five hundred times the distance of the nearest fixed star, or nearly two thousand billions of miles; a distance so great, that *light,* which flies at the rate of twelve millions of miles every minute, would require one thousand six hundred and forty years before it could traverse this mighty interval! The Milky Way is now, with good reason, considered

10 Who giveth rain upon the earth, and sendeth waters upon the [1] fields:

1 *out-places.*

11 To set up on high those that be low; that those which mourn may be exalted to safety.

to be the cluster of stars in which our sun is situated; and all the stars visible to the naked eye are only a few scattered orbs near the extremity of this cluster. Yet there is reason also to believe that the Milky Way, of which our system forms a part, is no more than a single *nebula*, of which several thousands have already been discovered, which compose the universe; and that it bears no more proportion to the whole siderial heavens than a small dusky speck which our telescopes enable us to descry in the heavens. *Three thousand nebulæ* have already been discovered. Suppose the number of stars in the whole Milky Way to be no more than ten millions, and that each of the nebulæ, at an average, contains the same number; supposing further, that only two thousand of the three thousand nebulæ are resolvable into stars, and that the other thousand are masses of a shining fluid, not yet condensed by the Almighty into luminous globes, the number of stars or *suns* comprehended in that portion of the firmament which is within the reach of our telescopes, is *twenty thousand millions.*" Yet all this may be as nothing compared with the parts of the universe which we are unable to discover. See in the Christian Keepsake for 1840, an article by Thomas Dick, entitled "An Idea of the Universe;' comp. Notes on chap. ix. 9.

10. *Who giveth rain upon the earth.* In the previous verse, Eliphaz had said, in general, that God did wonderful things—things which are fitted to lead us to put our trust in him. In this and the succeeding verses, he descends to particulars, and specifies those things which show that God is worthy to be confided in. This enunciation continues to ver. 16, and the general scope is, that the agency of God is seen everywhere; and that his providential dealings are adapted to impress man with elevated ideas of his justice and goodness. Eliphaz begins

with the *rain*, and says that the fact that God sends it upon the earth was fitted to lead man to confide in him. He means, that while the sun, and moon, and seasons have stated times, and are governed by settled laws, the rain seems to be sent directly by God, and is imparted at such times as are best. It is wholly under his control, and furnishes a constant evidence of his benevolence. Without it, every vegetable would dry up, and every animal on the earth would soon die. The word *earth* here refers probably to the cultivated part of the earth—the fields that are under tillage. Thus Eichhorn renders it, Angebauten Feldern. On the interest which the phenomena of rain excited among the ancient sages of Idumea, and the laws by which it is produced, see Notes on chap. xxxvii. 6, 15, 16; xxxviii. 22—28. ¶ *And sendeth waters.* That is, showers. ¶ *Upon the fields.* Marg. out-places. Heb. הוּצוֹת—out of doors, outside, abroad, meaning the fields out of cities and towns. Eichhorn renders it, "the pastures," auf Triften. The meaning is, that the whole country is watered; and the fact that God gives rain in this manner, is a reason why we should put confidence in him. It shows that he is a benevolent Being, since it contributes so essentially to human life and happiness, and since no other being but God can cause it.

11. *To set up on high.* That is, who sets up on high; or God exalts those who are low. From the works of nature, Eliphaz passes to the dealings of God with *men*, as designed to show that he was worthy of confidence. The first proof is, that he showed himself to be the friend of the humble and the afflicted, and often exalted those who were in lowly circumstances, in a manner which evinced his direct interposition. It is to be remembered here, that Eliphaz is detailing the result of his own observation, and stating the reasons which he had observed

12 He *a* disappointeth the devices of the crafty, so that their hands cannot perform *their* ¹ enterprise.

a Ne.4.15.   1 or, *any thing.*

13 He *a* taketh the wise in their own craftiness; and the counsel of the froward is carried headlong.

a 1 Co.3.19.

for putting confidence in God; and the meaning here is, that he had so often seen this done as to show that God was the friend of the humble and the poor. This sentiment was afterwards expressed with great beauty by Mary, the mother of the Lord Jesus:

He hath put down the mighty from their seats,
And exalted them of low degree;
He hath filled the hungry with good things,
And the rich he hath sent empty away.
Luke i. 52, 53.

¶ *That those which mourn may be exalted to safety.* Or rather, they who mourn are exalted to a place of safety. The sense is, that God did this; and that, therefore, there was ground of confidence in him. The word rendered, " those which mourn" (קֹדְרִים) is from קָדַר, to be turbid or foul as a torrent, Job vi. 16; hence to go about in filthy garments, like mourners, to mourn. The general sense of the Hebrew word, as in Arabic, is to be squalid, dark, filthy, dusky, obscure; and hence it denotes those who are afflicted, which is its sense here. The LXX. render it, ἀπολώλοτας, *the lost,* or those who are perished. The sense is plain. God raises up the bowed down, the oppressed, and the afflicted. Eliphaz undoubtedly referred to instances which had come under his own observation, when persons who had been in very depressed circumstances, had been raised up to situations of comfort, honour, and safety; and that in a manner which was a manifest interposition of his Providence. From this he argued that those who were in circumstances of great trial, should put their trust in him. Cases of this kind often occur; and a careful observation of the dealings of God with the afflicted, would undoubtedly furnish materials for an argument like that on which Eliphaz relied in this instance.

12. *He disappointeth the devices of the crafty.* He foils them in their schemes, or makes their plans vain.

This too was the result of close observation on the part of Eliphaz. He had seen instances where the plans of crafty, designing, and artful men had been defeated, and where the straightforward had been prospered and honoured. Such cases led him to believe that God was the friend of virtue, and was worthy of entire confidence. ¶ *So that their hands.* So that they. The hands are the instruments by which we accomplish our plans. ¶ Their *enterprise.* Marg. Or, *any thing.* Heb. תֻּשִׁיָּה. This word properly means *uprightness* from יָשַׁר; then help, deliverance, Job vi. 13; then purpose, undertaking, enterprise, *i. e.* what one wishes to set up or establish. *Gesenius.* This is its meaning here. Vulg. " Their hands cannot finish (*implere*) what they had begun." Sept. " Their hands cannot perform that which is true"— ἀληθές. The Chaldee Paraphrase refers this to the defeat of the purposes of the Egyptians: " Who made vain the thoughts of the Egyptians, who acted wisely [or cunningly—דְּהַכִּימוּ] that they might do evil to Israel, but their hands did not perform the work of their wisdom (ver. 13), who took the wise men of Pharaoh in their own wisdom, and the counsel of their perverse astrologers he made to return upon them." The general sense is, that artful and designing men —men who work in the dark, and who form secret purposes of evil, are disappointed and foiled. Eliphaz probably had seen instances of this, and he now attributes it to God as rendering him worthy of the confidence of men. It is still true. The crafty and the designing are often foiled in such a manner as to show that it is wholly of God. He exposes their designs in this way, and shows that he is the friend of the sincere and the honest; and in doing this, he shows that he is worthy the confidence of his people.

13. *He taketh the wise in their own craftiness.* This passage is quoted

14 They ¹ meet with darkness

1 or, *run into*, Is. 59.10 ; Am. 8.9.

in the day-time, and grope in the noon-day as in the night.

by the apostle Paul in 1 Cor. iii. 19, with the usual formula in referring to the Old Testament, γέγραπται γάρ, "for it is written," showing that he regarded it as a part of the inspired oracles of God. The word *wise* here undoubtedly means the cunning, the astute, the crafty, and the designing. It cannot mean those who are truly wise in the Scripture sense ; but the meaning is, that those who form plans which they expect to accomplish by cunning and craft, are often the victims of their own designs. The same sentiment not unfrequently occurs in the Scriptures and elsewhere, and has all the aspect of being a proverb. Thus in Ps. vii. 15 :

He made a pit and digged it,
And is fallen into the ditch which he made.

So Ps. ix. 15 :

The heathen are sunk down into the pit that
　　they made ;
In the net which they hid is their own foot
　　taken.

So Ps. xxxv. 8 :

Let his net that he hath hid catch himself
Into that very destruction let him fall.

So Ps. xxxvii. 15 :

Their sword shall enter into their own heart,
And their bow shall be broken.

Comp. Eurip. Med. 409 :

Κακῶν δὲ πάντων τέκτονες σοφώταται.

See also the same sentiment in Lucretius, v. 1151 :

Circumretit enim vis atque injuria quemque,
Atque.unde exorta est, ad eum plerumque revertit.

"For force and rapine in their craftiest nets
Oft their own sons entangle ; and the plague
Ten-fold recoils."

It is to be remembered that Eliphaz here speaks of his own observation, and of that as a reason for putting confidence in God. The sentiment is, that he had observed that a straightforward, honest, and upright course, was followed with the divine favour and blessing ; but that a man who attempted to carry his plans by intrigue and stratagem, would not be permanently successful. Sooner or later his cunning would recoil upon himself,

and he would experience the disastrous consequences of such a course. It is still true. A man is always sure of ultimate success and prosperity, if he is straightforward and honest. He never can be sure of it, if he attempts to carry his plans by management. Other men may evince as much cunning as himself ; and when his net *springs*, it may include himself as well as those for whom he set it. It will be well for him if it is not made to spring on him, while others escape. ¶ *And the counsel of the froward.* The design of the perverse. The word here rendered "froward," נִפְתָּלִים, is from פתל, to twist, to twine, to spin. It then means, to be twisted, crooked, crafty, deceitful. Here it means those who are crooked, artful, designing. Sept. πολυπλόκων, *the involved—the much-entangled.* ¶ *Is carried headlong.* Heb. is precipitated, or hastened. There is not time for it to be matured ; there is a development of the scheme before it is ripe, and the trick is detected before there is time to put it in execution. Nothing can be more true than this often is now. Something that could not be anticipated develops the design, and brings the dark plot out to mid-day ; and God shows that he is the foe of all such schemes.

14. *They meet with darkness in the day-time.* Marg. *run into ;* comp. Notes on Isa. lix. 10. The sense is, that where there is really no obstacle to the accomplishment of an honest plan—any more than there is for a man to walk in the day-time—*they* become perplexed and embarrassed, as much as a man would be, should sudden darkness come around him at mid-day. The same sentiment occurs in chap. xii. 25. A life of honesty and uprightness will be attended with prosperity, but a man who attempts to carry his plans by trick and art, will meet with unexpected embarrassments. The sentiment in all these expressions is, that God embarrasses the cunning, the crafty, and the artful, but gives success to those who are

15 But *a* he saveth the poor from the sword, from their mouth, and from the hand of the mighty.

a Ps. 107. 41.

16 So the poor hath hope, and iniquity stoppeth her mouth.

17 Behold, happy *b* is the man

b He. 12. 5 ; Ja. 1. 12.

upright ; and that, therefore, he is worthy of confidence.

15. *But he saveth the poor from the sword.* He shows himself to be the friend and protector of the defenceless. The phrase "from the sword, from their mouth," has been variously interpreted. Dr. Good renders it,

So he saveth the persecutors from their mouth,
And the helpless from the hand of the violent.

Noyes,

So he saveth the persecuted from their mouth,
The oppressed from the hand of the mighty.

This rendering is obtained by changing the points in the word מֵחֶרֶב, *from the sword,* to מֵחָרֵב, making it the Hophal participle from חָרַב, to make desolate. This was proposed by Capellus, and has been adopted by Durell, Michaelis, Dathe, Doederlein, and others. Rosenmüller pronounces it wholly unauthorized. Jerome renders it, *a gladio oris eorum*—"from the sword of their mouth." It seems to me that the whole verse may be literally rendered, "he saveth from the sword, from their mouth, and from the hand of the strong, the poor." According to this version, the phrase "from their mouth" may either mean from the mouth, *i. e.* the edge of the sword, using the plural for the singular, or from the mouth of oppressors, using it to represent their violence, and their disposition to devour the poor. The latter is more probably the true interpretation, and there is no need of a change in the points in the Hebrew. Thus interpreted, the sense is, that God preserves the poor from oppression ; or, in other words, that he befriends them, and is therefore worthy of confidence. This sentiment accords with what is found everywhere in the Bible.

16. *So the poor hath hope.* From the interposition of God. They are not left in a sad and comfortless condition. They are permitted to regard God as their protector and friend, and to look forward to another and a bet-

ter world. This sentiment accords with all that is elsewhere said in the Scriptures, that the offers of mercy are specially made to the poor, and that they are peculiarly the objects of the divine compassion. ¶ *And iniquity stoppeth her mouth.* That is, the wicked are confounded when they see all their plans foiled, and find themselves entangled in the snares which they have laid for others. A similar sentiment occurs in Ps. cvii. 41, 42 :

Yet setteth he the poor on high from affliction,
And maketh him families like a flock.
The righteous shall see it and rejoice,
And all iniquity shall stop her mouth.

It is to be remembered that Eliphaz states this as the result of his own observation, and as clearly demonstrating in his view that there is a superintending and overruling Providence. A careful observation of the course of events would undoubtedly lead to the same conclusion, and this has been embodied in almost every language by some proverbial sentiment. We express it by saying that "honesty is the best policy ;" a proverb that is undoubtedly founded in wisdom. The sentiment is, that if a man wishes long to prosper, he should pursue a straightforward and an honest course ; that cunning, intrigue, underhanded dealing, and mere management, will sooner or later defeat itself, and recoil on the head of him who uses it ; and that, therefore, if there were no higher motive than self-interest, a man should be honest, frank, and open. See this argument stated at greater length, and with great beauty, in Psalm xxxvii.

17. *Behold, happy is the man whom God correcteth.* This verse commences a new argument, designed to show that afflictions are followed by so important advantages as to make it proper that we should submit to them without a murmur. The sentiment in this verse, if not expressly quoted, is probably alluded to by the apostle Paul in Heb. xii. 5. The same thought frequently occurs in the Bible :

whom God correcteth; therefore despise not thou the chastening of the Almighty.

18 For [a] he maketh sore, and

a De. 32. 39.

bindeth up; he woundeth, and his hands make whole.

19 He [b] shall deliver thee in six troubles; yea, in seven there shall no evil touch thee.

b Ps. 91.

see James i. 12; Prov. iii. 11, 12. The sense is plain, that God confers a favour on us when he recalls us from our sins by the corrections of his paternal hand—as a father confers a favour on a child whom he restrains from sin by suitable correction. The *way* in which this is done, Eliphaz proceeds to state at length. He does it in most beautiful language, and in a manner entirely in accordance with the sentiments which occur elsewhere in the Bible. The word rendered *correcteth* (יכח) means to argue, convince, reprove, punish, and to judge. It here refers to any of the modes by which God calls men from their sins, and leads them to walk in the paths of virtue. The word "happy" here, means that the *condition* of such an one is blessed (אשרי); Gr. μακάριος—not that there is happiness in the suffering. The sense is, that it is *a favour* when God recalls his friends from their wanderings, and from the error of their ways, rather than to suffer them to go on to ruin. He does me a kindness who shows me a precipice down which I am in danger of falling; he lays me under obligation to him who even with violence saves me from flames which would devour me. Eliphaz undoubtedly means to be understood as implying that Job had been guilty of transgression, and that God had taken this method to recall him from the error of his ways. That he had sinned, and that these calamities had come as a consequence, he seems never once to doubt; yet he supposes that the affliction was meant in kindness, and proceeds to state that if Job would receive it in a proper manner, it might be attended still with important benefits. ¶ *Therefore despise not thou the chastening of the Almighty.* "Do not *regret* (תמאס). Sept. μὴ ἀπαναίνου—the means which God is using to admonish you." There is direct allusion here undoubtedly

to the feelings which Job had manifested (chap. iii.); and the object of Eliphaz is, to show him that there were important benefits to be derived from affliction which should make him willing to bear it without murmuring. Job had exhibited, as Eliphaz thought, a disposition to reject the lessons which afflictions were designed to teach him, and to spurn the admonitions of the Almighty. From that state of mind he would recall him, and would impress on him the truth that there were such advantages to be derived from those afflictions as should make him willing to endure all that was laid upon him without a murmur.

18. *For he maketh sore.* That is, he afflicts. ¶ *And bindeth up.* He heals. The phrase is taken from the custom of binding up a wound; see Notes on Isa. i. 6; xxxviii. 21. This was a common mode of healing among the Hebrews; and the practice of medicine appears to have been confined much to external applications. The meaning of this verse is, that afflictions come from God, and that he only can support, comfort, and restore. Health is his gift; and all the consolation which we need, and for which we can look, must come from him.

19. *He shall deliver thee in six troubles.* Six is used here to denote an indefinite number, meaning that he would support in *many* troubles. This mode of speech is not uncommon among the Hebrews, where one number is mentioned, so that an extreme number may be immediately added. The method is, to mention a number within the limit, and then to add one more, meaning that in *all* instances the thing referred to would occur. The *limit* here is seven, with the Hebrews a complete and perfect number; and the idea is, that in any succession of troubles, however numerous, God

20 In famine *a* he shall redeem thee from death ; and in war from the ¹ power of the sword.

a Ps. 37.19.   1 *hands.*

21 Thou shalt be hid ² from the scourge of the tongue ; *b* neither

2 or, *when the tongue scourgeth.*   *b* Ps.31.20.

---

was able to deliver. Similar expressions not unfrequently occur. Thus in Amos i. 3, 6, 9, 11, 13 ; ii. 1, 4, 6 :

Thus saith the LORD :   [four,
For three transgressions of Damascus, and for
I will not turn away the punishment thereof.
    Thus saith the LORD :
For three transgressions of Gaza, and for four,
I will not turn away the punishment thereof.
    Thus saith the LORD :
For three transgressions of Tyrus,an I for four,
I will not turn away the punishment thereof.

Thus in Prov. xxx. 15 :

There are three things that are never satisfied,
Yea, four things say not, It is enough.
There be three things that are too wonderful
    for me,
Yea, four which I know not. Ver.18.
For three things the earth is disquieted,
And for four which it cannot bear. Ver. 21.

There be three things that go well,
Yea, four are comely in going :
A lion which is strongest among beasts,
And turneth not away for any ;
A grey-hound ;
An he-goat also ;
And a king, against whom there is no rising up.
    Ver. 29–31.

Comp. Homer, Iliad vi. 174 :

Εννήμαρ ξείνισσε καὶ ἐννέα βοῦς ἱέρευσιν.

An enumeration, in regard to number similar to the one before us, occurs in Prov. vi. 16 :

These six things doth the Lord hate;
Yea, seven are an abomination to him.

¶ *There shall no evil touch thee.* That is, permanently ; for he could not mean that he would not be subjected to calamity at all, since by the very supposition he was a sufferer. But the sense is, that God would save from those calamities.

20. *In famine he shall redeem thee.* That is, will deliver thee from death. On the meaning of the word *redeem,* see Notes on Isaiah, chap. xliii. 1, 3. ¶ *From the power of the sword.* Marg. as in Heb. *hands.* That is, he should not be slain by armed men. A *mouth* is often attributed to the sword in the Scriptures, because it devours ; *hands* are attributed to it here, because it is by the hand that we perform an undertaking, and the sword is personified, and represented as acting

as a conscious agent ; comp. Ezek. xxxv. 5, *margin.* The meaning is, that God would protect those who put their trust in him, in times of calamity and war. Doubtless Eliphaz had seen instances enough of this kind to lead him to this general conclusion, where the pious poor had been protected in a remarkable manner, and where signal deliverances had been vouchsafed to the righteous in danger.

21. *Thou shalt be hid from the scourge of the tongue.* Marg. Or, *when the tongue scourgeth.* The word rendered "scourge" — שׁוֹט — means properly a whip. It is used of God when he *scourges* men by calamities and punishments; Isa. x. 26; Job ix. 23. See the use of the verb שׁוּט in chap. ii. 7. Here it is used to denote a *slanderous* tongue, as being that which inflicts a severe wound upon the reputation and peace of an individual. The idea is, that God would guard the reputation of those who commit themselves to him, and that they shall be secure from *slander*, "whose breath," Shakspeare says, "outvenoms all the worms of Nile." ¶ *Neither shalt thou be afraid when destruction cometh.* That is, your mind shall be calm in those calamities which threaten destruction. When war rages, when the tempest howls, when the pestilence breathes upon a community, then your mind shall be at peace. A similar thought occurs in Isa. xxvi. 3 : "Thou wilt keep him in perfect peace whose mind is stayed on thee;" and the same sentiment is beautifully illustrated at length in the ninety-first Psalm. The Chaldee Paraphrase applies all this to events which had occurred in the history of the Hebrews. Thus ver. 20: "In the famine in Egypt, he redeemed thee from death ; and in the war with Amalek, from being slain by the sword;" ver. 21: " In the injury inflicted by the tongue of Balaam thou wert hid among the clouds, and thou didst not fear from the desolation of the Midianites when

shalt thou be afraid of destruction when it cometh.

22 At destruction and famine

it came;" ver. 22: "In the desolation of Sihon, and in the famine of the desert, thou didst laugh; and of the camps of Og, who was like a wild beast of the earth, thou wert not afraid."

22. *At destruction and famine thou shalt laugh.* That is, thou shalt be perfectly safe and happy. They shall not come upon thee; and when they approach with threatening aspect, thou shalt smile with conscious security. The word here rendered famine (כָּפָן) is an unusual word, and differs from that occurring in ver. 20, רָעָב. This word is derived from כָּפֵן—to languish, to pine from hunger and thirst. It then means the languid and feeble state which exists where there is a want of proper nutriment. A sentiment similar to that which is here expressed occurs in Martial, iv. 19, 4.

Ridebis ventos hoc munere tectus, et imbres.

¶ *Neither shalt thou be afraid of the beasts of the earth.* Wild beasts in new countries are always objects of dread, and in the fastnesses and deserts of Arabia, they were especially so. They abounded there; and one of the highest images of happiness there would be, that there would be perfect safety from them. A similar promise occurs in Ps. xci. 13:

Thou shalt tread upon the lion and adder;
The young lion and the dragon shalt thou
   trample under foot.

And a promise similar to this was made by the Saviour to his disciples: "They shall take up serpents; and if they drink any deadly thing, it shall not hurt them." The sentiment of Eliphaz is, that they who put their trust in God would find protection, and have the consciousness that they were secure wherever they were.

23. *For thou shalt be in league with the stones of the field.* In the Hebrew, "There shall be a covenant between thee and the stones of the field." The sense is, they shall not harm thee. They are here spoken of as enemies that were made to be at peace, and that would not annoy or

thou shalt laugh: neither shalt thou be afraid of the beasts of the earth.

23 For thou shalt be in league

injure. It is to be remembered that this was spoken in Arabia, where rocks and stones abounded, and where travelling, from that cause, was difficult and dangerous. The sense here is, as I understand it, that he would be permitted to make his way in case and safety. Tindal renders it:

But the castels in the land shall be confederate
   with thee;
The beastes of the fealde shall give thee peace.

Some have supposed that the meaning is, that the land would be free from stones that rendered it barren, and would be rendered fertile if the favour of God was sought. Shaw, in his Travels, supposes that it refers to the custom of walking over stones, in which the feet are liable to be injured every moment, and that the meaning is, that that danger would be averted by the divine interposition. By others it has been conjectured that the allusion is to a custom which is known as *skopelism*, of which Egmont and Heyman (Reisen, II. Th. S. 156), give the following account: "that in Arabia, if any one is living at variance with another, he places on his land stones as a warning that no one should dare to plough it, as by doing it he would expose himself to the danger of being punished by him who had placed the stones there." This custom is also referred to by Ulpian (L. ix. de officio Proconsulis), and in the Greek Pandects, Lib. lx. Tit. xxii. Leg. 9. It may be doubted, however, whether this custom was as early as the time of Job, or was so common then as to make it probable that the allusion is to it. Rosenmüller supposes the meaning to be, "Thy field shall be free from stones, which would render it unfruitful." Alte u. neue Morgenland, *in loc.* Other explanations may be seen in Rosenmüller (Commentary), but it seems to me that the view presented above, that travelling would be rendered safe and pleasant, is the true one. Such a promise would be among the rich blessings in a country like Arabia.

with the stones of the field; and the beasts *a* of the field shall be at peace with thee.

24 And thou shalt know [1] that thy tabernacle *shall be* in peace;

a Is.11.9.   1 or, *that peace is thy tabernacle.*

and thou shalt visit thy habitation, and shalt not [2] sin.

25 Thou shalt know also that thy seed *shall be* [3] great, and thine off-spring as the grass of the earth.

2 or, *err.*   3 or, *much.*

24. *And thou shalt know that thy tabernacle* shall be *in peace.* Thy tent—אָהֳלֶךָ—showing that it was common then to dwell in tents. The sense is, that when he was away from home he would have confidence that his dwelling was secure, and his family safe. This would be an assurance producing no small degree of consolation in a country abounding in wild beasts and robbers. Such is the nature of the blessing which Eliphaz says the man would have who put his confidence in God, and committed his cause to him. To a certain extent this was, and is, undoubtedly true. A man cannot indeed have miraculous assurance when from home, that his wife and children are still alive, and in health ; nor can he be certain that his dwelling is not wrapped in flames, or that it has been preserved from the intrusion of evil-minded men. But he may feel assured that all is under the wise control of God ; that whatever occurs will be by his permission and direction, and will tend to ultimate good. He may also, with calmness and peace, commit his home with all that is dear to him to God, and feel that in his hands all is safe. ¶ *And thou shalt visit thy habitation.* That is, on the return from a journey. ¶ *And not sin.* This is a very unhappy translation. The true sense is, thou shalt not *miss* thy dwelling ; thou shalt not wander away lost, to return no more. The word here used, and which is rendered "sin" in our common version, is חָטָא, *hhâtâ.* It is true that it is commonly rendered *to sin,* and that it often has this sense. But it properly means *to miss;* that is, not to hit the mark, spoken of a slinger, Judges xx. 16 ; then to make a false step, to stumble or fall, Prov. xix. 2. It thus accords exactly in sense with the Greek ἁμαρτάνω. Here the original sense of the Hebrew word should be retained, meaning that he would not

miss the way to his dwelling ; that is, that he would be permitted to return to it in safety. Gesenius, however, renders it, " Thou musterest thy pasture (*flocks*), and missest naught:" that is, nothing is gone ; all thy flocks are there. But the more obvious sense, and a sense which the connection demands, is that which refers the whole description to a man who is on a journey, and who is exposed to the dangers of wild beasts, and to the perils of a rough and stony way, but who is permitted to visit his home without missing it or being disappointed. A great variety of interpretations have been given of the passage, which may be seen in Rosenmüller and Good. Many suppose it means that he should review his domestic affairs, and find all to his mind ; or should find that every thing was in its place, or was as it should be. It cannot be doubted that the Hebrew word "*visit*" (פָּקַד) will bear this interpretation, but that above proposed seems to me best to suit the connection. The margin correctly renders it, *err.*

25. *Thou shalt know also that thy seed* shall be *great.* Marg. *much.* That is, thy posterity shall be numerous. This was one of the blessings supposed to be connected with the favour of God ; see Notes on Isa. liii. 10. ¶ *And thine offspring as the grass of the earth.* On the meaning of the word here rendered *offspring,* see Notes on Isa. xlviii. 19. Nothing is more common in the Scriptures, than to compare a prosperous and a happy man to a green and flourishing tree ; see Ps. i. 3 ; xcii. 12—14. The idea here is, that the righteous would have a numerous and a happy posterity, and that the divine favour to them would be shown by the blessing of God on their children ; comp. Ps. cxxviii. 1, 3.

Blessed is every one that feareth the Lord,
That walketh in his ways.
Thy wife shall be a fruitful vine by the side of
    thine house ;

26 Thou shalt come to *thy* grave in a full age, *a* like as a shock of corn ¹ cometh in in his season.

27 Lo this, we have searched *b* it, so it *is ;* hear it, and know thou *it* for ² thy good.

a Pr.9.11.   1 *ascendeth.*
b Pr.2.3—5.   2 *thyself ;* Pr.9.12.

Thy children like olive-plants round about thy table.

26. *Thou shalt come to* thy *grave in full age.* That is, thou shalt have long life; thou shalt not be cut down prematurely, nor by any sudden calamity. It is to be remembered that long life was regarded as an eminent blessing in ancient times; see Notes on Isa. lxv. 22. ¶ *Like as a shock of corn cometh in in his season.* Marg. *ascendeth.* As a sheaf of grain is harvested when it is fully ripe. This is a beautiful comparison, and the meaning is obvious. He would not be cut off before his plans were fully matured; before the fruits of righteousness had ripened in his life. He would be taken away when he was ripe for heaven—as the yellow grain is for the harvest. Grain is not cut down when it is green; and the meaning of Eliphaz is, that it is as desirable that man should live to a good old age before he is gathered to his fathers, as it is that grain should be suffered to stand until it is fully ripe.

27. *Lo this.* All this that I have said; the truth of all the remarks which I have made. ¶ *We have searched it.* We have by careful observation of the course of events come to these conclusions. These are our views of the providence of God, and of the principles of his government, as far as we have had the opportunity of observing, and they are well worthy of your attention. The sentiments in these two chapters indicate close and accurate observation; and if we think that the observation was not always wholly accurate, or that the principles were carried farther than facts would warrant, or that Eliphaz applied them with somewhat undue severity to the case of Job, we are to remember that this was in the infancy of the world, that they had few historical records,

CHAPTER VI.

ANALYSIS OF CHAPTERS VI. AND VII.

These two chapters comprise the answer of Job to the speech of Eliphaz. There is much strong emotion in this reply; much that expresses the depth of his sorrow; much real piety; and much also that cannot be justified in his impatience, and in his remonstrances with God for afflicting him. He felt keenly the remarks of Eliphaz, and in the anguish of his soul, he gives vent to expressions which he himself afterwards sees to be improper.

and *that they had no written revelation.* If they were favoured with occasional revelations, as Eliphaz claimed (chap. iv. 12, seq.), yet they were few in number, and at distant intervals, and the divine communications pertained to but few points. Though it may without impropriety be maintained that some of the views of Eliphaz and his friends were not wholly accurate, yet we may safely ask, Where among the Greek and Roman sages can views of the divine government be found that equal these in correctness, or that are expressed with equal force and beauty? For profound and accurate observation, for beauty of thought and sublimity of expression, the sage of Teman will not fall behind the sages of Athens; and not the least interesting thing in the contemplation of the book of Job, is the comparison which we are almost of necessity compelled to make between the observations on the course of events which were made in Arabia, and those which were made by the philosophers of the ancient heathen world. Is it improper to suppose that one design of this book was to show how far the human mind could go, with the aid of occasional revelations on a few points, in ascertaining the principles of the divine administration, and to demonstrate that, after all, the mind needed a fuller revelation to enable man to comprehend the truths pertaining to the kingdom of God? ¶ *Hear it for thy good.* Marg. as in Heb. *thyself.* These principles are such that they are of importance for you to understand and to apply.

CHAPTER VI.

2. *O that my grief were thoroughly weighed.* The word rendered *grief* here (כעש) may mean either vexation, trouble, grief; Eccl. i. 18; ii. 23; or it may mean *anger ;* Deut. xxxii. 19; Ezek. xx. 28. It is rendered by the

proper, and for which, in the close, he makes humble and penitent acknowledgment to God. In reply to the harsh and severe insinuations of Eliphaz, he justifies the bitterness of his complaints by the severity of the affliction which he had been called to endure, chap. vi 2—13. This object leads him into a particular statement of the depth and extent of his sorrows, as if they had not been understood or appreciated by his friends. He wishes (ver. 2, 3) that his grief were thoroughly and attentively considered; says (ver. 4) that the arrows of the Almighty are in him, and that the terrors of God are arrayed against him, and that he did not complain without cause, any more than the wild ass or the ox when they were perishing, ver. 5—7; reiterates his request that God would suffer him to die, ver. 8, 9; repeats the thought that he would then have comfort in the grave, ver. 10; and complains bitterly that his strength was insufficient to bear these heavy trials. He then goes on to say, that a man in such circumstances ought to have the sympathy of his friends, but that *his* friends had deceived him, and had greatly aggravated his sufferings, ver. 14—23. They had shown themselves to be like a brook in the desert, where a company of travellers expected to find water, but which they found to be dried up, ver. 15—23. He then (ver. 24—30) earnestly requests his friends to consider more attentively his circumstances, and to see whether his strong expressions could not be justified. He evidently supposes that they did not understand the depth of his sorrows, and did not sympathize with him as they ought to do. In justification of his feelings (chap. vii. 1—11), he recapitulates his sufferings. Eliphaz had exhorted him to commit himself to God, and to bear all this with a calm and submissive mind. To all this he says (chap. vii. 1) that life was short, and that the days of man were like those of an hireling, who anxiously longed for the close of the day; that his was a life of toil and pain, where it was proper to look for the shades of the evening, ver. 2, 3; that his days and nights were filled with vanity and sorrow, ver. 3, 4. He describes his disease as filling his flesh with worms and clods of dust, ver. 5;

and says that his days are swift, and that he must soon vanish away like a cloud, and be known no more, ver. 10. How then, he asks, could he restrain his anguish? How could he help speaking in the bitterness of his soul? ver. 11. Hurried on by the deep sense of his sorrows, he now allows himself to expostulate in a very improper manner with God, and to remonstrate with him in great severity of language for thus afflicting him, ver. 12—19. He asks whether he was a sea or a whale, that God should watch him in this manner, ver. 12; says that when he would take rest on his bed, then God frightened him with distressing visions, ver. 13, 14; that such was his condition that he loathed and hated his life, ver. 15, 16, and demands with impatience what is man that God should thus visit him, and that he would not for the briefest time let him alone, ver. 17—19; and continuing the same bitter language of complaint, he asks with impatience why, supposing he *had* sinned, was he of so much consequence as to attract in a special manner, the attention of the Almighty? What injury had his offence done to God that he should visit him thus? Why did not God forgive the sin, and take his heavy hand from him? Why would he crush him down to the grave? ver. 20, 21. Substantially the same state of feeling is evinced in this speech of Job which was shown in chap. 3; and while there is great beauty, and much of the workings of the human heart developed, still there is much, as we shall see, which cannot be commended or approved.

CHAPTER VI.

BUT Job answered and said,
2 Oh that my grief were thoroughly weighed, and my calamity 1 laid in the balances together!
3 For now it would be heavier

1 *lifted up.*

LXX. here, ὀργὴ—*anger;* by Jerome, *peccata—sins.* The sense of the whole passage may either be, that Job wished his anger or his complaints to be laid in the balance with his calamity, to see if one was more weighty than the other—meaning that he had not complained unreasonably or unjustly (*Rosenmüller*); or that he wished that his afflictions might be put into one scale and the sands of the sea into another, and the one weighed against the other (*Noyes*); or simply, that he desired that his sorrows should be accurately estimated. This latter is, I think, the true sense of the passage. He supposed his friends had not understood and appreciated his sufferings; that they were disposed to blame him without understanding the extent of his sorrows, and he desires that they would estimate them aright before they condemned him. In particular, he seems to have supposed that Eliphaz had not done justice to the depth of his sorrows in the remarks which he

had just made. The figure of *weighing* actions or sorrows, is not uncommon or unnatural. It means to take an exact estimate of their amount. So we speak of *heavy* calamities, of afflictions that *crush* us by their weight, &c. ¶ *Laid in the balances.* Marg. *lifted up.* That is, raised up and put in the scales, or put in the scales and then raised up—as is common in weighing. ¶ *Together* (יחד). At the same time ; that *all* my sorrows, griefs, and woes, were piled on the scales, and then weighed. He supposed that only a partial estimate had been formed of the extent of his calamities.

3. *Heavier than the sand of the sea.* That is, they would be found to be insupportable. Who could bear up the sands of the sea? So Job says of his sorrows. A comparison somewhat similar is found in Prov. xxvii. 3.

Heavy is a stone, and weighty the sand of the sea,
But a fool's wrath is heavier than them both.

than the sand *a* of the sea : therefore ¹ my words are swallowed up.

4 For the arrows of the Almighty

a Pr. 27.3.   1 *i. e. I want words to express my grief;* Ps. 77.4.

¶ *My words are swallowed up.* Marg. *I want words to express my grief.* This expresses the true sense—but not with the same poetic beauty. *We* express the same idea when we say that we are *choked* with grief ; we are so overwhelmed with sorrow that we cannot speak. *Any* very deep emotion prevents the power of utterance. So in Ps. lxxvii. 4 :

Thou holdest mine eyes waking:
I am so troubled that I cannot speak.

So the well-known expressions in Virgil,

Obstupui, steteruntque comæ, et vox faucibus hæsit.

There has been, however, considerable variety in the interpretation of the word here rendered *swallowed up* —לֹעַי. Gesenius supposes that it means to speak rashly, to talk at random, and that the idea is, that Job now admits that his remarks had been unguarded—"therefore were my words rash." The same sense Castell gives to the Arabic word. Schultens renders it, " therefore are my words tempestuous or fretful." Rosenmüller, " my words exceed due moderation." Castellio, " my words fail." Luther, " therefore it is vain that I speak." The LXX., " but my words seem to be evil." Jerome, " my words are full of grief." In this variety it is difficult to determine the meaning ; but probably the old interpretation is to be retained, by which the word is derived from לוּעַ, *to absorb, to swallow up* ; comp. Prov. xx. 25 ; Obad. 16 ; Job xxxix. 30 ; Prov. xxiii. 2. The word does not elsewhere occur.

4. *For the arrows of the Almighty* are *within me.* That is, it is not a light affliction that I endure. I am wounded in a manner which could not be caused by man — called to endure a severity of suffering which shows that it proceeds from the Almighty. Thus called to suffer what man could not cause, he maintains that it is

are within me, the poison whereof drinketh up my spirit : the terrors *b* of God do set themselves in array against me.

b Ps. 88. 15, 16.

right for him to complain, and that the words which he employed were not an improper expression of the extent of the grief. ¶ *The p is n whereof drinketh up my spirit.* Takes away my vigour, my comfort, my life. He here compares his afflictions with being wounded with *p is ned* arrows. Such arrows were not unfrequently used among the ancients. The object was to secure certain death, even where the wound caused by the arrow itself would not produce it. Poison was made so concentrated, that the smallest quantity conveyed by the point of an arrow would render death inevitable. This practice contributed much to the barbarity of savage war. Thus Virgil speaks of poisoned arrows :

Ungere tela manu, ferrumque armare veneno
Æn. ix. 773.

And again, Æn. x. 140 :

Vulnera dirigere, et calamos armare veneno.

So Ovid, Lib. 1. de Ponto, Eleg. ii. of the Scythians :

Qui mortis sævo geminent ut vulnere causas,
    Omnia vipereo spicula felle linunt.

Comp. Justin, Lib. ii. c. 10. § 2 ; Grotius, de Jure Belli et Pacis ; and Virgil, Æn. xii. 857. In the Odyssey, i. 260, seq. we read of Ulysses that he went to Ephyra, a city of Thessaly, to obtain from Ilus, the son of Mermer, deadly poison, that he might smear it over the iron point of his arrows. The pestilence which produced so great a destruction in the Grecian camp is also said by Homer (Iliad i. 48) to have been caused by arrows shot from the bow of Apollo. The phrase " drinketh up the spirit" is very expressive. We speak now of the sword *thirsting for blood* ; but this language is more expressive and striking. The figure is not uncommon in the poetry of the East and of the ancients. In the poem of Zohair, the third of the Moallakat, or those transcribed in golden letters, and suspended in the temple of Mecca, the same

5 Doth the wild ass bray [1] when he hath grass? or loweth the ox over his fodder?

1 *at grass.*

6 Can that which is unsavoury be eaten without salt? or is there *any* taste in the white of an egg?

---

image occurs. It is thus rendered by Sir William Jones:

"Their javelins had no share in drinking the blood of Naufel."

A similar expression occurs in Sophocles in Trachinn. ver. 1061, as quoted by Schultens, when describing the pestilence in which Hercules suffered:

ἐκ δὲ χλωρὸν αἶμά μου
Πέπωκεν ἤδη—

This has been imitated by Cicero in Tusculan. Disp. ii. 8:

Hæc me irretivit veste furiali inscium,
Quæ lateri inhærens morsu lacerat viscera,
Urgensque graviter,pulmonum haurit spiritus,
Jam decolorem sanguinem omnem exsorbuit.

So Lucan, Pharsa. ix. 741, seq. gives a similar description:

Ecce subit virus tacitum, carpitque medullas
Ignis edax, calidaque incendit viscera tabe.
Ebibit humorem circa vitalia fusum
Pestis, et in sicco linguam torrere palato
Cœpit.

Far more beautiful, however, than the expressions of any of the ancient classics—more tender, more delicate, more full of pathos—is the description which the Christian poet Cowper gives of *the arrow* that pierces the side of the sinner. It is the account of his own conversion:

I was a stricken deer that left the herd
Long since. With many an arrow deep infix'd
My panting side was charged when I withdrew
To seek a tranquil death in distant shades.
There I was found by one, who had himself
Been hurt by the archers. In his side he bore,
And in his hands and feet, the cruel scars.
                              TASK, b. iii.

Of such wounding *he* did not complain. The arrow was extracted by the tender hand of him who alone had power to do it. Had Job known of him; had he been fully acquainted with the plan of mercy through him, and the comfort which a wounded sinner may find there, we should not have heard the bitter complaints which he uttered in his trials. Let us not judge him with the severity which we may use of one who is afflicted and complains under the full light of the

gospel. ¶ *The terrors of God do set themselves in array against me.* Those things which God uses to excite terror. The word which is rendered "set in array" (עָרַךְ) properly denotes the drawing up of a line for battle; and the sense is here, that all these terrors seem to be drawn up in battle array, as if on purpose to destroy him. No expression could more strikingly describe the condition of an awakened sinner, though it is not certain that Job used it precisely in this sense. The idea as he used it is, that all that God commonly employed to produce alarm seemed to be drawn up as in a line of battle against him.

5. *Doth the wild ass bray when he hath grass?* On the habits of the wild ass, see Notes on chap. xi. 12. The meaning of Job here is, that he did not complain without reason; and this he illustrates by the fact that the wild animal that had a plentiful supply of food would be gentle and calm, and that when its bray was heard it was proof that it was suffering. So Job says that there was a reason for his complaining. He was suffering; and perhaps he means that his complaint was just as natural, and just as innocent, as the braying of the ass for its food. He *should* have remembered however, that he was endowed with reason, and that he was bound to evince a different spirit from the brute creation. ¶ *Or loweth the ox over his fodder?* That is, the ox is satisfied and unmurmuring when his wants are supplied. The fact that he lows is proof that he is in distress, or there is a reason for it. So Job says that his complaints were proof that he was in distress, and that there was a reason for his language of complaint.

6. *Can that which is unsavoury.* Which is insipid, or without taste. ¶ *Be eaten without salt.* It is necessary to add salt in order to make it either palatable or wholesome. The *literal* truth of this no one can doubt,

Insipid food cannot be relished, nor
would it long sustain life. "The Orientals eat their bread often with mere
salt, without any other addition except some dry and pounded summer-
savory, which last is the common method at Aleppo." Russell's Natural
History of Aleppo, p. 27. It should
be remembered, also, that the bread
of the Orientals is commonly mere
unleavened cakes ; see Rosenmüller,
Alte u. neue Morgenland, on Gen.
xviii. 6. The idea of Job in this adage
or proverb is, that there was a fitness
and propriety in things. Certain
things went together, and were necessary companions. One cannot be expected without the other ; one is incomplete without the other. Insipid
food requires salt in order to make it
palatable and nutritious, and so it is
proper that suffering and lamentation
should be united. There was a reason
for his complaints, as there was for
adding salt to unsavoury food. Much
perplexity, however, has been felt in
regard to this whole passage ; ver. 6,
7. Some have supposed that Job
means to rebuke Eliphaz severely for
his harangue on the necessity of patience, which he characterizes as insipid, impertinent, and disgusting to
him ; as being in fact as unpleasant
to his soul as the white of an egg was
to the taste. Dr. Good explains it as
meaning, "Doth that which has nothing of seasoning, nothing of a pungent or irritating power within it, produce pungency or irritation ? I too
should be quiet and complain not, if
I had nothing provocative or acrimon-
ious ; but alas ! the food I am doomed to partake of is the very calamity
which is most acute to my soul, that
which I most loathe, and which is most
grievous or trying to my palate." But
the real sense of this first part of the
verse is, I think, that which is expressed above—that insipid food requires proper condiment, and that in
his sufferings there was a real ground
for lamentation and complaint — as
there was for making use of salt in
that which is unsavoury. I see no reason to think that he meant in this to
reproach Eliphaz for an insipid and
unmeaning address. ¶ Or is there

any *taste in the white of an egg?*
Critics and commentators have been
greatly divided about the meaning of
this. The LXX. render it, εἰ δὲ καὶ ἐστὶ
γεῦμα ἐν ῥήμασι κενοῖς ; *is there any taste
in vain words?* Jerome (Vulg.), "can
any one taste that which being tasted
produces death?" The Targums
render it substantially as it is in our
version. The Hebrew word rendered
"white" (ריר) means properly *spittle;*
1 Sam. xxi. 13. If applied to an egg,
it means the white of it, as resembling
spittle. The word rendered "egg"
(חלמית) occurs nowhere else in the
Scriptures. If it be regarded as derived
from חלם, *to sleep,* or *dream,* it may
denote somnolency or dreams, and then
fatuity, folly, or a foolish speech, as
resembling dreams ; and many have
supposed that Job meant to charac-
terize the speech of Eliphaz as of
this description. The word may mean,
as it does in Syriac, a species of herb,
the "purslain" (*Gesenius*), proverbial
for its insipidity among the Arabs,
Greeks, and Romans, but which was
used as a salad; and the whole phrase
here *may* denote *purslain-broth,* and
hence an insipid discourse. This is
the interpretation of Gesenius. But
the more common and more probable
explanation is that of our common
version, denoting the white of an egg.
But what is the point of the remark as
Job uses it? That it is a proverbial expression, is apparent; but in what way
Job meant to apply it, is not so clear.
The Jews say that he meant to apply it
to the speech of Eliphaz as being insipid and dull, without any thing to
penetrate the heart or to enliven the
fancy; a speech as disagreeable to the
mind as the white of an egg was insipid
to the taste. Rosenmüller supposes
that he refers to his afflictions, as being
as unpleasant to bear as the white of
an egg was to the taste. It seems to
me that the sense of all the proverbs
used here is about the same, and that
they mean, "there is a reason for every
thing which occurs. The ass brays
and the ox lows only when destitute
of food. That which is insipid is unpleasant, and the white of an egg is
loathsome. So with my afflictions.
They produce loathing and disgust.

7 The things *that* my soul refused to touch *are* as my sorrowful
meat.

8 Oh that I might have my request ; and that God would grant
me [1] the thing that I long for ;

1 *my expectation.*

9 Even that *a* it would please
God to destroy me ; that he would
let loose his hand and cut me off !

10 Then should I yet have comfort ; yea, I would harden myself
in sorrow : let him not spare ; for

a 1 Ki. 19.4 ; Jonah 4.3,8.

My very food (ver. 7) is disagreeable,
and *everything* seems tasteless as the
most insipid food would. Hence the
language which I have used—language
spoken not without reason, and expressive of this state of the soul."

7. *The things* that *my soul refused
to touch.* That *I* refused to touch—
the word *soul* here being used to denote himself. The idea here is, that
those things which formerly were objects of loathing to him, had become
his painful and distressing food. The
idea may be either that he was reduced to the greatest pain and distress in partaking of his food, since
he loathed that which he was obliged
to eat (comp. Notes, chap. iii. 24), or
more probably his calamity is described under the image of loathsome food
in accordance with the Oriental usage,
by which one is said to *eat* or *taste* any
thing ; *i. e.* to experience it. His
sorrows were as sickening to him as
the articles of food which he had
mentioned were to the stomach. The
LXX. render it strangely, "For my
wrath—μου ἡ ὀργή—cannot cease. For
I see my food offensive as the smell
of a lion '—ὥσπερ ὀσμὴν λέοντος.

8. *Oh that I might have my request.*
To wit, death. This he desired as the
end of his sorrows, either that he might
be freed from them, or that he might
be admitted to a happy world—or
both. ¶ *Would grant* me *the thing
that I long for.* Marg. *My expectation.* That is, death. He expected
it ; he looked out for it ; he was impatient that the hour should come.
This state of feeling is not uncommon
—where sorrows become so accumulated and intense that a man desires to
die. It is no evidence, however, of a
preparation for death. The wicked
are more frequently in this state than
the righteous. They are overwhelmed
with pain ; they see no hope of deliverance from it, and they impatiently

wish that the end had come. They
are stupid about the future world, and
either suppose that the grave is the
end of their being, or that in some un-
definable way they will be made happy
hereafter. The righteous, on the other
hand, are willing to wait until God
shall be pleased to release them, feeling that He has some good purpose in
all that they endure, and that they do
not suffer one pang too much. Such
sometimes were Job's feelings ; but
here, as in some other instances, no
one can doubt that he was betrayed
into unjustifiable impatience under his
sorrows, and that he expressed an improper wish to die.

9. *Even that it would please God to
destroy me.* To put me to death, and
to release me from my sorrows ; comp.
chap. iii. 20, 21. The word rendered
destroy here (דכא) means properly to
break in pieces, to crush, to trample
under foot, to make small by bruising.
Here the sense is, that Job wished
that God would *crush* him, so as to
take his life. The LXX. render it
wound—τρωσάτω. The Chaldee renders it, "Let God, who has begun to
make me poor, loose his hand and
make me rich." ¶ *That he would let
loose his hand.* Job here represents
the hand of God as bound or confined.
He wished that that fettered hand
were released, and were so free in its
inflictions that he might be permitted
to die. ¶ *And cut me off.* This expression, says Gesenius (Lex. in the
word בצע), is a metaphor derived from
a weaver, who, when his web is finished, cuts it off from the thrum by which
it is fastened to the loom ; see Notes
on Isa. xxxviii. 12. The sense is,
that Job wished that God would
wholly finish his work, and that as he
had begun to destroy him he would
complete it.

10. *Then should I yet have comfort.*
Dr. Good renders this, "then would

a I have not concealed the words of the Holy *b* One.

11 What *is* my strength, that I should hope? and what *is* mine end, that I should prolong my life?

a Ps.40.9; Ac.20.20,27.　　　　*b* Is. 57. 15.

I already take comfort." Noyes, "yet it should still be my consolation." The literal sense is, " and there would be to me yet consolation;" or " my consolation would yet be." That is, he would find comfort in the grave (comp. chap. iii. 13, seq.), or in the future world. ¶ *I would harden myself in sorrow.* Dr. Good renders this, " and I will leap for joy." In a similar way Noyes renders it, " I would exult." So Schultens understands the expression. The Hebrew word rendered " I would harden myself" (סלד) occurs nowhere else, and expositors have been divided in regard to its meaning. According to Castell, it means to strengthen, to confirm. The Chaldee כלד means to grow warm, to glow, to burn. The Arabic word is applied to a horse, and means to beat the earth with his feet, and then to leap, to exult, to spring up; and this is the idea which Gesenius and others suppose is to be retained here —an idea which certainly better suits the connection than the common one of hardening himself in sorrow. The LXX. render it ἡλλόμην — " I would leap," or exult, although they have sadly missed the sense in the other part of the verse. They render it, " Let but my city be a grave, upon whose walls I will leap; I will not spare, for I have not falsified the holy words of my God.' The Chaldee renders it, "and I will exult (ואשבין) when fury comes upon the wicked." The probable meaning is, that Job would exult or rejoice, if he was permitted to die; he would triumph even in the midst of his sorrow, if he might lie down and expire. ¶ *Let him not spare.* Let him not withhold or restrain those sufferings which would sink me down to the grave. ¶ *For I have not concealed the words of the Holy One.* I have openly and boldly maintained a profession of attachment to the cause of God, and to his truth. I have, in a public and solemn manner, professed attachment to my Maker; I have not refused to acknowledge

that I am his; I have not been ashamed of him and his cause. How much consolation may be found in such a reflection when we come to die! If there has been a consistent profession of religion; if there has been no shrinking back from attachment to God; if in all circles, high and low, rich and poor, gay and serious, there has been an unwavering and steady, though not ostentatious, attachment to the cause of God, it will give unspeakable consolation and confidence when we come to die. If there has been concealment, and shame, and shrinking back from a profession of religion, there will be shame, and regret, and sorrow; comp. Ps. xl. 9; Acts xx. 20—27.

11. *What is my strength, that I should hope?* Job had hitherto borne his trials without apprehension that he would lose his constancy of hope, or his confidence in God. He here seems to apprehend that his constancy might fail, and he therefore wishes to die before he should be left to dishonour God. He asks, therefore, what strength he had that he should hope to be able to sustain his trials much longer. ¶ *And what is mine end, that I should prolong my life?* Various interpretations have been given of this passage. Some suppose it means, " What is the limit of my strength? How long will it last?" Others, " What end is there to be to my miseries?" Others, " How distant is mine end? How long have I to live?" Noyes renders it, "And what is mine end that I should be patient?" Rosenmüller supposes that the word " end " here means the " end of his strength," or that he had not such fortitude as to be certain that he could long bear his trials without complaining or murmuring. The phrase rendered " prolong my life," probably means rather " to lengthen the patience," or to hold out under accumulated sorrows. The word rendered life (נפש) often means soul, spirit,

12 *Is* my strength the strength of stones? or *is* my flesh ¹ of brass? 13 *Is* not my help in me? and is wisdom driven quite from me?

1 *brazen.*

14 To him that ² is afflicted *a* pity *should be showed* from his friend; but he forsaketh the fear of the Almighty.

2 *melteth.*   *a* He. 13.3.

mind, as well as life, and the sense is, that he could not hope, from any strength that he had, to bear without murmuring these trials until the natural termination of his life; and hence he wished God to grant his request, and to destroy him. Feeling that his patience was sinking under his calamities, he says that it would be better for him to die than be left to dishonour his Maker. It is just the state of feeling which many a sufferer has, that his trials are so great that nature will sink under them, and that death would be a relief. *Then* is the time to look to God for support and consolation.

12. Is *my strength the strength of stones?* That is, like a rampart or fortification made of stones, or like a craggy rock that can endure assaults made upon it. A rock will bear the beatings of the tempest, and resist the floods, but how can frail man do it? The idea of Job is, that he had no strength to bear up against these accumulated trials; that he was afraid that he should be left to sink under them, and to complain of God; and that his friends were not to wonder if his strength gave way, and he uttered the language of complaint. ¶ *Or is my flesh of brass?* Marg. *brazen.* The comparison here used is not uncommon. So Cicero, Aca. Qu. iv. 31, says, Non enim est e saxo sculptus, aut e robore dolatus homo; habet corpus, habet animum; movetur mente, movetur sensibus:—" for man is not chiselled out of the rock, nor cut from a tree; he has a body, he has a soul; he is actuated by mind, he is swayed by senses." So Theocritus, in his description of Amycus, Idyll. xxii. 47:

Στήθεα δ' ἐσφαίρωτο πελώρια καὶ πλατὺ νῶτον,

Σαρχὶ σιδαρείη σφυρήλατος οἷα κολοσσός.

" Round as to his vast breast and broad back, and with iron flesh, he is as if a colossus formed with a hammer." So in Homer the expression frequently occurs—σιδήρειον ἦτορ—*an iron heart*

—to denote courage. And so, according to Schultens, it has come to be a proverb, οὐκ ἀπὸ δρυὸς, οὐκ ἀπὸ πέτρης—*not from a tree, not from a rock.* The meaning of Job is plain. He had flesh like others. His muscles, and nerves, and sinews, could not bear a constant force applied to them, as if they were made of brass or iron. They *must* give way; and he apprehended that he would sink under these sorrows, and be left to use language that might dishonour God. At all events, he felt that these great sorrows justified the strong expressions which he had already employed.

13. Is *not my help in me?* This would be better rendered in an affirmative manner, or as an exclamation. The interrogative form of the previous verses need not be continued in this. The sense is, "alas! there is no help in me!" That is, " I have no strength; I must give up under these sorrows in despair." So it is rendered by Jerome, Rosenmüller, Good, Noyes, and others. ¶ *And is wisdom quite driven from me?* This, also, should be read as an affirmation, "deliverance is driven from me." The word rendered *wisdom* (תושיה) means properly a setting upright; then help, deliverance; and then purpose, enterprise; see Notes on chap. v. 12. Here it means that all hope of deliverance had fled, and that he was sinking in despair.

14. *To him that is afflicted.* Marg. *melteth.* The word here used (מס) is from מסס, *mâsas,* to melt, flow down, waste away, and here means one who pines away, or is consumed under calamities. The design of this verse is, to reprove his friends for the little sympathy which they had shown for him. He had looked for consolation in his trials, and he had a right to expect it; but he says that he had met with just the opposite, and that his calamity was aggravated by the fact that they had dealt only in the language of severity. ¶ *Pity* should be showed

15 My brethren *a* have dealt deceitfully as a brook, *and* as the
stream of brooks they pass away ;

a Ps. 38. 11.

from his friend. Good renders this, "shame to the man who despiseth his friend." A great variety of interpretations have been proposed of the passage, but our translation has probably expressed the true sense. If there is any place where kindness should be shown, it is when a man is sinking under accumulated sorrows to the grave. ¶ *But he forsaketh the fear of the Almighty.* This may be either understood as referring to the language which Job says they had used of him—charging him with forsaking the fear of God, instead of consoling him ; or it may mean that *they* had forsaken the fear of God in reproaching him, and in failing to comfort him ; or it may mean that if such kindness were not shown to a friend in trial, he would be left to cast off the fear of God. This last interpretation is adopted by Noyes. Good supposes that it is designed to be a severe reproach of Eliphaz, for the course which he had pursued. It seems to me that this is probably the correct interpretation, and that the particle ך here is used in an adversative sense, meaning that while it was an obvious dictate of piety to show kindness to a friend, Eliphaz had forgotten this obligation, and had indulged himself in a strain of remark which could not have been prompted by true religion. This sentiment he proceeds to illustrate by one of the most beautiful comparisons to be found in any language.

15. *My brethren.* To wit, the three friends who had come to condole with him. He uses the language of *brethren,* to intimate what he had a right to expect from them. It is common in all languages to give the name *brethren* to friends. ¶ *Have dealt deceitfully.* That is, I have been sadly disappointed. I looked for the language of condolence and compassion ; for something to cheer my heart, and to uphold me in my trials—as weary and thirsty travellers look for water, and are sadly disappointed when they come to the place where they expected to find it, and find the stream dried

up. The simile here used is exquisitely beautiful, considered as a mere description of an actual occurrence in the deserts of Arabia. But its chief beauty consists in its exact adaptation to the case before him, and the point and pith of the reproof which it administers. " The fullness, strength, and noise of these temporary streams in winter, answer to the large professions made to Job in his prosperity by his friends. The dryness of the waters at the approach of summer, resembles the failure of their friendship in time of affliction." *Scott,* as quoted by Noyes. ¶ *As a brook.* That is, as a stream that is swelled by winter torrents, and that is dry in summer. Such streams abound in Arabia, and in the East generally. The torrents pour down from the hills in time of rain, or when swelled by the melting of the ice ; but in summer they are dry, or their waters are lost in the sand. Even large streams are thus absorbed. The river Barrady, which waters Damascus, after passing to a short distance to the south-east of the city towards the Arabian deserts, is lost in the sand, or evaporated by the heat of the sun. The idea here is, that travellers in a caravan would approach the place where water had been found before, but would find the fountain dried up, or the stream lost in the sand ; and when they looked for refreshment, they found only disappointment. In Arabia there are not many rivers. In Yemen, indeed, there are a few streams that flow the year round, and on the East the Euphrates has been claimed as belonging to Arabia. But most of the streams are winter torrents that become dry in summer, or rivulets that are swelled by heavy rains. An illustration of the verse before us occurs in Campbell's Travels in Africa. " In desert parts of Africa it has afforded much joy to fall in with a brook of water, especially when running in the direction of the journey, expecting it would prove a valuable companion. Perhaps before it

16 Which are blackish by reason of the ice, *and* wherein the snow
is hid :

17 What time they wax warm,

they [1] vanish : [2] when it is hot,
they are [3] consumed out of their
place.

1 *are cut off.* 2 *in the heat thereof.*
3 *extinguished.*

accompanied us two miles it became
invisible by sinking into the sand ;
but two miles farther along it would
reappear and raise hopes of its continuance ; but after running a few hundred yards, would sink finally into the
sand, no more again to rise." A
comparison of a man who deceives and
disappoints one to such a stream is
common in Arabia, and has given rise,
according to Schultens, to many proverbs. Thus they say of a treacherous
friend, "I put no trust in thy torrent ;"
and, "O torrent, thy flowing subsides."
So the Scholiast on Moallakat says,
" a pool or flood was called Gadyr, because travellers when they pass by it
find it full of water, but when they return they find nothing there, and it
seems to have treacherously betrayed
them. So they say of a false man,
that he is more deceitful than the appearance of water"—referring, perhaps, to the deceitful appearance of
the *mirage* in the sands of the desert ;
see Notes on Isa. xxxv. 7. ¶ And
*as the stream of brooks they pass
away.* As the valley stream—the
stream that runs along in the valley,
that is filled by the mountain torrent.
They pass away on the return of summer, or when the rain ceases to fall,
and the valley is again dry. So with
the consolations of false friends. They
cannot be depended on. All their
professions are temporary and evan-
escent.

16. *Which are blackish.* Or, rather,
which are *turbid.* The word here
used (קָדַר) means to be turbid, foul,
or muddy, spoken of a torrent, and
then to be of a dusky colour, to be
dark-coloured, as *e. g.* the skin scorched by the sun, Job xxx. 28 ; or to be
dark—as when the sun is obscured ;
Joel ii. 10 ; iii. 15. Jerome renders it,
Qui timent pruinam—"which fear the
frost, when the snow comes upon
them." The LXX. render it, "they
who had venerated me now rushed
upon me like snow or hoar-frost, which

melting at the approach of heat, it
was not known whence it was." The
expression in the Hebrew means that
they were rendered dark and turbid
by the accumulated torrents caused
by the dissolving snow and ice. ¶ *By
reason of the ice.* When it melts and
swells the streams. ¶ And *wherein
the snow is hid.* That is, says Noyes,
melts and flows into them. It refers
to the melting of the snow in the spring,
when the streams are swelled as a
consequence of it. Snow, by melting
in the spring and summer, would swell
the streams, which at other times were
dry. Lucretius mentions the melting
of the snows on the mountains of
Ethiopia, as one of the causes of the
overflowing of the Nile :

Forsitan Æthiopum penitus de montibus altis
Crescat, ubi in campos albas descendere nin-
 gues
Tabificis subigit radiis sol, omnia lustrans.
 vi. 734.
Or, from the Ethiop-mountains, the bright sun,
Now full matured, with deep-dissolving ray,
May melt the agglomerate snows, and down
 the plains
Drive them, augmenting hence the incipient
 stream. GOOD.

A similar description occurs in Homer, Il. xi. 492 :

'Ως δ' ὁπότε πλήθων ποταμὸς πεδίονδε κάτισι
Χειμάρρους κατ' ὄρεσφιν, κ.τ.λ.

And in Ovid also, Fast. ii. 219 :

Ecce, velut torrens undis pluvialibus auctus,
 Aut nive, quæ, Zephyro victa, repente fluit,
Per sata, perque vias, fertur ; nec, ut ante so-
 lebat,
Riparum clausas margine finit aquas.

17. *What time.* In the time ; or
after a time. ¶ *They wax warm.*
Gesenius renders this word (יְזֹרְבוּ)
when they became narrow, and this
version has been adopted by Noyes.
The word occurs nowhere else. Taylor
(Concord.) renders it, "to be dissolved by the heat of the sun." Jerome,
fuerint dissipati—"in the time in
which they are scattered." The LXX.
τακεῖσα θέρμης γινομένης—"melting at
the approach of heat." The Chaldee,
" In the time in which the generation
of the deluge sinned, they were scat-

18 The paths of their way are turned aside ; they go to nothing, and perish.

19 The troops of Tema *a* looked, the companies of Sheba waited for them.

a Ge.25.15.

tered." Castell says that the word רֵזב in Pihel, as the word in Chaldee (רֵזב) means to flow ; and also that it has the same signification as צרב, *tzârâbh,* to become warm. In Syriac the word means to be straitened, bound, confined. On the whole, however, the connection seems to require us to understand it as it is rendered in our common translation, as meaning, that when they are exposed to the rays of a burning sun, they evaporate. They pour down from the mountains in torrents, but when they flow into burning sands, or become exposed to the intense action of the sun, they are dried up, and disappear. ¶ *They vanish.* Marg. *are cut off.* That is, they wander off into the sands of the desert until they are finally lost. ¶ *When it is hot.* Marg. *in the heat thereof.* When the summer comes, or when the rays of the sun are poured down upon them. ¶ *They are consumed.* Marg. *extinguished.* They are dried up, and furnish no water for the caravan.

18. *The paths of their way are turned aside.* Noyes renders this, " The caravans turn aside to them on their way." Good, "The outlets of their channel wind about." Rosenmüller, " The bands of travellers direct their journey to them." Jerome, "Involved are the paths of their steps." According to the interpretation of Rosenmüller, Noyes, Umbreit, and others, it means that the caravans on their journey turn aside from their regular way in order to find water there ; and that in doing it they go up into a desert and perish. According to the other interpretation, it means that the channels of the stream wind along until they diminish and come to nothing. This latter I take to be the true sense of the passage, as it is undoubtedly the most poetical. It is a representation of the stream winding along in its channels, or making new channels as it flows from the mountain, until it diminishes by evaporation, and finally comes to nothing. ¶ *They go to no-*

thing. Noyes renders this very singularly, "into the desert,"— meaning that the caravans, when they suppose they are going to a place of refreshment, actually go to a desert, and thus perish. The word used here, however (תהו), does not occur in the sense of *a desert* elsewhere in the Scriptures. It denotes nothingness, emptiness, vanity (see Gen. i. 2), and very appropriately expresses the *nothingness* into which a stream vanishes when it is dried up or lost in the sand. The sense is, that those streams wander along until they become smaller and smaller, and then wholly disappear. They deceive the traveller who hoped to find refreshment there. Streams depending on snows and storms, and having no permanent fountains, cannot be confided in. Pretended friends are like them. In times of prosperity they are full of professions, and their aid is proffered to us. But we go to them when we need their assistance, when we are like the weary and thirsty traveller, and they disappear like deceitful streams in the sands of the desert.

19. *The troops of Tema looked.* That is, looked for the streams of water. On the situation of *Tema,* see Notes, chap. ii. 11. This was the country of Eliphaz, and the image would be well understood by him. The figure is one of exquisite beauty. It means that the caravans from Tema, in journeying through the desert, looked for those streams. They came with an expectation of finding the means of allaying their thirst. When they came there they were disappointed, for the waters had disappeared. Reiske, however, renders this, " Their tracks (the branchings of the flood) tend towards Tema ;"—a translation which the Hebrew will bear, but the usual version is more correct, and is more elegant. ¶ *The companies of Sheba waited for them.* The Sheba here referred to was probably in the southern part of Arabia ; see Notes on

20 They were confounded because they had hoped; they came thither, and were ashamed.

21 For now [1] ye are [2] nothing; ye see *my* casting down, and are afraid.

1 or, *ye are like to it, or, them.*

22 Did I say, Bring unto me? or, Give a reward for me of your substance?

23 Or, Deliver me from the enemy's hand? or, Redeem me from the hand of the mighty?

2 *not.*

Isa. xlv. 14. The idea is, that the caravans from that part of Arabia came and looked for a supply of water, and were disappointed.

20. *They were confounded because they had hoped.* The caravans of Tema and Sheba. The word "confounded" here means ashamed. It represents the state of feeling which one has who has met with disappointment. He is perplexed, distressed, and ashamed that he had entertained so confident hope; see Notes on Isa. xxx. 5. They were downcast and sad that the waters had failed, and they looked on one another with confusion and dismay. There are few images more poetic than this, and nothing that would more strikingly exhibit the disappointment of Job, that he had looked for consolation from his friends, and had not found it. He was downcast, distressed, and disheartened, like the travellers of Tema and of Sheba, because they had nothing to offer to console him; because he had waited for them to sustain him in his afflictions, and had been wholly disappointed.

21. *For now ye are as nothing.* Marg. "or, *Ye are like to it, or them.*" In the margin also the word *nothing* is rendered *not.* This variety arises from a difference of reading in the Hebrew text, many MSS. having instead of לֹא, *not,* לֹו, *to him, or to it.* Which is correct, it is not easy to determine. Rosenmüller supposes that it is only a variety in writing the word לֹא, where the י is often used for א. The probability is, that it means, that they were *as nothing*—like the stream that had disappeared. This is the point of the comparison; and this Job now applies to his friends. They had promised much by their coming—like the streams when swollen by rains and melted ice. But now they were found

to be nothing. ¶ *Ye see my casting down.* חתת — my being broken or crushed; my calamity. Vulg. *plagam.* LXX. τραῦμα, *wound.* ¶ *And are afraid.* Are timid and fearful. You shrink back; you dare not approach the subject boldly, or come to me with words of consolation. You came with a professed intention to administer comfort, but your courage fails.

22. *Did I say, Bring unto me?* Job proceeds to state that their conduct in this had been greatly aggravated by the fact that they had come *voluntarily.* He had not asked them to come. He had desired no gift; no favour. He had not applied to them in any way or form for help. They had come of their own accord, and when they came they uttered only the language of severity and reproach. If he had asked them to aid him, the case would have been different. That would have given them some excuse for interposing in the case. But now the whole was gratuitous and unasked. He did not desire their interference, and he implies by these remarks that if they could say nothing that would console him, it would have been kindness in them to have said nothing. ¶ *Or, Give a reward for me of your substance?* That is, did I ask a present from you out of your property? I asked nothing. I have on no occasion asked you to interpose and aid me.

23. *Or, Deliver me out of the enemy's hand?* At no time have I called on you to rescue me from a foe. ¶ *Or, Redeem me?* That is, rescue me from the hand of robbers. The meaning is, that he was in no way beholden to them; he had never called on them for assistance; and there was therefore no *claim* which they could now have to afflict me farther by their reflections. There seems to be

24 Teach me, and I will hold my tongue ; and cause me to understand wherein I have erred.

25 How forcible *a* are right words! but what doth your arguing reprove ?

a Ec.12.11.

26 Do ye imagine to reprove words, and the speeches of one that is desperate, *which are* as wind ?

27 Yea, ye [1] overwhelm the fatherless, and ye dig *a pit* for your friend.

1 *cause to fall upon.*

---

something peevish in these remarks ; and we need not attempt to justify the spirit which dictated them.

24. *Teach me, and I will hold my tongue.* That is, give me any real instruction, or show me what is my duty, and I will be silent. By this he means that Eliphaz had really imparted no instruction, but had dealt only in the language of reproof. The sense is, " I would willingly sit and listen where truth is imparted, and where I could be enabled to see the reason of the divine dealings. If I could be made to *understand* where I have erred, I would acquiesce."

25. *How forcible are right words!* How weighty and impressive are words of truth ! Job means that he was accustomed to feel their power, and to admit it on his soul. If their words were such, he would listen to them with profound attention, and in silence. The expression has a proverbial cast. ¶ *But what doth your arguing reprove?* Or rather, what doth the reproof from you reprove ? or what do your reproaches prove ? Job professes a readiness to listen to words of truth and wisdom ; he complains that the language of reproach used by them was not adapted to instruct his understanding or to benefit his heart. As it was, he did not feel himself convinced, and was likely to derive no advantage from what they said.

26. *Do ye imagine to reprove words ?* A considerable variety of interpretation has occurred in regard to this verse. Dr. Good, following Schultens, supposes that the word translated *wind* here (רוח) means sighs, or groans, and renders it,

Would ye then take up words for reproof,
The mere venting the moans of despair?

But Rosenmüller has well remarked that the word never has this signification. Noyes renders it,

Do ye mean to censure words ?
The words of a man in despair are but wind.

In this, he has probably expressed the true sense. This explanation was proposed by Ludov. de Dieu, and is adopted by Rosenmüller. According to this, the sense is, "Do you think it reasonable to carp at mere words ? Will you pass over weighty and important arguments and facts, and dwell upon the *words* merely that are extorted from a man in misery ? Do you not know that one in a state of despair utters many expressions which ought not to be regarded as the result of his deliberate judgment ? And will you spend your time in dwelling on those words rather than on the main argument involved ?" This is probably the true sense of the verse ; and if so it is a complaint of Job that they were disposed to make him " an offender for a word " rather than to enter into the real merits of the case, and especially that they were not disposed to make allowances for the hasty expressions of a man almost in despair.

27. *Yea, ye overwhelm the fatherless.* Job undoubtedly means that this should be applied to himself. He complains that they took advantage of his *words*, that they were disposed to pervert his meaning, and unkindly distorted what he said. The word rendered " fatherless " (יתום) properly denotes an orphan ; Ex. xxii. 22 ; Deut. x. 18 ; xiv. 29. But it is possible that it is not to be taken in this limited signification here. The word is still retained in the Arabic language —the language spoken in the country where Job lived,—where the word *yatham* means to be lonely, bereaved, &c. It may be that this idea occurs under the form of the word used here, that Job was lonely and bereaved ; that he was as desolate and helpless

28 Now, therefore, be content, look upon me : for *it is* [1] evident unto you if I lie.

29 Return, I pray you, let it

[1] *before your face.* [2] i.e. *this matter.* [3] *palate.*

not be iniquity ; yea, return again, my righteousness *is* in [2] it.

30 Is there iniquity in my tongue? can not my [3] taste discern perverse things ?

---

as a fatherless child ; and especially that they manifested a spirit like that of those who would oppress an orphan. The word " overwhelm " (תֵּפִּילוּ) means properly, " ye fall upon ;" that is, you deal with him violently. Or, it may mean here, in the Hiphil, "you cause to fall upon," referring to a *net,* and meaning, that they sprung a net for the orphan. So Rosenmüller and Noyes understand it. To do this was, in Oriental countries, regarded as a crime of peculiar enormity, and is often so spoken of in the Bible ; see Notes on Isa. i. 17. ¶ *And ye dig a pit for your friend.* You act toward your friend as hunters do toward wild beasts. They dig a pit and cover it over with brushwood to conceal it, and the hunted animal, deceived, falls into it unawares. So you endeavour to entrap your friend. You lay a plan for it. You conceal your design. You contrive to drive him into the pit that you have made, and urge him on till you have caught him in the use of unguarded language, or driven him to vent expressions that cover him with confusion. Instead of throwing a mantle of charity over his frailties and infirmities, you make the most of every word, take it out of its proper connection, and attempt to overwhelm him in shame and disgrace. On the method of hunting in ancient times, see Notes on chap. xviii. 8—10.

28. *Now, therefore, be content.* Rosenmüller has better rendered this, " if it please you." The sense is, " if you are willing, look upon me." That is, " if you are disposed, you may take a careful view of me. Look me in the countenance. You can see for yourselves whether I am sincere or false. I am willing that my whole demeanour should be subjected to the utmost scrutiny." ¶ *For it is evident unto you if I lie.* Marg. as in Heb. *before your face.* That is, "you yourselves can see by my whole de-

meanour, by my sufferings, my patience, my manifest sincerity, that I am not playing the hypocrite." Conscious of sincerity, he believed that if they would look upon him, they would be convinced that he was a sincere and an upright man.

29. *Return, I pray you.* That is, return to the argument. Give your attention to it again. Perhaps he may have discerned a disposition in them to turn away from what he was saying, and to withdraw and leave him. Job expresses his belief that he could convince them ; and he proposes more fully to state his views, if they would attend to him. ¶ *Let it not be iniquity.* Let it not be considered as wrong thus to come back to the argument. Or, let it not be assumed that my sentiments are erroneous, and my heart evil. Job means, that it should not be taken for granted that he was a hypocrite ; that he was conscious of sincerity, and that he was convinced that he could satisfy them of it if they would lend a listening ear. A similar sentiment he expresses in chap. xix. 28 :

But ye should say, Why persecute we him ? Seeing the root of the matter is found in me.

¶ *My righteousness is in it.* Marg. i. e. *this matter.* The sense is, " my complete vindication is in the argument which I propose to state. I am prepared to show that I am innocent." On that account, he wishes them to return and attend to what he proposed to say.

30. *Is there iniquity in my tongue ?* This is a solemn appeal to their consciences, and their own deep conviction that he was sincere. Iniquity *in the tongue* means falsehood, deceit, hypocrisy—that which would be expressed *by* the tongue. ¶ *Cannot my taste discern perverse things ?* Marg. *palate.* The word used here (חֵךְ) means properly the palate, together with the corresponding lower part of

CHAPTER VII.

*I*S *there* not ¹ an appointed*ᵃ* time to
man upon earth? *are not* his days
also like the days of an hireling?

1 or, *warfare.*   *a* chap. 14.5,14.

the mouth, the *inside mouth. Gesenius.* Hence it means the organ of
taste, residing in the mouth. The
meaning is, that Job was qualified to
discern what was true or false, sincere or hypocritical, just or unjust, in
the same manner as the palate is fitted to discern the qualities of objects,
whether bitter or sweet, pleasant or
unpleasant, wholesome or unwholesome. His object is to invite attention to what he had to state on the
subject. To this proposed vindication
he proceeds in the following chapter,
showing the greatness of his calamity,
and his right, as he supposes, to complain. Their attention was gained.
They did not refuse to listen to him,
and he proceeds to a fuller statement
of his calamity, and of the reasons
why he had allowed himself to use the
language of complaint. They listened
without interruption till he was done,
and then replied in tones of deeper
severity still.

CHAPTER VII.

1. Is there *not an appointed time to
man upon earth?* Marg. or, *warfare.*
The word here used (צָבָא) means properly a host, an army; see Notes, Isa.
i. 9; then it means *warfare,* or the
hard service of a soldier; Notes, Isa.
xl. 2. Here it means that man on
the earth was *enlisted,* so to speak,
for a certain time. He had a certain
and definite hard service to perform,
and which he must continue to dis-
charge until he was relieved by death.
It was a service of hazard, like the
life of a soldier, or of toil, like that of
one who had been hired for a certain
time, and who anxiously looked for the
period of his release. The object of
Job in introducing this remark evidently is, to vindicate himself for the
wish to die which he had expressed.
He maintains that it is as natural and
proper for man in his circumstances
to wish to be released by death, as
for a soldier to desire that his term of
service might be accomplished, or a

2 As a servant ² earnestly desireth the shadow, and as an hireling looketh for *the reward of* his
work:

2 *gapeth after.*

weary servant to long for the shades
of the evening. The LXX. render it,
" Is not the life of man upon the earth
πειρατήριον,"—explained by Schleusner
and rendered by Good, as meaning *a
band of pirates.* The Vulgate renders
it, *militia—military service.* The
sense is, that the life of man was like
the hard service of a soldier; and
this is one of the points of justification
to which Job referred in chap. vi. 29,
30. He maintains that it is not improper to desire that such a service
should close. ¶ *The days of an hireling.* A man who has been hired to
perform some service with a promise
of a reward, and who is not unnatur-
ally impatient to receive it. Job
maintained that such was the life of
man. He was looking forward to a
reward, and it was not unnatural or
improper to desire that that reward
should be given to him.

2. *As a servant earnestly desireth.*
Marg. *gapeth after.* The word here
(שָׁאַף) means to breathe hard, to pant,
to blow, and then to desire earnestly.
¶ *The shadow.* This may refer either
to a shade in the intense heat of the
day, or to the night. Nothing is more
grateful in oriental countries, when
the sun pours down intensely on burning sands, than the shadow of a tree,
or the shade of a projecting rock.
The editor of the Pictorial Bible on
this verse remarks, " We think we
can say, that next to water, the greatest and deepest enjoyment we could
ever realize in the hot climates of the
East was, when on a journey, any
circumstance of the road brought us
for a few minutes under some shade.
Its reviving influence upon the bodily
frame, and consequently upon the
spirits, is inconceivable by one who
has not had some experience of the
kind. Often also during the halt of a
caravan in the open air, when the
writer has been enabled to secure a
station for repose under the shelter
of a rock or of an old wall, has his

3 So am I made to possess months of vanity, and wearisome nights *a* are appointed to me.

4 When *b* I lie down, I say, When shall I arise, and the *1* night

a Ps. 6. 6.   *b* De. 28. 67.

be gone? and I am full of tossings to and fro unto the dawning of the day.

5 My flesh is clothed with worms and clods of dust; my

1 evening be measured.

own exultation and strong sense of luxurious enjoyment reminded him of this and other passages of Scripture, in which shade is mentioned as a thing panted for with intense desire." Probably here, however, the reference is to the shades of night, the time when darkness falls upon the earth, and the servant is released from his toil. It is common in all languages to speak of night as enveloped with shadows. Thus Virgil, Æn. iv. 7:

Humentemque aurora polo dimoverat umbram.

The meaning of Job is, that as a servant looked impatiently for the shades of the evening when he would be dismissed from toil, so he longed for death. ¶ *And as an hireling looketh.* That is, he anxiously desires his work to be finished, and expects the reward of his labours. So Job looked to the reward of a life of toil and piety. Is there not here an undoubted reference to a future state? Is it not manifest that Job looked to some recompense in the future world, as real and as sure, as a hired servant looks for the reward of his toils when his work is done?

3. *So am I made to possess.* Heb. I am made *to inherit.* The meaning is, that such sad and melancholy seasons now were his only portion. ¶ *Months of vanity.* That is, months which were destitute of comfort; in other words, months of affliction. How long his trials had continued before this, we have no means of ascertaining. There is no reason, however, to suppose that his bodily sufferings came upon him all at once, or that they had not continued for a considerable period. It is quite probable that his expressions of impatience were the result not only of the *intensity*, but the *continuance* of his sorrows. ¶ *And wearisome nights are appointed to me.* Even his rest was disturbed. The time when care is usually forgotten and toil ceases, was to him a period of sleepless anxiety and distress—עמל.

The LXX. render it, *nights of pangs* (νύκτες ὀδυνῶν), expressing accurately the sense of the Hebrew. The Hebrew word עמל is commonly applied to intense sorrow, to trouble and pain of the severest kind, such as the pains of parturition; see Notes on Isa. liii. 11.

4. *When I lie down.* I find no comfort and no rest on my bed. My nights are long, and I am impatient to have them passed, and equally so is it with the day. This is a description which all can understand who have been laid on a bed of pain. ¶ *And the night be gone.* Marg. *evening be measured.* Herder renders this, "the night is irksome to me." The word rendered *night* (ערב) properly means the early part of the night, until it is succeeded by the dawn. Thus in Gen. i. 5, "And the evening (ערב) and the morning were the first day." Here it means the portion of the night which is before the dawning of the aurora—the night. The word rendered "be gone" and in the margin "be measured" (מִדַּד), has been variously rendered. The verb מָדַד means to stretch, to extend, to measure; and, according to Gesenius, the form of the word here used is a noun meaning *flight*, and the sense is, "when shall be the flight of the night?" He derives it from נדד to move, to flee, to flee away. So Rosenmüller explains it. The expression is poetic, meaning, when shall the night be gone? ¶ *I am full of tossings to and fro* (נדודים). A word from the same root. It means uneasy motions, restlessness. He found no quiet repose on his bed. ¶ *Unto the dawning.* נֶשֶׁף, from נָשַׁף, *to breathe;* hence the evening twilight because the breezes blow, or seem to breathe, and then it means also the morning twilight, the dawn. Dr. Stock renders it, "till the morning breeze."

5. *My flesh is clothed with worms.* Job here undoubtedly refers to his diseased state, and this is one of the

skin is broken, and become loathsome.

6 My *a* days are swifter than a

weaver's shuttle, and are spent
without hope.

passages by which we may learn the
nature of his complaint ; comp. Notes
on chap. ii. 7. There is reference here
to the worms which are produced in
ulcers and in other forms of disease.
Michaelis remarks that such effects
are produced often in the elephantiasis.
Bochart, Hieroz. P. II., Lib. IV. c.
xxvi. pp. 619—621, has abundantly
proved that such effects occur in disease, and has mentioned several instances where death ensued from this
cause ; comp. Acts xii. 23. The same
thing would often happen—and particularly in hot climates—if it were
not for the closest care and attention
in keeping running sores as clean as
possible. ¶ *And clods of dust.* Accumulated on the ulcers which covered
his whole body. This effect would be
almost unavoidable. Dr. Good renders this, " worms and the imprisoning
dust," and supposes that the image is
taken from the grave, and that the idea
in the whole passage is that of one who
is " dead while he lives ;" that is, of
one who is undergoing putrefaction
before he is buried. But the more
common and correct interpretation is
that which refers it to the accumulated filth attending a loathsome disease ;
see chap. ii. 8. The word which is here
used and rendered *clods* (שׁוּג) means a
lump of earth or dust. Sept. βώλακας
γῆς ; Vulg. *sordes pulveris,* " clods of
earth." The whole verse is rendered
by the LXX., " My body swarms with
the putrefaction of worms, and I
moisten the clods of earth with the
ichor (ἰχῶρος) of ulcers." ¶ *My skin
is broken*—רגע. This word means, to
make afraid, to terrify ; and then to
shrink together from fear, or to contract. Here it means, according to
Gesenius, that " the skin came together and healed, and then broke
forth again and ran with pus." Jerome renders it, *aruit—dries up.* Herder, " my skin becometh closed." Dr.
Good, " my skin becometh stiff ;" and
carries out his idea that the reference
here is to the stiffened and rigid appearance of the body after death.

Doederlin supposes that it refers to
the rough and horrid appearance of
the skin in the elephantiasis, when it
becomes rigid and frightful by the disease. Jarchi renders it, *cutis mea
corrugata—my skin is rough,* or *filled
with wrinkles.* This seems to me to
be the idea, that it was filled with
wrinkles and corrugations ; that it
became stiff, fixed, frightful, and was
such as to excite terror in the beholder.
¶ *And become loathsome.* Gesenius,
" runs again with pus." The word
here used (מאם) means properly to reject, contemn, despise. A second
sense which it has is, to melt, to run
like water ; Ps. lviii. 7, " Let them
melt away (ימאסו) as waters." But
the usual meaning is to be preferred
here. His skin became abhorrent
and loathsome in the sight of others.

6. *My days are swifter than a
weaver's shuttle.* That is, they are
short and few. He does not here refer so much to the *rapidity* with which
they were passing away as to the fact
that they would soon be gone, and that
he was likely to be cut off without being permitted to enjoy the blessings of
a long life ; comp. Notes on Isa. xxxviii.
12. The weaver's shuttle is the instrument by which the weaver inserts the
filling in the woof. With us few things
would furnish a more striking emblem
of rapidity than the speed with which
a weaver throws his shuttle from one
side of the web to the other. It would
seem that such was the fact among the
ancients, though the precise manner
in which they wove their cloth, is unknown. It was common to compare
life with a web, which was filled up by
the successive days. The ancient
classic writers spoke of it as a web
woven by the Fates. We can all feel
the force of the comparison here used
by Job, that the days which we live
fly swift away. How rapidly is one
after another added to the web of life !
How soon will the whole web be filled
up, and life be closed ! A few more
shoots of the shuttle and all will be
over, and our life will be cut off, as

7 O remember that my life *is* wind : mine *a* eye shall [1] no more see [2] good.

8 The eye of him that hath seen me shall see me no *more:* thine eyes *are* upon me, and [3] I *am* not.

9 *As* the cloud is consumed and vanisheth away ; so he that goeth down to the grave shall come up no *more.*

a Ge. 42.36.   1 *not return.*   2 *to see,* i.e. *to enjoy.*   3 i.e. *I can live no longer.*

the weaver removes one web from the loom to make way for another. How important to improve the fleeting moments, and to live as if we were soon to see the rapid shuttle flying for the last time ! ¶ *And are spent without hope.* Without hope of recovery, or of future happiness on earth. It does not mean that he had no hope of happiness in the world to come. But such were his trials here, and so entirely had his comforts been removed, that he had no prospect of again enjoying life.

7. *O remember.* This is evidently an address to God. In the anguish of his soul Job turns his eye and his heart to his Maker, and urges reasons why he should close his life. The extent of his sufferings, and the certainty that he must die (ver. 9, 10), are the reasons on which he dwells why his life should be closed, and he released. The language is respectful, but it is the expression of deep anguish and sorrow. ¶ *That my life* is *wind.* Life is often compared with a vapour, a shadow, a breath. The language denotes that it is frail, and soon passed —as the breeze blows upon us, and soon passes by ; comp. Ps. lxxviii.39 :

For he remembered that they were but flesh ; A wind that passeth away and cometh not again.

¶ *Mine eye shall no more.* Marg. as in Heb. *not return.* The idea is, that if he was cut off, he would not return again to behold the pleasant scenes of this life. ¶ *See good.* Marg. *To see,* i. e. *to enjoy.* The sense is. that he would no more be permitted to look upon the things which now so much gratified the sight, and gave so much pleasure. There is some resemblance here to the feelings expressed by Hezekiah in his apprehension of death ; see Notes on Isa. xxxviii. 10, 11.

8. *The eye of him that hath seen me shall see me no* more. I shall be cut

off from all my friends—one of the things which most distresses men when they come to die. ¶ *Thine eyes* are *upon me, and I* am *not;* see ver. 21. Dr. Good renders this, " let thine eye be upon me, and I am nothing." Herder, " thine eye will seek me, but I am no more." According to this the sense is, that he was soon to be removed from the place where he had dwelt, and that should he be sought there he could not be found. He would seem to represent God as looking for him, and not finding him ; see ver. 21. The margin has, " I can live no longer." It may be possible that this is the meaning, that God had fixed an intense gaze upon him, and that he could not survive it. If this is the sense, then it accords with the descriptions given of the majesty of God everywhere in the Scriptures—that nothing could endure his presence, that even the earth trembles, and the mountains melt away, at his touch. Thus in Ps. civ. 32 :

He looketh on the earth, and it trembleth ; He toucheth the hills, and they smoke.

Compare the representation of the power of the *eye* in Job xvi. 9 :

He teareth me in his wrath who hateth me ; He gnasheth upon me with his teeth Mine enemy *sharpeneth his eyes* upon me.

On the whole, I think it probable that this is the sense here. There is an energy in the original which is greatly enfeebled in the common translation. God had fixed his eyes upon Job, and he at once disappeared ; comp. Rev. xx. 11 : " And I saw a great white throne, and him that sat upon it, from whose face the earth and the heaven fled away, and there was found no place for them."

9. As *the cloud is consumed and vanisheth away.* This image is taken from the light and fleecy clouds, which become smaller and smaller until they wholly vanish. For an illustration of a similar phrase, see Notes on Isa. xliv. 22. ¶ *To the grave —* שְׁאֹל,

10 He *a* shall return no more to his house, neither shall his place know him any *more.*

11 Therefore I will not re-

a Ps. 103.16.

frain my mouth; I will speak in the anguish of my spirit ; I will complain in the bitterness of my soul.

12 *Am* I a sea, or a whale,

Sheol. Sept. εἰς ᾅδην, to *Hades.* The word may mean *grave,* or the place of departed spirits; see Notes on Isa. v. 14 ; xiv. 9 ; comp. Notes on Job chap. x. 21, 22. Either signification will apply here. ¶ *Shall come up no* more. Shall no more live on the earth. It would be pressing this too far to adduce it as proving that Job did not believe in the doctrine of the resurrection. The connection here requires us to understand him as meaning only that he would not appear again on the earth.

10. *He shall return no more to his house.* He shall not revisit his family. Job is dwelling on the calamity of death, and one of the circumstances most deeply felt in the prospect of death is, that a man must leave his own house to return no more. The stately palaces that he has built ; the splendid halls which he has adorned ; the chamber where he slept ; the cheerful fireside where he met his family ; the place at the table which he occupied, he will revisit no more. His tread will be no more heard ; his voice will no more awaken delight in the happy family group ; the father and husband returning from his daily toil will no more give pleasure to the joyous circle. Such *is* death. It removes us from all earthly comforts, takes us away from home and kindred —from children and friends, and bids us go *alone* to an unknown world. Job felt that it was a sad and gloomy thing. And so it is, unless there is a well-founded hope of a better world. It is the gospel only that can make us willing to leave our happy dwellings, and the embraces of kindred and friends, and to tread the lonely path to the regions of the dead. The friend of God has a brighter home in heaven. He has more numerous and better friends there. He has there a more splendid and happy mansion than any here on earth. He will be engaged in more

blissful scenes there, than can be enjoyed by the most happy fireside here ; will have more cheerful employments there, than any which can be found on earth ; and will have higher and purer pleasures there, than can be found in parks, and lawns, and landscapes ; in splendid halls, in music, and the festive board ; in literary pursuits, and in the love of kindred. How far Job had the means of consolation from such reflections as these, it is not easy now to determine. The probability, however, is, that his views were comparatively dim and obscure.

11. *Therefore I will not refrain my mouth.* The idea in this verse is, "such is my distress at the prospect of dying, that I cannot but express it. The idea of going away from all my comforts, and of being committed to the grave, to revisit the earth no more, is so painful that I cannot but give vent to my feelings."

12. Am *I a sea ?* That is, "am I like a raging and tumultuous sea, that it is necessary to restrain and confine me ? The sense of the verse is, that God had treated him as if he were untamable and turbulent, as if he were like the restless ocean, or as if he were some monster, which could be restrained within proper limits only by the stern exercise of power. Dr. Good, following Reiske, renders this, "a savage beast," understanding by the Hebrew word ים a sea-monster instead of the sea itself, and then *any* ferocious beast, as the wild buffalo. But it is clear, I think, that the word never has this meaning. It means properly *the sea ;* then a lake or inland sea, and then it is applied to any great river that spreads out like the ocean. Thus it is applied both to the Nile, and to the Euphrates ; see Notes on Isa. xi. 15; xix. 5. Herder here renders it, "the river and its crocodile," and this it seems to me is probably the meaning. Job asks whether he is

that thou settest a watch over me?

13 When I say, My bed shall comfort me, my couch shall ease my complaint;

14 Then thou scarest me with

dreams, and terrifiest me through visions:

15 So that my soul chooseth strangling, *and* death rather than my [1] life.

1 *bones.*

---

like the Nile, overflowing its banks, and rolling on impetuously to the sea, and, unless restrained, sweeping every thing away. Some such flood of waters, and not a savage beast, is undoubtedly intended here. ¶ *Or a whale,* תנין, *tannin.* Jerome, *cetus—a whale.* The LXX. render it, δράκων, *a dragon.* The Chaldee paraphrases it, "Am I condemned as the Egyptians were, who were condemned and submerged in the Red sea; or as Pharaoh, who was drowned in the midst of it, in his sins, that thou placest over me a guard?" Herder renders it, "the crocodile." On the meaning of the word, see Notes on Isa. xiii. 22; li. 9. It refers here probably to a crocodile, or some similar monster, that was found either in the Nile or in the branches of the Red sea. There is no evidence that it means a whale. Harmer (Obs. iii. 536, Ed. Lond. 1808) supposes that the crocodile is meant, and observes that "Crocodiles are very terrible to the inhabitants of Egypt; when, therefore, they appear, they watch them with great attention, and take proper precautions to secure them, so as that they should not be able to avoid the deadly weapons the Egyptians afterwards make use of to kill them." According to this, the expression in Job refers to the anxious care which is evinced by the inhabitants of countries where crocodiles abound to destroy them. Every opportunity would be anxiously watched for, and great solicitude would be manifested to take their lives. In countries, too, which were subject to inundation from waters, great anxiety would be evinced. The rising waters would be carefully watched, lest they should burst over all barriers, and sweep away fences, houses, and towns. Such a constant vigilance Job represents the Almighty as keeping over

him—watching him as if he were a swelling, roaring, and ungovernable torrent, or as if he were a frightful monster of the deep, whom he was anxious to destroy. In both respects the language is forcible, and in both instances scarcely less irreverent than it is forcible. For a description of the crocodile, see Notes on chap. xli.

13. *When I say, My bed shall comfort me.* The idea in this verse and the following is, that there was no intermission to his sorrows. Even the times when men usually sought repose were to him times of distress. Then he was disturbed and alarmed by the most frightful dreams and visions, and sleep fled from him. ¶ *Shall ease my complaint.* The word rendered "shall ease" (ישא) means rather, *shall bear;* that is, shall lighten or sustain. The meaning is, that he sought relief on his bed.

14. *Then thou scarest me.* This is an address to God. He regarded him as the source of his sorrows, and he expresses his sense of this in language indeed very beautiful, but far from reverence. ¶ *With dreams;* see ver. 4. A similar expression occurs in Ovid:

Ut puto, cum requies medicinaque publica curæ,
Somnus adest, solitis nox venit orba malis,
Somnia me terrent, veros imitantia casus,
Et vigilant sensus in mea damna mei.
De Ponto, Lib. i. Eleg. 2.

¶ *And terrifiest me through visions;* see Notes on chap. iv. 13. This refers to the visions of the fancy, or to frightful appearances in the night. The belief of such night-visions was common in the early ages, and Job regarded them as under the direction of God, and as being designed to alarm him.

15. *So that my soul.* So that *I;* the soul being put for himself. ¶ *Chooseth strangling.* Dr. Good

16 I *a* loathe *it ;* I would not
live alway : let me alone ; for my
days *are* vanity.

renders it " suffocation," and supposes
that Job alludes to the oppression of
breathing, produced by what is commonly called the *night-mare,* and that
he means that he would prefer the
sense of suffocation excited at such
a time to the terrible images before
his mind. Herder renders it, *death.*
Jerome, *suspendium.* The LXX.,
" Thou separatest (ἀπαλλάξεις) my
life from my spirit, and my bones
from death ;" but what idea they attached to it, it is impossible now to
tell. The Syriac renders it, " Thou
choosest my soul from perdition, and
my bones from death." The word
rendered *strangling* (מֵחֶנֶק) is from
חנק, to be narrow, strait, close ; and
then means to strangle, to throttle,
Nah. ii. 12 ; 2 Sam. xvii. 23. Here
it means *death;* and Job designs to
say that he would prefer even the
most violent kind of death to the life
that he was then leading. I see no
evidence that the idea suggested by
Dr. Good is to be found in the passage. ¶ And *death rather than my life.*
Marg. as in Hebrew, *bones.* There
has been great variety in the exposition of this part of the verse. Herder
renders it, " death rather than this
frail body." Rosenmüller and Noyes,
" death rather than my bones ;" that
is, he preferred death to such an emaciated body as he then had, to the
wasted skeleton which was then all
that he had left to him. This is probably the true sense. Job was a sufferer in body and in soul. His flesh
was wasting away, his body was covered with ulcers, and his mind was harassed with apprehensions. By day
he had no peace, and at night he was
terrified by alarming visions and spectres ; and he preferred death in any
form to such a condition.
16. *I loathe* it. I loathe my life as
it is now. It has become a burden,
and I desire to part with it, and to go
down to the grave. There is, however, considerable variety in the interpretation of this. Noyes renders
it, " I am wasting away." Dr. Good
connects it with the previous verse,

and understands by it, " death in comparison with my sufferings do I despise." The Syriac is,—*it fails to me,*
i. e. I fail, or my powers are wasting
away. But the Hebrew word מאם
means properly to loathe and contemn
(See Note on chap. vii. 5), and the
true idea here is expressed in the common version. The sense is, " my life
is painful and offensive, and I wish to
die." ¶ *I would not live alway.* As
Job used this expression, there was
doubtless somewhat of impatience and
of an improper spirit. Still it contains a very important sentiment, and
one that may be expressed in the
highest state of just religious feeling.
A man who is prepared for heaven
should not and will not desire to live
here always. It is better to depart
and to be with Christ, better to leave
a world of imperfection and sin, and
to go to a world of purity and love.
On this text, fully and beautifully illustrating its meaning, the reader may
consult a sermon by Dr. Dwight.
Sermons, Edinburgh, 1828, vol. ii.
275, seq. This world is full of temptations and of sin ; it is a world where
suffering abounds ; it is the infancy of
our being ; it is a place where our
knowledge is imperfect, and where the
affections of the best are comparatively grovelling ; it is a world where the
good are often persecuted, and where
the bad are triumphant; and it is
better to go to abodes where all these
will be unknown. Heaven is a more
desirable place in which to dwell than
the earth ; and if we had a clear view
of that world, and proper desires, we
should pant to depart and to be there.
Most men live as though they *would*
live always here if they could do it,
and multitudes are forming their plans
as if they expected thus to live. They
build their houses and form their
plans as if life were never to end. It
is the privilege of the Christian, however, to EXPECT to die. Not wishing
to live always here, he forms his plans
with the anticipation that all which
he has must soon be left ; and he is
ready to loose his hold on the world

17 What *a is* man, that thou shouldest magnify him? and that

a Ps.8.4.

the moment the summons comes. So may we live ; so living, it will be easy to die. The sentiments suggested by this verse have been so beautifully versified in a hymn by Muhlenberg, that I will copy it here :

I would not live alway; I ask not to stay
Where storm after storm rises dark o'er the
 way; [here
The few fleeting mornings that dawn on us
Are enough for life's sorrows—enough for its
 cheer.

I would not live alway ; no, welcome the tomb;
Since Jesus hath lain there, I dread not its
 gloom;
There sweet be my rest, till he bid me arise,
To hail him in triumph descending the skies.

Who, who would live alway, away from his God,
Away from yon heaven, that blissful abode,
Where rivers of pleasure flow o'er the bright
 plains,
And the noontide of glory eternally reigns?

Where the saints of all ages in harmony meet,
Their Saviour and brethren transported to
 greet ;
While anthems of rapture unceasingly roll,
And the smile of the Lord is the feast of the
 soul.

¶ *Let me alone.* This is an address to God. It means, "cease to afflict me. Suffer me to live out my little length of life with some degree of ease. It is short at best, and I have no desire that it should always continue." This sentiment he illustrates in the following verses. ¶ *For my days* are *vanity.* They are as nothing, and are unworthy the notice of God. Life is a trifle, and I am not anxious that it should be prolonged. Why then may I not be suffered to pass my few days without being thus afflicted and pained?

17. *What is man, that thou shouldest magnify him?* That thou shouldst make him great, or that thou shouldst regard him as of so great importance as to fix thine eye attentively upon him. The idea here is, that it was unworthy the character of so great a being as God to bestow so much time and attention on a creature so insignificant as man ; and especially that man could not be of so much importance that it was necessary for God to watch all his defects with vigilance, and take special pains to mark and

thou shouldest set thine heart upon him?

punish all his offences. This question *might* be asked in another sense, and with another view. Man is so insignificant compared with God, that it may be asked why he should so carefully provide for his wants? Why make so ample provision for his welfare? Why institute measures so amazing and so wonderful for his recovery from sin? The answers to all these questions must be substantially the same. (1.) It is a part of the great plan of a condescending God. No insect is so small as to be beneath his notice. On the humblest and feeblest animalcula a care is bestowed in its formation and support as if God had nothing else to regard or provide for. (2.) Man *is* of importance. He has an immortal soul, and the salvation of that soul *is worth* all which it costs, even when it costs the blood of the Son of God. (3.) A creature who sins, *always* makes himself of importance. The murderer has an importance in the view of the community which he never had before. All good citizens become interested to arrest and punish him. There is no more certain way for a man to give consequence to himself, than to violate the laws, and to subject himself to punishment. An offending member of a family has an importance which he had not before, and all eyes are turned to him with deep interest. So it is with man—a part of the great family of God. (4.) A *sufferer* is a being of importance, and man as a sufferer is worthy of the notice of God. However feeble may be the powers of any one, or humble his rank, yet if he suffers, and especially if he is likely to suffer for ever, he becomes at once an object of the highest importance. Such is man ; a sufferer here, and liable to eternal pain hereafter ; and hence the God of mercy has interposed to visit him, and to devise a way to rescue him from his sorrows, and from eternal death. The Syriac renders this, "What is man, that thou shouldst *destroy* him?"—but the He-

18 And *that* thou shouldest visit him every morning, *and* try him every moment?

19 How long wilt thou not depart from me, nor let me alone till I swallow down my spittle?

brew means, "to magnify him, to make him great or of importance." ¶ *That thou shouldest set thine heart upon him?* Not with affection, but to punish him—for so the expression in this connection evidently means. The phrase itself might mean, "Why shouldst thou love him?"—implying that there was nothing in a creature so insignificant that could render him a proper object of the divine regard. But as used here by Job it means, "Why dost thou fix thy attention upon him so closely—marking the slightest offence, and seeming to take a special pleasure in inflicting pain and torture?" The Psalmist makes use of almost the same language, and not improbably copied it from this, though he employs it in a somewhat different sense. As used by him, it means that it was wonderful that the God who made the heavens should condescend to notice a creature so insignificant as man.

When I consider thy heavens, the work of thy
        fingers;
The moon and the stars, which thou hast or-
        dained;
What is man, that thou art mindful of him?
And the son of man, that thou visitest him?
                        Ps. viii. 3, 4.

18. *And* that *thou shouldest visit him?* That is, for the purpose of inflicting pain. This language Job intends undoubtedly to be applicable to himself, and he asks with impatience why God should take a pleasure in visiting with suffering each returning day a creature like him? ¶ *Every morning.* Why is there no intermission even for a day? Why does not God allow one morning, or one moment, to pass without inflicting pain on a creature so feeble and so frail? ¶ And *try him.* Or, prove him; to wit, by afflictions. ¶ *Every moment.* Constantly; without intermission.

19. *How long wilt thou not depart?* How long is this to continue? The same word occurs in chap. xiv. 6. The word rendered "*depart*" (שׁעה) means to look, to look around, and then to

look *away* from any one or any thing. The idea here is, that God had fixed his eyes upon Job, and he asks with anxiety, how long this was to continue, and when he would turn his eyes away; comp. Notes on ver. 8. Schultens supposes that the metaphor here is taken from combatants, who never take their eyes from their antagonists. ¶ *Till I swallow down my spittle.* For the shortest time. But there has been considerable variety in the explanation of this phrase. Herder renders it, "Till I draw my breath." Noyes, "Till I have time to breathe;" but he acknowledges that he has substituted this for the proverb which occurs in the original. The Hebrew is literally rendered in the common version, and the proverb is retained in Arabia to the present day. The meaning is, Give me a little respite; allow me a little time; as *we* would say, Suffer me to breathe. "This," says Burder, "is a proverb among the Arabians to the present day, by which they understand, Give me leave to rest after my fatigue. This is the favour which Job complains is not granted to him. There are two instances which illustrate this passage (quoted by Schultens) in Harris's Narratives entitled the Assembly. One is of a person, who, when eagerly pressed to give an account of his travels, answered with impatience, 'Let me swallow down my spittle, for my journey hath fatigued me.' The other instance is of a quick return made to a person who used the proverb. 'Suffer me,' said the person importuned, 'to swallow down my spittle;' to which the friend replied, 'You may, if you please, swallow down even the Tigris and the Euphrates;' that is, You may take what time you please." The expression is proverbial, and corresponds to ours when we say, "in the twinkling of an eye," or, "till I can catch my breath;" that is, in the briefest interval. Job addresses this language to God. There is

20 I have sinned ; *a* what shall I do unto thee, O thou Preserver *b* of men? why hast thou set me as a mark *c* against thee, so that I am a burden to myself?

a Ps.80.3.   *b* Ps.36 6.   *c* La.3.12.

much impatience in it, and much that a pious man should not employ ; but we are to remember that Job was beset with peculiar trials, and that he had not the views of the divine existence and perfections, the promises and the high hopes, which as Christians we have under the fuller light of revelation ; and before harshly condemning him we should put ourselves in his situation, and ask ourselves how *we* would be likely to think and feel and speak if we were in the same circumstances.

20. *I have sinned,* חָטָאתִי. This is a literal translation, and as it stands in the common version it is the language of a penitent— confessing that he had erred, and making humble acknowledgment of his sins. That such a confession became Job, and that he would be willing to admit that he was a sinner, there can be no doubt ; but the connection seems rather to require a different sense—a sense implying that *though* he had sinned, yet his offences could not be such as to require the notice which God had taken of them. Accordingly this interpretation has been adopted by many, and the Hebrew will bear the construction. It may be rendered as a question, " Have I sinned; what did I against thee?" *Herder.* Or, the sense may be, "I have sinned. I admit it. Let this be conceded. But what can that be to a being like God, that he should take such notice of it? Have I injured him? Have I deserved these heavy trials? Is it proper that he should make me a special mark, and direct his severest judgments against me in this manner?" comp. Notes on chap. xxxv. 6 — 8. The Syriac renders it in this manner, " If I have sinned, what have I done to thee?" So the Arabic, according to Walton. So the LXX. Εἰ ἐγὼ ἥμαρτον —" if I have sinned." This expresses the true sense. The object is not so much to make a penitent confession, as it is to say, that on the worst

construction of the case, on the admission of the truth of the charge, he had not deserved the severe inflictions which he had received at the hand of God. ¶ *What shall I do unto thee ?* Or, rather, what *have* I done unto thee? How can my conduct seriously affect thee ? It will not mar thy happiness, affect thy peace, or in any way injure a being so great as God. This sentiment is often *felt* by men— but not often so honestly *expressed.* ¶ *O thou Preserver of men.* Or, rather, " O thou that dost *watch* or *observe* men." The word rendered " Preserver " (נֹצֵר) is a participle from נָצַר which means, according to Gesenius, to watch, to guard, to keep, and is here used in the sense of observing one s faults ; and the idea of Job is, that God closely observed the conduct of men ; that he strictly marked their faults, and severely punished them ; and he asks with impatience, and evidently with improper feeling, why he thus closely watched men. So it is understood by Schultens, Rosenmüller, Dr. Good, Noyes, Herder, Kennicott, and others. The LXX. render it, " who knowest the mind of men ?" ¶ *Why hast thou set me as a mark?* The word rendered " mark " (מִפְגָּע), means properly that which one impinges against—from פָּגַע, to impinge against, to meet, to rush upon any one—and here means, why has God made me such an object of attack or assault ? The LXX. render it, κατεντευκτήν σου, " an accuser of thee." ¶ *So that I am a burden to myself.* The LXX. render this, ἐπὶ σοὶ φορτίον, *a burden to thee.* The copy from which they translated evidently had עָלֶיךָ—*to thee,* instead of עָלַי—*to me,* as it is now read in the Hebrew. " The Masorites also place this among the eighteen passages which they say were altered by transcribers." *Noyes.* But the received text is sustained by all the versions except the LXX. and by all the Hebrew MSS. hitherto examined, and is doubtless the true read-

21 And why dost thou not pardon my transgression, and take away *a* mine iniquity? for now

a Mi.7.18, 19 ; 1 John 1.9.

shall I sleep in the dust ; and thou shalt seek me in the morning, but I *b* *shall* not *be.*

b Ps.103.16.

ing. The sense is plain, that life had become a burden to Job. He says that God had made him the special object of his displeasure, and that his condition was insupportable. That there is much in this language which is irreverent and improper no one can doubt, and it is not possible wholly to vindicate it. Nor are we called to do it by any view which we have of the nature of inspiration. He was a good, but not a perfect man. These expressions are recorded, not for our imitation, but to show what human nature is. Before harshly condemning him, however, we should ask what *we* would be likely to do in his circumstances ; we should remember also, that he had few of the truths and promises to support him which we have.

21. *And why dost thou not pardon my transgression?* Admitting that I have sinned (ver. 20), yet why dost thou not forgive me? I shall soon pass away from the land of the living. I may be sought, but I shall not be found. No one would be injured by my being pardoned—since I am so short-lived, and so unimportant in the scale of being. No one can be benefited by pursuing a creature of a day, such as I am, with punishment. Such seems to be the meaning of this verse. It is the language of complaint, and is couched in language filled with irreverence. Still it is language such as awakened and convicted sinners often use, and expresses the feelings which often pass through their hearts. They admit that they are sinners. They know that they must be pardoned or they cannot be saved. They are distressed at the remembrance of guilt, and under this state of mind, deeply convicted and distressed, they ask with a murmuring spirit *why* God does not pardon them? Why does he allow them to remain in this state of agitation, suspense, and deep distress? Who could be injured by their being forgiven? Of what consequence

to others can it be that they should *not* be forgiven? How can God be benefited by his not pardoning them? It may not be easy to answer these questions in a manner wholly satisfactory ; but perhaps the following may be some of the reasons why *Job* had not the evidence of forgiveness which he now desired, and why the convicted sinner has not. *The main reason is, that they are not in a state of mind to make it proper to forgive them.* (1.) There is a feeling that they have a *claim* on God for pardon, or that it would be wrong for God *not* to pardon them. When men feel that they have a *claim* on God for pardon, they cannot be forgiven. The very notion of pardon implies that it must be when there is no *claim existing* or *felt.* (2.) There is no proper *submission* to God—to his views, his terms, his plan. In order that pardon may be extended to the guilty, there should be acquiescence in God's own terms, and time, and mode. The sinner must resign himself into his hands, to be forgiven or not as he pleases—feeling that the whole question is lodged in his bosom, and that if he should *not* forgive, still it would be right, and his throne would be pure. In particular, under the Christian method of pardon, there must be entire acquiescence in the plan of salvation by the Lord Jesus Christ ; a willingness to accept of forgiveness, not on the ground of personal claim, but on the ground of his merits ; and it is *because* the convicted sinner is not willing to be pardoned in this way, that he remains unforgiven. There should be a feeling, also, that it would be right for God to pardon others, if he pleases, even though *we* are not saved ; and it is often because the convicted sinner is not willing that that should be done, because he feels that it would be *wrong* in God to save others and not *him,* that he is not forgiven. The sinner is often suffered to remain in this state until he is brought to acquiesce in the right of a sovereign God to save whom he pleases. (3.) There is a murmuring spirit—and that is a reason why the sinner is not forgiven. That was manifestly the case with Job ; and when that exists, how can God forgive? How can a parent pardon an offending child, when he is constantly complaining of his injustice and of the severity of his government? This very spirit is a new offence, and a new reason why he should be punished. So the awakened sinner murmurs. He complains of the government of God as too severe ; of his law, as too strict; of his dealings, as harsh and unkind. He complains of his sufferings, and thinks they are wholly beyond his deserts. He complains of the doctrines of the Bible as mysterious, incomprehensible, and unjust. In this state how *can* he be forgiven ? God often suffers the awakened sinner, therefore, to remain under conviction for sin, until he is willing to acquiesce in all his claims, and to submit without a murmur; and then, and not till then, he extends forgiveness to the guilty and troubled spirit. ¶ *For now shall I sleep in the dust.* On the word *sleep,* as applied to death, see Notes chap. iii. 13. The meaning is, that he was soon to die. He urges the shortness of the time which remained to him as a reason why his afflictions should be lightened, and why he should be pardoned. If God had any thing that he could do for him, it must be done soon. But only a brief period remained, and Job seems to be impatient lest the whole of his life should be gone, and he should sleep in the dust without evidence that his sins were pardoned. Olympiodorus, as quoted by Rosenmller, expresses the sense in the following manner : "If, therefore, I am so short-lived [or momentary, πρόσκαιρος] and obnoxious to death, and must die after a short time, and shall no more arise, as if from sleep, why dost not thou suffer the little space of life to be free from punishment?" ¶ *And thou shalt seek me in the morning, but I shall not be.* That is, thou shalt seek to find me after I have slept in the dust, as if with the ex-

pectation that I should wake, but I shall not be found. My sleep will be perpetual, and I shall no more return to the land of the living The idea seems to be, that if God were to show him any favour, it must be done soon. His death, which *must* happen soon, would put it out of the power even of God to show him mercy on earth, if he should relent and be inclined to favour him. He seems not to doubt that God *would* be disposed yet to show him favour ; that he would be inclined to pardon him, and to relax the severity of his dealings with him, but he says that if it were done it must be done soon, and seems to apprehend that it would be delayed so long that it could not be done. The phrase "in the morning" here is used with reference to the *sleep* which he had just mentioned. We sleep at night, and awake and arise in the morning. Job says it would not be so with him in the sleep of death. He would awake no more; he could no more be found. —In this chapter there is much language of bitter complaint, and much which we cannot justify. It should not be taken as a model for our language when we are afflicted, though Job may have only *expressed* what has passed through the heart of many an afflicted child of God. We should not judge him harshly. Let us ask ourselves how *we* would have done if we had been in similar circumstances. Let us remember that he had comparatively few of the promises which we have to comfort us, and few of the elevated views of truth as made known by revelation, which we have to uphold us in trial. Let us be thankful that when we suffer, promises and consolations meet us on every hand. The Bible is open before us—rich with truth, and bright with promise. Let us remember that death is not as dark and dismal to us as it was to the pious in the time of the patriarchs—and that the grave is not now to us as dark and chilly, and gloomy, and comfortless an abode. To their view, the shadow of death cast a melancholy chillness over all the regions of the dead ; to us the tomb is enlightened by Christian hope. The empire of

CHAPTER VIII.

ANALYSIS OF THE CHAPTER.

This chapter contains the first reply which Bildad makes to Job. He is more severe and less argumentative than Eliphaz. Jahn, as quoted by the editor of the Pictorial Bible, thus characterizes him: "Bildad, less discerning and less polished than Eliphaz, breaks out at first into accusations against Job, and increases in vehemence as he proceeds. In the end, however, he is reduced to a mere repetition of his former arguments." Dr. Hales characterizes this speech, not unjustly, as "unkind." Dr. Good remarks that he commences his speech "with most provoking cruelty." There is evidently much harshness in the language, and much severity of reproof. He pursues substantially the same line of argumentation which Eliphaz had commenced, but he does it with much more severity. He takes it for granted, that the children of Job had sinned, and that they had been cut off on account of their crimes. Assuming that Job and his family had been guilty of great sins, the drift of the discourse is, to exhort him to repent and to humble himself before God. The speech comprises the following points:—

1. He compares the speech of Job to a sweeping and violent tempest which prostrates all before it. How long, he asks, is this to continue? ver 2.

2. He asks with earnestness whether the Almighty could pervert justice, as Job seems to have supposed? And in this question he implies, in the strongest manner, that God was just and right, ver 3.

3. He takes it for granted that the children of Job had sinned, and that God had cut them down in their iniquity (ver 4); but yet says, that if Job was an upright man, and would seek God in a humble and reverent manner, his favour might yet be obtained, and he would make his habitation prosperous, ver. 5—7. Though he should begin life again with none but himself, yet his end would be prosperous, and he would be blessed with a large increase. This part of the speech must have been particularly trying to Job. The assumption that his children had been cut down unpardoned, was one which would go at once to the heart of

the much afflicted father, and greatly aggravate his sorrows

4. In support of his views, Bildad appeals to the ancients, and especially to those who had lived much longer than they had done, and who had had an opportunity for more extended observation. He quotes from some ancient poem, representing by striking images the miserable condition of the wicked. The images in that ancient document are taken from what is observed in nature. The most succulent plants are soonest withered ; and, in like manner, the hope of the hypocrite would soon fail, ver. 8—18.

5. He concludes by saying that God would not cast away a perfect man, and by stating the happy effects which would result from putting confidence in God, ver. 19—22. Bildad thus agrees substantially with Eliphaz in the opinion that Job was a hypocrite, and that it was for his sins that he had been punished in this manner. There is great severity in his remarks, and much that is unkind in his manner, and uncharitable in his views. There is less, too, that is argumentative than in the speech of Eliphaz. Yet there is a beautiful appeal to the past (ver. 11, seq.); and if this is a fragment of a former poem, it is probably the oldest on record.

CHAPTER VIII.

THEN answered Bildad the Shu-hite, and said,

2 How long wilt thou speak these *things?* and *how long shall* the words of thy mouth *be like* a strong wind ?

3 Doth *a* God pervert judgment? or doth the Almighty pervert justice?

a chap. 34.12,17 ; De. 32.4 ; 2 Ch. 19.7 ; Ps. 89. 14 ; Da. 9 14 ; Ro. 3.5,6.

Death has been invaded, and his power has been taken away. Light has been shed around the tomb, and the grave to us is the avenue to immortal life ; the pathway on which the lamp of salvation shines, to eternal glory. Let us not complain, therefore, when we are afflicted, as if the blessing were long delayed, or as if it could not be conferred should we soon die. If withheld here, it will be imparted in a better world, and we should be willing to bear trials in this short life, with the sure promise that God will meet and bless us when we pass the confines of life, and enter the world of glory.

1. *Then answered Bildad the Shuhite ;* see Notes, chap. ii. 11.

2. *How long wilt thou speak these* things ? The things of murmuring and complaint, such as he had uttered in the previous chapters. ¶ *The words of thy mouth* be like *a strong wind ?* The Syriac and Arabic (ac-

cording to Walton) render this, " the spirit of pride fill thy mouth." The LXX. render it, " The spirit of thy mouth is profuse of words "—πολυ-ρῆμον. But the common rendering is undoubtedly correct, and the expression is a very strong and beautiful one. His language of complaint and murmuring was like a tempest. It swept over all barriers, and disregarded all restraint. The same figure is found in Aristophanes, Ran. 872, as quoted by Schultens, Τυφὼς ἐκζαίνειν παρασκευάζεται —a *tempest of words is preparing to burst forth.* And in Silius Italicus, xi. 581 :

————qui tanta superbo
Facta sonas ore, et spumanti turbine perflas
Ignorantum aures.

The Chaldee renders it correctly, א‫ר‬ א‫ע‬‫צ‬‫נ‬ —a *great tempest.*

3. *Doth God pervert judgment?* That is, Does God afflict men unjustly ? Does he show favour to the evil, and punish the good ? Bildad here

4 If thy children have sinned against him, and he have cast them away ¹ for their transgression ;

5 If ᵃ thou wouldest seek unto

1 *in the hand of their.*   ᵃ chap.11.
13; 22.23, &c.

God betimes, and make thy supplication to the Almighty ;

6 If thou *wert* pure and upright ; surely now he would awake for thee and make the habitation of thy righteousness prosperous.

undoubtedly refers to Job, and supposes that he had brought this charge against God. But he had not done it in so many words. He had complained of the severity of his sufferings, and had indulged in irreverent language towards God. But he had not advanced the charge openly that God had perverted right. Bildad strenuously maintains that God would do right. His argument is based on the supposition that God would deal with men in this life according to their character ; and thus he infers that Job must have been guilty of some great wickedness, that punishment should come upon him in this manner.

4. *If thy children have sinned against him.* Bildad here *assumes* that the children of Job had been wicked, and had been cut off in their sins. This must have cut him to the quick, for there was nothing which a bereaved father would feel more acutely than this. The meaning here is somewhat weakened by the word "if." The Hebrew אִם is rather to be taken in the sense of "*since*"—assuming it as an indisputable point, or taking it for granted. It was not a supposition that *if* they should now do it, certain other consequences would follow ; but the idea is, that since they *had been* cut off in their sins, if Job would even now seek God with a proper spirit, he might be restored to prosperity, though his beginning should be small ; ver. 7. ¶ *And he have cast them away.* Bildad supposes that they had been disowned by God, and had been put to death. ¶ *For their transgression.* Marg. *in the hand of their.* The Hebrew is, *by* the hand of their transgression ; *i. e.* their sin has been the cause of it, or it has been by the instrumentality of their sin. What foundation Bildad had for this opin-

ion, derived from the life and character of the sons of Job, we have no means of ascertaining. The probability is, however, that he had learned in general that they had been cut off ; and that, on the general principle which he maintained, that God deals with men in this life according to their character, he *inferred* that they must have been distinguished for wickedness. Men not unfrequently argue in this way when sudden calamity comes upon others.

5. *If thou wouldest seek unto God betimes.* If thou wouldest do it *now.* If even on the supposition that your sons have thus perished, and that God has come out in judgment against your family, you would look to God, you might be restored to favour. The word rendered "*seek betimes*" (שָׁחַר) means literally to seek in the morning, to seek early ; and then, to make it the first business. It is derived from the word meaning *aurora* (שַׁחַר) and has reference to the early light of the morning, and hence to an early seeking. It may be applied to seeking him in early life, or as the first thing—looking to him *immediately* when help is needed, or before we apply to any one else ; comp. Prov. vii. 15 ; viii. 17 ; xiii 24 ; Job xxiv. 5 ; Ps. lxiii. 1 ; lxxviii. 34 ; Isa. xxvi. 9 ; Hos. v. 15 ; comp. the advice of Eliphaz, chap. v. 8.

6. *If thou* wert *pure and upright.* There is something peculiarly severe and caustic in this whole speech of Bildad. He first assumes that the children of Job were cut off for impiety, and then takes it for granted that Job himself was not a pure and upright man. This inference he seems to have derived partly from the fact that he had been visited with so heavy calamities, and partly from the sentiments which Job had himself expressed. Nothing could be more unjust

7 Though thy beginning was small, yet thy latter end should greatly increase.

8 For inquire, I pray thee, of the former age, and prepare thyself to the search of their fathers :

and severe, however, than to take it for granted that he was a hypocrite, and then proceed to argue as if that were a settled point. He does not make it a supposition that *possibly* Job might have erred—which would not have been improper ; but he proceeds to argue as if it were a point about which there could be no hesitation. ¶ *He would awake for thee.* He would arouse or excite himself (יעיר) on thy account. The image is that of arousing one's self from sleep or inactivity to aid another ; and the idea is, that God had, as it were, slumbered over the calamities of Job, or had suffered them to come without interposing to prevent them, but that he would arouse himself if Job were pure, and would call upon him for aid. ¶ *And make the habitation of thy righteousness prosperous.* That is, if thy habitation should become righteous now, he would make it prosperous. Hitherto, is the idea of Bildad, it has been a habitation of wickedness. Thy children have been wicked, and are now cut off. Thou thyself hast been a wicked man, and in consequence art afflicted. If now thou wouldest become pure and seek unto God, then God would make thy habitation prosperous. What could more try the patience of a sufferer than such cold and unfeeling insinuations ? And what could more beautifully illustrate the nature of true courtesy, than to sit unmoved and hear such remarks ? It was by forbearance in such circumstances eminently that Job showed his extraordinary patience.

7. *Though thy beginning was small.* On the supposition that the children of Job had been cut off, his family now was small. Yet Bildad says, that if he were to begin life again, even with so small a family, and in such depressed and trying circumstances, if he were a righteous man he might hope for returning prosperity. ¶ *Yet thy latter end* From this, it is evident that Job was not now regarded as

an old man. He would still have the prospect of living many years. Some have supposed, however, that the meaning here is, that his former prosperity should *appear* small compared with that which he would hereafter enjoy if he were pure and righteous. So Noyes and Rosenm ller interpret it. But it seems to me that the former interpretation is the correct one. Bildad utters a general sentiment, that though when a man begins life he has a small family and little property, yet if he is an upright man, he will be prospered and his possessions will greatly increase ; comp. chap. xlii. 12 : " Jehovah blessed the latter end of Job more than the beginning."

8. *For inquire thee of the former age.* That is, attend to the results of observation. Ask the generations which have passed, and who in their poems and proverbs have left the records of their experience. The sentiment which Bildad proposes to confirm by this appeal is, that though the wicked should for a time flourish, yet they would be cut off, and that the righteous, though they may be for a time afflicted, yet if they seek God, they will ultimately prosper. It was common to make these appeals to the ancients. The results of observation were embodied in proverbs, parables fables, and fragments of poems ; and he was regarded as among the wisest of men who had the fruits of these observations most at command. To that Bildad appeals, and especially, as would appear, to the fragment of an ancient poem which he proceeds to repeat, and which, perhaps, is the oldest poem extant in any language. ¶ *And prepare thyself.* Make an effort, or give diligent attention to it. ¶ *To the search of their fathers.* Of the bygone generations, not only to the age immediately past, but to *their* ancestors. He would bring the results of the observation of far distant ages to confirm the sentiment which he had advanced.

9 (For we *a are but of* yesterday, and know [1] nothing, because

a Ps.39.5.   1 *not.*

our days upon earth *are* a *b* shadow :)

b 1 Ch. 29 15.

9. *For we* are but of *yesterday.*
That is, we are of short life. We
have had but few opportunities of observation compared with those who
have gone before us. There can be
no doubt that Bildad here refers to
the longevity of the antecedent ages
compared with the age of man at the
time when he lived; and the passage,
therefore, is of importance in order to
fix the date of the poem. It shows
that human life had been reduced in
the time of Job within comparatively
moderate limits, and that an important change had taken place in its du-
ration. This reduction began not long
after the flood, and was probably continued gradually until it reached the
present limit of seventy years. This
passage proves that Job could not
have lived in the time of the greatest
longevity of man ; comp. the Intro. §
3. ¶ *And know nothing.* Marg.
not. So the Hebrew literally, " we
do not know." The sense is, " we
have had comparatively few opportunities for observation. From the
comparative brevity of our lives, we
see but little of the course of events.
Our fathers lived through longer periods, and could mark more accurately
the result of human conduct." One
suggestion may be made here, perhaps
of considerable importance in explaining the course of argument in this
book. The friends of Job maintained
that the righteous would be rewarded
in this life, and that the wicked would
be overtaken by calamity. It may
seem remarkable that they should
have urged this so strenuously, when
in the actual course of events as we
now see them, there appears to be so
slender a foundation for it in fact.
But may this not be accounted for by
the remark of Bildad in the verse under
consideration ? They appealed to
their fathers. They relied on the results of experience in those ancient
times. When men lived nine hundred
or a thousand years ; when one generation was longer than twelve generations are now, this fact would be much

more likely to occur than as human
life is now ordered. Things would
have time to work themselves right.
The wicked in that long tract of time
would be likely to be overtaken by
disgrace and calamity, and the righteous would outlive the detractions
and calumnies of their enemies, and
meet in their old age with the ample
rewards of virtue. Should men now
live through the same long period,
the same thing substantially would
occur. A man's character, who is
remembered at all, is fully established
long before a thousand years have
elapsed, and posterity does justice to
the righteous and the wicked. If
men *lived* during that time instead of
being merely *remembered,* the same
thing would be likely to occur. Justice would be done to character, and
the world would, in general, render to
a man the honour which he deserved.
This fact may have been observed in
the long lives of the men before
the flood, and the result of the observation may have been embodied in
proverbs, fragments of poems, and in
traditionary sayings, and have been
recorded by the sages of Arabia as
indubitable maxims. With these maxims they came to the controversy
with Job, and forgetful of the change
necessarily made by the abbreviation
of human life, they proceed to apply
their maxims without mercy to him ;
and because he was overwhelmed with
calamity, they assumed that therefore
he *must* have been a wicked man.
¶ *Our days upon earth* are *a shadow.*
Comparisons of this kind are quite
common in the Scriptures ; see Notes
on chap. vii. 6. A similar figure occurs in 1 Chron. xxix. 15 :

For we are strangers before thee,
And sojourners, as were all our fathers:
Our days upon earth are as a shadow,
Yea, there is no abiding.

An expression similar occurs in Æschylus, Agam. v. 488, as quoted by
Drusius and Dr. Good :

—εἴδωλον σκιᾶς—
—the image or semblance of a shade—

10 Shall not they teach thee, *and* tell thee, and utter words out of their heart ?

11 Can the rush grow up without mire ? can the flag grow without water ?

So in Pindar, man is called σκιᾶς; ὄναρ — *the dream of a shade ;* and so by Sophocles, καπνοῦ σκιὰ—*the shadow of smoke.* All these mean the same thing, that the life of man is brief and transitory. Bildad designs to apply it not to man in general, but to the age in which he lived, as being disqualified by the shortness of life to make extended observations.

10. *Shall not they teach thee.* The results of human conduct, and the great principles on which God governs the world. ¶ *And utter words out of their heart.* Dr. Good renders this,

" And well forth the sayings of their wisdom,"

and supposes it means that the words of wisdom would proceed from them as water bubbles from a fountain. But this, I think, is a mere conceit. The true sense is, that they would not speak that merely which comes from the mouth, or that which comes uppermost, and without reflection—as the Greeks say, λέγειν πᾶν ὅ τι ἐπὶ στόμα ἔλθη ; or, as the Latins, *Quicquid in buccam venerit loqui—to speak whatever comes in the mouth ;* but they would utter that which came *from the heart*—which was sincere, and the result of deep and prolonged reflection. Perhaps, also, Bildad means to insinuate that Job had uttered what was uppermost in his mind, without taking time for reflection.

11. *Can the rush.* This passage has all the appearance of being a fragment of a poem handed down from ancient times. It is adduced by Bildad as an example of the views of the ancients, and, as the connection would seem to imply, as a specimen of the sentiments of those who lived before the life of man had been abridged. It was customary in the early ages of the world to communicate knowledge of all kinds by maxims, moral sayings, and proverbs ; by apothegms and by poetry handed down from generation to generation. Wisdom consisted much in the amount of maxims and proverbs which were thus treasured up ; as it

now consists much in the knowledge which we have of the lessons taught by the past, and in the ability to apply that knowledge to the various transactions of life. The records of past ages constitute a vast storehouse of wisdom, and the present generation is more wise than those which have gone before, only because the results of *their* observations have been treasured up, and we can act on *their* experience, and because we can begin where they left off, and, taught by their experience, can avoid the mistakes which they made. The word " *rush* " here (גֹּמֶא) denotes properly a bulrush, and especially the Egyptian *papyrus—papyrus Nilotica ;* see Notes on Isa. xviii. 2. It is derived from the verb גָּמָא, to absorb, to drink up, and is given to this plant because it absorbs or drinks up moisture. The Egyptians used it to make garments, shoes, baskets, and especially boats or skiffs ; Pliny, Nat. His. 13. 21—26 ; see Notes on Isa. xviii. 2. They also derived from it materials for writing—and hence our word *paper.* The LXX. render it here, πάπυρος, *papyrus* ¶ *Without mire.* Without moisture. It grew in the marshy places along the Nile. ¶ *Can the flag.* Another plant of a similar character. The word אָחוּ, *flag,* says Gesenius, is an Egyptian word, signifying *marsh-grass, reeds, bulrushes, sedge,* every thing which grows in wet grounds. The word was adopted not only into the Hebrew, but also into the Greek idiom of Alexandria, where it is written, ἄχι. ἄχει. Jerome says of it, " When I inquired of the learned what this word meant, I heard from the Egyptians, that by this name every thing was intended in their language which grew up in a pool." The word is synonymous with rush, or bulrush, and denotes a plant which absorbs a great quantity of water. What is the exact idea which this figure is designed to convey, is not very clear. I think it probable that the whole description is intended to represent a hypocrite, and that the

12 Whilst *a* it *is* yet in his greenness, *and* not cut down, it withereth before any *other* herb.

a Ps. 129.6 ; Mat. 13.6.

13 So *are* the paths of all that forget God ; and the hypocrite's hope *b* shall perish :

b chap. 11.20 ; 27.8 ; Pr.10.28.

meaning is, that he had in his growth a strong resemblance to such a rush or reed. There was nothing solid or substantial in his piety. It was like the soft, spongy texture of the water-reed, and would wilt under trial, as the papyrus would when deprived of water.

12. *Whilst it is yet in his greenness.* That is, while it seems to be in its vigour. ¶ And *is not cut down.* Even when it is not cut down. If suffered to stand by itself, and if undisturbed, it will wither away. The application of this is obvious and beautiful. Such plants have no self-sustaining power. They are dependent on moisture for their support. If that is withheld, they droop and die. So with the prosperous sinner and the hypocrite. His piety, compared with that which is genuine, is like the spongy texture of the paper-reed compared with the solid oak. He is sustained in his professed religion by outward prosperity, as the rush is nourished by moisture ; and the moment his prosperity is withdrawn, his religion droops and dies like the flag without water.

13. *So* are *the paths of all that forget God.* This is clearly a part of the quotation from the sayings of the ancients. The word *paths* here means ways, acts, doings. They who forget God are like the paper-reed. They seem to flourish, but they have nothing that is firm and substantial. As the paper-reed soon dies, as the flag withers away before any other herb, so it will be with the wicked, though apparently prosperous. ¶ *And the hypocrite's hope shall perish.* This important sentiment, it seems, was known in the earliest periods of the world ; and if the supposition above be correct, that this is a fragment of a poem which had come down from far distant times, it was probably known before the flood. The passage requires no particular philological explanation, but it is exceedingly important. We may remark on it, (1.) That there

were hypocrites even in that early age of the world. They are confined to no period, or country, or religious denomination, or profession. There *are* hypocrites in religion—and so there are in politics, and in business, and in friendship, and in morals. There are pretended friends, and pretended patriots, and pretended lovers of virtue, whose hearts are false and hollow, just as there are pretended friends of religion. Wherever there is genuine coin, it will be likely to be counterfeited ; and the fact of a counterfeit is always a tribute to the intrinsic worth of the coin—for who would be at the pains to counterfeit that which is worthless ? The fact that there are hypocrites in the church, is an involuntary tribute to the excellency of religion. (2.) The hypocrite has a hope of eternal life. This hope is founded on various things. It may be on his own morality ; it may be on the expectation that he will be able to practise a deception ; it may be on some wholly false and unfounded view of the character and plans of God. Or taking the word *hypocrite* in a larger sense to denote any one who pretends to religion and who has none, this hope may be founded on some change of feeling which he has had, and which he mistook for religion ; on some supposed vision which he had of the cross or of the Redeemer, or on the mere subsiding of the alarm which an awakened sinner experiences, and the comparative peace consequent on that. The mere cessation of fear produces a kind of peace—as the ocean is calm and beautiful after a storm—no matter what may be the cause, whether it be true religion or any other cause. Many a sinner, who has lost his convictions for sin in any way, mistakes the temporary calm which succeeds for true religion, and embraces the hope of the hypocrite. (3.) That hope will perish. This may occur in various ways. (*a*) It may die away insensibly, and leave the man to be *a mere pro-*

14 Whose hope shall be cut off, and whose trust *shall be* a spider's [1] web.

1 *house*; Is. 59.5,6.　　　*a* Mat.7.26.

15 He shall lean upon his house, but it *a* shall not stand: he shall hold it fast, but it shall not endure.

---

fessor of religion—a formalist, without comfort, usefulness, or peace. (*b*) It may be taken away in some calamity by which God tries the soul, and where the man will see that he has no religion to sustain him. (*c*) It may occur under the preaching of the gospel, when the hypocrite may be convinced that he is destitute of vital piety, and has no true love to God. (*d*) It may be on a bed of death — when God comes to take away the soul, and when the judgment-seat appears in view. (*e*) Or it will be at the bar of God. Then the hope of the hypocrite will certainly be destroyed. Then it will be seen that he had no true religion, and then he will be consigned to the awful doom of him who in the most solemn circumstances lived to deceive, and who assumed the appearance of that which he had the strongest reason to believe he never possessed. Oh! how important it is for every professor of religion to examine himself, that he may know what is the foundation of his hope of heaven!

14. *Whose hope shall be cut off.* Schultens supposes that the quotation from the ancients closes with ver. 13, and that these are the comments of Bildad on the passage to which he had referred. Rosenmüller and Noyes continue the quotation to the close of ver. 19; Dr. Good closes it at ver. 13. It seems to me that it is extended farther than ver. 13, and probably it is to be regarded as continued to the close of ver. 18. The beginning of this verse has been very variously rendered. Dr. Good says that it has never been understood, and proposes to translate it, "thus shall his support rot away." Noyes renders it, "whose expectation shall come to naught;" Gesenius, "shall be cut off." Jerome, *Non ei placebit vecordia sua,* "his madness [dotage, rage, or frenzy] shall not please him." The LXX., "his house shall be uninhabitable, and his

tent shall pass away as the spider." The Hebrew word translated "cut off" (יָקוֹט) is from קוֹט, *kūt*, usually meaning to loathe, to nauseate, to be offensive. Gesenius supposes that the word here is synonymous with the Arabic *to be cut off.* But this sense does not occur elsewhere in the Hebrew, and it is doubtful whether this is the true sense of the phrase. In the Hebrew word there is probably always the idea of loathing, of being offensive, irksome, or disgusting; see Ps. xcv. 10, I was grieved; Job x. 1, is weary; Ezek vi. 9, shall loathe; so Ezek. xx. 43; xxxvi. 31; Ezek. xvi. 47, a tiresome, or disgusting object. Taylor (Concord) renders it here, "Whom his hope shall loathe or abominate, *i. e.* who shall loathe or hate the thing that he hopes for." I have no doubt that the meaning here is, to be loathsome, offensive, or nauseous, and the correct sense is, "whose hope shall *rot.*" The figure is continued from the image of the paper-reed and the flag, which soon decay; and the idea is, that as such weeds grow offensive and putrid in the stagnant water, so shall it be with the hope of the hypocrite. ¶ *And whose trust.* Whose confidence, or expectation. ¶ *A spider's web.* Marg. *house.* So the Heb. בֵּית. The spider's house is the web which it forms, a frail, light, tenuous substance which will sustain almost nothing. The wind shakes it, and it is easily brushed away. So it will be with the hope of the hypocrite.

15. *He shall lean upon his house.* This is an *allusion* to the web or house of the spider. The hope of the hypocrite is called the *house* which he has built for himself, his home, his refuge, his support. But it shall fail him. In times of trial he will trust to it for support, and it will be found to be as frail as the web of the spider. How little the light and slender thread which a spider spins would avail a man for support in time of danger! So

16 He *is* green before the sun, and his branch shooteth forth in his garden.

17 His roots are wrapped about the heap, *and* seeth the place of stones.

---

frail and unsubstantial will be the hope of the hypocrite! It is impossible to conceive any figure which would more strongly describe the utter vanity of the hopes of the wicked. A similar comparison occurs in the Koran, Sur. 28, 40 : " They who assume any other patrons to themselves besides God, are like the spider building his house ; for the house of the spider is most feeble." ¶ *He shall hold it fast.* Or, he shall lay hold on it to sustain him, denoting the avidity with which the hypocrite seizes upon his hope. The figure is still taken from the spider, and is an instance of a careful observation of the habits of that insect. The idea is, that the spider, when a high wind or a tempest blows, seizes upon its slender web to sustain itself. But it is insufficient. The wind sweeps all away. So the tempest of calamity sweeps away the hypocrite, though he grasps at his hope, and would seek security in that, as a spider does in the light and tenuous thread which it has spun.

16. *He* is *green before the sun.* Vulg. *antequam veniat sol — before the sun comes.* So the Chaldee, "before the rising of the sun." So Eichhorn renders it. According to this, which is probably the true interpretation, the passage means that he is green and flourishing before the sun rises, but that he cannot bear its heat and withers away. A new illustration is here introduced, and the object is to compare the hypocrite with a vigorous plant that grows up quick and sends its branches afar, but which has no depth of root, and which, when the intense heat of the sun comes upon it, withers away. The comparison is not with a *tree*, which would bear the heat of the sun, but rather with those succulent plants which have a large growth of leaves and branches, like a gourd or vine, but which will not bear a drought or endure the intense heat of the sun. " This comparison of the transitory nature of human hope and prosperity to the sudden blight which

overthrows the glory of the forest and of the garden," says the Editor of the Pictorial Bible (on Ps. xxxvii. 35), " is at once so beautiful and so natural, as to have been employed by poets of every age." One such comparison of exquisite finish occurs in Shakspeare :

This is the state of man! To-day he puts forth
The tender leaves of hope; to-morrow blossoms,
And bears his blushing honours thick upon him:
The third day comes a frost, a killing frost,
And, when he thinks good easy man, full surely
His greatness is a ripening, nips his shoot,
And then he falls, as I do.

¶ *And his branch shooteth forth, &c.* A comparison of a prosperous person or nation with a *vine* which spreads in this manner, is common in the Scriptures. See Ps. lxxx. 11 :

She sent out her boughs unto the sea,
And her branches unto the river.

Comp. Note on Isa. xvi. 8. A similar figure occurs in Ps. xxxvii. 35 :

I have seen the wicked in great power,
And spreading himself like a green bay tree.

17. *His roots are wrapped about the heap.* There has been great diversity of opinion in the interpretation of this passage. Jerome renders it, "over the heap of stones his roots are condensed." Walton, *super fontem—over a fountain.* The LXX., "he lies down [or sleeps, κοιμᾶται] on a heap of stones ; and he lives in the midst of flint-stones.' According to some, the word rendered *heap* (בל) means a *fountain;* according to others, it means a heap or pile of stones ; according to Dr. Good, it means a rock. According to the view of the former, it refers to the flourishing condition of a hypocrite or sinner, and means that he is like a tree that sends its roots by a fountain, and is nourished by it. According to others, the reference is to the fact that the hypocrite is like a plant that has no depth of earth for its roots, that wraps its roots around any thing, even a heap of stones, to support itself: and that consequently will soon wither

under the intense heat of the sun. The word בַּל, rendered "*heap*," means either (1.) a heap, as a heap of stones, from בָּלַל—*to roll*, as *e. g.* stones. It may denote a heap of stones, Josh. vii. 26, but it commonly refers to the ruins of walls and cities, Jer. ix. 11 ; li. 37; Isa. xxv. 2. It means (2.) a fountain or spring, so called from the rolling or welling up of the waters, Cant. iv. 12, and hence rolling waves or billows, Ps. xlii. 7; lxxxix. 9 ; cvii. 25, 29. The *parallelism*, if nothing else, demands that the usual significa- tion should be given to it here; and the true sense is, that the prosperous wicked man or the hypocrite is like a plant which stands in the midst of rocks, rubbish, or old ruins, and not like one that stands in a fertile soil where it may strike its roots deep. The reference is to the fact that a tree or plant which springs up on a rock, or in the midst of rocks, will send its roots afar for nutriment, or will wrap them around the projecting points of rocks in order to obtain support. All have observed this in trees standing on rocks ; but the following extract from Silliman's Journal for January, 1840, will illustrate the fact referred to here more fully.

" About fifteen years ago, upon the top of an immense boulder of lime- stone, some ten or twelve feet in dia- meter, a sapling was found growing. The stone was but slightly imbedded in the earth ; several of its sides were raised from four to six feet above its surface ; but the top of the rock was rough with crevices, and its surface, which was sloping off, on one side, to the earth, was covered with a thin mould. From this mould the tree had sprung up, and having thrust its roots into the crevices of the rock, it had succeeded in reaching the height of some twelve or fifteen feet. But about this period the roots on one side became loosened from their attach- ment, and the tree gradually declined to the opposite side, until its body was in a parallel line with the earth. The roots on the opposite side, having ob- tained a firmer hold, afforded suffi- cient nourishment to sustain the plant; although they could not, alone, retain it in its vertical position. In this con- dition of things, the tree as if 'con- scious of its wants,' adopted (if the term may be used) an ingenious pro- cess, in order to regain its former up- right position. One of the most vig- orous of the detached roots sent out a branch from its side, which, passing round a projection of the rock, again united with the parent stalk, and thus formed a perfect *loop* around this pro- jection, which gave to the root an im- movable attachment.

" The tree now began to recover from its bent position. Obeying the natural tendency of all plants to grow erect, and sustained by this root, which increased with unwonted vigour, in a few years it had entirely regained its vertical position, elevated, as no one could doubt who saw it, by the aid of the root which had formed this sin- gular attachment. But this was not the only power exhibited by this re- markable tree.

" After its elevation it flourished vigorously for several years. Some of its roots had traced the sloping side of the rock to the earth, and were buried in the soil below. Others, having embedded themselves in its fur- rows, had completely filled these cre- vices with vegetable matter. The tree still continuing to grow, concentric layers of vegetable matter were annu- ally deposited between the alburnum and liber, until by the force of vege- table growth alone, the rock was split from the top to the bottom, into three nearly equal divisions, and branches of the roots were soon found, extending down, through the divisions into the earth below. On visiting the tree a few months since, to take a drawing of it, we found that it had attained an altitude of fifty feet, and was four and a half feet in circumference at its base."

The image here shows that the author of this beautiful fragment was a careful observer of nature, and the comparison is exceedingly pertinent and striking. What more beautiful illustration of a hypocrite can there be ? His roots do not strike into the earth. His piety is not planted in a rich soil. It is on the hard rock of

18 If he destroy him from his place, then *it* shall deny him, *saying,* 1 ^a have not seen thee.

a Ps.37.36.

19 Behold, this *is* the joy of his way, and out of the earth shall others ^b grow.

b Mat.3.9.

the unconverted human heart. Yet it sends out its roots afar; seems to flourish for a time; draws nutriment from remote objects; clings to a crag or a projecting rock, or to any thing for support—until a tempest sweeps it down to rise no more! No doubt the idea of Bildad was, that Job was just such a man. ¶ *Seeth the place of stones.* Sept., "and lives in the midst of flints," not an unapt rendering—and a very striking description of a hypocrite. So Castellio, *existit inter lapides.* Its only nutriment is derived from the scanty earth in the stony soil on which it stands, or in the crevices of the rocks.

18. *If he destroy him from his place.* The particle here which is rendered "if" (אם) is often used to denote emphasis, and means here *certainly*—"he shall be certainly destroyed." The word rendered *destroy,* from בלע, means literally to swallow (chap. vii. 19), to swallow up, to absorb; and hence to consume, lay waste, destroy. The sense is, that the wicked or the hypocrite shall be wholly destroyed from his place, but the image or figure of the *tree* is still retained. Some suppose that it means that *God* would destroy him from his place; others, as Rosenmller and Dr. Good, suppose that the reference is to the soil in which the tree was planted, that it would completely absorb all nutriment, and leave the tree to die; that is, that the dry and thirsty soil in which the tree is planted, instead of affording nutriment, acts as a "sucker," and absorbs itself all the juices which would otherwise give support to the tree. This seems to me to be probably the true interpretation. It is one drawn from nature, and one that preserves the *concinnity* of the passage. ¶ *Then* it *shall deny him.* That is, the soil, the earth, or the place where it stood. This represents a wicked man under the image of a tree. The figure is beautiful. The earth will be ashamed of it; ashamed

that it sustained the tree; ashamed that it ever ministered any nutriment, and will refuse to own it. So with the hypocrite. He shall pass away as if the earth refused to own him, or to retain any recollection of him. ¶ *I have not seen thee.* I never knew thee. It shall utterly deny any acquaintance with it. There is a striking resemblance here to the language which the Saviour says he will use respecting the hypocrite in the day of judgment: "and then will I profess to them, I never knew you;" Matth. vii. 23. The hypocrite has never been known as a pious man. The earth will refuse to own him as such, and so will the heavens.

19. *Behold, this* is *the joy of his way.* This is evidently sarcastic. "Lo! such is the joy of his course! He boasts of joy, as all hypocrites do, but his joy endures only for a little time. This is the end of it. He is cut down and removed, and the earth and the heavens disown him!" ¶ *And out of the earth shall others grow.* This image is still derived from the tree or plant. The meaning is, that such a plant would be taken away, and that others would spring up in its place which the earth would not be ashamed of. So the hypocrite is removed to make way for others who will be sincere, and who will be useful. Hypocrites and useless men in the church are removed to make way for others who will be active and devoted to the cause of the Redeemer. A similar sentiment occurs in chap. xxvii. 16, 17. This closes, as I suppose, the quotation which Bildad makes from the poets of the former age, and in the remainder of the chapter he states another truth pertaining to the righteous. This fragment is one of the most interesting that can be found any where. As a relic of the earliest times it is exceedingly valuable; as an illustration of the argument in hand, and of the course of events in this world, it is eminently beautiful. It is

20 Behold, God *a* will not cast away a perfect *man*, neither will he [1] help the evil doers;

21 Till he fill thy mouth with laughing, and thy lips with [2] rejoicing.

22 They that hate thee shall be clothed with *b* shame; and the dwelling-place of the wicked shall [3] come to nought.

a Ps.94.14.　1 *take the ungodly by the hand.*
2 *shouting for joy.*　*b* Ps.132.18.　3 *not be.*

as true now as it was when uttered before the flood, and may be used now as describing the doom of the hypocrite, with as much propriety as then, and it may be regarded as one of the way-marks in human affairs, showing that the government of God, and the manner of his dispensations, are always substantially the same.

20. *Behold, God will not cast away a perfect man.* On the meaning of the word *perfect*, see Note, chap. i. 1. The sentiment of Bildad, or the inference which he draws from the whole argument is, that God will be the friend of the pious, but that he will not aid the wicked. This accords with the general sentiment maintained in the argument of the friends of Job. ¶ *Neither will he help the evil doers.* Marg. *Take the ungodly by the hand.* This is in accordance with the Hebrew. The figure is that of taking one by the hand in order to assist him; see Isa. xlii. 6.

21. *Till he fill thy mouth with laughing.* Till he make thee completely happy. The word rendered "till" (עַד), is rendered by Dr. Good, "even yet." Noyes, following Houbigant, DeWette, and Michaelis, proposes to change the pointing, and to read עֹד, instead of עַד—meaning, "*while.*" The verse is connected with that which follows, and the particle here used evidently means "while," or "even yet"—and the whole passage means, "if you return to God, he will even yet fill you with joy, while those who hate you shall be clothed with shame. God will show you favour, but the dwelling of the wicked shall come to naught." The object of the passage is to induce Job

CHAPTER IX.

ANALYSIS OF CHAPTERS IX. AND X.

THIS chapter and the following comprise the answer of Job to the speech of Bildad. It may be remarked in general, that the object of Job in these arguments is not to prove that he was entirely faultless. He was charged with being a hypocrite, and his opponents in the argument proceeded on the presumption that he was a wicked man. Against this he protests, and maintains his own innocence of the charge. By this he does not mean absolute perfection. He means that he is free from the secret crimes of which he was accused; that he is not chargeable with uncommon guilt, such as they alleged; or, that he is a sincere and upright man. It may also be observed, that there are evidences in the speeches of Job that he is agitated with contending passions. Fear, hope, confidence, despair, and a sense

to return to God, with the assurance that if he did, he would show mercy to him, while the wicked should be destroyed. ¶ *With rejoicing.* Marg. *Shouting for joy.* The word used (תְּרוּעָה) is properly that which denotes the clangour of a trumpet, or the shout of victory and triumph.

22. *They that hate thee shall be clothed with shame.* When they see your returning prosperity, and the evidences of the divine favour. They will then be ashamed that they regarded you as a hypocrite, and that they reproached you in your trials. ¶ *And the dwelling-place of the wicked*, &c. The wicked shall be destroyed, and his family shall pass away. That is, God will favour the righteous, but punish the wicked. This opinion the friends of Job maintain all along, and by this they urge him to forsake his sins, repent, and return to God.

CHAPTER IX.

2. *I know it is so of a truth.* Job here refers, undoubtedly, to something that had been said before; but whether it is to the general strain of remark, or to some particular expression, may be doubted. Rosenmüller supposes that he refers to what was said by Eliphaz in chap iv. 17; but it seems more probable that it is to the general position which had been laid down and defended, that God was just and holy, and that his proceedings were marked with equity. Job admits this, and proceeds to show that it was a truth quite as familiar to him as it was to them. The object of his dwelling on it seems to be to show them that it was no new thing to him, and that he had some views on that im-

of the severity of his sufferings, by turns have possession of his mind, and he gives vent in turn to them all. There is, therefore, at times apparent inconsistency in his language and thoughts; but the object of the poem was to exhibit these contending emotions, and to show how the mind is agitated in scenes like these.

The substance of the reply of Job to Bildad here is the following:

He admits in general the truth of what Bildad had said, that no one can be just with God, and that if God should enter into judgment with man he could not answer him for one of a thousand of his offences. He thus shows that he had recovered his equanimity, and that he never meant in vindicating his own innocence to maintain that he was absolutely free from sin, ver. 1—3. He proceeds to argue that God is an absolute sovereign; that he distributes favours and judgments in accordance with his own inscrutable will; that men ought not to presume to sit in judgment on the doings of the Almighty; and that even if he had the fullest conviction of his own innocence, he would not presume to enter into an argument with him, but would make supplication to him, ver. 4—15. These thoughts are worthy of a man who had full confidence in God. They show the calm and deliberate judgment of Job, and prove that he was a pious man, though the severity of his sufferings, and the provocation which he met with, led him sometimes to express sentiments little in accordance with these. He proceeds to say (ver. 16—21), that he is so feeble that he could have no hope of prevailing in a controversy with God; and that though he were conscious of innocence, he would not set up a defence when God judged otherwise; for that in such a case his attempt to vindicate himself would prove that he was perverse. The principle here advanced is, that God must be right. He is great, and glorious, and holy; and men ought to believe, however much they may suffer, that the principles of his government are equitable and true. When he judges man to be a sinner, it *must* be so. The highest proof of human guilt is the fact that God regards man as a sinner. He proceeds (ver. 22—24) to advance the sentiment on which he so much insisted, that misery, so far from being proof of uncommon guilt, is equally the portion of the righteous and the wicked. He maintains that his sufferings do not prove that he is a bad man, for that calamities come upon all alike. He passes now to a contemplation of his own sufferings, and in the course of his description of his afflictions he is again led to give vent to feelings of a much less noble and elevated character than those

which he had just expressed. When arguing in the abstract about God, he is right; when his mind contemplates his own sorrows, he becomes impatient, and often uses language of murmuring and complaint. He says (ver. 25—28) that his days are swift and are full of sorrow, and that he cannot forget his sufferings and find comfort. He adds (ver. 29—35) that God is so great that he cannot enter into an argument with him; that he is reduced to silence by his mere power; that there is no days-man between him and God before whom the cause might be presented; and that if God would remove his calamity, he would then state his feelings fully, and without fear. But this could not be; and though he should say ever so much in his own vindication, and wash himself in snow-water, yet that God would plunge him into the ditch and overwhelm him with the consciousness of guilt, and hold him guilty still.

In chap. x. he prosecutes the argument, and indulges himself in a much greater latitude of expression and of feeling than he had done in chap. ix. In particular, he expostulates with great earnestness and pathos with God on account of his treating a creature – the work of his own hands—with such severity. He says (ver. 1) that he is weary of his life, for it is a burden; addresses God directly, and in a solemn manner, as his Maker, and asks why he deals thus with a poor, frail, and helpless creature whom he has made; acknowledges that all that he has is from God, appeals to God himself in proof that he is not a wicked man, and asks why he deals with him in this awful manner (ver. 2—12); and says that God marked him out and hunted him down as a lion, and multiplied the tokens of his indignation, so that he was utterly overwhelmed and confounded, ver. 13—17. As he proceeds he grows warmer; is roused to desperation at the idea that God is his enemy; and again vehemently wishes for death as a relief for his woes, asking only for a little respite before he goes down to the land of darkness and of shades, ver. 18—22. There are marks of great agitation of feeling, of deep emotion, of mingled sensibilities, in these chapters, and the whole is a remarkable illustration of the feelings which even pious men sometimes have in trials.

THEN Job answered and said,
  2 I know *it is* so of a truth;
but *a* how should man be just ¹ with
God?

a Ps. 143.2; Ro.3.20.   1 or, *before*

portant subject which were well worthy of attention. ¶ *But how should man be just with God?* Marg. *before.* The meaning is, that he could not be regarded as perfectly holy in the sight of God; or that so holy and pure a being as God must see that man was a sinner, and regard him as such; see the sentiment explained in the Notes on chap. iv. 17. The question here asked is, in itself, the most important ever propounded by man—"How shall sinful man be regarded and treated as righteous by his Maker?" This has been the great inquiry which has always been before the human mind. Man is conscious that he is a sinner. He feels that he must be regarded as such by God. Yet his happiness here and hereafter, his peace and all his hope, depend on his being treated *as*

if he were righteous, or regarded as just before God. This inquiry has led to all forms of religion among men; to all the penances and sacrifices of different systems: to all the efforts which have been made to devise some system that shall make it proper for God to treat men as righteous. The question has never been satisfactorily answered except in the Christian revelation, where a plan is disclosed by which God "may be just, and yet the justifier of him that believeth." Through the infinite merits of the Redeemer, man, though conscious that he is personally a sinner, may be treated as if he had never sinned; though feeling that he is guilty, he may consistently be for ever treated as if he were just. The question asked by Job implies that such is the

3 If he will contend with him, he cannot answer him one of a thousand.

4 He *a is* wise in heart, and mighty in strength : who hath hardened *himself* against him, and hath prospered ?

a Jude 24,25.

evidence and the extent of human guilt, that man can never justify himself. This is clear and indisputable. Man cannot justify himself by the deeds of the law. Justification, as a work of law, is this : A man is charged, for example, with the crime of murder. He sets up in defence that he did not kill, or that if he took life it was in self-defence, and that he had a right to do it. Unless the fact of killing be proved, and it be shown that he had no right to do in the case as he has done, he cannot be condemned, and the law acquits him. It has no charge against him, and he is just or justified in the sight of the law. But in this sense man can never be just before God. He can neither show that the things charged on him by his Maker were not done, or that being done, he had a right to do them ; and being unable to do this, he must be held to be guilty. He can never be justified therefore by the law, and it is only by that system which God has revealed in the gospel, where a conscious sinner may be treated *as if* he were righteous through the merits of another, that a man can ever be regarded as just before God ; see Notes on Rom. i. 17 ; iii. 24, 25.

3. *If he will contend with him.* That is, if God enters into a controversy with man. If he chooses to charge crime on him, and to hold him responsible for his deeds. The language here is taken from courts of justice, and means that if a *trial* were instituted, where God should submit charges, and the matter were left to adjudication, man could not answer the charges against him ; comp. Notes on Isa. xli. 1. ¶ *He cannot answer him one of a thousand.* For one of a thousand of the sins charged on him. The word *thousand* here is used to denote the largest number, or *all.* A man who could not answer for one charge brought against him out of a thousand, must be held to be guilty ; and the expression here is equivalent

to saying that he could not answer him at all. It may also be implied that God has *many* charges against man. His sins are to be reckoned by *thousands.* They are numerous as his years, his months, his weeks, his days, his hours, his moments ; numerous as his privileges, his deeds, and his thoughts. For not one of those sins can he answer. He can give no satisfactory account before an impartial tribunal for any of them. If so, how deeply guilty is man before God ! How glorious that plan of justification by which he can be freed from this long list of offences, and treated as though he had not sinned

4. He is *wise in heart.* Herder renders this,

Even the wise and the powerful,
Who hath withstood him and prospered ?

But the more common interpretation is to refer it to God. The meaning of Job appears to be, that God was a sagacious adversary ; that he was able to manage his cause ; that he could meet and refute all objections which could be urged ; and that it would be in vain to engage in a litigation before him. He so well understood the whole ground of debate, and was so entirely skilled in the merits of the controversy, and could so successfully meet all that could be alleged, that it was useless to attempt to hold an argument with him. ¶ *And mighty in strength.* He is able to execute all his designs, and to carry all his purposes into effect. Man is weak and feeble, and it is hopeless for him to attempt to contend with the Almighty. ¶ *Who hath hardened* himself *against him, and hath prospered?* To harden one's self, here means to resist or withstand him. It refers to the firmness or resolution which one is obliged to adopt who opposes another. Here it means the opposition which man makes to the law and government of the Most High ; and the affirmation is, that no one can make such opposition who will not be ultimately overcome.

5 Which removeth the mountains, and they know not ; which overturneth them in his anger ;

6 Which *a* shaketh the earth out of her place, and the pillars thereof tremble ;

a He.12.26.

God is so great, so powerful, and so just, that a successful resistance cannot be made. The arrangements of God *will* take their course, and man must yield to his claims and his government, or be prostrated. None can successfully resist God ; and the true policy of man, as well as his duty, is to yield to him, and be at peace with him. ¶ *And hath prospered.* Or been successful. He has failed in his opposition, and been obliged to yield. Prosperity is not found in opposing God. It is only by *falling in* with his arrangements and following his designs. A prosperous voyage is made by falling in with winds and currents, and not in opposing them ; prosperous agriculture is carried on by coinciding with the favourable seasons of the year, and taking advantage of the dews, and rains, and sunbeams that God sends, and not in opposing them ; prosperity in regard to health is found in taking advantage of the means which God gives to secure it, and not in opposing them. And the sinner in his course has no more chance of success and prosperity, than a man would have who should make it a point or principle of life always to sail against tides, and currents, and head winds ; or he who should set at defiance all the laws of husbandry, and plant on a rock, or in the dead of winter ; or he who should feed himself on poison rather than on nutritious food, and cultivate the nightshade rather that wheat. The great principle is, that if a man desires prosperity, he *must* fall in with the arrangements of God in his providence and grace ; and wisdom is seen in studying these arrangements, and in yielding to them.

5. *Which removeth the mountains.* In order to show how vain it was to contend with God, Job refers to some exhibitions of his power and greatness. The "removal of the mountains" here denotes the changes which occur in earthquakes and other violent convulsions of nature. This illustra-

tion of the power of God is often referred to in the Scriptures ; comp. Judges v. 5 ; 1 Kings xix. 11 ; Ps. lxv. 6 ; cxiv. 4 ; cxlv. 5 ; Isa. xl. 12 ; Jer. iv. 24. ¶ *And they know not.* This is evidently a Hebraism, meaning suddenly, or unexpectedly. He does it, as it were, before they are aware of it. A similar expression occurs in the Koran, "God overturns them, and they do not know it ;" *i. e.* he does it without their suspecting any such thing ; comp. Ps. xxxv. 8. "Let destruction come upon him at unawares," or, as it is in the Heb. and in the margin, *which he knoweth not of.* Tindal renders this, " He translateth the mountaynes *or ever they be aware.*" ¶ *Which overturneth them in his anger.* As if he were enraged. There could scarcely be any more terrific exhibition of the wrath of God than the sudden and tremendous violence of an earthquake.

6. *Which shaketh the earth out of her place.* This evidently refers to violent convulsions of nature, as if the earth were to be taken away. Objects on the earth's surface become displaced, and convulsion seems to seize the world. The LXX. render this, " who shaketh that which is under the heavens from its foundations"—ἐκ θεμελίων. The change in the Hebrew would be very slight to authorize this rendering. ¶ *And the pillars thereof tremble.* In this place the earth is represented as sustained like a building by pillars or columns. Whether this is a mere *poetic* representation, or whether it describes the actual belief of the speaker in regard to the structure of the earth, it is not easy to determine. I am inclined to think it is the former, because in another place where he is speaking of the earth, he presents his views in another form, and more in accordance with the truth (see Notes on chap. xxvi. 7) : and because here the illustration is evidently taken from the obvious and perceived effects of an

7 Which commandeth the sun, [a] and it riseth not, and sealeth up the stars ;

8 Which alone spreadeth out the [b] heavens, and treadeth [c] upon the [1] waves of the sea ;

a Jos.10.12. *b* Ps.104.2,3 ; Is.40.22,28. *c* Mat.14.25. [1] *heights.*

---

earthquake. It would convulse and agitate the pillars of the most substantial edifice, and *so* it seemed to shake the earth, as if its very supports would fall.

7. *Which commandeth the sun, and it riseth not.* Schultens supposes that all this is a description of the deluge —when the mountains were removed, when the fountains of the deep were broken up, and when the sun was obscured and seemed not to rise. Others have supposed that it refers to the fact that the sun is darkened by clouds and tempests, and appears not to rise and shine upon the earth. Others suppose that the allusion is to an eclipse ; and others, that it is to the power of God, and means that the rising of the sun depends on him, and that if he should choose to give the command, the heavenly bodies would rise and give light no more. It seems probable that the meaning is, that God has *power* to do this ; that the rising of the sun depends on him ; and that he could delay it, or prevent it, at his pleasure. His power over the sun was shown in the time of Joshua, when, at his command, it stood still ; but it is not necessary to suppose that there is any reference to this fact here. The whole meaning of the language is met by the supposition that it refers to the power of God, and affirms what he *could* do, or if it refer to any fact that had been observed, that the allusion is to the darkening of the sun by an eclipse or a tempest. No argument can be derived, therefore, from the expression, in regard to the age of the book. ¶ *And sealeth up the stars.* The word *seal* in the Scriptures (חתם) is used with considerable latitude of signification. It is employed in the sense of shutting, closing, making fast — as when any thing was sealed, it was shut up or made fast. The Hebrews often used a *seal* where we would use a *lock*, and depended on the protection derived from the belief that one would not

break open that which was sealed, where we are obliged to rely on the security of the lock against force. If there were honour and honesty among men everywhere, a seal would be as secure as a lock—as in a virtuous community a sealed letter is as secure as a merchant's iron " safe." To *seal up the stars*, means so to shut them up in the heavens, as to prevent their shining ; to hide them from the view. They are concealed, hidden, made close —as the contents of a letter, a package, or a room are by a seal, indicating that no one is to examine them, and concealing them from the view. So God hides from our view the stars by the interposition of clouds.

8. *Which alone spreadeth out the heavens.* As an expanse, or a curtain ; see Notes on Isa. xl. 22. ¶ *And treadeth upon the waves of the sea.* Marg. *Heights.* So it is in the Hebrew. It means the *high waves ;* that is, he walks upon the waves of the ocean when lifted up by a storm. This is spoken of here as a proof of the greatness of God ; and the meaning of all is. that he is seen in the storm, in the heaving ocean, when the heavens are black with tempest, and when the earth is convulsed. It may be added here, that the Lord Jesus walked amidst the howling winds on the lake, and thus gave evidence that he was God ; Matth. xiv. 25. " The Egyptian hieroglyphic for what was not possible to be done, was a man walking on the water." *Burder.* Dr. Good, and some others, render this, " on the mountains." But the more correct rendering is given in the common version. The Hebrew word rendered " waves " (במה) indeed properly means a height, a lofty place, a mountain ; but the comparison of waves with a mountain, is common in all languages. So we speak of waves " mountain-high," or as high as mountains. So Virgil, Æneid i. 105,

Insequitur cumulo præruptus aquæ mons.

9 Which ^a maketh ¹ Arcturus, Orion, and Pleiades, and the chambers of the south;

a Am.5.8.   1 *Ash, Cesil, and Cimah.*

Similar to this, is the expression occurring in Homer, κύματα ἴσα ὄρεσσιν; and so Apollonius, i. 521—ἁλὸς ἄκρα. The LXX. render it, "who walketh upon the sea as upon a pavement."

9. *Which maketh Arcturus.* This verse, with others of the same description in the book of Job, is of especial importance, as they furnish an illustration of the views which prevailed among the patriarchs on the subject of astronomy. There are frequent references to the sciences in this book (see the Introduction), and there is no source of illustration of the views which prevailed in the earliest times in regard to the state of the sciences, so copious as can be found in this poem. The thoughts of men were early turned to the science of astronomy. Not only were they led to this by the beauty of the heavens, and by the instinctive promptings of the human mind to know something about them, but the attention of the Chaldeans and of the other Oriental nations was early drawn to them by the fact that they were shepherds, and that they passed much of their time in the open air at night, watching their flocks. Having nothing else to do, and being much awake, they would naturally contrive to relieve the tediousness of the night by watching the movements of the stars; and they early gave employment to their talents, by endeavouring to ascertain the influence which the stars exerted over the fates of men, and to their imagination, by dividing the heavens into portions, having a fancied resemblance to certain animals, and by giving them appropriate names. Hence arose the arrangement of the stars into *constellations*, and the names which they still bear. The Hebrew word rendered *Arcturus*, is עשׁ, *ash.* The LXX render it, Πλειάδα—*the Pleiades.* Jerome, *Arcturum.* The Hebrew word usually means *a moth*, Job iv. 19; xiii. 28; xxvii. 18. It also denotes the splendid constellation in the northern hemisphere, which we call

Ursa Major, the Great Bear. Arcturus, or the Wain; comp. Niebuhr, Des. of Arabia, p. 114. The word עשׁ does not literally mean *a bear*, but is made by aphæresis from the Arabic *nas*, by the excision of the initial *n*—as is common in Arabic; see Bochart, Hieroz P. II. Lib. I. c. xvi. p. 113, 114. The word in Arabic means *a bier*, and is the name given to the constellation which we denominate Ursa Major, "because," says Bochart, "the four stars, which are a square, are regarded as a bier, on which a dead body is borne. The three following (the tail of the bear) are the daughters or sons which attend the funeral as mourners." This name is often given to this constellation in Arabic. The Arabic name is *Elna'sch*, the bier. "The expression," says Ideler, "denotes particularly the bier on which the dead are borne, and taken in this sense, each of the two biers [in the Ursa Major and Ursa Minor] is accompanied by three mourning-women. The biers and the mourning-women together, are called *Benâtna'sch*, literally, *daughters of the bier;* that is, those who pertain to the bier." Untersuchungen über den Ursprung und die Bedeutung der Sternnamen, S. 419; comp. chap. xxxviii. 32: "Canst thou guide Arcturus *with his sons?*" Schultens regards the word עשׁ as synonymous with the Arabic *asson, night-vigil,* from *assa to go about by night,* and supposes this constellation to be so called, because it always revolves around the pole, and never sets. The situation and figure of this constellation are well known. It is seen at all times in the northern part of the heavens, perpetually revolving around the North Star, and two of its principal stars point to the North Star always. Its resemblance to a *bear*, is quite fanciful—as it might be imagined as well to resemble any other object. The design of this fancy was merely to assist the memory. The only thing which seems to have suggested it was its slight resemblance to an animal followed by its young.   Thus the stars, now known as the " tail," might have been supposed to resemble the cubs of a bear following their dam.   The comparison of the constellation to a *bier*, and the movement to a funeral procession, with the sons or daughters of the deceased following on in the mourning train, is much more poetical and beautiful.   This constellation is so conspicuous, that it has been an object of interest in all ages, and has been one of the groups of stars most attentively observed by navigators, as a guide in sailing.   The reason was, probably, that as it constantly revolved around the North Pole, it could always be seen in clear weather, and thus the direction in which they were sailing, could always be told.   It has had a great variety of names.   The name Ursa Major, or the Great Bear, is that which is commonly given to it. It is a remarkable fact, also, that while this name was given to it in the East, a tribe of the American Indians—the Iroquois, also gave the same name of the Great Bear to it.   This is remarkable, because, so far as known, they had no communication with each other, and because the name is perfectly arbitrary.   Is this an evidence that the natives of our country [North America] derived their origin from some of the nations of the East?   In some parts of England the constellation is called " Charles' Wain," or Waggon, from its fancied resemblance to a waggon, drawn by three horses in a line. Others call it the *Plough*.   The whole number of visible stars in this constellation is eighty seven, of which one is of the first, three of the second, seven of the third, and about twice as many of the fourth magnitude.   The constellations of Ursa Major and Ursa Minor were represented by the ancients, under the image of a waggon drawn by a team of horses.   This is alluded to by the Greek poet, Aratus, in an address to the Athenians :

The one called Helix, soon as day retires,
Observed with ease lights up his radiant fires ;
The other smaller and with feebler beams,
In a less circle drives his lazy teams :
But more adapted for the sailor's guide,
Whene'er by night he tempts the briny tide.

Among the Egyptians these two constellations are represented by the figures of bears, instead of waggons. Whence the Hebrew name is derived is not quite certain ; but if it be from the Arabic, it probably means the same —a *bier*.   There seems no reason to doubt, however, that the Ursa Major is intended ; and that the idea here is, that the greatness of God is shown by his having made this beautiful constellation.   ¶ *Orion.*   The Vulgate renders this *Orion*, the LXX., Ἕσπερον, *Hesperus*—i. *e.* the evening star, Venus.   The word כסיל, *kesil*, is from כסל, *kâsîl*, to be fat or fleshy ; to be strong, lusty, firm ; and then to be dull, sluggish, stupid—as fat persons usually are.   Hence the word כסיל means *a fool*, Ps. xlix. 11 ; Prov. i. 32 ; x. 1. It is used here, however, to denote a constellation, and by most interpreters it is supposed to denote the constellation *Orion*, which the Orientals call *a giant.*   " They appear to have conceived of this constellation under the figure of an impious giant bound upon the sky." *Gesenius.*   Hence the expression, Job xxxviii. 31; " Canst thou loose the bands of Orion ?" According to the Eastern tradition, this giant was Nimrod, the founder of Babylon, afterwards translated to the skies ; see Notes on Isa. xiii. 10, where it is rendered *constellation.* Virgil speaks of it as the *Stormy Orion :*

Cum subito assurgens fluctu nimbosus Orion.
                                        Æn. i. 535.

And again :

Dum pelago desævit hiems, et aquoæus Orion.
                                        Æn. iv 52.

In another description of Orion by Virgil, it is represented as armed with gold, or surrounded by a yellow light :

Arcturum, pluviasque Hyadas, geminosque
        Triones,
Armatumque auro circumspicit Oriona.
                                        Æn. iii. 516, 517.

According to the fancy of the ancients, Orion was a mighty hunter, the attendant of Diana, who having offered violence to her was stung to death by a scorpion which she had provided for that purpose.   After his death he was translated to heaven, and made a constellation.   Others say that he was the son of Neptune and Queen Euryale, a famous Amazonian huntress ; and possessing the disposition of his mother, he became the greatest hunter in the world, and made a boast that there was no animal on earth that he could not subdue. To punish this vanity, it is said that a scorpion sprang out of the earth, and bit his foot, so that he died, but that at the request of Diana he was placed among the stars, and directly opposite to the scorpion that caused his death. On the names given to this constellation in Arabic, and the origin of the name *Orion* among the Greeks, see Ideler, Unter. über den Urs. u. die Bedeut. der Stern. s. 212—227, 331—336. The name *El-dscebbir, the giant,* or *hero,* is that which is commonly given to it in Arabic. The constellation Orion is usually mentioned by the ancients as connected with storms, and hence is called *nimbosus Orion* by Virgil, and *tristis Orion* by Horace. The reason of this was, that its rising usually occurred at those seasons of the year when storms prevailed, and hence it was supposed to be their cause—as we connect the rising of the dog-star with the idea of intense heat. The situation of Orion is on the equator, midway between the poles of the heavens. It comes to the meridian about the 23d of January. The whole number of visible stars in it is seventy-eight, of which two are of the first magnitude, four of the second, three of the third, and fifteen of the fourth. It is regarded as the most beautiful of the constellations, and when it is on the meridian there is then above the horizon the most magnificent view of the celestial bodies that the firmament exhibits. On the celestial maps it is represented by the figure of a man in the attitude of assaulting the Bull, with a sword in his belt, a huge club in his right hand, and a lion-skin in the left to serve him for a shield. The principal stars are four, in the form of a long square or parallelogram, intersected by the "Three Stars" in the middle called "The Ell and the Yard." The two upper ones are represented one on each shoulder, and of the two lower ones one is in the left foot, and the other on the right

knee. The position of the constellation may be seen by any one by remarking that the "Three Stars" in the belt are those which point to the Pleiades or seven stars on the one side, and to the dog-star on the other. This constellation is mentioned by Homer, as it is indeed by most of the classic writers :

Πληϊάδας ϑ᾽,᾽Υάδας τε, τό τε σθένος Ὠρίω-
νος.   Il. σ.

It may furnish an illustration of the *vastness* of the starry heavens to remark, that in the sword of the constellation Orion there is a *nebula* which is almost visible to the naked eye, which is computed to be 2,200,000,000,000,000,000, or two trillions, two hundred thousand billions times larger than the sun ! *Dr. Dick,* Chr. Keepsake for 1840, p. 184. If, then, Job, with his limited views of astronomy, saw in this constellation an impressive proof of the greatness of the Almighty, how much more sublime should be *our* views of God ! We see this constellation not merely as a beautiful object in the sky—a collection of bright and beautiful gems—but we see it as so vast as to surpass our comprehension, and behold in it a single *nebula,* or speck—not quite visible to the naked eye—that mocks all our powers of conception ! It may be added, that by the aid of a telescope about two thousand stars have been seen in this constellation. ¶ *And Pleiades.* The seven stars. The Hebrew word is כימה, *kimâ,* a heap or cluster. The name is given to the cluster of stars in the neck of the constellation *Taurus,* of which seven are the principal. Six or seven may be usually seen if the eye is directed towards it ; but if the eye be turned carelessly aside while the *attention* is fixed on the group, many more may be seen. For, " it is a very remarkable fact," says Sir John Herschell, " that the *centre* of the visual organ is by far less sensible to feeble impressions of light than the exterior portion of the retina." *Ast.* p. 398. Telescopes show fifty or sixty large stars there crowded together into a small space. Rheita affirms that he counted two hundred stars in this small cluster. In regard to the Pleiades, Ideler makes the following remarks. " These stars were by the ancients sometimes denoted by the singular, Πλειὰς, *Pleias*, and sometimes by the plural, Πλειάδες (in metrical composition, Πληϊάδες), *Pleiades*. They are mentioned by Homer, Ili. σ. 486, Od. s. 272, and by Hesiod, ῾Εργ. 383, 615. Hesiod mentions the cluster as *the daughter of Atlas*—᾿Ατλαγενεῖς. The name *Atlantides*, which so often occurs among the Romans, signifies the same thing. Their mythological names are Alcyone, Merope, Celæno, Electra, Sterope or Asterope, Taygete, and Maia. There is some uncertainty among the ancient writers whence the name *Pleiades* is derived. Among most etymologists, the name has respect to navigation, and the derivation is from ἀπὸ τοῦ πλεῖν—because the time of navigation commenced with the rising of the Pleiades in the first part of May, and ended with their setting in the first part of November. But perhaps the name is derived simply from πλέος, πλεῖος, *full*, so that it merely denotes a condensed assemblage of stars, which Manilius, iv. 523, expresses by *glomerabile sidus*. Aratus, v. 257, says that the Pleiades were called ἑπτάποροι—*those which walked in seven paths*, although but six stars can be seen. In a similar sense Ovid, speaking of the Pleiades, says,

Quæ septem dici, sex tamen esse solent.
FAST. iv.170.

Hipparchus, on the contrary, affirms that in a clear night, when there is no moon, seven stars can be seen. The difference of these views is easily explained. The group consists of one star of the third magnitude, three of the fifth, two of the sixth, and many smaller stars. It requires a very keen vision to be able to distinguish in the group more than six stars. Since, therefore, among the ancients, it was commonly believed that there were no more than six, and yet among them, as with us, the name *the seven stars* was given to them, the opinion arose that one star of the seven had been lost. Some supposed that it had been

smitten by lightning, others that it had united itself to the middle star in the tail of the Ursa Major, and others gave to the belief a mythic signification, as is mentioned by Ovid in the place above referred to. The Romans called the Pleiades *Vergiliæ*, because they arose in the spring. The Arabians called those stars *El-thoreja*—meaning *abundant, copious*, and answering to the Greek Πλειὰς, *Pleias*. The Asiatic poets Sadi, Hafiz, and others, always mention these stars as a beautiful *rosette*, with one brilliant. Sadi, in the description of a beautiful garden, says " The ground was strewed with pieces of enamel, and bands of Pleiades appeared to hang on the branches of the trees." Hafiz says, " The heavens bear up thy poems—the pearly rosette of the Pleiades as the seal of immortality." Beigel, who has translated these poets, adds, " In this genuine Oriental spirit must we understand the words of Job, ' Canst thou bind the brilliant rosettes of the Pleiades?' that is, Who can say that he has placed this collection of brilliants as a rosette in the sky ?" *Ideler*, Untersuchungen ü. den Urs. u. die Bedeut. der Sternnamen, s. 143—147. ¶ *And the chambers of the south.* What is the exact idea to be attached to this expression, it is not easy to say. Probably it means the remote regions of the south, or the part of the heavens which is not visible to the inhabitants of the northern hemisphere. The word rendered *chambers* means in the Scriptures a private apartment of a dwelling ; a part that is separated from the rest by a curtain ; a harem, &c. Hence it may mean the abodes of the stars in the south—comparing the heavens with an immense *tent*, and regarding it as divided into separate apartments. It may mean here the stars which are hidden, as it were, in the recesses of the southern hemisphere, like the private apartments of a house, which all were not allowed to enter. There are *some* intimations in the book of Job that the true structure of the earth was not unknown at that remote period of the world (comp. Notes, chap. xxvi. 7) ; and if so, then this may re-

10 Which doeth great things past finding out ; yea, and wonders without number.

11 Lo, he goeth by me, and I see *him* not : he passeth on also, but I perceive him not.

12 Behold, he taketh away,

who can hinder [1] him ? who [a] will say unto him, What doest thou ?

13 *If* God will not withdraw his anger, the [2] proud helpers do stoop under him.

1 *turn him away ?* chap. 11.10.   a Da.4.35.
2 *helpers of pride.* or, *strength.*

---

fer to the constellations in the south which are invisible to an inhabitant of the northern hemisphere. There is no impropriety at any rate, in supposing that those who had travelled into the south had brought reports of stars and constellations seen there which are invisible to an inhabitant of northern Arabia.

10. *Which doeth great things.* This is almost the sentiment which had been expressed by Eliphaz ; see Notes, chap. v. 9. It was evidently a proverb. and as such was used by both Eliphaz and Job.

11. *Lo, he goeth by me.* That is, he passes along – as in the silent movements of the heavenly bodies. " I see the evidence of his existence. I can see that God must be there — moving along by me in the orbs of night and in the march of the constellations, but I cannot see God himself. He passes *by*, or rather he passes *over* me (עָלַי), as in the majestic movement of the heavenly bodies over my head." This is, I think, the idea, and the image is exceedingly poetic and beautiful. The heavens are seen to move in silent grandeur. The northern constellation rolls around the pole. The others move on as a marshalled army. They go in silent and solemn order, *and God must be there.* But, says Job, I cannot see him. I can feel that he must be there, and I look out on the heavens to see him, but my eyes fail, and I cannot behold him. He passes on, and I see him not. Who has ever looked upon the heavens in the still night, and seen the silent grandeur of such movements of the heavenly host, without some such feeling—some emotion of inexpressible awe—as if he, if I may so express it, COULD ALMOST SEE GOD ?

12. *Behold, he taketh away.* Property, friends, or life. ¶ *Who can*

hinder him ? Marg. *turn him away.* Or, rather, " who shall cause him to restore ?" *i. e.* who can bring back what he takes away ? He is so mighty, that what he removes, it is impossible for us to recover. ¶ *Who will say unto him, What doest thou ?* A similar expression occurs in Dan. iv. 35. The meaning is plain. God has a right to remove any thing which we possess. Our friends, property, health, and lives, are his gift. and he has a right to them all. When he takes them away, he is but taking that which is his own, and which has been lent to us for a little time, and which he has a right to remove when it seems good to him. This truth Job fully admits, and in the calm contemplation of all his losses and his sorrows, he acknowledges that God had a right to do as he had done ; see Note, chap. i. 21.

13. *If God will not withdraw his anger.* That is, if he perseveres in inflicting punishment. He will not turn aside his displeasure by any opposition or resistance made to him. ¶ *The proud helpers.* Marg. *Helpers of pride*, or, *strength.* Jerome renders this, " under whom they who bear up the world bow down." The LXX., not less singularly, " by him the whales [or monsters—κήτη] which are under heaven, are bowed down." Codurcus renders it, " aids of pride," and understands by it all the things on which proud men rely, as wealth, health, rank, talent. So Dr. Good renders it, " the supports of the proud.' The meaning is, probably, that all those things which contribute to the support of *pride*, or all those persons who are allied together to maintain the dominion of pride on the earth, must sink under the wrath of God. Or it may refer to those who sustain the pride of state and empire—the men who stand around the thrones of

14 How much less shall I answer him, *and* choose out my words *to reason* with him ?

15 Whom, though I were right-

eous, *yet* would I not answer, *but* [a] I would make supplication to my judge.

a chap. 34. 31.

---

monarchs, and who contribute, by their talent and power, to uphold the pomp and magnificence of courts. On the meaning of the word here rendered *pride* (רֹהַב), see Notes on Isa. xxx. 7.

14. *How much less shall I answer him?* I, who am so feeble, how can I contend with him ? If the most mighty objects in the universe are under his control ; if the constellations are directed by him ; if the earth is shaken, and mountains moved from their places, by his power, and if the men of most exalted rank are prostrated by him, how can I presume to contend with God ? This is the common view which is given of the passage, and is evidently that which our translators entertained. But I have given in the translation what appears to me to be a more literal version, and to express a better sense —though, I confess, the translation differs from all that I have seen. According to this, the sense is simply, that such was the veneration which Job had for the character of God, that should he attempt to answer him, he would select his words with the utmost care and attention.

15. *Whom, though I were righteous.* That is, if I felt the utmost confidence that I was righteous, yet, if God judged otherwise, and regarded me as a sinner, I would not reply to him, but would make supplication to him *as a* sinner. I would have so much confidence in him, and would feel that he was so much better qualified than I am to judge, and that I am so liable to be deceived, that I would come to him as a sinner, if *he* judged and declared me to be one, and would plead for pardon. The meaning is, that God is a much better judge of our character than we can possibly be, and that *his* regarding us as sinners is the highest proof that we *are* such, whatever may be *our* views to the contrary. This shows the extent of the confidence which Job had in God,

and is an indication of true piety. And it is founded in *reason* as well as in *piety.* Men often suppose that they are righteous, and yet they know that God adjudges otherwise, and regards them as sinners. He offers them pardon as sinners. He threatens to punish them as sinners. The question is, whether they shall act on their own feelings and judgment in the case, or on his ? Shall they adhere obstinately to their views, and refuse to yield to God, or shall they act on the truth of *his* declarations ? Now that Job was right in his views of the case, may appear from the following considerations. (1.) God knows the heart. *He* cannot be deceived ; *we* may be. In nothing are we more liable to be deceived than in regard to our own character. We should, therefore, distrust our own judgment in this case, but we should never distrust God. (2.) God is infinitely benevolent, and will not judge unkindly. He has no wish to find us sinners ; he will have no pleasure in making us out to be transgressors. A heart of infinite benevolence would prefer to find all men holy, and would look on every favourable circumstance in the case with all the kindness which it would deserve. No being would be so likely to make a favourable decision in our case as the infinitely benevolent God ; none would so delight to find that we were free from the charge of guilt. (3.) God will act on his own views of our character, and not on ours ; and it is prudent and wise, therefore, for us to act on *his* views now. He will judge us in the last day according to *his* estimate of our character, and not according to the estimate which *we* may form. (4.) At the same time, we cannot but accord with *his* views of our own character. Our reason and conscience tell us that we have violated his laws, and that we have no claim to his mercy. No man can persuade himself that he is wholly righteous ; and being conscious of guilt, though in the slightest degree,

16 If I had called, and he had answered me, *yet* would I not believe that he had hearkened unto my voice.

17 For he breaketh me with a tempest, and multiplieth my wounds without cause.

18 He will not suffer me to take my breath, but filleth me with bitterness.

19 If *I speak* of strength, lo, *he is* strong : and if of judgment, who shall set me a time *to plead ?*

---

he should make supplication to his Judge.

16. *If I had called, and he had answered me.* It is remarked by Schultens, that the expressions in these verses are all taken from courts of justice. If so, the meaning is, that even if Job should call the Almighty to a judicial action, and he should respond to him, and consent to submit the great question about his innocence, and about the justice of the divine dealings with him, to trial, yet that such was the distance between God and him, that he could not hope successfully to contend with him in the argument. He would, therefore, prostrate himself in a suppliant manner, and implore his mercy and compassion—submitting to him as having all power, and as being a just and righteous Sovereign. ¶ *Would I not believe.* I cannot believe that he would enter into my complaint. He deals with me in a manner so severe ; he acts towards me so much as a sovereign, that I have no reason to suppose that he would not continue to act towards me in the same way still.

17. *For he breaketh me.* He is overwhelming me with a tempest ; that is, with the storms of wrath. He shows me no mercy. The idea seems to be, that God acted towards him not as a *judge* determining matters by rule of law, but as a *sovereign*—determining them by his own will. If it were a matter of law ; if he could come before him as a judge, and maintain his cause there ; if the case could be fairly adjudicated whether he deserved the calamities that came upon him, he would be willing to enter into such a trial. But where the matter was determined solely by will, and God acted as a sovereign, doing as he pleased, and giving no account of his matters to any one, then it

would be useless to argue the cause. He would not know what to expect, or understand the principles on which an adjudication would be made. It *is* true that God acts as a sovereign, but he does not act without reference to law. He dispenses his favours and his judgments as he pleases, but he violates none of the rules of right. The error of Job was the common error which men commit, that if God acts as a *sovereign*, he must of course act regardless of *law*, and that it is vain to plead with him or try to please him. But sovereignty is not necessarily inconsistent with respect for law ; and He who presides with the most absolute power over the universe is He who is most directed by the rule of right. In Him sovereignty and law coincide ; and to come to Him as a sovereign, is to come with the assurance that supreme rectitude will be done. ¶ *And multiplieth my wounds without cause.* That is, without sufficient reason. This is in accordance with the views which Job had repeatedly expressed. The main ground of his complaint was, that his sufferings were disproportionate to his faults.

18. *He will not suffer me to take my breath;* see Notes on chap. vii. 19.

19. *If I speak of strength, lo,* he is *strong.* There has been a considerable variety in the interpretation of this passage. The meaning seems to be this. It refers to a judicial contest, and Job is speaking of the effect if he and God were to come to a trial, and the cause were to be settled before judges. He is urging reasons why he would have no hope of success in such a case. He says, therefore, "If the matter pertained only to *strength,* or if it were to be determined *by* strength, lo, he is more mighty than I am, and I could have no hope of success in

20 If I justify myself, mine own mouth shall condemn me : *if I say,* I *am* perfect, it shall also prove me perverse.

such a controversy : and if the controversy was one of *judgment, i. e.* of justice or right, I have no one to manage my cause—no one that could cope with him in the pleadings—no one who could equal him in setting forth my arguments, or presenting my side of the case. It would, therefore, be wholly an unequal contest, where I could have no hope of success; and I am unwilling to engage in such a controversy or trial with God. My interest, my duty, and the necessity of the case, require me to submit the case without argument, and I will not attempt to plead with my Maker.'' That there was a want of right feeling in this, must be apparent to all. There was evidently the secret belief that God had dealt with him severely; that he had gone beyond his deserts in inflicting pain on him, and that he was under a necessity of submitting not so much to justice and right as to mere power and sovereignty. But who has not had something of this feeling when deeply afflicted? And yet who, when he has had it, has not felt that it was far from being what it should be? Our feeling *should* be, ''we deserve all that we suffer, and more than we have yet endured. God is a sovereign; but He is right. Though he afflicts *us* much, and others *little*, yet it is not because he is unjust, but because he sees that there is some good reason why we should suffer. That reason may be seen yet by us, but if not, we should never doubt that it exists.'' ¶ *Who shall set me a time* to plead? Noyes renders this, ''Who shall summon me to trial?'' Dr. Good, ''Who should become a witness for me?'' The sense is, ''Who would summon witnesses for me? If it was a mere trial of strength, God is too mighty for me; if it were a question of justice, who would compel witnesses to come on my side? Who could make them willing to appear against God, and to bear testimony for me in a controversy with the Almighty?'

20. *If I justify myself, mine own mouth shall condemn me.* That is,

referring still to the form of a judicial trial, if I should undertake to manage my own cause, I should lay myself open to condemnation even in my argument on the subject, and should show that I was far from the perfection which I had undertaken to maintain. By passionate expressions; by the language of complaint and murmuring; by a want of suitable reverence; by showing my ignorance of the principles of the divine government; by arguments unsound and based on false positions; or by contradictions and self-refutations, I should show that my position was untenable, and that God was right in charging me with guilt. In some or in all of these ways Job felt, probably, that in an argument before God he would be self-condemned, and that even an attempt to justify himself, or to prove that he was innocent, would prove that he was guilty. And is it not always so? Did a man ever yet undertake to repel the charges of guilt brought against him by his Maker, and to prove that he was innocent, in which he did not himself show the truth of what he was denying? Did not his false views of God and of his law; his passion, murmuring, and irreverence; his unwillingness to admit the force of the palpable considerations urged to prove that he was guilty, demonstrate that he was at heart a sinner, and that he was insubmissive and rebellious? The very attempt to enter into such an argument against God, shows that the heart is not right; and the manner in which such an argument is commonly conducted demonstrates that he who does it is sinful. ¶ If I say, *I* am *perfect.* Should I attempt to maintain such an argument, the very attempt would prove that my heart is perverse and evil. It would do this because God had adjudged the contrary, and because such an effort would show an insubmissive and a proud heart. This passage shows that Job did not regard himself as a man absolutely free from sin. He was indeed said (chap. i. 1.) to be ''perfect and upright;'' but this

21 *Though* I *were* perfect, *yet* would I not know my soul: I would despise my life.

22 This *is* one *thing*, therefore I said *it*, He *a* destroyeth the perfect and the wicked.

a Eze.21.3.

verse proves that that testimony in regard to him was not inconsistent with *his* consciousness of guilt. See the Notes on that verse. And is not the claim to absolute perfection in this world always a proof that the heart is perverse? Does not the very setting up of such a claim in fact indicate a pride of heart, a self-satisfaction, and an ignorance of the true state of the soul, which is full demonstration that the heart is far from being perfect? God adjudges man to be exceedingly sinful; and if I do not mistake the meaning of the Scriptures, this is his testimony of every human heart—*totally* until renewed—*partially* ever onward till death. If this be the account in the Scriptures, then the claim to absolute perfection is *prima facie*, if not full proof, that the heart is in some way perverse. It has come to a different conclusion from that of God. It sets up an argument against him—and there can be no more certain proof of a want of perfection than such an attempt. There is in this verse an energy in the original which is very feebly conveyed by our translation. It is the language of strong and decided indignation at the very idea of asserting that he was perfect. אני תם—"*perfect I!*" or, "*I perfect!*" The thought is absurd! It can only prove that I am perverse to attempt to set up any such claim!" Stuhlman renders this,

"However good I may be, I must condemn myself;
However free from guilt, I must call myself evil:"

and explains it as meaning, "God can through the punishments which he inflicts constrain me to confess, against the clear consciousness of my *inno*cence, that I am guilty."

21. Though *I* were *perfect.* The same mode of expression occurs here again. "I perfect! I would not know it, or recognize it. If this were my view, and God judged otherwise, I would seem to be ignorant of it. I would not mention it." ¶ Yet *would*

I not know my soul. Cr, "I could not know my soul. If I should advance such a claim, it must be from my ignorance of myself." Is not this true of all the claims to perfection which have ever been set up by man? Do they not demonstrate that he is ignorant of his own nature and character? So clear does this seem to me, that I have no doubt that Job expressed more than three thousand years ago what will be found true to the end of time—that if a man advances the claim to absolute perfection, it is conclusive proof that he does not know his own heart. A superficial view of ourselves, mingled with pride and vanity, may lead us to think that we are wholly free from sin. But who can tell what he would be if placed in other circumstances? Who knows what latent depravity would be developed if he were thrown into temptations? ¶ *I would despise my life.* Dr. Good, I think, has well expressed the sense of this. According to his interpretation, it means that the claim of perfection would be in fact disowning all the consciousness which he had of sinfulness; all the arguments and convictions pressed on him by his reason and conscience, that he was a guilty man. Schultens, however, has given an interpretation which slightly differs from this, and one which Rosenmüller prefers. "Although I should be wholly conscious of innocence, yet that clear consciousness could not sustain me against the infinite splendour of the divine glory and majesty; but I should be compelled to appear ignorant of my own soul, and to reprobate, condemn, and despise my life passed with integrity and virtue." This interpretation is in accordance with the connection, and may be sustained by the Hebrew.

22. *This* is *one* thing, *therefore I* said it. This may mean, "it is all the same thing. It makes no difference whether a man be righteous or wicked. God treats them substantially

23 If the scourge slay suddenly, he will laugh at the trial of the innocent.

24 The earth is given into the hand of the wicked : he covereth the faces of the judges thereof ; if not, where, *and* who *is* he ?

alike ; he has one and the same rule on the subject. Nothing can be argued certainly about the character of a man from the divine dealings with him here." This was the point in dispute, this the position that Job maintained—that God did *not* deal with men here in strict accordance with their character, but that the righteous and the wicked in this world were afflicted alike. ¶ *He destroyeth the perfect and the wicked.* He makes no distinction among them. That Job was right in this his main position there can be no doubt ; and the wonder is, that his friends did not all see it. But it required a long time in the course of events, and much observation and discussion, before this important point was made clear. With *our* full views of the state of retribution in the future world, *we* can have no doubt on the subject. Heavy and sudden judgments do not necessarily prove that they who are cut off are peculiarly guilty, and long prosperity is no evidence that a man is holy. Calamity, by fire and flood, on a steamboat, or in the pestilence, does not demonstrate the peculiar and eminent wickedness of those who suffer (comp. Luke xiii. 1—5), nor should those who escape from such calamities infer that of necessity they are the objects of the divine favour.

23. *If the scourge slay suddenly.* If calamity comes in a sudden and unexpected manner. Dr. Good, following Reiske, translates this, " if he suddenly slay the oppressor," understanding the word *scourge* (שׁוֹט) as meaning an oppressor, or one whom God employs as a scourge of nations. But this is contrary to all the ancient versions. The word שׁוֹט means properly a whip, a scourge (comp. Notes on chap. v. 21), and then calamity or affliction sent by God upon men. Such is clearly the case here. ¶ *He will laugh at the trial of the innocent.* That is, he seems to disregard or to be pleased with their trials. He does not interpose to rescue them. He

seems to look calmly on, and suffers them to be overwhelmed with others. This is a poetic expression, and cannot mean that God *derides* the trials of the innocent, or *mocks* their sufferings. It means that he seems to be inattentive to them ; he suffers the righteous and the wicked to be swept away together as if he were regardless of character.

24. *The earth is given into the hand of the wicked.* This is evidently designed as an illustration of the sentiment that Job was maintaining—that there was not a distribution of rewards and punishments in this life according to character. In illustration of this, he says that the wicked are raised to places of trust and power. They exercise a wide dominion over the earth, and the world is under their control. Of the truth of this there can be no doubt. Rulers have been, in general, eminent for wickedness, and the affairs of nations have thus far been almost always under the control of those who are strangers to God. At the present time there is scarcely a pious man on any throne in the world, and the rulers of even Christian nations are in general eminent for any thing rather than for personal religion. ¶ *He covereth the faces of the judges thereof.* There has been considerable variety in the exposition of this expression. Some suppose that it refers to the wicked, meaning that they cover the faces of the judges under them so that they connive at and tolerate crime. Others, that it means that God blinds the eyes of wicked rulers, so that they connive at crime, and are partial and unjust in their decisions. Others, that it means that God covers the faces of the judges of the earth with shame and confusion, that though he admits them to prosperity and honour for a time, yet that he overwhelms them at length with calamities and sorrows. Dr. Good supposes it to mean that the earth is given over into the hands of INJUSTICE, and that *this* hoodwinks the faces of

25 Now my days are swifter than a post: they flee away, they see no good.

26 They are passed away as the ¹ swift ships; as the eagle *that* hasteth to the prey.

1 *ships of desire,* or *ships of Ebeh.*

the judges. The phrase properly means, to hoodwink, to blind, to conceal the face. It seems to me that the true sense is not expressed by either of the views above. The parallelism requires us to understand it as meaning that while the wicked had dominion over the earth, the righteous were in obscurity, or were not advanced to honour and power. The word *"judges,"* therefore, I think, is to be understood of the *righteous* judges, of those who are qualified to administer justice. Their face is covered. They are kept in concealment. The wicked have the sway, and they are doomed to shame, obscurity, and dishonour. This interpretation accords with the tenor of the argument, and may be sustained by the Hebrew, though I have not found it in any of the commentaries which I have consulted. ¶ *If not, where,* and *who* is *he?* If this is not a just view, who *is* God? What *are* his dealings? Where is he to be seen, and how is he to be known? Or, it may mean, "if it is not God who does these strange things, who is it that does them?" *Rosenmüller.* But I prefer the former interpretation. "Tell me who and what God is, if this is not a fair and just account of him. These things in fact are done, and if the agency of God is not employed in them, who is God? And where is his agency seen?' 25. *Now my days are swifter than a post.* Than a courier, runner, or racer, רץ. Vulg. *cursore;* LXX., δρομίως, a racer. The word is not unfrequently applied to the runners or couriers, that carried royal commands in ancient times. It is applied to the mounted couriers of the Persians who carried the royal edicts to the distant provinces, Est. iii. 13, 15; viii. 14, and to the body-guard and royal messengers of Saul and of David, 1 Sam. xxii. 17; 2 Kings x. 25. The common rate of travelling in the East is exceedingly slow. The caravans move little more than two miles an hour.

Couriers are however employed who go either on dromedaries, on horses, or on foot, and who travel with great rapidity. Lady Montague says that "after the defeat at Peterwaradin, they [the couriers on dromedaries] far outran the fleetest horses, and brought the first news of the battle at Belgrade." The messengers in Barbary who carry despatches, it is said, will run one hundred and fifty miles in twenty-four hours (Harmer's Observa. ii. 200, ed. 1808), and it has been said that the messengers among the American savages would run an hundred and twenty miles in the twenty-four hours. In Egypt, it is a common thing for an Arab on foot to accompany a rider, and to keep up with the horse when at full gallop, and to do this for a long time without apparent fatigue. The meaning of Job here is, that his life was short, and that his days were passing swiftly away, not like the slow caravan, but like the most fleet messenger; comp. Note chap. vii. 6. ¶ *They see no good.* I am not permitted to enjoy happiness. My life is a life of misery. 26. *They are passed away as the swift ships.* Marg. *Ships of desire;* or *ships of Ebeh.* Heb. אניות אבה. Vulg. *Naves poma portantes.* Sept. "Is there any track left by ships in their passage?" The Chaldee renders it as the Vulgate, "Ships bearing good fruit;" that is, as such fruit was perishable, haste was required in order to reach the place of destination. Our translators were evidently perplexed by the word אבה—*ebeh,* as appears by their placing two different phrases in the margin. "Ships of desire," denotes the value or *desirableness* of such ships; and the phrase, "Ships of Ebeh," denotes their confession of ignorance as to the meaning of the word. Gesenius explains the word to mean reed, bulrush, or papyrus—from an Arabic use of the word, and supposes that the reference is to the light vessels made of the papyrus,

27 If I say, I will forget my complaint, I will leave off my heaviness, and comfort *myself;*

28 I am afraid of all my sorrows,

Je.2. 22.

which were used on the Nile; see Notes on Isa. xviii. 2. Such vessels would be distinguished for the ease with which they might be rowed, and the rapidity of their motion. Chardin supposes that the reference is to vessels that were made to go on the Euphrates or the Tigris, and that were borne along with the rapid current. The supposition of an allusion to any boat or vessel under full sail, will be in accordance with the language here, though the probability is, that the reference is to the light vessels, made of reeds, that might be propelled with so much fleetness. Sails were frequently used, also, for such vessels. ¶ *As the eagle* that *hasteth to the prey* A striking emblem of rapidity. Few things can be more rapid than the motion of the eagle, as he darts upon his victim.

27. *If I say, I will forget my complaint.* If I resolve that I will leave off complaining, and will be more cheerful, I find it all in vain. My fears and sorrows return, and all my efforts to be cheerful are ineffectual ¶ *I will leave off my heaviness.* The word rendered "my heaviness" here (פני) denotes literally *my face;* and the reference is to the sad and sorrowful countenance which he had. "If I should lay that aside, and endeavour to be cheerful." ¶ *And comfort* myself. The word rendered *comfort* here (בלג) in Arabic means to be bright, to shine forth; and it would here be better rendered by *brighten up.* We have the same expression still when we say to one who is sad and melancholy, "brighten up; be cheerful.' The meaning is, that Job endeavoured to appear pleasant and cheerful, but it was in vain. His sorrows pressed heavily on him, and weighed down his spirits in spite of himself, and made him sad.

28. *I am afraid of all my sorrows.* My fears return. I dread the continuance of my griefs, and cannot close

I know that thou wilt not hold me innocent.

29 *If* I be wicked, why then labour I in vain?

30 If I wash myself with snow

my eye to them. ¶ *Thou wilt not hold me innocent.* God will not remove my sorrows so as to furnish the evidence that I am innocent. My sufferings continue, and with them continue all the evidence on which my friends rely that I am a guilty man. In such a state of things, how can I be otherwise than sad? He was held to be guilty; he was suffering in such a way as to afford them the proof that he was so, and how could he be cheerful?

29. If *I be wicked, why then labour I in vain?* The word "if," here introduced by our translators, greatly obscures the sense. The meaning evidently is, "I am held to be guilty, and cannot answer to that charge. God regards me as such, and if I should attempt to meet him on the charge, it would be a vain attempt; and I must admit its truth. It would be labour in vain to deny it against one so mighty as he is." This interpretation accords with the argument in the whole chapter. Job maintains that it would be in vain to contend with God, and he gives up the argument in despair. It is quite evident, however, that he does not do it so much because he is *convinced* himself, as because he knows that God is great, and that it would be useless to contend with him. There is evidently implied all along the feeling that if he was able to cope with God in the argument, the result would be different. As it is, he submits—not because he is *convinced*, but because he is *weak;* not because he sees that God is *right,* but because he sees that he is *powerful.* How much submission of this kind is there in the world—submission, not to *right,* but to *power;* submission to God, not because he is seen to be wise and good, but because he is seen to be almighty, and it is vain to attempt to oppose him! It is needless to say that such feelings evince no true submission.

30. *If I wash myself with snow*

water, and make my hands never
so clean ;
  31 Yet shalt thou plunge me
  1 *make me to be abhorred.*

in the ditch, and mine own clothes
shall [1] abhor me.
  32 For *he is* not a man, as I *am,*

water. If I should make myself as
pure as possible, and should become,
in my view, perfectly holy. Snow
water, it seems, was regarded as peculiarly pure. The whiteness of snow
itself perhaps suggested the idea that
the water of melted snow was better
than other for purification. Washing
the hands formerly was an emblem of
cleansing from guilt. Hence Pilate,
when he gave up the Saviour to death,
took water and washed his hands
before the multitude, and said that he
was innocent of his blood ; Matth.
xxvii. 24. The expression here used
by Job, also is imitated by the Psalmist, to denote his innocence :
I will wash mine hands in innocency :
So will I compass thine altar, O Lord.
                              Ps. xxvi. 6.
Verily I have cleansed my heart in vain,
And washed my hands in innocency.
                              Ps. lxxiii. 13.
So in Shakspeare, Richard III. :
How fain, like Pilate, would I wash my hands
Of this most grievous, guilty murder done !
¶ *And make my hands never so clean.*
Or, rather, should I cleanse my hands
with lye, or alkali. The word בֹּר, *bor,*
means properly purity, cleanliness,
pureness ; and then it is used to denote that which cleanses, alkali, lye,
or vegetable salt. The ancients made
use of this, mingled with oil, instead
of soap, for the purpose of washing,
and also in smelting metals, to make
them melt more readily ; see Notes
on Isa. i. 25. The Chaldee renders it
accurately, באאלב—*in soap.* I have
no doubt that this is the sense, and
that Job means to say, if he should
make use of the purest water and of
soap to cleanse himself, still he would
be regarded as impure. God would
throw him at once into the ditch, and
he would be covered with moral filth
and defilement again in his sight.
  31. *Yet shalt thou plunge me in the
ditch.* God would treat me as if he
should throw me into the gutter, and
as if I were wholly defiled and polluted.
The meaning is, God would not admit
the proofs which I should adduce of

my innocence, but would overwhelm me
with the demonstrations of my guilt.
I doubt not that Job urged this with
some degree of impatience, and with
some improper feelings. *He* felt,
evidently, that God was so great and
powerful, that it was vain to contend
with him. But it *is* true in a higher
and more important sense than he
seems to have understood it. After
all the efforts which we can make to
justify, vindicate, or purify ourselves,
it is in the power of God to overwhelm
us with the *consciousness* of guilt. He
has access to the heart. He can show
us our past sins. He can recall what
we have forgotten, and overwhelm us
with the remembrance of our deep
depravity. It is in vain, therefore, for
any man to attempt to justify himself
before God. After the most laboured
argument to prove his own innocence,
after all the confidence which he can
repose in his own morality and his own
righteousness, still God can with infinite ease overwhelm him with the
consciousness of guilt. How many
men that were once relying on their
own morality for their salvation, have
been bowed down with a consciousness
of guilt in a revival of religion ! How
many who have been trusting to their
own righteousness have been overwhelmed with deep and awful conviction, when they have been brought to
lie on a bed of death ! Let no man,
therefore, rely on his own righteousness, when God accuses him with being
a sinner. Let no one trust to his own
morality for salvation—for soon it
will all be seen to be insufficient, and
the soul must appear covered over
with the consciousness of guilt at the
awful bar of God. ¶ *And mine own
clothes shall abhor me.* Marg. *Make
me to be abhorred.* That is, they shall
be filthy and offensive—like one who
has been rolled in the mire. God has
power to make me seem defiled and
loathsome, notwithstanding all my efforts to cleanse myself.
  32. *For* he is *not a man as I* am.

that I should answer him, *and* we should come together in judgment.

33 Neither is there [1] any [2] days- man betwixt [a] us, *that* might lay his hand upon us both.

1 *one that should argue.*   2 *or, umpire.*
a Ps. 106. 23.

He is infinitely superior to me in majesty and power. The idea is, that the contest would be unequal, and that he might as well surrender without bringing the matter to an issue. It is evident that the disposition of Job to yield, was rather because he saw that God was superior *in power* than because he saw that he was *right,* and that he felt that if he had ability to manage the cause as well as God could, the matter would not be so much against him as it was then. That there was no little impropriety of feeling in this, no one can doubt ; but have *we* never had feelings like this when we have been afflicted? Have we never submitted to God because we felt that he was Almighty, and that it was vain to contend with him, rather than because he was seen to be *right*? True submission is always accompanied with the belief that that God is RIGHT—whether we can see him to be right or not. ¶ And *we should come together in judgment.* For trial, to have the case adjudicated. That is, that we should meet face to face, and have the cause tried before a superior judge. *Noyes.*

33. *Neither is there any daysman.* Marg. *One that should argue,* or, *umpire.* The word *daysman* in English means "an umpire or arbiter, a mediator." *Webster.* Why such a man is called a *daysman* I do not know. The Hebrew word rendered *daysman* (מוכיח) is from יכח, not used in Kal, to be before, in front of; and then to appear, to be clear, or manifest ; and in Hiphil, to cause to be manifest, to argue, prove, convince ; and then to argue down, to confute, reprove ; see the word used in chap. vi. 25 : "What doth your arguing reprove ?" It then means to make a cause clear, to judge, determine, decide, as an arbiter, umpire, judge, Isa. xi. 3 ; Gen. xxxi. 37. Jerome renders it, "Non est qui utrumque valeat arguere." The LXX., "if there were. or, O that there were a mediator (ὁ μεσίτης), and a reprover (καὶ ἐλέγχων), and one to hear us both" (καὶ διακούων ἀναμέσον ἀμφοτέρων). The word as used by Job does not mean mediator, but *arbiter, umpire,* or *judge;* one before whom the cause might be tried, who could lay the hand of restraint on either party. who could confine the pleadings within proper bounds, who could preserve the parties within the limits of order and propriety, and who had power to determine the question at issue. Job complains that there could be no such tribunal. He feels that God was so great that the cause could be referred to no other, and that he had no prospect of success in the unequal contest. It does not appear, therefore, that he desired a *mediator,* in the sense in which we understand that word—one who shall come between us and God, and manage our cause *before* him, and be our advocate at his bar. He rather says that there was no one *above* God, or no umpire uninterested in the controversy, before whom the cause could be argued, and who would be competent to decide the matter in issue between him and his Maker. He had no hope, therefore, in a cause where one of the parties was to be the judge, and where that party was omnipotent ; and he must give up the cause in despair. It is not with strict propriety that this language is ever applied to the Lord Jesus, the great Mediator between God and man. He is not an umpire to settle a dispute, in the sense in which Job understood it ; he is not an arbiter, to whom the cause in dispute between man and his Maker is to be referred ; he is not a judge to listen to the arguments of the respective parties, and to decide the controversy. He is a *mediator* between us and God, to make it proper or possible that God should be reconciled to the guilty, and to propose to man the terms of reconciliation ; to plead our cause before God, and to communicate to us the favours which he proposes to bestow on man. ¶ *That might lay his hand upon us both.* It

34 Let him take ^a his rod away from me, and let not his fear terrify me :

35 *Then* would I speak, and not fear him : but 1 *it is* not so with me.

a Ps. 39.10. 1 *I am not so with myself.*

is not improbable that this may refer to some ancient ceremony in courts where, for some cause, the umpire or arbiter laid his hand on both the parties. Or, it may mean merely that the umpire had the power of control over both the parties ; that it was his office to restrain them within proper limits, to check any improper expressions, and to see that the argument was fairly conducted on both sides. The meaning of the whole here is, that if there were such an umpire, Job would be willing to argue the cause. As it was, it was a hopeless thing, and he could do nothing more than to be silent. That there was irreverence in this language must be admitted ; but it is language taken from courts of law, and the substance of it is, that Job could not hope to maintain his cause before one so great and powerful as God.

34. *Let him take his rod away from me.* Let him suspend my sufferings, and let us come together on equal terms. His terror now is upon me, and I can do nothing. I am oppressed, and broken down, and crushed under his hand, and I could not hope to maintain my cause with any degree of success. If my sufferings were lightened, and I could approach the question with the vigour of health and the power of reasoning unweakened by calamity, I could then do justice to the views which I entertain. Now there would be obvious disparity, while one of the parties has crushed and enervated the other by the mere exercise of power.

35. Then *would I speak, and not fear him.* I should then be able to maintain my cause on equal terms, and with equal advantages. ¶ *But* it is *not so with me.* Marg. *I am not so with myself.* Noyes, "I am not so at heart." Good, "but not thus could I in my present state." Literally, "for not thus I with myself." The Syriac renders it, "for neither am I his adversary." Very various interpretations have been given of

JOB I.

this phrase. The Jews, with Aben Ezra, suppose it means, " for I am not such as you suppose me to be. You take me to be a guilty man ; but I am innocent, and if I had a fair opportunity for trial, I could show that I am." Others suppose it to mean, "I am held to be guilty by the Most High. and am treated accordingly. But I am not so. I am conscious to myself that I am innocent." It seems to me that Dr. Good has come nearer the true sense than any other interpreter, and certainly his exposition accords with the connection. According to this the meaning is, "I am not able thus to vindicate myself in my present circumstances. I am oppressed and crushed beneath a load of calamities. But if these were removed, and if I had a fair opportunity of trial, then I could so state my cause as to make it appear to be just." In this whole chapter, there is evidently much insubmission and improper feeling. Job submits to *power*, not to *truth* and *right.* He sees and admits that God is *able* to overwhelm him, but he does not seem disposed to admit that he is *right* in doing it. He supposes that if he had a fair and full opportunity of trial, he could make his cause good, and that it would be seen that he did not deserve his heavy calamities. There is much of this kind of submission to God even among good people. It is submission because they cannot help it, not because they see the divine dealings to be right. There is nothing cheerful or confiding about it. There is often a secret feeling in the heart that the sufferings are beyond the deserts, and that if the case could be fairly tried, the dealings of God would be found to be harsh and severe. Let us not blame Job for his impatience and irreverent language, until we have carefully examined our own hearts in the times of trial like those which he endured. Let us not infer that he was worse than other men, until *we* are placed in similar circumstances, and are able

CHAPTER X.

MY soul is ¹ weary of my life ; I will leave my complaint upon myself ; 1 will speak in the bitterness of my soul.

2 I will say unto God, Do not *a*

1 or, *cut off while I live.*   *a* Ps.143.2 ; Ro 8.1.
b La.5.20.   2 *labour.*

condemn me ; show me wherefore *b* thou contendest with me.

3 *Is it* good unto thee that thou shouldest oppress, that thou shouldest despise the ² work of thine hands, and shine upon the counsel of the wicked ?

---

to manifest better feelings than he did.

CHAPTER X.

1. *My soul is weary of my life;* comp. Notes on chap. vii. 16. The margin here is, Or, *cut off while I live.* The meaning in the margin is in accordance with the interpretation of Schultens. The Chaldee also renders it in a similar way : נְפְשִׁי אתגזרת—*my soul is cut off.* But the more correct interpretation is that in our common version; and the sense is, that his soul, *i. e.* that he himself was disgusted with life. It was a weary burden, and he wished to die. ¶ *I will leave my complaint upon myself.* Noyes, " I will give myself up to complaint." Dr. Good, " I will let loose from myself my dark thoughts." The literal sense is, " I will leave complaint upon myself;" that is, I will give way to it ; I will not restrain it ; comp. chap. vii. 11. ¶ *I will speak in the bitterness of my soul;* see Notes, chap. vii. 11.

2. *I will say unto God, Do not condemn me.* Do not *hold me to be wicked* — אל תרשיעני. The sense is, " Do not simply hold me to be wicked, and treat me as such, without showing me the reasons why I am so regarded." This was the ground of Job's complaint, that God by mere sovereignty and power held him to be a wicked man, and that he did not see the reasons why he was so considered and treated. He now desired to know in what he had offended, and to be made acquainted with the cause of his sufferings. The idea is, that it was unjust to treat one as guilty who had no opportunity of knowing the nature of the offence with which he was charged, or the reason why he was condemned.

3. Is it *good unto thee that thou shouldest oppress.* The sense of this is, that it could not be with God a

matter of personal gratification to inflict pain wantonly. There *must* be a reason why he did it. This was clear to Job, and he was anxious, therefore, to know the reason why he was treated in this manner. Yet there is evidently here not a little of the spirit of complaining. There is an insinuation that God was afflicting him beyond what he deserved; see ver. 7. The state of his mind appears to have been this: he is conscious to himself that he is a sincere friend of God, and he is unwilling to believe that God can wantonly inflict pain—and yet he has no other way of accounting for it. He is in a sort *driven* to this painful conclusion—and he asks with deep feeling, whether it *can* be so? Is there no *other* solution than this ? Is there no way of explaining the fact that he suffers so much, than either the supposition that he is a hypocrite —which he feels assured he is not; or that God took a wanton pleasure in inflicting pain—which he was as little disposed to believe, if he could avoid it ? Yet his mind *rather* verges to this latter belief, for he seems more disposed to believe that God was severe than that he himself was a hypocrite and a wicked man. Neither of these conclusions was necessary. If he had taken a middle ground, and had adverted to the fact *that God might afflict his own children for their good,* the mystery would have been solved. He could have retained the consciousness of his integrity, and at the same time his confidence in God. ¶ *That thou shouldest despise the work of thine hands.* Marg. *labour.* That is, despise *man,* or treat him as if he were of no value. The idea is, that it would be natural for God to love his own work, and that his treatment of Job seemed as if he regarded his own workmanship—*man*—as of no value. ¶ *And*

4 Hast thou eyes of flesh? or *a* seest thou as man seeth?

5 *Are* thy days as the days of man? *are* thy years as man's days,

6 That *b* thou inquirest after

a 1 Sa.16.7.   b Ps.139.1.   c Ps.10.15.
1 It is *upon thy knowledge.*   d John 21.17.

mine iniquity, and searchest *c* after my sin?

7 Thou [1] knowest *d* that I am not wicked; and *there is* none that can deliver out of thine hand.

8 Thine hands [2] have made me,
2 *took pains about me.*

---

shine upon the counsel of the wicked. By giving them health and prosperity.

4. *Hast thou eyes of flesh?* Eyes like man. Dost thou look upon man with the same disposition to discern faults; the same uncharitableness and inclination to construe every thing in the severest manner possible, which characterizes man? Possibly Job may have reference here to the harsh judgment of his friends, and means to ask whether it could be possible for God to evince the same feelings in judging of him which they had done.

5. Are *thy days as the days of man.* Does thy life pass on like that of man? Dost thou expect soon to die, that thou dost pursue me in this manner, searching out my sins, and afflicting me as if there were no time to lose? The idea is, that God seemed to press this matter as if he were soon to cease to exist, and as if there were no time to spare in accomplishing it. His strokes were unintermitted, as if it were necessary that the work should be done soon, and as if no respite could be given for a full and fair development of the real character of the sufferer. The whole passage (ver. 4—7) expresses the settled conviction of Job that God *could not* resemble man. Man was short lived, fickle, blind; he was incapable, from the brevity of his existence, and from his imperfections, of judging correctly of the character of others. But it could not be so with God. He was eternal. He knew the heart. He saw every thing as it was. Why, then, Job asks with deep feeling, did he deal with him *as if* he were influenced by the methods of judgment which were inseparable from the condition of imperfect and dying man?

6. *That thou inquirest after mine iniquity.* Art thou governed by human passions and prejudices, that thou dost thus seem to search out every

little obliquity and error? Job here evidently refers to the conduct of man in strictly marking faults, and in being unwilling to forgive; and he asks whether it is possible that God could be governed by such feelings as these.

7. *Thou knowest that I am not wicked.* That is, that I am not a hypocrite, or an impenitent sinner. Job did not claim perfection (see Notes on chap. ix. 20), but he maintained through all this argument that he was not a wicked man, in the sense in which his friends regarded him as such, and for the truth of this he could boldly appeal to God. The margin is, " It is *upon thy knowledge.*" This is a literal translation of the Hebrew, but the sense is well expressed in the text. The meaning of the verse is, " Why dost thou thus afflict me, when thou knowest that I am not wicked? Why am I treated as if I were the worst of men? Why is occasion thus furnished for my friends to construct an argument as if I were a man of singular depravity?" ¶ There is *none that can deliver out of thine hand.* I have no power to release myself. Job felt that God had almighty power; and he seems to have felt that his sufferings were rather the simple exertion of *power,* than the exercise of justice. It was this that laid the foundation for his complaint.

8. *Thine hands have made me.* Job proceeds now to state that he had been made by God, and that he had shown great skill and pains in his formation. He argues that it would seem like caprice to take such pains, and to exercise such amazing wisdom and care in forming him, and then, on a sudden, and without cause, dash his own work to pieces. Who makes a beautiful vase only to be destroyed? Who moulds a statue from marble only to break it to pieces? Who builds a splendid edifice only to pull it down?

and fashioned me together round about ; yet thou dost destroy me.

9 Remember, I beseech thee, that thou hast made me as the ^a clay ; and wilt thou bring me into dust again ?

10 Hast thou not poured me

a Je.18.6 ; Ro.9.21.

Who plants a rare and precious flower only to have the pleasure of plucking it up ? The statement in ver. 8—12, is not only beautiful and forcible as an argument, but is peculiarly interesting and valuable, as it may be presumed to embody the views in the patriarchal age about the formation and the laws of the human frame. No inconsiderable part of the value of the book of Job, as was remarked in the Introduction, arises from the incidental notices of the sciences as they prevailed at the time when it was composed. If it is the oldest book in the world, it is an invaluable record on these points. The expression, "thine hands have made me," is in the margin, " took pains about me." Dr. Good renders it, " have wrought me ;" Noyes, " completely fashioned me ;" Rosenmüller explains it to mean, " have formed me with the highest diligence and care." Schultens renders it, Manus tuæ nervis colligarunt —" thy hands have bound me with nerves or sinews ;" and appeals to the use of the Arabic as authority for this interpretation. He maintains (De Defectibus hodiernis Ling. Hebr. pp. 142, 144, 151), that the Arabic word atzaba denotes "the body united and bound in a beautiful form by nerves and tendons ;" and that the idea here is, that God had so constructed the human frame. The Hebrew word here used (עָצַב) means properly to work, form, fashion. The primary idea, according to Gesenius, is, that of cutting, both wood and stone, and hence to cut or carve with a view to the forming of an image. The verb also has the idea of labour, pain, travail, grief; perhaps from the labour of cutting or carving a stone or a block of wood. Hence it means, in Piel, to form or fashion, with the idea of labour or toil ; and the sense here is undoubtedly, that God had elaborated the bodies of men with care and skill, like that bestowed on a carved image or statue. The margin expresses the

idea not badly—took pains about me. ¶ And fashioned me. Made me. The Hebrew here means simply to make. ¶ Together round about. יַחַד סָבִיב. Vulg. totum in circuitu. Sept. simply, "made me." Dr. Good, "moulded me compact on all sides." The word יַחַד rendered "together," has the notion of oneness, or union. It may refer to the oneness of the man—the making of one from the apparently discordant materials, and the compact form in which the body, though composed of bones, and sinews, and blood-vessels, is constructed. A similar idea is expressed by Lucretius, as quoted by Schultens. Lib. iii. 358 :

——Qui cœtu, conjugioque
Corporis atque animæ consistimus uniter apti.

¶ Yet thou dost destroy me. Notwithstanding I am thus made, yet thou art taking down my frame, as if it were of no consequence, and formed with no care.

9. Remember, I beseech thee, that thou hast made me as the clay. There is evident allusion here to the creation of man, and to the fact that he was moulded from the dust of the earth —a fact which would be preserved by tradition; see Gen. ii. 7. The fact that God had moulded the human form as the potter moulds the clay, is one that is often referred to in the Scriptures ; comp. Rom. ix. 20, 21. The object of Job in this is, probably, to recall the fact that God, out of clay, had formed the noble structure, man, and to ask whether it was his intention to reduce that structure again to its former worthless condition — to destroy its beauty, and to efface the remembrance of his workmanship ? Was it becoming God thus to blot out every memorial of his own power and skill in moulding the human frame ?

10. Hast thou not poured me out as milk ? The whole image in this verse and the following, is designed to furnish an illustration of the origin and growth of the human frame. The

out as milk, and curdled me like cheese?

11 Thou ^a hast clothed me with skin and flesh, and hast fenced ¹ me with bones and sinews.

a Ps.139.13.   *1 hedged.*

12 Thou hast granted me life and favour, and thy visitation hath preserved my spirit.

13 And these *things* hast thou hid in thine heart: I know that this *is* with thee.

Note of Dr. Good may be transcribed, as furnishing an illustration of what may have *possibly* been the meaning of Job. "The whole of the simile is highly correct and beautiful, and has not been neglected by the best poets of Greece and Rome. From the well tempered or mingled milk of the chyle, every individual atom of every individual organ in the human frame, the most compact and consolidated, as well as the soft and pliable, is perpetually supplied and renewed, through the medium of a system of *lacteals* or *milk vessels*, as they are usually called in anatomy, from the nature of this common chyle or milk which they circulate. Into the delicate stomach of the infant it is introduced in the form of milk; but even in the adult it must be reduced to some such form, whatever be the substance he feed upon, by the conjoint action of the stomach and other chylifactive organs, before it can become the basis of animal nutriment. It then circulates through the system, and either continues fluid as milk in its simple state, or is rendered solid as milk is in its caseous or cheese-state, according to the nature of the organ which it supplies with its vital current." True as this is, however, as a matter of physiology, now well understood, a doubt may arise whether Job was acquainted with the method thus described, in which man is sustained. The idea of Job is, that God was the author of the human frame, and that that frame was so formed as to evince his wonderful and incomprehensible wisdom. A consultation of the works on physiology, which explain the facts about the formation and the growth of the human body, will show that there are few things which more strikingly evince the wisdom of God than the formation of the human frame, alike at its origin, and in every stage of its development.

It is a subject, however, which cannot, with propriety, be pursued in a work of this kind.

11. *Thou hast clothed me with skin and flesh.* This refers, undoubtedly, to the formation of man in his fœtal existence, and is designed to denote that the whole organization of the human frame was to be traced to God. Grotius remarks that this is the order in which the infant is formed— that the skin appears first, then the flesh, then the harder parts of the frame. On this subject, the reader may consult Dunglison's Physiology, vol. ii. p. 340, seq. ¶ *And hast fenced me.* Marg. *Hedged.* Literally, *Hast covered me.* The sense is plain. God had formed him as he was, and to him he owed his life, and all that he had. Job asks with the deepest interest whether God would take down a frame formed in this manner, and reduce it again to dust? Would it not be more for his honour to preserve it still—at least to the common limit of human life?

12. *Thy visitation hath preserved my spirit.* Thy constant care; thy watchful providence; thy superintendence. The word rendered *visitation* (פקדה) means properly the *mustering* of an army, the care that is manifested in looking after those who are enlisted; and then denotes care, vigilance, providence, custody, watch. The idea is, that God had watched over him and preserved him, and that to his constant vigilance he owed the preservation of his life.

13. *And these* things *hast thou hid in thine heart.* This may either refer to the arrangements by which God had made him, or to the calamities which he had brought upon him. Most expositors suppose that the latter is intended. Such is the opinion of Rosenmüller, Good, Noyes, and Scott. According to this the idea is, that

14 If I sin, then thou markest me, and thou wilt not acquit me from mine iniquity.

15 If I be wicked, woe *a* unto

a Is.6.5.

me; and *if* I be righteous, *yet* will I not lift up my head. *I am* full of confusion; therefore see thou mine affliction;

God had purposed in his heart to bring these calamities upon him. They were a part of his counsel and design. To hide in the heart, or to lay up in the heart, is a phrase expressive of a secret purpose. I see no reason to confine it, however, to the calamities which Job had experienced. It may refer to *all* the plans and doings of the Most High, to which Job had just referred. *All* his acts in the creation and preservation of man, were a part of his secret counsel. He had formed the plan in his heart, and was now executing it in the various dispensations of his providence. ¶ *I know that this* is *with thee.* That all this is a part of thy purpose. It has its origin in thee, and is according to thy counsel. This is the language of piety, recognizing the great truth that all things are in accordance with the purposes of God, or that his plans embrace all events—a doctrine which Job most assuredly held.

14. *If I sin.* The object of this verse and the following is, evidently, to say that he was wholly perplexed. He did not know how to act. He could not understand the reason of the divine dealings, and he was wholly unable to explain them, and hence he did not know how to act in a proper manner. It is expressive of a state of mind where the individual *wishes* to think and feel right, but where he finds so much to perplex him, that he does not know what to do. Job was sure that his friends were not right in the position which they maintained— that he was a sinner of enormous character, and that his sufferings were proof of this, and yet he did not know how to answer their arguments. He desired to have confidence in God, and yet he knew not how to reconcile his dealings with his sense of right. He felt that he was a friend of God, and be did not know why he should visit one who had this consciousness in this distressing and painful manner. His

mind was perplexed, vacillating, embarrassed, and he did not know what to do or say. The truth in this whole argument was, that he was more often right than his friends, but that he, in common with them, had embraced some principles which he was compelled to admit to be true, or which he could not demonstrate to be false, which gave them greatly the advantage in the argument, and which they pressed upon him now with overwhelming force. ¶ *Then thou markest me.* Dost carefully observe every fault. *Why* he did this, Job could not see. The same difficulty he expressed in chap. vii. 17—19; see the Notes on that place. ¶ *And wilt not acquit me.* Wilt not pardon me. Job did not understand why God would not do this. It was exceedingly perplexing to him that God held him to be guilty, and would not pardon him if he had sinned. The same perplexity he expressed in chap. vii. 21; see Notes on that verse.

15. *If I be wicked, woe unto me.* The meaning of this in this connection is, " I am full of perplexity and sorrow. Whether I am wicked or righteous, I find no comfort. *Whatever* is my character, my efforts to be happy are unavailing, and my mind is full of anguish. Woe follows if I have been guilty of sin; and if I am not a sinful man, I am equally incapable of enjoyment. In every way I am doomed to wretchedness." *And if I be righteous,* yet *will I not lift up my head.* That is, with confidence and cheerfulness. The meaning is, that though he was conscious that he was not a hypocrite, yet he did not know what to do. God treated him as if he were wicked, and his friends regarded him as such, and he was overwhelmed with the perplexities of his situation. He could not lift up his head with confidence, though he was certain that he was not a sinner in the sense in which they charged him with being such; and yet

16 For it increaseth. Thou huntest me as a fierce *a* lion ; and

a La.3.10 ; Hos.13.7,8.   1 that is, *plagues.*

again thou showest thyself marvellous upon me.

17 Thou renewest thy [1] wit-

---

since he was treated by God in a manner so similar to the mode in which the wicked are treated, he felt ashamed and confounded. Who has not felt the same thing? Who has not experienced a sense of shame and mortification at being *sick,*—a proof of guilt, and an expression of the hatred of God against sin? Who has not felt *humbled* that he must die, as the most vile of the race must die, and that his body must become the "prey of corruption" and "the banquet of worms," as a demonstration of guilt? Such humiliation Job experienced. He was treated as if he were the vilest of sinners. He endured from God sufferings such as they endure. He was so regarded by his friends. He felt humbled and mortified that he was brought into this situation, and was ashamed that he could not meet the arguments of his friends. ¶ I am *full of confusion.* Shame, ignominy, distress, and perplexity. On every side there was embarrassment, and he knew not what to do. His friends regarded him as vile, and he could not but admit that he was so treated by God. ¶ *Therefore see thou mine affliction.* The word rendered here "*see*" (ראה) in the imperative, Rosenmüller, Gesenius, and others suppose should be regarded as in the infinitive absolute, the finite verb being understood ; "seeing I see my affliction," that is, I certainly see it. So the Chaldee and the Syriac render it, and this agrees better with the connection of the passage. "I see the depth of my affliction. I cannot hide it from myself. I see, and must admit, that God treats me *as if* I were a sinner, and I am greatly perplexed and embarrassed by that fact. My mind is in confusion, and I know not what to say.'

16. *For it increaseth.* Our translators understand this as meaning that the calamities of Job, so far from becoming less, were constantly increasing, and thus augmenting his perplexity and embarrassment. But a

somewhat different explanation is given to it by many interpreters. The word rendered "increaseth" (יגאה) means properly, to lift up, to lift up one's self, to rise ; and Gesenius supposes that it refers here to *the head,* and that the meaning is, "if it lift up itself (sc. my head), thou huntest me as a lion." It cannot be denied that the notion of pride, elation, haughtiness, is usually connected with the use of the word, but it is not necessary here to depart from the common interpretation, meaning that the increase of his affliction greatly augmented his perplexity. Jerome, however, renders it, "and on account of pride, thou dost seize me as a lioness." The idea is, "my affliction, as it were, *exalts itself,* or, becomes more and more prominent." This is a better interpretation than to refer it to the raising up of his head. ¶ *Thou huntest me as a fierce lion.* On the meaning of the word here rendered "fierce lion" (שחל, *shăhhăl*), see Notes on chap. iv. 10. The sense here is, that God hunted or followed him as a fierce lion pursued his prey. ¶ *And again thou showest thyself marvellous.* Or rather, "thou turnest, and art wonderful towards me." The meaning is, that he did not at once spring upon his prey and then leave it, but he came back as if it had not been put to death when first seized, as if a lion should come back and torture his victim again. The meaning of the phrase "showest thyself marvellous" is, that the dealings of God towards him were wonderful. They were wholly incomprehensible. He had no means of finding out the reasons of his doings. On the word here used, comp. Notes on Isa. ix. 6.

17. *Thou renewest thy witnesses against me.* Marg. " that is, *plagues.*" The Hebrew is, *thy witnesses*—עדיך. So the Vulgate. The LXX. is, "renewing against me my examination," τὴν ἐξέτασίν μου. Rabbi Levi supposes that the plague of the leprosy is intended. But the true meaning seems

nesses against me, and increasest thine indignation upon me; changes and war *are* against me.

18 Wherefore then hast thou brought me forth out of the womb? Oh *a* that I had given up the ghost, and no eye had seen me!

19 I should have been as though I had not been; I should have been carried from the womb to the grave.

20 *Are* not my days few? *b* cease *then, and* let me alone, that I may take comfort a little,

21 Before I go *whence* I shall

to be, that God sent upon him calamities which were regarded by his friends as *proofs* or *witnesses* that he was wicked, the public and solemn attestation of God, as they supposed, to the truth that he was eminently a bad man. New proofs of this kind were constantly occurring in his augmenting and protracted sorrows, and he could not answer the arguments which were brought from them by his friends. ¶ *Changes and war* are *against me.* Or rather, are *with me,* עמי. There were with him such reverses of condition as laid the foundation for the argument which they had urged with so much pertinacity and force that he was punished by God. The word rendered *changes* (חליפות) means properly *changes,* or exchanges, and is applied to garments, 2 Kings v. 5, 22, 23. It may be used also of soldiers keeping watch until they are relieved by a succeeding guard; see Note on chap. xiv. 14. Here it is not improbably employed in the sense of a *succession* of attacks made on him. One succeeds another, as if platoon after platoon, to use the modern terms, or phalanx after phalanx, should come up against him. As soon as one had discharged its arrows, another succeeded in its place; or as soon as one became exhausted, it was followed by a fresh recruit. All this Job could not endure. The *succession* wearied him, and he could not bear it. Dr. Good supposes that the word refers to the skirmishes by which a battle is usually introduced, in which two armies attempt to gall each other before they are engaged. But the true idea, as it seems to me, is, that afflictions succeeded each other as soldiers on a watch, or in a battle, relieve each other. When one set is exhausted

on duty, it is succeeded by another. Or, when in battle one company has discharged its weapons, or is exhausted, it is succeeded by those who are brought fresh into the field. The word rendered "war" (צבא) properly means an army or a host; see Note chap. vii. 1. Here it means that a whole *host* had rushed upon him. Not only had he been galled by the *succession,* the *relief-guard* of calamities, the attacks which had followed each other from an advanced guard, or from scouts sent out to skirmish, but the *whole army* was upon him. A whole host of calamities came rushing upon him alone, and he could not endure them.

18. *Wherefore then hast thou brought me forth;* see Notes on chap. iii. 11.

19 *I should have been carried from the womb to the grave;* see Notes on chap. iii. 16.

20. Are *not my days few?* My life is short, and hastens to a close. Let not then my afflictions be continued to the last moment of life, but let thine hand be removed, that I may enjoy some rest before I go hence to return no more. This is an address to God, and the meaning is, that as life was necessarily *so* short, he asked to be permitted to enjoy *some* comfort before he should go to the land of darkness and of death; comp. Note on chap. vii. 21. A somewhat similar expression occurs in Ps. xxxix. 13:

O spare me, that I may recover strength,
Before I go hence, and be no more.

21. *Before I go* whence *I shall not return.* To the grave, to the land of shades, to

"That undiscovered country, from whose bourne
No traveller returns."

¶ *To the land of darkness.* This passage is important as furnishing an

not return, *even* to the land [a] of darkness and the shadow [b] of death;

22 A land of darkness, as

[a] Ps.88.12.

darkness *itself; and* of the shadow of death, without any order, and *where* the light *is* as darkness.

[b] Ps.23.4.

illustration of what was early understood about the regions of the dead. The essential idea here is, that it was a land of *darkness*, of total and absolute night. This idea Job presents in a great variety of forms and phrases. He amplifies it, and uses apparently all the epithets which he can command to represent the *utter* and *entire* darkness of the place. The place referred to is not the grave, but the region beyond, the abode of departed spirits, the Hades of the ancients; and the idea here is, that it is a place where not a clear ray of light ever shines. That this was a common opinion of the ancients in regard to the world of departed spirits, is well known. Virgil thus speaks of those gloomy regions:

Dii, quibus imperium est animarum, umbræque
    silentes,   [late,
Et Chaos, et Phlegethon, loca nocte tacentia
Sit mihi fas audita loqui; sit numine vestro
Pandere res alta terra et caligine mersas.
Ibant obscuri sola sub nocte per umbram,
Perque domos Ditis vacuas, et inania regna:
Quale per incertam lunam sub luce maligna
Est iter in silvis: ubi cœlum condidit umbra
Jupiter, et rebus nox abstulit atra colorem
                        Æn. vi. 259, seq.

A similar view of Hades was held by the Greeks. Thus *Theognis*, 1007:

Ὡς μάκαρ εὐδαίμων τε καὶ ὄλβιος, ὅστις
    ἄπειρος
Ἄθλων, εἰς Ἅδου δῶμα μέλαν κατέβη.

There is nowhere to be found, however, a description which for intensity and emphasis of expression surpasses this of Job. ¶ *Shadow of death;* see this phrase explained in the Note on chap. iii. 5.

22. *A land of darkness.* The word here used (עֵיפָתָה) is different from that rendered *darkness* (חֹשֶׁךְ) in the previous verse. That is the common word to denote darkness; this seldom occurs. It is derived from עוּף, to fly; and then to cover as with wings; and hence the noun means that which is shaded or dark; Amos iv. 13; comp. Job xvii. 13; Isa. viii. 22; ix. 1.

¶ *As darkness* itself. This is still another word (אֹפֶל) though in our common version but one term is used. We have not the means in our language of marking different degrees of obscurity with the accuracy with which the Hebrews did it. The word here used (אֹפֶל) denotes a *thick* darkness—such as exists when the sun is set—from אָפֵל, to go down, to set. It is poetic, and is used to denote intense and deep darkness; see chap. iii. 6. ¶ And *of the shadow of death.* I would prefer reading this as connected with the previous word—"the deep darkness of the shadow of death." The Hebrew will bear this, and indeed it is the obvious construction. ¶ *Without any order.* The word rendered *order* (סְדָרִים) is in the plural. It is from סָדַר, obsolete, to place in a row or order, to arrange. The meaning is, that every thing was mingled together as in chaos, and all was confusion. Milton has used similar language:

    —"a vast immeasurable abyss."
    —"dark, wasteful, wild."

Ovid uses similar language in speaking of chaos: "Unus chaos, rudis indigestaque moles.". ¶ *And* where the light is *as darkness*. This is a very striking and graphic expression. It means that there is no pure and clear light. Even all the light that shines there is dark, sombre, gloomy—like the little light of a total eclipse, which *seems* to be darkness itself, and which only serves to render the darkness more distressing. Compare Milton:

" A dungeon horrible on all sides round,
    As one great furnace flamed, *yet from those
    flames*
No *light;* but rather *darkness visible*
Served only to discover sights of woe."
                        PAR. LOST, I.

The Hebrew here literally is, " And it shines forth (וַתֹּפַע) as darkness:" *i. e.* the very shining of the light there, if there is any, is like darkness ! Such

CHAPTER XI.

ANALYSIS OF THE CHAPTER.

This chapter contains the first speech of Zophar. In regard to this person, see Note on chap. ii. 11. It is generally agreed that he has less ability, gentleness, and refinement than either of the other speakers. The Editor of the Pictorial Bible says, "Zophar seems inferior even to Bildad in discernment, temper, and charitable consideration." Jahn says, " His first address is characterized by rusticity, his second adds but little to the first, and in the third dialogue he has no reply to make." Hales says, " He, without any reserve, taxes Job openly with loquacity, arrogance, and iniquity, and as justly punished for his sins; and exhorts him to repentance as the only means of recovering his prosperity." Analy. vol. ii. p. 70. Rosenmuller characterizes him as *ceteris immodestior et inhumanior*. I do not see the evidence, however, unless it be in the commencement of his discourse, that he is more rude and severe than Eliphaz or Bildad. Like them, he takes it for granted that Job had sinned, and assures him that if he would return to God, he should have prosperity and happiness again. This is the current strain of all their speeches; and in this they all agree. All are severe in their remarks, and it may be admitted that Zophar is much less argumentative than Eliphaz, and that his speeches are in fact little more than a repetition of what his friends had before said.

The speech in this chapter properly comprises three parts.

I. He accuses Job of garrulity, of arrogance, and of impiety, in maintaining his own innocence in the circumstances in which he then was. The *ground* of this was that Job maintained his innocence, and held that he was pure in the sight of God, ver. 1—4.

II. He says that he wishes that God would speak to Job and acquaint him with *his* estimate of what he was. He affirms that God exacted of him less than his iniquity deserved; and then goes into a sublime descrip-

tion of Go 1, as vast, and as unfathomable in his counsels and plans. He declares not only that God is *great*, but that he knows the heart of man, and knows exactly what he deserves. Man, he says, however, would arraign the divine counsels and plans, though he was born like a wild ass's colt. Zophar does not attempt to explain the equity of the divine dealings, but he dwells on the greatness and the sovereignty of God, and on the duty of man to *submit* with humility, ver. 5—12.

III. He assures Job that if he would repent and turn to God, he should be prospered again. He would forget his misery; his age would be clear as noonday; he would lie down in safety, and would again become an honoured and respected man. If he persevered in his wickedness, however, he must expect to be destroyed, for that was the lot of all the wicked, ver. 13—20.

It cannot be denied that there was much that was unkind in this speech, and much that Job would feel keenly. To *assume* that a man is wicked; that he is a hypocrite and abandoned by God, and then to exhort him *as if* it were so, and as if it did not admit a moment's debate or excite a doubt in the mind of the speaker, is a mode of address that will find its way to the heart of any man. Job felt it, as who would not? Yet th's was the error of all the friends of Job, and in a particular manner that of Zophar. To sit and hear this was one of the severe trials of that much afflicted patriarch, and if he answered occasionally with severity and sarcasm we must remember what human nature's, and think of the severity of the provocation before we severely censure him.

THEN answered Zophar the Naamathite, and said,

2 Should not the multitude of words be *a* answered? and should a man 1 full of talk be justified?

a Pr. 10. 19.   1 *of lips.*

---

was the view of Job of the abodes of the dead—even of the pious dead. No wonder he shrank back from it, and wished to live. Such is the prospect of the grave to man, till Christianity comes and reveals a brighter world beyond the grave—a world that *is all light.* That darkness is now scattered A clear light shines even around the grave, and beyond there is a world where *all* is light, and where " there is no night," and where all is one bright eternal day; Rev. xxi. 23; xxii. 5. O had Job been favoured with these views of heaven, he would not have thus feared to die !

CHAPTER XI.

2. *Should not the multitude of words be answered?* As if all that Job had said had been mere words ; or as if he was remarkable for mere garrulity ¶ *And should a man full of talk be justified ?* Marg. as in Heb. *of lips.* The phrase is evidently a Hebraism. to denote a great talker—a man of *mere* lips, or empty sound. Zophar

asks whether such a man could be justified or vindicated. It will be recollected that taciturnity was with the Orientals a much greater virtue than with us, and that it was regarded as one of the proofs of wisdom. The wise man with them was he who sat down at the feet of age, and desired to learn ; who carefully collected the maxims of former times ; who diligently observed the course of events ; and who deliberated with care on what others had to say. Thus Solomon says, "In the multitude of words there wanteth not sin : but he that refraineth his lips is wise ;" Prov. x. 19 : so James (i. 19), " let every man be swift to hear, slow to speak." It was supposed that a man who said much would say some foolish or improper things, and hence it was regarded as a proof of prudence to be distinguished for silence. In Oriental countries, and it may be added also, in all countries that *we* regard as uncivilized, it is unusual and disrespectful to be hasty in offering

3 Should thy · lies make men hold their peace? and when thou mockest, shall no man make thee ashamed?

4 For *a thou* hast said, My

doctrine *is* pure, and I am clean in thine eyes.

5 But oh that God would speak and open his lips against thee;

1 or, *devices.*   *a* chap.6.30;10 7.

counsel, to be forward to speak, or to be confident and bold in opinion; see Notes on chap. xxxii. 6, 7. It was for reasons such as these that Zophar maintained that a man who was full of talk could not be justified in it; that there was presumptive proof that he was not a safe man, or a man who could be vindicated in all that he said.

3. *Should thy lies.* Marg. *devices.* Rosenmüller renders this, "should men bear thy boastings with silence?" Dr. Good, "before thee would mankind keep silence?" Vulg. *tibi soli tacebunt homines?* "Shall men be silent before thee alone? The LXX. tender the whole passage, "he who speaketh much should also hear in turn; else the fine speaker (εὔλαλος) thinketh himself just.—Blessed be the short-lived offspring of woman. Be not profuse of words, for there is no one that judges against thee, and do not say that I am pure in works and blameless before him." How this was made out of the Hebrew, or what is its exact sense, I am unable to say. There can be no doubt, I think, that our present translation is altogether too harsh, and that Zophar by no means designs to charge Job with uttering *lies.* The Hebrew word commonly used for *lies,* is wholly different from that which is used here. The word here (בד) denotes properly *separation;* then *a part;* and in various combinations as a preposition, *alone, separate, besides.* Then the noun means empty talk, vain boasting; and then it may denote lies or falsehood. The leading idea is that of *separation* or of remoteness from *any thing,* as from prudence, wisdom, propriety, or truth. It is a *general* term, like our word *bad,* which I presume has been derived from this Hebrew word בד—*badh,* or from the Arabic *bad.* In the plural (בדים) it is rendered *liars* in Isa. xliv. 25; Jer. l. 36; *lies* in Job xi. 3; Isa. xvi. 6; Jer. xlviii. 30; and *parts* in Job xli. 12. It is also often rendered

staves, Ex. xxvii. 6; xxv. 14, 15, 28, *et sæp, al.* That it *may* mean "lies" here I admit, but it may also mean talk that is *aside* from propriety, and may refer here to a kind of discourse that was destitute of propriety, empty. vain talk. ¶ *And when thou mockest.* That is, "shalt thou be permitted to use the language of reproach and of complaint, and no one attempt to make thee sensible of its impropriety?" The complaints and arguments of Job he represented as in fact *mocking* God. ¶ *Shall no man make thee ashamed?* Shall no one show thee the impropriety of it, and bring thy mind to a sense of shame for what it has done? .This was what Zophar now proposed to do.

4. *My doctrine is pure.* The LXX. instead of the word *doctrine* here read *deeds,* ἔργοις; the Syriac, "thou sayest I have acted justly." But the word here used (לקח) means properly *fair speech* or *taking arguments,* that by which one is *taken* or captivated, from לקח, *to take.* Then it means doctrine, or instruction, Prov. i. 5; ix 9. Here it means the views which Job had expressed. Dr. Good supposes that it means *conduct,* a word which would suit the connection, but the Hebrew is not used in this sense. ¶ *And I am clean in thine eyes.* In the eyes of God, or in his sight. This was a false charge. Job had never maintained that he was perfect (comp. Notes on chap. ix. 20); he had only maintained that he was not such a sinner as his friends maintained that he was, a hypocrite, and a man eminent for guilt. His want of absolute perfection he was ever ready to admit and mourn over.

5. *But oh that God would speak.* Heb., "and truly, who will give that God should speak." It is the expression of an earnest wish that God would address him, and bring him to a proper sense of his ill desert. The mean-

6 And that he would show thee the secrets of wisdom, that *they are* double to that which is! Know,

a Ezr.9.13.

therefore, that God exacteth of thee *less* *a* than thine iniquity *deserveth.*

7 Canst thou by searching *b* find

b Is.40.28 ; Ro.11.33.

ing is, that if God should speak to him he would by no means find himself so holy as he now claimed to be.

6. *And that he would show thee the secrets of wisdom.* The hidden things that pertain to wisdom. The reference here is to the wisdom of God himself. The sense is this, "you now think yourself pure and holy. You have confidence in your own wisdom and integrity. But this apprehension is based on a short-sighted view of God, and on ignorance of him. If he would speak and show you his wisdom ; if he would express *his* sense of what purity is, you would at once see how far you have come from perfection, and would be overwhelmed with a sense of your comparative vileness and sin." ¶ *That* they are *double to that which is !* Noyes renders this, " his wisdom which is unsearchable." Dr. Good, strangely enough, "for they are intricacies to iniquity." The expression, as it stands in our common version, is not very intelligible ; and indeed it is difficult to attach any idea to it. Of the *words* used in the Hebrew, the sense is not difficult. The word כפלים, *double,* is from כפל *to fold, to double;* and means a doubling (Job xli. 5); and then two folds, or double folds, and the sense here is, that the wisdom of God is *double-fold ;* that is, complicated, inexplicable, or manifold. It is not spread out and plain, but is infolded, so that it requires to be unrolled to be understood. The word rendered " that which is" (תושיה), means properly a setting upright, uprightness—from ישה. Hence it means help, deliverance, Job vi. 13; purpose, undertaking, Notes on Job v. 12 ; and then counsel, wisdom, understanding, Job xii. 16 ; Isa. xxviii. 29. It means here, I suppose, *understanding ;* and the idea is, that the wisdom of God is " double of understanding ;" that is, it is so infolded, so complex, that it greatly surpasses our comprehension. What we see is a small part of it ; and the " secrets" of his wisdom—the parts

of his wisdom which are not unfolded, are far above our grasp. His wisdom is like a vast *roll* or volume, only the first and a very small part of which is unrolled so that we can read it. But who can look into that that remains unopened, and penetrate between the involutions, so as to perceive and read it all ? It is but little that is now unrolled of the mighty volume—the remainder will be unfolded as years and ages shall pass on, and the entire unfolding of the book will be reserved for eternity. ¶ *Know, therefore, that God exacteth of thee* less *than thine iniquity deserveth.* The word here rendered " exacteth" (ישה) more properly means *to forget*—from נשה. It also means to loan on usury, or to borrow ; but the sense here is rather that of forgetting It is not used in the sense of *exacting.* The true meaning is, " know, therefore, that for thee God hath caused to be forgotten a part of thy iniquity." That is, he has treated you as if he had caused a part of your sins to be out of mind, or as if they were not remembered. Instead of treating you, as you complain, with severity, he has by no means inflicted on you the calamities which you deserve. The *ground* of this unfeeling assertion is the abstract proposition that God is infinitely wiser than men ; that he has a deeper insight into human guilt than men can have ; and that if he should disclose to us *all* that he sees of the heart, we should be amazed at the revelations of our own sins. This sentiment is undoubtedly true, and accords almost exactly with what Job had himself said (chap. ix.19—22), but there is something very harsh and severe in the manner in which Zophar applies it.

7. *Canst thou, by searching, find out God ?* In order to illustrate the sentiment which he had just expressed, that the secrets of divine wisdom must be far above our comprehension, Zophar introduces here this sublime description of God—a description which seems to have the form and force of a

out God? canst thou find out the Almighty unto perfection?

8 *It is* [1] as high as heaven; what

1 *the heights of heaven.*

canst thou do? deeper than hell; what canst thou know?

9 The measure thereof *is* longer

proverb. It seems to have been a settled opinion that man could not find out the Almighty to perfection by his own powers—a sentiment, which is as true now, as it was then, and which is of the utmost importance in all our inquiries about the Creator. The sentiment is expressed in a most beautiful manner; and the language itself is not unworthy of the theme. The word "searching," חֵקֶר, is from חָקַר to search, to search out, to examine; and the primary sense, according to Gesenius, lies in searching in the earth by boring or digging—as for metals. Then it means to search with diligence and care. Here it means that by the utmost attention in examining the works of God, it would be impossible for man to find out the Almighty to perfection. All the investigations which have been made of God, have fallen short of the object; and at the present time it is as true as it was in the days of Job, that we cannot, by searching, find him out. Of much that pertains to him and his plans we must be content to remain in ignorance, until we are admitted to the revelations of a higher world—happy and thankful now that we are permitted to know so much of him as we do, and that we are apprized of the existence of ONE INFINITE AND PERFECT MIND. It is an inexpressible privilege to know *any thing* of God; and it is proof of the exalted nature of man, that he is now capable of becoming in any degree acquainted with the divine nature.

8. It is *as high as heaven.* That is, the knowledge of God; or the subject is as high as heaven. The idea is, that man is incompetent to examine, with accuracy, an object that is as far off as the heavens; and that as the knowledge of God *must* be of that character, it is vain for him to attempt to investigate it fully. There is an energy in the Hebrew which is lost in our common translation. The Hebrew is abrupt and very emphatic : " The heights of the heavens !" It is the

language of one looking up with astonishment at the high heavens, and overpowered with the thought that the knowledge of God must be higher even than those distant skies. Who can hope to understand it? Who can be qualified to make the investigation? It is a matter of simple but sublime truth, that God *must be* higher than these heavens; and when we take into view the amazing distances of many of the heavenly bodies, as now known by the aid of modern astronomy, we may ask with deeper emphasis by far than Zophar did. " Can we, by searching, find out God?" ¶ *Deeper than hell.* Heb. " Than Sheol"—משאול. The LXX. render this, "the heaven is high, what canst thou do? And there are things deeper than in Hades —βαθύτερα τῶν ἐν ᾅδου—what dost thou know?" On the meaning of the word *Sheol,* see Notes on Isa. chap. v. 14; xiv. 9. It seems to have been supposed to be as deep as the heavens are high; and the idea here is, that it would be impossible for man to investigate a subject that was as profound as Sheol was deep. The idea is not that God was in Sheol, but that the subject was as profound as the abode of departed spirits was deep and remote. It is possible that the Psalmist may have had this passage in his eye in the similar expression, occurring in Psalm cxxxix.:

If I ascend into heaven, thou art there;
If I make my bed in hell, behold thou art there.

9. *The measure thereof* is *longer than the earth.* The measure of the knowledge of God. The extent of the earth would be one of the longest measures known to the ancients. Yet it is now impossible to ascertain what ideas were attached, in the time of Job, to the extent of the earth—and it is not necessary to know this in order to understand this expression. It is morally certain that the prevailing ideas were very limited, and that a small part of the earth was then known. The general belief seems to have been,

than the earth, and broader than the sea.

10 If ^a he ¹ cut off, and shut up,

or gather together, then who can ² hinder him?

a Re.3.7.　　1 or, *make a change.*
2 *turn him away.*

---

that it was a vast plain, surrounded by water—but how supported, and what were its limits, were evidently matters to them unknown. The earliest knowledge which we have of geography, as understood by the Arabs, represents the earth as wholly encompassed by an ocean, like a zone. This was usually characterized as a " Sea of Darkness;" an appellation usually given to the Atlantic ; while to the Northern Sea was given the name of " The Sea of Pitchy Darkness." Edrisi imagined the land to be floating in the sea, and only part appearing above, like an egg in a basin of water. If these views prevailed so late as the tenth and eleventh centuries of the Christian era, it is reasonable to conclude that the views of the figure and size of the earth must have been extremely limited in the time of Job. On the ancient views of geography, see Notes on chap. xxvi. 7—10, and the maps there, also Murray's Encyclopædia of Geography, Book I., and Eschenberg's Manual of Classical Literature, by Prof. Fiske, Part I. ¶ *And broader than the sea.* What was the idea of the breadth of the sea, which was supposed to surround the earth, it is now wholly impossible to determine. Probably there were *no* ideas on the subject that could be regarded as settled and definite. The ancients had no means of ascertaining this, and they perhaps supposed that the ocean extended to an unlimited extent—or, perhaps, to the far-distant place where the sky and the water appeared to meet. At all events it was an illustration then, as it is now, of a vast distance, and is not inappropriately used here to denote the impossibility of fully understanding God. This illustration would be far more striking then than now. *We* have crossed the ocean ; and we do not deem it an impracticable thing to explore the remotest seas. But not so the ancients. They kept close to the shore. They seldom ventured out of sight of land. The enterprise of ex-

ploring and crossing the vast ocean, which they supposed encompassed the globe, was regarded by them as *wholly impracticable*—and equally so they correctly supposed it was to find out God.

10. *If he cut off.* Marg. *Make a change.* But neither of these phrases properly expresses the sense of the original. The whole image here is probably that of arresting a criminal and bringing him to trial, and the language is taken from the mode of conducting a prosecution. The word rendered " cut off"—יחלף, from חלף—means properly to pass along; to pass on; then to pass *against* any one, to rush on, to assail; and in a remote sense in Piel and Hiphil, to *cause* to pass on or away, that is, to change. This is the sense expressed in the margin. The idea is not that of cutting off, but is that of making *a rush* upon a man, for the purpose of arresting him and bringing him to trial. There are frequent references to such trials in the book of Job. The Chaldee renders this, "if he pass on and shut up the heavens with clouds"—but the paraphrast evidently did not understand the passage. ¶ *And shut up.* That is, imprison or detain with a view to trial. Some such detention is always practised of necessity before trial. ¶ *Or gather together.* Gather together the parties for trial; or rather call the individual into court for trial. The word קהל means properly to call together, to convoke, as a people ; and is used to denote the custom of assembling the people for a trial—or, as we would say, to " call the court," which is now the office of a crier. ¶ *Then who can hinder him?* Marg. *Who can turn him away?* He has all power, and no one can resist him. No one can deliver the criminal from his hands. Zophar here is in fact repeating in another form what Job had himself said (chap. ix. 3, seq.), and the sentiment seems to be proverbial. The idea here is, that if God should

11 For *a* he knoweth vain men : he seeth wickedness also : will he not then consider *it ?*

a Ps.10.14.

12 For [1] vain man would be wise, though man be born *like* a wild ass's colt.

[1] *empty.*

call a man into judgment, and hold him guilty, he could neither answer nor resist him. God is so great ; he so intimately knows the human heart; he has so thorough an acquaintance with all our past sins, that we cannot hope to answer him or escape. Zophar argues on this principle : "God holds you to be guilty. He is punishing you accordingly. You do not feel it so, or suppose that you deserve all this. But he sees your heart, and knows all your life. If he holds you to be guilty, it is so. You cannot answer him, and you should so regard it, and submit."

11. *For he knoweth vain men.* He is intimately acquainted with the heart; he knows men altogether. The word *vain* here (שׁיא), means properly vanity, emptiness, falsehood, a lie, iniquity. " Men of vanity," here may mean men whose opinions are valueless, or it may mean men of deceit, falsehood, hypocrisy. Most probably it means the latter, and the indirect reference may be to such men as Job. The sense is, that God is intimately acquainted with such men. They cannot deceive him, and their wickedness will be found out. ¶ *Will he not then consider* it ? Various ways have been proposed of explaining this. By some it is supposed to mean, " He seeth iniquity, where they do not observe it ;" that is, he perceives it, where men do not themselves. This would express a thought which would accord well with the connection, but it is doubtful whether the Hebrew will bear this construction. By another explanation it is supposed to mean, as in our common version, " Will not God observe it, and bring it to trial? Will he suffer it to pass unnoticed?" This makes good sense, and the Hebrew will admit of this interpretation. But there is another view still, which is preferable to either. According to this it means, that God perceives the iniquity in man, though he does not *seem* to

notice it; see Notes on ver. 6. He appears to pass over a part of it, but he sees it notwithstanding, and is intimately acquainted with all the depravity of the heart. The main reference here is to Job, and the object is to show him that he was guilty, though he had asserted his innocence in so decided a manner. Though he seemed to himself to be innocent, yet Zophar labours to show him that he must be guilty, and that he had seen but a small part of his sins.

12. *For vain man.* Marg. *empty.* נבוב, according to Gesenius, from the root נבב, to bore through, and then to be hollow; metaphorical, *empty, foolish.* The LXX., strangely enough, render this. " but man floats about with words." The Hebrew here means, manifestly, hollow, empty; then insincere and hypocritical. Zophar refers to a hollow-hearted man, who, though he was in fact like a wild ass's colt, attempted to *appear* mild and gentle, and *to have a heart.* The meaning is, that man by nature has a spirit untamed and unsubdued, and that *with* this, he *assumes* the appearance of gentleness and tenderness, and attempts to *appear* as if he was worthy of love and affection. God, seeing this hollow-heartedness, treats him accordingly. The reference here is to men like Job, and Zophar undoubtedly meant to say that he was hollow-hearted and insincere, and yet that he wished to appear to be a man having a *heart,* or, having true piety. ¶ *Would be wise.* Various interpretations have been given to this expression. The most simple and obvious seems to be the true one, though I have not seen it noticed by any of the commentators. The word rendered "would be wise " (ילבב) is from לבב, or לב, meaning *heart,* and the sense here, as it seems to me, is, "vain, hollow, and insincere, man would *wish to seem to have a heart;* " that is, would desire to appear sincere, or pious. Destitute of that truly, and false and hollow

13 If thou prepare *a* thine heart,

a 1 Sa. 7. 3.

he would nevertheless wish to appear different, and would put on the aspect of sincerity and religion. This is the most simple exposition, and this accords with the drift of the passage exactly, and expresses a sentiment which is unquestionably true. Gesenius, however, and some others render it, " *but man is hollow and wanteth understanding; yea, man is born like a wild ass's colt,* signifying the weakness and dullness of the human understanding in comparison with the divine wisdom." Others render it, " but the foolish man becometh wise when the wild ass's colt shall become a man," i. e. *never*, a most forced and unnatural construction. Dr. Good renders it :

                       [son ?
Will he then accept the hollow-hearted per-
Or shall the wild ass-colt assume the man?

Schultens and Dathe translate it :

Let then vain man be wise,
And the wild ass's colt become a man.

¶ *Though man be born.* Though man by nature, or in connection with his birth, is untamed, lawless, rebellious. The wild ass is a striking image of that which is untamed and unsubdued ; comp. Notes on chap. xxxix. 5. Thus Jeremiah describes it, " a wild ass used to the wilderness, that snuffeth up the wind at her pleasure," Jer. ii. 24. Thus it is said of Ishmael (Gen. xvi. 12), " and he will be *a wild man,*" פרא אדם—*a wild ass of a man.* So Job xxxix. 5 :

Who hath sent out the wild ass free ?
Or who hath loosed the bands of the wild ass ?

It is not quite easy for us to understand these allusions, for with us the *ass* is the proverbial image of stupidity, dullness, obstinacy, and immobility. But it was not so with the ancients. It is mentioned as distinguished for velocity, for wildness, and for an unsubdued spirit. Thus Oppian, as quoted by Bochart, Hieroz. Lib. i. c. ix. p. 63, says :

Κραιπνὸν, ἀελλοπόδην, κρατερώνυχον, ὀξύ-
    τατον θεῖν.

Swift, rapid, with strong hoofs, and most fleet in his course. And Aristotle mentions wild asses as τὴν ταχυ-

and stretch out thine hands toward him ;

τῆτα διαφέροντες, *Hist.* Lib. vi. 6 c. 36. So Ælian says of them, ὠκιστοι δραμεῖν, *fleet in their course.* And Xenophon says of them, πολὺ τοῦ ἵππου θᾶττον ἔτρεχον, they run much swifter than a horse. In describing the march of the younger Cyrus through Syria, he says, " The wild ass, being swifter of foot than our horses, would, in gaining ground upon them, stand still and look around ; and when their pursuers got nearly up to them, they would start off, and repeat the same trick ; so that there remained to the hunters no other method of taking them but by dividing themselves into dispersed parties which succeeded each other in the chase ;" comp. Bochart, Hieroz. P. I. Lib. iii. c. xvi. pp. 867—879. A similar statement is made by Ælian (Lib. xiv. cap. 10, as quoted by Bochart), "The wild asses of Maurusius (ὄνα Μαυρούσιοι) are most fleet in their course, and at the commencement of their course they seem to be borne along by the winds, or as on the wings of a bird." " In Persia," says the Editor of the Pictorial Bible, " the wild ass is prized above all other animals as an object of chase, not only from its fleetness, but the delicacy of its flesh, which made it an article of luxury even at the royal tables." " They are now most abundantly found in the deserts of Tartary, and of the countries between the Tigris and the Indus, more particularly in the central parts of the regions thus defined. We know that they were also anciently found in the regions of Mesopotamia, Asia Minor, Syria, and Arabia Deserta ; but from these regions they seem to have been, in the course of ages, almost entirely expelled or extirpated." *Pict. Bib.* on Job xxxix. 5. The idea in the passage before us is, that man at his birth has a strong resemblance to a wild and untamed animal ; and the passage undoubtedly indicates the early belief of the native proneness of man to wander away from God, and of his possessing by nature an insubmissive spirit.

13. *If thou prepare thine heart.* Zo-

14 If iniquity *be* in thine hand, put it far away, and let not wickedness dwell in ^a thy tabernacles.

15 For then shalt thou lift up

a Ps. 101. 3, 4.

thy face without spot ; yea, thou shalt be steadfast, and shalt not fear :

16 Because thou shalt forget *thy* misery, *and* remember *it* as waters *that* pass away :

phar now proceeds to state that if Job even yet would return to God, he might hope for acceptance. Though he had sinned, and though he was now, as he supposed, a hollow-hearted and an insincere man, yet, if he would repent, he might expect the divine favour. In this he accords with the sentiment of Eliphaz, and he concludes his speech in a manner not a little resembling his; see chap. v. 17 —27. ¶ *And stretch out thine hands toward him.* In the attitude of supplication. To stretch out or spread forth the hands, is a phrase often used to denote the act of supplication ; see 1 Tim. ii. 8, and the Notes of Wetstein on that place. Horace, 3 Carm. xxiii. 1, Cœlo supinas si tuleris manus. Ovid, M. ix. 701, Ad sidera supplex Cressa manus tollens. Trist. i. 10, 21, Ipse gubernator, tollens ad sidera palmas ; comp. Livy v. 21. Seneca, Ep. 41 ; Ps. lxiii. 4 ; cxxxiv. 2 ; cxli. 2 ; Ezra ix. 5.

14. *If iniquity* be *in thine hand.* If you have in your possession any thing that has been unjustly obtained. If you have oppressed the poor and the fatherless, and have what properly belongs to them, let it be restored. This is the obvious duty of one who comes to God to implore his favour ; comp. Luke xix. 8.

15. *For then shalt thou lift up thy face without spot.* That is, thy face shall be bright, clear, and cheerful. Thus we speak of a bright and happy countenance. Zophar undoubtedly designs to show what his appearance would be, contrasted with what it then was. Now his countenance was dejected and sad. It was disfigured by tears, and terror, and long continued anguish. But if he would put away iniquity, and return to God, his face would be cheerful again, and he would be a happy man. ¶ *Yea, thou shalt be steadfast, and shalt not fear.* The word rendered "steadfast" (מֻצָק) is from יָצַק, to pour, to pour out, and

is applied to liquids, or to metals which are fused and poured into a mould, and which then become hard. Hence it is used in the sense of firm, solid, intrepid. *Gesenius.* Schultens supposes that the reference here is to metallic mirrors, made by casting, and then polished, and that the idea is, that his face would shine like such a mirror. But it may be doubted whether this interpretation is not too refined. The other and more common explanation well suits the sense, and should probably be retained.

16. And *remember* it *as waters that pass away.* As calamity that has completely gone by, or that has rolled on and will return no more. The comparison is beautiful. The water of the river is borne by us, and returns no more. The rough, the swollen, the turbid stream, we remember as it foamed and dashed along, threatening to sweep every thing away ; but it went swiftly by, and will never come back. So with afflictions. They are soon gone. The most intense pain soon subsides. The days of sorrow pass quickly away. There is an outer limit of suffering, and even ingenuity cannot prolong it far. The man disgraced, and whose life is a burden, will soon die. On the cheeks of the solitary prisoner doomed to the dungeon for life, a "mortal paleness" will soon settle down, and the comforts of approaching death will soothe the anguish of his sad heart. The rack of torture cheats itself of its own purpose, and the exhausted sufferer is released. "The excess [of grief] makes it soon mortal." "No sorrow but killed itself much sooner." *Shakspeare.* When we look back upon our sorrows, it is like thinking of the stream that was so much swollen, and was so impetuous. Its waters rolled on, and they come not back again ; and there is a kind of pleasure in thinking of that time of danger, of that flood that was then so fearful, and that has

17 And *thine* age shall [1] be clearer than the noon-day; thou shalt shine [a] forth, thou shalt be as the morning.

18 And thou shalt be secure, because there is hope; yea, thou shalt dig *about thee, and* thou shalt take thy rest in safety.

1 *arise above the noon-day.*
a Pr.4.18; Is.58.8,10.

19 Also thou shalt lie down, and none shall make *thee* afraid; yea, many [2] shall make suit unto thee.

20 But the eyes [b] of the wicked shall fail, and [3] they shall not escape, and their [c] hope *shall be as* [4] the giving up of the ghost.

2 *intreat thy face.*　b De.28.65.
3 *flight shall perish from them.*　c Pr.11.7.
4 or, *a puff of breath.*

now swept on to come back no more. So there is a kind of peaceful joy in thinking of the days of sorrow that are now fled for ever; in the assurance that those sad times will never, never recur again.

17. *And thine age.* Thy life. This does not mean old age, but the idea is, that his *life* would be cheerful and happy. ¶ *Clearer than the noon-day.* Marg. *Arise above the noon-day.* The margin is a literal rendering; but the sense is clear in the text. The idea is, that the remainder of his life would be bright as the sun if he would return to God. ¶ *Thou shalt shine forth.* Or rather, "thou art now in darkness, but thou shalt be as the morning." The word here used—תעופה is from עוף, to cover—as with wings, to fly, to cover with darkness. In no instance does it mean to shine, or to be clear and bright; and why our translators attached that idea to it, it is now difficult to conjecture. The Chaldee and Syriac read the word as a noun, and render the passage, "and thy *darkness* shall be as the aurora." The Vulgate renders it, "and meridian splendour, as it were, shall arise upon thee at the evening." The LXX., "and thy prayer shall be like the morning star, and life shall rise upon thee from noon-day." The sense in the Hebrew is plain. He was then in darkness. Clouds and calamities were round about him, but if he would return to God, he would be permitted to enjoy a bright day of prosperity. Such a day would return to him like the morning after a long and gloomy night.

18. *And thou shalt be secure.* You will feel confident that your prosperity will be permanent, and you will be free from the distressing anxieties and fears which you now have. ¶ *Thou shalt dig* about thee. The Chaldee renders this, "thou shalt prepare for thyself a sepulchre, and shalt lie down in safety." The word here used (חפר) has two significations. It means, (1.) *to dig*—as, *e. g.* a well, and under this signification to search out, to explore; and, (2.) to be ashamed, to blush, Isa. i. 29. According to Gesenius, the latter here is the signification. "Now thou art ashamed, then thou shalt dwell in quiet." *Lex.* So Noyes renders it. Dr. Good translates it, "yea, thou shalt look around;" Rosenmüller, "thou art suffused with shame." This is, probably, the true sense; and the idea is, that though he was now covered with shame, yet he would lie down in peace and safety if he would return to the Lord.

19. *Many shall make suit unto thee.* Many shall come in a suppliant manner to ask counsel and advice. The meaning is, that he would be a man of distinction, to whom many would look for counsel. This was evidently an honour highly valued in the East, and one on which Job had formerly prided himself; see chap. xxix. 7—13.

20. *But the eyes of the wicked shall fail.* That is, they shall be wearied out by anxiously looking for relief from their miseries. *Noyes.* Their expectation shall be vain, and they shall find no relief. *Perhaps* Zophar here means to apply this to Job, and to say to him that with his present views and character, his hope of relief would fail. His only hope of relief was in a change—in turning to God — since it was a settled maxim that the wicked would look for relief in vain. This *assumption* that he was a wicked man, must have been among the most trying things that Job had

CHAPTER XII.

ANALYSIS OF CHAPTERS XII. XIII. XIV.

THESE three chapters, which comprise the reply of Job to the speech of Zophar, and in general to what had been advanced by his friends, embrace the following points :—

I. He commences the reply with a severe sarcasm—the first in which he had indulged—on the superiority which they assumed. They were "*the people*," he said, and wisdom would die with them, chap. xii. 2.

II. He affirms that he understood the points on which they had insisted as well as they ; that they had advanced nothing that was new to him, or which he had not often reflected on ; that by urging these plain maxims and common-place topics, they had done him an unkindness by undervaluing his understanding, and complains that they had added to his sorrows by inflicting on him these truisms, and compelling him to hear sentiments with which he was so familiar, but which they supposed were profound and novel discoveries, chap. xii. 3—5.

III. He then re-affirms his main position (ver. 6), maintaining that the worst of men, so far from receiving the punishment which was their due, were in fact prospered ; and then proceeds to show them what *he* knew of God. They had spoken of his wisdom and power, as if he were ignorant on the subject. He proceeds, therefore, to discourse of the Most High in a manner calculated to make them ashamed of their comparatively obscure and narrow views, and to show that he had reflected on that point much more than they had, chap. xii. 7—25 ; xiii. 1, 2. This part of the discourse may be regarded somewhat as a trial of skill ; or an attempt to show that he could speak of God in strains as sublime as they could, and that the maxims which I e had treasured up were quite as well calculated to exalt God as theirs were. He speaks of the universal sovereignty of God ; says that the knowledge of him is to be learned from the beasts, the earth, and the whole course of events ; admits that his agency is seen every where, but maintains that his dispensations are not in

exact accordance with the character of man, and that men are not treated according to their deserts in this life.

IV. He expresses his earnest desire to transfer his cause to the tribunal of the Almighty. This he wishes because he believes that God would be just, and because his friends were manifestly so severe in their judgments, chap. xiii. 3—13. In the course of this part of the argument, he accuses them of injustice and unkindness, and concludes it by desiring that they would hold their peace. Their arguments, he said, were such as to dishonour God, and to expose them to the divine displeasure, and he counsels them if they would be wise to be silent.

V. In chap xiii. 14—28, he makes his appeal, in the most solemn manner, to God. He urges the most earnest protestations of his innocence, and affirms that it is his intention to trust in God, though he should slay him ; but in connection with this, he remonstrates in the most pathetic manner with God for afflicting him as he was doing.

VI. The argument of Job is closed in chapter xiv. by a description of the shortness of human life, of exquisite beauty. This is a part of his address to God, and is the expression of the deep feelings of his soul. It is full of mingled emotions of fear, and hope, and despondency, exhibiting doubts respecting the future state, with occasionally a slight hope of it, until his mind sinks into utter despondency, and he wishes that he were in the grave. This beautiful chapter contains the following parts, viz. :—

(1.) An affirmation that man is born to trouble, and must soon be cut down, ver. 1, 2.

(2.) Since such must be the lot of man, Job asks why God should afflict him ? Why not suffer him to enjoy his few days here in peace, and let him pass through his brief existence without annoyance ? ver. 3—6.

3 He then adverts with the deepest feeling to the fact that a man when he is dead will not be suffered to live again on the earth, ver. 7—12. A tree when it is cut down will spring up again, and if it were so with man, he might well bear to be afflicted. But he was

to endure. Indeed nothing could be more provoking than to have others *take it for granted* as a matter that did not admit of argument, that he was a hypocrite, and that God was dealing with him as an incorrigible sinner. ¶ *And they shall not escape.* Marg. *Flight shall perish from them.* The margin is a literal translation of the Hebrew. The sense is, escape for the wicked is out of the question. They must be arrested and punished. ¶ *And their hope* shall be as *the giving up of the ghost.* Literally, "the breathing out of the life or soul." Their hope shall leave them as the breath or life does the body. It is like death. The expression does not mean that their hope would always expire *at* death, but that it would certainly expire *as* life leaves the body. The meaning is, that whatever hope a wicked man has of future happiness and salvation, must fail. The time must come when it will cease to comfort and support him.

The hope of the pious man lives until it is lost in fruition in heaven. It attends him in health ; supports him in sickness ; is with him at home ; accompanies him abroad ; cheers him in solitude ; is his companion in society ; is with him as he goes down into the shades of adversity, and it brightens as he travels along the valley of the shadow of death. It stands as a bright star over his grave—and is lost only in the glories of heaven, as the morning star is lost in the superior brightness of the rising sun. Not so the hypocrite and the sinner. His hope dies —and he leaves the world in despair. Sooner or later the last ray of his delusive hopes shall take its departure from the soul, and leave it to darkness. No matter how bright it may have been ; no matter how long he has cherished it ; no matter on what it is founded—whether on his morals, his prayers, his accomplishments, his learning ; if it be not based on true

cut down, and never again while the heavens endured would he be allowed to revisit the earth.

4. He then expresses the earnest wish that God would hide him in the grave, until his wrath should be overpast ; and that then if He would call him forth, he would answer him, and would vindicate himself. Now while thus suffering under the expressions of the divine displeasure, he was unequal to it. God watched him, and as waters wash away stones, and even the mountain is wasted away, so man *must* waste away under long-continued trials. With this language of mingled complaint, remonstrance, despondency and doubt, Job closes the first series of the controversy. He is evidently in deep perplexity. He knows not what to do, or what to think ; but on the whole his language is

conversion, and the promised mercy of God through a Redeemer, it must soon cease to shine, and will leave the soul to the gloom of black despair.

CHAPTER XII.

2. *No doubt but ye are the people.* That is, the only wise people. You have engrossed all the wisdom of the world, and all else are to be regarded as fools. This is evidently the language of severe sarcasm ; and it shows a spirit fretted and chafed by their reproaches. Job felt contempt for their reasoning, and meant to intimate that their maxims, on which they placed so much reliance, were common-place, and such as every one was familar with. ¶ *And wisdom shall die with you.* This is ironical, but it is language such as is common perhaps everywhere. "The people of the East," says Roberts, "take great pleasure in irony, and some of their satirical sayings are very cutting. When a sage intimates that he has superior wisdom, or when he is disposed to rally another for his meagre attainments, he says, ' Yes, yes, you are the man !' ' Your wisdom is like the sea.' ' When you die, whither will wisdom go ?' " In a serious sense, language like this is used by the classic writers to describe the death of eminently great or good men. They speak of wisdom, bravery, piety, or music, as dying with them. Thus Moschus, Idyll. iii. 12.

Ὅττι βίων τέθνηκεν ὁ βώκολος, ἔττι σὺν αὐτῷ
Καὶ τὸ μέλος τέθνακε, καὶ ὤλετο Δωρὶς ἀειδός.

"Bion the swain is dead, and with him song has died, and the Doric muse has perished."

Expressions like these are common. Thus in the "Pleasures of Hope" it is said :

And Freedom shrieked when Kosciusko fell.

that of one who felt that God and man were alike against him, and that he had no comforter.

AND Job answered and said,
2 No doubt but ye *are* the people and wisdom shall die with you.
3 But I have ¹ understanding as well as you ; I ² *am* not inferior to you : yea, ³ who knoweth not such things as these ?

1 *an heart.*   2 *fall not lower than.*
3 *with whom* are *not such as these ?*

3. *But I have understanding as well as you.* Marg. as in the Heb. *an heart.* The word *heart* in the Scriptures is often used to denote the understanding or mind. It seems to have been regarded as the source of that which was called life or soul. Indeed, I do not recollect a single instance in the Scriptures in which the word "*head*" is used, as with us, as the seat of the intellect, or where the distinction is adverted to that is so common with us, between the head and the heart. With us, the heart is the seat of the affections and emotions ; with the Hebrews, it was the seat of understanding, and the σπλάγχνα – the viscera, the bowels, were the seat of the emotions ; see Notes on Isa. xvi. 11. A more correct physiology has taught us that the brain is the organ of the intellect, and we now speak of *the heart* as the seat of the affections. The Romans regarded the *breast* as the seat of the soul. Thus Virgil, speaking of the death of Lucagus by the hand of Æneas, says :

Tum *latebras animæ pectus* mucrone recludit.
Æn. x. 601.

¶ *I* am *not inferior to you.* Marg. *fall not lower than.* This is the literal translation : " I do not fall beneath you." Job claims to be equal to them in the power of quoting the sayings of the ancients ; and in order to show this, he proceeds to adduce a number of proverbial sayings, occupying the remainder of this chapter, to show that he was familiar with that mode of reasoning, and that in this respect he was fully their equal. This may be regarded as a trial of skill, and was quite common in the East. Wisdom consisted in storing up a large amount

4 I am *as* one mocked of his neighbour, who calleth upon God, and he answereth him : the just upright *man is* laughed to scorn.

5 He that is ready to slip with *his* feet *is as* a lamp despised in the thought of him that is at ease.

---

of proverbs and maxims, and in applying them readily and pertinently on all public occasions ; and in this controversy, Job was by no means disposed to yield to them. ¶ *Yea, who knoweth not such things as these?* Marg. *With whom* are *not such as these?* The meaning is, that instead of being original, the sentiments which they advanced were the most common-place imaginable. Job not only said that *he* knew them, but that it would be strange if every body did not know them.

4. *I am* as *one mocked of his neighbour.* There has been considerable variety in the interpretation of this verse. The general sense is, that Job felt himself to be a mere laughing-stock for his neighbours. They treated him as if he were not worth regarding. They had no sympathy for him in his sorrows, and they showed no respect for his opinions. Dr. Good understands this and the following verses as a part of the controversy in which Job proposes to show his skill in debate, and to adduce proverbs after the manner of his friends. But it is more probably an allusion to himself, and is designed to state that he felt that he was not treated with the respect which was due to him. Much difficulty has been felt in understanding the connection. Reiske contends that ver. 2 has no connection with ver. 3, and that ver. 11, 12, should be interposed between them. The connection seems to me to be this : Job complains that he was not treated with due deference. They had showed no respect for his understanding and rank. They had urged the most common-place topics ; advanced stale and trite apothegms, as if he had never heard them ; dwelt on maxims familiar even to the meanest persons ; and had treated him in this manner as if he were a mere child in knowledge. Thus to be approached with vague common-places, and with remarks such as would be used in addressing children, he regarded as

insult and mockery. ¶ *Who calleth upon God, and he answereth him.* This phrase has given occasion to great variety in the interpretation. Umbreit renders it, " I, who once called upon God, and he answered me ;" that is, I, who once was a happy man, and blessed of God. Schultens renders it, " I, who call upon God," *i. e.* for trial, " and am ready to answer him.' Rosenmüller supposes that Job has reference to the assurances of his friends, that if he would call upon God, he would answer him, and that in view of that suggestion he exclaims, " Shall a man who is a laughing-stock to his neighbour call upon God, and will he answer him !" The probable meaning is, that he had been a man who had had constant communion with God. He had been a favourite of the Almighty, for he had lent a listening ear to his supplications It was now a thing of which he might reasonably complain, that a man who had enjoyed such manifest tokens of the divine favour, was treated with reproach and scorn.

5. *He that is ready to slip with* his *feet.* The man whose feet waver or totter ; that is, the man in adversity ; see Prov. xxv. 19. A man in prosperity is represented as standing firm ; one in adversity as wavering, or falling; see Ps. lxxiii. 2.

But as for me, my feet were almost gone ;
My steps had well nigh slipped.

There is much difficulty in this passage, and it has by no means been removed by the labour of critics. The reader may consult Rosenmüller, Good, and Schultens, on the verse, for a more full attempt to illustrate its meaning. Dr. Good, after Reiske and Parkhurst, has offered an explanation by rendering the whole passage thus :

The just, the perfect man is a laughing-stock to the proud,
A derision amidst the sunshine of the prosperous,
While ready to slip with his foot.

6 The tabernacles of robbers prosper, ^a and they that provoke God are secure ; into whose hand God bringeth *abundantly.*

a Ps. 73. 12, &c. Je. 12. 1, &c.

It does not appear to me, however, that this translation can be fairly educed from the Hebrew text, and I am disposed to acquiesce in the more common and obvious interpretation. According to that, the idea is, that a man in adversity, when falling from a high condition of honour, is regarded as an almost extinguished lamp, that is now held in contempt, and is cast away. When the torch was blazing, it was regarded as of value ; when nearly extinguished, it would be regarded as worthless, and would be cast away. So when a man was in prosperity, he would be looked up to as a guide and example. In adversity, his counsels would be rejected, and he would be looked upon with contempt. Nothing can be more certain or more common than the *fact* here adverted to. The rich and the great are looked up to with respect and veneration. Their words and actions have an influence which those of no other men have. When they begin to fall, others are willing to hasten their fall. Long cherished but secret envy begins to show itself ; those who wish to rise rejoice in their ruin, and they are looked upon with contempt in proportion to their former honour, rank, and power. They are regarded as an extinguished torch—of no value, and are cast away. ¶ *In the thought.* In the mind, or the view. ¶ *Of him that is at ease.* In a state of comfort and prosperity. He finds no sympathy from them. Job doubtless meant to apply this to his friends. They were then at ease, and were prosperous. Not suffering pain, and not overwhelmed with poverty, they now looked with the utmost composure on him—as they would on a torch which was burnt out, and which there would be no hope of rekindling.

6. *The tabernacles of robbers prosper.* The tents or dwellings of robbers are safe and secure. This is Job's original proposition, to which he all along adheres. It is, that God does not deal with men in this life

according to their character ; and in support of this he now appeals to the fact that the tents or dwellings of robbers are safe. Arabia would furnish many illustrations of this, which could not be unknown to the friends of Job. The Arabs dwelt in tents, and they were then, as now, wandering, predatory tribes. They lived, to a great extent, by plunder, and doubtless Job could appeal to the observation of his friends for the proof of this. He affirms that so far from dealing with men according to their character, God often seemed to protect the public robber, and the blasphemer of his name. ¶ *Prosper.* They are secure, tranquil, at rest—for so the Hebrew word means. They are not disturbed and broken in upon. ¶ *And they that provoke God.* Or rather, "the tents are secure to those who provoke God." Dr. Good renders it, "and are fortresses to those who provoke God ;" but the true idea is, that the tents of those who provoke God by their conduct are safe. God does not seem to notice them, or to come out in judgment against them. ¶ *Into whose hand God bringeth* abundantly. Dr. Noyes renders this, "who carry their God in their hand ;" but with much less accuracy, as it seems to me, than commonly characterizes his version. Eichhorn renders it in a sense somewhat similar :

Die ihre Faust fur ihre Gottheit achten—

"who regard their fist as their God." And so Stuhlman renders it :

Und wem die Faust fur Gottheit gilt—

" and to whom the fist avails for their God ;" that is, says he, Job means that this is the course of the world. Dr. Good renders it, "of him who hath created all these things with his hand"—still less accurately. In order to this, he is obliged to suppose an error in the text, but without the slightest authority. Jerome renders it as in our version. The LXX., " who provoke the Lord as if there would be

7 But ask now the beasts, and they shall teach thee ; and the fowls of the air, and they shall tell thee ;

8 Or speak to the earth, and it shall teach thee ; and the fishes of the sea shall declare unto thee.

no trial to them—*ἴτασις αὐτῶν*—hereafter ;" which certainly makes sense, but it was never obtained from the Hebrew. Rosenmüller renders it, "who have their own hand, i. e. *power for God ;*" a description, says he, of a wicked and violent man who thinks it right for him to do as he pleases. It seems to me, however, that the common interpretation, which is the most simple, is most in accordance with the Hebrew, and with the drift of the passage. According to this it means, that there is security to the man who lives to provoke that God who is constantly bringing to him in abundance the tokens of kindness. This is the fact on which Job is insisting—that God does not treat men in this world according to their real character, but that the wicked are prospered and the righteous are afflicted.

7. *But ask now the beasts.* Rosenmüller supposes that this appeal to the inferior creation should be regarded as connected with ver. 3, and that the intermediate verses are parenthetic. Zophar had spoken with considerable parade of the wisdom of God. He had said (chap. xi. 7, seq.) that the knowledge of God was higher than the heavens, and had professed (ver. 6) to have himself exalted views of the Most High.   In reply to this, Job says that the views which Zophar had expressed, were the most commonplace imaginable. He need not pretend to be acquainted with the more exalted works of God, or appeal to them as if his knowledge corresponded with them.   Even the lower creation —the brutes—the earth—the fishes— could teach him knowledge which he had not now. Even from their nature, properties, and modes of life, higher views might he obtained than Zophar had.   Others suppose, that the meaning is, that in the distribution of happiness, God is so far from observing moral relations, that even among the lower animals, the rapacious and the violent are prospered, and the gentle

and the innocent are the victims. Lions, wolves, and panthers are prospered—the lamb, the kid, the gazelle, are the victims. Either of these views may suit the connection, though the latter seems to me to be the more probable interpretation.   The object of Job is to show that rewards and punishments are not distributed according to character.   This was so plain in his view as scarcely to admit of argument.   It was seen all over the world not only among men, but even in the brute creation.   Every where the strong prey upon the weak ; the fierce upon the tame ; the violent upon the timid.   Yet God does not come forth to destroy the lion and the hyæna, or to deliver the lamb and the gazelle from their grasp.   Like robbers (ver. 6),—lions, panthers, and wolves prowl upon the earth ; and the eagle and the vulture from the air pounce upon the defenceless, and the great robbers of the deep prey upon the feeble, and still are prospered.   What a striking illustration of the course of events among men, and of the relative con dition of the righteous and the wicked. Nothing could be more pertinent to the design of Job than this appeal, and nothing was more in accordance with the whole structure of the argument in the poem, where wisdom is seen mainly to consist in the result of careful observation. ¶ *And they shall teach thee.*   Shall teach thee that God does not treat all according to their character.   He does not give security to the gentle, the tame, and the innocent, and punish the ferocious, the blood-thirsty, and the cruel. ¶ *And the fowls.*   They shall give thee information of the point under discussion. Those that prey upon others—as the eagle and the vulture—are not exposed at once to the divine displeasure, and the tender and harmless are not protected.   The general principle is illustrated in them, that the dealings of God are not always in exact accordance with character.

8. *Or speak to the earth, and it shall*

9 Who knoweth not in all these, that the hand of the LORD hath wrought this?

10 In whose hand *is* the ¹ soul

1 or, *life.*

of every living thing, and the breath of all ² mankind.

11 Doth not the ear try words? and the ³ mouth taste his meat?

2 *flesh of man.*   3 *palate.*

teach thee. Perhaps this appeal to the *earth* may mean, as Stuhlman supposes, that the same thing is shown in the productions of the earth, as in the case of fierce animals. Noxious weeds and useless plants are more thrifty than the plants which are useful, and the growth of poisonous or annoying things on the earth illustrates the same thing as the dealings of God with men—that his dealings are not in accordance with the real nature of objects. ¶ *And the fishes of the sea.* The same thing is manifested in the sea, where the mighty prey upon the feeble, and the fierce and the ferocious overcome the defenceless. The sentiment is, that it is a great principle which pervades all things, that the ferocious, the strong, the wicked, are often prospered, while the weak, the defenceless, the innocent, the pious, are subject to calamities, and that God does not apportion his dealings to the exact character of his creatures. Undoubtedly Job was right in this, and this general principle might be seen then, as now, to pervade the world.

9. *Who knoweth not in all these.* Who cannot see in all these the proofs of the same divine and sovereign agency? Who cannot see the hand of the same God and the same great principles of administration? The meaning of Job is, that the position which he defends is so plain, that it may be learned from the very earth and the lowest orders of animals which God has made. ¶ *That the hand of the* LORD *hath wrought this.* In this place the original word is ‏יהוה‎—JEHOVAH. On the meaning of the word see Notes on Isaiah, chap. i. 2. The Chaldee also renders it here ‏יה‎—JAH. It is remarkable that this is the only place where the name JEHOVAH occurs in poetical parts of the book of Job, in the printed editions. In chap. xxviii. 28, JEHOVAH is found in some manuscripts, though the word *Adonai* is in the printed copies. Eichhorn,

Einleit. § 644, *Note.* In chap. xii. 9, the word JEHOVAH, though found in the printed editions, is wanting in nine ancient manuscripts. Dr. J. P. Wilson on the "Hope of Immortality," p. 57. The word JEHOVAH constantly occurs in the historical parts of the book. On the argument derived from this, in regard to the antiquity of the book of Job, see the Introduction, § 4. iii. 3.

10. *In whose hand* is *the soul of every living thing.* Marg. *Life.* The margin is the more correct rendering. The idea is, that all are under the control of God. He gives life, and health, and happiness when he pleases, and when he chooses he takes them away. His sovereignty is manifested, says Job, in the inferior creation, or among the beasts of the field, the fishes of the sea, and the fowls of heaven. ¶ *And the breath of all mankind.* Marg. *Flesh of man.* The margin is in accordance with the Hebrew. The meaning is, that man is subjected to the same laws as the rest of the creation. God is a sovereign, and the same great principles of administration may be seen in all his works.

11. *Doth not the ear try words?* The *literal* meaning of this, which is evidently a proverbial expression, is plain; but about its bearing here there is more difficulty. The literal sense is, that it is the office of the ear to mark the distinction of sounds, and to convey the sense to the soul. But in regard to the exact bearing of this proverb on the case in hand, commentators have not been agreed. Probably the sense is, that there ought to be a diligent attention to the signification of words, and to the meaning of a speaker, as one carefully tastes his food; and Job, perhaps, may be disposed to complain that his friends had not given that attention which they ought to have done to the true design and signification of his remarks. Or it may mean that man is endowed with the faculty of attending to the nature

12 With the ancient ^{*a*} is wisdom; and in length of days understanding.

13 With ¹ him *is* wisdom and strength, he hath counsel ^{*b*} and understanding.

14 Behold, he breaketh down, and it cannot be built again; he shutteth ² up a man, and there can be no opening.

a chap. 32.7.   1 i. e. *God*.
b Pr.8.14.   2 *upon.*

and qualities of objects, and that he ought to exercise that faculty in judging of the lessons which are taught respecting God or his works. ¶ *And the mouth.* Marg. as in the Heb. חך —*palate.* The word means not merely the palate, but the lower part of the mouth (*Gesenius*), and is especially used to designate the organ or the seat of taste; Ps. cxix. 103; Job vi. 30. ¶ *His meat.* Its food—the word *meat* being used in old English to denote all kinds of food. The sense is, man is endowed with the faculty of distinguishing what is wholesome from what is unwholesome, and he should, in like manner, exercise the faculty which God has given him of distinguishing the true from the false on moral subjects. He should not suppose that all that had been said, or that could be said, must necessarily be true. He should not suppose that merely to string together proverbs, and to utter common-place suggestions, was a mark of true wisdom. He should separate the valuable from the worthless, the true from the false, and the wholesome from the injurious. Job complains that his friends had not done this. They had shown no power of discrimination or selection. They had uttered common-place apothegms, and they gathered adages of former times, without any discrimination, and had urged them in their arguments against him, whether pertinent or not. It was by this kind of irrelevant and miscellaneous remark that he felt that he had been mocked by his friends, ver. 4.

12. *With the ancient is wisdom.* With the aged. The word ישיש here used, means an old man, one gray-headed. It is used chiefly in poetry, and is commonly employed in the sense of one who is decrepit by age. It is rendered *very aged* in Job xv. 10; "*him that stooped for age.*" 2 Chron. xxxvi. 17; "*very old,*" Job

xxxii. 6; and *the aged,* Job xxix. 8. The LXX. render it, Ἐν πολλῷ χρόνῳ *in much time.* The sense is, that wisdom might be expected to be found with the man who had had a long opportunity to observe the course of events; who had conversed with a former generation, and who had had time for personal reflection. This was in accordance with the ancient Oriental views, where knowledge was imparted mainly by tradition, and where wisdom depended much on the opportunity of personal observation; comp. chap. xxxii. 7.

13. *With him is wisdom.* Marg. correctly, "*God.*" However much wisdom there may seem to be with aged men, yet the true wisdom—that which was supreme and worthy of the name—was to be found in God alone. The object of Job was to lead the thoughts up to God, and to bring his friends to a contemplation of the wisdom which he manifests in his works. Accordingly he goes on in the remainder of this chapter to state some of the illustrations of wisdom and power which God had exhibited, and particularly to show that he was a sovereign, and did his pleasure every where. He made all things; he sustains all things; he reverses the condition of men at his pleasure; he sets up whom he pleases, and when he chooses he casts them down. His works are contrary in many respects to what we should anticipate; and the sense of all is, that God was a holy and a righteous sovereign, and that such were the reverses under his administration that we could not argue that he treated all according to their character on earth.

14. *Behold, he breaketh down.* None can repair what he pulls down. Cities and towns he can devote to ruin by fire, or earthquake, or the pestilence, and so completely destroy them that they can never be rebuilt. *We may* now refer to such illustrations as So-

15 Behold, he withholdeth the waters, and they dry up ; also he sendeth them out, and they overturn the earth.

16 With him *is* strength and wisdom : the deceived *a* and the deceiver *are* his.

17 He leadeth counsellors away spoiled, and maketh the judges *b* fools.

18 He looseth the bond of kings, and girdeth their loins with a girdle.

a Eze.14.9.   b Is.19.13.

---

dom, Babylon, Petra, Tyre, Herculaneum, and Pompeii, as full proof of what is here affirmed. ¶ *He shutteth up a man.* He can shut up a man in such difficulties and straits that he cannot extricate himself; see chap. xi. 10. The Chaldee renders this, "he shuts up a man in the grave (בקבר־א) and it cannot be opened." But the more correct idea is, that God has complete control over a man, and that he can so hedge up his way that he cannot help himself.

15. *He withholdeth the waters.* From the clouds and springs. He has control over the rains and the fountains ; and when these are withheld, rivers and lakes become dry. The Syriac renders this, — *if he rebuke the waters,* supposing that there might perhaps be an allusion to the drying up of the Red Sea, or the formation of a passage for the Israelites. But it is remarkable that in the argument here there is no allusion to any *historical* fact, not to the flood, or to the destruction of Sodom and Gomorrah, or to the passage through the Red Sea, though these occurrences would have furnished so appropriate illustrations of the points under discussion. Is it to be inferred that Job had never heard of any of those events? Or may it have been that the lessons which they were adapted to teach had been actually embodied in the proverbs which he was using, and furnished well-known illustrations or the *basis* of such apothegms? ¶ *He sendeth them out, and they overturn the earth.* Such inundations may have occurred in the swollen torrents of Arabia, and indeed are so common everywhere as to furnish a striking illustration of the power and sovereign agency of God.

16. *The deceived and the deceiver*

are *his.* This is designed to teach that all classes of men are under his control. All are dependent on him, and all are subject to him. He has power to keep them, and he can destroy them when he pleases. Dr. Good supposes that Job refers here to himself and his friends who had beguiled him into expressions of impatience and complaint. But it is more probably a *general* declaration that all classes of men were under the control of God.

17. *He leadeth counsellors away spoiled.* Plundered or captive. That is, the counsels of wise and great men do not avail against God. Statesmen who promised themselves victory as the result of their plans he disappoints, and leads away into captivity. The object of this is to show that God is superior over all, and also that men are not dealt with in exact accordance with their character and rank. God is a sovereign, and he shows his sovereignty when defeating the counsels and purposes of the wisest of men, and overturning the plans of the mighty. ¶ *And maketh the judges fools.* He leaves them to distracted and foolish plans. He leaves them to the adoption of measures which result in their own ruin. He is a sovereign, having control over the minds of the great, and power to defeat all their counsels, and to render them infatuated. Nothing can be clearer than this. Nothing has been more frequently illustrated in the history of nations. In accordance with this belief is the well-known expression :

Quem Deus vult perdere prius dementat.

" Whom God purposes to destroy, he first infatuates."

18. *He looseth the bond of kings*
The bond of kings (מוסר) here means that by which they bind others. Their

19 He *a* leadeth princes away spoiled, and overthroweth the mighty.

20 He removeth *b* away the [1] speech of the trusty, and taketh

away the understanding of the aged.

21 He *c* poureth contempt upon princes, and [2] weakeneth the strength of the mighty.

a Is 45.1.   *b* Is.3.1-3.   [1] *lip of the faithful.*   *c* Da.2.21.   [2] or, *looseth the girdle of the strong.*

power over others he loosens or takes away. ¶ *And girdeth their loins with a girdle.* That is, he girds them with a rope or cord, and leads them away as prisoners. The whole series of remarks here refers to the reverses and changes in the conditions of life. The meaning here is, that the bonds of authority which they imposed on others are unbound, and that their own loins are bound with a girdle, not a girdle of royal dignity and ornament, but such a one as they are bound with who are servants, or who travel. *Pict. Bib.*

19. *He leadeth princes away spoiled.* That is, plundered. The word here rendered "princes" (כהנים) means properly *priests*, and it is usually so rendered in the Scriptures. The ancient Hebrew interpreters suppose that the word sometimes also means *prince.* The Chaldee Paraphrast has not unfrequently so rendered it, using the word רבא to express it ; Gen. xli. 45 ; Ps. cx. 4. In this place, the Vulgate renders it, *sacerdotes;* and the LXX., ἱερεῖς, *priests.* So Luther renders it, *Priester.* So Castellio. It can be applied to princes or statesmen only because *priests* were frequently engaged in performing the functions of civil officers, and were in fact to a certain extent officers of the government. But it seems to me that it is to be taken in its usual signification, and that it means that even the ministers of religion were at the control of God, and were subject to the same reverses as other men of distinction and power. ¶ *And overthroweth.* The word here used (כלף) has the notion of slipping, or gliding. So in Arabic, the word means to slip by, and to besmear ; see Prov. xiii. 6 : "Wickedness overthroweth (תסלף), causes to slip) the sinner ;" comp. Prov. xxi. 12 ; xxii. 12. Here it means to overthrow, to prostrate. The most mighty chieftains cannot stand firm

before him, but they glide away and fall.

20 *He removeth away the speech of the trusty.* Marg. *lip of the faithful.* "He takes away the lip," *i. e.* he takes away the power of giving safe counsel or good advice. The "trusty" or "faithful" here refer to those of age and experience, and on whose counsel men are accustomed to rely. The meaning here is, that their most sagacious anticipations are disappointed, their wisest schemes are foiled. They fail in their calculations of the course of events, and the arrangements of Providence are such that they could not anticipate what was to occur. ¶ *The understanding of the aged.* To whom the young were accustomed to look up with deference and respect. The meaning here is, that they who were accustomed to give wise and sound advice, if left by God, give vain and foolish counsels.

21. *He poureth contempt upon princes.* He has power to hurl them from their thrones, and to overwhelm them with disgrace. ¶ *And weakeneth the strength of the mighty.* Marg. as in Heb. *looseth the girdle of the strong.* The Orientals wore loose flowing robes, which were secured by a girdle around the loins. When they laboured, ran, or travelled, their robes were girded up. But this is common everywhere. Wrestlers, leapers, and runners, put a girdle around them, and are able thus to accomplish much more than they otherwise could. To loosen that, is to weaken them. So Job says that God had power to loosen the strength of the mighty. He here seems to labour for expressions, and varies the form of the image in every way to show the absolute control which God has over men, and the fact that his power is seen in the reverses of mankind. Lucretius has a passage strongly resembling this in the general sentiment :

22 He discovereth *a* deep things out of darkness, and bringeth out to light the shadow *b* of death.

23 He increaseth *c* the nations, and destroyeth them; he enlargeth the nations, and ¹ straiteneth them *again*.

a 1 Co.4.5.   b chap.34.22.   c Ps.107.38.
1 *leadeth in.*   d Da.4.16,33.

24 He taketh way the heart *d* of the chief of the people of the earth, and causeth them to wander in a wilderness *where there is* no way.

25 They grope *e* in the dark without light, and he maketh them to ² stagger like *a* drunken *man*.

e De.28.29.   2 *wander.*

Usque adeo res humanas vis abdita quædam
Obterit; et pulchros fasces, sævasque secures,
Proculcare, atque ludibrio sibi habere, videtur.
                                   Lib. v. 1232.

So from his awful shades, some Power unseen
O'erthrows all human greatness! Treads to dust
Rods, ensigns, crowns—the proudest pomps of state;
And laughs at all the mockery of man!
                                   GOOD.

22. *He discovereth deep things out of darkness.* That is, God discloses truths which are wholly beyond the power of man to discover—truths that seem to be hidden in profound night. This may refer either to the revelation which God was believed to have furnished, or to his power of bringing out the most secret thoughts and purposes, or to his power of predicting future events by bringing them out of darkness to the clear light of day, or to his power of detecting plots, intrigues, and conspiracies. ¶ *And bringeth out to light the shadow of death.* On the meaning of the word rendered "shadow of death," see Notes on chap. iii. 5. It here denotes whatever is dark or obscure. It is rather a favourite expression with the author of this poem (see chap. x. 22; xvi. 16; xxiv. 17; xxxiv. 22; xxxviii. 17), though it occurs elsewhere in the Scriptures. The deepest darkness, the obscurest night, are represented by it; and the idea is, that even from the most dark and impenetrable regions God could bring out light and truth. All is naked and open to the mind of God.

23. *He increaseth the nations, and destroyeth them.* He has entire control over them. The sources of prosperity are in his hand, and at his pleasure he can visit them with famine, pestilence, or war, and diminish their numbers and arrest their prosperity. Dr. Good renders this very

improperly, "He letteth the nations grow licentious;" but the word שׂגא never has this sense. It means, to make great; to multiply; to increase. ¶ *And straiteneth them* again. Marg. *leadeth in.* So the word נחה means. The idea is, that he increases a nation so that it spreads abroad beyond its usual limits, and then at his pleasure *leads* them back again, or *confines* them within the limits whence they had emigrated.

24. *He taketh away the heart.* The word *heart* here evidently means mind, intelligence, wisdom; see Notes on ver. 3. ¶ *Of the chief of the people.* Heb. "*Heads* of the people;" that is, of the rulers of the earth. The meaning is, that he leaves them to infatuated and distracted counsels. By withdrawing from them, he has power to frustrate their plans, and to leave them to an entire want of wisdom; see Notes on ver. 17. ¶ *And causeth them to wander in a wilderness.* They are like persons in a vast waste of pathless sands without a waymark, a guide, or a path. The perplexity and confusion of the great ones of the earth could not be more strikingly represented than by the condition of such a lost traveller.

25. *They grope in the dark.* They are like persons who attempt to feel their way along in the dark; comp. Notes on Isa. lix. 10. ¶ *And he maketh them to stagger like* a drunken man. Marg. *wander.* Their unstable and perplexed counsels are like the reelings of a drunken man; see Notes on Isa. xix. 14; xxiv. 20. This closes the chapter, and with it the controversy in regard to the ability to adduce pertinent and striking proverbial expressions; see Notes on ver. 3. Job had showed them that he was as familiar with proverbs re-

CHAPTER XIII.

L O, mine eye hath seen all *this,* mine ear hath heard and understood it.

2 What ye know, *the same* do I know also ; I *am* not inferior unto you.

3 Surely I would speak to the Almighty, *a* and I desire to reason *b* with God.

4 But ye *are* forgers of lies, ye *are* all physicians of no *c* value.

5 Oh that ye would altogether hold your peace ! and *d* it should be your wisdom.

6 Hear now my reasoning, and hearken to the pleadings of my lips.

7 Will ye speak wickedly *e*

a chap.23.3; 31.35. *b* Is 1.18; Mi.6.2, &c.
c chap.16.2. *d* Pr.17.28 ; Am.5.13.
e chap.32.21,22.

---

specting God as they were, and that he entertained as exalted ideas of the control and government of the Most High as they did. It may be added, that these *are* sublime and beautiful expressions respecting God. They surpass all that can be found in the writings of the heathen ; and they show that somehow in the earliest ages there prevailed views of God which the human mind for ages afterwards, and in the most favourable circumstances, was not capable of originating. These proverbial sayings were doubtless fragments of revealed truth, which had come down by tradition, and which were thus embodied in a form convenient to be transmitted from age to age.

CHAPTER XIII.

1. *Lo, mine eye hath seen all this.* I have seen illustrations of all that I have said, or that you have said about the methods of divine providence.

2. *What ye know,* &c.; see Note on chap. xii. 3.

3. *Surely I would speak to the Almighty.* I would desire to carry my cause directly up to God, and spread out my reasons before him. This Job often professed to desire ; see chap. ix. 34, 35. He felt that God would appreciate the arguments which he would urge, and would do justice to them. His friends he felt were censorious and severe. They neither did justice to his feelings, nor to his motives. They perverted his words and arguments ; and instead of consoling him, they only aggravated his trials, and caused him to sink into deeper sorrows. But he felt if he could carry his cause to God, he would do ample justice to him and his cause. The views which he entertained of his

friends he proceeds to state at considerable length, and without much reserve, in the following verses.

4. *But ye* are *forgers of lies.* The word *lies* here seems to be used in a large sense, to denote sophisms, false accusations, errors. They maintained false positions ; they did not see the exact truth in respect to the divine dealings, and to the character of Job. They maintained strenuously that Job was a hypocrite, and that God was punishing him for his sins. They maintained that God deals with men in exact accordance with their character in this world, all of which Job regarded as false doctrine, and asserted that they defended it with sophistical arguments invented for the purpose, and thus they could be spoken of as "forgers of lies." ¶ *Physicians of no value.* The meaning is, that they had come to give him consolation, but nothing that they had said had imparted comfort. They were like physicians sent for to visit the sick, who could do nothing when they came ; comp. chap. xvi. 2.

5. *Oh that ye would altogether hold your peace !* You would show your wisdom by silence. Since you can say nothing that is adapted to give comfort, or to explain the true state of the case, it would be wise to say nothing ; comp. Prov. xvii. 28 : "Even a fool when he holdeth his peace is counted wise."

7. *Will ye speak wickedly for God?* That is, will you maintain unjust principles with a view to honour or to vindicate God? Job refers doubtless to the positions which they had defended in regard to the divine administration—principles which he regarded as unjust, though they had employed them

254 JOB.

a 2 Co.4.2.

8 Will ye accept his person? will ye contend for God?

professedly in vindicating God. The sense is, that unjust principles ought not to be advanced to vindicate God. The great cause of truth and justice should always be maintained, and even in attempting to vindicate the divine administration, we ought to make use of no arguments which are not based on that which is right and true. Job means to reproach his friends with having, in their professed vindication of God, advanced sentiments which were at war with truth and justice, and which were full of fallacy and sophistry. And is this never done now? Are sophistical arguments never employed in attempting to vindicate the divine government? Do we never state principles in regard to him which we should esteem to be unjust and dishonourable if applied to man? Do not good men sometimes feel that that government must be defended at all events; and when they can see no reason for the divine dealings, do they not make attempts at vindicating them, which are merely designed to throw dust in the eyes of an opponent, and which are known to be sophistical in their nature? It is wrong to employ a sophistical argument on any subject; and in reasoning on the divine character and dealings, when we come, as we often do, to points which we cannot understand, it is best to confess it. God asks no weak or sophistical argument in his defence; still less can he be pleased with an argument, though in defence of his government, which is based on unjust principles. ¶ *And talk deceitfully for him.* Use fallacies and sophisms in attempting to vindicate him. Every thing in speaking of God, should be true, pure, and sound. Every argument should be free from any appearance of sophism, and should be such as will bear the test of the most thorough examination. No honour is done to God by sophistical arguments, nor can he be pleased when such arguments are employed even to vindicate and honour his character.

8. *Will ye accept his person?* That is, will you be partial to him? The language is such as is used in relation to courts of justice, where a judge shows favour to one of the parties on account of birth, rank, wealth, or personal friendship. The idea here is, "will you, from partiality to God, maintain unjust principles, and defend positions which are really untenable?" There was a controversy between Job and God. Job maintained that he was punished too severely; that the divine dealings were unequal and disproportioned to his offences. His friends, he alleges, have not done justice to the arguments which he had urged, but had taken sides with God against *him*, no matter what he urged or what he said. So little disposed were they to do justice to him and to listen to his vindication, that no matter what he said, they set it all down to impatience, rebellion, and insubmission. They assumed that he was wrong, and that God was wholly right in all things. Of this position that God was right, no one could reasonably complain, and in his sober reflections Job himself would not be disposed to object to it; but his complaint is, that though the considerations which he urged were of the greatest weight, they would not allow their force, simply because they were *determined* to vindicate God. Their position was, that God dealt with men strictly according to their character; and that no matter what they suffered, their sufferings were the exact measure of their ill desert. Against this position, they would hear nothing that Job could say; and they maintained it by every kind of argument which was at their command—whether sound or unsound, sophistical or solid. Job says that this was showing *partiality* for God, and he felt that he had a right to complain. We need never show "partiality" even for God. He can be vindicated by just and equal arguments; and we need never injure others while we vindicate him. Our

9 Is it good that he should search you out? or as one man mocketh another, do ye *so* mock *a* him?

a Ga.6.7.

arguments for him should indeed be reverent, and we should *desire* to vindicate his character and government; but the considerations which we urge need not be those of mere partiality and favour. ¶ *Will ye contend for God?* Language taken from a court of justice, and referring to an argument in favour of a party or cause. Job asks whether *they* would undertake to maintain the cause of God, and he may mean to intimate that they were wholly disqualified for such an undertaking. He not only reproves them for a want of candour and impartiality, as in the previous expressions, but he means to say that they were unfitted in all respects to be the advocates of God. They did not understand the principles of his administration. Their views were narrow, their information limited, and their arguments either common-place or unsound. According to this interpretation, the emphasis will be on the word "*ye*"—"will YE contend for God?" The whole verse may mean, "God is not to be defended by mere partiality, or favour. Solid arguments only should be employed in his cause. Such you have not used, and you have shown yourselves to be entirely unfitted for this great argument." The practical inference which *we* should draw from this is, that our arguments in defence of the divine administration, should be solid and sound. They should not be mere declamation, or mere assertion. They should be such as will become the great theme, and such as will stand the test of any proper trial that can be applied to reasoning. There *are* arguments which will "vindicate all God's ways to men;" and to search them out should be one of the great employments of our lives. If ministers of the gospel would always abide by these principles, they would often do much more than they do now to commend religion to the sober views of mankind. No men are under greater temptations to use weak or unsound arguments than they are.

They feel it to be their duty at all hazards to defend the divine administration. They are in circumstances where their arguments will not be subjected to the searching process which an argument at the bar will be, where a keen and interested opponent is on the alert, and will certainly sift every argument which is urged. Either by inability to explain the difficulties of the divine government, or by indolence in searching out arguments, or by presuming on the ignorance and dullness of their hearers, or by a pride which will not allow them to confess their ignorance on any subject, they are in danger of attempting to *hide* a difficulty which they cannot explain, or of using arguments and resorting to reasoning, which would be regarded as unsound or worthless any where else. A minister should always remember that sound reasoning is *as* necessary in religion as in other things, and that there are always *some* men who can detect a fallacy or see through sophistry. With what diligent study then should the ministers of the gospel prepare for their work! How careful should they be, as the advocates of God and his cause in a world opposed to him, to find out solid arguments, to meet with candour every objection, and to convince men by sound reasoning, that God is right! Their work is to *convince*, not to *denounce;* and if there is any office of unspeakable responsibility on earth, it is that of undertaking to be the advocates of God.

9. *Is it good that he should search you out?* Would it be well for you if he should go into an investigation of your character, and of the arguments which you adduce? The idea is, that if God should make such an investigation, the result would be highly unfavourable to them. Perhaps Job means to intimate that, if they were subjected to the kind of trial that he had been, it would be seen that *they* could not bear it. ¶ *Or as one man mocketh another.* The idea here is, "it is pos-

10 He will surely reprove you, if ye do secretly accept *a* persons.

11 Shall not his excellency make

you afraid: *b* and his dread fall upon you ?

12 Your remembrances *are* like

a Ps.82.1,2.

b Je.5.22 ; 10.7,10.

sible to delude or deceive man, but God cannot be deceived. You may conceal your thoughts and motives from man, but you cannot from God. You may use arguments that may impose upon man—you may employ fallacies and sophisms which he cannot detect, but every such effort is vain with God;" comp. Gal. vi. 7.

10. *He will surely reprove you, if ye do secretly accept persons.* If you show partiality, you will incur his disapprobation. This seems to have much of a proverbial cast, and to mean that under no possible circumstances was it right to show partiality. No matter for whom it may be done, it will be displeasing to God. Even if it be in favour of the righteous, the widow, the fatherless, or *of himself*, if there is not a disposition to judge according to truth and evidence, God will frown upon you. No matter who the parties might be ; no matter what their rank; no matter what friendship there might be for one or the other of them, it was never to be assumed that one was right and the other wrong without evidence. The exact truth was to be sought after, and the judgment made up accordingly. Even when God was one of the parties, the same course was to be pursued. His character was capable of being successfully vindicated, and he would not be pleased to have his cause defended or decided by partiality, or by mere favour. Hence he encourages men to bring forth their strong reasons, and to adduce all that can be said against his government and laws. See Notes on Isa. xli. 1—21.

11. *Shall not his excellency.* His exaltation (שׂאֵת from נשׂא to exalt, to lift up), or his majesty, Gen. xlix. 3. ¶ *Make you afraid.* Fill you with awe and reverence. Shall it not restrain you from fallacy, from sophisms, and from all presumptuous and unfounded reasoning? The sense here is, that a sense of the greatness and

majesty of God should fill the mind with solemnity and reverence, and make us serious and sincere ; should repress all declamation and mere assertion, and should lead us to adduce only those considerations which will bear the test of the final trial. The *general* proposition, however, is not less clear, that a sense of the majesty and glory of God should at all times fill the mind with solemn awe, and produce the deepest veneration. See Jer. v. 22 ; x. 7—10; Gen. xxviii. 17. ¶ *And his dread.* The fear of him. You should so stand in awe of him as not to advance any sentiments which he will not approve, or which will not bear the test of examination. Rosenmüller, however, and after him Noyes, supposes that this is not so much a declaration of what *ought* to be, implying that the fear of God *ought* to produce veneration, as a declaration of what actually occurred—implying that they were actually influenced by this slavish fear in what they said. According to this it means that they were actuated only by a dread of what God would do to them that led them to condemn Job without proof, and not by a regard to truth. But the common interpretation seems to me most in accordance with the meaning of the passage.

12. *Your remembrances* are *like unto ashes.* There has been a considerable variety in the interpretation of this verse. The meaning in our common version is certainly not very clear. The Vulgate renders it, Memoria vestra comparabitur cineri. The LXX., Ἀποβήσεται δὲ ὑμῶν τὸ γαυρίαμα ἴσα σποδῷ —your boasting shall pass away like ashes. Dr. Good renders it, "Dust are your stored-up sayings." Noyes, " Your maxims are words of dust." The word rendered *remembrances* (זכּרֹן) means properly *remembrance, memory*, Josh. iv. 7; Ex. xii. 14; then *a memento*, or *record ;* then *a memorable saying, a maxim.* This is

unto ashes, your bodies to bodies of clay.

13 Hold [1] your peace, let me

1 *be silent from me.*

---

alone, that I may speak, and let come on me what *will.*

14 Wherefore do I take my flesh

---

probably the meaning here; and the reference is to the apothegms or proverbs which they had so profusely uttered, and which they regarded as so profound and worthy of attention, but which Job was disposed to regard as most common-place, and to treat with contempt. ¶ Are *like unto ashes.* That is, they are valueless. See Notes on Isa. xliv. 20. Their maxims had about the same relation to true wisdom which ashes have to substantial and nutritious food. The Hebrew here (משלי־אפר) is rather, "are parables of ashes;"—the word משל meaning similitude, parable, proverb. This interpretation gives more force and beauty to the passage. ¶ *Your bodies.* —גביכם Vulg. *cervices.* Sept. τὸ δὲ σῶμα πήλινον—*but the body is clay.* The Hebrew word גב, *gabh,* means something *gibbous* (whence the word *gibbous* is derived), convex, arched; hence the *back* of animals or men, Ezek. x. 12; the boss of a shield or buckler—the *gibbous,* or exterior convex part—Job xv. 26; and then, according to Gesenius, an entrenchment, a fortress, a strong-hold. According to this interpretation, the passage here means, that the arguments behind which they entrenched themselves were like clay. They could not resist an attack made upon them, but would be easily thrown down, like mud walls. Grotius renders it, " Your towers [of defence] are tumuli of clay." Rosenmuller remarks on the verse, that the ancients were accustomed to inscribe sentences of valuable historical facts on pillars. If these were engraved on stone, they would be permanent; if on pillars covered with clay, they would soon be obliterated. On a pillar or column at Alexandria, the architect cut his own name at the base deep in the stone. On the plaster or stucco with which the column was covered. he inscribed the name of the person to whose honour it was reared. The consequence was, that that name became soon obliterated;

his own then appeared, and was permanent. But the meaning here is rather, that the apothegms and maxims behind which they entrenched themselves were like mud walls, and could not withstand an attack.

13. *Hold your peace.* Marg. *Be silent from me* ; see ver. 5. It is possible that Job may have perceived in them some disposition to interrupt him in a rude manner in reply to the severe remarks which he had made, and he asked the privilege, therefore, of being permitted to go on, and to say what he intended, let come what would. ¶ *And let come on me what* will. Any thing, whether reproaches from you, or additional sufferings from the hand of God. Allow me to express my sentiments, whatever may be the consequences to myself. One cannot but be forcibly reminded by this verse of the remark of the Greek philosopher, " Strike, but hear me."

14. *Wherefore do I take my flesh in my teeth.* The meaning of the proverbial expressions in this verse is not very clear. They indicate a state of great danger ; but the exact sense of the proverbs it has been difficult to ascertain. Some have supposed that the phrase " to take the flesh in the teeth," is significant of a state of famine, where a man dying from this cause would cease upon his own flesh and devour it ; others, that it refers to the contentions of voracious animals, struggling for a piece of flesh ; others, that it refers to the fact that what is borne in the teeth is liable to be dropped, and that Job regarded his life as in such a perilous condition. Schultens regards it as denoting that bold courage in which a man exposes his life to imminent peril. He supposes that it is to be taken in connection with the previous verse, as intimating that he would go forward and speak at any rate, whatever might be the result. He translates it, " Whatever may be the event, I will take my flesh in my teeth, and my life in my hand."

in my teeth, and put my life in mine hand?

15 Though *a* he slay me, yet

will I trust in him; but I will [1] maintain mine own ways before him.

1 *prove, or, argue.*

In this interpretation Rosenmüller concurs. Noyes renders it, " I will count it nothing to bear my flesh in my teeth." Good, " Let what may— I will carry my flesh in my teeth ;" and supposes that the phrase is equivalent to saying, that he would incur any risk or danger. The proverb he supposes is taken from the contest which so frequently takes place between dogs and other carnivorous quadrupeds, when one of them is carrying a bone or piece of flesh in his mouth, which becomes a source of dispute and a prize to be fought for. The Vulgate renders it, *Quare lacero carnes meas dentibus meis.* The LXX., " Taking my flesh in my teeth, I will put my life in my hand." It seems to me, that the language is to be taken in connection with the previous verse, and is not to be regarded as an interrogatory, but as a declaration. " Let come upon me any thing—whatever it may be—מה—(ver. 13) on account of that, or in reference to that—על־מה —(ver. 14), I will take my life in my hand, braving any and every danger." It is a firm and determined purpose that he would express his sentiments, no matter what might occur—even if it involved the peril of his life. The word "*flesh*" I take to be synonymous with *life*, or with his best interests ; and the figure is probably taken from the fact that animals thus carry their prey or spoil in their teeth. Of course, this would be a poor protection. It would be liable to be seized by others. It might even tempt and provoke others to seize it : and would lead to conflict and perils. So Job felt that the course he was pursuing would lead him into danger, but he was determined to pursue it, let come what might. ¶ *And put my life in mine hand.* This is a proverbial expression, meaning the same as, I will expose myself to danger. Any thing of value taken in the hand is liable to be rudely snatched away. It is like taking a casket of jewels, or a purse

of gold, in the hand, which may at any moment be seized by robbers. The phrase is not uncommon in the Scriptures to denote exposure to great peril ; comp. Ps. cxix. 109, " My soul is continually in my hand ;" 1 Sam. xix. 5, " For he did put his life in his hand, and slew the Philistine ;" Judges xii. 3, " I put my life in my hands, and passed over against the children of Ammon." A similar expression occurs in the Greek classics denoting exposure to imminent danger—ἐν τῇ χειρὶ τὴν ψυχὴν ἔχει—*he has his life in his hand ;* see Rosenmüller on Ps. cxix. 109. The Arabs have a somewhat similar proverb, as quoted by Schultens, " His flesh is upon a butcher's block."

15. *Though he slay me.* " God may so multiply my sorrows and pains that I cannot survive them. I see that I may be exposed to increased calamities, yet I am willing to meet them. If in maintaining my own cause, and showing that I am not a hypocrite (ver. 16), it should so happen that my sufferings should be so increased that I should die, yet I will do it." The word *slay*, or *kill*, here refers to temporal death. It has no reference to punishment in the future world, or to the death of the soul. It means merely that Job was determined to maintain his cause and defend his character, though his sufferings should be so increased that life would be the forfeit. Such was the extent of his sufferings, that he had reason to suppose that they would terminate in death; and yet notwithstanding this, it was his fixed purpose to confide in God ; comp. Notes on chap. xix. 25—27. This was spoken in Job's better moments, and was his deliberate and prevailing intention. This deliberate purpose expresses what was really the character of the man, though occasionally, when he became impatient, he gave utterance to different sentiments and feelings. We are to look to the prevailing and habitual tenor of

a man's feelings and declared principles, in order to determine what his character is, and not to expressions made under the influence of temptation, or under the severity of pain. On the sentiment here expressed, comp. Ps. xxiii. 4 ; Prov. xiv. 32. ¶ *Yet will I trust in him.* The word here used (יחל) means properly to wait, stay, delay ; and it usually conveys the idea of *waiting* on one with an expectation of aid or help. Hence it means to hope. The sense here is, that his expectation or hope was in God ; and if the sense expressed in our common version be correct, it implies that even *in* death, or *after* death, he would confide in God. He would adhere to him, and would still feel that beyond death he would bless him. ¶ *In him.* In God. But there is here an important variation in the reading. The present Hebrew is לא—*not.* The *keri,* or marginal reading, is ו —*in him.* Jerome renders it as if it were לו—*in ipso,* that is, in him. The LXX. followed some reading which does not now appear in any copies of the Hebrew text, or which was the result of mere imagination : " Though the Almighty, as he hath begun, may subdue me—χειρώσεται—yet will I speak, and maintain my cause before him." The Chaldee renders it, קדמוי אצלי — *I will pray before him;* evidently reading it as if it were לו *in him.* So the Syriac, *in him.* I have no doubt, therefore, that this was the ancient reading, and that the true sense is retained in our common version ; though Rosenmüller, Good, Noyes, and others, have adopted the other reading, and suppose that it is to be taken as a negative. Noyes renders it, " Lo ! he slayeth me, and I have no hope !" Good, much worse," Should he even slay me, I would not delay." It may be added, that there are frequent instances where לא and לו are interchanged, and where the copyist seems to have been determined by the *sound* rather than by a careful inspection of the letters. According to the Masorites, there are fifteen places where לא, *not,* is written for לו, *to him.* Ex. xxi. 8 ; Lev. xi. 21 ; xxv. 30 ; 1 Sam. ii. 3 ; 2 Sam. xvi. 18 ; Ps. c. 4 ; cxxxix. 16 ; Job xiii. 15 ; xli. 4 ; Ezra iv. 2 ; Prov. xix. 7 ; xxvi. 2 ; Isa. ix. 2 ; lxiii. 9. On the other hand, לו is put for לא in 1 Sam. ii. 16 ; xx. 2 ; Job vi. 21. A mistake of this kind may have easily occurred here. The *sentiment* here expressed is one of the noblest that could fall from the lips of man. It indicates unwavering confidence in God, even in death. It is the determination of a mind to adhere to him, though he should strip away comfort after comfort, and though there should be no respite to his sorrows until he should sink down in death. This is the highest expression of piety, and this it is the privilege of the friends of God to experience. When professed earthly friends become cold towards us, our love for them also is chilled. Should they leave and forsake us in the midst of suffering and want, and especially should they leave us on a bed of death, we should cease to confide in them. But not so in respect to God. Such is the nature of our confidence in him, that though he takes away comfort after comfort, though our health is destroyed and our friends are removed, and though we are led down into the valley and the shadow of death, yet still we never lose our confidence in him. We feel that all will yet be well. We look forward to another state, and anticipate the blessedness of another and a better world. Reader, can *you* in sincerity lift the eye toward God, and say to him, " Though Thou dost slay me, though comfort after comfort is taken away, though the waves of trouble roll over me, and though I go down into the valley of the shadow of death, yet I will trust in Thee ;— Thine I will be even then, and when all is dark I will believe that God is right, and just, and true, and good, and will never doubt that he is worthy of my eternal affection and praise?" Such is religion. Where else is it found but in the views of God and of his government which the Bible reveals ? The infidel may have apathy in his sufferings, the blasphemer may be stupid, the moralist or the formalist may be unconcerned ; but that is not to have *confidence in God.* That

16 He also *shall be* my salvation; for an hypocrite *b* shall not come before him.

17 Hear diligently my speech, and my declaration with your ears.

18 Behold now, I have ordered

my cause ; I know that I shall be justified.

19 Who *c is* he *that* will plead with me ? for now, if I hold my tongue, I shall give up the ghost.

a Ps. 27. 1.　　　　*b* Is. 33.14.
c Is.50.8 ; Ro 8.33, 34.

results from religion alone. ¶ *But I will maintain mine own ways before him.* Marg. *prove,* or *argue.* The sense is, I will *vindicate* my ways, or myself. That is, I will maintain that I am his friend, and that I am not a hypocrite. His friends charged him with insincerity. They were not able, Job supposed, to appreciate his arguments and to do justice to him. He had, therefore, expressed the wish to carry his cause directly before God (ver. 3) ; and he was assured that He would do justice to his arguments. Even should he slay him, he would still stand up as his friend. and would still maintain that his calamities had not come upon him, as his friends supposed, because he was a hypocrite and a secret enemy of his Maker.

16. *He also* shall be *my salvation.* See Notes on Is. xii. 2. Literally, " He is unto me for salvation," that is, " I put my trust in him, and he will save me. The opportunity of appearing before God, and of maintaining my cause in his presence, will result in my deliverance from the charges which are alleged against me. I shall be able there to show that I am not a hypocrite, and God will become my defender." ¶ *For an hypocrite shall not come before him.* This seems to be a proverb, or a statement of a general and indisputable principle. Job admitted this to be true. Yet he expected to be able to vindicate himself before God, and this would *prove* that he was not an hypocrite—on the general principle that a man who was permitted to stand before God and to obtain his favour, could not be an unrighteous man. To God he looked with confidence ; and God, he had no doubt, would be his defender. *This fact* would prove that he could not be an hypocrite, as his friends maintained.

17. *Hear diligently my speech.*

That which I *have* made ; that is, the declaration which I have made of my innocence. He refers to his solemn declaration, (ver. 15, 16,) that he had unwavering confidence in God, and that even should God slay him he would put confidence in him. This solemn appeal he wished them to attend to as one of the utmost importance.

18. *I have ordered* my *cause.* Literally. " judgment ? " — משפט. The LXX. render it, " I am near (ἐγγύς εἰμι) to my judgment," or my trial. The meaning may be, that he had gone through the pleading, and had said what he wished in self-vindication, and he was willing to leave the cause with God, and did not doubt the issue. Or more probably, I think, the word עיכתי should be taken, as the word ידעתי is, in the *present* tense, meaning " I now set in order my cause ; I enter on the pleading ; I am confident that I shall so present it as to be declared righteous." ¶ *I know that I shall be justified.* I have no doubt as to the issue. I shall be declared to be an holy man, and not a hypocrite. The word rendered " I shall be justified " (אצדק) is used here in the proper and literal sense of the word *justify.* It is a term of law ; and means, " I shall be *declared* to be righteous. I shall be shown not to be guilty in the form charged on me, and shall be acquitted or vindicated." This sense is different from that which so often occurs in the Scriptures when applied to the doctrine of the justification of a sinner. Then it means, *to treat one* AS IF *he were righteous, though he is personally guilty and undeserving.*

19. *Who* is *he that will plead with me?* That is, " who is there now that will take up the cause, and enter into an argument against me? I have set my cause before God. I appeal now to all to take up the argument against me, and have no fear if they do as to

20 Only do not two *things* unto me : then will I not hide myself from thee.

21 Withdraw *a* thine hand far

a Ps.39.10.   *b* chap.38.3.

from me: and let not thy dread make me afraid.

22 Then call *b* thou, and I will answer: or let me speak, and answer thou me.

the result. I am confident of a sucessful issue, and await calmly the divine adjudication." ¶ *For now, if I hold my tongue, I shall give up the ghost.* This translation, in my view, by no means expresses the sense of the original, if indeed it is not exactly the reverse. According to this version, the meaning is, that if he did not go into a vindication of himself he would die. The Hebrew, however is, "for now I will be silent, and die." That is, " I have maintained my cause, I will say no more. If there is any one who can successfully contend with me, and can prove that my course cannot be vindicated, then I have no more to say. I will be silent, and die. I will submit to my fate without further argument, and without a murmur. I have said all that needs to be said, and nothing would remain but to submit and die."

20. *Only do not two* things *unto me.* The two things which are specified in the following verse. This is an address to God as Job argues his cause before him, and the request is, that he would remove every obstacle to his presenting his cause in the most favourable manner, and so that he may be on equal terms with him. See Notes chap. ix. 34, 35. He was ready to present his cause, and to plead before God, as (ver. 18) he had the utmost confidence that he would be able so to present it as to vindicate himself ; and he asks of God that he would withdraw his hand for a time (ver. 21) and not terrify him (ver. 21), so that he could present his case with the full vigour of his mind and body, and so that he need not be overawed by the sense of the majesty and glory of the Most High. He wished to be free to present his cause without the impediments arising from a deeply distressing and painful malady. He wished to have his full intellectual and bodily vigour restored for a time to him, and then he was confident that he could successfully defend himself. He felt

that he was now enfeebled by disease, and incapacitated from making the effort for self-vindication and for maintaining his cause, which he would have been enabled to make in his palmy days. ¶ *Then will I not hide myself from thee.* From God. I will stand forth boldly and maintain my cause. I will not attempt to conceal myself, or shun the trial and the argument. See chap. ix. 34, 35.

21. *Withdraw thine hand far from me.* Notes chap. ix. 34. The *hand* of God here is used to denote the calamity or affliction which Job was suffering. The meaning is, " Remove my affliction; restore me to health, and I will then enter on the argument in vindication of my cause. I am now oppressed, and broken down, and enfeebled by disease, and I cannot present it with the vigour which I might evince if I were in health." ¶ *And let not thy dread make me afraid.* " Do not so overpower me by thy severe majesty, that I cannot present my cause in a calm and composed manner." See Notes chap. ix. 34. Job felt that God had power to overawe him, and he asked, therefore, that he might have a calm and composed mind, and then he would be able to do justice to his own cause.

22. *Then call thou, and I will answer.* Call me to trial; summon me to make my defence. This is language taken from courts of justice, and the idea is, that if God would remove his calamity, and not overawe him, and would then call on him to make a defence, he would be ready to respond to his call. The language means, " be thou *plaintiff* in the case, and I will enter on my defence." He speaks now to God not as to *a judge* but as *a party,* and is disposed to go to trial. See Notes on chap. ix. 33—35. ¶ *Or let me speak, and answer thou me.* " Let me be the plaintiff, and commence the cause. In any way, let the cause come to an issue. Let me open the

---

23 How many *are* mine iniquities and sins? make me to know *a* my transgression and my sin.

24 Wherefore hidest *b* thou thy face, and holdest me for thine enemy? *c*

a chap.34.32; John 16.8,9.   *b* Ps.102.2.

25 Wilt thou break *d* a leaf driven to and fro? and wilt thou pursue the dry stubble?

26 For thou writest bitter things against me, and makest me to possess the iniquities of my youth.*e*

c La.2.5.   *d* Is.42.3.   *e* Ps.25.7.

cause, adduce my arguments, and defend my view of the subject; and then do thou respond." The idea is, that Job desired a fair trial. He was willing that God should select his position, and should either open the cause, or respond to it when he had himself opened it. To our view, there is something that is quite irreverent in this language, and I know not that it can be entirely vindicated. But perhaps, when the idea of a *trial* was once suggested, all the rest may be regarded as the mere *filling up*, or as language fitted to carry out that single idea, and to preserve the concinnity of the poem. Still, to address God in this manner is a wide license even for poetry. There is the language of complaint here: there is an evident feeling that God was not right; there is an undue reliance of Job on his own powers; there is a disposition to blame God which we can by no means approve, and which we are not required to approve. But let us not too harshly blame the patriarch. Let him who has suffered much and long, who feels that he is forsaken by God and by man, who has lost property and friends, and who is suffering under a painful bodily malady, if he has never had any of those feelings, cast the first stone. Let not those blame him who live in affluence and prosperity, and who have yet to endure the first severe trial of life. *One* of the objects, I suppose, of this poem is, to show *human nature* as it is; to show how good men often feel under severe trial; and it would not be true to nature if the representation had been that Job was always calm, and that he never cherished an improper feeling or gave vent to an improper thought.

23. *How many are mine iniquities and sins?* Job takes the place of the plaintiff or accuser. He opens the cause. He appeals to God to state the catalogue of his crimes, or to bring forward his charges of guilt against him. The meaning, according to Schultens, is, "That catalogue ought to be great which has called down so many and so great calamities upon my head from heaven, when I am conscious to myself of being guilty of no offence." God sorely afflicted him. Job appeals to him to show *why* it was done, and to make a statement of the number and the magnitude of his offences. ¶ *Make me to know.* I would know on what account and why I am thus held to be guilty, and why I am thus punished.

24. *Wherefore hidest thou thy face.* To hide the face, or to turn it away, is expressive of disapprobation. We turn away the face when we are offended with any one. See Notes on Isa. i. 15. ¶ *And holdest me for thine enemy.* Regardest and treatest me as an enemy.

25. *Wilt thou break a leaf driven to and fro?* Job here means to say that the treatment of God in regard to him was like treading down a leaf that was driven about by the wind—an insignificant, unsettled, and worthless thing. "Wouldst thou show thy power against such an object?"—The sense is, that it was not worthy of God thus to pursue one so unimportant, and so incapable of offering any resistance. ¶ *And wilt thou pursue the dry stubble?* Is it worthy of God thus to contend with the driven straw and stubble of the field? To such a leaf, and to such stubble, he compares himself; and he asks whether God could be employed in a work such as that would be, of pursuing such a flying leaf or driven stubble with a desire to overtake it, and wreak his vengeance on it.

26. *For thou writest bitter things against me.* Charges or accusations of severity. We use the word *bitter* now in a somewhat similar sense. We speak of bitter sorrow, bitter cold, &c. The language here is all taken from courts of justice, and Job is carrying

out the train of thought on which he had entered in regard to a trial before God. He says that the accusations which God had brought against him were of a bitter and severe character; charging him with aggravated offences, and recalling the sins of his youth, and holding him responsible for them. Rosenmüller remarks that the word *write* here is a judicial term, referring to the custom of writing the sentence of a person condemned (as in Ps. cxlix. 9; Jer. xxii. 30); that is, decreeing the punishment. So the Greeks used the expression γράφεσθαι δίκην, meaning to declare a judicial sentence. So the Arabs use the word *kitāb, writing*, to denote a judicial sentence. ¶ *And makest me to possess.* Heb. Causest me to inherit— תורישני. He was *heir* to them; or they were now his as a possession or an inheritance. The Vulgate renders it, *consumere me vis*, etc. "thou wishest to consume me with the sins of my youth." The LXX., " and thou dost charge against me"—περιέθηκας. ¶ *The iniquities of my youth.* The offences which I committed when young. He complains now that God recalled all those offences; that he went into days that were past, and raked up what Job had forgotten; that, not satisfied with charging on him what he had done as a man, he went back and collected all that could be found in the days when he was under the influence of youthful passions, and when, like other young men, he might have gone astray. But why should he not do it? What impropriety could there be in God in thus recalling the memory of long-forgotten sins, and causing the results to meet him now that he was a man? We may remark here, (1.) That this is often done. The sins and follies of youth seem often to be passed over or to be unnoticed by God. Long intervals of time or long tracts of land or ocean may intervene between the time when sin was committed in youth, and when it shall be punished in age. The man may himself have forgotten it, and after a youth of dissipation and folly he *may* perhaps have a life of prosperity for many years. But those sins are not forgotten by God. Far

on in life the results of early dissipation, licentiousness, folly, will meet the offender, and overwhelm him in disgrace or calamity. (2.) God has power to recall all the offences of early life. He has access to the soul. He knows all its secret springs. With infinite ease he can reach the memory of a long-forgotten deed of guilt; and he can overwhelm the mind with the recollection of crimes that have not been thought of for years. He can fix the attention with painful intensity on some slight deed of past criminality; or he can recall forgotten sins in groups; or he can make the remembrance of one sin suggest a host of others. No man who has passed a guilty youth can be certain that his mind will not be overwhelmed with painful recollections, and however calm and secure he may now be, he may in a moment be harassed with the consciousness of deep criminality, and with most gloomy apprehensions of the wrath to come. (3.) A young man should be pure. He has otherwise no security of respectability in future life, or of pleasant recollections of the past, should he reach old age. He who spends his early days in dissipation must expect to reap the fruits of it in future years. Those sins will meet him in his way, and most probably at an unexpected moment, and in an unexpected place. If he ever becomes a good man, he will have many an hour of bitter and painful regret at the follies of his early life; if he does not, he will meet the accumulated results of his sin on the bed of death and in hell. Somewhere, and somehow, every instance of folly is to be remembered hereafter, and will be remembered with sighs and tears. (4.) God rules among men. There is a moral government on the earth. Of this there is no more certain proof than in this fact. The power of summoning up past sins to the recollection; of recalling those that have been forgotten by the offender himself, and of placing them in black array before the guilty man; and of causing them to seize with a giant's grasp upon the soul, is a power such as God alone can wield, and

27 Thou puttest my feet also in the stocks, *a* and 1 lookest narrowly

a chap.33.11.　　1 *observest.*

unto all my paths ; thou settest a print upon the 2 heels of my feet.

2 *roots.*

---

shows at once that there *is* a God, and that he *rules* in the hearts of men. And (5.) If God holds this power now, he will hold it in the world to come. The forgotten sins of youth, and the sins of age, will be remembered then. The sinner walks over a volcano. It may be now calm and still. Its base may be crowned with verdure, its sides with orchards and vineyards; and far up its heights the tall tree may wave, and on its summit the snow may lie undisturbed. But at any moment that mountain may heave, and the burning torrent spread desolation every where. So with the sinner. He knows not how soon the day of vengeance may come; how soon he may be made to inherit the sins of his youth.

27. *Thou puttest my feet also in the stocks.* The word rendered *stocks* (ס), denotes the wooden frame or block in which the feet of a person were confined for punishment. The whole passage here is designed to describe the feet as so confined in a clog or clogs, as to preclude the power of motion. Stocks or clogs were used often in ancient times as a mode of punishment. Prov. vii. 22. Jeremiah was punished by being confined in the stocks. Jer. xx. 2 ; xxix. 2,6. Paul and Silas were in like manner confined in the prison in stocks; Acts xvi. 24. Stocks appear to have been of two kinds. They were either *clogs* attached to one foot or to both feet, so as to embarrass, but not entirely to prevent walking, or they were fixed frames to which the feet were attached so as entirely to preclude motion. The former were often used with runaway slaves to prevent their escaping again when taken, or were affixed to prisoners to prevent their escape. The fixed kinds—which are probably referred to here—were of different sorts. They consisted of a frame, with holes for the feet only; or for the feet and the hands; or for the feet, the hands, and the neck. At Pompeii, stocks have been found so contrived that ten prisoners might be

chained by the leg, each leg separately by the sliding of a bar. *Pict. Bible.* The instrument is still used in India, and is such as to confine the limbs in a very distressing position, though the head is allowed to move freely. ¶ *And lookest narrowly unto all my paths.* This idea occurs also in chap. xxxiii. 11, though expressed somewhat differently, " He putteth my feet in the stocks, he marketh all my paths. ' Probably the allusion is to the paths by which he might escape. God watched or observed every way—as a sentinel or guard would a prisoner who was hampered or clogged, and who would make an attempt to escape. ¶ *Thou settest a print upon the heels of my feet.* Marg. *roots.* Such also is the Hebrew — שׁרשׁי רגלי. Vulg. *vestigia.* Sept. "Upon the roots — εἰς δὲ ῥίζας of my feet thou comest." The word שׁרשׁ means properly *root;* then the *bottom,* or the lower part of a thing ; and hence the soles of the feet. The word rendered " settest a print," from חקה, means to cut in, to hew, to hack ; then to engrave, carve, delineate, portray ; then to dig. Various interpretations have been given of the passage here. Gesenius supposes it to mean, " Around the roots of my feet thou hast digged, ' that is, hast made a trench so that I can get no farther. But though this suits the connection, yet it is an improbable interpretation. It is not the way in which one would endeavour to secure a prisoner, to make a ditch over which he could not leap. Others render it, " Around the soles of my feet thou hast drawn lines," *i. e.* thou hast made marks how far I may go Dr. Good supposes that the whole description refers to some method of clogging a wild animal for the purpose of taming him, and that the expression here refers to a mark on the hoof of the animal by which the owner could designate him. Noyes accords with Gesenius. The editor of the Pictorial Bible supposes that it may refer to the manner in which the stocks were

28 And he, as a rotten thing, consumeth, as a garment that is moth-eaten.

CHAPTER XIV.

MAN *that is* born of a woman, *is* [1] of few days, and full *a* of trouble.

1 *short of.*   *a* Ec.2.23.

made, and that it means that a *seal* was affixed to the parts of the plank of which they were constructed, when they were joined together. He adds that the Chinese have a portable pillory of this kind, and that offenders are obliged to wear it around their necks for a given period, and that over the place where it is joined together a piece of paper is pasted, that it may not be opened without detection. Rosenmüller supposes that it means, that Job was confined within certain prescribed limits, beyond which he was not allowed to go. This restraint he supposes was effected by binding his feet by a cord to the stocks, so that he was not allowed to go beyond a certain distance. The *general* sense is clear, that Job was confined within certain limits, and was observed with very marked vigilance. But I doubt whether either of the explanations suggested is the true one. Probably some custom is alluded to of which we have no knowledge now—some mark that was affixed to the feet to prevent a prisoner from escaping without being detected. What that was, I think, we do not know. Perhaps Oriental researches will yet disclose some custom that will explain it.

28. *And he, as a rotten thing, consumeth.* Noyes renders this, " And I, like an abandoned thing, shall waste away." Dr. Good translates it, " Well may he dissolve as corruption." Rosenmüller supposes that Job refers to himself by the word אוה—*he,* and that having spoken of himself in the previous verses, he now changes the mode of speech, and speaks in the third person. In illustration of this, he refers to a passage in Euripides, *Alcestes,* ver. 690. The Vulgate renders it in the first person, *Qui quasi putredo consumendus sum.* The design seems to be, to represent himself as an object not worthy such constant *surveillance* on the part of God. God set his mark upon him; watched him with a close vigilance

and a steady eye—and yet he was watching one who was turning fast to corruption, and who would soon be gone. He regarded it as unworthy of God, to be so attentive in watching over so worthless an object. This is closely connected with the following chapter, and there should have been no interruption here. The allusion to himself as feeble and decaying, leads him into the beautiful description in the following chapter of the state of man in general. The connection is something like this :—" I am afflicted and tried in various ways. My feet are in the stocks ; my way is hedged up. I am weak, frail, and dying. But so it is with man universally. My condition is like that of the man at large, for

" Man, the offspring of a woman,
  Is short-lived, and is full of trouble."

¶ *As a rotten thing,* רקב. The word רקב means rottenness, or *caries* of bones ; Prov. xii. 4 ; xiv. 30 ; Hos. v. 12. Here it means any thing that is going to decay, and the comparison is that of man to any thing that is thus constantly decaying, and that will soon be wholly gone. ¶ *Consumeth.* Or rather *decays,* יבלה. The word בלה is applied to that which falls away or decays, which is worn out and waxes old—as a garment ; Deut. viii. 4 ; Isa. l. 9 ; li. 6. ¶ *As a garment that is moth-eaten.* " As a garment the moth consumes it." Heb. On the word *moth,* and the sentiment here expressed, see Notes on chap. iv. 19.

CHAPTER XIV.

1. *Man that is born of a woman.* see Notes on chap. xiii. 28. The object of Job in these verses, is to show the frailty and feebleness of man. He, therefore, dwells on many circumstances adapted to this, and this is one of the most stirring and beautiful. He alludes to the delicacy and feebleness of the female sex, and says that the offspring of one so frail must himself be frail ; the child of one so feeble

2 He ^a cometh forth like a flow-er, and is cut down: he fleeth also
as a shadow, and continueth not.

a Ps.90.5-10.

---

must himself be feeble. Possibly also
there may be an allusion here to the
prevailing opinion in the Oriental
world of the inferiority of the female
sex. The following forcible lines
by Lord Bacon, express a similar
sentiment:

The world's a bubble, and the life of man
　　Less than a span,
In his conception wretched, from the womb
　　So to the tomb.
Curst from the cradle, and brought up toyears
　　With cares and fears.
　Who then to frail mortality shall trust,
　But limns the water, or but writes in dust.

¶ *Of few days.* Heb. "Brief of
days;" comp. Ps. xc. 10 ; Gen. xlvii.
9. ¶ *And full of trouble;* comp.
Notes on chap. iii. 17. Who cannot
bear witness to this ? How expressive
a description is it of life ! And even
too where life seems most happy ;
where the sun of prosperity seems to
shine on our way, and where blessings
like drops of dew seem to descend on
us, how true is it still that life is full
of trouble, and that the way of man is
a weary way ! Despite all that he can
do—all his care, and skill, and learning
and wealth, life is a weary pilgrimage,
and is burdened with many woes.
" Few and evil have the days of the
years of my pilgrimage been,' said
the patriarch Jacob, and they who
have advanced near the same number
of years with him can utter with deep
emotion the same beautiful language.
Goethe, the celebrated German, said
of himself in advanced age, " They
have called me a child of fortune, nor
have I any wish to complain of the
course of my life. Yet it has been
nothing but labour and sorrow, and I
may truly say that in seventy-five
years I have not had four weeks of
true comfort. It was the constant
rolling of a stone that was always to
be lifted anew. When I look back
upon my earlier and middle life, and
consider how few are left of those that
were young with me, I am reminded
of a summer visit to a watering-place.
On arriving one makes the acquaintance of those who have been already
some time there, and leave the week

following. This loss is painful. Now
one becomes attached to the second
generation, with which one lives for a
time and becomes intimately connected. But this also passes away and
leaves us solitary with the third, which
arrives shortly before our own departure, and with which we have no desire
to have much intercourse."—Rauch's
Psychology, p. 343.

2. *He cometh forth like a flower, and
is cut down.* Nothing can be more
obvious and more beautiful than this,
and the image has been employed by
writers in all ages, but nowhere with
more beauty, or with more frequency
than in the Bible; see Isa. xl. 6 ; Ps.
xxxvii. 2 ; xc. 6 ; ciii. 15. Next to the
Bible, it is probable that Shakspeare
has employed the image with the most
exquisite beauty of any poet :

This is the state of man ; to-day he puts forth
The tender leaves of hope, to-morrow blossoms,
And bears his blushing honours thick upon him;
The third day comes a frost, a killing frost,
And—when he thinks, good easy man, full
　　surely
His greatness is a ripening—nips his root,
And then he falls. Henry viii. Act iii. Sc. 2.

¶ *He fleeth also as a shadow.* Another
exquisite figure, and as true as it is
beautiful. So the Psalmist :

My days are like a shadow that declineth.
　　　　　　　　　　　　Ps. cii. 11.
Man is like to vanity ;
His days are as a shadow that passeth away.
　　　　　　　　　　　　Ps. cxliv. 4.

The idea of Job is, that there is no
substance, nothing that is permanent.
A shadow moves on gently and silently, and is soon gone. It leaves no
trace of its being, and returns no more.
They who have watched the beautiful
shadow of a cloud on a landscape, and
have seen how rapidly it passes over
meadows and fields of grain, and rolls
up the mountain side and disappears,
will have a vivid conception of this
figure How gently yet how rapidly
it moves. How soon it is gone. How
void of impression is its course. Who
can track its way ; who can reach it ?
So man moves on. Soon he is gone ;
he leaves no trace of his being, and
returns no more.

3 And *a* dost thou open thine eyes upon such an one, and bringest *b* me into judgment with thee ?

4 Who ¹ can bring a clean *c thing* out of an unclean ? Not one.

5 Seeing his days *are* determined, the number of his months *are* with thee, thou hast appointed *d* his bounds that he cannot pass.

a Ps.144.3.   b Ps. 143.2.   1 *will give*
c Ps.51.5,10 ; John 3.6.   d ver.14 ; He.9.27

3. *And dost thou open thine eyes upon such an one?* Is one so weak, so frail, so short-lived, worthy the constant vigilance of the infinite God? In Zech. xii. 4, the expression " to open the eyes " upon one, means to look angrily upon him. Here it means to observe or watch closely. ¶ *And bringest me into judgment with thee* Is it equal or proper that one so frail and feeble should be called to a trial with one so mighty as the infinite God? Does God seek a trial with one so much his inferior, and so unable to stand before him ? This is language taken from courts of justice, and the meaning is, that the parties were wholly unequal, and that it was unworthy of God to maintain a controversy in this manner with feeble man. This is a favourite idea with Job, that there was no equality between him and God, and that the whole controversy was, therefore, conducted on his part with great disadvantage ; comp. Notes on chap. ix. 34, 35.

4. *Who can bring a clean thing out of an unclean?* This is evidently a proverb or an adage ; but its connection here is not very apparent. Probably, however, it is designed as a plea of mitigation for his conscious frailties and infirmities. He could not but admit that he had faults. But he asks, how could it be expected to be otherwise ? He belonged to a race that was sinful and depraved. Connected with such a race, how could it be otherwise than that he should be prone to evil ? Why then did God follow him with so much severity, and hold him with a grasp so close and so unrelenting ? Why did he treat him as if he *ought* to be expected to be perfectly pure, or as if it were reasonable to suppose he would be otherwise than unholy ? This passage is of great value as showing the early opinion of the world in regard to the native charac-

ter of man. The sentiment was undoubtedly common—so common as to have passed into a proverb—that man was a sinner ; and that it could not be expected that any one of the race should be pure and holy. The sentiment is as true as it is obvious—like will beget like all over the world. The nature of the lion, the tiger, the hyæna, the serpent is propagated, and so the same thing is true of man. It is a great law, that the offspring will resemble the parentage ; and as the offspring of the lion is not a lamb but a young lion ; of a wolf is not a kid but a young wolf, so the offspring of man is not an angel, but is a man with the same nature, the same moral character, the same proneness to evil with the parent. The Chaldee renders this : " Who will give one pure from a man polluted in sin, except God, who is one, and who forgiveth him ?" But this is manifestly a departure from the sense of the passage. Jerome, however, has adopted nearly the same translation. As a historical record, this passage proves that the doctrine of original sin was early held in the world. Still it is true that the same great law prevails, that the offspring of woman is a sinner—no matter where he may be born, or in what circumstances he may be placed. No art, no philosophy, no system of religion can prevent the operation of this great law under which we live, and by which we die ; comp. Notes on Rom. v. 19.

5. *Seeing his days* are *determined.* Since man is so frail, and so short-lived, let him alone, that he may pass his little time with some degree of comfort and then die ; see Notes on chap. vii. 19—21. The word *determined* here means *fixed, settled.* God has fixed the number of his days, so that they cannot be exceeded ; comp. Notes on Isa. x. 23, and Ps. xc. 10. ¶ *The number of his months* are *with thee.*

6 Turn from him, that he may
¹ rest, till he shall accomplish, as
an hireling, his day.

1 cease.

7 For there is hope of a tree, if
it be cut down, that it will sprout
again, and that the tender branch
thereof will not cease.

Thou hast the ordering of them, or they are determined by thee. ¶ *Thou hast appointed his bounds.* Thou hast fixed a limit, or hast determined the time which he is to live, and he cannot go beyond it. There is no elixir of life that can prolong our days beyond that period. Soon we shall come to that outer limit of life, and then we MUST DIE. *When* that is we know not, and it is not desirable to know. It is better that it should be concealed. If we knew that it was near, it would fill us with gloom, and deter us from the efforts and the plans of life altogether. If it were remote, we should be careless and secure, and should think there was time enough yet to prepare to die. As it is, we know that the period is not *very* far distant; we know not but that it may be very near at hand, and we would be always ready.

6. *Turn from him—*שעה. Look away from; or turn away the eyes; Isa. xxii. 4. Job had represented the Lord as looking intently upon him, and narrowly watching all his ways. He now asks him that he would look away and suffer him to be alone, and to spend the little time he had in comfort and peace. ¶ *That he may rest.* Marg. *Cease.* "Let him be ceased from"—ויחדל. The idea is not that of *rest*, but it is that of having God *cease* to afflict him; or, in other words, leaving him to himself. Job wished the hand of God to be withdrawn, and prayed that he might be left to himself. ¶ *Till he shall accomplish—*ירצה. Sept. εὐδοκήσῃ τὸν βίον—"and comfort his life," or make his life pleasant. Jerome renders it, "until his desired day—*optata dies—*shall come like that of an hireling." Dr. Good, "that he may fill up his day." Noyes, "that he may enjoy his day." The word here used (רצה) means properly to delight in, to take pleasure in, to satisfy, to pay off; and there can be no doubt that there was couched under the use of this word the notion of *enjoyment*, or *pleasure.*

Job wished to be spared, that he might have comfort yet in this world. The comparison of himself with a *hireling,* is not that he might have comfort *like* a hireling—for such an image would not be pertinent or appropriate—but that his life was like that of an hireling, and he wished to be let alone until the time was completed. On this sentiment, see Notes on chap. vii. 1.

7. *For there is hope of a tree.* This passage to ver. 12, is one of exquisite beauty. Its object is to state reasons why man should be permitted to enjoy this life. A tree, if cut down, might spring up again and flourish; but not man. He died to rise no more; he is cut down and lives not again. The passage is important as expressing the prevalent sentiment of the time in which Job lived about the future condition of man, and is one that deserves a close examination. The great question is, whether Job believed in the future state, or in the resurrection of the dead? On this question one or two things are clear at the outset. (1.) He did not believe that man would spring up from the grave in any sense similar to the mode in which the sprout or germ of a tree grows up when the tree is cut down. (2.) He did not believe in the doctrine of metempsychosis, or transmigration of souls; a doctrine that was so common among the ancients. In this respect the patriarchal religion stood aloof from the systems of heathenism, and there is not to be found, that I know of, any expression that would lead us to suppose that they had ever embraced it, or had even heard of it. The general sentiment here is, that if a tree is cut down, it may be expected to shoot up again, and another tree will be found in its place—as is the case with the chestnut, the willow, the oak. But Job says that there was nothing like this to happen to man. There was no root, no germ, no seminal principle from which he would be made to live again on the

earth. He was to be finally cut off from all his pleasures and his friends here, and to go away to return no more. Still, that Job believed in his continued existence beyond the grave —his existence in the dark and gloomy world of shades, is apparent from the whole book, and indeed from the very passage before us; see ver. 13 — comp. chap. x. 21, 22. The image here is one that is very beautiful, and one that is often employed by poets. Thus Moschus, in his third Idyl, as translated by Gisborne:

The meanest herb we trample in the field,
Or in the garden nurture, when its leaf
At winter's touch is blasted, and its place
Forgotten, soon its vernal bud renews,
And from short slumber wakes to life again.
Man wakes no more! Man, valiant, glorious, wise,
When death once chills him, sinks in sleep profound.
A long, unconscious, never-ending sleep.

See also Beattie's Hermit:

'Tis night, and the landscape is lovely no more;
I mourn, but ye woodlands, I mourn not for you;
For morn is approaching, your charms to restore,
Perfumed with fresh fragrance, and glittering with dew.
Nor yet for the ravage of winter I mourn;
Kind nature the embryo blossom will save;
But when shall spring visit the mouldering urn?
O when shall it dawn on the night of the grave?

The same image, also, has been beautifully employed by Dr. Dwight, though urged by him as an argument to prove the doctrine of the resurrection:

In those lone, silent realms of night,
Shall peace and hope no more arise?
No future morning light the tomb,
Nor day-star gild the darksome skies?
Shall spring the faded world revive?
Shall waning moons their light renew?
Again shall setting suns ascend,
And chase the darkness from our view?

The feeling of Job here is, that when man was removed from the earth, he was removed finally; that there was no hope of his revisiting it again, and that he could not be employed in the dark abode of departed spirits in the cheerful and happy manner in which he might be in this world of light. This idea is expressed, also, in a most tender manner by the Psalmist:

Wilt thou show wonders to the dead?
Shall the dead arise and praise thee?

Shall thy loving-kindness be declared in the grave?
Or thy faithfulness in destruction?
Shall thy wonders be known in the dark?
And thy righteousness in the land of forgetfulness?   Ps. lxxxviii. 10—12.

And the same feelings were evinced by Hezekiah, the pious king of Israel:

For Sheol cannot praise thee;
Death cannot celebrate thee;
They that go down into the pit cannot hope for thy truth.
The living, the living, he shall praise thee, as I do this day;
The father to the children shall make known thy faithfulness.   Isa. xxxviii. 18, 19.

All these gloomy and desponding views arose from the imperfect conception which they had of the future world. It was to them a world of dense and gloomy shades—a world of night—of conscious existence indeed —but still far away from light, and from the comforts which men enjoyed on the earth. We are to remember that the revelations then made were very few and obscure; and we should deem it a matter of inestimable favour that *we* have a better hope, and have far more just and clear views of the employments of the future world. Yet probably our views of that world, with all the light which we have, are much farther from the reality than the views of the patriarchs were from those which we are permitted to cherish. Such as they are, however, they are fitted to elevate and cheer the soul. We shall not, indeed, live again on the earth, but we shall enter a world of light and glory, compared with which all that is glorious here shall fade away. Not far distant is that blessed world; and in *our* trials we may look to it not with dread, as Job did to the land of shades, but with triumph and joy. ¶ *Will not cease.* Will not fail, or be wanting. It will spring up and live.

8. *Though the root thereof wax old.* Though life becomes almost extinct. The idea is, though the root of the tree be *very old*, yet it does not become wholly lifeless. It is not like an old man, when life goes out altogether. In the very aged root there will be vitality still; but not so in man. ¶ *Though the stock thereof.* The *stump*—literally that which is

8 Though the root thereof wax old in the earth, and the stock thereof die in the ground ;

9 *Yet* through the scent of water it will bud, and bring forth boughs like a plant.

10 But man dieth, and [1] wasteth away : yea, man giveth up the ghost, and where *is* he ?

11 *As* the waters fail from the sea, and the flood decayeth and drieth up :

[1] *is weakened,* or, *cut off.*

---

cut off— זֶגַע. The meaning is, that when the trunk of the tree is cut down and dies altogether, life remains in the root ; but when man falls, life is wholly extinct.

9. Yet *through the scent of water.* The word here rendered *scent* (רִיחַ) means properly the odour or fragrance which any thing exhales or emits ; Cant. ii. 13; vii. 13 ; Gen. xxvii. 27. The idea is very delicate and poetic. It is designed to denote a gentle and pleasant contact—not a *rush* of water —by which the tree is made to live. It *inhales,* so to speak, the vital influence from the water—as we are refreshed and revived by grateful odorifics when we are ready to faint. ¶ *It will bud.* Or, rather, it will *germinate,* or spring up again—יַפְרִֽחַ; see Notes on Isa. lv. 10. ¶ *And bring forth boughs*—קָצִיר. This word usually means a harvest ; Gen. viii. 22 ; xxx. 14 ; xlv. 6. It also means, as here, a bough, or branch; comp. Ps. lxxx. 11 ; Job xviii. 16; xxix. 19. ¶ *Like a plant.* Like a young plant—as fresh and vigorous as a plant that is set out.

10. *But man dieth and wasteth away.* Marg. *Is weakened,* or *cut off.* The Hebrew word (חָלַשׁ) means to overthrow, prostrate, discomfit ; and hence to be weak, frail, or waste away. The LXX. render it 'Ανὴρ δὲ τελευτή-σας ᾤχετο—*man dying goes away.* Herder renders it, "his power is gone." The idea is, he entirely vanishes. He leaves nothing to sprout up again. There is no germ ; no shoot ; no living root ; no seminal principle. Of course, this refers wholly to his living again on the earth, and not to the question about his future existence. That is a different inquiry. The main idea with Job here is, that when man dies there is no germinating principle, as there is in a tree that is cut down. Of the truth of this there can be no doubt ; and this comparison of man

with the vegetable world, must have early occurred to mankind, and hence led to the inquiry whether he would not live in a future state. Other things that are cut down, spring up again and live. But man is cut down, and does not spring up again. Will he not be likely, therefore, to have an existence in some future state, and to spring up and flourish there ? " The Romans," says Rosenmüller, "made those trees to be the symbol of death, which, being cut down, do not live again, or from whose roots no germs arise, as the pine and cypress, which were planted in burial-places, or were accustomed to be placed at the doors of the houses of the dead." ¶ *Man giveth up the ghost.* Expires, or dies. This is all that the word (גָוַע) means. The notion of giving up the spirit or the ghost—an idea not improper in itself—is not found in the Hebrew word, nor is it in the corresponding Greek word in the New Testament ; comp. Acts v. 10.

11. As *the waters fail from the sea.* As the waters evaporate wholly, and leave the bottom wholly dry, so it is with man, who passes entirely away, and leaves nothing. But to what *fact* Job refers here, is not known. The sea or ocean has never been dried up, so as to furnish a ground for this comparison. Noyes renders it, " the lake." Dr. Good, without the slightest authority, renders it, " as the billows pass away with the tides." Herder supposes it to mean that *till* the waters fail from the sea man will not rise again, but the Hebrew will not bear this interpretation. Probably the true interpretation is, that which makes the word rendered *sea* (יָם) refer to a *lake,* or a stagnant pool ; see Notes on Isa. xi. 15 ; xix. 5. The word is applied not unfrequently to a *lake,* as to the lake of Genesareth, Num. xxxiv. 11 ; to the Dead sea, Gen. xiv.

12 So man lieth down, and riseth not: till the heavens *a* be no more, they shall not awake nor be raised out of their sleep.

a Ps.102.26; Is.51.6; 2 Pe.3.10,12; Re.20.11.

3; Deut. iv. 49; Zech. xiv. 8. It is used, also, to denote the Nile, Isa. xix. 5, and the Euphrates, Isa. xxvii. 1. It is also employed to denote the brazen sea that was made by Solomon, and placed in front of the temple ; 2 Kings xxv. 13. I see no reason to doubt, therefore, that it may be used here to denote the collections of water, which were made by torrents pouring down from the mountains, and which would after a little while wholly eva- porate. ¶ *And the flood decayeth.* The river—נהר. Such an occurrence would be common in the parched countries of the East ; see Notes on chap. vi. 15, seq. As such torrents van- ish wholly away, so it was with man. Every vestige disappeared ; comp. 2. Sam. xiv. 14.

12. *So man lieth down, and riseth not.* He lies down in the grave and does not rise again on the earth. ¶ *Till the heavens be no more.* That is, never ; for such is the fair inter- pretation of the passage, and this ac- cords with its design. Job means to say, undoubtedly, that man would never appear again in the land of the living; that he would not spring up from the grave, as a sprout does from a fallen tree; and that when he dies, he goes away from the earth never to return. Whether he believed in a *future* state, or in the future resur- rection, is another question, and one that cannot be determined from this passage. His complaint is, that the present life is short, and that man when he has once passed through it cannot return to enjoy it again, if it has been unhappy ; and he asks, there- fore, why, since it was so short, man might not be permitted to enjoy it without molestation. It does not fol- low from this passage that he believed that the heavens ever *would* be no more, or would pass away. The hea- vens are the most permanent and en- during objects of which we have any knowledge, and are therefore used to

13 Oh that thou wouldest hide me in the grave, that thou would- est keep me secret, until thy wrath be past, that thou wouldest appoint me a set time, and remember me !

denote permanency and eternity ; see Psalm lxxxix. 36, 37. This verse, therefore, is simply a solemn declara- tion of the belief of Job that when man dies, he dies to live no more on the earth. Of the truth of this, no one can doubt—and the truth is as important and affecting as it is un- doubted. If man could come back again, life would be a different thing. If he could revisit the earth to repair the evils of a wicked life, to repent of his errors, to make amends for his faults, and to make preparation for a future world, it would be a different thing to live, and a different thing to die. But when he travels over the road of life, he treads a path which is not to be traversed again. When he neglects an opportunity to do good, it cannot be recalled. When he com- mits an offence, he cannot come back to repair the evil. He falls, and dies, and lives no more. He enters on other scenes, and is amidst the retri- butions of another state. How im- portant then to secure the passing moment, and to be prepared to go hence, to return no more ! The idea here presented is one that is common with the poets. Thus Horace says :

Nobis, cum semel occidit brevis lux,
Nox est perpetua una dormienda.

13. *Oh that thou wouldest hide me in the grave;* comp. Notes on chap. iii. 11, seq. Heb. *in Sheol*—בשאול. Vulg. *in inferno.* Sept. ἐν ᾅδῃ—*in Hades.* On the meaning of the word *Sheol,* see Notes on Isaiah v. 14. It does not mean here, I think, the grave. It means the region of departed spirits, the place of the dead, where he wished to be, until the tempest of the wrath of God should pass by. He wished to be shut up in some place where the fury of that tempest would not meet him, and where he would be safe. On the meaning of this passage, however, there has been considerable variety of opinion among expositors. Many sup- pose that the word here properly

14 If a man die, shall ^a he live *again?* all the days of my appointed

a 1 Ti.4.14—16.

means *the grave,* and that Job was willing to wait there until the wrath of God should be spent, and then that he desired to be brought forth in the general resurrection of the dead. So the Chaldee interprets it of the grave —קבורתא. There is evidently a desire on the part of Job to be hid in some secret place until the tempest of wrath should sweep by, and until he should be safe. There is an expectation that he would live again at some future period, and a desire to live after the present tokens of the wrath of God should pass by. It is probably a wish for a safe retreat or a hiding-place—where he might be secure, as from a storm. A somewhat similar expression occurs in Isa. ii. 19, where it is said that men would go into holes and caverns until the storm of wrath should pass by, or in order to escape it. But whether Job meant the grave, or the place of departed spirits, cannot be determined, and is not material. In the view of the ancients the one was not remote from the other. The entrance to Sheol was the grave; and either of them would furnish the protection sought. It should be added, that the grave was with the ancients usually a cave, or an excavation from the rock, and *such* a place might suggest the idea of a hiding-place from the raging storm. ¶ *That thou wouldest appoint me a set time.* When I should be delivered or rescued. Herder renders this, "Appoint me then a new term." The word rendered "a set time"—חק—means, properly, something decreed, prescribed, appointed; and here an appointed time when God would remember or revisit him. It is the expression of his lingering love of life. He had wished to die. He was borne down by heavy trials, and desired a release. He longed even for the grave; comp. chap. iii. 20—22. But there is the instinctive love of life in his bosom, and he asks that God would appoint a time, though ever so remote, in which he would return to him, and permit him to live again.

time will I wait, till my change ^b come.

b 1 Co.15.51—54.

There is the secret hope of some future life—though remote; and he is willing to be hid for any period of time until the wrath of God should pass by, if he might live again. Such is the lingering desire of life in the bosom of man in the severest trials, and the darkest hours; and so instinctively does man look on even to the most remote period with the hope of life. Nature speaks out in the desires of Job; and one of the objects of the poem is to describe the workings of nature with reference to a future state in the severe trials to which he was subjected. We cannot but remark here, what support and consolation would he have found in the clear revelation which we have of the future world, and what a debt of gratitude do we owe to that gospel which has brought life and immortality to light!

14. *If a man die, shall he live* again? This is a sudden transition in the thought. He had unconsciously worked himself up almost to the belief that man *might* live again even on the earth. He had asked to be hid somewhere—even in the grave—until the wrath of God should be overpast, and then that God would remember him, and bring him forth again to life. Here he checks himself. It cannot be, he says, that man *will* live again on the earth. The hope is visionary and vain, and I will endure what is appointed for me, until some change shall come. The question here "shall he live again?" is a strong form of expressing negation. He will *not* live again on the earth. Any hope of that kind is, therefore, vain, and I will wait until the change come—whatever that may be. ¶ *All the days of my appointed time.* צבאי—my warfare; my enlistment; my hard service. See Notes on chap. vii. 1. ¶ *Will I wait.* I will endure with patience my trials. I will not seek to cut short the time of my service. ¶ *Till my change come.* What this should be, he does not seem to know. It might be relief from sufferings, or it might be happiness in

15 Thou shalt call, and I will answer thee: thou wilt have a desire to the work of thine hands.

16 For ᵃ now thou numberest

a Pr.5.21.

my steps: dost thou not watch over my sin?

17 My transgression *is* sealed up in a bag, and thou sewest up mine iniquity.

---

some future state. At all events, this state of things could not last always, and under his heavy pressure of wo, he concluded to sit down and quietly wait for any change. He was certain of one thing—that life was to be passed over but once—that man could not go over the journey again—that he could not return to the earth and go over his youth or his age again. Grotius, and after him Rosenmüller and Noyes, here quotes a sentiment similar to this from Euripides, *in Supplicibus,* vs. 1080, seq.

Οἴμοι· τί δὴ βροτοῖσιν οὐκ ἔστιν τόδε,
Νέους δὶς εἶναι, καὶ γέροντας αὖ πάλιν; κ. τ. λ.

The whole passage is thus elegantly translated by Grotius:

Proh fata! cur non est datum mortalibus
Duplici juventa, duplici senio frui?
Intra penates siquid habet incommode,
Fas seriore corrigi sententia;
Hoc vita non permittit; at qui bis foret
Juvenis senexque, siquid erratum foret
Priore, id emendaret in cursu altero.

The thought here expressed cannot but occur to every reflecting mind. There is no one who has not felt that he could correct the errors and follies of his life, if he were permitted to live it over again. But there is a good reason why it should not be so. What a world would this be if man *knew* that he might return and repair the evils of his course by living it over again! How securely in sin would he live! How little would he be restrained! How little concerned to be prepared for the life to come! God has, therefore, wisely and kindly put this out of the question; and there is scarcely any safeguard of virtue more firm than this fact. We may also observe that the feelings here expressed by Job are the appropriate expressions of a pious heart. Man *should* wait patiently in trial till his change comes. To the friend of God those sorrows will be brief. A change will soon come—the last change—and a change for the better. Beyond that, there shall be no change; none will

JOB I.

be desirable or desired. For that time we should patiently wait, and all the sorrows which may intervene *before* that comes, we should patiently bear.

15. *Thou shalt call, and I will answer thee.* This is language taken from courts of justice. It refers, probably, not to a future time, but to the present. "Call thou now, and I will respond." It expresses a desire to come at once to trial; to have the matter adjusted before he should leave the world. He could not bear the idea of going out of the world under the imputations which were lying on him, and he asked for an opportunity to vindicate himself before his Maker; comp. Notes on chap. ix. 16. ¶ *Thou wilt have a desire to the work of thine hands.* To me, one of thy creatures. This should, with more propriety, be rendered in the imperative, "do thou have a desire." It is the expression of an earnest wish that God would show an interest in him as one of his creatures, and would bring the matter to a speedy issue. The word here rendered, "have a desire" (תִּכְסֹף), means literally to be or become *pale* (from כֶּסֶף, *silver,* so called from its paleness, like the Greek ἄργυρος from ἀργὸς, *white);* and then the verb means to pine or long after any thing, so as to become pale.

16. *For now thou numberest my steps.* Thou dost make strict inquiry into all my conduct, that thou mayest mark my errors, and hold me bound to punishment. The sense is, that God treated him now with severity; and he besought him to have pity on him, and bring him to trial, and give him an opportunity to vindicate himself.

17. *My transgression is sealed up.* The verb rendered *sealed up* (חָתֻם) means to seal, to close, to shut up; see Notes on Isa. viii. 16; comp. Notes on Job ix. 7. It was common with the ancients to use a seal where we use a lock. Money was counted and put into a bag, and a seal was attached to

18 And surely the mountain falling [1] cometh to nought, and the
rock is removed out of his place.

19 The waters wear the stones:

1 *fadeth.*

it. Hence a seal might be put to a
bag, as a sort of certificate of the
amount, and to save the necessity of
counting it again. ¶ *In a bag*—בצרור.
So Jerome, *in sacculo.* So the LXX,
ἐν βαλαντίῳ. The word צרור means
usually *a bundle* (1 Sam. xxv. 29;
Cant. i. 13), or any thing bound up
(comp. Job xxvi. 8; Hos. xiii. 12;
Ex. xii. 34; Prov. xxvi. 8; Isa. viii.
16; Gen. xlii. 35; Cant. i. 13; Prov.
vii. 20); but here it is not improperly
rendered a bag. The idea is, that they
were counted and numbered like money,
and then sealed up and carefully put
away. God had made an accurate estimate of their number, and he seemed
carefully to guard and observe them—
as a man does bags of gold—so that
none might be lost. His sins seemed
to have become a sort of valuable treasure to the Almighty, none of which
he allowed now to escape his notice.
¶ *And thou sewest up mine iniquity.*
Noyes renders this, "and thou addest
unto mine iniquity." Good, "thou
tiest together mine iniquity." The
word here used (טפל) means properly
to patch ; to patch together ; to sew ;
to join together as carpenters do their
work ; and then to devise or forge—
as a falsehood ;—to *join* a malicious
charge to a person. Thus in Ps. cxix.
69, " The proud have *forged a lie* (שקר
טפלו) against me," that is, they have
joined a lie to me, or devised this story
about me. So in Job xiii. 4, " Ye are
forgers of lies." The word does not
occur elsewhere. The Greeks have a
similar expression in the phrase ῥάπτειν
ἔπη—whence the word ῥαψῳδός. The
word here, it seems to me, is used in
the sense of *sewing up* money in a bag,
as well as sealing it. This is done
when there are large sums, to avoid
the inconvenience of counting it. The
sum is marked on the bag, and a seal
affixed to it to authenticate it, and it
is thus passed from one to another
without the trouble of counting. If a
seal is placed on the bag, it will cir-

thou [2] washest away the things
which grow *out* of the dust of the
earth ; and thou destroyest the hope
of man.

2 *overflowest.*

culate for its assigned value, without
being opened for examination. It is
usual now in the East for a bag to contain five hundred piastres, and hence
such a sum is called "a purse," and
amounts are calculated by so many
"purses;" see Harmer, ii. 285, Chardin, and Pict. Bible *in loc.* The sense
here is, that God had carefully numbered his sins, and marked them, and
meant that none of them should escape. He regarded them as very
great. They could now be referred
to in the *gross*, without the trouble of
casting up the amount again. The
sins of a man's past life are summed
up and marked with reference to the
future judgment.

18. *And surely the mountain falling.*
Marg. *Fadeth.* The sense of this
is, that the hope of man in regard to
living again, must certainly fail—as a
mountain falls and does not rise again ;
as the rock is removed, and is not re-
placed; or as the waters wear away the
stones, and they disappear. The hope
of dying man was not like the tree
that would spring up again (ver. 7—
9); it was like the falling mountain,
the wasting waters (ver. 11), the rock
that was removed. The reference in
the phrase before us is, probably, to a
mountain that settles down and disappears—as is sometimes the case in
violent convulsions of nature. It does
not rise again, but is gone to re-ap-
pear no more. So Job says it was of
man. ¶ *And the rock is removed.* An
earthquake shakes it, and removes it
from its foundation, and it is not re-
placed.

19. *The waters wear the stones.* By
their constant attrition they wear away
even the hard rocks, and they disappear, and return no more. The sense
is, that constant changes are going on
in nature, and man resembles those
objects which are removed to appear
no more, and not the productions of
the vegetable world that spring up
again. It is *possible* that there may

20 Thou prevailest for ever against him, and he passeth: thou changest his countenance, and sendest him away.

21 His sons come to honour, and he knoweth *it* not ; and they are brought low, but he perceiveth *it* not of them.

---

also be included the idea here, that the patience, constancy, firmness, and life of any man must be worn out by long continued trials, as even hard rocks would be worn away by the constant attrition of waters. ¶ *Thou washest away.* Marg. *Overflowest.* This is literally the meaning of the Hebrew תשטף. But there is included the sense of washing away *by* the inundation. ¶ *The things which grow out of the dust of the earth.* Herder and Noyes translate this, "the floods overflow the dust of the earth," and this accords with the interpretation of Good and Rosenmüller. So Castellio renders it, and so Luther— *Tropfen flossen die Erde weg.* This is probably the true sense. The Hebrew word rendered "the things which grow out" (ספיח), means properly that which *is poured out*—from ספה, to pour out, to spread out—and is applied to grain produced spontaneously from kernels of the former year, without new seed. Lev. xxv. 5—11; 2 Kings xix. 29. See Notes on Isa. xxxvii. 30. But here it probably means a flood—that which flows out—and which washes away the earth. ¶ *The dust of the earth.* The earth or the land on the margin of streams. The sense is, that as a flood sweeps away the soil, so the hope of man was destroyed. ¶ *Thou destroyest the hope of man.* By death—for so the connection demands. It is the language of despondency. The tree would spring up, but man would die like a removed rock, like land washed away, like a falling mountain, and would revive no more. If Job had at times a hope of a future state, yet that hope seems at times, also, wholly to fail him, and he sinks down in utter despondency. At best, his views of the future world were dark and obscure. He seems to have had at no time clear conceptions of heaven—of the future holiness and blessedness of the righteous; but he anticipated, at best, only a residence in the world of disembodied spirits—dark, dreary, sad;—a world to which the grave was the entrance, and where the light was as darkness. With such anticipations, we are not to wonder that his mind sank into despondency; nor are we to be surprised at the expressions which he so often used, and which seem so inconsistent with the feelings which a child of God ought to cherish. In our trials let us imitate his patience, but not his despondency; let us copy his example in his better moments, and when he was full of confidence in God, and not his language of complaint, and his unhappy reflections on the government of the Most High.

20. *Thou prevailest for ever against him.* Thou dost always show that thou art stronger than he is. He never shows that he is able to contend with God. ¶ *And he passeth.* He cannot stand before thee, but is vanquished, and passes off the stage of being. ¶ *Thou changest his countenance.* Possibly the allusion is to the change produced by death. The countenance that glowed with health and was flushed with beauty and hope—blooming as the rose—is made pale as the lily under the hand of God. What an affecting exhibition of the power of God! ¶ *And sendest him away.* This language *seems* to be that of expectation that man would still live though he was sent away; but all his hopes on earth were blasted, and he went away from his friends and possessions to return no more.

21. *His sons come to honour, and he knoweth it not.* He is unacquainted with what is passing on the earth. Even should that occur which is most gratifying to a parent's heart; should his children rise to stations of honour and influence, he would not be permitted to enjoy the happiness which every father feels when his sons do well. This is suggested as one of the evils of death. ¶ *They are brought low, but he perceiveth it not of them.*

22 But his flesh upon him shall have pain, and his soul within him shall mourn.

CHAPTER XV.

ANALYSIS OF THE CHAPTER.

This chapter contains the second speech of Eliphaz, and begins the second series of the controversy, which continues to the close of chap. xxi. As in the other series of the arguments, Eliphaz is the first speaker. See an account of his character in the Notes on chap. ii. 11, and on chap. iv., v. He is the most argumentative, calm, and reasonable of those who maintain the argument against Job. His speech here consists of two parts. I. The first extends to ver. 13. In this he accuses Job of vanity and unprofitable talk (ver. 2, 3); reproaches him with having cast off the fear of God, and with pursuing a train of argument that was full proof that he had done it (ver. 3); says that the positions which he had maintained about the government of God were ample demonstration of his guilt (ver. 5, 6); accuses him of arrogance and self-confidence, for speaking as if he had been the first man that was born, or was made before the hills, or understood the secret of God (ver. 7, 8); says that they had had more ample opportunities for observation than he had, since there were men among them old enough to be his father (ver. 9, 10); and asks him why he suffers himself to give utterance to expressions like these (ver. 11—13). II. In the second part (ver. 14—35), he gives a graphic description of the misery which in various ways will pursue a wicked man. This part is made up, apparently, either of a string of apothegms, or is a fragment of an ancient poem, which he now quotes as fully sustain-

He is not permitted to sympathize with them, or to sustain them in their trials. This is another of the evils of death. When his children need his counsel and advice, he is not permitted to give it. He is taken away from his family, and revisits them no more.

22. *But his flesh upon him shall have pain.* Dr. Good renders this. "his flesh shall drop away from him." This is evidently a representation of the state of the man after he was dead. He would be taken away from hope and from his friends. His body would be committed to the grave, and his spirit would go to the world of shades. The image in the mind seems to have been, that his flesh would *suffer*. It would be cold and chill, and would be devoured by worms. There seems to have been an impression that the soul would be conscious of this in its distant and silent abode, and the description is given of the grave *as if* the body were conscious there, and the turning back to dust were attended with pain. This thought is that which makes the grave so gloomy now. We think of *ourselves* in its darkness and chilliness. We insensibly suppose that we shall be conscious there. And hence we dread so much the lonely, sad, and gloomy residence in the tomb. The meaning of the word rendered "shall have pain"—באב— is *to be sore, to be grieved, afflicted, sad.* It is by the imagination, that pain is here attributed to the dead body. But Job was not alone in this. We all feel the same thing when we think of death. ¶ *And his soul within him shall mourn.* The soul that is within him shall be sad; that is, in the land of shades. So Virgil, speaking of the death of Lausus, says,

Tum vita per auras
Concessit *mœsta* ad manes, corpusque reliquit.
Æn. x. 819.

The idea of Job is, that it would leave all the comforts of this life; it would be separate from family and friends ; it would go lonely and sad to the land of shades and of night. Job dreaded it. He loved life ; and in the future world, as it was presented to his view, there was nothing to charm and attract. There he expected to wander in darkness and sadness ; and from that gloomy world he expected to return no more for ever. Eichhorn, however, has rendered this verse so as to give a different signification, which may perhaps be the true one.

Nur uber sich ist er betrubt;
Nur sich betrauert er.

" His troubles pertain only to himself ; his grief relates to himself alone. " According to this, the idea is that he must bear all his sorrows alone, and for himself. He is cut off from the living, and is not permitted to share in the joys and sorrows of his posterity, nor they in his. He has no knowledge of any thing that pertains to them, nor do they participate in his griefs. What a flood of light and joy would have been poured on his soul by the Christian hope, and by the revelation of the truth that there is a world of perfect light and joy for the righteous—in heaven ! And what thanks do we owe to the Great Author of our religion—to him who is "the Resurrection and the Life"—that we are permitted to look upon the grave with hearts full of peace and joy !

ing the position that the calamities of Job are proofs of guilt. The argument is, that calamity will overtake the wicked; and that, therefore, when calamities exist, there is proof of guilt that may be measured by the calamity. As Job had been afflicted in an uncommon degree, the inference in the mind of Eliphaz from this principle was unavoidable, that he was a man of uncommon guilt. In illustrating this position, he urges the following considerations: (1.) He repeats the solemn truth which had been communicated to him in the fearful vision which he describes in chap. iv., that man could not be pure before God, and that even the angels are chargeable with folly, ver. 14—16. (2.) He appeals to the fathers, and professes to quote the sentiments of the observing men of former times in proof of what would be the consequences of eminent wickedness, ver. 17--19. (3.) He then states, more particularly, what would be the condition of the guilty man. He would travail in pain; he would be subject to alarms; he would have no security in prosperity; he would be compelled to wander abroad for bread, and trouble and anguish would come upon him, ver. 20—24. (4.) He states as a *reason* for this, that he makes an assault on God, and rushes upon his buckler; he impinges on the great principles of the divine government and law, and he cannot prosper, ver. 25—27. (5.) He then shows that such a man *must* be desolate; he could neither be rich, nor honoured, nor long-lived, ver. 28—30. (6.) And he concludes his discourse by an exhortation not

to trust in vanity, and not to rely on the hope of the hypocrite; for in the midst of his confidence and security he would be cut down before his time—like unripe fruit, or like a fading flower, ver. 31—35. All this was so applicable to the circumstances of Job, and was so obviously designed to be a description of his condition, though his name is not mentioned, that there is no wonder that he replied with so much severity in the following chapter. The conclusions of Eliphaz were the more deeply felt by Job, because they were communicated as the result of long observation, and strengthened by the undisputed maxims of antiquity.

THEN answered Eliphaz the Temanite, and said,

2 Should a wise man utter [1] vain knowledge, and fill his belly with the east wind?

3 Should he reason with unprofitable talk? *a* or with speeches wherewith he can do no good?

4 Yea, thou [2] castest off fear and restrainest [3] prayer before God.

1 *knowledge of wind.*   *a* 1 Ti.6.4,5.
2 *makest void.*   3 or, *speech.*

CHAPTER XV.

2. *Should a wise man.* Referring to Job, and to his claims to be esteemed wise; see chap. xii. 3; xiii. 2, 6. The argument of Eliphaz here is, that the sentiments which Job had advanced were a sufficient refutation of his pretensions to wisdom. A wise man would not be guilty of *mere talk*, or of using language that conveyed no ideas. ¶ *Utter.* Literally, *answer.* It refers to the replies which Job had made to the arguments of his friends. ¶ *Vain knowledge.* Marg. *Knowledge of wind.* So the Hebrew; see chap. vi. 26; vii. 7. The *wind* is used to denote what is unsubstantial, vain, changing. Here it is used as an emblem of remarks which were vain, empty, and irrelevant. ¶ *And fill his belly.* Fill his mind with unsubstantial arguments or sentiments—as little fitted for utility as the east wind is for food. The image is, "he fills himself with mere wind, and then blows it out under pretence of delivering the maxims of wisdom." ¶ *With the east wind* The *east* wind was not only tempestuous and vehement, but sultry, and destructive to vegetation. It passed over vast deserts, and was characterized by great dryness and heat. It is used here to denote a manner of discourse that had in it nothing profitable.

3. *Should he reason with unprofitable talk?* It does not become a man professing to be wise to make use of words that are nothing to the purpose. The sense is, that what Job said amounted to just nothing.

4. *Yea, thou castest off fear.* Marg. *Makest void. Fear* here means the fear or reverence of God; and the idea is, that Job had not maintained a proper veneration or respect for his Maker in his argument. He had defended principles and made assertions which implied great disrespect for the Deity. If those doctrines were true; if he was right in his views about God, then he was not a being who could be reverenced. No confidence could be placed in his government; no worship of such a being could be maintained. Eliphaz does not refer here so much to what was *personal* with Job, as to his *principles.* He does not mean so much to affirm that he himself had lost all reverence for God, as that his *arguments* led to that. Job had maintained that God did not in this life reward and punish men strictly according to their deserts. If this was so, Eliphaz says, then it would be impossible to honour him, and religion and worship would be at an end. The Hebrew word rendered "castest off"—more accurately rendered in the margin "makest void" (רֵפָהַו)—implies this.

5 For thy mouth [1] uttereth thine iniquity, and thou choosest the tongue of the crafty.

6 Thine [a] own mouth condemn-

eth thee, and not I; yea, thine own lips testify against thee.

7 *Art* thou the first man *that*

1 *teacheth.*   a Lu.19.22.

¶ *And restrainest prayer before God.* Marg. *speech.* The Hebrew word (שׂיחָה) means properly *meditation*—and particularly meditation about divine things: Ps. cxix. 97. Then it means *devotion*—as to meditate on divine things is a part of devotion. It may be applied to any part of devotion, and seems to be not improperly rendered *prayer.* It is that devotion which finds utterance in the language of prayer. The word rendered *restrainest*—תִּגְרַע—means to *shave off*—like the beard; then to cut off, to take away, detract, withhold; and the idea here is, that the views which Job maintained were such as *to sap the very foundations of religion.* If God treated the righteous and the wicked alike, the one would have nothing to hope and the other nothing to fear. There could be no ground of encouragement to pray to him. How could the righteous pray to him, unless there was evidence that he was the friend of virtue? How could they hope for his special blessing, if he were disposed to treat the good and the bad alike? Why was it not just as well to live in sin as to be holy? And how could such a being be the object of confidence or prayer? Eliphaz mistook the meaning of Job, and pressed his positions farther than he intended; and Job was not entirely able to vindicate his position, or to show how the consequences stated by Eliphaz could be avoided. *They both wanted the complete and full view of the future state of retribution revealed in the gospel, and that would have removed the whole difficulty.* But I see not how the considerations here urged by this ancient sage of the tendency of Job's doctrine can be avoided, if it be applied to the views of those who hold that all men will be saved at death. If *that* be the truth, then who can fail to see that the tendency must be to make men cast off the fear of God, and to undermine all devotion and prayer? Why should men pray, if all

are to be treated alike at death? How can men worship and honour a being who will treat the good and the bad alike? How can we have confidence in a being who makes no distinction in regard to character? And what inducement can there be to be pious, when all men shall be made as happy as they can be for ever whether they are pious or not? We are not to wonder, therefore, that the system tends every where to sap the foundations of virtue and religion; that it makes no man better; and that where it prevails, it banishes religion and prayer from the world.

5. *For thy mouth uttereth thine iniquity.* Marg. *teacheth.* That is, "your whole argument shows that you are a guilty man. A man who can defend such positions about God cannot be a pious man, or have any proper veneration for the Most High." A man *may* pursue an argument, and defend positions, that shall as certainly show that he is destitute of religion as though he lived an abandoned life; and he who holds opinions that are dishonourable to God, can no more be a pious man than if he dishonoured God by violating his law. ¶ *Thou choosest the tongue of the crafty.* Instead of pursuing an argument with candour and sincerity, you have resorted to miserable sophisms, such as cunning disputants use. You have not showed a disposition to ascertain and defend the truth, but have relied on the arts and evasions of the subtle disputant and the rhetorician. His whole discourse, according to Eliphaz, was a work of mere art, designed to blind his hearers; to deceive them with a favourable opinion of his piety; and to give some plausible, but delusive view of the government of God.

6. *Thine own mouth condemneth thee.* That is, the sentiments which you have uttered show that you cannot be a pious man.

7. Art *thou the first man that was born?* Hast thou lived ever since the

was born? or wast thou made before *a* the hills?

8 Hast *b* thou heard the secret of God? and dost thou restrain wisdom to thyself?

a Ps.90.2 ; Pr.8.25.   b Ro.11.34 ; 1 Co.2.11.

9 What *c* knowest thou that we know not? *what* understandest thou which *is* not in us?

10 With us *are* both the gray-

c chap. 13.2.

creation, and treasured up all the wisdom of past times, that thou dost now speak so arrogantly and confidently? This question was asked, because, in the estimation of Eliphaz and his friends, wisdom was supposed to be connected with long life, and with an opportunity for extended and varied observation; see ver. 10. Job they regarded as comparatively a young man. ¶ *Wast thou made before the hills?* The mountains and the hills are often represented as being the oldest of created objects, probably because they are the most ancient things that appear on earth. Springs dry up, and waters change their beds; cities are built and decay; kingdoms rise and fall, and all the monuments of human skill and art perish; but the hills and mountains remain the same from age to age. Thus in Psalm xc. 2:

Before the mountains were brought forth,
Or ever thou hadst formed the earth and the world,
Even from everlasting to everlasting thou art God.

So in Prov. viii. 25, in the description of wisdom:

Before the mountains were settled,
Before the hills was I brought forth.

So the hills are called "everlasting" (Gen. xlix. 26), in allusion to their great antiquity and permanence. And so we, in common parlance, have a similar expression when we say of any thing that "it is as old as the hills." The question which Eliphaz intends to ask here of Job is, whether he had lived from the creation, and had observed every thing?

8. *Hast thou heard the secret of God?* Literally, "*in* the secret of God hast thou heard"—הבסוד. The word rendered *secret* (סוד) means properly a *couch* or *cushion*, on which one reclines—whether for sleep or at a table, or as a divan. Hence it means a divan, or circle of persons sitting together for familiar conversation, Jer. vi. 11; xv. 17; or of judges, counsel-

lors, or advisers for consultation, as the word *divan* is now used in Oriental countries; Ps. lxxxix. 7; Jer. xxxiii. 18. Then it means any consultation, counsel, familiar intercourse, or intimacy; Ps. lv. 14; Prov. xv. 22. Here God is represented in Oriental language as seated in a *divan*, or council of state: there is deliberation about the concerns of his government; important questions are agitated and decided; and Eliphaz asks of Job whether *he* had been admitted to that council, and had heard those deliberations; and whether, if he had not, he was qualified to pronounce as he had done, on the plans and purposes of the Almighty. ¶ *And dost thou restrain wisdom to thyself?* Having obtained the secret of that council, art thou now keeping it wholly to thyself—as a prime minister might be supposed to keep the purposes resolved on in the divan? "Hast thou listened in the council of Jehovah, and dost thou now reserve all wisdom to thyself?"

9. *What knowest thou that we know not?* What pretensions or claims to wisdom have you which we have not? We have had, at least, equal advantages, and may be *presumed* to know as much as you.

10. *With us* are *both the gray-headed.* That is, *some* of us who are here are much older than thy father; or we express the sentiments of such aged men. Job had admitted (chap. xii. 12), that with the aged was wisdom, and in length of days understanding; and Eliphaz here urges that on that principle he and his friends had a claim to be heard. It would seem from this, that Job was very far from being regarded as an old man, and would probably be esteemed as in middle life. The Targum (Chaldee) refers this to Eliphaz himself and his two friends. "Truly Eliphaz, who is hoary-headed (דקיב), and Bildad, the long-lived (דקשישו), are with us, and

headed *a* and very aged men, much elder than thy father.

11 *Are* the consolations of God

a chap.32.6-9.

Zophar, who is older than thy father." But it is not certain that he meant to confine the remark to them. It seems to me probable that this whole discussion occurred in the presence of others, and perhaps was a *public* contest. It is clear, I think, that Elihu was present, and heard it all (see chap. xxxii. 4), and it would accord well with Oriental habits to suppose that this was a trial of skill, which many were permitted to witness, and which was continued for a considerable time. Eliphaz may, therefore, have meant to say, that among his friends who had assembled to hear this debate, there were not a few who coincided with him in sentiment, who were much more aged than Job, and who had had much longer experience in the world.

11. Are *the consolations of God small with thee ?* The "consolations of God" here refer probably to those considerations which had been suggested by Eliphaz and his friends, and which he takes to be the "*consolations*" which God had furnished for the afflicted. He asks whether they were regarded by Job as of little value? Whether he was not willing to take such consolations as God had provided, and to allow them to sustain him instead of permitting himself to inveigh against God? The LXX. render this, "thou hast been chastised less than thy sins deserve. Thou hast spoken with excessive haughtiness !" But the true idea seems to be, that Eliphaz regarded the considerations adduced by him and his friends, as the gracious consolations which God had provided for men in affliction, and as the results of all former reflections on the design of God in sending trial. He now represents Job as regarding them as of no value, and maintaining sentiments directly at variance with them. ¶ *Is there any secret thing with thee ?* Noyes renders this, " and words so full of kindness to thee," that is, are *they* of no account to you ? So

small with thee ? is there any secret thing with thee ?

12 Why doth thine heart carry

Dr. Good and Wemyss, "or the addresses of kindness to thyself?" Luther translates it, "but thou hast, perhaps, yet a secret portion with thee." Rosenmüller, "and words most guilty spoken towards thee." The LXX. render it, "and thou hast spoken proudly beyond measure"— μεγάλως ὑπερβαλλόντας λελάληκας. The word which occurs in the Hebrew— לאט, *lâât*, when it is a single word, and used as a verb, means to wrap around, to muffle, to cover, to conceal, and then to be *secret*—whence the Greek λάθω, and λανθάνω, and the Latin *lateo*. In this sense it is understood here by our translators. But it may be also a compound word—from אט—a gentle sound, murmur, whisper; whence it is used adverbially—לְאַט and כְּאַט— gently, softly, slowly—as of the slow gait of a mourner, 1 Kings xxi. 27 ; and of water gently flowing, as the water of Siloam, Isa. viii. 6. And hence, also, it may refer to *words* flowing kindly or gently towards any one ; and this seems to be the meaning here. Eliphaz asks whether Job could despise or undervalue the words spoken *so gently* and *kindly* towards him? A singular illustration, to be sure, of kindness, but still showing how the friends of Job estimated their own remarks.

12. *Why doth thine heart carry thee away?* Why do you allow your *feelings* to control you in spite of the decisions of the understanding? Eliphaz means to represent him as wholly under the influence of passion, instead of looking calmly and coolly at things as they were, and listening to the results of past experience and observation. ¶ *And what do thy eyes wink at.* This expression has given considerable perplexity to commentators. Rosenmüller (and after him Noyes) remarks that the expression indicates pride, haughtiness, and arrogance In Ps. xxxv. 19, it is an indication of joyfulness or triumph over a prostrate foe :

thee away? and what do thine eyes wink at,

13 That thou turnest thy spirit against God, *a* and lettest *such* words go out of thy mouth?

14 What *is* man, that he should

a Mal.3.13.

Let not them that are mine enemies wrongfully rejoice over me; Neither let them wink with the eye that hate me without a cause.

In Prov. vi. 13, it is an indication of a haughty, froward, self-confident person:

A haughty person, a wicked man,
Walketh with a froward mouth;
He winketh with his eyes,
He speaketh with his feet,
He teacheth with his fingers.

The Hebrew word (רזם) occurs nowhere else, and it is therefore difficult to determine its true signification. The most probable meaning is, to wink with the eyes as a gesture of pride and insolence; comp. Notes on Isa. iii. 16. The Vulgate renders it, *attonitos habes oculos?*—" Why, as though meditating great things, hast thou eyes of astonishment"? Sept. " Why are thine eyes elevated?" Schultens renders it, " Why do thine eyes roll fury?"— *Quid fremitum volvunt oculi tui?* Luther, " Why art thou so proud?" There can be no reasonable doubt that the word conveys the idea of pride and haughtiness manifested in some way by the eyes.

13. *That thou turnest thy spirit.* That your mind is turned against God instead of acquiescing in his dealings. The views of Job he traces to pride and to overweening self-confidence, and perhaps not improperly.

14. *What is man that he should be clean?* The *object* of Eliphaz in this is to overturn the positions of Job that he was righteous, and had been punished beyond his deserts. He had before maintained (chap. iv. 7), that no one ever perished being innocent, and that the righteous were not cut off. This was with him a favourite position; and indeed the whole drift of the argument maintained by him and his friends was, to prove that uncommon calamities were proof of uncommon guilt. Job had insisted on

be clean?*b* and *he which is* born of a woman, that he should be righteous?

15 Behold, he putteth no trust in his saints; yea, the *c* heavens are not clean in his sight.

b Ps.14,3; Pr.20.9; Ep.2.3; 1Jn.1.8,10. *c* chap.25.5.

it that he was a righteous man, and had not deserved the calamities which had come upon him—a position which Eliphaz seems to have regarded as an assertion of innocence. To meet this he now maintains that *no one* is righteous; that all that are born of women are guilty; and in proof of this he goes back to the oracle which had made so deep an impression on his mind, and to the declaration then made to him that no one was pure before God; chap. iv. He does not repeat it exactly as the oracle was then delivered to him, but adverts to the substance of it, and regards it as final and indisputable. The meaning is, " What are all the pretensions of man to purity, when even the angels are regarded as impure and the heavens unclean?" ¶ He which is *born of a woman.* Another mode of denoting *man.* No particular *argument* to maintain the doctrine of man's depravity is couched in the fact that he is born of a woman. The sense is, simply, how can any one of the human family be pure?

15. *Behold, he putteth no trust in his saints.* In chap. iv. 18, it is, " in his *servants,*" but no doubt the same thing is intended. The reference is to the *angels,* called there *servants,* and here *saints* (קדשים), *holy ones;* see Notes on chap. iv. 18. ¶ *Yea, the heavens are not clean in his sight.* In chap. iv. 18, " and his angels he charged with folly." The general idea is the same. God is so holy that all things else seem to be impure. The very heavens seem to be unclean when compared with him. We are not to understand this as meaning that the heavens are defiled; that there is sin and corruption there, and that they are loathsome in the sight of God. The object is to set forth the exceeding purity of God, and the greatness of his holiness. This sentiment seemed to

16 How much more abominable and filthy *a is* man, which drinketh *b* iniquity like water!

17 I will show thee, hear me; and that *which* I have seen I will declare;

a Ps.53 3.   b chap.20.12; Pr.19.28.

18 Which wise men have told from their fathers, and have not hid *it;*

19 Unto whom *c* alone the earth was given, and no stranger *d* passed among them.

c De. 32.8.   d Joel 3.17.

---

be a kind of proverb, or a *common-place* in theology among the sages of Arabia. Thus it occurs in chap. xxv. 5, in the speech of Bildad, when he had nothing to say but to repeat the most common-place moral and theological adages—

Behold even to the moon, and it shineth not;
Yea, the stars are not pure in his sight:
How much less man, that is a worm,
And the son of man, which is a worm!

16. *How much more abominable and filthy is man.* How much more than the angels, and than the heavens. In chap. iv. 19, the image is somewhat different. There it is, how can man be the object of the divine confidence since he lives in a house of clay, and is so frail? Here the image is more striking and forcible. The word rendered *filthy* (אלח) means, in Arabic, to be *sour,* as milk, and then to be corrupt, in a moral sense; Ps. xiv. 3; liii. 4. Here it means that man is defiled and polluted, and this declaration is a remarkable illustration of the ancient belief of the depravity of man. ¶ *Which drinketh iniquity like water!* This is still a true, though a melancholy account of man. He loves sin, and is as greedy of it as a thirsty man is of water. He practises it as if it were his very nature—as much so as it is to drink. Perhaps too there may be an allusion, as Dr. Good supposes, to the large draught of water which the camel makes, implying that man is exceedingly greedy of iniquity; comp. chap. xx. 12; xxxiv. 7; Prov. xix. 28.

17. *I will show thee,* &c. The remainder of this chapter is a violent declamation, designed to overwhelm Job with the proofs of personal guilt. Eliphaz professes to urge nothing which had not been handed down from his ancestors, and was the result of careful observation. What he says

is made up of apothegms and maxims that were regarded as containing the results of ancient wisdom, all meaning that God would punish the wicked, or that the wicked would be treated according to their deserts. The implied inference all along was, that Job, who had had so many proofs of the divine displeasure, must be a wicked man.

18. *Which wise men have told from their fathers.* Which they have received from their ancestors and communicated to others. Knowledge among the ancients was communicated chiefly by tradition from father to son. They had few or no written records, and hence they embodied the results of their observation in brief, sententious maxims, and transmitted them from one generation to another. ¶ *And have not hid* it. They have freely communicated the result of their observations to others.

19. *Unto whom alone the earth was given.* The *land;* the land or country where they dwelt. He refers to the period before they became intermingled with other nations, and before they imbibed any sentiments or opinions from strangers. The meaning is, " I will give you the result of the observations of the *golden age* of the world when our fathers dwelt alone, and it could not be pretended that they had been corrupted by foreign philosophy; and when in morals and in sentiment they were pure." Probably all nations look back to such times of primeval simplicity, and freedom from corruption, when the sentiments on morals and religion were comparatively pure, and before the people became corrupt by the importation of foreign opinions. It is a pleasing delusion to look back to such times—to some innocent Arcadia, or to a golden age—but usually all such retrospections are the mere

20 The wicked man travaileth *a* with pain all *his* days, and the number *b* of years is hidden to the oppressor.

21 [1] A dreadful sound *is* *c* in his ears : in prosperity *d* the destroyer shall come upon him.

a Ec.9.3.   *b* Pr.10,27.   1 *A sound of fears.*
c Le.26.36.   *d* 1 Th.5. 3.

work of fancy. The world really grows wiser as it grows older ; and in the progress of society it is a rare thing when the present is not more pure and happy than its early stages. The comforts, privileges, and intelligence, of the patriarchal age were not to be compared with those which *we* enjoy—any more than the condition of the wandering Arab is to be preferred to the quiet, peace, intelligence, and order of a calm, Christian home. ¶ *No stranger passed among them.* No foreigner came to corrupt their sentiments by an admixture of strange doctrines. " Eliphaz here speaks like a genuine Arab, whose pride is in his tongue, his sword, and his pure blood." *Umbreit.* It is *possible,* as Rosenmüller suggests, that Eliphaz means to insinuate that Job had been corrupted by the sentiments of the Chaldeans and Sabeans, and had departed from the pure doctrines of earlier times.

20. *Travaileth with pain.* That is, his sorrows are like the pains of parturition. Eliphaz means to say that he is a constant sufferer. ¶ *All his days.* It seems difficult to see how they could have ever formed this universal maxim. It is certainly not literally true now ; nor was it ever. But in order to convey the doctrine that the wicked would be punished in as pointed and striking a manner as possible, it was made to assume this universal form—meaning that the life of the wicked would be miserable. There is some reason to think that this and what follows to the close of the chapter, is an ancient fragment which Eliphaz rehearses as containing the sentiments of a purer age of the world. ¶ *And the number of years is hidden to the oppressor.* Wemyss renders this, " and a reckoning of years is laid up for the violent." So, also, Dr. Good. The Vulgate renders it, " and the number of the years of his tyranny is uncertain." Rosenmüller,

Cocceius, Drusius, and some others suppose that there should be understood here and repeated the clause occurring in the first hemistich, and that it means, " and in the number of years which are laid up for the violent man, he is tortured with pain." Luther renders it, " and to a tyrant is the number of his years concealed." It is difficult to tell what the passage means. To me, the most probable interpretation is one which I have not met with in any of the books which I have consulted, and which may be thus expressed, " the wicked man will be tormented all his days." To one who is an oppressor or tyrant, the number of his years is hidden. He has no *security* of life. He cannot calculate with any certainty on its continuance. The end is hid. A righteous man may make *some* calculation, and can see the probable end of his days. He may expect to see an honoured old age. But tyrants are so often cut down suddenly ; they so frequently perish by assassination, and robbers are so often unexpectedly overcome, that there is *no* calculation which can be formed in respect to the termination of their course. *Their* end is hid. They die suddenly and disappear. This suits the connection ; and the sentiment is, in the main, in accordance with facts as they occur.

21. *A dreadful sound* is *in his ears.* Marg. *A sound of fears.* He hears sudden, frightful sounds, and is alarmed. Or when he thinks himself safe, he is suddenly surprised. The enemy steals upon him, and in his fancied security he dies. This sentiment might be illustrated at almost any length by the mode of savage warfare in America, and by the sudden attacks which the American savage makes, in the silence of the night, on his unsuspecting foes. The Chaldee renders this, " the fear of the terrors in Gehenna are in his ears ; when the righteous dwell in peace and eternal life, destruction

22 He believeth not that he shall return out of darkness, and he is waited for of the sword.

23 He wandereth abroad for bread, *saying*, Where *is it?* he knoweth that the day of darkness is ready at his hand.

24 Trouble and anguish shall make him afraid ; they shall pre-

vail against him, as a king ready to return to the battle.

25 For *a* he stretcheth out his hand against God, and strengtheneth himself against *b* the Almighty.

26 He runneth upon him, *even* on *his* neck, upon the thick bosses of his bucklers :

a Ps. 10.13.   b chap. 9.4.

comes upon him." ¶ *In prosperity the destroyer shall come upon him.* When he supposes he is safe, and his affairs seem to be prosperous, then sudden destruction comes ; see 1 Th. v. 3. The history of wicked men, who have encompassed themselves with wealth, and as they supposed with every thing necessary to happiness, and who have been suddenly cut off, would furnish all the instances which would be necessary to illustrate this sentiment of Eliphaz. See an exquisitely beautiful illustration of it in Ps. xxxvii. 35, 36 :

I have seen the wicked in great power,
And spreading himself like a green bay-tree.
Yet he passed away, and lo he was not ;
Yea, I sought him, but he could not be found.

So, also, in Ps. lxxiii. 18—20 :

Surely thou didst set them in slippery places ;
Thou castedst them down into destruction.
How are they brought into desolation as in
    a moment !
They are utterly consumed with terrors.
As a dream when one awaketh,
O Lord, when thou awakest, thou shalt de-
    spise their image.

22. *He believeth not that he shall return out of darkness. Darkness* is used in the Bible, as elsewhere, to denote calamity ; and the meaning here is, that the wicked man has not confidence (לא יאמין), that he shall return safely from impending danger. He is in constant dread of assassination, or of some fearful evil. He is never secure ; his mind is never calm; he lives in constant dread. This is still an accurate description of a man with a guilty conscience ; for such a man lives in constant fear, and never feels any security that he is safe. ¶ *And he is waited for of the sword.* That is, he is destined for the sword. *Gesenius.*

23. *He wandereth abroad for bread.*

The LXX. render this, " he is destined to be food for vultures "— κατατέτακται δὲ εἰς σῖτα γυψίν. The meaning of the Hebrew is, simply, that he will be reduced to poverty, and will not know where to obtain a supply for his returning wants. ¶ *He knoweth that the day of darkness is ready at his hand.* He is assured that the period of calamity is not far remote. It must come. He has no security that it will not come immediately. The whole design of this is to show that there is no calmness and security for a wicked man ; that in the midst of apparent prosperity his soul is in constant dread.

24. *As a king ready to the battle.* Fully prepared for a battle ; whom it would be vain to attempt to resist. So mighty would be the combined forces of trouble and anguish against him, that it would be vain to attempt to oppose them.

25. *For he stretcheth out his hand against God.* The hand is stretched out for battle. It wields the spear or the sword against an enemy. The idea here is, that the wicked man makes *God* an adversary. He does not contend with his fellow-man, with fate, with the elements, with evil angels, but with God. His opponent is an Almighty Being, and he cannot prevail against him ; comp. Notes on Isa. xxvii. 4. ¶ *And strengtheneth himself.* As an army does that throws up a rampart, or constructs a fortification. The whole image here is taken from the practice of war ; and the sense is, that a wicked man is really making war on the Almighty, and that in that war he *must* be vanquished ; comp. chap. ix. 4.

26. *He runneth upon him.* That is, upon God. The image here is

taken from the mode in which men rushed into battle. It was with a violent concussion, and usually with a shout, that they might intimidate their foes, and overcome them at first, with the violence of the shock. The mode of warfare is now changed, and it is the vaunted excellency of modern warfare that armies now go deliberately and calmly to put each other to death. ¶ Even *on* his *neck.* Literally, "with the neck"—בְּצַוָּ֫אר. Vulg. *With erect neck—erecto collo.* Sept. Contemptuously, or with pride—ὕβρει. The idea seems to be, not that he ran *upon the neck* of his adversary—as would seem to be implied in our translation—but that he ran in a firm, haughty, confident manner; with a head erect and firm, as the indication of self-confidence, and a determined purpose to overcome his foe. See *Schultens in loc.* ¶ *Upon the thick bosses.* The word *boss* with us means a knob—a protuberant ornament of silver, brass, or ivory on a harness or a bridle; then a protuberant part, a prominence, or a round or swelling body of any kind. The Hebrew word here used (גַּב) means properly any thing gibbous, convex, arched; and hence *the back*—as of animals. Applied to a shield, it means the convex part or the back of it—the part which was presented to an enemy, and which was made swelling and strong, called by the Greeks ὀμφαλὸς, or μεσομφάλιον. Gesenius supposes that the metaphor here is taken from soldiers, who joined their shields together, and thus rushed upon an enemy. This was one mode of ancient warfare, when an army or a phalanx united their shields in front, so that nothing could penetrate them, or so united them over their heads when approaching a fortress, that they could safely march under them as a covering. This, among the Romans and Greeks, was commonly practised when approaching a besieged town. One form of the *testudo*—the χελώνη στρατιωτῶν of the Greeks, was formed by the soldiers, pressed close together and holding their shields over their heads in such a manner as to form a compact covering. J. H. Eschenburg, Manual of Classical Literature, by N.

W. Fiske, pt. III. § 147. The Vulgate renders this, " and he is armed with a fat neck"—*pingui cervice armatus est.* Schultens expresses the idea that is adopted by Gesenius, and refers to Arabic customs to show that shields were thus united in defending an army from a foe, or in making an attack on them. He says, also, that it is a common expression—a proverb—among the Arabs, " he turns the back of his shield " to denote that one is an adversary; and quotes a passage from Hamasa, " When a friend meets me with base suspicions, I turn to him the back of my shield—a proverb, whose origin is derived from the fact, that a warrior turns the back of his shield to his foes." Paxton supposes that the expression here is taken from single combat, which early prevailed. But the idea here is not that which our translation would seem to convey. It is not that he rushes upon or against the hard or thick shield *of the Almighty*—and that, therefore, he must meet resistance and be overcome; it is that he rushes upon God WITH his own shield. He puts himself in the attitude of a warrior. He turns the boss of his own shield against God, and becomes his antagonist. He is his enemy. The omission of the word *with* in the passage—or the preposition which is in the Hebrew (ב), has led to this erroneous translation. The passage is often quoted in a popular manner to denote that the sinner rushes upon God, *and must meet resistance* from his shield, or be overcome. It should be quoted only to denote that the sinner places himself in an attitude of opposition to God, and is his enemy. ¶ *Of his bucklers.* Of his shields (מָגִנָּיו), that is, of the shields which the sinner has; not the shields of God. The shield was a well-known instrument of war, usually made with a rim of wood or metal, and covered with skins, and carried on the left arm; see Notes on Isa. xxi. 5. The outer surface was made rounding from the centre to the edge, and was smoothly polished, so that darts or arrows would glide off and not penetrate.

27. *Because he covereth his face with his fatness.* That is, he not only

27 Because *a* he covereth his face with his fatness, and maketh collops of fat on *his* flanks.

28 And he dwelleth in desolate cities, *and* in houses which no man inhabiteth, which are ready to become heaps.

a Ps. 73.7, &c.

---

stretches out his hand against God (ver. 25) and rushes upon him as an armed foe (ver. 26), but he gives himself up to a life of luxury, gluttony, and licentiousness ; and *therefore* these calamities must come upon him. This is designed to be a description of a luxurious and licentious person—a man who is an enemy of God, and who, therefore, must incur his displeasure. ¶ *And maketh collops of fat.* Like an ox that is fattened. The word *collop* properly means "a small slice of meat, a piece of flesh" (*Webster*), but here it means a thick piece, or a mass. The word is used in this sense in New England. The sense is, that he becomes excessively fat and gross —as they usually do who live in sensual indulgence and who forget God.

28. *And he dwelleth.* Or rather, "therefore he shall dwell." As a consequence of his opposing God, and devoting himself to a life of sensuality and ease, he shall dwell in a desolate place. Instead of living in affluence and in a splendid city, he shall be compelled to take up his abode in places that have been deserted and abandoned. Such places—like Petra or Babylon now—became the temporary lodgings of caravans and travellers, or the abodes of outcasts and robbers. The meaning here is, that the proud and wicked man shall be ejected from his palace, and compelled to seek a refuge far away from the usual haunts of men. ¶ *Which are ready to become heaps.* Which are just ready to tumble into ruin.

29. *He shall not be rich.* That is, he shall not continue rich ; or he shall not again become rich. He shall be *permanently* poor. ¶ *Neither shall his substance continue.* His property. ¶ *Neither shall he prolong the perfection thereof.* Noyes renders this,

29 He shall not be rich, neither shall his substance continue, neither shall he prolong the perfection thereof upon the earth.

30 He shall not depart out of darkness : the flame shall dry up his branches, and by the breath of his mouth shall he go away.

" And his possessions shall not be extended upon the earth." Wemyss, " Nor shall he be master of his own desires." Good, " Nor their success spread abroad in the land." Luther, Und sein Gluck wird sich nicht ausbreiten im Lande—" And his fortune shall not spread itself abroad in the land." Vulg. " Neither shall he send his root in the earth "—nec mittet in terra radicem suam. The LXX. οὐ μὴ βάλῃ ἐπὶ τὴν γῆν σκιάν—" and shall not cast a shadow upon the earth." The word rendered *perfection* (מִנְלָה) is commonly supposed to be from מִנְלָה, from נלה to finish, to procure, and hence the noun may be applied to that which is *procured*—and thus may denote possessions. According to this the correct rendering is, " and he does not extend their possessions abroad in the land ;" that is, his possessions do not extend abroad. Gesenius supposes, however, that the word is a corruption for מִבְלָם—*their flocks.* I see no objection, however, to its being regarded as meaning *possessions*—and then the sense is, that he would fail in that which is so much the object of ambition with every avaricious man— that his possessions should extend through the land ; comp. Notes on Isa. v. 8.

30. *He shall not depart out of darkness.* He shall not escape from calamity ; see ver. 22. He shall not be able to rise again, but shall be continually poor. ¶ *The flame shall dry up his branches.* As the fire consumes the green branches of a tree, so shall punishment do to him. This comparison is very forcible, and the idea is, that the man who has been prospered as a tree shall be consumed—as the fire consumes a tree when it passes through the branches. The comparison of a prosperous man with a tree is

31 Let not him that is deceived trust *a* in vanity ; for vanity shall be his recompense.

32 It shall be ¹ accomplished

a Is.59.4. 1 or, *cut off.* *b* Ps.55.23.

before *b* his time, and his branch shall not be green.

33 He shall shake off his unripe grape as the vine, and shall cast off his flower as the olive.

---

very common, and very beautiful. Thus the Psalmist says,

I have seen the wicked in great power,
And spreading himself like a green bay tree.
Ps. xxxvii. 35.

Comp. Ps. xcii. 12, 13. The aged Skenandoah—a chief of the Oneida tribe of Indians, said, " I am an aged hemlock. The winds of an hundred winters have whistled through my branches. I am dead at the top. My branches are falling," &c. ¶ *And by the breath of his mouth shall he go away.* That is, by the breath of the mouth of God. God is not indeed specified, but it is not unusual to speak of him in this manner. The image here seems to be that of the destruction of a man by a burning wind or by lightning. As a tree is dried up, or is rent by lightning, or is torn up from the roots by a tempest sent by the Deity, so the wicked will be destroyed.

31. *Let not him that is deceived trust in vanity.* The sense is, " Let him not trust in vanity. He will be deceived. Vanity will be his recompense." The idea is, that a man should not confide in that which will furnish no support. He should not rely on his wealth and rank ; his houses and lands ; his servants, his armies, or his power, if he is wicked, for all this is vain. He needs some better reliance, and that can be found only in a righteous life. The word *vanity* here means that which is unsubstantial; which cannot uphold or sustain; which will certainly give way. ¶ *For vanity will be his recompense.* He will find only vanity. He will be stripped of all his honours and possessions.

32. *It shall be accomplished before his time.* Marg. *cut off.* The image here is that of a tree, which had been suggested in ver. 30. Here it is followed up by various illustrations drawn from the flower, the fruit, &c., all of which are designed to denote the same thing—that a wicked man will not be

permanently prosperous ; he will not live and flourish as he would if he were righteous. He will be like a tree that is cut down before its proper time, or that casts its flowers and fruits and brings nothing to perfection. The phrase here literally is, " It shall not be filled up in its time ;" that is, a wicked man will be cut off before he has filled up the measure of his days, like a tree that decays and falls before its proper time. A similar idea occurs in Ps. lv. 23. " Bloody and deceitful men shall not live out half their days." As a general fact this is all true, and the observation of the ancient Idumeans was correct. The temperate live longer than the intemperate ; the chaste longer than the licentious ; he that controls and governs his passions longer than he who gives the reins to them ; and he who leads a life of honesty and virtue longer than he who lives for crime. Pure religion makes a man temperate, sober, chaste, calm, dispassionate, and equable in his temper ; saves from broils, contentions, and strifes ; subdues the angry passions, and thus tends to lengthen out life. ¶ *His branch shall not be green.* It shall be dried up and withered away —retaining the image of a tree.

33. *He shall shake off his unripe grape as the vine.* The idea here is, that the wicked man shall be like a vine that casts off its grapes while they are yet sour and green, and brings none to perfection ; comp. Notes on Isa. xviii. 5. Scott renders this,

" As when the vine her half-grown berries showers,
Or poisoned olive her unfolding flowers."

It would seem from this passage that the vine might be so blasted by a hot wind or other cause, as to cast its unripe grapes to the earth. The employment of a figure of this kind supposes that such a case was familiar to those who were addressed. It is well known that in the East the grape and the olive might

34 For the congregation of *a* hypocrites *shall be* desolate, and

a chap.27.8 ; 1s.33.14.

fire shall consume the tabernacles of *b* bribery.

b Am.5.11,12.

be blasted while in blossom, or when the fruit was *setting*, as all fruit may be. The injury is usually done in the flower, or when the fruit is just forming. Yet our observations of the effects of the burning winds that pass over the deserts on fruit that is half formed, in blasting it and causing it to fall, are too limited to allow us to come to any definite conclusion in regard to such effects in general. Any one, however, can see the *beauty* of this image. The plans and purposes of wicked men are immature. Nothing is carried to perfection. They are cut off, their plans are blasted, and all the results of their living are like the sour, hard, crabbed, and useless fruit that falls from the tree before it is ripe. The results of the life of the righteous, on the other hand, are like a tree loaded with ripe and mellow fruit—their plans are brought to maturity, and resemble the rich and heavy clusters of grapes, or the abundant fruits of the olive when ripe. ¶ *And shall cast off his flower as the olive.* The olive is a well-known tree that abounds in the East. The fruit is chiefly valuable for the oil which it produces; comp. Notes Rom. xi. 17. The olive is liable to be blasted while the fruit is setting, or while the tree is in blossom. In Greece, a north-east wind often proves destructive to the olive, and the same may be true of other places. Dr. Chandler, speaking of Greece, says, " The olive groves are now, as anciently, a principal source of the riches of Athens. The crops had failed five years successively when we arrived; the cause assigned was a northerly wind, called Greco-tramontane, which destroyed the flower. The fruit is set in about a fortnight, when the apprehension from this unpropitious quarter ceases. The bloom in the following year was unhurt, and we had the pleasure of leaving the Athenians happy in the prospect of a plentiful harvest." A wicked man is here elegantly compared with such a tree that casts its flowers and produces no fruit.

34. *For the congregation of hypocrites.* The word rendered "congregation" here (עֵדָה) means properly an appointed meeting; a meeting convened by appointment or at stated times (from יָעַד), and hence an assembly of any kind. It is commonly applied to an assembly for public worship; but it may refer to a more private company—a family, or circle of friends, dependents, &c. It refers here, I suppose, to such a community that a man can get around him in his own dwelling—his family, servants, dependents, &c. The word rendered "hypocrites" (חָנֵף) is in the singular number, and should be so rendered here. It does not mean that a worshipping assembly composed of hypocrites would be desolate—which may be true —but that the community which a man *who is a hypocrite* can gather around him shall be swept away. His children, his dependents, and his retinue of servants, shall be taken away from him, and he shall be left to solitude. Probably there was an allusion here to Job, who had been stripped in this manner ; or at any rate the remark was one, if it were a quotation from the ancient sayings of the Arabians, which Job could not but regard as applied to himself. ¶ *And fire shall consume.* This has all the appearance of being a proverb. The meaning is, that they who received a bribe would be certainly punished. ¶ *The tabernacles of bribery.* The tents or dwellings of those who receive bribes, and who therefore are easily corrupted, and have no solid *principles.* There is probably an allusion here to Job ; and no doubt Eliphaz meant to apply this severe remark to him. Job was a *Sheik*, an *Emir*, a head of a tribe, and, therefore, a magistrate ; see chap. xxix. 7, seq. Yet a part of his possessions and servants had been cut off by fire from heaven (chap. i. 16) ; and Eliphaz means probably to imply that it had been because he had been guilty of receiving a bribe. This ancient proverb declared that the

35 They *a* conceive mischief, and bring forth 1 vanity, and their belly prepareth deceit.

CHAPTER XVI.

ANALYSIS OF CHAPTERS XVI. AND XVII.

CHAPTERS XVI. and XVII. contain the reply of Job to the speech of Eliphaz, and should not have been separated. This speech of Job is full of the language of complaint and of solemn appeals to God. It is the language of bitterness and distress, where he felt that he was called to suffer almost beyond the power of endurance. In his former speech (chap. iv., v.), Eliphaz had shown *some* tenderness. He had exhorted him to return to God; he had assured him that his favour might be found if he would return. But now he had argued as if it were a settled point that Job was a wicked man, and as if there were no possibility that he could find favour. In reply to this, Job in the following speech dwells on the following points. He says that he had heard many such things, and that they imparted to him no consolation (ver. 2, 3); that it was no difficult matter to speak as they did, and that if they were to change places, he *could* use similar language, but *would not* do it; he would comfort them, and assuage their grief (ver. 4–7). He then goes on with an affecting description of his calamities. God had made him weary; he had filled him with wrinkles; he had torn him in his wrath; he had delivered him to the ungodly; he had come upon him when he was at ease; he had compassed him about; and he had rushed upon him like a giant (ver. 8–14). Of this he now makes complaint. He knew not why it was; he felt that he was innocent, and that his prayers had been pure (ver. 15 —17). Overcome with deep emotion, he appeals to the earth, and asks that it would not cover his blood, or suffer him to go unavenged, but that it would disclose

a Ho.10.13; Ga.6.7,8.   1 or, *iniquity.*

his guilt, and prays that his very blood might cry out from the ground, attesting his innocence (ver. 18). He then expresses the earnest desire that he might plead his cause before God; that as his friends scorned him, he might have the privilege of presenting his cause to One by whom he might hope to have justice done (ver. 19–21). He goes on to say that in a little time it would all be over—he would go down to the grave, where he would sleep in peace (ver. 22). In chap. xvii. he goes on in the language of complaint, especially of the conduct of his friends. There are mockers, he says, with him (ver. 2). God had hid their heart from understanding, and *they* never could be exalted (ver. 4). He was now made a by-word, but the time would come when upright men would be astonished at the course of things in regard to him; that God had afflicted him in this manner, and had suffered his friends to rail on him thus, and had not come forth for his vindication (ver. 5–8). He says that it was a great truth that the righteous should hold on his way, but that among them there was not one wise man (ver. 9, 10). And he closes by saying, that in such a series of calamities his only hope was in the grave. There was rest. He was prepared to embrace corruption as his father, and to say to the worm that it was his mother and his sister (ver. 11 —16).

THEN Job answered and said,

2 I have heard many such 2 things: miserable *b* comforters *are* ye all.

3 Shall 3 vain words have an end? or what emboldeneth thee that thou answerest?

4 I also could speak as ye *do:* if

2 or, *troublesome.*   *b* chap.13.4.
3 *words of wind,* chap.15.2.

---

dwellings of the man who could be bribed would be consumed by fire; and now he presumes that the fact that Job had been visited by the fire of heaven was full proof that he had been guilty in this manner. It was about on principles such as these that the reasoning of the friends of Job was conducted.

35. *They conceive mischief.* The meaning of this verse is, that they form and execute plans of evil. It is the characteristic of such men that they form such plans and live to execute them, and they must abide the consequences. All this was evidently meant for Job; and few things could be more trying to a man's patience than to sit and hear those ancient apothegms, designed to describe the wicked, applied so unfeelingly to himself.

CHAPTER XVI.

2. *Many such things.* That is, either things fitted to provoke and irritate, or sentiments that are common-place. There was nothing new in what they

said, and nothing to the purpose. ¶ *Miserable comforters;* comp. chap. xiii. 4. They had come professedly to condole with him. Now all that they said was adapted only to irritate, and to deepen his distress. He was disappointed; and he was deeply wounded and grieved.

3. *Shall vain words?* Marg. As in Heb. *words of wind;* that is, words which were devoid of thought—light, trifling. This is a retort on Eliphaz. He had charged Job (chap. xv. 2, 3) with uttering only such words. Such forms of expression are common in the East. "His promise, it is only wind." "Breath, breath; all breath." *Roberts.* ¶ *Or what emboldeneth thee?* "What provokes or irritates thee, that thou dost answer in this manner? What have I said, that has given occasion to such a speech—a speech so severe and unkind?" The Syriac reads this, "do not afflict me any more with speeches; for if you speak any more, I will not answer you."

4. *I also could speak as ye do.* In

your soul were in my soul's stead,
I could heap up words against you,
and shake *a* mine head at you.

5 *But* I would strengthen you
with my mouth, *b* and the moving

a Ps.22.7.　　　　　*b* Pr.27.9.

the same reproachful manner, and
stringing together old proverbs and
maxims as you have. ¶ *If your soul
were in my soul's stead.* If you were
in my place. The idea is, that there
is no difficulty in finding arguments to
overwhelm the afflicted—a truth which
most persons who have been unfortunate, have had opportunity to experience. ¶ *I could heap up words
against you.* Or, rather, "I could
string together words against you."
The idea is not that of *heaping up,*
or *accumulating;* it is that of tying
together, or uniting; and refers here
to stringing together old maxims,
saws, and proverbs, in the form of a
set argument or discourse. The idea
of Job is, that their discourses were
nothing but ancient proverbs, thrown
together, or strung along without regard to order, pertinency, or force.
The Hebrew word used here (חבר)
means to bind, to bind together, to
associate, to be confederate. It may
be applied to friends—united in friendship; to nations—united in an alliance,
&c. Gesenius supposes that it means
here that he "would make a league
with words against them;" but the
above seems to be the more probable
interpretation. The LXX. render it,
"then I could *insult* you—ἐναλοῦμαι—
with words." Jerome (Vulg.) "I
would *console* you with words, and
move my head over you." The Chaldee is as the Hebrew—אחבר. Dr.
Good renders it, "against you will I
string together old sayings." ¶ *And
shake mine head at you.* An action
common to all countries and ages,
expressive of contempt, or of threatening; comp. Jer. xviii. 16 ; Lam. ii.
15 ; Zeph. ii. 15 ; Mat. xxvii. 39. So
Lucretius ii. 1163 :

Jamque caput quassans grandis suspirat arator
Crebrius incassum magnum cecidisse laborem.

In like manner Virgil, Æn. vii. 292:

Tum quassans caput, hæc effudit pectore dicta.

of my lips should assuage *your
grief.*

6 Though I speak, my grief is not
assuaged; and *though* I forbear,
what [1] am I eased ?

1 *goeth from me ?*

So, also, Homer, Odys. ε:

Κινήσας δὲ κάρη προτὶ ὃν μυθήσατο θυμόν.

The meaning of Job here is, that he
could as easily have expressed contempt, reproach, and scorn, as they
did. It required no uncommon talent
to do it, and he felt that he would
have been fully sufficient for the task.
5. But *I would strengthen you with
my mouth.* With that which proceeds
from the mouth—*words.* ¶ *And the
moving of my lips.* My speaking—
implying that it would have been done
in a mild, gentle, kind manner—so that
the lips would appear just to move.
Others, however, have given a different interpretation. Thus Dr. Good
renders it :

"With my own mouth will I overpower you,
Till the quivering of my lips shall fail."

But the common interpretation is to
be preferred. The word rendered
"*moving*" (ניד), is from נוד—to move,
agitate, and hence denotes motion. It
denotes here the motion of the lips
when we speak. Gesenius renders it,
consolation, comfort—because this is
expressed by a motion of the head.
¶ *Should assuage* your grief. The
word here used (יחשׂך) means properly
to hold back, to restrain ; Job vii. 11.
Here it is correctly rendered, meaning that he would *hold back,* or *check*
their sorrows. In other words, he
would *sustain* them.
6. *Though I speak, my grief is not
assuaged.* "But for me, it makes now
no difference whether I speak or am
silent. My sufferings continue. If I
attempt to vindicate myself before
men, I am reproached ; and equally
so if I am silent. If I maintain my
cause before God, it avails me nothing,
for my sufferings continue. If I am
silent, and submit without a murmur,
they are the same. Neither silence,
nor argument, nor entreaty, avail me
before God or man. I am doomed to
suffering." ¶ *What am I eased ?*

7 But now he hath made me weary: thou hast made desolate all my company.

8 And thou hast filled me with

a wrinkles, *which* is a witness *against me;* and my leanness rising up in me beareth witness to my face.

a Ps. 102.4.

Marg. Goeth from me. Literally, "what goeth from me?" The sense is, that it all availed nothing.

7. *But now he hath made me weary.* That is, God has exhausted my strength. This verse introduces a new description of his sufferings; and he begins with a statement of the woes that *God* had brought on him. The first was, that he had taken away all his strength. ¶ *All my company.* The word rendered "*company*" (עדה) means properly an assembly that comes together by appointment, or at stated times; but here it is evidently used in the sense of the little community of which Job was the head and father. The sense is, that all his family had been destroyed.

8. *And thou hast filled me with wrinkles.* Noyes renders this, "and thou hast seized hold of me, which is a witness against me." Wemyss, "since thou hast bound me with chains, witnesses come forward." Good, "and hast cut off myself from becoming a witness." Luther, "he has made me *kuntzlich* (skilfully, artificially, cunningly,) and bears witness against me." Jerome, "my wrinkles bear witness against me." Sept., "my lie has become a witness, and is risen up against me." From this variety of explanations, it will be seen that this passage is not of easy and obvious construction. The Hebrew word which is here used and rendered, "thou hast filled me with wrinkles" (הקמטני), from קמט—*kâmăt*, occurs only in one other place in the Bible; Job xxii. 16. It is there in the *Pual* form, and rendered "were cut down." According to Gesenius, it means, to lay fast hold of, to seize with the hands, and answers to the Arabic *to bind.* The word in Chaldee (קמט) means to wrinkle, or collect in wrinkles; and is applied to any thing that is *contracted,* or rough. It is applied in the form קומט to the pupil of the eye as being *contracted,* as in

the declaration in Derec Erez, c. 5, quoted by Castell. "The world is like the eye; where the ocean that surrounds the world is white; the world itself is black; the pupil is Jerusalem, and the image in the pupil is the sanctuary." Probably the true notion of the word is to be found in the Arabic. According to Castell, this means, to tie together the four feet of a sheep or lamb, in order that it might be slain; to bind an infant in swaddling clothes before it is laid in a cradle; to collect camels into a group or herd; and hence the *noun* is used to denote a cord or rope twisted of wool, or of leaves of the palm, or the bandages by which an infant is bound. This idea is not in use in the Hebrew; but I have no doubt that this was the original sense of the word, and that this is one of the numerous places in Job where light may be cast upon the meaning of a word from its use in Arabic. The Hebrew word may be applied to the *collecting* or *contraction* of the face in wrinkles by age, but this is not the sense here. We should express the idea by "being *drawn up* with pain or affliction; by being straitened, or compressed." The meaning is that of *drawing together*—as the feet of a sheep when tied, or twisting—as a rope; and the idea here is, that Job was drawn up, compressed, bound by his afflictions—and that this was a witness against him. The word *compressed* comes as near to the sense as any one that we have. ¶ *Which is a witness* against me. That is, "this is an argument against my innocence. The fact that God has thus compressed, and fettered, and fastened me; that he has bound me as with a cord—as if I were tied for the slaughter, is an argument on which my friends insist, and to which they appeal, as a proof of my guilt. I cannot answer it. They refer to it constantly. It is the burden of their de-

9 He teareth *a me* in his wrath, who hateth me; he gnasheth upon

me with his teeth; mine *b* enemy sharpeneth his eyes upon me.

a chap.10.16,17.

b chap.13.24.

monstration, and how can I reply to it?" The position of mind here is, that he could appeal to God for his uprightness, but these afflictions stood in the way of his argument for his innocence with his friends. They were the *usual* proofs of God's displeasure, and he could not well meet the argument which was drawn from them in his case, for in all his protestations of innocence there stood these afflictions—the usual proofs of God's displeasure against men—as evidence against him, to which they triumphantly appealed. ¶ *And my leanness rising up in me.* Dr. Good renders this, "my calumniator." Wemyss, "false witnesses." So Jerome, "falsiloquus." The LXX. render it, "my lie—τὸ ψευδός μου—rises up against me." The Hebrew word (כחש) means properly *a lie, deceit, hypocrisy.* But it cannot be supposed that Job would formally admit that he was a liar and a hypocrite. This would have been to concede the whole point in dispute. The word, therefore, it would seem, *must* have some other sense. The verb כחש is used to denote not only to *lie,* but also to *waste away, to fail.* Ps. cix. 24, "My flesh *faileth* of fatness." The idea seems to have been, that a person whose flesh had wasted away by sickness, as it were, *belied himself;* or it was a *false testimony* about himself; it did not give *a fair representation* of him. That could be obtained only when he was in sound health. Thus in Hab. iii. 17, "the labour of the olive *shall fail.*" Heb. shall *lie* or *deceive;* that is, it shall belie itself, or shall not do justice to itself; it shall afford no fair representation of what the olive is fitted to produce. So the word is used in Hos. ix. 2. It is used here in this sense, as denoting *the false appearance of Job*—his present aspect—which was no proper representation of himself; that is, his emaciated and ulcerated form. This, he says, was a " witness" against him. It was one of the proofs to which they appealed, and he did not

know how to answer it. It was usually an evidence of divine displeasure, and he now solemnly and tenderly addresses God, and says, that he had furnished this testimony against him—and he was overwhelmed.

9. *He teareth* me *in his wrath.* The language here is all taken from the ferocity of wild beasts; and the idea is, that his enemy had come upon him as a lion seizes upon its prey. Rosenmüller, Reiske, and some others suppose that this refers to God. Cocceius refers it to Satan. Schultens, Dr. Good, and some others, to Eliphaz, as the leading man among his adversaries. I have no doubt that this is the true reference. The connection seems to demand this; and we ought not to suppose that Job would charge this upon God, unless there is the clearest evidence. The whole passage is a description of the manner in which Job supposed his friends had come upon him. He says they had attacked him like wild beasts. Yet it must be admitted that he sometimes attributes these feelings to God, and says that he came upon him like a roaring lion; see chap. x. 16, 17. ¶ *Who hateth me.* Or rather, " and persecutes me, or is become my adversary," for so the word here used (שׂטם) means; see Notes on chap. xxx. 21. ¶ *He gnasheth upon me with his teeth.* As an enraged wild animal does when about to seize upon its prey. A similar figure occurs in Otway, in his " Orphan:"

—— for my Castalio's false;
False as the wind, the water, or the weather;
Cruel as tigers o'er their trembling prey;
I feel him in my breast, he tears my heart,
And at each sigh he drinks the gushing blood.

And so Homer, when he describes the wrath of Achilles as he armed himself to avenge the death of Patroclus, mentions among other signs of wrath his gnashing his teeth:

Τοῦ καὶ ὀδόντων μὲν καναχὴ πέλε.
Il. xix. 364.

So Virgil describes his hero as

furens animis, dentibus infrendens.
Æn. viii. 228.

10 They have gaped upon me with their mouth; they have smitten [a] me upon the cheek reproachfully; they have [b] gathered themselves together against me.

11 God [c] hath [1] delivered me to the ungodly, and turned me over into the hands of the wicked.

12 I was at ease, but he hath broken me asunder; he hath also taken *me* by my neck, and shaken me to pieces, and set me [c] up for his mark.

13 His archers compass me round about; he cleaveth my reins asunder, and doth not spare; he poureth out my gall upon the ground.

a La.3.30.   b Ps.35.15.   c chap.1.15,17.

1 *shut me up*.   c chap.7.20.

¶ *Mine enemy sharpeneth his eyes upon me.* Looks fiercely; watches me narrowly—as an animal does his victim when about to seize upon it. The image is probably drawn from the intense gaze of the lion when about to pounce upon his prey. "He darts piercing looks at me; or looks at me with a fierce and penetrating eye."

10. *They have gaped upon me.* Changing the form from the singular to the plural, and including *all* his pretended friends. Such a change in the number is not uncommon. His mind seems to have passed from the particular instance which he was contemplating, to *all* his friends, and he suddenly felt that *all* had treated him alike. The meaning is, that, like wild beasts, they open their mouth to devour me. ¶ *They have gathered themselves together.* They have entered into a conspiracy, and have *agreed* to oppose me. They are united in this thing, and all feel and act alike.

11. *God hath delivered me.* Marg. *shut me up.* The meaning is, that God had committed him to their hands as a prisoner or captive. They had power over him to do as they pleased. ¶ *To the ungodly.* Into the hands of wicked men—meaning undoubtedly his professed friends. ¶ *And turned me over.* The word here used (from יָרַט) means to throw head long, to precipitate, to cast down. Here it means, "he has thrown me headlong into the hands of the wicked."

12. *I was at ease.* I was in a state of happiness and security. The word here used (שָׁלֵו) means sometimes to be *at ease* in an improper sense; that is, to be in a state of "carnal security," or living unconcerned in sin (Ezek. xxiii. 42; comp. Prov. i. 32); but here it is used in the sense of comfort. He had every thing desirable around him. ¶ *But he hath broken me asunder.* He has crushed me. ¶ *He hath also taken* me *by my neck.* Perhaps as an animal does his prey. We have all seen dogs seize upon their prey in this manner. ¶ *And set me up for his mark.* Changing the figure, and saying that God had directed his arrows against him; so Jeremiah, Lam. iii. 12 :

He hath bent his bow,
And set me as a mark for the arrow.

13. *His archers.* He does not come alone to shoot at me; he has employed a company of bowmen, who also direct *their* arrows against me. The word here used (רַב) means properly *much, large,* great; and is applied to that which is powerful or mighty. It is nowhere else used in the sense of *archers,* and might be rendered "*his many;*" i. e. his bands, hosts, or armies. But as all the ancient versions render it *arrows,* or *archers,* probably that sense is to be retained. Allusion is here made to those who claimed to be the friends of Job, but who now showed to his apprehension that they were merely sharp-shooters under the control of God, to deepen his woes. ¶ *He cleaveth my reins asunder.* With his arrows. They penetrate quite through me. ¶ *He poureth out my gall.* The word *gall* means the *bile*—the yellowish-green bitter fluid secreted in the liver. A similar figure occurs in Lam. ii. 11, "My liver is poured upon the earth." Among the heathen poets, also, the *liver* is represented as pierced, and as pouring out gore. Thus Æsch. Agam.

14 He breaketh me with breach upon breach ; [a] he runneth upon me like a giant.

a Jer. 14.17.

15 I have sewed sackcloth upon my skin, and defiled my horn in the [b] dust.

b chap. 30.19.

442 : Θιγγάνει πρὸς ἧπαρ. So also 801: Δῆγμα λύπης ἐφ' ἧπαρ προσικνεῖται. So in the Iliad xiii. 412, xx. 469, 470. The meaning here is, "I am transfixed with a deadly wound, and must die. God has come upon me as an armed man, and has pierced my vitals."

14. *He breaketh me.* He crushes me. ¶ *With breach upon breach.* He renews and repeats the attack, and thus completely overwhelms me. One blow follows another in such quick succession, that he does not give me time to recover. ¶ *He runneth upon me like a giant.* With great and irresistible force—as some strong and mighty warrior whom his adversary cannot resist. The Hebrew is גבור—*a mighty one.* Sept. " The mighty—δυνάμενοι—run upon me." Vulg. *gigas* —a giant.

15. *I have sewed sackcloth.* I have put on the badges of humiliation and grief; see Notes on Isa. iii. 24. This was the usual emblem of mourning. In order more deeply to express it, or to make it a *permanent* memorial of sorrow, it would seem that it was *sewed* around the body—as we sew crape on the hat. ¶ *And defiled my horn in the dust.* The word rendered *defiled* (from עלל) has, according to Gesenius, the notion of *repetition,* derived from the use of the Arabic word. The Arabic means, to drink again, *i. e.* after a former draught ; and then, to drink deep. Hence the word is applied to any action which is repeated —as to the second blow by which one already struck down is killed ; to an after-harvest, or to gleaning in the fields. Here Gesenius supposes it means to *maltreat,* to *abuse ;* and the idea according to him is, that he had covered his whole head in the dust. The word *horn* is used in the Scriptures to denote strength and power. The figure is taken from horned animals, whose strength resides in their horns ; and hence, as the horn is the means of defence, the word comes to denote that on which one relies ; his strength, honour, dignity. A *horn,* made of silver, was also worn as an ornament, or as an emblem, on the forehead of females or warriors. It was probably used at first by warriors a a symbol of *power, authority,* or *strength ;* and the idea was undoubtedly derived from the fact that the strength of animals was seen to lie in the horn. Then it came to be a mere ornament, and as such is used still in the vicinity of Mount Lebanon. Oriental customs do not undergo those changes which are so common in the Western world, and it is possible that this custom prevailed in the time of Job. The *horn* was usually worn by females ; it is also a part of the ornament on the head of a male, and as such would be regarded doubtless as an emblem of honour. The custom is prevalent at the present day among the Druses of Lebanon, the Egyptian cavalry, and in some parts of Russia bordering on Persia. Dr. Macmichael, in his " Journey," says : " One of the most extraordinary parts of the attire of their females (Drusus of Lebanon), is a silver horn, sometimes studded with jewels, worn on the head in various positions, *distinguishing their different conditions.* A married woman has it affixed to the right side of the head, a widow on the left, and a virgin is pointed out by its being placed on the very crown. Over this silver projection the long veil is thrown, with which they so completely conceal their faces as to rarely have more than an eye visible." The horn worn by females is a conical tube, about twelve inches long. Col. Light mentions the horn of the wife of an emir, made of gold, and studded with precious stones. Horns are worn by Abyssinian chiefs in military reviews, or on parade after a victory. They are much shorter than those of the females, and are about the size and shape of a candle extinguisher, fastened by a strong fillet to the head, which is often made of met-

16 My face is foul with weeping, and on my eyelids *is* the shadow of death ;

17 Not *a* for *any* injustice in mine

a Ps.44.17-21.

al ; they are not easily broken off. This peculiar kind of horn is undoubtedly the kind made by the false prophet Zedekiah for Ahab, to whom he said, when Ahab was about to attack the enemy, "With these shalt thou push the Syrians, until thou hast conquered them;" 1 Kings xxii. 11 ; 2 Chron. xviii. 10 ; comp. Deut. xxxiii. 17. The idea here is, that whatever once constituted the reliance or the glory of Job, was now completely prostrate. It was as if it were buried in the earth.

16. *My face is foul with weeping.* Wemyss, "swelled." Noyes, "red." Good, "tarnished." Luther, "ist geschwollen"—is swelled. So Jerome. The LXX., strangely enough, ἡ γαστήρ μου συνκέκαυται, κ. τ. λ. "my belly is burned with weeping." The Hebrew word (חֳמַר) means to boil up, to ferment, to foam. Hence it means to be red, and the word is often used in this sense in Arabic—from the idea of becoming heated or inflamed. Here it probably means either to be *swelled*, as any thing does that *ferments*, or to be *red* as if *heated*—the usual effect of weeping. The idea of being *defiled* is not in the word. ¶ *And on my eyelids is the shadow of death.* On the meaning of the word rendered "shadow of death," see Notes on chap. iii. 5. The meaning is, that darkness covered his eyes, and he felt that he was about to die. One of the usual indications of the approach of death is, that the sight fails, and every thing seems to be dark. Hence Homer so often describes death by the phrase, "and darkness covered his eyes;" or the form "a cloud of death covered his eyes"—θανάτου νέφος ὄσσι ἐκάλυψη. The idea here is, that he experienced the indications of approaching death.

17. *Not for any injustice,* &c. Still claiming that he does not deserve his sorrows, and that these calamities had not come upon him on account of any

hands : also my prayer *b is* pure.

18 O earth, cover not thou my blood, and let my cry have no place.

b Ps.66.18,19.

enormous sins, as his friends believed. ¶ *My prayer* is *pure.* My devotion ; my worship of God is not hypocritical —as my friends maintain.

18. *O earth.* Passionate appeals to the earth are not uncommon in the Scriptures ; see Notes on Isa. i. 2. Such appeals indicate deep emotion, and are among the most animated forms of personification. ¶ *Cover not thou my blood.* Blood here seems to denote the wrong done to him. He compares his situation with that of one who had been murdered, and calls on the earth not to conceal the crime, and prays that his injuries may not be hidden, or pass unavenged. Aben Ezra, Dr. Good, and some others, however, suppose that he refers to blood shed *by* him, and that the idea is, that he would have the earth reveal any blood if he had ever shed any; or in other words, that it is a strong protestation of his innocence. But the former interpretation seems to accord best with the connection. It is the exclamation of deep feeling. He speaks as a man about to die, but he says that he would die as an innocent and a much injured man, and he passionately prays that his death may not pass unavenged. God had crushed him, and his friends had wronged him, and he now earnestly implores that his character may yet be vindicated. "According to the saying of the Arabs, the blood of one who was unjustly slain remained upon the earth without sinking into it until the avenger of blood came up. It was regarded as a proof of innocence." Eichhorn, *in loc.* That there is much of irreverence in all this must, I think, be conceded. It is not language for us to imitate. But it is not more irreverent and unbecoming than what often occurs, and it is designed to show what the human heart *will* express when it is allowed to give utterance to its real feelings. ¶ *And let my cry have no place.* Let it not be hid or concealed. Let there

19 Also now, behold, my witness *is* in heaven, and my record *is* [1] on high.

20 My friends [2] scorn me ; *but* mine eye poureth out *tears* unto God.

1 *in the high places*, Ep.1.3.
2 are *my scorners*.

21 Oh [a] that one might plead for a man with God, as a man *pleadeth* for his [3] neighbour !

22 When [4] a few years are come, then I shall go [b] the way *whence* I shall not return.

a Is. 45.9.   3 or, *friend*.
4 *years of number*.   b Ec.12. 5.

be nothing to hinder my cry from ascending to heaven. The meaning is, that Job wished his solemn protestations of his innocence to go abroad. He desired that all might hear him. He called on the nations and heaven to hear. He appealed to the universe. He desired that the earth would not conceal the proof of his wrongs, and that his cry might not be confined or limited by any bounds, but that it might go abroad so that all worlds might hear.

19. *My witness is in heaven.* That is, I can appeal to God for my sincerity. He is my witness ; and he will bear record for me. This is an evidence of returning confidence in God—to which Job always returns even after the most passionate and irreverent expressions. Such is his real trust in God, that though he is betrayed at times into expressions of impatience and irreverence, yet he is sure to return to calmer views, and to show that he has true confidence in the Most High. The strength, the power, and the point of his expressions of passion and impatience are against his *friends;* but they *sometimes* terminate on God, as if even he was leagued with them against him. But he still had *permanent* or *abiding* confidence in God. ¶ *My record* is *on high.* Marg. *in the high places.* It means, in heaven. Luther renders this, und der mich kennet, ist in der Höhe—and he who knows me is on high. The Hebrew is שָׂהֲדִי—*my witness ;* properly an eye-witness. The meaning is, that he could appeal to God as a witness of his sincerity.

20. *My friends scorn me.* Marg. *are my scorners.* That is, his friends had him in derision and mocked him, and he could only appeal with tears to God. ¶ *Mine eye poureth out* tears *unto God.* Despised and mocked by his friends, he made his appeal to one who he

knew would regard him with compassion. This shows that the heart of Job was substantially right. Notwithstanding all his passionate exclamations ; and notwithstanding his expressions, when he was urged on by his sorrows to give vent to improper emotions in relation to God ; yet he had a firm confidence in him, and always returned to right feelings and views. The heart may sometimes err. The best of men may sometimes give expression to improper feelings. But they will return to just views, and will ultimately evince unwavering confidence in God.

21. *Oh that one might plead for a man.* A more correct rendering of this would be, " Oh that it might be for a man to contend with God ;" that is, in a judicial controversy. It is the expression of an earnest desire to carry his cause at once before God, and to be permitted to argue it there. This desire Job had often expressed ; see Notes on chap. xiii. 3, 18—22. On the grammatical construction of the passage, see Rosenmüller. ¶ *As a man* pleadeth *for his neighbour.* Heb. "the son of man ;" that is, the offspring of man. Or, rather, as a man contendeth with his neighbour ; as one man may carry on a cause with another. He desired to carry his cause directly before God, and to be permitted to argue the case with him, as one is permitted to maintain an argument with a man ; see Notes on chap. xiii. 20, 21.

22. *When a few years are come.* Marg. *years of number;* that is, numbered years, or a few years. The same idea is expressed in chap. vii. 21 ; see Notes on that place. The idea is, that he must soon die. He desired, therefore, before he went down to the grave, to carry his cause before God, and to have, as he did not doubt he

CHAPTER XVII.

M Y ¹ breath is corrupt, my days are extinct, the graves ª *are ready* for me.

2 *Are there* not mockers with

1 or, *spirit is spent.*   a Ps.88.3,4.

me? and doth not mine eye,² con-tinue in their provocation?

3 Lay down now, put me in a surety with thee; who *is* he *that* will strike hands ᵇ with me?

2 *lodge.*   b Pr.6.1.

should have, the divine attestation in his favour; comp. Notes on chap. xix. 25—27. Now he was overwhelmed with calamities and reproaches, and was about to die in this condition. He did not wish to die thus. He wished that the reproaches might be wiped off, and that his character might be cleared up and made fair. He believ-ed assuredly that if he could be per-mitted to carry his cause directly be-fore God, he might be able to vindicate his character, and to obtain the divine verdict in his favour; and if he ob-tained that, he was not unwilling to die. It is the expression of such a wish as every man has, that his sun may not go down under a cloud; that whatever aspersions may rest on his character may be wiped away; and that his name, if remembered at all when he is dead, may go untarnished down to future times, and be such that his friends may repeat it without a blush.

CHAPTER XVII.

1. *My breath is corrupt.* Marg. or *spirit is spent.* The idea is, that his vital powers were nearly extinct; his breath failed; his power was weaken-ed, and he was ready to die. This is connected with the previous chapter, and should not have been separated from it. There was no necessity of making a new chapter here, and we have one of those unfortunate breaks in the middle of a paragraph, and al-most of a sentence, which are too common in the Scriptures. ¶ *The graves* are ready *for me.* The Hebrew is plural, but why so used I know not. The Vulgate is singular—*sepulchrum.* The LXX. render it, "I pray for a tomb (sing. ταφῆς), but I cannot ob-tain it." Possibly the meaning is, "I am about to be united *to the graves,* or *to tombs.*" Schultens re-marks that the plural form is common in Arabic poetry, as well as in poe-try in general.

2. *And doth not mine eye continue in their provocation?* Marg. *lodge.* This is the meaning of the Hebrew word here used—חלן. It properly denotes to pass the night, or to lodge in a place, as distinguished from a permanent residence. The idea here seems to be, that his eye *rested* on their provocations. It remained fixed on them. It was not a mere glance, a passing notice, but was such a view as resulted from a careful observation. It was not such a view as a traveller would obtain by passing hastily by, but it was such as one would obtain who had encamped for a time, and had an opportunity of looking around him with care, and seeing things as they were. Thus explained, there is much poetic beauty in the passage. The Vulgate, however, renders it, "I have not sinned, and mine eye remains in bitterness." The LXX., "I suppli-cate in distress — κάμνων — yet what have I done? Strangers came, and stole my substance: who is the man?" The simple meaning is, that Job had a calm view of their wickedness, and that he could not be deceived.

3. *Lay down now.* This is evidently an address to God—a repetition of the wish which he had so often expressed, that he might be permitted to bring his cause directly before him; see chap. xiii. 3. The whole passage here is ob-scure, because we are in a great measure ignorant of the ancient practices in courts of law, and of the ancient forms of trial. The general sense seems to be, that Job desires the Deity to en-ter into a judicial investigation, and to give him a *pledge*—or, as we should say, a *bond,* or *security*—that he would not avail himself of his almighty power, but would place him on an equality in the trial, and allow him to plead his cause on equal terms; see Notes on chap. xiii. 20—22. The phrase "lay down now" means, lay down a pledge,

4 For thou hast hid their heart from understanding : therefore shalt thou not exalt *them*.

5 He that speaketh flattery *a* to *his* friends, even the eyes of his children shall fail.

a Ps. 12. 3.

---

or something of that kind ; and may have referred to some ancient custom of giving security on going to trial, that no advantage would be taken, or that the parties would abide by the decision in the case. ¶ *Put me in a surety with thee.* The word used here (ערבני) is from ערב, to mix, mingle ; to exchange, to barter ; and then to become surety for any one—that is, to *exchange* places with him, or to stand in his place; Gen. xliii. 9 ; xliv. 32. Here the idea seems to be, that Job wished the Deity to give him some pledge or security that justice would be done, or that he would not take advantage of his power and majesty to overawe him. Or, as has been remarked, it may refer to some custom of furnishing security on a voluntary trial or arbitration, that the award of the referees would be observed. I think it most probable that this is the idea. The controversy here was to be voluntary. In a voluntary trial, or an arbitration, there is a necessity of some security by the parties that the decision shall be submitted to—a pledge to each other that they will abide by it. Such a pledge Job desired in this case. All this is language taken from courts, and should not be pressed too much, nor should Job be hastily charged with irreverence. Having once suggested the idea of *a trial* of the cause, it was natural for him to use the language which was commonly employed in reference to such trials ; and these expressions are to be regarded as thrown in for the sake of *keeping*, or verisimilitude. ¶ *Who is he that will strike hands with me ?* Striking hands then, as now, seems to have been one mode of confirming an agreement, or ratifying a compact. The idea here is, " Who is there that will be surety to me for thee ?" that is, for the faithful observance of right and justice. There is an appearance of irreverence in this language, but it arises from carrying out the ideas pertaining to a form of trial in a

court. In entering into *sureties*, it was usual to unite hands; see Prov. vi. 1 :

My son, if thou be surety for thy friend,
If thou hast stricken thy hand with a stranger.

So Prov. xvii. 18 :

A man void of understanding striketh hands,
And becometh surety in the presence of his friend.

Comp. Prov. xi. 15 ; xxii. 26. The same custom prevailed in the times of Homer and of Virgil. Thus Homer (Iliad, β. 341) says :

Πoῦ δὴ ——————
—— δεξιαί ἧς ἐπέπιθμεν—

And so Virgil (Æneid iv. 597) says ;

——en dextra fidesque.

4. *For thou hast hid their heart from understanding.* That is, the heart of his professed friends. Job says that they were blind and perverse, and indisposed to render him justice ; and he therefore pleads that he may carry his cause directly before God. He attributes their want of understanding to the agency of God in accordance with the doctrine which prevailed in early times, and which is so often expressed in the Scriptures, that God is the source of light and truth, and that when men are blinded it is in accordance with his wise purposes ; see Isa. vi. 9, 10. It is *because* they were thus blind and perverse, that he asks the privilege of carrying the cause at once up to God—and who could blame him for such a desire ? ¶ *Therefore thou shalt not exalt* them. By the honour of deciding a case like this, or by the reputation of wisdom. The name of sage or *wise man* was among the most valued in those times; but Job says that that would not be awarded to his friends. God would not exalt or honour men thus devoid of wisdom.

5. *He that speaketh flattery to* his *friends.* Noyes renders this, " He that delivers up his friend as a prey, the eyes of his children shall fail." So Wemyss, " He who delivers up his friends to plunder." Dr. Good, " He that rebuketh his friends with mild-

6 He hath made me also a by-word of the people, and [1] aforetime I was as a tabret.

[1] or, *before them.*

7 Mine eye also is dim by reason of sorrow, and all my [2] members *are* as a shadow.

[2] or, *thoughts.*

ness, even the eyes of his children shall be accomplished." The LXX., " He announces evil for his portion ; his eyes fail over his sons." The Vulg. "He promises spoil to his companions, and the eyes of his sons fail." The word rendered "flattery" (חֵלֶק) properly means *that which is smooth, smoothness* (from חָלַק to be smooth) ; and thence it denotes *a lot or portion,* because *a smooth stone* was anciently used to cast lots in dividing spoils; Deut. xviii. 8. Here it is synonymous with plunder or spoil ; and the idea is, that he who betrayeth his friends to the spoil or to the spoiler, the eyes of his children shall fail. The meaning in this connection is, that the friends of Job had acted as one would who should announce the residence of his neighbours to robbers, that they might come and plunder them. Instead of defending him, they had acted the part of a traitor. Schultens says that this verse is " a Gordian knot ;" and most commentators regard it as such ; but the above seems to give a clear and consistent meaning. It is evidently a proverb, and is designed to bear on the professed friends of Job, and to show that they had acted a fraudulent part towards him. In ver. 4, he had said that God had hid their heart from understanding, and that wisdom had failed them. He *here* says that in addition to a want of wisdom, they were like a man who should betray his neighbours to robbers. ¶ *Even the eyes of his children shall fail.* He shall be punished. To do this is a crime, and great calamity shall come upon him, represented by the failure of the eyes of his children. Calamity is not unfrequently expressed by the loss of the eyes; see Prov. xxx. 17.

6. *He hath also.* That is, God has done this. ¶ *Also a by-word.* A proverb (מָשָׁל) ; a term of reproach, ridicule, or scorn. He has exposed me to derision. ¶ *And aforetime.* Marg. *before them.* The margin is

the correct translation of the Hebrew, לִפְנֵי. It means, in their presence, or in their view. ¶ *I was as a tabret.* This is an unhappy translation. The true meaning is, " I am become *their abhorrence,* or am to them an object of contempt." Vulg. " I am an example *(exemplum)* to them." Sept. " I am become a laughter (γέλως;) to them." The Chaldee renders it, " Thou hast placed me for a proverb to the people, and I shall be *Gehenna* (גֵּיהִנָּם) to them." The Hebrew word תֹּפֶת—*thopheth,* or *Tophet,* is the name which is often given in the Scriptures to the valley of Hinnom—the place where children were sacrificed to Moloch ; see Notes on Matth. v. 22. But there is no evidence or probability that the word was so used in the time of Job. It is never used in the Scriptures in the sense of a *tabret,* that is a tabor or small drum ; though the word תֹּף—*toph* is thus used ; see Notes on Isa. v. 12. The word here used is derived, probably, from the obsolete verb תּוּף—*to spit out ;* and then to spit out with contempt. The verb is so used in Chaldee. *Castell.* The meaning of the word probably still lives in the Arabic. The Arabic word means to spit out with contempt ; and the various forms of the nouns derived from the verb are applied to any thing detested, or detestable ; to the parings of the nails ; to an abandoned woman ; to a dog, &c. See *Castell* on this word. I have no doubt that is the sense here, and that we have here a word whose true signification is to be sought in the Arabic; and that Job means to say that he was treated as the most loathsome and execrable object.

7. *Mine eye is dim by reason of sorrow.* Schultens supposes that this refers to his external appearance in general, as being worn down, exhausted, *defaced* by his many troubles; but it seems rather to mean that his eyes failed on account of weeping. ¶ *And all my members are as a sha-*

8 Upright *men* shall be astonied at this, and the innocent shall stir up himself against the hypocrite.

9 The righteous *a* also shall hold

on his way, and he that hath clean *b* hands shall be stronger and [1] stronger.   *a* Ps.84.7.11; Pr.14.16.

b Ps. 24 4.   [1] *add strength.*

---

dow. " I am a mere skeleton, I am exhausted and emaciated by my sufferings." It is common to speak of persons who are emaciated by sickness or famine as mere *shadows.* Thus Livy (L. xxi. 40) says, Effigies, imo, *umbræ hominum ;* fame, frigore, illuvie, squalore enecti, contusi, debilitati inter saxa rupesque. So Æschylus calls Œdipus—Οἰδίπου σκιαν—*the shadow of Œdipus.*

8. *Upright* men *shall be astonished at this.* At the course of events in regard to me. They will be amazed that God has suffered a holy man to be plunged into such calamities, and to be treated in this manner by his friends. The fact at which he supposes they would be so much astonished was, that the good were afflicted in this manner, and that no relief was furnished. ¶ *And the innocent shall stir up himself.* Shall rouse himself, or assume vigour to resist the wicked. ¶ *The hypocrite.* The wicked—alluding probably to his professed friends. The idea of *hypocrisy* which the sentence conveys arises from the fact, that they professed to be *his* friends, and had proved to be false ; and that they had professed to be the friends *of God,* and yet had uttered sentiments inconsistent with any right views of him. He now says, that that could not go unnoticed. The world would be aroused at so remarkable a state of things, and a just public indignation would be the result.

9. *The righteous also shall hold on his way.* The meaning of this verse is plain ; but the connection is not so apparent. It seems to me that it refers to *Job himself,* and is a declaration that *he,* a righteous man, who had been so grievously calumniated, would hold on his way, and become stronger and stronger, while *they* would sink in the public esteem, and be compelled to abandon their position. It is the expression of a confident assurance that *he* would be more and more confirmed in his integrity, and would be-

come stronger and stronger in God. Though Job intended, probably, that this should be applied to himself, yet he has expressed it in a general manner, and indeed the whole passage has a proverbial cast ; and it shows that even then it was the settled belief that the righteous would persevere. As an expression of the early faith of the pious in one of the now settled doctrines of Christianity, "the perseverance of the saints," this doctrine is invaluable. It shows that that doctrine has travelled down from the earliest ages. It was one of the elementary doctrines of religion in the earliest times. It became a proverb ; and was admitted among the undisputed maxims of the wise and good, and it was such a sentiment as was just adapted to the circumstances of Job—a much tried and persecuted man. He was in all the danger of apostacy to which the pious are usually exposed ; he was tempted to forsake his confidence in God ; he was afflicted for reasons which he could not comprehend ; he was without an earthly friend to sustain him, and he seemed to be forsaken by God himself ; yet he had the fullest conviction that he would be enabled to persevere. The great principle was settled, that if there was true religion in the heart, it would abide ; that if the path of righteousness had been entered, he who trod it would keep on his way. ¶ *And he that hath clean hands.* The innocent ; the friend of God ; the man of pure life ; see Notes chap. ix. 30 ; comp. Ps. xxiv. 4. " Clean hands" here, are designed to denote a pure and holy life. Among the ancients they were regarded as indicative of purity of heart. Porphyry remarks (de antro Nympharum) that in the "mysteries," those who were initiated were accustomed to wash their hands with honey instead of water, as a pledge that they would preserve themselves from every impure and unholy thing ; see Burder, in Rosenmüller's Alte u. neue Morgen-

10 But as for you all, do you return, and come now: for I cannot find *one* wise *man* among you.

a Pr.16.9; 19.21.

11 My days are past, my purposes *a* are broken off, *even* the ¹ thoughts of my heart.

1 *possessions.*

land, *in loc.* ¶ *Shall be stronger and stronger.* Marg. as in Heb. *add strength.* He shall advance in the strength of his attachment to God. This is true. The man of pure and blameless life shall become more and more established in virtue; more confirmed in his principles; more convinced of the value and the truth of religion. Piety, like every thing else, becomes stronger by exercise. The man who speaks truth only, becomes more and more attached to truth; the principle of benevolence is strengthened by being practised; honesty, the more it is exhibited, becomes more the settled rule of the life; and he who prays, delights more and more in his approaches to God. The *tendency* of religion in the heart is to grow stronger and stronger; and God *intends* that he who has once loved him, shall continue to love him for ever.

10. *But as for you all, do you return.* This may mean, either, "return to the debate;" or, "return from your unjust and uncharitable opinion concerning me." The former seems to accord best with the scope of the passage. Tindal renders it, "Get you hence." Dr. Good, "Get ye hence, and begone, I pray." Wemyss, "Repeat your discourses as often as you may, I do not find a wise man among you." It is doubtful, however, whether the Hebrew will bear this construction. ¶ *For I cannot find* one *wise* man *among you.* Perhaps the idea here is, "I have not yet found one wise man among you, and you are invited, therefore, to renew the argument. Hitherto you have said nothing that indicates wisdom. Try again, and see if you can say any thing now that shall deserve attention." If this is the meaning, it shows that Job was willing to hear all that they had to say, and to give them credit for wisdom, if they ever evinced any.

11. *My days are past.* "I am about to die." Job relapses again into sadness—as he often does. A sense of

his miserable condition comes over him like a cloud, and he feels that he must die. ¶ *My purposes are broken off.* All my plans fail, and my schemes of life come to an end. No matter what they could say now, it was all over with him. and he must die; comp. Isa. xxxviii. 12:

" My habitation is taken away, and is removed from me like a shepherd's tent;
My life is cut off as by a weaver
Who severeth the web from the loom;
Between the morning and the night thou wilt make an end of me."

¶ *Even the thoughts of my heart.* Marg. *possession.* Noyes, "*treasures.*" Dr. Good, "*resolves.*" Dr. Stock, "*the tenants of my heart.*" Vulg., "*torquentes cor meum.*" Sept., τὰ ἄρθρα τῆς καρδίας μου—*the string of my heart.* The Hebrew word (מורשׁ) means properly *possession* (from ירשׁ, *to inherit*); and the word here means the dear possessions of his heart; his cherished plans and schemes; the delights of his soul—the purposes which he had hoped to accomplish. All these were now to be broken on by death. This is to man one of the most trying things in death. All his plans must be arrested. His projects of ambition and gain, of pleasure and of fame, of professional eminence and of learning, all are arrested midway. The farmer is compelled to leave his plough in the furrow; the mechanic, his work unfinished; the lawyer, his brief half prepared; the student, his books lying open; the man who is building a palace, leaves it incomplete; and he who is seeking a crown, is taken away when it seemed just within his grasp. How many *unfinished* plans are caused by death every day! How many unfinished books, sermons, houses, does it make! How many schemes of wickedness and of benevolence, of fraud and of kindness, of gain and of mercy, are daily broken in upon by death! Soon, reader, all *your* plans and *mine* will be ended—mine, perhaps, before these lines meet your eye; yours soon afterwards. God

12 They change the night into day: the light *is* [1] short because of darkness.

13 If I wait, the grave *is* mine

1 *near.*   2 *cried, or, called.*

grant that our purposes of life may be such that we shall be *willing* to have them broken in upon—all so subordinate to the GREAT PLAN of being prepared for heaven, that we may cheerfully surrender them at any moment, at the call of the Master summoning us into his awful presence!

12. *They change.* The word "they" in this place, some understand as referring to his friends; others, to his thoughts. Rosenmüller supposes it is to be taken *impersonally*, and that the meaning is, "night is become day to me." Wemyss translates it, "night is assigned me for day." So Dr. Good renders it. The meaning may be, that the night was to him as the day. He had no rest. The period when he had formerly sought repose, was now made like the day, and all was alike gloom and sadness. ¶ *The light* is *short because of darkness.* Marg. *near.* The meaning is, probably, "even the day has lost its usual brilliancy and cheerfulness, and has become gloomy and sad. It seems to be like night. Neither night nor day is natural to me; the one is restless and full of cares like the usual employments of day, and the other is gloomy, or almost night, where there is no comfort and peace. Day brings to me none of its usual enjoyments. It is short, gloomy, sad, and hastens away, and a distressing and restless night soon comes on."

13. *If I wait.* Or more accurately, "truly I expect that the grave will be my home." The word rendered "if" (אם) is often used in such a sense. The meaning is, " I look certainly to the grave as my home. I have made up my mind to it, and have no other expectation." ¶ *The grave.* Heb. שאול. It may mean here either the grave, or the region of departed spirits, to which he expected soon to descend. ¶ *Mine house.* My home; my permanent abode. ¶ *I have made my bed.* I am certain of making my bed there. I shall soon lie down there. ¶ *In the*

house: I have made my bed in the darkness.

14 I have [2] said to corruption, Thou *art* my father: to the worm, *Thou art* my mother and my sister.

darkness. In the grave, or in the dark world to which it leads; see Notes on chap. x. 21, 22.

14. *I have said.* Marg. *cried,* or *called.* The sense is, " I say," or " I thus address the grave." ¶ *To corruption.* The word here used (שחת) means properly *a pit,* or *pit-fall,* Ps. vii. 15 ; ix. 15 ; a *cistern,* or *a ditch,* Job ix. 31 ; or *the sepulchre,* or *grave,* Ps. xxx. 9 ; Job xxxiii. 18, 30. The LXX. render it here by θανάτον—*death.* Jerome (Vulg.), *putredini dixi.* According to Gesenius *(Lex.),* the word never has the sense of *corruption.* Schultens, however, Rosenmüller, and others, understand it in the sense of corruption or putrefaction. This accords, certainly, with the other hemistich, and better constitutes a parallelism with the "worm" than the word "*grave*" would. It seems probable that this is the sense here ; and if the proper meaning of the word is *a pit,* or *the grave,* it here denotes the grave, as containing a dead and mouldering body. ¶ *Thou* art *my father.* "I am nearly allied to it. I sustain to it a relation like that of a child to a father." The idea seems to be that of *family likeness;* and the object is to present the most striking and impressive view of his sad and sorrowful condition. He was so diseased, so wretched, so full of sores and of corruption (see chap. vii. 5), that he might be said to be the child of one mouldering in the grave, and was kindred to a family in the tomb ! ¶ *To the worm.* The worm that feeds upon the dead. He belonged to that sad family where the body was putrifying, and where it was covered with worms ; see Notes on Isa. xiv. 11. ¶ *My mother.* I am so nearly allied to the worms, that the connection may be compared to that between a mother and her son. ¶ *And my sister.* "The sister here is mentioned rather than the brother, because the noun rendered *worm* in the Hebrew, is in the feminine gender."

15 And where *is* now my hope? as for my hope, who shall see it?

a Jonah 2. 6.

16 They shall go down to the bars *a* of the pit, when *our* rest *b* together *is* in the dust.

b chap. 3. 17-19.

Rosenmüller. The sense of the whole is, that Job felt that he belonged to the grave. He was destined to corruption. He was soon to lie down with the dead. His acquaintance and kindred were there. So corrupt was his body, so afflicted and diseased, that he seemed to belong to the family of the putrifying, and of those covered with worms! What an impressive description; and yet how true is it of all! The most vigorous frame, the most beautiful and graceful form, the most brilliant complexion, has a near relationship to the worm, and will soon belong to the mouldering family beneath the ground! Christian reader! such are you; such am I. Well, let it be so. Let us not repine. Be the grave our home; be the mouldering people there our parents, and brothers, and sisters. Be our alliance with the worms. There is a brighter scene beyond—a world where we shall be kindred with the angels, and ranked among the sons of God. In that world we shall be clothed with immortal youth, and shall know corruption no more. Then our eyes will shine with undiminished brilliancy for ever; our cheeks glow with immortal health; our hearts beat with the pulsations of eternal life. Then our hands shall be feeble and our knees totter with disease or age no more; and then the current of health and joy shall flow on through our veins for ever and ever! Allied now to worms we are, but we are allied to the angels too; the grave is to be our home, but so also is heaven; the worm is our brother, but so also is the Son of God! Such is man; such are his prospects here, such his hopes and destiny in the world to come. He dies here, but he lives in glory and honour hereafter for ever.

Shall man, O God of light and life,
  For ever moulder in the grave?
Canst thou forget thy glorious work,
  Thy promise and thy power to save?

Shall life revisit dying worms,
  And spread the joyful insects' wing;

And O shall man awake no more,
  To see thy face, thy name to sing?

Faith sees the bright, eternal doors,
  Unfold to make her children way;
They shall be clothed with endless life,
  And shine in everlasting day.

The trump shall sound, the dead shall wake,
  From the cold tomb the slumberers spring;
Through heaven with joy these myriads rise,
  And hail their Saviour and their King.
                              DR. DWIGHT.

15. *And where* is *now my hope?* What hope have I of life? What possibility is there of my escape from death? ¶ *Who shall see it?* That is, who will see any hopes that I may now cherish fulfilled. If I cherish any, they will be disappointed, and no one will see them accomplished.

16. *They shall go down.* That is, *my hopes* shall go down. All the expectations that I have cherished of life and happiness, will descend with me. We have a similar expression when we say, that a man "has buried his hopes in the grave," when he loses an only son. ¶ *To the bars of the pit.* "*Bars of Sheol*"—בדי שאל. Vulg., "*Profoundest deep.*" Sept., εἰς ᾅδην—*to Hades.* Sheol, or Hades, was supposed to be under the earth. Its entrance was by the grave as a gate that led to it. It was protected by *bars* —as prisons are—so that those who entered there could not escape; see Notes on Isa. xiv. 9. It was a dark, gloomy dwelling, far away from light, and from the comforts which men enjoy in this life; see Job x. 21, 22. To that dark world Job expected soon to descend; and though he did not regard that as properly a place of *punishment,* yet it was not a place of positive joy. It was a gloomy and wretched world—the land of darkness and of the shadow of death; and he looked to the certainty of going there not with joy, but with anguish and distress of heart. Had Job been favoured with the clear and elevated views of heaven which *we* have in the Christian revelation, death to him would have lost its gloom. We wonder, often, that so good a man expressed

CHAPTER XVIII.

ANALYSIS OF THE CHAPTER.

This second discourse of Bildad is made up almost entirely of a string of proverbial expressions, showing what must befall the wicked. The design is to prove that the wicked must be punished, and to portray the various kinds of calamities that will come upon them. The *inference* which he manifestly designs should be drawn from his discourse is, that where great calamities come upon a man, there is the most conclusive evidence that he is wicked. The speech contains some particulars peculiarly adapted to the circumstances of Job, and were doubtless intended to be applied to him; and they are such as to leave no doubt that he regarded Job as an eminently wicked man.

The speech consists of two parts.

1. A reproof of Job for the manner in which he had spoken; ver. 1—4. He accuses him of being *long-minded* and interminable in his speech; ver. 2. He complains that he and his friends had been overlooked and despised, and had been regarded as beasts, ver. 3. He accuses Job of insufferable pride and arrogance, as if even the most firm principles of the divine administration were to be changed to accommodate him, ver. 4.

II. A highly wrought description of the calamities which must come upon a wicked man, ver. 5-21. His light in his dwelling would be put out (ver. 5, 6);

his own plans would destroy him, and he would be taken in a net which he himself had spread (ver. 7, 8); he would soon be seized by robbers, who would spring a net unexpectedly upon him (ver. 9, 10); terrors on every side would alarm him (ver. 11); his strength would be wasted (ver. 12, 13); he would be brought to the king of terrors, and brimstone would be sprinkled on his dwelling (ver. 14, 15); he would be like a tree whose roots and branches were dead (ver. 16); his memory would perish from the earth (ver. 17), and he would be chased out of the world (ver. 18); his family and name would become extinct, so that there would be no one to perpetuate his memory on earth (ver. 19); and they who should come after him would be astonished at the total ruin which had come upon the wicked man. That Bildad meant to apply all this to Job, there can be no doubt; and that it would add greatly to his trials is equally clear. He felt it; and his reply in the following chapter is replete with expressions indicative of his intolerable anguish.

THEN answered Bildad the Shuhite, and said,

2 How long *will it be ere* ye make an end of words? mark, and afterwards we will speak.

such a dread of death, and that he did not look more calmly into the future world. But to do him justice, we should place ourselves in his situation. We should lay aside all that is cheerful and glad in the views of heaven which Christianity has given us. We should look upon the future world as the shadow of death; a land of gloom and spectres; a place beneath the ground—dark, chilly, repulsive; and we shall cease to wonder at the expressions of even so good a man at the prospect of death. When we look at *him*, we should remember with thankfulness the different views which *we* have of the future world, and the source to which we owe them. To us, if we are pious in any measure as Job was, death is the avenue, not to a world of gloom, but to a world of light and glory. It opens into heaven. There is *no* gloom, no darkness, no sorrow. There all are happy; and where all that is mysterious in this life is made plain—all that is sad is succeeded by eternal joy. These views we owe to that gospel which has brought life and immortality to light; and when we think of death and the future world, when from the midst of woes and sorrows we are compelled to look out on eternity, let us rejoice that we are not constrained to look forward with the sad forebodings of the Sage of Uz, but

that we may think of the grave cheered by the strong consolations of Christian hope of the glorious resurrection. ¶ *When our rest together is in the dust.* The rest of me and my hopes. My hopes and myself will expire together.

CHAPTER XVIII.

2. *How long* will it be ere *ye make an end of words?* It has been made a question to whom this is addressed. It is in the plural number, and it is not usual in Hebrew when addressing an individual to make use of the plural form. Some have supposed that it is addressed to Job and to Eliphaz, as being both "long-winded" and tedious in their remarks. Others have supposed that it refers to Job *and the members of his family*, who possibly interposed remarks, and joined Job in his complaints. Others suppose that it refers to Eliphaz and Zophar, as being silent during the speech of Job, and not arresting his remarks as they ought to have done. Rosenmüller supposes that it refers to Job and those similar to him, who were mere feigners of piety, and that Bildad means to ask how long it would be before they would be effectually silenced, and their complaints hushed. I see no great difficulty in supposing that the reference is to Job. The whole strain of the discourse evidently

3 Wherefore are we counted as beasts, *and* reputed vile in your sight ?

4 He *a* teareth ¹ himself in his

anger ; shall the earth be forsaken for thee ? and shall the rock be removed out of his place ?

a chap. 13.14.   1 *his soul.*

---

supposes it ; and there is no evidence that any of the family of Job had spoken, nor does it seem at all probable that Bildad would reprove his own friends either for the length of their speeches, or for not interrupting another. The custom in the East is to allow a man to utter all that he has to say without interruption. ¶ *Mark.* Heb. *understand ;* or *be intelligent—* תבינו ; that is, either speak distinctly, clearly, intelligently ; or consider and weigh our arguments. The former is the interpretation of Schultens, and seems to me to be the true one. The idea is this : " You, Job, have been uttering mere *words.* They are words of complaint, without argument. Speak now in a different manner ; show that you understand the case ; advance *arguments* that are worthy of attention, and then we will reply."

3. *Wherefore are we counted as beasts ?* " Why are we treated in your remarks as if we had no sense, and were unworthy of sound argument in reply to what we say ?" It is *possible* that there may be reference here to what Job said (chap. xii. 7)—that even the *beasts* could give them information about God. But the general idea is, that Job had not treated their views with the attention which they deserved, but had regarded them as unworthy of notice. ¶ And *reputed vile.* The word here used (נמה) means to be unclean, or polluted ; and the idea is, that Job regarded them as worthless or impious.

4. *He teareth himself.* More correctly, " thou that tearest thyself in anger !" It is not an affirmation *about* Job, but it is a direct address *to* him. The meaning is, that he was in the paroxysms of a violent rage ; he acted like a madman. ¶ *Shall the earth be forsaken for thee ?* A reproof of his pride and arrogance. " Shall every thing be made to give way for you ? Are you the only man in the world, and of so much importance, that the

earth is to be made vacant for you to dwell in ? Are the interests of all others to be sacrificed for you, and is every thing else to give place for you ? Are all the laws of God's government to be made to yield rather than that you should be punished ?" Similar modes of expression to denote the insignificance of any one who is proud and arrogant, are still used among the Arabs. " Since Mohammed died, the Imams govern." " The world will not suffer loss on your account." " The world is not dependent on any one man." T. Hunt, in Lowth's Lectures on Hebrew Poetry. Rosenmüller's Morgenland, *in loc.* ¶ *And shall the rock be removed out of his place ?* " Shall the most firm and immutable things give way for your special accommodation ? Shall the most important and settled principles of the divine administration be made to bend on your account ?" These were *not* the principles and feelings of Job ; and great injustice was done to him by this supposition. He was disposed to be submissive in the main to the divine arrangement. But this will describe the feelings of many a man of pride, who supposes that the divine arrangements should be made to *bend* for his special accommodation, and that the great, eternal principles of justice and right should give way rather than that he should be dealt with as common sinners are, and rather than that he should be cast into hell. Such men wish a special place of salvation for themselves. They are too proud to be saved as others are. They complain in their hearts that they are made to suffer, to lose their property, to be sick, to die—as others do. They would wish to be treated with special mercy, and to have special enactments in their favour, and would have the eternal laws of right made to bend for their special accommodation. Such is the pride of the human heart !

5 Yea, the light of the wicked shall a be put out, and the spark of his fire shall not shine.

6 The light shall be dark in his

a Pr.24.20.   1 or, *lamp.*   b Pr.1.30-32.

tabernacle, and his [1] candle shall be put out with him.

7 The steps of his strength shall be straitened, and his own b counsel shall cast him down.

---

5. *Yea.* Truly; or, behold. Bildad here commences his remarks on the certain destiny of the wicked, and strings together a number of apparently proverbial sayings, showing that calamity in various forms would certainly overtake the wicked. There is nothing particularly new in his argument, though the use of the various images which he employs shows how deep was the conviction of this doctrine at that time, and how extensively it prevailed. ¶ *The light of the wicked shall be put out.* *Light* here is an emblem of prosperity. ¶ *The spark of his fire.* Heb. *the flame* of his fire. There may be an allusion here to the customs of Arabian hospitality. This was, and is, their national glory, and it is their boast that no one is ever refused it. The emblem of *fire* or *flame* here may refer to the custom of kindling a fire on an eminence, near a dwelling, to attract the stranger to share the hospitality of the owner of it; or it may refer to the fire *in* his tent, which the stranger was always at liberty to share. In the collection of the Arabian poems, called the Hamasa, this idea occurs almost in the words of Bildad. The extract was furnished me by the Rev. Eli Smith. It is a boast of Salamiel, a prince of Tema. In extolling the virtues of his tribe, he says, "No fire of ours was ever extinguished at night without a guest; and of our guests never did one disparage us." The idea here is, that the wicked would attempt to show hospitality, but the means would be taken away. He would not be permitted to enjoy the coveted reputation of showing it to the stranger, and the fire which might invite the traveller, or which might confer comfort on him, would be put out in his dwelling. The inability to extend the offer of a liberal hospitality would be equivalent to the deepest poverty or the most trying affliction.

6. *And his cand'e.* Marg. *lamp.* The reference is to a lamp that was suspended from the ceiling. The Arabians are fond of this image. Thus they say, "Bad fortune has extinguished my lamp." Of a man whose hopes are remarkably blasted, they say, "He is like a lamp which is immediately extinguished if you let it sink in the oil." See *Schultens.* The putting out of a lamp is to the Orientals an image of utter desolation. It is the universal custom to have a light burning in their houses at night. "The houses of Egypt, in modern times, are never without lights; they burn lamps all the night long, and in every occupied apartment. So requisite to the comfort of a family is this custom reckoned, and so imperious is the power which it exercises, that the poorest people would rather retrench part of their food than neglect it." *Paxton.* It is not improbable that this custom prevailed in former times in Arabia, as it does now in Egypt; and this consideration will give increased beauty and force to this passage.

7. *The steps of his strength.* Strong steps. "Steps of strength" is a Hebraism, to denote firm or vigorous steps. ¶ *Shall be straitened:* Shall be compressed, embarrassed, hindered. Instead of walking freely and at large, he shall be compressed and limited in his goings. "Large steps," "free movement," &c. are proverbial expressions among the Arabs, to denote freedom, prosperity. &c. *Rosenmüller.* Schultens quotes the following illustrations from the Arabic poets. From Ibn Doreid, "He who does not confine himself within human limits, his vast strides shall be straitened." And from Taurizius, "After the battle of Bedrense, the steps were straitened." The meaning here is, that he would be greatly impeded in his movements, instead of going forth at large and in full vigour as he had formerly

8 For he is cast into a net *a* by his own feet, and he walketh upon a snare.

9 The gin shall take *him* by the

a Pr.5.22;29.6.   1 *hidden.*

heel, *and* the robber shall prevail against him.

10 The snare *is* [1] laid for him in the ground, and a trap for him in the way.

done. ¶ *And his own counsel.* His own plans shall be the means of his fall.

8. *For he is cast into a net by his own feet.* He is caught in his own tricks, as if he had spread a net or dug a pitfall for another, and had fallen into it himself. The meaning is, that he would bring ruin upon himself while he was plotting the ruin of others; see Ps. ix. 16, "The wicked is snared by the work of his own hands;" comp. Note chap. v. 13. The phrase "by his own feet" here means, that he walks there *himself.* He is not led or driven by others, but he goes himself into the net. Wild animals are sometimes driven, but *he* walks along of his own accord into the net, and has no one to blame but himself. ¶ *And he walketh upon a snare.* Or a *pitfall.* This was formerly the mode of taking wild beasts. It was done by excavating a place in the earth, and covering it over with turf, leaves, &c. supported in a slender manner ; so that the lion, or elephant or tiger that should tread on it, would fall through. These methods of taking wild beasts have been practised from the earliest times, and are practised every where.

9. *The gin.* Another method of taking wild beasts. It was a snare so made as to spring suddenly on an animal, securing him by the neck or feet. We use a *trap* for the same purpose. The Hebrew word (פַּח) may denote any thing of this kind—a snare, net, noose, &c. with which birds or wild animals are taken. ¶ *By the heel.* By the foot. ¶ *And the robber shall prevail.* He shall be overpowered by the highwayman ; or the plunderer shall make a sudden descent upon him, and strip him of his all. The meaning is, that destruction would suddenly overtake him. There can be no doubt that Bildad meant to apply all this to Job.

10. *The snare is laid.* All this language is taken from the modes of taking wild beasts ; but it is not pos-

sible to designate with absolute certainty the methods in which it was done. The word here used (הֶבֶל) means a *cord,* or *rope;* and then a snare, gin, or toil, such as is used by hunters. It was used in some way as a *noose* to secure an animal. This was *concealed* (Hebrew) "in the earth" —so covered up that an animal would not perceive it, and so constructed that it might be made to spring upon it suddenly. ¶ *And a trap.* We have no reason to suppose that at that time they employed *steel* to construct traps as we do now, or that the word here has exactly the sense which we give to it. The Hebrew word (מַלְכֹּדֶת) is from לכד—*to take, to catch,* and means a noose, snare, spring—by which an animal was seized. It is a *general* term ; though undoubtedly used to denote a particular instrument, then well known. The general idea in all this is, that the wicked man would be suddenly seized by calamities, as a wild animal or a bird is taken in a snare. Independently of the interest of the entire passage (ver. 8—10) as a part of the argument of Bildad, it is interesting from the view which it gives of the mode of securing wild animals in the early periods of the world. They had no guns as we have ; but they early learned the art of setting gins and snares by which they were taken. In illustrating this passage, it will not be inappropriate to refer to some of the modes of hunting practised by the ancient Egyptians, and to introduce here some cuts which may illustrate that mode. The cuts will show that substantially the same methods were practised then in catching birds and taking wild beasts as now, and that there is little novelty in modern practices. The ancients had not only traps, nets, and springs, but also bird-lime smeared upon twigs, and made use of stalking-horses, setting-dogs, &c. The various methods in which this was done, may be seen described at length in Wilkinson's Manners and Customs of the Ancient Egyptians, vol. iii. pp. 1—81. The noose was employed to catch the wild ox, the antelope, and other animals. The following cuts taken from drawings at Beni Hassan, will illustrate some of these methods.

Catching a Gazelle with the Noose.

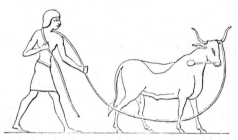

Catching a Wild Ox with the Noose or *lasso*.

The following specimens of *bird-traps* are also found in drawings at Beni Hassan. This seems to be a self-acting net, so constructed that the birds, when coming in contact with it, close it upon themselves.

Egyptian Catching Birds.

[This trap appears as if in a verti-cal position, although, doubtless, it is intended to represent a trap lying upon the ground.]

The following figure (2.) is very similar to this, except that it is oval; it had probably a net like the former. It is composed of two arcs, which, being kept open by machinery in the middle, furnish the oval frame of the net; but when the bird flies in, and knocks out the pin in the centre, the arcs collapse, as is shown in fig. 1, inclosing the bird in the net.

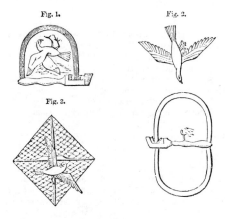

Egyptian Bird Traps.

Fig. 1.—Trap closed, and the bird caught in it; the net work of the trap being effaced.
Fig. 2.—An open Trap similar to Fig. 1; also having the net work effaced.
Fig. 3.—Square Trap of different construction from the preceding, showing the net work entire.

One instance occurs, in a painting at *Thebes*, of a *trap*, in which a hyæna is caught, and carried on the shoulders of two men.

Hyena caught in a Trap.

It was a common method of hunting to enclose a large tract of land by a circle of nets, or to station men at convenient distances, and gradually to contract the circle by coming near to each other, and thus to drive all the wild animals into a narrow enclosure, where they could be easily slain. Some idea

11 Terrors *a* shall make him afraid on every side, and shall [1] drive him to his feet.

12 His strength shall be hunger-bitten, and destruction *shall be* ready at his side.

13 It shall devour the [2] strength of his skin : *even* the first-born of death shall devour his strength.

14 His confidence *b* shall be rooted out of his tabernacle; and it shall bring him to the king of terrors.

of the extent of those enclosures may be formed from the by no means incredible circumstance related by Plutarch, that when the Macedonian conquerors were in Persia, Philotos, the son of Armenio, had hunting-nets that would enclose the space of an hundred furlongs. The Oriental sovereigns have sometimes employed whole armies in this species of hunting. *Pict. Bib.*

11. *Terrors shall make him afraid.* He shall be constantly subject to alarms, and shall never feel secure. "Terrors here are represented as allegorical persons, like the Furies in the Greek poets." *Noyes.* The idea here is substantially the same as that given by Eliphaz, chap. xv. 21, 22. ¶ *And shall drive him to his feet.* Marg. *scatter.* This is a literal translation of the Hebrew. The idea is, that he will be alarmed by such terrors: his self-composure will be dissipated, and he will "take *to his heels.*"

12. *His strength shall be hunger-bitten.* Shall be exhausted by hunger or famine. ¶ *And destruction* shall be *ready at his side.* Heb. "Shall be fitted" (נָכוֹן) "to his side." Some have supposed that this refers to some disease, like the pleurisy, that would adhere closely to his side. So Jerome understands it. Schultens has quoted some passages from Arabic poets, in which calamities are represented as *breaking the side.* Bildad refers, probably, to some heavy judgments that would crush a man ; such that the *ribs,* or the human frame, could not bear; and the meaning is, that a wicked man would be certainly crushed by misfortune.

13. *It shall devour the strength of his skin.* Marg. *bars.* The margin is a correct translation of the Hebrew. The word used (בַּד, construct with עוֹר—*his skin*) means *bars, staves, branches,* and here denotes his limbs, members ; or, more literally, *the bones,*

as *supports* of the skin, or the human frame. The bones are regarded as the *bars,* or the *framework,* holding the other parts of the body in their place, and over which the skin is stretched. The word "it" here refers to the "first-born of death" in the other hemistich of the verse ; and the meaning is, that the strength of his body shall be entirely exhausted. ¶ *The first-born of death.* The "first-born" is usually spoken of as distinguished for vigour and strength ; Gen. xlix. 3, "Reuben, thou art my first-born, my might, and the beginning of my strength ;" and the idea conveyed here by the "first-born of death" is the most fearful and destructive disease that death has ever engendered ; comp. Milton's description of the progeny of sin, in Paradise Lost. Diseases are called "the sons or children of death" by the Arabs, (see Schultens *in loc.,*) as being begotten by it.

14. *His confidence shall be rooted out of his tabernacle.* Security shall forsake his dwelling, and he shall be subject to constant alarms. There shall be nothing there in which he can confide, and all that he relied on as sources of safety shall have fled. ¶ *And it shall bring him.* That is, he shall be brought. ¶ *To the king of terrors.* There has been much variety in the explanation of this verse. Dr. Noyes renders it, "Terror pursues him like a king." Dr. Good, "Dissolution shall invade him like a monarch." Dr. Stock says. "I am sorry to part with a beautiful phrase in our common version, *the king of terrors,* as descriptive of death, but there is no authority for it in the Hebrew text." Wemyss renders it, "Terror shall seize him as a king." So Schultens translates it, "Gradientur in eum, instar regis, terrores." Rosenmüller renders it as it is in our version. The Vulgate, *Et calcet super eum, quasi*

15 It shall dwell in his tabernacle, because *it is* none of his: brimstone shall be scattered upon his habitation.

16 His roots [a] shall be dried up beneath, and above shall his branch be cut off.

a Is.5.24.

rex, interitus — "destruction shall tread upon him as a king." The LXX. " and distress shall lay hold on him with the authority of a king "— αἰτία βασιλική. The Chaldee renders it, " shall be brought to the king of terrors"—למלך רגישתא. It is not evident, therefore, that we are to give up the beautiful phrase, *the king of terrors.* The fair construction of the Hebrew, as it seems to me, is that which is conveyed in our common version—meaning, that the wicked man would be conducted, not merely to death. but to that kind of death where a fearful king would preside—a monarch infusing terrors into his soul. There *is* something singularly beautiful and appropriate in the phrase, " *the king of terrors.*" Death *is* a fearful monarch. All dread him. He presides in regions of chilliness and gloom. All fear to enter those dark regions where he dwells and reigns, and an involuntary shudder seizes the soul on approaching the confines of his kingdom. Yet all must be brought there ; and though man dreads the interview with that fearful king, there is no release. The monarch reigns from age to age—reigns over all. There is but one way in which he will cease to appear as a terrific king.— It is by confidence in Him who came to destroy death ; that great Redeemer who has taken away his " sting," and who can enable man to look with calmness and peace even on the chilly regions where he reigns. The idea here is not precisely that of the Roman and Grecian mythologists, of a terrific king, like Rhadamanthus, presiding over the regions of the dead ; but it is of death personified—of death represented as a king fitted to inspire awe and terror.

15. *It shall dwell in his tabernacle.* It is uncertain what is to be understood as referred to here. Some suppose that the word to be understood is *soul,* and that the meaning is " his soul," *i. e.* he himself, " shall dwell

in his tent." Rosenmüller, Noyes, Wemyss, and others, suppose that the word is *terror.* " Terror (בכלה) shall dwell in his tent," the same word which is used in the plural in the previous verse. This is undoubtedly the correct sense ; and the idea is, that his forsaken tent shall be a place of terror—somewhat, perhaps, as we speak of a forsaken house as *haunted.* It *may be* that Bildad refers to some such superstitious fear as we sometimes, and almost always in childhood, connect with the idea of a house in which nobody lives. ¶ *Because* it is *none of his.* It is no longer his. It is a forsaken, tenantless dwelling. ¶ *Brimstone shall be scattered.* Brimstone has been always the image of desolation. Nothing will grow on a field that is covered with sulphur ; and the meaning here is, that his house would be utterly desolate and forsaken. Rosenmüller and Noyes suppose that there is an allusion here to a sudden destruction, such as was that of Sodom and Gomorrha. Grotius doubts whether it refers to that or to lightning. Others suppose that lightning is referred to both here and in Gen. xix. 24 ; Deut. xxix. 23. I can see no evidence here, however, that there is any reference to Sodom and Gomorrha, or that there is any allusion to lightning. If the allusion had been to Sodom, it would have been more full. That was a case *just in point* in the argument ; and the fact that it was exactly in point, and would have furnished to the friends of Job such an irrefragable proof of the position which they were defending, and that it is not inwrought into the very texture of their argument, is full demonstration, to my mind, that that remarkable event is not referred to in this place. The only thing necessarily implied in the language before us is, that sulphur, the emblem of desolation, would be scattered on his dwelling, and that his dwelling would be wholly desolate.

17 His remembrance *a* shall perish from the earth, and he shall have no name in the street.

18 ¹ He shall be driven from light into darkness, and chased out of the world.

a Ps.34.16.   1 *They shall drive him.*
        b Is.14.22.

19 He shall neither *b* have son nor nephew among his people, nor any remaining in his dwellings.

20 They that come after *him* shall be astonied at his day, *c* as they that ² went before ³ were affrighted.

c Ps.37.13.   2 or, *lived with him.*
        3 *laid hold on horror.*

16. *His roots shall be dried up.* Another image of complete desolation—where he is compared to a *tree* that is dead—a figure whose meaning is obvious, and which often occurs; see Notes, chap. xv. 30 ; viii. 12, 13. ¶ *Above his branch.* Perhaps referring to his children or family. All shall be swept away—an allusion which Job could not well hesitate to apply to himself.

17. *His remembrance shall perish.* His name—all recollection of him. Calamity shall follow him even after death ; and that which every man desires, and every good man has, an honoured name when he is dead, will be denied him. Men will hasten to forget him as fast as possible ; comp. Prov. x. 7, " The name of the wicked shall rot." ¶ *No name in the street.* Men when they meet together in highways and places of concourse—when traveller meets traveller, and caravan caravan, shall not pause to speak of him and of the loss which society has sustained by his death. It is one of the rewards of virtue that the good will speak of the upright man when he is dead ; that they will pause in their journey, or in their business, to converse about him ; and that the poor and the needy will dwell with affectionate interest upon their loss. *This* blessing, Bildad says, will be denied the wicked man. The world will not feel that they have any loss to deplore when he is dead. No great plan of benevolence has been arrested by his removal. The poor and the needy fare as well as they did before. The widow and the fatherless make no grateful remembrance of his name, and the world hastens to forget him as soon as possible. There is no man, except one who is lost to all virtue, who does not desire to be remembered when he is dead—by his children, his

neighbours, his friends, and by the stranger who may read the record on the stone that marks his grave. Where this desire is *wholly* extinguished, man has reached the lowest possible point of degradation, and the last hold on him in favour of virtue has expired.

18. *He shall be driven from light into darkness.* Marg. *They shall drive him.* The meaning is, that he should be driven from a state of prosperity to one of calamity. ¶ *And chased out of the world.* Perhaps meaning that he should not be conducted to the grave with the slow and solemn pomp of a respectful funeral, but in a hurry—as a malefactor is driven from human life, and hastily committed to the earth. The living would be glad to be rid of him, and would *chase* him out of life.

19. *He shall neither have son,* &c. All his family shall be cut off. He shall have no one to perpetuate his name or remembrance. All this Job could not help applying to himself, as it was doubtless intended he should. The *facts* in his case were just such as were supposed in these proverbs about the wicked ; and hence his friends could not but conclude that he was a wicked man ; and hence, too, since these were undisputed maxims, Job felt so much embarrassment in answering them.

20. *They that come after* him. Future ages ; they who may hear of his history and of the manner in which he was cut off from life. So the passage has been generally rendered ; so, substantially, it is by Dr. Good, Dr. Noyes, Rosenmüller, and Luther. The Vulgate translates it *novissimi;* the Sept. ἔσχατοι—" *the last* "—meaning those that should live after him, or at a later period. But Schultens supposes that the word here used denotes those in *the West,* and the corresponding word

21 Surely such *are* the dwellings of the wicked, and this *is* the place *of him that* knoweth not [a] God.

a 2 Th.1.8.

rendered " went before," denotes those in *the East*. With this view Wemyss concurs, who renders the whole verse,

" The West shall be astonished at his end ;
The East shall be panic-struck."

According to this, it means that those who dwelt in the remotest regions would be astonished at the calamities which would come upon him. It seems to me that this accords better with the scope of the passage than the other interpretation, and avoids some difficulties which cannot be separated from the other view. The word translated in our version, " that come after him " (אחרנים) is from אחר, to be after, or behind ; to stay behind, to delay, remain. It then means *after*, or *behind ;* and as in the geography of the Orientals the face was supposed to be turned to *the East*, instead of being turned to the North, as with us —a much more natural position than ours—the word *after*, or *behind*, comes to denote the West, the right hand the South, the left the North ; see Notes on chap. xxiii. 8, 9.

Thus the phrase הים האחרון—*the sea behind*, denotes the Mediterranean sea—the West ; Deut. xxiv. 3 ; see also Deut. xi. 24 ; xxxiv. 2 ; Joel xi. 20, where the same phrase in Hebrew occurs. Those who dwelt in the *West*, therefore, would be accurately referred to by this phrase. ¶ *Shall be astonied.* Shall be *astonished*—the old mode of writing the word being *astonied;* Isa. lii. 14. It is not known, however, to be used in any other book than the Bible. ¶ *As they that went before.* Marg. or *lived with him.* Noyes, " his elders shall be struck with horror." Vulg. " et primos invadet *horror*." Sept. " amazement seizes *the first*"—πρώτους. But the more correct interpretation is that which refers it to the people of the East. The word קדמני is from קדם to precede, to go before ; and then the derivatives refer to that which goes before, which is in front, &c. ; and as

the face was turned to the East by geographers, the word comes to express that which is in the East, or near the sun-rising ; see Joel ii. 20 ; Job xxiii. 8 ; Gen. ii. 8 ; xii. 8. Hence the phrase בני קדם—*Benē kēdĕm*— *sons of the East*—meaning the persons who dwelt east of Palestine ; Job i. 3. Isa. xi. 14 ; Gen. xxv. 6 ; xxix. 1. The word here used, (קדמנים—*kădmōnīm*,) is used to denote the people or the regions of the East ; in Ezek. xlvii. 8, 18 ; Zech. xiv. 8. Here it means, as it seems to me, the people of the East ; and the idea is that men every where would be astonished at the doom of the wicked man. His punishment would be so sudden and entire as to hold the world mute with amazement. ¶ *Were affrighted.* Marg. *laid hold on horror.* This is a more literal rendering. The sense is, they would be struck with horror at what would occur to him.

21. *Surely such* are *the dwellings of the wicked.* The conclusion or sum of the whole matter. The meaning is, that the habitations of all that knew not God would be desolate—a declaration which Job could not but regard as aimed at himself; comp. chap. xx. 29. This is the close of this harsh and severe speech. It is no wonder that Job should feel it keenly, and that he *did* feel it is apparent from the following chapter. A string of proverbs had been presented, having the appearance of proof, and as the result of the long observation of the course of events, evidently bearing on his circumstances, and so much in point that he could not well deny their pertinency to his condition. He was stung to the quick, and gave vent to his agonized feelings in the following chapter.

CHAPTER XIX.

2. *How long will ye vex my soul?* Perhaps designing to reply to the taunting speech of Bildad ; chap. xviii. 2. *He* had asked " how long it would be ere Job would make an end of

CHAPTER XIX.

ANALYSIS OF THE CHAPTER.

This exceedingly beautiful chapter consists of the following parts :

I. Job complains in the most pathetic manner of the

want of feeling in nis friends, and of their regarding his calamities as undoubted proof of his guilt, ver. 1—4.

II. He maintains in the most earnest manner, that his calamities had been brought on him by a sovereign God, for some cause unknown to him, but which was not to be regarded as proof of his guilt. Though he could not *answer* the plausible reasoning of his friends, yet he maintained that God, and not his sins, had been the cause of his afflictions, ver. 5—20. He then goes into a pathetic description of the afflictions which God had brought upon him, designed to show that such sufferings *ought* to excite the compassion of his friends, and not to be the occasion of reproach. God had overthrown him (ver. 6); he had refused to hear him (ver. 7); he had hedged up his way (ver. 8); he had stripped him of his glory (ver. 9); he had destroyed him on every side (ver. 10); he had kindled his wrath against him (ver. 11, 12); he had made him an alien and a stranger to his own family, and even children had refused to render him the respect due to age and rank (ver. 13—20)

III In view of the afflictions which he had suffered at the hand of God, he calls on his friends, in the most pathetic manner, to have pity on him. He asks them why *they* join with God in accumulating sorrows upon him, ver 21, 22.

IV. Perceiving that the representations of his sufferings had no effect on his friends, and that he was unable to rouse them to any sense of his wrongs, or to obtain justice from them, he suddenly turns from them, and expresses the earnest desire that all that he had said might be engraven on the solid rock for ever, that his case might go down to future times, and that he might obtain in distant ages the justice which was denied him in his own, ver. 23, 24.

V. Yet he is not satisfied with the slow and tardy justice which posterity would render him, but makes his appeal to God, and says that *he* would vindicate his cause. He expresses the firmest assurance that he would come forth in his favour, and rescue his name from the charges which had been brought against it. These sufferings might continue; disease might wholly waste him away; all his flesh might be consumed by worms; and the circumstances on which his friends so confidently relied in proof that he was a hypocrite, might be more aggravated still; yet he had the utmost confidence that God would come forth to vindicate him, and that every thing that was dark would be cleared away, ver. 25—27.

VI. He closes by saying, that their treatment of him *ought* to have been different, ver. 28, 29. They could not but have perceived that he had the elements of piety in him, though he was thus overwhelmed; and they had reason to dread the wrath of Heaven for the manner in which they had treated a pious sufferer.

THEN Job answered and said,
2 How long will ye vex my soul, and break me in pieces with words ?

3 These ten *a* times have ye reproached me : you are not ashamed *that* you ¹ make yourselves strange to me.

4 And be it indeed *that* I have

a Ge.31.7.   ¹ or, *harden yourselves against me.*

empty talk ?" *Job* asks, in reply, *how long* they would torture and afflict his soul ? Or whether there was no hope that this would ever come to an end ! ¶ *And break me in pieces.* Crush me, or bruise me—like breaking any thing in a mortar, or breaking rocks by repeated blows of the hammer. *Noyes.* He says they had crushed him, as if by repeated blows.

3. *These ten times.* Many times; the word *ten* being used as we often say, *ten, a dozen,* or *twenty,* to denote many; see Gen. xxxi. 7, "And your father hath changed my wages *ten times.*" Lev. xxvi. 26, "And when I have broken your staff of bread, *ten women* shall bake your bread in one oven ;" comp. Num. xiv. 22 ; Neh. iv. 6. ¶ *You are not ashamed that you make yourselves strange to me.* Marg. *harden yourselves against me.* Gesenius, and after him Noyes, renders this, "Shameless ye stun me." Wemyss, "Are ye not ashamed to treat me thus cruelly ? The word here used (-כה—*hâkhir*) occurs no where else, and hence it is difficult to determine its meaning. The Vulgate renders it, "*oppressing me.*" The LXX., "and you are not ashamed to press upon me."—ἐπίκεισθέ μοι. Schultens has gone into an extended examination of its meaning, and supposes that the primary idea is that of being *stiff,* or *rigid.* The word in Arabic, he says, means to be *stupid with wonder.* It is applied, he supposes, to those who are *stiff* or *rigid* with stupor ; and then to those who have a stony heart and an iron fore-head—and who can look on the suffering without feeling or compassion. This sense accords well with the connection here. Gesenius, however, supposes that the primary idea is that of beating or pounding ; and hence of stunning by repeated blows. In either case the sense would be substantially the same—that of *stunning.* The idea given by our translators of making themselves "*strange*" was derived from the supposition that the word might be formed from כר—*nâkhir*—to be strange, foreign ; to estrange, alienate, &c. For a more full examination of the word, the reader may consult Schultens, or Rosenmüller *in loco.*

4. *And be it indeed* that *I have erred.* Admitting that I have erred, it is my own concern. You have not a right

erred, mine error remaineth with myself.

5 If indeed ye will magnify *a* *yourselves* against me, and plead against me my reproach ;

6 Know now that God hath

a Ps.38.16.

to reproach and revile me in this manner. ¶ *Mine error abideth with myself.* I must abide the consequences of the error. The design of this seems to be to reprove what he regarded as an improper and meddlesome interference with his concerns. Or it may be an expression of a willingness to bear all the consequences himself. He was willing to meet all the fair results of his own conduct.

5. *If, indeed, ye will magnify* your-selves *against me.* This is connected with the next verse. The sense is, " all these calamities came from God. He has brought them upon me in a sudden and mysterious manner. In these circumstances you *ought* to have pity upon me ; ver. 21. Instead of magnifying yourselves against me, setting yourselves up as censors and judges, overwhelming me with reproaches and filling my mind with pain and anguish, you ought to show to me the sympathy of a friend." The phrase, " magnify yourselves," refers to the fact that they had assumed a tone of superiority and an authoritative manner, instead of showing the compassion due to a friend in affliction. ¶ *And plead against me my reproach.* My calamities as a cause of reproach. You urge them as a proof of the displeasure of God, and you join in re-proaching me as a hypocrite. Instead of this, you should have shown compassion to me as a man whom God had greatly afflicted.

6. *Know now that God.* Understand the case ; and in order that they might, he goes into an extended description of the calamities which God had brought upon him. He wished them to be *fully* apprised of all that he had suffered at the hand of God. ¶ *Hath overthrown me.* The word here used (עוה) means to bend, to make crooked or curved ; then to distort, pervert : then to overturn, to de-

overthrown me, and hath compassed me with his net.

7 Behold, I cry out of [1] wrong, but I am not heard : I cry aloud, but *there is* no judgment.

8 He hath fenced up my way

[1] or, *violence*.

stroy ; Isa. xxiv. 1 ; Lam. iii. 9. The meaning here is, that he had been in a state of prosperity, but that God had completely *reversed* every thing. ¶ *And hath compassed me with his net.* Has sprung his net upon me as a hunter does, and I am caught. Perhaps there may be an allusion here to what Bildad said in chap. xviii. 8, seq.: that the wicked would be taken in his own snares. Instead of that, Job says that *God* had sprung the snare upon him—for reasons which he could not understand, but in such a manner as should move the compassion of his friends.

7. *Behold, I cry out of wrong.* Marg. or *violence.* The Hebrew word (חמס) means properly *violence.* The violence referred to is that which was brought upon him by God. It is, indeed, harsh language ; but it is not quite sure that he means to complain of God for doing him injustice. God had dealt with him in a severe or violent manner, is the meaning, and he had cried unto him for relief, but had cried in vain. ¶ *No judgment.* No justice. The meaning is, that he could obtain justice from no one God would not interpose to remove the calamities which he had brought upon him, and his friends would do no justice to his motives and character.

8. *He hath fenced up my way.* This figure is taken from a traveller, whose way is obstructed by trees, rocks, or fences, so that he cannot get along, and Job says it was so with him. He was travelling along in a peaceful manner on the journey of life, and all at once obstructions were put in his path, so that he could not go farther. This does not refer, particularly, to his spiritual condition, if it does at all. It is descriptive of the obstruction of his plans, rather than of spiritual darkness or distress. ¶ *And he hath set darkness in my paths.* So that I can-

that I cannot pass, and he hath set darkness in my paths.

9 He hath stripped me of my glory, and taken the crown *from* my head.

10 He [a] hath destroyed me on every side, and I am gone: and mine hope hath he removed like a tree.

a La.2.5,6.

11 He hath also kindled his wrath against me, and he counteth me unto him as *one of* his enemies.

12 His troops come together, and raise up their way against me, and encamp round about my tabernacle.

13 He hath put my brethren far from me, and mine acquaintance are verily estranged from me.

not see—as if all around the traveller should become suddenly dark, so that he could not discern his way. The *language* here would well express the spiritual darkness which the friends of God sometimes experience, though it is by no means certain that Job referred to that. All the dealings of God are to them mysterious, and there is no light in the soul—and they are ready to sink down in despair.

9. *He hath stripped me of my glory.* Every thing which I had that contributed to my respectability and honour, he has taken away. My property, my health, my family, the esteem of my friends—all is gone. ¶ *And taken the crown* from *my head.* The crown is an emblem of honour and dignity—and Job says that God had removed all that contributed to his former dignity; comp. Prov. iv. 9; xvii. 6; Ezek. xvi. 12; Lam. v. 16.

10. *He hath destroyed me on every side.* He has left me nothing. The word which is here used is that which is commonly applied to destroying cities, towns, and houses. *Rosenmüller.* ¶ *And I am gone.* That is, I am near death. I cannot recover myself. ¶ *And mine hope hath he removed like a tree.* A tree, which is plucked up by the roots, and which does not grow again. That is, his hopes of life and happiness, of an honoured old age, and of a continuance of his prosperity, had been wholly destroyed. This does not refer to his *religious* hope—as the word *hope* is often used now—but to his desire of future comfort and prosperity in this life. It does not appear but that his religious hope, arising from confidence in God, remained unaffected.

11. *He hath also kindled his wrath.* He is angry. Wrath in the Scriptures

is usually represented as burning or inflamed—because like fire it destroys every thing before it. ¶ *And he counteth me unto him as* one *of his enemies.* He treats me as he would an enemy. The same complaint he elsewhere makes; see chap. xiii. 24; perhaps also in chap. xvi. 9. We are not to understand Job here as admitting that *he* was an enemy of God. He constantly maintained that he was not, but he was constrained to admit that God *treated him* as if he were his enemy, and he could not account for it. *On this ground,* therefore, he now maintains that his friends ought to show him compassion, instead of trying to prove that he *was* an enemy of God; they ought to pity a man who was so strangely and mysteriously afflicted, instead of increasing his sorrows by endeavouring to demonstrate that he was a man of eminent wickedness.

12. *His troops.* The calamities which he had sent, and which are here represented as *armies* or *soldiers* to accomplish his work. It is not probable that he refers here to the bands of the Chaldeans and the Sabeans, that had robbed him of his property, but to the calamities that had come upon him, *as if* they were bands of robbers. ¶ *And raise up their way.* As an army that is about to lay siege to a city, or that is marching to attack it, casts up a way of access to it, and thus obtains every facility to take it; see Notes on Isa. xl. 3; lvii. 14. ¶ *And encamp round about my tabernacle.* In the manner of an army besieging a city. Often an army is encamped in this manner for months or even years, in order to reduce the city by famine. ¶ *My tabernacle.* My tent; my dwelling.

13. *He hath put my brethren.* This

CHAPTER XIX. 317

14 My ^a kinsfolk have failed, and my familiar friends have forgotten me.

15 They that dwell in mine house, and my maids, count me for a stranger: I am an alien in their sight.

16 I called my servant, and he gave me no answer : I entreated him with my mouth.

a Ps. 38. 11.

is a new source of affliction that he had not adverted to before, that God had caused all his children to be estranged from him—a calamity which he regarded as the crown of all his woes. The word rendered "my brethren" (אחי) means properly *my brothers*—but whether he means literally his brothers, or whether he designs it to be taken in a figurative sense as denoting his intimate friends, or those of the same rank in life or calling, it is impossible now to determine. ¶ *And mine acquaintance.* My friends—on whom I relied in time of calamity. ¶ *Are verily estranged.* They have forgotten me, and treat me as a stranger. What an accurate description is this of what often occurs! In prosperity a man will be surrounded by friends; but as soon as his prosperity is stripped away, and he is overwhelmed with calamity, they withdraw, and leave him to suffer alone. Proud of his acquaintance before, they now pass him by as a stranger, or treat him with cold civility, and when he *needs* their friendship, they are gone.

14. *My kinsfolk have failed.* My neighbours (קרובי), those who were near to me. It may refer to *nearness* of affinity, friendship, or residence. The essential idea is that of *nearness*—whether by blood, affection, or vicinity. In Ps. xxxviii. 11, it denotes near friends. ¶ *And my familiar friends.* Those who knew me—מידעי. The allusion is to those who were *intimately* acquainted with him, or who were his bosom friends.

15. *They that dwell in mine house.* The trials came to his very dwelling, and produced a sad estrangement there. The word here used (גרי from גור) means properly those who *sojourn* in a house for a little time. It may refer to guests, strangers, servants, clients, or tenants. The essential idea is, that they were not *permanent* re-

sidents, though for a time they were inmates of the family. Jerome renders the place, *Inquilini domûs meæ—the tenants of my house.* The LXX., Γείτονες οικίας—*neighbours.* Schultens supposes it means *clients,* or those who were taken under the protection of a great man. He quotes from the Arabian poets to show that the word is used in that sense, and particularly a passage from the *Hamasa,* which he thus translates :

Descendite sub alas meas, alasque gentis meæ,
Ut sim præsidium vobis quum pugna conseritur.
Namque testamento injunxit mihi pater, ut reciperem vos hospites,
Omnemque oppressorem a vobis propulsarem.

There can be no doubt that Job refers to *dependents,* but whether in the capacity of servants, tenants, or clients, it is not easy to determine, and is not material. Dr. Good renders it " *sojourners,*" and this is a correct rendering of the word. This would be clearly the sense if the corresponding member of the parallelism were not "maids," or female servants. *That* requires us to understand here persons who were *somehow* engaged in the service of Job. Perhaps his clients, or those who came for protection, were under obligation to some sort of service as the return for his patronage. ¶ *And my maids.* Female domestics. The Chaldee, however, renders this אמהתי—*my concubines ;* but the correct reference is to female servants. ¶ *I am an alien.* That is, to them. They cease to treat me as the head of the family.

16. *I called my servant.* He lost all respect for me, and paid me no attention. ¶ *I entreated him.* I ceased to expect *obedience,* and tried to see what *persuasion* would do. I ceased to be master in my own house.

17 *My breath is strange to my wife.* Schultens renders this, "my breath

17 My breath is strange to my wife, though I entreated for the children's *sake* of ¹ mine own body.

1 *my belly.*					2 or, *the wicked.*
3 *The men of my secret.*

18 Yea, ² young children despised me ; I arose, and they spake against me.

19 All ³ my inward friends ab-

is loathsome to my wife," and so also Noyes. Wemyss translates it, "my own wife turns aside from my breath." Dr. Good, "my breath is scattered away by my wife." The literal meaning is, " my breath is *strange* (זרה) to my wife ;" and the idea is, that there had been such a change in him from his disease, that his breath was not that which she had been accustomed to breathe without offence, and that she now turned away from it as if it were the breath of a stranger. Jerome renders it, *Halitum meum exhorruit uxor mea—my wife abhors my breath.* It may be worthy of remark here, that but *one* wife of Job is mentioned—a remarkable fact, as he probably lived in an age when polygamy was common. ¶ *I entreated her.* I appealed to her by all that was tender in the domestic relation, but in vain. From this it would seem that even his wife had regarded him as an object of divine displeasure. and had also left him to suffer alone. ¶ *For the children's sake of mine own body.* Marg. *my belly.* There is considerable variety in the interpretation of this passage. The word rendered " my own body" (בטני) means literally, *my belly,* or *womb ;* and Noyes, Gesenius, and some others, suppose it means the children of his own mother ! But assuredly this was scarcely an appeal that Job would be likely to make to his wife in such circumstances. There can be no impropriety in supposing that Job referred to himself, and that the word is used somewhat in the same sense as the word *loins* is in Gen. xxxv. 11 ; xlvi. 26 ; Ex. i. 5 ; 1 Kings viii. 19. Thus understood, it would refer to his own children, and the appeal to his wife was founded on the relation which they had sustained to them. Though they were now dead, he referred to their former united attachment to them, to the common affliction which they had experienced in their loss ; and in view of all their former love to them, and

all the sorrow which they had experienced in their death, he made an appeal to his wife to show him kindness, but in vain. Jerome renders this, " Orabam filios uteri mei." The LXX., not understanding it, and trying to *make* sense of it, introduced a statement which is undoubtedly false, though Rosenmüller accords with it. " I called affectionately (κολακευων) the sons of my concubines "—υἱους παλλακιδων μου. But the whole meaning is evidently that he made a solemn and tender appeal to his wife, in view of all the joys and sorrows which they had experienced as the united head of a family of children now no more. What would reach the heart of an estranged wife, if such an appeal would not ?

18. *Yea, young children.* Marg. or *the wicked.* This difference between the text and the margin arises from the ambiguity of the original word— עוילים. The word עויל (whence our word *evil*) means sometimes the wicked, or the ungodly, as in Job xvi. 11. It may also mean a child, or suckling, (from עול—to give milk, to suckle, 1 Sam. vii. 7—10 ; Gen. xxiii. 13 ; Ps. lxxviii. 71 ; Isa. xl. 11 ; comp. Isa. xlix. 15 ; lxv. 20,) and is doubtless used in this sense here. Jerome, however, renders it *stulti—fools.* The LXX., strangely enough, " They renounced me for ever." Dr. Good renders it, "Even the dependents." So Schultens, Etiam clientes egentissimi —*even the most needy clients.* But the reference is probably to children who are represented as withholding from him the respect which was due to age. ¶ *I arose, and they spake against me.* "When I rise up, instead of regarding and treating me with respect, they make me an object of contempt and sport." Comp. the account of the respect which had formerly been shown him in chap. xxix. 8.

19. *All my inward friends.* Marg. *the men of my secret.* The meaning is,

horred me : and they whom I loved are turned against me.

20 My*a* bone cleaveth to my

a Ps.102.5.

those who were admitted to the intimacy of friendship or who were permitted to be acquainted with his
secret thoughts, purposes, and plans.
The word here used (סוֹד) denotes
properly a *couch, cushion, pillow,* on
which one reclines ; then a *divan,* a
circle of persons sitting together for
consultation or conversation ; and
hence it refers to those who are sitting together in intimate counsel,
(see Notes on chap. xv. 8; xxix. 4,)
and then familiar intercourse, intimacy. Here the phrase " men of my
intimacy " (סוֹדִי) denotes those who
were admitted to intimate friendship.
All such persons had now forsaken
him, and turned against him.

20. *My bone cleaveth to my skin
and to my flesh.* The meaning of this
probably is, " my skin and flesh are
dried up so that the bone seems to adhere to the skin, and so that the form
of the bone becomes visible." It is
designed to denote a state of great
emaciation, and describes an effect
which we often see. ¶ *And I am
escaped with the skin of my teeth.* A
very difficult expression, and which has
greatly perplexed commentators, and
on whose meaning they are by no means
agreed. Dr. Good renders it, "and
in the skin of my teeth am I dissolved;"
but what that means is as difficult of
explanation as the original. Noyes,
" and I have scarcely escaped with
the skin of my teeth." Herder, (as
translated by Marsh,) " and scarcely
the skin in my teeth have I brought
away as a spoil." He says that " the
figure is taken from the prey which
wild beasts carry in their teeth ; his
skin is his poor and wretched body,
which alone he had escaped with. His
friends are represented as carnivorous
animals which gnaw upon his skin,
upon the poor remnant of life ;" but
the Hebrew will not bear this construction. Poole observes, quaintly enough,
that it means, " I am scarcely sound
and whole and free from sores in any
part of my skin, except that of my

skin and to my flesh, and I am
escaped with the skin of my
teeth.

jaws, which holdeth and covereth the
roots of my teeth. This being, as
divers observe, the devil's policy, to
leave his mouth untouched, that he
might more freely express his mind,
and vent his blasphemies against God,
which he supposed sharp pain would
force him to do." Schultens has mentioned four different interpretations
given to the phrase, none of which
seems to be perfectly satisfactory.
They are the following : (1.) That it
means that the skin *about* the teeth
alone was preserved, or the gums and
the lips, so that he had the power of
speaking, though every other part was
wasted away, and this exposition is
given, accompanied with the suggestion that his faculty of speech was
preserved entire by Satan, in order
that he might be *able* to utter the language of complaint and blasphemy
against God. (2.) That he was emaciated and exhausted completely, *except* the skin about his teeth, that is,
his lips, and that by them he was kept
alive; that if it were not for them he
could not breathe, but must soon expire. (3.) That the teeth themselves
had fallen out by the force of disease,
and that nothing was left but the
gums. This opinion Schultens himself
adopts. The image, he says, is taken
from pugilists, whose teeth are knocked
out by each other; and the meaning
he supposes to be, that Job had been
treated by his disease in the same manner. So violent had it been that he
had lost all his teeth, and nothing was
left but his gums. (4.) A fourth opinion is, that the reference is to the
enamel of the teeth, and that the
meaning is, that such was the force
and extent of his afflictions that all his
teeth became hollow and were decayed,
leaving only the enamel. It is difficult
to determine the true sense amidst a
multitude of learned conjectures ; but
probably the most simple and easy interpretation is the best. It may mean
that he was *almost* consumed. Disease
had preyed upon his frame until he was

21 Have pity upon me, have pity upon me, O ye my friends; for the hand of God hath touched me.

22 Why do ye persecute *a* me

a Ps. 69. 26.

as God, and are not satisfied with my flesh?

23 Oh [1] that my words were now written! Oh that they were printed in a book!

[1] *who will give.*

---

wasted away. Nothing was left but his lips, or his gums; he was just able to speak, and that was all. So Jerome renders it, delicta sunt tantummodò labia circa dentes meos. Luther renders it, und kann meine Zähne mit der Haut nicht bedecken—" and I cannot cover my teeth with the skin;" that is, with the lips.

21. *Have pity on me.* A tender, pathetic cry for sympathy. " God has afflicted me, and stripped me of all my comforts, and I am left a poor, distressed, forsaken man. I make my appeal to you, my friends, and entreat you to have pity; to sympathize with me, and to sustain me by the words of consolation." One would have supposed that these words would have gone to the heart, and that we should hear no more of their bitter reproofs. But far otherwise was the fact. ¶ *The hand of God hath touched me.* Hath smitten me; or is heavy upon me. The meaning is, that he had been subjected to great calamities by God, and that it was right to appeal now to his friends, and to expect their sympathy and compassion. On the usual meaning of the word here rendered, " *hath touched* " (נגעה from נגע), see Notes on Isa. liii. 4.

22. *Why do ye persecute me as God?* As God has done. That is, without giving me any reason for it; accusing me of crimes without proof, and condemning me without mitigation. That there is here an improper reflection on God, will be apparent to all. It accords with what Job frequently expresses where he speaks of him as judging him severely, and is one of the instances which prove that he was not entirely perfect. ¶ *And are not satisfied with my flesh.* That is, are not contented that my *body* is subjected to inexpressible torments, and is wholly wasting away, but add to this the torment of the soul. Why is it not enough that my *body* is thus

tormented without adding the severer tortures of the mind?

23. *Oh that my words were now written!* Marg. as in Heb., " *Who will give;*" a common mode of expressing desire among the Hebrews. This expression of desire introduces one of the most important passages in the book of Job. It is the language of a man who felt that injustice was done him by his friends, and that he was not likely to have justice done him by that generation. He was charged with hypocrisy; his motives were called in question; his solemn appeals, and his arguments to assert his innocence, were disregarded; and in this state of mind he expresses the earnest wish that his expressions might be permanently recorded, and go down to far distant times. He desired that what he had said might be preserved, that future ages might be able to judge between him and his accusers, and to know the justice of his cause. The desire thus expressed has been granted, and a more permanent record has been made than if, in accordance with his request, his sentiments had been engraved on lead or stone. ¶ *Oh that they were printed!* It is clear that this expression may convey wholly an erroneous idea. The art of *printing* was then unknown; and the passage has no allusion to that art. The original word (חקק) means properly, to cut in, to hew; then to cut—*e. g.* a sepulchre in a rock, Isa. xxii. 16; then to cut, or engrave letters on a tablet of lead or stone, Isa. xxx. 8; Ezek. iv. 1; and generally it implies the notion of engraving, or inscribing on a plate with an engraving tool. Anciently books were made of materials which allowed of this mode of making a record. Stone would probably be the first material; and then plates of metal, leaves, bark, skins, &c. The notion of *engraving*, however, is the proper idea here. ¶ *In*

a book—־ספר. The word ־ספ is derived from ־ספ. In Arabic the kindred word *shafar* means to scratch, to scrape; and hence to engrave, write, record—and the idea was originally that of insculping or engraving on a stone. Hence the word comes to denote a book, of any materials, or made in any form. Pliny, speaking of the materials of ancient books, says, Olim in palmarum foliis scriptitatum, et libris quarundam arborum ; postea publica monumenta plumbeis voluminibus, mox et privata linteis confici cœpta aut ceris. *Lib.* xiii. 11. " At first men wrote on the leaves of the palm, or the bark of certain trees; but afterwards public documents were preserved in leaden volumes [or rolls], and those of a private nature on wax or linen." " Montfaucon purchased at Rome, in 1699, an ancient book entirely composed of lead. It was about four inches long, and three inches wide: and not only were the two pieces that formed the cover, and the leaves, six in number, of lead, but also the stick inserted through the rings to hold the leaves together, as well as the hinges and nails. It contained Egyptian Gnostic figures and unintelligible writing. Brass, as more durable, was used for the inscriptions designed to last the longest, such as treaties, laws, and alliances. These public documents were, however, usually written on large tablets. The style for writing on hard substances was sometimes tipped with diamond." The meaning of the word here is evidently a record made on stone or lead—for so the following verses indicate. The art of writing or engraving was known in the time of Job; but I do not know that there is evidence that the art of writing on leaves, bark, or vellum was yet understood. As *books* in the form in which they are now were then unknown ; as there is no evidence that at that time anything like *volumes* or *rolls* were possessed ; as the records were probably preserved on tablets of stone or lead ; and as the entire description here pertains to something that was *engraved ;* and as this sense is conveyed by the Arabic verb from which the word ־ספ, *book,* is derived, the word *tablet,* or some kindred word, will better express the sense of the original than *book*—and I have, therefore, used it in the translation. It may be interesting, however, to see a specimen of the mode of writing on papyrus, and accordingly I insert one in this place.—*See next page.*

Assyrian records are found generally in stone or clay; and the latter being more easily and speedily engraven with a triangular instrument, was more frequently employed. (1) Assyrian terra-cotta cylinder, from Khorsabad, containing the annals of the reign of Sargon, about 721 B.C.——(2) Hexagonal terra-cotta cylinder, from Koyunjik, containing the annals of the first eight years of the reign of Sennacherib (B.C. 702 to 694), with an account of the expedition against Hezekiah.——(3) Assyrian scribes making notes of prisoners, heads of slain, spoils, &c., from Koyunjik.

24 That they were graven with an iron pen and lead in the rock forever!

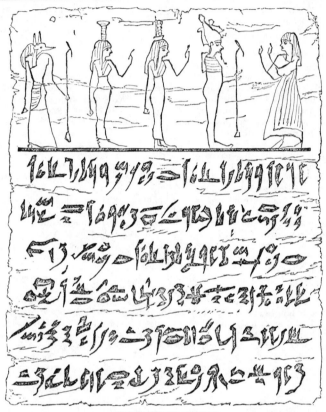

Facsimile of Writing on Papyrus.

24. *That they were graven.* Cut in, or sculptured—as is done on stones. That they might become thus a permanent record. ¶ *With an iron pen.* A stylus, or an engraving tool—for so the word (ט‎ע‎) means. The instrument formerly used for writing or engraving was a small, sharp-pointed piece of iron or steel, that was employed to mark on lead or stone—somewhat in the form of small graving tools now. When the writing was on wax, the instrument was made with a flat head, that it could be obliterated by pressing it on or passing it over the wax.

The reason why Job mentions the *iron pen* here is, that he wished a *permanent* record. He did not desire one made with paint or chalk, but one which would convey his sentiments down to future times. ¶ *And lead.* That is, either engraved on lead, or more probably with lead. It was customary to cut the letters deep in stone, and then to fill them up with lead, so that the record became more permanent. This I take to be the meaning here. The Hebrew will scarcely allow of the supposition that Job meant that the records should be made on plates of lead—

The following cut from Montfaucon's Paleographia Græca, will illustrate the ancient use of the stylus :

though such plates were early used, but perhaps not until after the time of Job. ¶ *In the rock.* It was common, at an early period, to make inscriptions on the smooth surface of a rock. Perhaps the first that were made were on stones, which were placed as way-marks, or monuments over the dead—as we now make such inscriptions on grave-stones. Then it became common to record any memorable transaction—as a battle—on stones or rocks ; and perhaps, also, sententious and apothegmatical remarks were recorded in this manner, to admonish travellers, or to transmit them to posterity. Numerous inscriptions of this kind are found by travellers in the East, on tombs, and on rocks in the desert. All that can be appropriate here is a notice of such early inscriptions of that kind in Arabia, as would render it probable that they existed in the time of Job, or such as indicate great antiquity. Happily we are at no loss for such inscriptions on rocks in the country where Job lived.

The Wady Mokatta, the cliffs of which bear these inscriptions, is a valley entering Wady Sheikh, and bordering the upper regions of the Sinai mountains. It extends for about three hours' march, and in most places its rocks present abrupt cliffs, twenty or thirty feet high. From these cliffs large masses have separated, and lie at the bottom of the valley. The cliffs and rocks are thickly covered with inscriptions, which are continued at intervals of a few hundred paces only, for at least the distance of two hours and a half. Burckhardt, in his travels from Akaba to Cairo, by Mount Sinai, observed many inscriptions on the rocks, part of which he has copied. See his Travels in Syria, Lond. Ed. pp. 506, 581, 582, 606, 613, 614. Pococke, who also visited the regions of Mount Sinai in 1777, has given a description of the inscriptions which he saw on the rocks at Mount Sinai. Vol. i. 148, he says, "There are on many of the rocks, both near these mountains and in the road, a great many inscriptions in an ancient

25 For I know *that* my Redeemer liveth, and *that* he shall
stand at the latter *day* upon the
earth:

character; many of them I copied, and observed that most of them were not cut, but stained, making the granite of a lighter colour, and where the stone had scaled, I could see the stain had sunk into the stone." Numerous specimens of these inscriptions may be seen in Pococke, vol. i. p. 148. These inscriptions were also observed by Robinson and Smith, and are described by them in Biblical Researches, vol. i. 108, 118, 119, 123, 161, 167. They are first mentioned by Cosmas, about A.D. 535. He supposed them to be the work of the ancient Hebrews, and says that certain Jews, who had read them, explained them to him as noting "the journey of such an one, out of such a tribe, in such a year and month." They have also been noticed by many early travellers, as Neitzschitz, p. 149; Moncongs, i. p 245; and also by Niebuhr in his Reisebeschr. i. p. 250. The copies of them given by Pococke and Niebuhr are said to be very imperfect; those by Seetzen are better, and those made by Burckhardt are tolerably accurate. Rob. Bib. Research. i. 553. A large number of them have been copied and published by Mr. Grey, in the Transactions of the Royal Society of Literature, vol. iii. pt. 1, Lond. 1832; consisting of one hundred and seventy-seven in the unknown character, nine in Greek, and one in Latin. These inscriptions, which so long excited the curiosity of travellers, have been recently deciphered (in the year 1839) by Professor Beer, of the University of Leipzig. He had turned his attention to them in the year 1833, but without success. In the year 1839 his attention was again turned to them, and after several months of the most persevering application, he succeeded in making out the alphabet, and was enabled to read all the inscriptions which have been copied, with a good degree of accuracy. According to the results of this examination, the *characters* of the Sinaitic inscriptions belong to a distinct and independent

alphabet. Some of the letters are wholly peculiar; the others have more or less affinity with the Palmyrene, and particularly with the Estrangelo and the Cufic. They are written from right to left. The *contents* of the inscriptions, so far as examined, consist only of proper names, preceded by a word which is usually שלם, *peace*, though occasionally some other word is used. In one or two instances the name is followed by a sentence which has not yet been deciphered. The names are those common in Arabic. It is a remarkable fact that not one Jewish or Christian name has been found. The question, as to the *writers* of these inscriptions, receives very little light from their contents. A word at the end of some of them may be so read as to affirm that they were *pilgrims*, and this opinion Professor Beer adopts; but this is not certain. That the writers were *Christians*, seems apparent from many of the crosses connected with the inscriptions. The *age*, also, of the inscriptions, receives no light from their contents, as no date has yet been read. Beer supposes that the greater part of them could not have been written earlier than the fourth century. Little light, therefore, is cast upon the question who wrote them; what was their design; in what age they were written, or who were the *pilgrims* who wrote them. See Rob. Bib. Research. i. 552—556. That there were such records in the time of Job, is probable.

25. *For I know that my Redeemer liveth.* There are few passages in the Bible which have excited more attention than this, or in respect to which the opinions of expositors have been more divided. The importance of the passage (ver. 25—27) has contributed much to the anxiety to understand its meaning—since, if it refers to the Messiah, it is one of the most valuable of all the testimonials now remaining of the early faith on that subject. The importance of the passage will justify a somewhat more extended examina-

tion of its meaning than it is customary to give in a commentary of a single passage of Scripture; and I shall (1.) give the views entertained of it by the translators of the ancient and some of the modern versions; (2.) investigate the meaning of the *words* and *phrases* which occur in it; and (3.) state the arguments, *pro* and *con*, for its supposed reference to the Messiah. The Vulgate renders it, "For I know that my Redeemer—*Redemptor meus*—lives, and that in the last day I shall rise from the earth; and again, I shall be enveloped—*circumdabor*—with my skin, and in my flesh shall I see my God. Whom I myself shall see, and my eyes shall behold, and not another—this, my hope, is laid up in my bosom." The LXX. translate it, "For I know that he is Eternal who is about to deliver me—ὁ ἐκλύειν με μέλλων—to raise again upon earth this skin of mine, which draws up these things—τὸ ἀναντλοῦν ταῦτα—[the meaning of which, I believe, no one has ever been able to divine.] For from the Lord these things have happened to me of which I alone am conscious, which my eye has seen, and not another, and which have all been done to me in my bosom." *Thompson's trans. in part.* The Syriac is in the main a simple and correct rendering of the Hebrew. "I know that my Redeemer liveth, and in the consummation he will be revealed upon the earth, and after my skin I shall bless myself in these things, and after my flesh. If my eyes shall see God, I shall see light." The Chaldee accords with our version, except in one phrase. "And afterwards my skin shall be inflated, (אֶתְהַפֵּ֫ת מִשְׁכִּי) —then in my flesh shall I see God." It will be seen that some perplexity was felt by the authors of the ancient versions in regard to the passage. Much more has been felt by expositors. Some notices of the views of the moderns, in regard to particular words and phrases, will be given in the exposition. ¶ *I know.* I am certain. On that point Job desires to express the utmost confidence. His friends might accuse him of hypocrisy—they might charge him with want of piety, and he might not be able to refute all that they

said; but in the position referred to here he would remain fixed, and with this firm confidence he would support his soul. It was this which he wished to have recorded in the eternal rocks, that the record might go down to future times. If after ages should be made acquainted with his name and his sufferings—if they should hear of the charges brought against him and of the accusations of impiety which had been so harshly and unfeelingly urged, he wished that *this* testimony might be recorded, to show that he *had* unwavering confidence in God. He wished this eternal record to be made, to show that he was not a rejecter of truth; that he was not an enemy of God; that he had a firm confidence that God would yet come forth to vindicate him, and would stand up as his friend. It was a testimony worthy of being held in everlasting remembrance, and one which has had, and will have, a permanency much greater than he anticipated. ¶ That *my Redeemer.* This important word has been variously translated. Rosenmüller and Schultens render it, *vindicem;* Dr. Good, *Redeemer;* Noyes and Wemyss, *vindicator;* Herder, *avenger,* Luther, Erlöser—*Redeemer;* Chaldee and Syriac, *Redeemer.* The Hebrew word, גֹּאֵל—*goël,* is from גָּאַל—*gáál,* to redeem, to ransom. It is applied to the redemption of a farm sold, by paying back the price, Lev. xxv. 25; Ruth iv. 4, 6; to any thing consecrated to God that is redeemed by paying its value, Lev. xxvii. 13, and to a slave that is ransomed, Lev. xxv. 48, 49. The word גֹּאֵל—*goël,* is applied to one who redeems a field, Lev. xxv. 26; and is often applied to God, who had redeemed his people from bondage, Ex. vi. 6; Isa. xliii. 1. See Notes on Isa. xliii. 1; and on the general meaning of the word, see Notes on Job iii. 5. Among the Hebrews, the גֹּאֵל—*goël* occupied an important place, as a *blood-avenger,* or a vindicator of violated rights. See Numb. xxxv. 12, 19, 21, 24, 25, 27; Deut. xix. 6—12; Ruth iv. 1, 6, 8; Josh. xx. 3. The word גֹּאֵל—*goël,* is rendered *kinsman,* Ruth iv. 1, 3, 6, 8; *near kinsman,* Ruth iii. 9, 12;

avenger, Num. xxxv. 12; Josh. xx. 3; *Redeemer,* Job xix. 25; Ps. xix. 14; Isa. xlvii. 4; lxiii. 16; xliv. 24; xlviii. 17; liv. 8; xli. 14; xlix. 26; lx. 16; *kin,* Lev. xxv. 25, *et al.* Moses *found* the office of the goël, or avenger, already instituted, (see Michaelis's Commentary on laws of Moses, § cxxxvi.) and he adopted it into his code of laws. It would seem, therefore, not improbable that it prevailed in the adjacent countries in the time of Job, or that there may have been a reference to this office in the place before us. The *goël* is first introduced in the laws of Moses, as having a right to redeem a mortgaged field, Lev. xxv. 25, 26; and then as having a right, as kinsman, to the restoration of any thing which had been iniquitously acquired, Num. v. 8. Then he is often referred to in the writings of Moses as the blood-avenger, or the kinsman of one who was slain, who would have a right to pursue the murderer, and to take vengeance on him, and whose *duty* it would be to do it. This right of a near relative to pursue a murderer, and to take vengeance, seems to have been one that was early conceded every where. It was so understood among the American Indians, and probably prevails in all countries before there are settled laws for the trial and punishment of the guilty. It was a right, however, which was liable to great abuse. Passion would take the place of reason, the innocent would be suspected, and the man who had slain another in self-defence was as likely to be pursued and slain as he who had been guilty of wilful murder. To guard against this, in the unsettled state of jurisprudence, Moses appointed *cities of refuge,* where the man-slayer might flee until he could have a fair opportunity of trial. It was impossible to put an end at once to the office of the *goël.* The kinsman, the near relative, would feel himself called on to pursue the murderer; but the man-slayer might flee into a sacred city, and remain until he had a fair trial; see Num. xxxv; Deut. xix. 6, 7. It was a humane arrangement to appoint cities of refuge, where the man who had slain another might be secure until he

had an opportunity of trial—an arrangement which eminently showed the wisdom of Moses. On the rights and duties of the *goël,* the reader may consult Michaelis's Com. on the laws of Moses, art. 136, 137. His essential office was that of a *vindicator*—one who took up the cause of a friend, whether that friend was murdered, or was oppressed, or was wronged in any way. Usually, perhaps always, this pertained to the nearest male kin, and was instituted for the aid of the defenceless and the wronged. In times long subsequent, a somewhat similar feeling gave rise to the institution of chivalry, and the voluntary defence of the innocent and oppressed. It cannot now be determined whether Job in this passage has reference to the office of the *goël,* as it was afterwards understood, or whether it existed in his time. It seems probable that the office would exist at the earliest periods of the world, and that in the rudest stages of society the nearest of kin would feel himself called on to vindicate the wrong done to one of the feebler members of his family. The word properly denotes, therefore, either *vindicator,* or *redeemer;* and so far as the *term* is concerned, it may refer either to God, as an avenger of the innocent, or to the future Redeemer—the Messiah. The meaning of this *word* would be met, should it be understood as referring to God, coming forth in a public manner to vindicate the cause of Job against all the charges and accusations of his professed friends; or to God, who would appear as his vindicator at the resurrection; or to the future Messiah—the Redeemer of the body and the soul. No *argument* in favour of either of these interpretations can be derived from the use of the *word.* ¶ *Liveth.* Is alive—חי Sept. *immortal—ἀϊναός.* He *seems* now to have forsaken me as if he were dead, but my faith is unwavering in him as a *living* vindicator. A similar expression occurs in ch. xvi. 19, "My witness is in heaven, and my record is on high." It is a declaration of entire confidence in God, and will beautifully convey the emotions of the sin-

26 And [1] *though* after my skin

1 or, *after I shall awake, though this body be destroyed, yet out of my flesh shall I see God.*

worms destroy this *body*, yet in my flesh [a] shall I see [b] God :

a 1 Co.15.53.　　b 1 John 3.2.

cere believer in all ages. He may be afflicted with disease, or the loss of property, or be forsaken by his friends, or persecuted by his foes, but if he can look up to heaven and say, " I know that my Redeemer *lives*," he will have peace. ¶ *And that he shall stand.* He will stand up, as one does who undertakes the cause of another. Jerome has rendered this as though it referred to Job, " And in the last day *I shall rise from the earth* "—de terra surrecturus sum—as if it referred to the resurrection of the body. But this is not in accordance with the Hebrew, (יָקוּם)—" *he* shall stand." There is clearly no necessary reference in *this* word to the resurrection. The simple meaning is, " he shall appear, or manifest himself, as the vindicator of my cause." ¶ *At the latter* day. The word " day " here is supplied by the translators. The Hebrew is, וְאַחֲרוֹן —and *after, afterwards, hereafter, at length.* The word *literally* means, hinder, hinder part—opposite to foremost, former. It is applied to the Mediterranean sea, as being behind when the eye of the geographer was supposed to be turned to the East ; (see Notes on ch. xviii. 20 ;) then it means after, later, applied to a generation or age. Ps. xlviii. 14, to a day —to future times—(יוֹם אַחֲרוֹן), Prov. xxxi. 25 ; Isa. xxx. 8. All that this word necessarily expresses here is, that *at some future period* this would occur. It does not determine *when* it would be. The *language* would apply to any future time, and might refer to the coming of the Redeemer, to the resurrection, or to some subsequent period in the life of Job. The meaning is, that however long he was to suffer, however protracted his calamities were, and were likely to be, he had the utmost confidence that God would *at length*, or *at some future time*, come forth to vindicate him. The phrase, " the latter day," has now acquired a kind of technical meaning, by which we naturally refer it to the day of judgment. But there

is no evidence that it has any such reference here. On the general meaning of phrases of this kind, however, the reader may consult my Notes on Isaiah, ch. ii. 2. ¶ *Upon the earth.* Heb. עַל־עָפָר —*upon the dust.* Why the word *dust* is used, instead of (אֶרֶץ) *earth*, is unknown. It may be because the word *dust* is emphatic, as being contrasted with heaven, the residence of the Deity. *Noyes.* What *kind* of an appearance God would assume when he should thus come forth, or how he would manifest himself as the vindicator and Redeemer of Job, he does not intimate, and conjecture would be useless. The *words* do not necessarily imply any *visible* manifestation—though such a manifestation would not be forbidden by the fair construction of the passage. I say, they do not necessarily imply it ; see Psalms xii. 5, " For the sighing of the needy, now will I arise, (Heb. *stand up* — אָקוּם), saith the Lord." Ps. xliv. 26, " Arise (Heb. קוּמָה—*stand up*) for our help." Whether this refers to any *visible* manifestation in behalf of Job is to be determined in other words than by the mere meaning of this word.

26. *And though.* Marg. Or, *after I shall awake, though this body be destroyed, yet out of my flesh shall I see God.* This verse has given not less perplexity than the preceding. Noyes renders it,

And though with this skin this body be wasted away,
Yet in my flesh shall I see God.

Dr. Good renders it,

And, after the DISEASE hath destroyed my skin,
That in my flesh I shall see God.

Rosenmüller explains it, " And when after my skin (*scil.* is consumed and destroyed) they consume (*scil.* those corroding, or consuming, *i.e.* it is corroded, or broken into fragments) *this*, that is, this structure of my bones— my body (which he does not mention, because it was so wasted away that it did not deserve to be called a body) —yet without my flesh—with my whole

27 Whom I shall see for my-

self, and mine eyes shall behold,

body consumed, shall I see God." He translates it,

Et quum post cutem meam hoc fuerit consumptum,
Tamen absque carne mea videbo Deum.

The Hebrew is literally, "and after my skin." Gesenius translates it, "After they shall have destroyed my skin, this shall happen—that I will see God." Herder renders it,

Though they tear and devour this my skin,
Yet in my living body shall I see God.

The fair and obvious meaning, I think, is that which is conveyed by our translation. Disease had attacked his skin. It was covered with ulcers, and was fast consuming ; comp. ch. ii. 8, vii. 5. This process of corruption and decay he had reason to expect would go on until all would be consumed. But if it did, he would hold fast his confidence in God. He would believe that he would come forth as his vindicator, and he would still put his trust in him. ¶ Worms. This word is supplied by our translators. There is not a semblance of it in the original. That is, simply, "they destroy ;" where the verb is used impersonally, meaning that it would be destroyed. The *agent* by which this would be done is not specified. The word rendered "destroy" (נִקְּפוּ from נָקַף), means to cut, to strike, to cut down (comp. Notes on ch. i. 5, for the general meaning of the word), and here means *to destroy;* that is, that the work of destruction might go on until the frame should be wholly wasted away. It is not quite certain that the word here would convey the idea that he expected *to die.* It *may* mean that he would become entirely emaciated, and all his flesh be gone. There is nothing, however, in the word to show that he did not expect to die—and perhaps that would be the most obvious and proper interpretation. ¶ *This* body. The word *body* is also supplied by the translators. The Hebrew is simply זֹאת—*this.* Perhaps he *pointed* to his body—for there can be no doubt that his body or flesh is intended. Rosenmüller supposes that he did not mention it, because it

was so emaciated that it did not deserve to be called a body. ¶ *Yet in my flesh.* Heb. " From my flesh "—מִבְּשָׂרִי. Herder renders this, " In my living body." Rosenmüller, *absque carne mea*—" without my flesh ;" and explains it as meaning, " my whole body being consumed, I shall see God." The literal meaning is, " from, or out of, my flesh shall I see God." It does not mean *in* his flesh, which would have been expressed by the preposition בְּ—but there is the notion that *from* or *out* of his flesh he would see him ; that is, clearly, as Rosenmüller has expressed it, tho' my body be consumed, and I *have no flesh,* I shall see him. Disease might carry its fearful ravages through all his frame, until it utterly wasted away, yet he had confidence that he would see his vindicator and Redeemer on the earth. It cannot be *proved* that this refers to the resurrection of that body, and indeed the natural interpretation is against it. It is, rather, that though *without* a body, or though his body should all waste away, he would see God as his vindicator. He would not always be left overwhelmed in this manner with calamities and reproaches. He would be permitted to see God coming forth as his Goël or Avenger, and manifesting himself as his friend. Calmly, therefore, he would bear these reproaches and trials, and see his frame waste away, for it would not always be so—God would yet undertake and vindicate his cause. ¶ *Shall I see God.* He would be permitted to behold him as *his* friend and avenger. What was the nature of the vision which he anticipated, it is not possible to determine with certainty. If he expected that God would appear in some remarkable manner to judge the world, and to vindicate the cause of the oppressed ; or that he would come forth in a special manner to vindicate *his* cause ; or if he looked to a general resurrection, and to the trial on that day, the *language* would apply to either of these events.

27. *Whom I shall see for myself.* It will not come to be by mere report.

and not [1] another ; *though* [2] my

1 *a stranger*.   [2] *or, my reins within me are consumed with earnest desire* for that day.

I shall not merely hear of the decision of God in my favour, but I shall myself behold him. He will at length come forth, and I shall be permitted to see him, and shall have the delightful assurance that he settles this controversy in my favour, and declares that I am his friend. Job *was* thus permitted to see God (ch. xlii. 5), and hear his voice in his favour. He spake to him from the whirlwind (ch. xxxviii. 1), and pronounced the sentence in his favour which he had desired. ¶ *And not another*. Marg. *a stranger*. So in the Hebrew. The meaning is. that *his own* eyes would be permitted to see him. He would have the satisfaction of seeing God himself, and of hearing the sentence in his favour. That expectation he deemed worthy of a permanent record, and wished it transmitted to future times, that in his darkest days and severest trials —when God overwhelmed him, and man forsook him, he still firmly maintained his confidence in God, and his belief that he would come forth to vindicate his cause. ¶ Though *my reins*. The margin renders this, "*my reins within me are consumed with earnest desire* for that day." Noyes translates it. " For this my soul panteth within me." Herder,

I shall see him as my deliverer,
Mine eyes shall behold him, as mine,
For whom my heart so long fainted.

So Wemyss, " My reins faint with desire of his arrival." Jerome renders it *(Vulgate), reposita est hæc spes mea in sinu meo* — " this, my hope. is laid up in my bosom." The LXX., " All which things have been done —συντετέλεσται— in my bosom," but what they understood by this it is difficult to say. The word rendered *reins* (כליה —or in the plural כליות— in which form only it is found), means properly the reins, or the kidneys (Job xvi. 13), and then comes to denote the inward parts, and then the seat of the desires and affections, *because* in strong emotions the inward parts are affected. *We* speak of the *heart* as the seat of the affections, but

reins be consumed [3] within me.

3 *in my bosom*.

with no more propriety than the Hebrews did of the upper viscera in general, or of the reins. In the Scriptures the heart and the reins are united as the seat of the affections. Thus, Jer. xi. 20, God " trieth the reins and the heart ;" Jer. xvii. 10 ; xx. 12 ; Ps. vii. 10. I see no reason why the word here may not be used to denote the *viscera* in general, and that the idea may be, that he felt that his disease was invading the seat of life, and his body, in all its parts, was wasting away. Our word *vitals*, perhaps, expresses the idea. ¶ *Be consumed*. Gesenius renders this, " Pine away." So Noyes, Wemyss, and some others. But the proper meaning of the word is, to consume, to be wasted, to be destroyed. The word (כלה) *strictly* means to finish, complete, render entire ; and thence has the notion of *completion* or *finishing*—whether by making a thing perfect, or by destroying it. It is used with reference to the *eyes* that fail or waste away with weeping, Lam. ii. 11, or to the spirit or heart as fainting with grief and sorrow. Ps. lxxxiv. 3 ; cxliii. 7 ; lxix. 4. It is used often in the sense of *destroying*. Jer. xvi. 4 ; Ezra v. 13; Ps. xxxix. 11 ; Isa. xxvii. 10 ; xlix. 4 ; Gen. xli. 30 ; Jer. xiv. 12 ; *et sæpe al*. This, I think, is the meaning here. Job affirms that his whole frame, external and internal, was wasting away, yet he had confidence that he would see God. ¶ *Within me*. Marg. *in my bosom*. So the Hebrew. The word *bosom* is here used as we use the word *chest*— and is not improperly rendered " within me." In view of this exposition of the words, I would translate the whole passage as follows :

For I know that my Avenger liveth,
And that hereafter he shall stand upon the earth ;
And though after my skin this [flesh] shall be destroyed,
Yet even without my flesh shall I see God:
Whom I shall see for myself,
And mine eyes shall behold, an I not another,
Though my vitals are wasting away within me

It has already been observed, that

very various views have been entertained of this important passage of Scripture. The great question has been, whether it refers to the Messiah, and to the resurrection of the dead, or to an expectation which Job had that God would come forth as his vindicator in some such way as he is declared afterwards to have done. It may be proper, therefore, to give a summary of the arguments by which these opinions would be defended. I have not found many *arguments* stated for the former opinion, though the belief is held by many, but they would be probably such as the following :—

I. Arguments which would be adduced to show that the passage refers to the Messiah and to the future resurrection of the dead. (1.) The *language* which is used is such as would appropriately describe such events. This is undoubted, though more so in our translation than in the original : but the original would appropriately express such an expectation. (2.) The impression which it would make on the mass of readers, and particularly those of plain, sober sense, who had no theory to defend. It is probably a fact, that the great body of the readers of the Bible suppose that it has such a reference. It is usually a very strong presumptive proof of the correctness of an interpretation of Scripture when this can be alleged in its favour, though it is not an infallible guide. (3.) The probability that some knowledge of the Messiah would prevail in Arabia in the time of Job. This must be admitted, though it cannot be certainly demonstrated ; comp. Num. xxiv. 17. The amount of this is, that it could not be regarded as so improbable that any such knowledge would prevail as to demonstrate certainly that this could not be referred to the Messiah. (4.) The probability that there would be found in this book some allusion to the Redeemer—the great hope of the ancient saints, and the burden of the Old Testament. But this is not conclusive or very weighty, for there are several of the books of the Old Testament which contain no distinct allusion to him. (5.) The pertinency of

such a view to the case, and its adaptedness to give to Job the kind of consolation which he needed. There can be no doubt of the truth of this; but the question is, not what *would* have imparted consolation, but what knowledge he actually had. There are many of the doctrines of the Christian religion which would have been eminently fitted to give comfort in such circumstances to a man in affliction, which it would be exceedingly unreasonable to expect to find in the book of Job, and which it is certain were wholly unknown to him and his friends. (6.) The importance which he himself attached to his declaration, and the solemnity of the manner in which he introduced it. His profession of faith on the subject he wished to have engraved in the eternal rocks. He wished it transmitted to future times. He wished a permanent record to be made, that succeeding ages might read it, and see the ground of his confidence and his hope. This, to my mind, is the strongest argument which has occurred in favour of the opinion that the passage refers to the Redeemer and to the resurrection. These are all the considerations which have occurred to me, or which I have found stated, which would go to sustain the position that the passage referred to the resurrection. Some of them have weight ; but the prevailing opinion, that the passage has such a reference, will be found to be sustained, probably, more *by the feelings of piety* than by solid argument and sound exegesis. It is favoured, doubtless, by our common version, and there can be no doubt that the translators supposed that it had such a reference.

II. On the other hand, weighty considerations are urged to show that the passage does not refer to the Messiah, and to the resurrection of the dead. They are such as the following :

(1.) The language, fairly interpreted and translated, does not necessarily imply this. It is admitted that our translators had this belief, and without doing intentional or actual violence to the passage, or designing to make a forced translation, they have allowed their feelings to give a complexion to their language which the original does not necessarily convey. Hence, the word " Redeemer," which is now used technically to denote the Messiah, is employed, though the original *may*, and commonly *does*, have a much more general signification ; and hence, the phrase " at the latter day," also a technical phrase, occurs, though the original means no more than *afterwards* or *after this ;* and hence, they have employed the phrase " in my flesh," though the original means no more than " though my flesh be all wasted away." The following I believe to express fairly the meaning of the Hebrew : " I know that my deliverer, or avenger, lives, and that he will yet appear in some public manner on the earth ; and though after the destruction of my skin, the process of corruption shall go on till *all* my flesh shall be destroyed, yet when my flesh is entirely wasted away, I shall see God ; I shall have the happiness of seeing him for myself, and beholding him with my own eyes, even though my very vitals shall be consumed. He will come and vindicate me and my cause. I have such confidence in his justice, that I do not doubt that he will yet show himself to be the friend of him who puts his trust in him."

(2.) It is inconsistent with the argument, and the whole scope and connection of the book, to suppose that this refers to the Messiah and to the resurrection of the body after death. The book of Job is strictly an *argument*—a train of clear, consecutive reasoning. It discusses a great inquiry about the doctrines of divine Providence and the divine dealings with men. The three friends of Job maintained that God deals with men strictly according to their character in this life—that eminent wickedness is attended with eminent suffering ; and that when men experience any great calamity, it is proof of eminent wickedness. All this they meant to apply to Job, and all this Job denied. Yet he was perplexed and confounded. He did not know what to do with *the facts* in the case; but still he felt embarrassed. All that he could say

was, that God would *yet* come forth and show himself to be the friend of those who loved him, and that though they suffered now, yet he had confidence that he would appear for their relief. Now, had they possessed the knowledge of the doctrine of the *resurrection of the dead*, it would have ended the whole debate. It would not only have met all the difficulties of Job, but we should have found him perpetually recurring to it —placing it in every variety of form —appealing to it as relieving his embarrassments, and as demanding an answer from his friends. But, on the supposition that this refers to the resurrection, it is remarkable that the passage here stands alone. Job never adverted to it before, but allowed himself to be greatly embarrassed for the want of just such an argument, and he never refers to it again. He goes on to argue again *as if* he believed no such doctrine. He does not ask his friends to notice this; he expresses no surprise that they should pass by, in entire neglect, an argument which *must have been seen* to be decisive of the controversy. It is equally unaccountable that his friends should not have noticed it. If the doctrine of the resurrection was true, it settled the case. It rendered all their arguments worthless, and would have met the case just as we meet similar cases now. It was incumbent on them to show that there was no evidence of the truth of any such doctrine as the resurrection, and that this could not be urged to meet their arguments. Yet they never allude to so important and unanswerable an argument, and evidently did not suppose that Job referred to any such event. It is equally remarkable that neither Elihu nor God himself, in the close of the book, make any such allusion, or refer to the doctrine of the resurrection at all, as meeting the difficulties of the case. In the argument with which the Almighty is represented as closing the book, the whole thing is resolved into a matter of *sovereignty*, and men are required to submit because God is great, and is inscrutable in his ways —not because the dead will be raised, and the inequalities of the present life will be recompensed in a future state. The doctrine of a *resurrection*—a great and glorious doctrine, such as, if once suggested, could not have escaped the profound attention of these sages—would have solved the whole difficulty; and yet, confessedly, it is never alluded to by them—never introduced—never examined—never admitted or rejected—never becomes a matter of inquiry, and is never referred to by God himself as settling the matter—never occurs in the book in any form, unless it be in this. This is wholly unaccountable on the supposition that this refers to the resurrection.

(3.) The interpretation which refers this to the resurrection of the dead, is inconsistent with numerous passages where Job expresses a contrary belief. Of this nature are the following: ch. vii. 9, "As the cloud is consumed, and vanisheth away, so he that goeth down to the grave shall come up no more;" vii. 21, "I shall sleep in the dust—thou shalt seek me in the morning, but I shall not be;" see ch. x. 21, 22, "I go whence I shall not return—to the land of darkness, and the shadow of death; a land of darkness as darkness itself;" ch. xiv. throughout, particularly vs. 7, 9, 11, 12, "For there is hope of a tree, if it be cut down, that it will sprout again, and that the tender branch thereof will not cease. But man dieth, and wasteth away; yea, man giveth up the ghost, and where is he? As the waters fail from the sea, and the flood decayeth and drieth up, so man lieth down and riseth not: till the heavens be no more, they shall not awake, nor be raised out of their sleep." Ch. xvi. 22, "When a few years are come, then I shall go the way whence I shall not return." These passages all imply that when he should die, he would not appear again on the earth. This is not such language as one would use who believed in the resurrection of the dead. It is true, that in the discourses of Job, various and sometimes apparently contradictory feelings are expressed. He was a severe sufferer; and under strong conflicting emotions he sometimes expressed himself in a manner which he at other times regrets, and gives vent to feelings which, on mature reflection, he confesses to have been wrong. But how is it *possible* to believe that a man, in his circumstances, would ever deny the doctrine of the resurrection if he held it? How could he forget it? How could he throw out a remark that *seemed* to imply a doubt of it? If he had known of this, it would have been a sheet-anchor to his soul in all the storms of adversity—an unanswerable argument to all that his friends advanced—a topic of consolation which he could never have lost sight of, much less denied. He would have clung to that hope as the refuge of his soul, and not for one moment would he have denied it, or expressed a doubt of its truth.

(4.) I may urge as a distinct argument what has before been hinted at, that this is not referred to as a topic of consolation by either of the friends of Job, by Elihu, or by God himself. Had it been a doctrine of those times, his friends would have understood it, and it would have reversed all their theology. Had it been understood by Elihu, he would have urged it as a reason for resignation in affliction. Had God designed that it should be known in that age, no more favourable opportunity could be conceived for the purpose than at the end of the arguments in this book. What a flood of light would it have thrown on the design of afflictions! How effectually would it have rebuked the arguments of the friends of Job! And how clear is it, therefore, that God did not *intend* that it should then be revealed to man, but meant that it should be reserved for a more advanced state of the world, and particularly that it should be reserved as the grand doctrine of the Christian revelation.

(5.) A fifth consideration is, that on the supposition that it refers to the resurrection, it would be inconsistent with the views which prevailed in the age when Job is supposed to have lived. It is wholly in advance of that age. It makes little difference in regard to this whether we suppose him to have lived in the time of Abraham, Jacob, or Moses, or even at a later period—such a supposition would be equally at variance with the revelations which had then been given. The clear doctrine of the resurrection of the dead, is one of the peculiar doctrines of Christianity—one of the last truths of revelation, and is one of the glorious truths which seem to have been reserved for the Redeemer himself to make known to man. There are, indeed, obscure traces of it in the Old Testament. Occasionally we meet with a hint on the subject that was sufficient to excite the hopes of the ancient saints, and to lead them to suppose that more glorious truths were in reserve to be communicated by the Messiah. But those hints occur at distant intervals ; are obscure in their character, and perhaps if all in the Old Testament were collected, they would not be sufficient to convey any very intelligible view of the resurrection of the dead. But on the supposition that the passage before us refers to that doctrine, we have here one of the most clear and full revelations on the subject, laid far back in the early ages of the world, originating in Arabia, and entirely in advance of the prevailing views of the age, and of all that had been communicated by the Spirit of inspiration to the generations then living. It is admitted, indeed, that it was *possible* for the Holy Spirit to communicate that truth in its fulness and completeness to an Arabian sage ; but it is not the way in which revelation, in other respects, has been imparted. It has been done *gradually.* Obscure intimations are given at first—they are increased from time to time — the light becomes clearer, till some prophet discloses the whole truth, and the doctrine stands complete before us. Such a course we should expect to find in regard to the doctrine of the resurrection, and such is exactly the course pursued, unless *this* passage teaches what was in fact the highest revelation made by the Messiah.

(6.) All which the words and phrases fairly convey, and all which the argument demands, is fully met by the supposition that it refers to some such event as is recorded in the close of the book. God appeared in a manner corresponding to the meaning of the words here upon the earth. He came as the Vindicator, the Redeemer, the *Goël,* of Job. He vindicated his cause, rebuked his friends, expressed his approbation of the sentiments of Job, and blessed him again with returning prosperity and plenty. The disease of the patriarch may have advanced, as he supposed it would. His flesh may have wasted away, but his confidence in God was not misplaced, and he came forth as his vindicator and friend. It was a noble expression of faith on the part of Job; it showed that he *had* confidence in God, and that in the midst of his trials he truly relied on him; and it was a sentiment worthy to be engraved in the eternal rock, and to be transmitted to future times. It was an invaluable lesson to sufferers, showing them that confidence could, and should be placed in God in the severest trials. So far as I can see, all that is fairly implied in the passage, when properly interpreted, is fully met by the events recorded in the close of the book. Such an interpretation meets the exigency of the case, accords with the strain of the argument and with the result, and is the most simple and natural that has been proposed. These considerations are so weighty in my mind that they have conducted me to a conclusion, contrary I confess to what I had *hoped* to have reached, that this passage has no reference to the Messiah and the doctrine of the resurrection. We do not *need* it—for all the truths respecting the Messiah and the resurrection which we need, are fully revealed elsewhere; and though this is an exquisitely beautiful passage, and piety would love to retain the belief that it refers to the resurrection of the dead, yet *truth* is to be preferred to indulgence of the wishes and desires of the heart, however amiable or pious, and the *desire* to find certain doctrines in the Bible should yield to what we are constrained to believe the Spirit of inspiration actually taught. I confess

28 But ye should say, Why persecute we him? [1] seeing the root of the matter is found in me.

[1] or, *and what root of matter is found in me.*

Then shall ye say, "How did we persecute him?"
When the root of the matter is disclosed in me.

---

that I have never been so pained at any conclusion to which I have come in the interpretation of the Bible, as in the case before us. I would like to have found a distinct prophecy of the Messiah in this ancient and venerable book. I would like to have found the faith of this eminent saint sustained by such a faith in his future advent and incarnation. I would like to have found evidence that this expectation had become incorporated in the piety of the early nations, and was found in Arabia. I would like to have found traces of the early belief of the doctrine of the resurrection of the dead sustaining the souls of the patriarchs then, as it does ours now, in trial. But I cannot. Yet I can regard it as a most beautiful and triumphant expression of confidence in God, and as wholly worthy to be engraved, as Job desired it might be, in the solid rock for ever, that the passing traveller might see and read it; or as worthy of that more permanent record which it has received by being "*printed in a book*"—by an art unknown then, and sent down to the end of the world to be read and admired in all generations.

The opinion which has now been expressed, it is not necessary to say, has been held by a large number of the most distinguished critics. Grotius says that the Jews never applied it to the Messiah and the resurrection. The same opinion is held by Grotius himself, by Warburton, Rosenmüller, Le Clerc, Patrick, Kennicott, Dalthe, and Jahn. Calvin seems to be doubtful—sometimes giving it an interpretation similar to that suggested above, and then pursuing his remarks as if it referred to the Messiah. Most of the fathers, and a large portion of modern critics, it is to be admitted, suppose that it refers to the Messiah, and to the future resurrection.

28. *But ye should say.* Noyes renders this, "Since ye say, 'How may we persecute him, and find grounds of accusation against him?'" Dr. Good,

The Vulgate, "Why now do ye say, let us persecute him, and find ground of accusation-*radicem verbi*-against him?" The LXX., "If you also say, What shall we say against him? and what ground of accusation—ῥίζαν λόγου—shall we find in him?" Rosenmüller renders it, "When you say, let us persecute him, and see what ground of accusation we can find in him, then fear the sword." Most critics concur in such an interpretation as implies that they had sought a ground of accusation against him, and that they would have occasion to fear the divine displeasure on account of it. It seems to me, however, that our translators have given substantially the fair sense of the Hebrew. A slight variation would, perhaps, better express the idea: "For you will yet say, Why did we persecute him? The root of the matter was found in him—and since this will be the case, fear now that justice will overtake you for it, for vengeance will not always slumber when a friend of God is wronged." ¶ *Seeing the root of the matter.* Marg. *and what root of matter is found in me.* The word rendered *matter* (דבר) means, properly, *word* or *thing*—and may refer to *any* thing. Here it is used in one of the two opposite senses, *piety* or *guilt*—as being *the thing* under consideration. The interpretation to be adopted must depend on the view taken of the other words of the sentence. To me it seems that it denotes piety, and that the idea is, that the root of true piety was in him, or that he was not a hypocrite. The word *root* is so common as to need no explanation. It is used sometimes to denote the *bottom*, or the lowest part of any thing—as *e. g.* the foot (see chap. xiii. 27, *margin*), the bottom of the mountains (Job xxviii. 9), or of the sea, Job xxxvi. 30, *margin.* Here it means the foundation, support, or source—as the root is of a tree; and

29 Be ye afraid of the sword: for wrath *bringeth* the punishments of the sword, that *a* ye may know *there is* a judgment.

CHAPTER XX.

ANALYSIS OF THE CHAPTER.

Zophar, the third of the friends of Job, replies. He is not moved to compassion by the tender appeals of Job in the previous chapter, but seems rather provoked and urged on by the solemn warning with which Job concluded his discourse. He begins (ver. 1—3) by stating the reasons which induced him to reply at all, the principal of which was, the injurious reproach and threat with which Job had concluded his speech, and then proceeds with the main topic of the argument, that calamity must be, and always had been, the lot of the wicked, ver. 4—29. He says, that it had been the settled course of events from the beginning of the world that the triumphing of the wicked would be short, and then proceeds to show this by striking images and examples. The point of his remarks is, that it was no matter how high a wicked man was exalted, he would be suddenly brought low; no matter what comforts he drew around him, they would be suddenly stripped away; no matter

a Ps.58.10,11.

the sense, I suppose, is, that he was not a dead trunk, but he was like a tree that had a root, and consequently support and life. Many critics, however, among whom is Gesenius, suppose that it means that the root of the controversy, that is, the ground of strife, was in *him*, or that he was the cause of the whole dispute.

29. *Be ye afraid of the sword.* Of the sword of justice, of the wrath of God. In taking such views, and using such language, you ought to dread the vengeance of God, for he will punish the guilty. ¶ *For wrath* bringeth *the punishments of the sword.* The word " *bringeth* " is supplied by the translators, and as it seems to me improperly. The idea is, that wrath or anger, such as they had manifested, was proper for punishment; that such malice as they had shown was a crime that God would not suffer to escape unpunished. They had, therefore, every thing to dread. Literally it is, " for wrath the iniquities of the sword;" that is, wrath is a crime for the sword. ¶ *That ye may know that there is a judgment.* That there is justice; that God punishes injuries done to the character, and that he will come forth to vindicate his friends. Probably Job anticipated that when God should come forth to vindicate *him*, he would inflict exemplary punishment on *them;* and

how much he obtained by oppression and fraud, he would not be permitted to enjoy it; and no matter how much he endeavoured to conceal his guilt, the heavens would reveal it, and would show his true character to the world. All this he doubtless intended should be applied to Job, and the application was so obvious to the circumstances of the case, that it could not fail to be made. The speech is remarkable for severity, and remarkable because it does not notice the solemn profession of confidence in God which Job had made in the previous chapter, (ver. 25—27,) further than that it is implied all along in this speech that his belief was, that the wicked, once cast down, would not be restored. Had the solemn profession of Job there referred to the Messiah and the resurrection, it is hardly conceivable that it should not have been noticed in this reply. It is, indeed, remarkable, on any supposition, that he did not refer to it, or that even Job did not refer to it again.

THEN answered Zophar the Naamathite, and said,

2 Therefore do my thoughts cause me to answer, and for *this* [1] I make haste.

[1] *my haste* is *in me.*

that this would be not only by words, but by some heavy judgment, such as he had himself experienced. The vindication of the just is commonly attended with the punishment of the unjust; the salvation of the friends of God is connected with the destruction of his foes. Job seems to have anticipated this in the case of himself and his friends; it will certainly occur in the great day when the affairs of this world shall be wound up in the decisions of the final judgment. See Matth. xxv.

CHAPTER XX.

2. *Therefore.* לכן. In view of what has been just said. Or perhaps the word means merely *certainly, truly.* ¶ *Do my thoughts cause me to answer.* This is variously rendered. The Vulgate renders it, Idcirco cogitationes meæ variæ succedunt sibi, et mens in diversa rapitur—" Therefore my various thoughts follow in succession, and the mind is distracted." The LXX., " I did not suppose that thou wouldst speak against these things, and you do not understand more than I." How this was ever made from the Hebrew it is impossible to say. On the word *thoughts*, see Notes on ch. iv. 13. The word denotes thoughts which divide and distract the mind ; not calm and collected reflections, but those which disturb, disconcert, and

3 I have heard the check of my reproach, and the spirit of my understanding causeth me to answer.

1 *from near.*　　　*a* Mat.7.21.

4 Knowest thou *not* this of old, since man was placed upon earth,

5 That the triumphing of the wicked *is* short, ¹and the joy of the hypocrite *but* for a *ᵃ*moment?

trouble. He acknowledges that it was not calm reflection which induced him to reply, but the agitating emotions produced by the speech of Job. The word rendered " cause me to answer" (ישׁיבני) means " cause me to return "—and Jerome understood it as meaning that his thoughts returned upon him in quick and troublesome succession, and says in his Commentary on Job, that the meaning is, " I am troubled and agitated because you say that you sustain these evils from God without cause, when nothing evil ought to be suspected of God." ¶ *And for* this *I make haste.* Marg. *my haste* is *in me.* The meaning is, " the impetuosity of my feelings urges me on. I reply on account of the agitation of my soul, which will admit of no delay." His heart was full, and he hastened to give vent to his feelings in impassioned and earnest language.

3. *I have heard the check of my reproach.* I have heard your violent and severe language reproaching us. Probably he refers to what Job had said in the close of his speech (ch. xix. 29), that they had occasion to dread the wrath of God, and that they might anticipate heavy judgments as the result of their opinions. Or it may be, as Schultens supposes, that he refers to what Job said in ch. xix. 2, and the rebuke that he had administered there. Or possibly, and still more probably, I think, he may refer to what Job had said in reply to the former speech of Zophar (ch. xii. 2), where he tauntingly says that " they were the people, and that wisdom would die with them." The Hebrew literally is, " the correction of my shame" (מוסר כלמתי), that is, the castigation or rebuke which tends to cover me with ignominy. The sense is, " you have accused me of that which is ignominious and shameful, and under the impetuous feelings caused by such a charge, I cannot refrain from replying." ¶ *And the spirit of my un-*

derstanding. Meaning, perhaps, "the emotion of his mind." The word *mind* or *soul* would better express the idea than the word *understanding;* and the word *spirit* here seems to be used in the sense of violent or agitating emotions—perhaps in allusion to the primary signification of the word (רוח) *mind.*

4. *Knowest thou* not *this of old.* That is, dost thou not know that this has always happened from the beginning of the world, or that this is the invariable course of events. His purpose is to show that it was the settled arrangement of Providence that the wicked would be overtaken with signal calamity. It was *so* settled that Job ought not to be surprised that it had occurred in *his* case. Zophar goes on to show that though a wicked man might rise high in honour, and obtain great wealth, yet that the fall would certainly come, and he would sink to a depth of degradation corresponding to the former prosperity. ¶ *Since man was placed upon earth.* Since the creation ; that is, it has always been so.

5. *That the triumphing.* The word "triumphing" here (רננ) means shouting, rejoicing—such a shouting as men make after a victory, or such as occurred at the close of harvesting. Here it means that the occasion which the wicked had for rejoicing would be brief. It would be but for a moment, and he then would be overwhelmed with calamity or cut off by death. ¶ *Short.* Marg. as in Heb. *from near.* That is, it would be soon over. ¶ *And the joy of the hypocrite but for a moment?* This probably means, as used by Zophar, that the happiness of a hypocrite would be brief—referring to the happiness arising from the possession of health, life, property, friends, reputation. Soon God would take away all these, and leave him to sorrow. This, he said, was the regular course of events as they had been observed from the earliest times. But

6 Though *a* his excellency mount
a Is.14.13,14.   1 *cloud.*

up to the heavens, and his head reach unto the [1] clouds;

the *language* conveys most important truths in reference to the spiritual joys of the hypocrite at all times, though it is not certain that Zophar used it in this sense. The truths are these. (1.) There is a kind of *joy* which a hypocrite may have — the counterfeit of that which a true Christian possesses. The word *hypocrite* may be used in a large sense to denote the man who is a professor of religion, but who has none, as well as him who intentionally imposes on others, and who makes pretensions to piety which he knows he has not. Such a man *may* have joy. He supposes that his sins are forgiven, and that he has a well-founded hope of eternal life. He may have been greatly distressed in view of his sin and danger, and when he supposes that his heart is changed, and that the danger is passed, from the nature of the case he will have a species of enjoyment. A man is confined in a dungeon under sentence of death. A forged instrument of pardon is brought to him. He does not know that it is forged, and supposes the danger is past, and his joy will be as real as though the pardon were genuine. So with the man who *supposes* that his sins are forgiven. (2.) The joy of the self-deceiver or the hypocrite will be short. There is no genuine religion to sustain it, and it soon dies away. It may be at first very elevated, just as the joy of the man who supposed that he was pardoned would fill him with exultation. But in the case of the hypocrite it soon dies away. He has no true love to God; he has never been truly reconciled to him; he has no real faith in Christ; he has no sincere love of prayer, of the Bible, or of Christians; and soon the temporary excitement dies away, and he lives without comfort or peace. He may be a professor of religion, but with him it is a matter of form, and he has neither love nor zeal in the cause of his professed Master. Motives of pride, or the desire of a reputation for piety, or some other selfish aim may keep him

in the church, and he lives to shed blighting on all around him. Or if, under the illusion, he should be enabled to keep up some emotions of happiness in his bosom, they must soon cease, for to the hypocrite death will soon end it all. How much does it become us, therefore, to inquire whether the peace which we seek and which we may possess in religion, is the genuine happiness which results from true reconciliation to God and a well-founded hope of salvation. Sad will be the disappointment of him who has cherished a hope of heaven through life, should he at last sink down to hell! Deep the condemnation of him who has professed to be a friend of God, and who has been at heart his bitter foe; who has endeavoured to keep up the forms of religion, but who has been a stranger through life to the true peace which religion produces!

6. *Though his excellency mount up to the heavens.* Though he attain to the highest pitch of honour and prosperity. The LXX. render this, "Though his gifts should go up to heaven, and his sacrifice should touch the clouds;" a sentence conveying a true and a beautiful idea, but which is not a translation of the Hebrew. The phrases, to go up to heaven, and to touch the clouds, often occur to denote any thing that is greatly exalted, or that is very high. Thus in Virgil,

It clamor cœlo.

So Horace,

Sublimi feriam sidera vertice.

And again,

Attingit solium Jovis.

Comp. Gen. xi. 4, "Let us build us a tower whose top may reach unto heaven." In Homer the expression not unfrequently occurs, τοῦ γὰρ κλέος οὐρανὸν ἵκει. In Seneca (Thyest. Act. v. ver. 1, 2, 4,) similar expressions occur:
Æqualis astris gradior, et cunctos super
Altum superbo vertice attingens polum,
Dimitto superos: summa votorum attigi.
The *language* of Zophar would also well express the condition of many a

7 *Yet* he shall perish for ever, like *a* his own dung: they which have seen him shall say, Where *is* he?

8 He shall fly away as a dream, *b* and shall not be found; yea, he shall be chased away as a vision of the night.

9 The eye also *which* saw him

a 1 Ki.14.10. *b* Ps.83.10. 1 or, *the poor shall*

shall *see him* no more; neither shall his place any more behold him.

10 His [1] children shall seek to please the poor, and his hands shall restore their *c* goods.

11 His bones are full *of the sin d* of his youth, which shall lie down with him in the dust.

oppress his children. *c* ver.18. *d* chap.13.26.

---

hypocrite whose piety seems to be of the most exalted character, and who appears to have made most eminent attainments in religion. Such a man may *seem* to be a man of uncommon excellence. He may attract attention as having extraordinary sanctity. He may seem to have a remarkable spirit of prayer, and yet all may be false and hollow. Men who design to be hypocrites, aim usually to be *eminent* hypocrites; they who have true piety often, alas, aim at a much lower standard. A hypocrite cannot keep himself in countenance, or accomplish his purpose of imposing on the world, without the appearance of extraordinary devotedness to God; many a sincere believer is satisfied with much less of the appearance of religion. He is sincere and honest. He is conscious of true piety, and he attempts to impose on none. At the same time he makes no attempt scarcely *to be* what the hypocrite wishes *to appear* to be; and hence the man that shall appear to be the most eminently devoted to God *may* be a hypocrite—yet usually not long. His zeal dies away, or he is suffered to fall into open sin, and to show that he had no true religion at heart.

8. *He shall fly away as a dream.* As a dream wholly disappears or vanishes. This comparison of man with a dream is not uncommon, and is most impressive. See Psalm lxxiii. 20; Notes on Isa. xxix. 7, 8. ¶ *As a vision of the night.* As when one in a dream seems to see objects which vanish when he awakes. The parallelism requires us to understand this of what appears in a dream, and not of a spectre. In our dreams we *seem* to see objects, and when we awake they vanish.

9. *The eye also* which *saw him.* This is almost exactly the language which Job uses respecting himself. See chap. vii. 8, 10, and the Notes on those verses.

10. *His children shall seek to please the poor.* Marg. or, *the poor shall oppress his children.* The idea in the Hebrew seems to be, that his sons shall be reduced to the humiliating condition of asking the aid of the most needy and abject. Instead of being in a situation to assist others, and to indulge in a liberal hospitality, they themselves shall be reduced to the necessity of applying to the poor for the means of subsistence. There is great strength in this expression. It is usually regarded as humiliating to be compelled to ask aid at all; but the idea here is, that they would be reduced to the necessity of asking it of those who themselves needed it, *or would be beggars of beggars.* ¶ *And his hands shall restore their goods.* Noyes renders this, " And their hands shall give back his wealth." Rosenmüller supposes it means, " And their hands shall restore his iniquity;" that is, what their father took unjustly away. There can be but little doubt that this refers to his *sons*, and not to himself—though the singular suffix in the word (ידיו) "*his hands*" is used. But the singular is sometimes used instead of the plural. The word rendered "*goods*" (און) means *strength, power,* and then *wealth;* and the idea here is, that the hands of his sons would be compelled to give back the property which the father had unjustly acquired. Instead of retaining and enjoying it, they would be compelled to make restitution, and thus be reduced to penury and want.

11. *His bones are full* of the sin *of*

12 Though wickedness be sweet in *a* his mouth, *though* he hide it under his tongue ;

a chap.15.16.

13 *Though* he spare it, and forsake it not, but keep it still [1] within his mouth ;

[1] *in the midst of his palate.*

his youth. The words " of the sin" in our common translation are supplied by the translators. Gesenius and Noyes suppose that the Hebrew means, " His bones are full of youth;" that is, full of vigour and strength, and the idea according to this would be, that he would be cut off in the fulness of his strength. Dr. Good renders it forcibly,

" His secret lusts shall follow his bones,
Yea, they shall press upon him in the dust."

The Vulgate renders it, " His bones are full of the sins of his youth." The LXX., " His bones are full of his youth." The Chaldee Paraphrase, " His bones are full of his strength." The Hebrew literally is, " His bones are full of his secret things" (עלומיו)—referring, as I suppose, to the *secret, long-cherished* faults of his life; the corrupt propensities and desires of his soul which had been seated in his very nature, and which would adhere to him, leaving a withering influence on his whole system in advancing years. The effect is that which is so often seen, when vices corrupt the very physical frame, and where the results are seen long in future life. The effect would be seen in the diseases which they engendered in his system, and in the certainty with which they would bring him down to the grave. The Syriac renders it, *marrow,* as if the idea were that he would die full of vigour and strength. But the sense is rather that his secret lusts would work his certain ruin. ¶ *Which shall lie down with him.* That is, the results of his secret sins shall lie down with him in the grave. He will never get rid of them. He has so long indulged in his sins; they have so thoroughly pervaded his nature, and he so delights to cherish them, that they will attend him to the tomb. There is truth in this representation. Wicked men often indulge in secret sin so long that it seems to pervade the whole system. Nothing will remove it; and it lives and acts until the body is com-

mitted to the dust, and the soul sinks ruined into hell.

12. *Though wickedness be sweet in his mouth.* Though he has pleasure in committing it, as he has in pleasant food. The sense of this and the following verses is, that though a man may have pleasure in indulgence in sin, and may find happiness of a certain kind in it, yet that the consequences will be bitter—as if the food which he ate should become like gall, and he should cast it up with loathing. There are many sins which, from the laws of our nature, are attended with a kind of pleasure. Such, for illustration, are the sins of gluttony and of intemperance in drinking; the sins of ambition and vanity; the sins of amusement and of fashionable life. To such we give the name of *pleasures.* We do not speak of them as *happiness.* That is a word which would not express their nature. It denotes rather substantial, solid, permanent joy—such joy as the " pleasures of sin for a season" do not furnish. It is this temporary *pleasure* which the lovers of vanity, fashion and dress, seek, and which, it cannot be denied, they often find. As long ago as the time of Zophar, it was admitted that such pleasure might be found in some forms of sinful indulgence, and yet even in his time that was seen, which all subsequent observation has proved true, that such indulgence must lead to bitter results. ¶ *Though he hide it under his tongue.* It is from this passage, probably, that we have derived the phrase, " to roll sin as a sweet morsel under the tongue," which is often quoted as if it were a part of Scripture. The *meaning* here is, that a man would find pleasure in sin, and would seek to prolong it, as one does the pleasure of eating that which is grateful to the palate by holding it long in the mouth, or by placing it under the tongue.

13. Though *he spare it.* That is, though he retains it long in his mouth,

14 *Yet* his meat in his bowels is turned, *it is* the gall of asps within him.

15 He hath swallowed down

riches, and he shall vomit them up again : God shall cast them out of his belly.

16 He shall suck the poison *a* of

a Ro.3.13.

that he may enjoy it the more. ¶ *And forsake it not.* Retains it as long as he can. ¶ *But keep it still within his mouth.* Marg. as in Heb. *in the midst of his palate.* He seeks to enjoy it as long as possible.

14. Yet *his meat.* His food. ¶ *In his bowels is turned.* That is, it is as if he had taken food which was exceedingly pleasant, and had retained it in his mouth as long as possible, that he might enjoy it, but when he swallowed it, it became bitter and offensive ; comp. Rev. x. 9, 10. Sin may be pleasant when it is committed, but its consequences will be bitter. ¶ It is *the gall of asps.* On the meaning of the word here rendered *asps* (פתן), see Notes on Isa. xi. 8. There can be little doubt that the *asp*, or aspic, of antiquity, which was so celebrated, is here intended. The bite was deadly, and was regarded as incurable. The sight became immediately dim after the bite—a swelling took place, and pain was felt in the stomach, followed by stupor, convulsions, and death. It is probably the same as the *boetan* of the Arabians. It is about a foot in length, and two inches in circumference—its colour being black and white. *Pict. Bib.* The word *gall* (מרירה), means *bitterness, acridness* (compare Job xiii. 26); and hence bile or gall. It is not improbable that it was formerly supposed that the poison of the serpent was contained in the gall, though it is now ascertained that it is found in a small sack in the mouth. It is here used as synonymous with the *poison* of asps—supposed to be *bitter* and *deadly.* The meaning is, that sin, however pleasant and grateful it may be when committed, will be as destructive to the soul as food would be to the body, which, as soon as it was swallowed, became the most deadly poison. This is a fair account still of the effects of sin.

15. *He hath swallowed down riches.* He has *glutted* down riches—or gor-

mandized them—or devoured them greedily. The Hebrew word בלע, means to absorb, to devour with the idea of greediness. It is descriptive of the voracity of a wild beast, and means here that he had devoured them eagerly, or voraciously. ¶ *And he shall vomit.* As an epicure does that which he has drunk or swallowed with delight. *Noyes.* The idea is, that he shall lose that which he has acquired, and that it will be attended with loathing. All this is to a great extent true still, and may be applied to those who aim to accumulate wealth, and to lay up ill-gotten gold. It will be ruinous to their peace ; and the time will come when it will be looked on with inexpressible loathing. Zophar meant, undoubtedly, to apply this to Job, and to infer, that since it was a settled maxim that such would be the result of the ill-gotten gain of a wicked man, where a result like this *had* happened, that there must have been wickedness. How cutting and severe this must have been to Job can be easily conceived. The LXX. renders this, "Out of his house let an angel drag him."

16. *He shall suck the poison of asps.* That which he swallowed as pleasant nutriment, shall become the most deadly poison ; or the consequence shall be as if he had sucked the poison of asps. It would seem that the ancients regarded the poison of the serpent as deadly, however it was taken into the system. They seem not to have been aware that the poison of a wound may be sucked out without injury to him who does it ; and that it is necessary that the poison should mingle with the blood to be fatal. ¶ *The viper's tongue shall slay him.* The early impression probably was, that the injury done by a serpent was by the fiery, forked, and brandished tongue, which was supposed to be sharp and penetrating. It is now known, that the injury is done by the

asps: the viper's tongue shall slay him.

17 He shall not see the rivers,

the floods, [1] the brooks of honey and butter.

[1] or, *streaming brooks.*

---

poison ejected through a groove, or orifice in one of the teeth, which is so made as to lie flat on the roof of the mouth, except when the serpent bites, when that tooth is elevated, and penetrates the flesh. The word *viper* here (אֶפְעֶה), is probably the same species of serpent that is known among the Arabs by the same name still—*El Effah.* See Notes on Isa. xxx. 6. It is the most common and venomous of the serpent tribe in Northern Africa and in South-western Asia. It is remarkable for its quick and penetrating poison. It is about two feet long, as thick as a man's arm, beautifully spotted with yellow and brown, and sprinkled over with blackish specks. They have a large mouth, by which they inhale a large quantity of air, and when inflated therewith, they eject it with such force as to be heard a considerable distance.   *Jackson.* Capt. Riley, in his "Authentic Narrative," (New York, 1817,) confirms this account. He describes the viper as the "most beautiful object in nature," and says that the poison is so virulent as to cause death in fifteen minutes.

17. *He shall not see the rivers.* That is, he shall not be permitted to enjoy plenty and prosperity. Rivers or rills of honey and butter are emblems of prosperity; comp. Ex. iii. 17; Job xxix. 6. A land flowing with milk, honey, and butter, is, in the Scripture, the highest image of prosperity and happiness. The word rendered "rivers" (פְּלַגּוֹת), means rather *rivulets,* small streams—or brooks, such as were made by *dividing* a large stream (from פָּלַג—to *cleave, divide*), and would properly be applied to canals made by separating a large stream, or dividing it into numerous watercourses for the purpose of irrigating lands. The word rendered *floods,* and in the margin, *streaming brooks* (נַחֲלֵי נִחֲלֵי), means "the rivers of the valley," or such as flow through a valley when it is swelled by the melting of snow, or by torrents of

rain. A flood, a rapid, swollen, full stream, would express the idea. These were ideas of beauty and fertility among the Orientals; and where butter and honey were represented as flowing in this manner in a land, it was the highest conception of plenty. The word rendered *honey* (דְּבַשׁ) may, and commonly does, mean honey; but it also means the juice of the grape, boiled down to about the consistency of molasses, and used as an article of food. The Arabs make much use of this kind of food now, and in Syria, nearly two-thirds of the grapes are employed in preparing this article of food. It is called by the Arabs *Dibs,* which is the same as the Hebrew word used here. May not the word mean this in some of the places where it is rendered *honey* in the Scriptures? The word rendered *butter* (חֶמְאָה) probably means, usually, *curdled milk.* See Notes on Isa. vii. 15. It is not certain that the word is ever used in the Old Testament to denote *butter.* The article which is used still by the Arabs is chiefly curdled milk, and probably this is referred to here. It will illustrate this passage to remark, that the inhabitants of Arabia, and of those who live in similar countries, have no idea of *butter,* as it exists among us, in a solid state. What they call *butter,* is in a fluid state, and is hence compared with flowing streams. An abundance of these articles was regarded as a high proof of prosperity, as they constitute a considerable part of the diet of Orientals. The same image, to denote plenty, is often used by the sacred writers, and by classic poets; see Isa. vii. 22:

And it shall come to pass in that day
That a man shall keep alive a young cow and
   two sheep,
And it shall be that from the plenty of milk
   which they shall give, he shall eat butter.
For butter and honey shall every one eat,
Who is left alone in the midst of the land.

See also in Joel iii. 18:

And it shall come to pass in that day,
The mountains shall drop down new wine,

18 That which he laboured for shall he restore, and shall not swallow *it* down: according to [1]*his* substance *shall* the restitution *be,* and he shall not rejoice *therein.*

1 *the substance of his exchange.*

And the hills shall flow with milk,
And all the rivers of Judah shall flow with
    water.

Thus also Ovid, Metam. iii.

Flumina jam lactis, jam flumina nectaris ibant.

Comp. Horace Epod. xvi. 41.

Mella cava manant ex ilice ; montibus altis
    Levis crepante lympha desilit pede.

From oaks pure honey flows, from lofty hills
Bound in light dance the murmuring rills.
                                BOSCAWEN.

See also Euripides, Bacch. 142 ; and Theoc. Idyll. 5, 124. Compare Rosenmüller's Alte u. neue Morgenland on Ex. iii. 8, No. 194.

18. *That which he laboured for shall he restore.* This means that he shall give back the profit of his labour. He shall not be permitted to enjoy it or to consume it. ¶ *And shall not swallow it down.* Shall not enjoy it ; shall not eat it. He shall be obliged to give it to others. ¶ *According to his substance* shall *the restitution* be. Literally, according to Gesenius, " As a possession to be restored in which one rejoices not." The sense is, that all that he has is like property which a man has, which he feels not to be his own, but which belongs to another, and which is soon to be given *up.* In such property a man does not find that pleasure which he does in that which he feels to be his own. He cannot dispose of it, and he cannot look on it and feel that it is his. So Zophar says it is with the wicked man. He can look on his property only as that which he will soon be compelled to part with, and not having any security for retaining it, he cannot rejoice in it as if it were his own. Dr. Lee, however, renders this, " As his wealth is, so shall his restitution be ; and he shall not rejoice." But the interpretation proposed above, seems to me to accord best with the sense of the Hebrew.

19. *Because he hath oppressed.* Marg. *crushed.* Such is the Hebrew. ¶ *And forsaken the poor.* He has

19 Because he hath [2] oppressed *and* hath forsaken the poor; *because* he hath violently taken away an house which he builded not;

20 Surely he shall not [3] feel

2 *crushed.*   3 *know.*

plundered them, and then forsaken them—as robbers do. The meaning is, that he had done this by his oppressive manner of dealing, and then left them to suffer and pine in want. ¶ *He hath violently taken away an house which he builded not.* That is, by overreaching and harsh dealings he has come in possession of dwellings which he did not build, or purchase in any proper manner. It does not mean that he had done this by violence—for Zophar is not describing a robber, but he means that he took advantage of the wants of the poor and obtained their property. This is often done still. A rich man takes advantage of the wants of the poor, and obtains their little farm or house for much less than it is worth. He takes a mortgage, and then forecloses it, and buys the property himself for much less than its real value, and thus practises a species of the worst kind of robbery. Such a man, Zophar says, must expect punishment—and if there is any man who has occasion to dread the wrath of heaven it is he.

20. *Surely he shall not feel quietness.* Marg. as in the Heb. *know.* The sense is, he shall not know peace or tranquillity. He shall be agitated and troubled. Wemyss, however, renders this, " Because his appetite could not be satisfied." Noyes, " Because his avarice was insatiable." So Rosenmüller explains it. So the Vulgate renders it, *Nec est satiatus venter ejus.* The LXX., " Neither is there safety to his property, nor shall he be saved by his desire." But it seems to me that the former is the sense, and that the idea is, that he should not know peace or tranquillity after he had obtained the things which he had so anxiously sought. ¶ *In his belly.* Within him ; in his mind or heart. The viscera in general in the Scriptures are regarded as the seat of the

quietness in his belly, he shall not save of that which he desired.

21 There shall [1]none of his meat be [a]left; therefore shall no man look for his goods.

22 In the fulness of his suffici-

1 or, *be none left for his meat.*   a Ec.5. 13 14.

ency he shall be in straits: every hand of the [2] wicked shall come upon him.

23 *When* he is about to fill his belly, *God* shall cast the fury of his wrath upon him, and shall rain *it* upon him [b] while he is eating.

2 or, *troublesome.*   b Ps.78.30,31.

---

affections. We confine the idea now to the *heart.* ¶ *He shall not save of that which he desired.* Literally, he shall not *escape* with that which was an object of desire. He shall not be *delivered* from the evils which threaten him by obtaining that which he desired. All this shall be taken from him.

21. *There shall none of his meat be left.* Marg. " or, *be none left for his meat.*" Noyes renders it, " Because nothing escaped his greatness." Prof. Lee, "no surviver shall remain for his provision." But the meaning, probably, is, nothing shall remain of his food, or it shall all be wasted, or dissipated. ¶ *Therefore shall no man look for his goods.* Or rather, his goods or his property shall not endure. But a great variety of interpretations has been given to the passage. The Hebrew word rendered " shall look," יהיל, is from הול, which means to turn round, to twist, to whirl; and thence arises the notion of being firm, stable, or strong—as a rope that is twisted is strong. That is the idea here; and the sense is, that his property should not be secure or firm; or that he should not prosper. Jerome renders it, " Nothing shall remain of his goods." The LXX., " Therefore his good things— αὐτοῦ τὰ ἀγκαθά—shall not flourish" —ἀνθήσει.

22. *In the fulness of his sufficiency.* When he seems to have an abundance. ¶ *He shall be in straits.* Either by the dread of calamity, or because calamity shall come suddenly upon him, and his property shall be swept away. When every thing seemed to be abundant he should be reduced to want. ¶ *Every hand of the wicked shall come upon him.* Marg. " or, *troublesome.*" The meaning is, that all that the wretched or miserable endure

should come suddenly upon him. Rosenmüller suggests, however, that it means that all the poor, and all who had been oppressed and robbed by him, would suddenly come upon him to recover their own property, and would scatter all that he had. The general meaning is clear, that he would be involved in misery from every quarter, or on every hand.

23. When *he is about to fill his belly.* Or rather, " there shall be enough to fill his belly." But what *kind* of food it should be, is indicated in the following part of the verse. *God* would fill him with the food of his displeasure. It is spoken sarcastically, as of a gormandizer, or a man who lived to enjoy eating, and the meaning is, that he should for once have enough. So Rosenmüller interprets it. ¶ God *shall cast the fury.* This is the kind of food that he shall have. God shall fill him with the tokens of his wrath—and he shall have enough. ¶ *And shall rain it upon him while he is eating.* Noyes renders this, " And rain it down upon him for his food.' The meaning is, that God would pour down his wrath like a plentiful shower while he was in the act of eating. In the very midst of his enjoyments God would fill him with the tokens of his displeasure. There can be no doubt that Zophar designed that this should be understood to be applicable to Job. Indeed no one can fail to see that his remarks are made with consummate skill, and that they are such as would be fitted *to cut deep,* as they were doubtless intended to do. The speaker does not, indeed, make a direct application of them, but he so makes his selection of proverbs that there could be no difficulty in perceiving that they were designed to apply to him, who, from such a height of

24 He shall flee from the iron weapon, *and* the bow of steel shall strike him through.

25 It is drawn, and cometh out of the body; yea, the glittering

a Ps. 73.19.　　　*b* Ps.21.8; Mat.3.12.

sword cometh out of his gall: terrors *a are* upon him.

26 All darkness *shall be* hid in his secret places; a fire *b*not blown shall consume him; it shall go ill with him that is left in his tabernacle.

---

prosperity, had been so suddenly plunged into so deep calamity.

24. *He shall flee from the iron weapon.* The sword, or the spear. That is, he shall be exposed to attacks, and shall flee in cowardice and alarm. Bands of robbers shall come suddenly upon him, and he shall have no safety except in flight. Prof. Lee explains this as meaning, " *While* he flees from the iron weapon, the brazen bow shall pierce him through." Probably the expression is proverbial, like that in Latin, Incidit in Scyllam cupiens vitare Charybdin. ¶ *The bow of steel shall strike him through.* That is, the *arrow* from the bow of steel shall strike him down. Bows and arrows were commonly used in hunting and in war. To a considerable extent they are still employed in Persia, though the use has been somewhat superseded by the gun. *Bows* were made of various materials. The first were, undoubtedly, of wood. They were inlaid with horn, or ivory, or were made in part of metal. Sometimes, it would seem that the whole bow was made of metal, though it is supposed that the metal bow was not in general use. The *weight*, if nothing else, would be an objection to it. The word which is here rendered *steel* (נחושה), means properly *brass* or *copper*—but it is certain that brass or copper could never have been used to form the main part of the bow, as they are destitute of the elasticity which is necessary. Jerome renders it, et irruet in arcum æreum—*he rushes on the brazen bow.* So the LXX., τόξον χάλκειον. So the Chaldee, (דקיבתא קשתא)—*the bow of brass.* There is no certain proof that *steel* was then known—though *iron* is often mentioned. It is possible, however, that though the whole bow was not made of brass or copper, yet that such quantities of these metals were employed

in constructing bows, that they might, without impropriety, be called bows of brass. The Oriental bow consists of three parts. The handle, or middle part—that on which the arrow rested—was straight, and might be made of wood, brass, copper, or any other strong substance. To this was affixed, at each end, pieces of horn, or of any other elastic substance,

in this form, ⌒————⌐

and to the ends of these horns the string was applied. The straight piece might have been of brass, and so without impropriety it might be called a brazen bow. It is not properly rendered *steel* at any rate, as the word here used is never employed to denote iron or steel.

25. *It is drawn.* Or rather, " he draws"—that is, he draws out the arrow that has been shot at him ; or it may mean, as Prof. Lee supposes, that he draws, that is, *some one* draws the arrow from its quiver, or the sword from its sheath, in order to smite him. The object is to describe his death, and to show that he should be certainly overtaken with calamity. Zophar, therefore, goes through the process by which he would be shot down, or shows that he could not escape. ¶ *And cometh out of the body.* That is, the arrow, or the glittering blade. It has penetrated the body, and passed through it. He shall be pierced through and through. ¶ *The glittering sword.* Heb. ברק—the *glittering;* scil. thing, or weapon, and is given to the sword, because it is kept bright. ¶ *Cometh out of his gall.* Supposed to be the seat of life. See Notes, ch. xvi. 13. ¶ *Terrors* are *upon him.* The terrors of death.

26. *All darkness* shall be *hid in his secret places.* The word *darkness*

27 The heaven shall reveal his iniquity; and the earth shall rise up against him.

28 The increase of his house shall depart, *and his goods* shall flow away in the day of his wrath.

here, as is common, means evidently calamity. The phrase *is hid*, means is treasured up for him. The phrase *in his secret places*, may mean " for his treasures," or instead of the great treasures which he had laid up for himself. The Apostle Paul has a similar expression, in which, perhaps, he makes an allusion to this place. Rom. ii. 5, " But, after thy hardness and impenitent heart, treasurest up unto thyself wrath against the day of wrath." Treasures formerly were laid up in secret places, or places of darkness, that were regarded as inaccessible ; see Notes on Isa. xlv. 3. ¶ *A fire not blown.* A fire unkindled. Probably the meaning is, a fire that man has not kindled, or that is of heavenly origin. The language is such as would convey the idea of being consumed by lightning, and probably Zophar intended to refer to such calamities as had come upon the family of Job, chap. i. 16. There is much *tact* in this speech of Zophar, and in the discourses of his friends on this point. They never, I believe, refer expressly to the calamities that had come upon Job and his family. They never in so many words say, that those calamities were proof of the wrath of heaven. But they go on to mention a great many similar *cases* in the abstract; to prove that the wicked would be destroyed in that manner; that when such calamities came upon men, it was proof that they were wicked, and they leave Job himself to make the application. The allusion, as in this case, was too broad to be misunderstood, and Job was not slow in regarding it as intended for himself. Prof. Lee (*in loc.*) supposes that there may be an allusion here to the "fire that shall not be quenched," or to the future punishment of the wicked. But this seems to me to be foreign to the design of the argument, and not to be suggested or demanded by the use of the word. The argument is not conducted on the supposition that men will be punished in the future world.

That would at once have given a new phase to the whole controversy, and would have settled it at once. The question was about the dealings of God *in this life*, and whether men are punished according to their deeds here. Had there been a knowledge of the future world of rewards and punishments, the whole difficulty would have vanished at once, and the controversy would have been ended. ¶ *It shall go ill with him in his tabernacle.* Heb. ירע שריד—" It shall be ill with whatever survives or remains in his tent." That is, all that remains in his dwelling shall be destroyed. Prof. Lee renders it, " In his tent shall his survivor be broken"—supposing that the word ירע is from רעע—*to break.* But it is more probably from רוע—*to be evil; to suffer evil; to come off ill;* and the sense is, that evil, or calamity, would come upon all that should remain in his dwelling.

27. *The heaven shall reveal his iniquity.* The meaning here is, that the whole creation would conspire against such a man. Heaven and earth would be arrayed against him. The course of events would be so ordered as to seem designed to bring his character out, and to show what he was. He would attempt to conceal his sin, but it would be in vain. He would hide it in his bosom, but it would be developed. He would put on the air of piety and innocence, but his secret sin would be known. This seems to be the general sense of the verse ; and it is not necessary to attempt to show *how* it would be done—whether by lightning from heaven, as Noyes supposes, or whether by some direct manifestation from the skies. Probably the meaning is, that the divine dispensations towards such a man—the overwhelming calamities which he would experience, would show what he was. The word *heaven* is not unfrequently put for God himself. Dan. iv. 23, " The heavens do rule." Luke xv. 21, " I have sinned against heaven." ¶ *The earth shall rise up against him.*

29 This *is* the portion of a wicked man from God, and the heritage [1] appointed unto him by God.

CHAPTER XXI.

ANALYSIS OF THE CHAPTER.

In this chapter, Job takes up the subject which had been under discussion, and replies, not only to Zophar, but to Eliphaz and Bildad, who had maintained the same opinions. They had asserted, and endeavoured to prove at great length, that the wicked are punished in this life, and had inferred that when a man suffers much, it is full proof that he is eminently wicked. This point they had argued as the result of their own observation, and had maintained that it was the doctrine which had been settled by the course of events, and embodied in numerous proverbs. It was time to examine that position, and to see whether it was so, and Job enters on that task in this chapter. The chapter comprises the following points:

(1.) The exordium, in which he asks their patient attention to what he had to say, and says, that when he had spoken, they might mock on, ver. 1—3.

(2.) He says that his complaint is not to man, and that his condition was such as to excite commiseration, and should, at least, have led them to be silent, and not to have overwhelmed him with reproaches, ver. 4—6.

(3.) He then enters on the great question. He takes up the inquiry, whether it is a matter of fact that the wicked suffer in this life, and are overwhelmed with calamity, as his friends maintained. He defends the contrary opinion, and shows that so far was this from being a fact, that they were often eminently prosperous, and that their just doom must be in another state, ver. 7—34. This important argument comprises the following particulars, viz.—(*a*) He states *as a fact* that they are prosperous, ver. 7—15. They live to a great age; they are mighty; their houses are secure; they are successful in business; they have instruments of joy in their dwellings; they and their families live in thoughtless mirth; they die without long-continued pain; and all this, when the effect of their whole lives has been to

1 *of his decree from.*

exclude God from their dwellings, and they have been saying to him depart from us. (*b*) It might be said, that calamity came often upon the wicked, and that their candle was suddenly put out, and that woes were laid up for their children (ver. 16—21); but Job maintains that this is no certain rule of judging. This happened not to them alone. Of two persons of the same character, one might be seen dying in the midst of comforts, his breasts full of milk, and his bones moistened with marrow, and another in the bitterness of his soul; and how could any certain inference be drawn respecting their character from the dispensations of Providence towards them? How could it be certainly inferred that the man who suffered much was a wicked man, and that the other was a favourite of heaven? They lie down alike in the dust, after the various dispensations in regard to them, and both come to the same end in the grave, ver. 22—26. (*c*) Job seems to have supposed, from something in their manner, that his friends were not satisfied still, ver. 27. They would ask, Where were the dwelling places of the mighty men of wickedness? What became of princes, and the great and proud oppressors? Were they not cut off, and prematurely consigned to the grave? To these questions, which they might be disposed to ask, Job states what he supposes to be the true doctrine in regard to the wicked, and what would accord with all the facts, as far as we can observe them. This doctrine he professes to have learned from travellers, and says that it was the result of their careful inquiries on this important subject in foreign lands. He maintains, therefore (ver. 29—34), that the true doctrine was, the wicked were reserved for future destruction. Now, he maintains, they were prospered. No one dares attack them to their face; no one punishes them. They live in prosperity, and they lie down peacefully in the grave, and the clods of the valley are as sweet to them as to other men. They are accompanied to the grave by multitudes; they drew numbers after them by their example; and in their death they are publicly bemoaned. Their punishment must be beyond the tomb. Job thus, with boldness, attacks the main principle—a principle which they regarded as settled. He carried the war into their camp, and the controversy after this became feebler, until his opponents were wholly silenced, and they ceased to attempt to answer him.

Calamities from the earth. The course of events here. Want of success—sterility of soil—blight and mildew, would rise up against such a man and show what he was. His real character would in some way be brought out, and it would be seen that he was a wicked man; comp. Judges, v. 20.

They fought from heaven; The stars in their courses fought against Sisera.

28. *The increase of his house shall depart.* Sept. "Destruction shall bring his house to an end." The word rendered "*depart*" (יבל-from כלה), means, properly, *shall go into captivity.* The sense is, that whatever he had laid up in his house would entirely disappear. ¶ His goods *shall flow away.* What he had gained would seem to flow away like water. ¶ *In the day of his wrath.* The wrath of God—for so the connection demands.

29. *This* is *the portion of a wicked man.* This conclusion is similar to that which Bildad drew at the close of his speech, chap. xviii. 21. Zophar intended, undoubtedly, that Job should apply it to himself, and that he should draw the inference, that one who had been treated in this manner, must be a wicked man. ¶ *And the heritage appointed.* Marg. *of his decree from.* The Hebrew is, "Of his word" (אמרו) —that is, of his *purpose.* The idea is, that this is the divine rule, or arrangement. It is not a matter of chance. It is the result of appointment, and when men are afflicted in this manner, we are to conclude that *God* regards them as guilty. The whole object of the discussion was to arrive at the principles of the divine administration. Nothing is attributed to chance; and nothing is ascribed to second causes, except as indicating the

B UT Job answered and said,
2 Hear diligently my speech;
and let this be your consolations.
3 Suffer me that I may speak ;

1 *shortened.*

and after that I have spoken, mock
on.
4 As for me, *is* my complaint to
man? and if *it were so,* why should
not my spirit be [1] troubled?

will of God. It is assumed, that the
course of events in the world was a
sufficient exponent of the divine intention, and that when they understood
how God *treated* a man, they could
clearly understand how he regarded
his character. The principle is a
good one, when *the whole of existence*
is taken into the account; the fault
here was in taking in only a small part
of existence—this short life—and hastening to the conclusion, that the
character could be certainly determined by the manner in which God
deals with men here.

2 *Hear diligently.* Heb. "Hearing hear"—that is, hear attentively.
What he was about to say was worthy
of their solemn consideration. ¶ *And
let this be your consolations.* That is,
"You came to me for the professed
purpose of giving *me* consolation. In
that you have wholly failed. You
have done nothing to sustain or comfort me ; but all that you have said
has only tended to exasperate me, and
to increase my sorrow. If you will
now hear me attentively, I will take
that as a consolation, and it shall be
in the place of what I had a right to
expect from you. It will be *some*
comfort if I am permitted to express
my sentiments without interruption,
and I will accept it as a proof of kindness on your part."

3. *Suffer me that I may speak.*
Allow me to speak without interruption, or bear with me while I freely
express my sentiments—it is all that
I now ask. ¶ *And after that I have
spoken, mock on.* Resume your reproaches, if you will, when I am done.
I ask only the privilege of expressing
my thoughts on a very important point,
and when that is done, I will allow you
to resume your remarks as you have
done before, and you may utter your
sentiments without interruption. Or
it may be, that Job utters this in a
kind of triumph, and that he feels that
what he was about to say was so im-

portant that it would end the *argument;* and that all they could say after
that would be mere mockery and re-
viling. The word rendered *mock on*
(לעג) means, originally, to stammer, to
speak unintelligibly—then, to speak in
a barbarous or foreign language—then,
to deride or to mock, to ridicule or
insult. The idea is, that they might
mock his woes, and torture his feelings
as they had done, if they would only
allow him to express his sentiments.

4. *As for me,* is *my complaint to
man?* There is some difficulty in the
interpretation of this verse, and considerable variety of explanation may
be seen among expositors. The *object* of the verse is plain. It is to
state a reason why they should hear
him with patience and without interruption. The meaning of this part of
the verse probably is, that his principal difficulty was not with his friends,
but with God. It was not so much
what they had said, that gave him
trouble, as it was what God had done.
Severe and cutting as were their re-
bukes, yet it was far more trying to
him to be treated as he had been by
God, *as if* he were a great sinner.
That was what he could not understand. Perplexed and troubled, therefore, by the mysteriousness of the divine dealings, his friends ought to be
willing to listen patiently to what he
had to say; and in his anxiety to find
out *why* God had treated him so, they
ought not at once to infer that he was
a wicked man, and to overwhelm him
with increased anguish of spirit. It
will be recollected that Job repeatedly
expressed the wish to be permitted to
carry his cause at once up to God, and
to have his adjudication on it. See
Notes on chap. xiii. 3, 18, seq. It is
that to which he refers when he says
here, that he wished to have the cause
before God, and not before man. It
was a matter which he wished to refer
to the Almighty, and he ought to be
allowed to express his sentiments with

5 Mark [1] me, and be astonished, and lay [a] *your* hand upon *your* mouth.

6 Even when I remember, I am

1 *look unto.*   a chap.40.4.   b Je.12.1,2.

afraid, and trembling taketh hold on my flesh.

7 Wherefore [b] do the wicked live, become old, yea, are mighty in power?

---

entire freedom. One of the difficulties in understanding this verse arises from the word *complaint*. We use it in the sense of *murmuring*, or *repining;* but this, I think, is not its meaning here. It is used rather in the sense of *cause, argument, reasoning,* or *reflections.* The Hebrew word שׂיחַ means, properly, that which is *brought out*—from שׂיחַ, to bring out, to put forth, to produce—as buds, leaves, flowers; and then it means *words*—as brought out, or spoken; and then, meditations, reflections, discourses, speeches; and then it *may* mean complaint. But there is no evidence that the word is used in that sense here. It means his reflections, or arguments. They were not to man. He wished to carry them at once before God, and he ought, therefore, to be allowed to speak freely. Jerome renders it, *disputatio mea.* The LXX., ἔλεγξίς—used here, probably, in the sense of an argument to produce conviction, as it is often. ¶ *And if* it were so, *why should not my spirit be troubled?* Marg. *shortened,* meaning the same as troubled, afflicted, or impatient. A more literal translation will better express the idea which is now lost sight of, " And if so, why should not my spirit be distressed?" That is, since my cause is with God—since my difficulty is in understanding his dealings with me—since I have carried my cause up to him, and all now depends on him, why should I not be allowed to have solicitude in regard to the result? If I manifest anxiety, who can blame me? Who would not, when his all was at stake, and when the divine dealings towards him were so mysterious?

5. *Mark me.* Marg. *look unto.* Literally, " Look upon me. That is, attentively look on me, on my sufferings, on my disease, and my losses. See if I am a proper object of reproach and mockery—see if I have not abundant reason to be in deep distress

when God has afflicted me in a manner so unusual and mysterious. ¶ *And be astonished.* Silent astonishment should be evinced instead of censure. You should wonder that a man whose life has been a life of piety, should exhibit the spectacle which you now behold, while so many proud contemners of God are permitted to live in affluence and ease. ¶ *And lay* your *hand upon* your *mouth.* As a token of silence and wonder. So Plutarch, de Iside et Osiride, " Wherefore, he had laid his finger on his mouth as a symbol of silence and admiration—ἐχεμυθίας καὶ σιωπῆς σύμβολον."

6. *Even when I remember, I am afraid.* I have an internal shuddering and horror when I recall the scenes through which I have passed. I am myself utterly overwhelmed at the magnitude of my own sufferings, and they are such as should excite commiseration in your hearts. Some, however, have connected this with the following verse, supposing the idea to be, that he was horror-stricken when he contemplated the prosperity of wicked men. But there seems to me to be no reason for this interpretation. His object is undoubtedly to show them that there was enough in his case to awe them into silence; and he says, in order to show that, that the recollection of his sufferings perfectly overwhelmed *him*, and filled him with horror. They who have passed through scenes of peculiar danger, or of great bodily suffering, can easily sympathize with Job here. The very recollection will make the flesh tremble.

7. *Wherefore do the wicked live?* Job comes now to the main design of his argument in this chapter, to show that it is a fact, that the wicked often have great prosperity; that they are not treated in this life according to their character; and that it is not a fact that men of eminent wickedness, as his friends maintained, would meet, in this life, with proportionate suffer-

8 Their seed is established in their sight with them, and their offspring before their eyes.

9 Their houses are [1] safe from fear, neither is the rod of God upon them.

[1] peace from.

ings. He says, that the fact is, that they enjoy great prosperity; that they live to a great age; and that they are surrounded with the comforts of life in an eminent degree. The meaning is, "If you are positive that the wicked are treated according to their character in this life—that great wickedness is followed by great judgments, how is it to be accounted for that they live, and grow old, and are mighty in power?" Job assumes the fact to be so, and proceeds to argue as if that were indisputable. It is remarkable, that the fact was not adverted to at an earlier period of the debate. It would have done much to settle the controversy. The *question*, "Why do the wicked live?" is one of great importance at all times, and one which it is natural to ask, but which it is not even yet always easy to answer. *Some* points are clear, and may be easily suggested. They are such as these—They live (1) to show the forbearance and long-suffering of God; (2) to furnish a full illustration of the character of the human heart; (3) to afford them ample space for repentance, so that there shall not be the semblance of a ground of complaint when they are called before God, and are condemned; (4) because God intends to make some of them the monuments of his mercy, and more fully to display the riches of his grace in their conversion, as he did in the case of Paul, Augustine, John Bunyan, and John Newton; (5) they may be preserved to be the instruments of his executing some important purpose by them, as was the case with Pharaoh, Sennacherib, and Nebuchadnezzar; or, (6) he keeps them, that the great interests of society may be carried on; that the affairs of the commercial and the political world may be forwarded by their skill and talent. For some, or all of these purposes, it may be, the wicked are kept in the land of the living, and are favoured with great external prosperity, while many a

Christian is oppressed, afflicted, and crushed to the dust. Of the *fact*, there can be no doubt; of the *reasons* for the fact, there will be a fuller development in the future world than there can be now. ¶ *Become old.* The friends of Job had maintained that the wicked would be cut off. Job, on the other hand, affirms that they live on to old age. The *fact* is, that many of the wicked are cut off for their sins in early life, but that some live on to an extreme old age. The argument of Job is founded on the fact, that *any* should live to old age, as, according to the principles of his friends, *all* were treated in this life according to their character. ¶ *Yea, are mighty in power.* Or, rather, *in wealth*—היל. Jerome, "Are comforted in riches"—*confortatique divitiis.* So the LXX., ἐν πλούτῳ. The idea is, that they become very rich.

8. *Their seed.* Their children—their posterity. ¶ *Is established in their sight.* Around them, where they may often see them—where they may enjoy their society. The friends of Job had maintained, with great positiveness and earnestness, that the children of wicked men would be cut off. See chap. xviii. 19; xx. 28. This position Job now directly controverts, and says that it is a fact, that so far from being cut off, they are often established in the very presence of their ungodly parents, and live and prosper. How, he asks, is this consistent with the position, that God deals with men in this life according to their character?

9. *Their houses* are *safe from fear.* Marg. *peace from.* The friends of Job had maintained just the contrary; see chap. xx. 27, 28; xv. 21—24. Their idea was, that the wicked man would never be free from alarms. Job says, that they lived in security and peace, and that their houses are preserved from the intrusions of evil-minded men. ¶ *Neither is the rod of God upon them.* The *rod* is an em-

10 Their bull gendereth, and faileth not; their cow calveth, and casteth not her calf.

11 They send forth their little ones like a flock, and their children dance.

12 They take the timbrel and harp, and rejoice at the sound of the organ.

---

blem of punishment. The idea is, that they were free from the chastisements which their sins deserved. There can be no doubt that there are cases enough in which the wicked live in security, to justify Job in all that he here affirms, as there are instances enough in which the wicked are cut off for their sins, to make what his friends said plausible. The truth is, good and evil are intermingled. There is a *general* course of events by which the wicked are involved in calamity in this life, and the righteous are prospered; but still, there are so many exceptions as to show the necessity of a future state of rewards and punishments. To us, who look to that future world, all is clear. But that view of the future state of retribution was not possessed by Job and his friends.

10. *Their bull gendereth.* See Rosenmüller and Lee on this verse; comp Bochart, Hieroz. P. 1, Lib. ii. c. xxx. The general idea is, that the wicked were prospered as well as the pious. God did not interpose by a miracle to cut off their cattle, and to prevent their becoming rich.

11. *They send forth their little ones.* Their numerous and happy children they send forth to plays and pastimes. ¶ *Like a flock.* In great numbers. This is an exquisitely beautiful image of prosperity. What can be more so than a group of happy children around a man's dwelling? ¶ *And their children dance.* Dance for joy. They are playful and sportive, like the lambs of the flock. It is the skip of playfulness and exultation that is referred to here, and not the set and formal dance where children are instructed in the art; the sportiveness of children in the fields, the woods, and on the lawn, and not the set step taught in the dancing-school. The word here used (רקד) means to leap, to skip—as from joy, and then to dance. Jerome has well rendered it, *exultant lusibus*— "they leap about in their plays." So

the LXX., προσπαίζουσιν—*they frolick* or *play.* There is no evidence here that Job meant to say that they taught their children to dance; that they caused them to be trained in any thing that now corresponds to dancing-schools; and that he meant to say that such a training was improper and tended to exclude God from the heart. The image is one simply of health, abundance, exuberance of feeling, cheerfulness, prosperity. The houses were free from alarms; the fields were filled with herds and flocks, and their families of happy and playful children were around them. The object of Job was not to say that all this was in itself wrong, but that it was a plain matter of fact that God did not take away the comforts of all the wicked and overwhelm them with calamity. Of the impropriety of training children in a dancing-school, there ought to be but one opinion among the friends of religion (see National Preacher for January 1844), but there is no evidence that Job referred to any such training here, and *this* passage should not be adduced to prove that dancing is wrong. It refers to the playfulness and the cheerful sports of children, and God has made them so that they *will* find pleasure in such sports, and so that they are benefited by them. There is not a more lovely picture of happiness and of the benevolence of God any where on earth than in such groups of children, and in their sportiveness and playfulness there is no more that is wrong than there is in the gambols of the lambs of the flock.

12. *They take the timbrel.* They have instruments of cheerful music in their dwellings; and this is an evidence that they are not treated as the friends of Job had maintained. Instead of being, as they asserted, overwhelmed with calamity, they are actually happy. They have all that can make them cheerful, and their houses exhibit all that is usually the emblem

13 They spend their days in
  1 or, *mirth.*

1 wealth, and in a moment go down
to the grave.

of contentment and peace. Rosenmüller and Noyes suppose this to
mean, "They sing to the timbrel and
harp;" that is, "they raise up" (ישׂאוּ)
scil. *the voice* to accompany the timbrel. Dr. Good renders it, "They
rise up to the tabor and harp, and trip
merrily to the sound of the pipe." So
Wemyss. It is literally, "They rise
up with the tabor;" and the word
voice may be understood, and the
meaning may be that they accompany
the timbrel with the voice. The
Vulg. and the LXX., however, render
it, they "Take up the timbrel." Dr.
Good supposes that the allusion is to
the modes of dancing; to their raising
themselves in an erect position, and
then changing their position—advancing and retreating as in alternate
dances, and quotes the following exquisite piece of poetry as illustrating
it :

" Now pursuing, now retreating,
  Now in circling troops they meet;
To brisk notes, in cadence meeting,
  Glance their many-twinkling feet."

Still, it seems to me, that the exact
idea has not been expressed. It is
this, "They raise, or elevate (ישׂאוּ)
scil. THEMSELVES;" that is, they become
exhilarated and excited at the sound
of music. It is in their dwellings,
and it is one of the indications of joy.
Instead of lamentations and wo, as his
friends said there would be in such
dwellings, Job says that there was
there the sound of music and mirth;
that they exhilarated themselves, and
were happy. On the word rendered
"timbrel" (תֹּף) and the word "harp"
(כִּנּוֹר), see Notes on Isa. v. 12. ¶ *At
the sound of the organ.* The word
organ we now apply to an instrument
of music which was wholly unknown in
the time of Job. With us it denotes
an instrument consisting of pipes,
which are filled with wind, and of stops
touched by the fingers. It is the largest and most harmonious of the wind
instruments, and is blown by bellows.
That such an instrument was known
in the time of Job, is wholly improbable, and it is not probable that it

would be used for the purposes here
referred to if it were known. Jerome
renders it, *organ;* the LXX., ψαλμοῦ—
"the sound of a song;" Noyes, *pipe;*
Lee, *lyre;* Good and Wemyss, *pipe.*
The Hebrew word (עוּגָב) is derived
from עָגַב—to breathe, to blow; and it
is manifest that the reference is to
some wind instrument. Various forms
of wind instruments were early invented, and this is expressly mentioned
as having been early in use. Thus it
is said of Jubal (Gen. iv. 21), "He
was the father of all such as handle
the harp and *organ*"—עוּגָב. It was
probably at first a rude reed or pipe,
which came ultimately to be changed
to the fife and flute. It is here mentioned merely as an instrument exciting hilarity, and in the mere use of
such an instrument there can be nothing improper. Job does not mean,
evidently, to complain of it as wrong.
He is simply showing that the wicked
live in ease and prosperity, and are
not subjected to trials and calamities
as his friends maintained.

13. *They spend their days in wealth.*
Marg. or, *mirth.* Literally, "they
wear out their days *in good*"—בַטּוֹב.
Vulg. *in bonis.* Sept. ἐν ἀγαθοῖς,—*in
good things ;* in the enjoyment of good.
They are not oppressed with the evils
of poverty and want, but they have
abundance of "the good things" of
life. ¶ *And in a moment go down to
the grave.* Heb. to *Sheol*—but here
meaning evidently the grave. The
idea is, that when they die they are
not afflicted with lingering disease,
and great bodily pain, but having lived
to an old age in the midst of comforts,
they drop off suddenly and quietly,
and sleep in the grave. God gives
them prosperity while they live, and
when they come to die he does not
come forth with the severe expressions
of his displeasure, and oppress them
with long and lingering sickness. The
author of the LXXIII. Psalm had a
view of the death of the wicked remarkably similar to this, when he said,

For I was envious at the foolish,
When I saw the prosperity of the wicked.

14 Therefore ᵃ they say unto God, Depart from us; for we desire not the knowledge of thy ways.

15 What ᵇ *is* the Almighty, that

we should serve him? and what profit ᶜ should we have, if we pray unto him?

a Hab.1.15.   b Ex.5.2.   c Mal.3.14.

For there are no bands in their death,
But their strength is firm.   Ver. 3, 4.

All that Job says here is predicated on the supposition that such a sudden removal is preferable to death accompanied with long and lingering illness. The idea is, that it is in itself *desirable* to live in tranquillity; to reach an honourable old age surrounded by children and friends, and then quietly and suddenly to drop into the grave without being a burden to friends. The wicked, he says, often live such a life, and he infers, therefore, that it is not a fact that God deals with men according to their character in this life, and that it is not right to draw an inference respecting their moral character from his dealings with them in this world. There are instances enough occurring in every age like those supposed here by Job, to justify the conclusion which he draws.

14. *Therefore.* This would seem to indicate that the *result* of their living in this manner was that they rejected God, or that one of the consequences of their being prospered would be that they would cast off his government and authority; that they renounced him *because* they were thus prosperous, or because they wished to train up their children in merriment and dancing. All this may be true in itself, but that idea is not in the Hebrew. That is simply "*and* they say"—וַיֹּאמְרוּ. So the Vulgate; the LXX.; the Chaldee —וְאָמְרוּ; and the Syriac. The word "*therefore*" should not have been inserted. Job is not affirming that their mode of life is a *reason* why they reject the claims of God, but that it is a simple *fact* that they *do* live, even in this prosperity, in the neglect of God. This is the gist of what he is saying, that being thus wicked they were in fact prospered, and not punished as his friends had maintained. ¶ *They say unto God.* This is the language of their conduct. Men do not often formally and openly say this; but it is the language of their deportment. ¶ *De-*

part from us. This is about all that the wicked say of God. *They wish him to let them alone.* They do not desire that he would come into their habitations; they would be glad never more to hear his name. Yet what a state of mind is this! What must be the condition and character of the human heart when this desire is felt? ¶ *We desire not the knowledge of thy ways.* We have no wish to become acquainted with God. His "ways" here mean his government, his law, his claims—whatever God does. Never was there a better description of the feelings of the human heart than is here expressed. The ways of God are displeasing to men, and they seek to crowd from their minds all respect to his commandments and claims. Yet, if this is the character of man, assuredly he is very far from being a holy being. What higher proof of depravity CAN there be, than that a man has no desire to know any thing about a pure and holy God; no pleasure in becoming acquainted with his Maker!

15. *What* is *the Almighty, that we should serve him?* comp. for similar expressions, Ex. v. 2; Prov. xxx. 9. The meaning here is, "What claim has the Almighty, or who is he, that we should be bound to obey and worship him? What authority has he over us? Why should we yield our will to his, and why submit to his claims?" This is the language of the human heart everywhere. Man seeks to deny the authority of God over him, and to feel that he has no claim to his service. He desires to be independent. He would cast off the claims of God. Forgetful that he made, and that he sustains him; regardless of his infinite perfections and of the fact that he is dependent on him every moment, he asks with contempt, what right God has to set up a dominion over him. Such is man—a creature of a day—dependent for every breath he draws on that Great Being, whose government and authority he so con-

16 Lo, their good *is* not in their

a Ps.1.1.

hand: the counsel *a* of the wicked is far from me.

temptuously disowns and rejects! ¶ *And what profit should we have, if we pray unto him?* What advantage would it be to us should we worship him? Men still ask this question, or, if not openly asked, they *feel* the force of it in their hearts. Learn hence, (1.) That wicked men are influenced by a regard to *self* in the inquiry about God, and in meeting his claims. They do not ask what is *right*, but what *advantage* will accrue to them. (2.) If they see no immediate benefit arising from worshipping God, they will not do it. Multitudes abstain from prayer, and from the house of God, because they cannot see how their self-interest would be promoted by it. (3.) Men *ought* to serve God, without respect to the immediate, selfish, and personal good that may follow to themselves. It is a good in itself to worship God. It is what is *right;* what the conscience says *ought* to be done: yet (4.) It is not difficult to answer the question which the sinner puts. There *is* an advantage in calling upon God. There is (*a*) the possibility of obtaining the pardon of sin by prayer—an immense and unspeakable "profit" to a dying and guilty man; (*b*) a peace which this world cannot furnish—worth more than all that it costs to obtain it; (*c*) support in trial in answer to prayer—in a world of suffering of more value than silver and gold; (*d*) the salvation of friends in answer to prayer —an object that should be one of intense interest to those who love their friends; (*e*) eternal life—the "profit" of which who can estimate? What are the few sacrifices which religion requires, compared with the infinite and immortal blessings which may be obtained by *asking* for them? 'Profit!' What can be done by man that will be turned to so good an account as to pray? Where can man make so good an investment of time and strength as by calling on God to save his soul, and to bless his friends and the world?

16. *Lo, their good* is *not in their hand.* Schultens, Rosenmuller, and Noyes, suppose, I think, correctly, that

this is to be understood ironically, or as referring to what *they* had maintained. "Lo! you say, that their good is not in their hand! They do not enjoy prosperity, do they? They are soon overwhelmed with calamity, are they? How often have *I* seen it otherwise! How often is it a fact that they continue to enjoy prosperity, and live and die in peace!" The common interpretation, which Prof. Lee has adopted, seems to me to be much less probable. According to that it means that "their prosperity was not brought about or preserved by their own power. It was by the power of God, and was under his control. An inscrutable Providence governs all things." But the true sense is, that Job is replying to the arguments which they had advanced, and one of those was, that whatever prosperity they had was not at all secure, but that in a moment it might be, and often was, wrested from them. Job maintains the contrary, and affirms that it was a somewhat unusual occurrence (ver. 17), that the wicked were plunged into sudden calamity. The phrase "in their hand" means *in their power*, or under their control, and at their disposal. ¶ *The counsel of the wicked is far from me.* Or, rather, "far be it from me!" Perhaps the meaning is this, "Do not misunderstand me. I maintain that the wicked are often prospered, and that God does not in this life deal with them according to their deserts. They have life, and health, and property. But do not suppose that I am their advocate. Far be it from me to defend them. Far from me be their counsels and their plans. I have no sympathy with them. But I maintain merely that your position is not correct that they are *always* subjected to calamity, and that the character of men can *always* be known by the dealings of Providence towards them." Or, it may mean, that he was not disposed to be united with them. They were, in fact, prospered; but though they were prospered, he wished to have no part in their plans and counsels.

17 How oft is the [1] candle of the wicked put out? and *how oft* cometh their destruction upon them? *God* distributeth sorrows in his anger.

18 They are as stubble before the wind, and as chaff that the storm [2] carrieth away.

19 God layeth up [3] his iniquity for his children: *a* he rewardeth him, and he shall know *it.*

20 His eyes shall see his destruction, and he shall drink of the wrath of the Almighty.

[1] or, *lamp.* [2] *stealeth away.* [3] i. e. *the punishment of iniquity.* *a* Ex.20.5; Eze.18.14.

He would prefer a holy life with all the ills that might attend it.

17. *How oft is the candle of the wicked put out?* Marg. *lamp.* A light, or a lamp, was an image of prosperity. There is, probably, an allusion here to what had been maintained by Bildad, chap. xviii. 5, 6, that the light of the wicked would be extinguished, and their dwellings made dark; see Notes on those verses. Job replies to this by asking how often it occurred. He inquires whether it was a frequent thing. By this, he implies that it was not universal; that it was a less frequent occurrence than they supposed. The meaning is, "How often does it, in fact, happen that the light of the wicked is extinguished, and that God distributes sorrows among them in his anger? Much less frequently than you suppose, for he bestows upon many of them tokens of abundant prosperity." In this manner, by an appeal to *fact* and *observation,* Job aims to convince them that their position was wrong, and that it was not true that the wicked were invariably overwhelmed with calamity, as they had maintained. ¶ *God distributeth sorrows.* The word *God* here, is understood, but there can be no doubt that it is correct. Job means to ask, how often it was true in fact that God *apportioned* the sorrows which he sent on men in accordance with their character. How often, in fact, did he treat the wicked as they deserved, and overwhelm them with calamity. It was not true that he did it, by any means, as often as they maintained, or so as to make it a certain rule in judging of character.

18. *They are as stubble before the wind.* According to the interpretation proposed of the previous verse, this may be read as a question, "How

often is it that the wicked are made like stubble? You say that God deals with men exactly according to their characters, and that the wicked are certainly subjected to calamities; but how often does this, in fact, occur? Is it a uniform law? Do they not, in fact, live in prosperity, and arrive at a good old age?" It is not uncommon in the Scriptures to compare the wicked with stubble, and to affirm that they shall be driven away, as the chaff is driven by the wind; see Notes on Isa. xvii. 13. ¶ *The storm carrieth away.* Marg. *stealeth away.* This is a literal translation of the Hebrew. The idea is that of stealing away before one is aware, as a thief carries off spoil.

19. *God layeth up his iniquity for his children.* Marg. i. e. *the punishment of iniquity.* This is a reference evidently to the opinion which *they* had maintained. It may be rendered, "*You say* that God layeth up iniquity," &c. They had affirmed that not only did God, as a great law, punish the wicked in this life, but that the consequences of their sins passed over to their posterity; or, if *they* were not punished, yet the calamity would certainly come on their descendants; see chap. xviii. 19, 20; xx. 10, 28. This is the objection which Job now adverts to. The statement of the objection, it seems to me, continues to ver. 22, where Job says, that no one can teach God knowledge, or prescribe to him what he should do, and then goes on to say, that the *fact* was far different from what they maintained; that there was no such exact distribution of punishments; but that one died in full strength, and another in the bitterness of his soul, and both laid down in the dust together. This view seems to me to give better sense than

21 For what pleasure *hath* he in his house after him, when the number of his months is cut off in the midst?

22 Shall *a* any teach God knowledge? seeing he judgeth those that are high.

23 One dieth in his ¹ full strength, being wholly at ease and quiet:

a Ro.11.34.

¹ *very perfection,* or, *in the strength of his perfection.*

any other interpretation which I have seen proposed. ¶ *He rewardeth him, and he shall know it.* That is, you maintain that God will certainly reward him in this life, and that his dealings with him shall so exactly express the divine view of his conduct, that he shall certainly know what God thinks of his character. This opinion they had maintained throughout the argument, and this Job as constantly called in question.

20. *His eyes shall see his destruction.* That is, his own eyes shall see his destruction, or the calamities that shall come upon him. That is, "You maintain that, or this is the position which you defend." Job designs to meet this, and to show that it is not always so. ¶ *And he shall drink of the wrath of the Almighty.* Wrath is often represented as a cup which the wicked are compelled to drink. See Notes, Isa. li. 17.

21. *For what pleasure* hath *he,* &c. That is, what happiness shall he have in his family? This, it seems to me, is designed to be a reference to their sentiments, or a statement by Job of what *they* maintained. They held, that a man who was wicked, could have none of the comfort which he anticipated in his children, for he would himself be cut off in the midst of life, and taken away. ¶ *When the number of his months is cut off in the midst?* When his *life* is cut off—the word *months* here being used in the sense of *life,* or *years.* This they had maintained, that a wicked man would be punished, by being cut off in the midst of his way; comp. chap. xiv. 21.

22. *Shall any teach God knowledge?* This commences the reply of Job to the sentiments of his friends to which he had just adverted. The substance of the reply is, that no one could prescribe to God how he should deal with men, and that it was not *a fact* that

men were treated as they had supposed. Instead of its being true, as they maintained, that wicked men would all be cut down in some fearful and violent manner, as a punishment for their sins, Job goes on (ver. 23—26) to show that they died in a great variety of ways—one in full age and prosperity, and another in another manner. This, he says, God directs as he pleases. No one can teach him knowledge; no one can tell him what he ought to do. The reasoning of his friends, Job seems to imply, had been rather an attempt to teach God how he *ought* to deal with men, than a patient and candid inquiry into the *facts* in the case, and he says the facts were not as they supposed they ought to be. ¶ *Seeing he judgeth those that are high.* Or rather, he judges *among the things* that are high. He rules over the great affairs of the universe, and it is presumptuous in us to attempt to prescribe to him how he shall govern the world. The design of this and the following verses is to show, that, from the manner in which men actually die, no argument can be derived to determine what was their religious condition, or their real character. Nothing is more fallacious than that kind of reasoning.

23. *One dieth in his full strength.* Marg. *very perfection,* or, *in the strength of his perfection.* The meaning is, that he dies in the very prime and vigour of life, surrounded with every thing that can contribute to comfort. Of the truth of this position, no one can doubt; and the wonder is, that the friends of Job had not seen or admitted it. ¶ *Being wholly at ease and quiet.* That is, having every thing to make them happy, so far as external circumstances are concerned. He is borne down by no calamities; he is overwhelmed by no sudden and heavy judgments. The phrase in this

24 His [1] breasts are full of milk, and his bones are moistened with marrow.

1 or, *milk pails.*

25 And another dieth in the bitterness of his soul, and never eateth with pleasure.

verse rendered "full strength" המו בעצמ), is literally, "in the bone of his perfection." It means full prosperity.

24. *His breasts.* Marg. *milk-pails.* The marginal translation is much the most correct, and it is difficult to understand why so improbable a statement has been introduced into our common version. But there has been great variety in the translation. The Vulgate renders it, Viscera ejus plena sunt adipe—"*his viscera are full of fat.*" So the LXX. τὰ ἔγκατα ἀυτοῦ πλήρη στέατος. The Syraic, *his sides;* Prof. Lee, *his bottles;* Noyes, *his sides;* Luther, *sein milkfass — his milk-pail;* Wemyss, *the stations of his cattle;* Good, *his sleek skin.* In this variety of rendering, what hope is there of ascertaining the meaning of the word? It is not easy to account for this variety, though it is clear that Jerome and the LXX. followed a different reading from the present, and instead of עטיניו, they read בטיניו — from בטנ —*the belly;* and that instead of the word חלב, as at present pointed, meaning *milk,* they understood it as if it were pointed חֵלֶב—meaning *fat—* the same letters, but different vowels. The word which is rendered *breast* (עטין) occurs nowhere else in the Hebrew Scriptures. It has become necessary, therefore, to seek its meaning in the ancient versions, and in the cognate languages. For a full examination of the word, the reader may consult Bochart, Hieroz. P. 1, Lib. ii. c. xliv., pp. 455, 458; or Rosenmüller, where the remarks of Bochart are abridged; or Lee on Job, *in loc.* The Chaldee renders it בריזוי—*his breasts.* So Junius et Tre. Piscator, and others. Among the Rabbins, Moses Bar. Nackman, Levi, and others, render it as denoting the breasts, or *mulctralia* —*milk-vessels,* denoting, as some have supposed, *the lacteals.* This idea would admirably suit the connection, but it is doubtful whether it can be maintained; and the presumption is,

that it would be in advance of the knowledge of physiology in the times of Job. Aben Ezra explains it of the places where camels lie down to drink —an idea which is found in the Arabic, and which will well suit the connection. According to this, the sense would be, that those places abounded with milk—that is, that he was prospered and happy. The Hebrew word עטין, as has been observed, occurs nowhere else. It is supposed to be derived from an obsolete root, the same as the Arabic *atana, to lie down around water, as cattle do ;* and then the derivative denotes a place where cattle and flocks lie down around water ; and then the passage would mean, " the resting places of his herds are full, or abound with milk." Yet the primary idea, according to Castell, Golius, and Lee, is that of saturating with water ; softening, *scil.* a skin with water, or dressing a skin, for the purpose of using it as a bottle. Perhaps the word was used with reference to the place where camels came to drink, because it was a place that was *saturated* with water, or that abounded with water. The Arabic verb, also, according to Castell, is used in the sense of freeing a skin from wool and hairs—a lana pilisve levari pellem—so that it might be dressed for use. From this reference to a *skin* thus dressed, Prof. Lee supposes that the word here means *a bottle,* and that the sense is, that his bottles were full of milk ; that is, that he had great prosperity and abundance. But it is very doubtful whether the word will bear this meaning, and whether it is ever used in this sense. In the instances adduced by Castell, Schultens, and even of Prof. Lee, of the use of the word, I find no one where it means a *skin,* or denotes a bottle made of a skin. The application of the *verb* to a skin is only in the sense of saturating and dressing it. The leading idea in all the forms of the word, and its common use in Arabic,

26 They shall lie down alike in the dust, and the worms shall cover them.

27 Behold, I know your thoughts, and the devices *which* ye wrongfully imagine against me.

28 For ye say, Where *is* the house of the prince ? and where *are* the [1] dwelling places of the wicked ?

29 Have ye not asked them that

[1] *tent of the tabernacles.*

is *that of a place where cattle kneel down for the purpose of drinking,* and then a place well watered, where a man might lead his camels and flocks to water. The noun would then come to mean a watering place—a place that would be of great value, and which a man who had large flocks and herds would greatly prize. The thought here is, therefore, that the places of this kind, in the possession of the man referred to, would abound with milk—that is, he would have abundance. ¶ *Are full of milk.* Milk, butter and honey, are, in the Scriptures, the emblems of plenty and prosperity. Many of the versions, however, here render this *fat.* The change is only in the pointing of the Hebrew word. But, if the interpretation above given be correct, then the word here means *milk.* ¶ *And his bones are moistened with marrow.* From the belief, that bones full of marrow are an indication of health and vigour.

26. *They shall lie down alike in the dust.* The emphasis here is on the word *alike*—יחד. The idea is, that they should die *in a similar manner.* There would be no such difference in the mode of their death as to determine anything about their character, or to show that one was the friend of God, and that the other was not. The friends of Job had maintained, that that could be certainly known by the divine dealings with men, either in their life, or in their death. Job combats this opinion, and says, that there is no such marked distinction in their life, nor is there any certain indication of their character in their death. Prosperity often attends the wicked as well as the righteous, and the death of the righteous and the wicked resemble each other. ¶ *And the worms shall cover them.* Cover them *both.* They shall alike moulder back to dust. There is no distinction in the grave. There is no difference in the manner

in which they moulder back to dust. No argument can be drawn respecting their character from the divine dealings towards them when in life—none from the manner of their death—none from the mode in which they moulder back to dust. On the reference to the *worm* here, see Notes on ch. xiv. 11

27. *Behold, I know your thoughts.* That is, " I see that you are not satisfied, and that you are disposed still to maintain your former position. You will be ready to ask, Where *are* the proofs of the prosperity of the wicked? Where *are* the palaces of the mighty? Where *are* the dwelling places of ungodly men !" ¶ *And the devices* which *ye wrongfully imagine against me.* The course of sophistical argument which you pursue, the tendency and design of which is to prove that I am a wicked man. You artfully lay down the position, that the wicked must be, and are in fact, overwhelmed with calamities, and then you infer, that because *I* am overwhelmed in this manner, I *must be* a wicked man.

28. *For ye say, Where* is *the house of the prince ?* That is, you maintain that the house of the wicked man, in a high station, will be certainly over thrown. The parallelism, as well as the whole connection, requires us to understand the word *prince* here as referring to a *wicked* ruler. The word used (נדיב) properly means, one willing, voluntary, prompt ; then, one who is liberal, generous, noble ; then, one of noble birth, or of elevated rank ; and then, as princes often had that character, it is used in a bad sense, and means a *tyrant.* See Isa. xiii. 2. ¶ *And where* are *the dwelling places of the wicked?* Marg. *tent of the tabernacles.* The Hebrew is, " The tent of the dwelling places." The dwelling place was usually a *tent.* The meaning is, that such dwelling places would be certainly destroyed, as an expression of the divine displeasure.

go by the way? and do ye not know their tokens,

30 That the wicked is reserved to the day of destruction? they shall be brought forth to the day of [1] wrath.

[1] wraths.

---

29. *Have ye not asked them that go by the way?* Travellers, who have passed into other countries, and who have had an opportunity of making observations, and of learning the opinions of those residing there. The idea of Job is, that they might have learned from such travellers that such men were *reserved* for future destruction, and that calamity did not immediately overtake them. Information was obtained in ancient times by careful observation, and by travelling, and they who had gone into other countries would be regarded as peculiarly well qualified to bear testimony on a point like this. They could speak of what they had observed of the actual dealings of God there, and of the sentiments of sages there. The idea is, that *they* would confirm the truth of what Job had said, that the wicked were often prosperous and happy. ¶ *And do ye not know their tokens.* The signs, or intimations which they have given of the actual state of things in other countries, perhaps by the inscriptions, records, and proverbs, by which they had *signified* the result of their inquiries.

30. *That the wicked is reserved to the day of destruction?* He is not punished, as you maintain, at once. He is *kept* with a view to future punishment; and though calamity will certainly overtake him at some time, yet it is not immediate. This was Job's doctrine in opposition to theirs, and in this he was undoubtedly correct. The only wonder is, that they had not at all seen it sooner, and that it should have been necessary to make this appeal to the testimony of travellers. Rosenmüller, Noyes, and Schultens, understand it as meaning that the wicked are *spared* in the day of destruction, that is, in the day when destruction comes upon other men. This accords well with the argument which Job is maintaining. Yet the word (חשׂך) rather means, especially when followed by ל, to hold

back, reserve, or retain *for* something future; and this is the sentiment which Job was maintaining, that the wicked were not cut off at once, or suddenly overwhelmed with punishment. He did not deny that they would be punished at some period; and that exact justice would be done them. The point of the controversy turned upon the inquiry whether this would come *at once*, or whether the wicked might not live long in prosperity. ¶ *They shall be brought forth,* יובלו. They shall be led or conducted—as one is to execution. This appears as if Job held to the doctrine of *future* retribution. But when that time would be, or what were his exact views in reference to the future judgment, is not certainly intimated. It is clear, however, from this discussion, that he supposed it would be *beyond* death, for he says that the wicked are prospered in this life; that they go down to the grave and sleep in the tomb; that the clods of the valley are sweet unto them, (ver. 32, 33), yet that the judgment, the just retribution, would certainly come. This passage, therefore, seems to be decisive to prove that he held to a state of retribution beyond the grave, where the inequalities of the present life would be corrected, and where men, though prospered here, would be treated as they deserved. This, he says, was the current opinion. It was that which was brought by travellers, who had gone into other lands. What impropriety is there in supposing that he may refer to some travellers who had gone into the country where Abraham, Isaac, or Jacob had lived, or then lived, and that they had brought this back as the prevalent belief there? To this current faith in that foreign land, he may now appeal as deserving the attention of his friends, and as meeting all that they had said. It *would* meet all that they said. It was the exact truth. It accorded with the course of events. And sustained, as Job says it was, by the prevailing

31 Who shall declare his way to his face? and who shall repay him *what* he hath done?

1 graves.

32 Yet shall he be brought to the ¹ grave, and shall ² remain in the tomb.

2 watch in the heap.

opinion in foreign lands, it was regarded by him as settling the controversy. It is as true now as it was then; and this solution, which could come only from revelation, settles all inquiries about the rectitude of the divine administration in the dispensation of rewards and punishments. It answers the question, "How is it consistent for God to bestow so many blessings on the wicked, while his own people are so much afflicted?" The answer is, they have *their* good things in this life, and in the future world all these inequalities will be rectified. ¶ *Day of wrath.* Marg. as in Heb. *wraths.* The plural form here is probably employed to denote emphasis, and means the same as *fierce wrath.*

31. *Who shall declare his way to his face?* That is, the face of the wicked. Who shall dare to rise up and openly charge him with his guilt? The idea is, that none would dare to do it, and that, therefore, the wicked man was not punished according to his character here, and was reserved to a day of future wrath. ¶ *And who shall repay him* what *he hath done?* The meaning is, that many wicked men lived without being punished for their sins. No one was able to recompense them for the evil which they had done, and consequently they lived in security and prosperity. Such were the tyrants and conquerors, who had made the world desolate.

32. *Yet shall he be brought to the grave.* Marg. *graves.* That is, he is brought with honour and prosperity to the grave. He is not cut down by manifest divine displeasure for his sins. He is conducted to the grave as other men are, notwithstanding his enormous wickedness. The *object* of this is clearly to state that he would not be overwhelmed with calamity, as the friends of Job had maintained, and that nothing could be determined in regard to his character from the divine dealings toward him in this life. ¶ *And shall remain*

in the tomb. Marg. *watch in the heap.* The marginal reading does not make sense, though it seems to be an exact translation of the Hebrew. Noyes renders it, "Yet he still survives upon his tomb." Prof. Lee, "For the tomb was he watchful;" that is, his anxiety was to have an honoured and a splendid burial. Wemyss, "They watch over his tomb;" that is, he is honoured in his death, and his friends visit his tomb with affectionate solicitude, and keep watch over his grave. So Dr. Good renders it. Jerome translates it; *et in congerie mortuorum vigilabit.* The LXX., "And he shall be borne to the graves, and he shall watch over the tombs;" or, he shall cause a watch to be kept over his tomb—ἐπὶ σωρῶν ἠγρύπνησεν. Amidst this variety of interpretation, it is not easy to determine the true sense of the passage. The *general* meaning is not difficult. It is, that he should be honoured even in his death; that he would live in prosperity, and be buried with magnificence. There would be nothing in his death or burial which would certainly show that God regarded him as a wicked man. But there is considerable difficulty in determining the exact sense of the original words. The word rendered *tomb* in the text and *heap* in the margin (גדיש) occurs only in the following places, Ex. xxii. 6; Job v. 26; Judges xv. 5, where it is rendered *a shock of corn,* and in this place. The *verb* in the Syriac, Arabic, and in Chaldee, means *to heap up* (see Castell), and the noun may denote, therefore, a stack, or a heap of grain, or a tomb, that was made by a pile of earth, or stones. The ancient *tumuli* were mere heaps of earth or stone, and probably such a pile was made usually over a grave as a monument. On the meaning of the word here used, the reader may consult Bochart, Hieroz. P. i. L. iii. c. xiii. p. 853. There can be little doubt that it here means a tomb, or a monument raised over a tomb. There is more difficulty about

33 The clods of the valley shall be sweet unto him, and every *a* man shall draw after him, as *there are* innumerable before him.

a He.9.27.

---

the word rendered "shall remain" (יִשְׁקֹד). This properly means, to wake, to be watchful, to be sleepless. So the Chaldee שְׁקַד, and the Arabic *dakash.* The verb is commonly rendered in the Scriptures, *watch,* or *waketh.* See Ps. cxvii. 1; cii. 7; Jer. xxxi. 28; i. 12; v. 6; xliv. 27; Isa. xxix. 20; Ezra viii. 29; Dan. ix. 14. There is usually in the word the notion of *watching,* with a view to guarding, or protecting, as when one watches a vineyard, a house, or other property. The sense here is, probably, that his tomb should be carefully *watched* by friends, and the verb is probably taken impersonally, or used to denote that *some one* would watch over his grave. This might be either as a proof of affection, or to keep it in repair. One of the most painful ideas might have been then, as it is now among American savages (Bancroft's History of the United States, vol. iii. p. 299), that of having the grave left or violated, and it may have been regarded as a peculiar honour to have had friends, who would come and watch over their sepulchre. According to this view, the meaning is, that the wicked man was often honourably buried; that a monument was reared to his memory; and that every mark of attention was paid to him after he was dead. Numbers followed him to his burial, and friends came and wept with affection around his tomb. The argument of Job is, that there was no such distinction between the lives and death of the righteous and the wicked as to make it possible to determine the character; and is it not so still? The wicked man often dies in a palace, and with all the comforts that every clime can furnish to alleviate his pain, and to soothe him in his dying moments. He lies upon a bed of down ; friends attend him with unwearied care ; the skill of medicine is exhausted to restore him, and there is every indication of grief at his death. So, in the place of his burial, a monument of finest marble, sculptured with all the skill of art, is reared over his

grave. An inscription, beautiful as taste can make it, proclaims his virtues to the traveller and the stranger. Friends go and plant roses over his grave, that breathe forth their odours around the spot where he lies. Who from the dying scene, the funeral, the monument, the attendants, would suppose that he was a man whom God abhorred, and whose soul was already in hell? This is the argument of Job, and of its solidity no one can doubt.

33. *The clods of the valley shall be sweet unto him.* That is, he shall lie as calmly as others in the grave. The language here is taken from that delusion of which we all partake when we reflect on death. We think of *ourselves* in the grave, and it is almost impossible to divest our minds of the idea, that we shall be conscious there, and be capable of understanding our condition. The idea here is, that the person who was thus buried, might be sensible of the quiet of his abode, and enjoy, in some measure, the honours of the beautiful or splendid tomb, in which he was buried, and the anxious care of his friends. So we *think* of our friends, though we do not often *express* it. The dear child that is placed in the dark vault, or that is covered up in the ground—we feel as if we could not have him there. We insensibly shudder, as if *he* might be conscious of the darkness and chilliness, and *a part* of our trial arises from this delusion. So felt the American savage—expressing the emotions of the heart, which, in other cases, are often concealed. " At the bottom of a grave, the melting snows had left a little water ; and the sight of it chilled and saddened his imagination. ' You have no compassion for my poor brother'—such was the reproach of an Algonquin—'the air is pleasant, and the sun so cheering, and yet you do not remove the snow from the grave, to warm him a little,' and he knew no contentment till it was done."—Bancroft's History, U. S. iii. 294. 295. The

34 How then comfort ye me in *a* vain, seeing in your answers there remaineth 1 falsehood ?

a chap.16.2.   1 *transgression.*

same feeling is expressed by Fingal over the grave of Gaul:

Prepare, ye children of musical strings,
The bed of Gaul, and his sun-beam by him;
Where may be seen his resting place from afar
Which branches high overshadow,
Under the wing of the oak of greenest flourish,
Of quickest growth, and most durable form,
Which will shoot forth its leaves to the breeze
    of the shower,
While the heath around is still withered.
Its leaves, from the extremity of the land,
Shall be seen by the birds in Summer;
And each bird shall perch, as it arrives,
On a sprig of its verdant branch;
Gaul in this mist shall hear the cheerful note,
While the virgins are singing of Evirchoma.

Thus, also, Knolles (History of the Turks, p. 332) remarks of the Sultan Murad II., that "after his death, his son raised the siege, and returned back to Adrianople. He caused the dead to be buried with great solemnity in the Western suburbs of Broosa, in a chapel without a roof, in accordance with the express desire of the Sultan, in order that the mercy and blessing of God might descend on him, that the sun and the moon might shine on his grave, and the rain and the dew of heaven fall upon it." Rosenmüller's Alte u. neue Morgenland, *in loc.* The word *clods* here, is rendered *stones* by Prof. Lee, but the more general interpretation is that of *sods*, or *clods.* The word is used only here, and in Job xxxviii. 38, where it is also rendered clods. The word *valley* (בהנ) means usually a stream, brook, or rivulet, and then a valley where such a brook runs. Notes chap. vi. 15. It is not improbable that such valleys were chosen as burial places, from the custom of planting shrubs and flowers around a grave, because they would flourish best there. The valley of Jehoshaphat, near Jerusalem, was long occupied as a burial place. ¶ *And every man shall draw after him.* Some suppose that this means, that he shall share the common lot of mortals—that innumerable multitudes have gone thither before him—and that succeeding generations shall follow to the same place appointed for all the living. *Noyes.* Others, however, suppose that this

refers to a funeral procession and that the meaning is, that all the world is drawn out after him, and that an innumerable multitude precedes him when he is buried. Others, again, suppose it means, that his example shall attract many to follow and adopt his practices, as many have done before him in imitating similar characters. *Lee.* It is clear, that there is some notion of honour, respect, or pomp in the language; and it seems to me more likely that the meaning is, that he would draw out every body to go to the place where he was buried, that they might look on it, and thus honour him. What multitudes would go to look on the grave of Alexander the Great! How many have gone to look on the place where Cæsar fell! How many have gone, and will go, to look on the place where Nelson or Napoleon is buried! This, I think, is the idea here, that the man who should thus die, would draw great numbers to the place where he was buried, and that before him, or in his presence, there was an innumerable multitude, so greatly would he be honoured.

34. *How then comfort ye me in vain,* &c. That is, how can you be qualified to give me consolation in my trials, who have such erroneous views of the government and dealings of God? True consolation could be founded only on correct views of the divine government; but such views, Job says, they had not. With their conceptions of the divine administration, they could not administer to him any real consolation. We may learn hence, (1.) That all real consolation in trial must be based on correct apprehensions of the divine character and plans. Falsehood, delusion, error, can give no permanent comfort. (2.) They whose office it is to administer consolation to the afflicted, should seek after the *truth* about God and his government. They should endeavour to learn why he afflicts men, what purpose he proposes to accomplish, and what are the proper ends of trial. They should have an unwavering conviction that he

is right, and should see as far as possible *why* he is right, before they attempt to comfort others. Their own souls should be imbued with the fullest conviction that all the ways of God are holy, and then they should go and endeavour to pour their convictions into other hearts, and make them feel so too. A minister of the gospel, who has unsettled, erroneous, or false views of the character and government of God, is poorly qualified for his station, and will be a *"miserable comforter"* to those who are in trial. Truth alone sustains the soul in affliction. Truth only can inspire confidence in God. Truth only can break the force of sorrow, and enable the sufferer to look up to God and to heaven with confidence and joy.

SUPPLEMENTARY NOTE TO CHAP. V. Ver. 9.

The labours of astronomers, aided by instruments of remarkable accuracy and power, and by improved methods of observation, are ever adding to our knowledge of the "wonderful things without number" which render the mechanism of the heavens such a spectacle of sublimity. Among the most interesting and beautiful of the celestial phenomena are the star-clusters and nebulæ. A small number of the star-clusters are bright enough to be distinguished by the naked eye, to which they appear as a faint cloudlike patch of light; but it is only when the telescope is used that their real character becomes known, and they are then seen to be vast agglomerations of stars—connected systems of suns. The greater number are of a rounded and apparently globular form, the stars being densely crowded together in the centre; though others are very irregular in shape. Those of a globular form often consist of an astonishingly great number of stars. "Herschel has calculated that many clusters contain 5000 collected in a space, the apparent dimensions of which are scarcely the tenth part of the surface of the lunar disk." "The beautiful cluster in Aquarius, which Sir J. Herschel's drawing exhibits as fine luminous dust, when examined through the Earl of Rosse's powerful reflector, appeared like a magnificent globular cluster, entirely separated into stars. But the most beautiful specimen of this kind is without doubt the splendid cluster in Toucan, quite visible to the naked eye, in the vicinity of the smaller Magellanic cloud, in a region of the southern sky entirely void of stars. The condensation at the centre of this cluster is extremely decided; there are three perfectly distinct gradations, and the orange red colour of the central agglomeration contrasts wonderfully with the white light of the concentric envelopes." It was formerly supposed by many that all nebulæ were resolvable into star-clusters, and that it was only the want of instruments of sufficient power that prevented this from being done; but spectrum analysis has now demonstrated what was before conjectured, that although there may be many nebulæ that would appear as distinct stars if more powerful instruments were brought to bear upon them, there are others of a different nature, consisting, namely, of glowing masses of gaseous matter. The forms assumed by nebulæ are extremely varied, and some of them very remarkable. The round or globular form is very common; others resemble rings, circular or oval; others are conical or fan-shaped, resembling the tail of a comet; some consist of spirals, radiating from a common nucleus; while many assume forms so irregular and bizarre as to be difficult to describe. The names given to some of them, such as the Crab Nebula, the Dumb-bell Nebula, the Fish-mouth Nebula (Nebula in Orion, see Plate), sufficiently intimate the striking aspects that they sometimes present. Many of the nebulæ, in which the separate stars could not previously be distinguished, have been resolved by Lord Rosse's great telescope; while others as seen by it have very different shapes from what less powerful instruments gave them. This is the case with the Dumb-bell Nebula in particular, its form as described and figured by Sir John Herschel being considerably different from that in our engraving, which shows its aspect under Lord Rosse's telescope. "Two luminous masses symmetrically placed and bound together by a rather short neck, the whole surrounded with a light nebulous envelope of oval form, gave it a very marked appearance of regularity. This aspect was however modified by Lord Rosse's telescope of three feet aperture, and the nebulous masses showed a decided tendency to resolvability. Later still, with the six-feet telescope, numerous stars were observed standing out, however, on a nebulous ground. The general aspect retains its primitive shape, less regular, but striking nevertheless." With regard to the nebula in Orion we extract the following passage from Guillemin's *The Heavens*, edited by J. N. Lockyer, F.R.A.S., the work from which the above passages are taken:—"Sir J. Herschel compares the brightest portion to the head of a monstrous animal, the mouth of which is open, and the nose of which is in the form of a trunk. Hence its name, the Fish-mouth Nebula. It is at the edge of the opening, in a space free from nebula that the four brightest of the components of θ [a sevenfold star, *i. e.* a connected system of seven stars which appear to the naked eye a single luminous point] are to be found; around, but principally above the trapezium formed by these four stars is a luminous region, with a *mottled* appearance, which Lord Rosse and Bond have partly resolved. This region is remarkable on account, not only of the brilliancy of its lights, but also of the numerous centres where this light is condensed, and each of which appears to form a stellar cluster. The rectangular form of the whole is also worthy of attention. The nebulous masses surrounding it, the light of which is much fainter than that of the central region, are lost gradually; according to Bond they assume a spiral form as indicated in the drawing executed by that astronomer" (from which our engraving is taken). Writing soon after Lord Rosse's observation had resolved the nebula of Orion, Dr. Nichol says:—"The great cluster in Hercules has long dazzled the heart with its splendours; but we have learned now, that among circular and compact galaxies, a class to which the nebulous stars belong, there are multitudes which infinitely surpass it; nay, that schemes of being rise above it, sun becoming nearer to sun, until their skies must be one blaze of light, a throng of burning activities! But far aloft stands Orion, the pre-eminent glory and wonder of the starry universe!—It would seem almost that if all other clusters, hitherto gauged, were collected and compressed into one, they would not surpass this mighty group, in which every wisp, every wrinkle, is a SAND HEAP of stars. There are cases in which, though imagination has quailed, reason may still adventure inquiry, and prolong its speculations; but at times we are brought to a limit across which no human faculty has the strength to penetrate, and where, as if at the very footstool of the secret THRONE, we can only bend our heads, and silently ADORE!" "These facts furnish a most impressive commentary upon the words of Eliphaz—which doeth great things and unsearchable, *marvellous things till there be no number* (margin)—and become the more significant from their connection with the constellation of ORION, which is more than once mentioned in the book of Job" (ch. ix. 9; xxxviii. 31).